The Legacy of Milton Friedman as Teacher
Volume II

Intellectual Legacies in Modern Economics

Series Editor: Steven G. Medema
Associate Professor, University of Colorado at Denver, USA

Associate Editors: Roger Backhouse
Reader in the History of Economic Thought
University of Birmingham, UK

A.W. Coats
Professor Emeritus of Economic History
University of Nottingham, UK

Wherever possible, the articles in these volumes have been reproduced as originally published using facsimile reproduction, inclusive of footnotes and pagination to facilitate ease of reference.

For a list of all Edward Elgar published titles visit our site on the World Wide Web at
http://www.e-elgar.co.uk

The Legacy of Milton Friedman as Teacher Volume II

Edited by

J. Daniel Hammond

Professor of Economics
Wake Forest University, USA

INTELLECTUAL LEGACIES IN MODERN ECONOMICS

An Elgar Reference Collection
Cheltenham, UK • Northampton, MA, USA

Published by
Edward Elgar Publishing Limited
Glensanda House
Montpellier Parade
Cheltenham
Glos GL50 1UA
UK

Edward Elgar Publishing, Inc.
136 West Street
Suite 202
Northampton
Massachusetts 01060
USA

A catalogue record for this book is available from the British Library.

Library of Congress Cataloguing in Publication Data

The legacy of Milton Friedman as teacher / edited by J. Daniel Hammond.
    (Intellectual legacies in modern economics: 2)
    (An Elgar reference collection)
    Includes bibliographical references and index.
    1. Friedman, Milton, 1912–   . 2. Economists—United States—Biography.
  I. Hammond, J. Daniel. II. Series. III. Series.
  HB119.F84L44   1999
  330'.092—dc21
                                              99–14858
                                              CIP

ISBN 1 85898 423 8 (2 volume set)

Printed and bound in Great Britain by Biddles Ltd, Guildford and King's Lynn

Contents

Acknowledgements

The editor and publishers wish to thank the authors and the following publishers who have kindly given permission for the use of copyright material.

Douglas K. Adie for his own article: (1970), 'English Bank Deposits before 1844', *Economic History Review*, **XXIII** (2), August, 285–97.

American Economic Association for articles: Miguel Sidrauski (1967), 'Rational Choice and Patterns of Growth in a Monetary Economy', *American Economic Review*, **LVII** (2), May, 534–44; Michael R. Darby (1972), 'The Allocation of Transitory Income Among Consumers' Assets', *American Economic Review*, **LXII** (5), December, 928–41; Benjamin Klein (1974), 'Competitive Interest Payments on Bank Deposits and the Long-Run Demand for Money', *American Economic Review*, **LXIV** (6), December, 931–49; James R. Lothian (1976), 'The Demand for High-Powered Money', *American Economic Review*, **LXVI** (1), March, 56–68.

American Finance Association and Blackwell Publishers, Inc. for articles: Warren L. Coats, Jr. (1973), 'Regulation D and the Vault Cash Game', *Journal of Finance*, **XXVIII** (3), June, 601–7; Richard V.L. Cooper (1974), 'Efficient Capital Markets and the Quantity Theory of Money', *Journal of Finance*, **XXIX** (3), June, 887–908.

Blackwell Publishers Ltd for article: Gerald P. Dwyer, Jr. (1984), 'The Gibson Paradox: A Cross-Country Analysis', *Economica*, **51** (202), May, 109–27.

Journal of Law and Economics, University of Chicago Law School for article: Sam Peltzman (1965), 'Entry in Commercial Banking', *Journal of Law and Economics*, **VIII**, October, 11–50.

Ohio State University Press for article: Robert D. Laurent (1974), 'Currency in Circulation and the Real Value of Notes', *Journal of Money, Credit, and Banking*, **VI** (2), May, 213–26.

Prentice-Hall, Inc. for excerpt: Edgar L. Feige (1964), 'Estimation of Demand Functions for Financial Assets', 'Conclusions' and 'Appendix A', *The Demand for Liquid Assets: A Temporal Cross-Section Analysis*, Chapters 3 and 4, 16–42, 43–4 and 45–64.

University of Chicago Press for articles and excerpts: George R. Morrison (1966), 'The Theory and Its Implementation', in *Liquidity Preferences of Commercial Banks*, Chapter II, 8–20; William E. Gibson (1970), 'Interest Rates and Monetary Policy', *Journal of Political Economy*, **78** (3), May/June, 431–55; Adolfo Cesar Diz (1970), 'Money and Prices in Argentina, 1935–1962', in David Meiselman (ed.), *Varieties of Monetary Experience*, Chapter II, 71–130, 133–9, 143–62; Michael W. Keran (1970), 'Monetary Policy and the Business Cycle in Postwar Japan', in David Meiselman (ed.), *Varieties of Monetary Experience*, Chapter III, 165–245, references; Morris Perlman (1970), 'International Differences in Liquid Assets Portfolios', in David Meiselman (ed.), *Varieties of Monetary Experience*, Chapter V, 299–337; Edi Karni (1972), 'Inflation and Real Interest Rate: A Long-Term Analysis', *Journal of Political Economy*, **80** (2), March/April, 365–74; Leonardo Auernheimer (1974), 'The Honest Government's Guide to the Revenue from the Creation of Money', *Journal of Political Economy*, **82** (3), May/June, 598–606; Benjamin Eden (1976), 'On the Specification of the Demand for Money: The Real Rate of Return versus the Rate of Inflation', *Journal of Political Economy*, **84** (6), December, 1353–9; Jo Anna Gray (1978), 'On Indexation and Contract Length', *Journal of Political Economy*, **86** (1), February, 1–18; Alan C. Stockman (1980), 'A Theory of Exchange Rate Determination', *Journal of Political Economy*, **88** (4), August, 673–98.

Western Economic Association International for article: Michael David Bordo (1975), 'The Income Effects of the Sources of Monetary Change: An Historical Approach', *Economic Inquiry*, **XIII** (4), December, 505–25.

Every effort has been made to trace all the copyright holders but if any have been inadvertently overlooked the publishers will be pleased to make the necessary arrangement at the first opportunity.

In addition the publishers wish to thank the Library of the London School of Economics and Political Science and Marshall Library of Economics, Cambridge University for their assistance in obtaining these articles.

[1]

Estimation of Demand Functions for Financial Assets

Variables Affecting the Demand for Financial Assets

Many financial assets are described as being *liquid*. The adjective *liquid* refers to a particular non-pecuniary service flow rendered by this particular subset of assets. Other non-pecuniary services may include salability, safety, convenience, defense against misfortune, etc. When one considers the demand for such assets, the relevant relationship involves the bundle of non-pecuniary service flows rendered by these assets. The emphasis on flows, rather than on stocks, permits utilization of the analytic framework provided by the traditional theory of consumer behavior.

The theory of consumer behavior classifies those variables which affect the individual's demand for a particular commodity. The traditional demand hypothesis asserts that the demand for a commodity depends upon the price of the commodity, income, the prices of related commodities, and tastes. Analogously, the demand for the non-pecuniary services of an asset depends upon the price of the services, income, prices of related services, and tastes. The problem then is to define the quantity dimensions of the service flows, the prices of these flows, and to specify the other related variables.

A given stock of a financial asset yields a stream of various non-

16

pecuniary services. One may define the quantity dimension of this stream in terms of the dollar value of the stock that yields the services, so that one can speak of the services per unit time rendered by a dollar of a particular financial asset. The appropriate price of the service is the number of dollars required to buy the particular service stream, per unit time, of a dollar's worth of the asset. Although the value of the service stream cannot be observed, the value of the stock is directly measurable. Assuming a fixed relationship between the stock and the flow of services rendered by the given stock permits utilization of the stock quantity as a proxy measure of the flow. We can thus use the terms *the demand for a financial asset* and the *demand for the non-pecuniary services* yielded by a financial asset interchangeably.

The price of the service flow rendered by a particular asset is the alternative income foregone by purchasing a specific service flow. This price is the difference between the pecuniary return of an asset which yields no non-pecuniary service and the net pecuniary return on the asset in question. Thus, if these returns are expressed as a fraction of the value of the asset,

(3.1) $$P_i = r_0 - r_i^n,$$

where P_i is the price of the non-pecuniary service rendered by the ith asset, r_0 is the pecuniary rate of return on an asset yielding no non-pecuniary services, and r_i^n is the net pecuniary rate of return on the ith asset. If r_0 is considered fixed, the price of the service flow rendered by the ith asset varies inversely with the net pecuniary return on the ith asset.

The net pecuniary rate of return on the ith asset equals the sum of all pecuniary returns, minus the costs associated with the acquisition of the asset and its yield. For convenience, these costs and returns can be expressed as a fraction of the value of the asset so that,

(3.2) $$r_i^n = r_i^i + r_i^g - r_i^c,$$

where r_i^i is the pecuniary interest return per dollar per year, r_i^g is the non-interest pecuniary return per dollar per year (this may include additional gifts and premiums which are distributed with some assets), and r_i^c is the acquisition cost per dollar per year.

The asset holder's behavior will be influenced by the net pecuniary rates of return on other assets. If the rate of return on an asset increases, the individual has an incentive to rearrange his asset portfolio in such a way as to substitute this asset for other assets whose relative yields are lower.

The income of the asset holder will affect the total stock of assets desired as well as the mix of particular assets in his portfolio.

The foregoing classification of variables suggested by consumer theory can be regarded as a hypothesis which specifies that the demand for a particular liquid asset will depend upon the interest return on the asset, the interest returns on alternative assets, non-interest pecuniary returns, convenience costs associated with the acquisition of assets, income, and tastes.

In order to estimate the demand functions for liquid assets, it is desirable to choose a sample with the following attributes: the variables measured should correspond to those postulated by the theoretical model; the sample size should be large enough to permit statistical inferences; the observed quantities should exhibit sufficient variation to provide a basis for the inferences desired. Cross-sectional state data for the United States provide these desirable sample characteristics. State data were collected for the eleven-year period 1949–59. Each year provides a cross-sectional sample of 49 observations, taken from the then 48 states plus the District of Columbia.

Measurement of the Variables

Quantity Variables. In order to estimate demand functions for liquid assets held by *individuals*, it is desirable to derive measures of quantity which exclude the holdings of partnerships, corporations, and state, local, and Federal governments. Data for individual holdings of demand deposits, time deposits, and savings and loan association shares cannot be obtained directly. The finest available breakdown of deposits by ownership class is the sum of deposits held by individuals, partnerships, and corporations.

Because corporations and partnerships hold a small fraction of time deposits and savings and loan association shares, the individual, corporation, and partnership ownership classification is a close approximation to the desired measure of individual holdings, and no additional adjustment seems warranted.

For demand deposits, the aggregation of corporation and partnership balances with individual balances poses a more serious problem. The Federal deposit ownership survey indicates that almost 50 per cent of commercial bank demand deposits are held by corporations. If the demand functions for corporate balances and individual balances were very similar, use of the aggregated balances as the dependent variable would not significantly alter the estimates of the structural parameters. If, on the other hand, the demand functions for individual and corporate balances differed substantially, use of aggregative balances could yield distorted estimates of the structural parameters of the individual demand functions.

In order to reduce the possible error stemming from the inclusion of business balances, an adjustment of the deposit figures has been attempted, to separate out the individual holdings. For the past few years, the Federal Reserve Board has conducted an ownership survey of demand deposit holdings throughout the United States. Although this survey was designed to provide national estimates, it was possible to estimate individuals' holdings on a state basis from the 1960 survey data. Estimates of the fraction of total deposits held by individuals in each state were computed from the original survey data. It was assumed that the fraction of total deposits held by individuals varies considerably more among states than over time for a given state: the state ratios derived from the 1960 survey were therefore included as an independent variable in the demand deposit equation for the 1949–59 period. Because the ownership survey was not designed for this particular type of breakdown, it is difficult to estimate the reliability of this variable.

Interest Returns. The interest returns on time deposits, mutual savings bank deposits, and savings and loan association shares can be measured by taking either the announced nominal rate of return or the actual interest rate paid. The two rates differ because of institutional arrangements regarding compounding of interest and different payment schedules. Since the actual rate represents more clearly the real market opportunities affecting the consumer, this is the rate used in the analysis. The actual interest rate is computed by dividing the total interest payments in a particular period (derived from the consolidated income and expense data of the various institutions) by the average balance of the assets held during the period. The same procedure is used with regard to demand deposits: in this case, however, the interest return is negative and is represented by total service charges divided by average demand deposit balances for the period.

Non-interest Returns. Non-interest returns, such as gifts and premiums offered by savings and loan associations, have become commonplace in the postwar period as a method of attracting new depositors. Since these returns affect the attractiveness of savings and loan association shares, they should be included in the demand function. Unfortunately, it is impossible to estimate accurately the amounts of such non-interest returns, because they are included in the income and expense statements under the general category of advertising expenditures. Although some commercial banks, as well as some mutual savings banks, utilize this method of increasing the effective return, the practice has been carried out on a large scale only by savings and loan associations. Recent literature attributes the rapid growth in savings and loan associations in the postwar period in part to their aggressive advertising policies. Advertising expenditures are therefore included in the demand function for savings and loan association shares in order to test this particular hypothesis as well as clearly to specify the market opportunities facing individual consumers. Advertising expenditures of savings and loan associations were also included as a variable in the demand functions for demand deposits and time deposits. The parameters of the advertising variable did not differ significantly from zero in the preliminary estimates; therefore the variable was excluded from the demand deposit and time deposit equations in the final analysis.

Convenience Costs. The costs associated with the acquisition of a particular asset and its service yield may vary among states. Since the major convenience cost appears to be the value of the individual's time spent in acquiring an asset or utilizing the non-pecuniary services of the asset, a proxy variable for convenience cost was considered for inclusion in the analysis. The per capita number of offices of commercial banks, savings and loan associations, and mutual savings banks was introduced as arguments of the demand functions for the various assets considered. The preliminary regression results indicated that the parameters of these variables were not significantly different from zero when regional shift variables were included in the analysis. The role of convenience costs in affecting the demand for liquid assets, however, deserves further explicit investigation.

Income. Personal income data are available on a state basis. The personal income data were adjusted in order to derive a series of "permanent personal income." *Permanent personal income* is a weighted average of present and past values of personal income; the weights are adopted from Friedman's study of the consumption function.[1] The

---

[1] Milton Friedman, *A Theory of the Consumption Function* (Princeton: Princeton University Press, 1957).

"permanent" and the "measured" series are highly correlated because the Department of Commerce obtained the estimates of personal income by states by using interpolation between benchmark years.

Single Equation Least Squares Estimation

In a particular year, the $S \times 1$ vector y describes the collection of observations on the per capita quantity of liquid asset y in the S states where $s = 1, 2, \ldots, 49$. Similarly, the $S \times j$ matrix X describes a collection of observations on a set of independent variables, J in number, observed in the S states. The observations are assumed to be generated in the following fashion:

$$(3.3) \qquad\qquad y = X\beta + e,$$

where β is a $J \times 1$ coefficient vector and e is a $S \times 1$ vector of disturbances. A typical equation in the system is

$$(3.4) \qquad\qquad y_s = \beta_1 x_{1s} + \beta_2 x_{2s} +, \ldots, + \beta_j x_{js} + e_s.$$

The demand functions for various liquid assets are estimated by the method of least squares, from the cross-sectional sample previously described. The derived regression estimates are based on the following assumptions:

1. The form of the demand functions is linear and the slope coefficients of the variables included in the demand function for a particular liquid asset are the same for all states.

2. The intercepts of the demand functions for a particular liquid asset can vary among geographic areas and among states with important financial centers. Dummy variables were included in the X matrix such that each of the geographic areas (West, South, Central, Northeast) and each of the states which contain the main financial centers of the respective geographic area (California, Washington, D.C., Illinois, New York) was allowed a free intercept.

3. The level of the supply curve of a particular asset differs between states, and is independent of the variables which shift the demand curve. The level of the supply curve in each state is determined primarily by state laws and regulations governing the

22 ***Estimation of Demand Functions for Financial Assets***

activities of financial intermediaries. The rates of return are therefore considered as exogenous variables.

4. Consumer behavior in any given state is affected only by economic conditions in that state.

The notations and definitions of the variables used in the estimation procedure are as follows:

Notation	*Definition*
D	Per capita commercial bank demand deposits held by individuals, partnerships, and corporations
T	Per capital commercial bank time deposits
S	Per capita savings and loan association shares
Y	"Permanent" per capita personal income
r_d	Actual interest rate on commercial bank demand deposits (negative)
r_t	Actual interest rate on commercial bank time deposits
r_s	Actual interest rate on savings and loan association shares
r_m	Actual interest rate on mutual savings bank deposits
D_m	Dummy variable (1 for mutual savings bank states, 0 for non-mutual savings bank states)
I	Survey estimate of the ratio of commercial bank demand deposits held by individuals to total commercial bank demand deposits
A	Per capita advertising expenditures by savings and loan associations
Cal	Dummy variable (1 for California; 0 for all other states)
DC	Dummy variable (1 for Washington, D.C.; 0 for all other states)
Ill	Dummy variable (1 for Illinois; 0 for all other states)
NY	Dummy variable (1 for New York; 0 for all other states)
W	Dummy variable (1 for Western states excluding California; 0 for all other states)
S	Dummy variable (1 for Southern states excluding Washington, D.C.; 0 for all other states)
C	Dummy variable (1 for Central states excluding Illinois; 0 for all other states)
NE	Dummy variable (1 for Northeastern states excluding New York; 0 for all other states)

Single Equation Least Squares Estimates— Demand Deposits

The single equation least squares estimates of the demand functions for demand deposits for the individual years 1949–59 are listed in Table 4 in Appendix A. A summary of the own price and cross substitution terms is found in Table 7 and the estimated elasticities are listed in Table 8. The Durbin-Watson statistic was computed for each of the equations in order to test the functional form implied by (3.4).[1] In each of the eleven equations, it was impossible to reject the hypothesis that the linear form implied by (3.4) was the correct specification.

The coefficients of income in all the equations are highly significant.[2] The income elasticities (estimated at the respective means) do not significantly differ from unity. The coefficients of the interest rate on demand deposits are significant and have the expected sign for all years. These coefficients imply that a reduction in service charges will significantly increase the quantity of demand deposits demanded.

The coefficients of the interest rates on time deposits and savings and loan association shares do not differ significantly from zero, implying that these assets are not as substitutable for demand deposits as has been assumed in much of the monetary literature.

The relationship between demand deposits and mutual savings bank deposits is somewhat ambiguous. The coefficients of the mutual savings bank rate are positive, implying a complementary relationship between demand deposits and mutual savings bank deposits. The coefficient of the mutual savings bank dummy variable is, on the other hand, significantly negative. These results may be interpreted as implying a short-run complementary relationship, but a long-run substitution relationship between demand deposits and mutual savings bank deposits.

The coefficients of the geographic areas and the coefficients of financial centers with the exception of New York do not differ significantly from zero. The New York coefficients are positive and significant, as might be expected, owing to the errors of measurement in the dependent variable for the New York observation.

---

[1] See S. Prais and H. Houthakker, *The Analysis of Family Budgets* (Cambridge: The University Press, 1955), 51–53; also J. Durbin and G. S. Watson, "Testing for Serial Correlation in Least Squares Regression," *Biometrika*, **XXXVIII** (1951), 159–78.

[2] The .05 level was selected as the criterion for all significance tests.

24 **Estimation of Demand Functions for Financial Assets**

The most remarkable feature of the estimated demand functions is the apparent stability of the coefficients over the time period considered. It is possible to test the stability of the demand functions over the entire time period by computing a pooled regression which constrains the coefficients to be equal over time. The sum of squared errors from the pooled regression can be compared to the sum of the sum of squared errors from the individual year regressions in order to test the hypothesis that the demand functions were stable over the period.[1] The appropriate F-statistic,

$$F\, p(K - 1)\,(n - pK) = .705,$$

where p is the number of independent variables, K the number of categories (years), and n the number of observations in the sample. The test indicates that one cannot reject the hypothesis that the demand functions were stable over the time period considered. This latter result implies that financial innovation had no significant effect on reducing the stability of the demand function for demand deposits in the time period considered.

Pooling the individual cross sections for the entire period 1949–59, and constraining the coefficients to be constant over time, yielded the following regression equation:

$$D = .365\ Y + 535\ r_d - 35\ r_t + 53\ r_s + 25\ r_m - 126\ D_m + 405\ I$$
$$(.080) \quad\ (48) \quad\ (13) \quad\ (13) \quad\ (15) \quad\quad (34) \quad\quad (71)$$

$$+ 4\ \text{Cal} + 283\ \text{DC} + 151\ \text{Ill} + 734\ \text{NY} + 10\ \text{W}$$
$$ (57) \quad\quad (55) \quad\quad\ (48) \quad\quad (48) \quad\quad (43)$$

$$- 103\ \text{S} + .2\ \text{C} - 32\ \text{NE}.$$
$$ (42) \quad\quad (43) \quad\quad (45)$$

The coefficient of multiple determination adjusted for degrees of freedom is .978. The own price elasticity, the cross-elasticities, and the income elasticity (all estimated at the means) are listed on the first line of Table 1.

The results of the pooled single equation least squares estimates may be summarized as follows:

1. The income elasticity of demand deposits does not differ significantly from unity.

---

[1] This test is described by S. Kullback and H. M. Rosenblatt, "On the Analysis of Multiple Regression in k Categories," *Biometrika*, **XLIV** (1957), 67–83.

Estimation of Demand Functions for Financial Assets   **25**

TABLE 1. MATRIX OF OWN PRICE, CROSS AND INCOME ELASTICITIES

Pooled Single Equation Least Squares Estimates

1949–59

Dependent variable	Elasticity Estimates at the Mean				
	η_{xd}	η_{xt}	η_{xs}	η_{xm}	η_{xy}
Demand deposits	−.31	.10	−.30	−.04	.92
Time deposits	.13	−.49	.55	.28	.69
Savings and loan association shares	.10	.003	−.18	.08	.63

2. The own price coefficient is more than ten times its standard error and suggests that increases in the service charges on demand deposits will substantially reduce the quantity of demand deposits demanded.

3. Demand deposits and time deposits in commercial banks appear to be weak substitutes.

4. Demand deposits and savings and loan association shares appear to be complements in the pooled equation although the individual cross-section regressions indicate that the two assets are roughly independent in demand.

The possibility of finding complementarity relationships among liquid assets has been suggested by Tobin and Brainard, who argue that an increase in the rate of return on the liabilities of a financial intermediary may have the direct effect of reducing individuals' demand for demand deposits, but the indirect effect of increasing the demand for demand deposits as reserves for the intermediary.[1]

If the indirect effect outweighs the direct effect, complementarity rather than substitution will be observed. As Tobin and Brainard state: "Even though the substitution assumption applies to the portfolio choices of the public, and of every intermediary, taken separately, it is possible that assets will be complements in the systems as a whole. This can happen whenever the public and intermediaries hold the same

---

[1] J. Tobin and W. C. Brainard, "Financial Intermediaries and the Effectiveness of Monetary Controls." Unpublished paper delivered at the meetings of the Econometric Society, December, 1962.

assets or whenever one intermediary holds as assets the liabilities of another intermediary."

Since it was not possible completely to separate individual holdings of demand deposits from holdings of financial intermediaries, it is possible that this error of measurement in the dependent variable accounts for the complementarity result. It is interesting to note that the pooled single equation least squares estimate of the demand function for savings and loan association shares indicates that demand deposits and savings and loan association shares are weak substitutes. Both the complementarity result from the demand deposit equation and the substitution result from the savings and loan association equations are consistent with the Tobin-Brainard hypothesis. The savings and loan demand function is not subject to the measurement error found in the demand deposit equation and thus suggests that demand deposits and savings and loan deposits are weak substitutes in the asset portfolios of individuals. The complementarity result from the demand deposit equation implies that the indirect effect of an increase in the rate of return on savings and loan association shares outweighed the direct effect, since the demand for demand deposits on the part of savings and loan associations is included in the measurement of the dependent variable.

5. Mutual savings bank deposits and demand deposits appear to be independent in the short run and substitutes in the long run. The weak complementary relationship between mutual savings deposits and demand deposits may be explained by a hypothesis similar to that previously described.

Single Equation Least Squares Estimates—Time Deposits

The single equation least squares estimates of the demand functions for time deposits for the individual years 1949–59 are listed in Table 5. The own price and cross substitution terms are summarized in Table 7, and the elasticities estimated at the means are listed in Table 8.

The Durbin-Watson statistic was employed to test the functional form, and the test revealed no significant departures from linearity.

The coefficients of the time deposit equations were tested for stability over time, and it was not possible to reject the hypothesis that the demand functions were stable over the time period. The appropriate F-statistic was,

$$F\ (p(k-1)(n-pk)\ =\ .555.$$

Pooling the individual cross sections for the entire period 1949–59, and constraining the coefficients to be constant over time yielded the following regression equation:

$$T = .122\ Y - 101\ r_d + 76\ r_t - 44\ r_s - 82\ r_m + 235\ D_m$$
$$\quad (.037) \qquad (37) \qquad (10) \qquad (10) \qquad (11) \qquad (25)$$

$$+\ 304\ \text{Cal} + 86\ \text{DC} + 204\ \text{Ill} + 69\ \text{NY} + 39\ \text{W}$$
$$\quad (40) \qquad\quad (39) \qquad\quad (35) \qquad\quad (32) \qquad\quad (28)$$

$$+\ 7\ \text{S} + 57\ \text{C} + 57\ \text{NE}.$$
$$(27) \quad\ (27) \quad\ (27)$$

The coefficient of multiple determination adjusted for degrees of freedom is .942. The own price elasticity, the cross elasticities, and the income elasticity are listed on the second line of Table 1.

The results of the pooled single equation least squares estimates may be summarized as follows:

1. The income elasticity of time deposits is .69, which is considerably lower than the income elasticity estimated for demand deposits. Inspection of Table 8 reveals that the income elasticity of time deposits was greater than the income elasticity of demand deposits in the early years of the period, but dropped sharply in the later years. This result sheds some light on the recent discussion concerning the income elasticity of the demand for money.

Milton Friedman has estimated a demand function for money and concludes that the income elasticity of the demand for money is approximately 1.8, implying that money is a "luxury" asset.[1] Friedman's estimates of the income elasticity are not strictly comparable to those of the present study insofar as different definitions of *money* and *income* were used in the two studies. Friedman's money series included time deposits in addition to currency and demand deposits, and Friedman's income series was adjusted net national product as opposed to the personal income series utilized in the present study. Friedman's inclusion of currency would tend to have the effect of reducing his income elasticity estimate, for Philip Cagen has demonstrated that the income elasticity of currency is less than that of demand deposits.[2]

---

[1] Milton Friedman, "The Demand for Money: Some Theoretical and Empirical Results," National Bureau of Economic Research, *Occasional Paper* 68, 1959.

[2] Philip Cagen, "The Demand for Currency Relative to the Total Money Supply " *Journal of Political Economy*, **LXVI** (August, 1958), 303–28.

The results listed in Table 8 suggest that the income elasticity of time deposits exceeded the income elasticity of demand deposits from 1949–53. If the income elasticity of time deposits had been substantially higher than that of demand deposits and currency in the period prior to 1949, the inclusion of time deposits in the definition of money may have been responsible for Friedman's high income elasticity. The period from 1954–59 shows a marked decline in the income elasticity of time deposits, and this might also explain why Friedman's demand function does a poor job of predicting the demand for money in this latter period.

2. The own price coefficient of time deposits is more than seven times its standard error and implies that an increase in the rate of return on time deposits will substantially increase the demand for time deposits. The interest elasticity estimated at the means is approximately +.50, implying an own price elasticity of −.50.

This result helps to clarify some of the apparent conflicts in the findings of various economists who have estimated demand functions for money, using different definitions of money. Friedman's findings suggest that the demand for money (defined as currency plus demand deposits plus time deposits in commercial banks) depends primarily upon income and is unaffected by changes in the rate of interest.[1] Latané, on the other hand, suggests that the rate of interest has a significant impact on the demand for money (defined as currency plus demand deposits).[2] Carl Christ in re-estimating Latané's demand function for money found that the interest rate impact was significantly reduced when time deposits were included in the definition of money.[3]

These apparently conflicting results can be reconciled by recognizing the dual role played by the rate of interest. When money is defined narrowly, the rate of interest represents the opportunity cost of holding money and the coefficient of the interest rate in the demand function for money narrowly defined is expected to be negative. Latané's estimate of this interest elasticity is approximately −.50. The interest rate, however, also assumes the role of a proxy variable for the yield on time deposits, and the estimate of the own interest elasticity for time deposits has been shown to be approximately +.50. Thus when money is defined to include time deposits, the two separate effects are likely to

[1] Milton Friedman, *op. cit.*
[2] H. A. Latané, *op. cit.*
[3] Carl F. Christ, *op. cit.*

be offsetting, resulting in a weak or insignificant relationship between the rate of interest and money broadly defined.

3. Demand deposits and time deposits appear to be substitutes, implying that an increase in service charges on demand deposits will increase the demand for time deposits. The cross elasticity estimated from the time deposit equation is .13, and does not differ significantly from the cross elasticity estimated from the demand deposit equation. The individual cross-section regressions indicate that demand deposits and time deposits are very weak substitutes and that the degree of substitutability declined over time.

4. The pooled regression equation implies that time deposits and savings and loan association shares are substitutes.

5. Mutual savings bank deposits and time deposits appear to be short-run substitutes.

Single Equation Least Squares Estimates—Savings and Loan Association Shares

The single equation least squares estimates of the demand functions for savings and loan association shares for the individual years 1949–59 are listed in Table 6. The own price and cross substitution terms are summarized in Table 7 and the elasticities estimated at the means are listed in Table 8.

The Durbin-Watson statistic was employed to test the functional form, and the test revealed no significant departures from linearity.

The coefficients of the savings and loan association demand functions were tested for stability over time, and it was not possible to reject the hypothesis that the demand functions were stable over time. The savings and loan demand functions, however, exhibit less stability than the demand functions for demand deposits and time deposits, implying that qualitative changes in the characteristics of the savings and loan association liabilities may have had some effect on reducing the stability of the demand functions over time. The value of the F-statistic employed in the stability test was

$$F \, p(k-1)(n-pk) \, = 1.14.$$

Pooling the individual cross sections for the entire period 1949–59,

30   **Estimation of Demand Functions for Financial Assets**

and constraining the coefficients to be constant over time yielded the following regression equation:

$$S = .069 \; Y - 48 \; r_d + .25 \; r_t + 9 \; r_s - 14 \; r_m + 66 \; D_m + .48 \; A$$
$$\quad (.008) \quad (19) \quad (5.39) \quad (5) \quad (6) \quad (14) \quad (.01)$$

$$- 177 \; \text{Cal} + 125 \; \text{DC} - 128 \; \text{Ill} - 118 \; \text{NY} - 114 \; \text{W}$$
$$\quad (21) \qquad\quad (21) \qquad\quad (18) \qquad\quad (17) \qquad\quad (15)$$

$$- 69 \; \text{S} - 94 \; \text{C} - 116 \; \text{NE.}$$
$$(14) \quad\;\; (14) \quad\;\; (16)$$

The coefficient of multiple determination adjusted for degrees of freedom is .968. The own price elasticity, the cross elasticities, and the income elasticity are listed on the third line of Table 1.

The results of the pooled single equation least squares estimates may be summarized as follows:

1. The income elasticity of savings and loan association shares appears to be very similar to that of time deposits and less than the income elasticity of demand deposits.

2. The own price coefficient has the expected sign, but the own price elasticity of savings and loan association shares is substantially lower than the own price elasticities of demand and time deposits.

3. Demand deposits and savings and loan association shares appear to be weak substitutes, but the substitution relationship appears to have strengthened over time.

4. Savings and loan association shares and time deposits appear to be independent of one another.

5. The demand for savings and loan association shares appears to be most strongly affected by the per capita advertising expenditures of savings and loan associations. The advertising coefficient is highly significant for all cross sections and is fifty times its standard error in the pooled regression.

A possible explanation for this significant relationship is that a supply rather than a demand phenomenon is observed in the regression coefficients. Assume, for example, that savings and loan associations determined the size of their advertising budget by a rule of thumb, which allocated a fixed percentage of total shares outstanding to advertising expenditures. If such a practice prevailed, the highly significant coefficient of per capita advertising expenditures would be misleading, in that it would reflect a supply phenomenon. In order to test this possible explanation, advertising expenditures were deflated by average savings and loan association shares outstanding, and the regressions recomputed. If the significant relationship between per capita advertising expenditures and savings and loan association shares was purely a supply phenomenon, one would expect a coefficient equal to zero for the adjusted advertising variable in the recomputed regression. The resulting regression indicated a coefficient which was positive and highly significant in all cross sections. This test suggests that the significant relationship observed in the original regression is indeed a demand phenomenon. It must be recalled that advertising expenditures include such items as gifts and premiums doled out by the associations. The results indicate that gifts and premiums in addition to the informational services provided by advertising have a significant effect on the demand for savings and loan association shares.

It is interesting to note that advertising expenditures by savings and loan associations had no significant effect on the demand for demand deposits and time deposits. This result, coupled with the weak substitution coefficients derived from the savings and loan association equations, suggests that demand deposits and time deposits are not as close substitutes for savings and loan association shares as it is usually assumed. The significant advertising coefficient in the savings and loan association demand equation suggests that assets other than demand deposits and time deposits have been substituted for savings and loan association shares.

Efficient Estimation of the Demand Functions for Liquid Assets

The data described in the preceding section lend themselves to an estimation procedure developed by Arnold Zellner which yields coefficient estimators which are asymptotically more efficient than single equation least squares estimators.[1]

The demand function for a particular asset may be considered as a single equation from a system of equations consisting of demand func-

---

[1] Arnold Zellner, "An Efficient Method of Estimating Seemingly Unrelated Regressions and Tests for Aggregation Bias," *Journal of American Statistical Association*, **LVII** (June, 1962), 348–68. The estimates presented in this section were computed from a Fortran program developed by Arnold Zellner and Arthur Stroud at the University of Wisconsin.

tions for various assets. Thus one may regard

(3.5) $$y_\mu = X_\mu \beta_\mu + e_\mu$$

as the μth equation of an M equation regression system with y_μ a $S \times 1$ vector of observations on the μth asset, X_μ a $S \times j$ matrix of observations on the J "independent" variables, β_μ a $J \times 1$ vector of regression coefficients, and e_μ a $S \times 1$ vector of random disturbances. The system of which (3.5) is an equation may be written as

(3.6)
$$
\begin{bmatrix} y_1 \\ y_2 \\ \vdots \\ y_M \end{bmatrix}
=
\begin{bmatrix} X_1 & 0 & \cdots & 0 \\ 0 & X_2 & \cdots & 0 \\ \vdots & \vdots & & \vdots \\ 0 & 0 & \cdots & X_M \end{bmatrix}
\begin{bmatrix} \beta_1 \\ \beta_2 \\ \vdots \\ \beta_M \end{bmatrix}
+
\begin{bmatrix} e_1 \\ e_2 \\ \vdots \\ e_M \end{bmatrix} ;
$$

(3.7) $$y = X\beta + e,$$

where $y \equiv [y_1', y_2', \ldots, y_M']'$, $\beta \equiv [\beta_1', \beta_2', \ldots, \beta_M']'$, $e \equiv [e_1', e_2', \ldots, e_M']'$, and X is the block-diagonal matrix of (3.6).

The $M \times 1$ disturbance vector of (3.7) is assumed to have the following variance-covariance matrix.

(3.8)
$$
\Sigma = V(e) =
\begin{bmatrix}
\sigma_{11}I & \sigma_{12}I & \cdots & \sigma_{1M}I \\
\sigma_{21}I & \sigma_{22}I & \cdots & \sigma_{2M}I \\
\vdots & & & \vdots \\
\sigma_{M1}I & \sigma_{M2}I & \cdots & \sigma_{MM}I
\end{bmatrix}
$$

$$
=
\begin{bmatrix}
\sigma_{11} & \sigma_{12} & \cdots & \sigma_{1M} \\
\sigma_{21} & \sigma_{22} & \cdots & \sigma_{2M} \\
\vdots & & & \vdots \\
\sigma_{M1} & \sigma_{M2} & \cdots & \sigma_{MM}
\end{bmatrix} \cdot I,
$$

where I is a $S \times S$ unit matrix and $\sigma_{\mu\mu}' = E(e_{\mu s}e_{\mu's})$ for $s = 1, \ldots, S$ and $\mu, \mu' = 1. \ldots, M$.

For the data described in the preceding section, (3.6) reduces to

$$(3.9) \qquad \begin{bmatrix} y_d \\ y_t \\ y_{\bar{s}} \end{bmatrix} = \begin{bmatrix} X_d & 0 & 0 \\ 0 & X_t & 0 \\ 0 & 0 & X_{\bar{s}} \end{bmatrix} \begin{bmatrix} \beta_d \\ \beta_t \\ \beta_{\bar{s}} \end{bmatrix} + \begin{bmatrix} e_d \\ e_t \\ e_{\bar{s}} \end{bmatrix},$$

where the subscripts d, t, $\bar{s}$, refer respectively to the assets, demand deposits, time deposits, and savings and loan association shares. The variance-covariance matrix (3.8) reduces to

$$(3.10) \qquad \Sigma = V(e) = \begin{bmatrix} \sigma_{dd}I & \sigma_{dt}I & \sigma_{d\bar{s}}I \\ \sigma_{td}I & \sigma_{tt}I & \sigma_{t\bar{s}}I \\ \sigma_{\bar{s}d}I & \sigma_{\bar{s}t}I & \sigma_{\bar{s}\bar{s}}I \end{bmatrix} = \begin{bmatrix} \sigma_{dd} & \sigma_{dt} & \sigma_{ds} \\ \sigma_{td} & \sigma_{tt} & \sigma_{ts} \\ \sigma_{\bar{s}d} & \sigma_{\bar{s}t} & \sigma_{\bar{s}\bar{s}} \end{bmatrix} \cdot I.$$

The form of (3.10) is such that there are correlations between the disturbances or dependent variables relating to a particular state, but no such correlations are assumed to exist among states. Moreover, the form of (3.10) implies that disturbance variances and covariances are assumed to be constant from state to state.

Given the regression system in (3.9), it is possible to construct the "pure" Aitken estimator of the coefficient vector which is

$$(3.11) \qquad b^* = (X' \Sigma^{-1} X)^{-1} X' \Sigma^{-1} y$$

and its covariance matrix,

$$(3.12) \qquad V(b^*) = (X' \Sigma^{-1} X)^{-1}.$$

As Σ is generally unknown, an estimate of the disturbance variance-covariance matrix is formed from the single equation least squares residuals. The resulting estimator of β has the property of being asymptotically more efficient than the single equation least squares estimator. The gain in efficiency occurs because the Aitken estimator of the coefficients of a single equation takes account of the zero restrictions on the coefficients of the other equations. If the non-zero submatrices of X in (3.6) are all equal; that is, $X_1 = X_2 = \ldots = X_M$, then the Aitken estimator reduces to the single equation least squares estimator.

The coefficients of the demand functions for demand deposits, time deposits, and savings and loan association shares, derived from the efficient estimation technique, are listed in Tables 9–11. The summaries

34   **Estimation of Demand Functions for Financial Assets**

of the own and cross price terms are listed in Table 12; and income, own price, and cross elasticities are listed in Table 13.

The resulting coefficients do not significantly differ from the single equation least squares estimates because the non-zero submatrices of X in (3.9) are nearly identical. As the demand for different liquid assets is affected by roughly the same set of independent variables, the number of zero restrictions implicit in (3.9) is substantially reduced, with the result that the potential gain in efficiency from the Aitken estimator cannot be exploited.

Restricted Efficient Estimation

The estimates of the demand functions derived in the preceding section suggest the possibility of subjecting the theory of rational consumers' behavior to empirical test. In particular, one may inquire whether or not the traditional theory of consumers' choice can be usefully applied to behavioral decisions regarding the choice of liquid assets. The theory of consumer choice postulates the familiar "Slutsky condition" that

$$(3.13) \qquad X_{ji} = \frac{\partial x_j}{\partial p_i} + x_i \frac{\partial x_j}{\partial Y} = \frac{\partial x_i}{\partial p_j} + x_j \frac{\partial x_i}{\partial Y} = X_{ij}.$$

This equation separates the effects of a change in the price of the non-pecuniary services rendered by the ith asset on the quantity demanded of the non-pecuniary services rendered by the jth asset into a income effect and a substitution effect, where X_{ji} represents the substitution effect, $-x_i \, \partial x_j/\partial Y$ represents the income effect, and the total effect is given by $\partial x_j/\partial p_i$. Traditional consumer theory postulates that the substitution effects of a change in the price of the ith service flow on the demand for the jth service is symmetrical with the substitution effect of a change in the price of the jth service flow on the demand for the ith service.

The simpler "Hotelling condition,"

$$(3.14) \qquad \frac{\partial x_j}{\partial p_i} = \frac{\partial x_i}{\partial p_j} = \frac{\partial x_j}{\partial (r_0 - r_i)} = \frac{\partial x_i}{\partial (r_0 - r_j)}$$

is approximately satisfied if the income effects are either negligible, as compared with the substitution effects, or are of equal importance for the service flows considered.

The theoretical conditions, (3.13) and (3.14), related to the demand of a single individual, whereas the statistical results of the preceding sections are the aggregated demands of a large number of individuals. As Herman Wold points out, the "Slutsky condition" has no direct analogue for aggregated market demands unless very rigid assumptions are employed.[1] It can, however, be shown that the simpler "Hotelling condition" has the property that, if it is satisfied for all individuals, it will also be satisfied for the market as a whole.[2] It is therefore possible to test the hypothesis that the Hotelling symmetry condition holds for the appropriate coefficients of the demand functions for liquid assets, by assuming that r_0 is constant. If r_0 is constant, then

$$(3.15) \qquad \frac{\partial x_i}{\partial r_j} = \frac{\partial x_j}{\partial (r_0 - r_j)} \frac{\partial (r_0 - r_j)}{\partial r_j} = -\frac{\partial x_i}{\partial (r_0 - r_j)},$$

and

$$(3.16) \qquad \frac{\partial x_i}{\partial r_j} = \frac{\partial x_j}{\partial r_i}.$$

Letting q_{ij} denote $\partial x_i/\partial r_j$, the "Hotelling condition" as applied to the preceding estimates suggests the following linear restrictions on the coefficients of the regression system described in (3.9):

$$(3.17) \qquad \begin{aligned} q_{dt} &= q_{td} \\ q_{d\bar{s}} &= q_{\bar{s}d} \\ q_{t\bar{s}} &= q_{\bar{s}t}. \end{aligned}$$

The test of the "Hotelling condition" is simply a test of a general linear hypothesis involving the β vector, and may be described by

$$(3.18) \qquad C\beta = 0,$$

where C is an arbitrary matrix and β is the coefficient vector described in (3.9).

We wish to test the hypothesis that particular elements of the β vector are equal. The relevant elements are the corresponding cross price terms. We wish particularly to test the hypothesis that the effect

---

[1] Herman Wold, *Demand Analysis* (New York: John Wiley & Sons, Inc., 1953), chap. 7.

[2] See Henry Schultz, *The Theory and Measurement of Demand* (Chicago: University of Chicago Press, 1938), chap. **XIX,** 628–35.

of a change in the price of the ith asset on the demand for the jth asset is equal to the effect of a change in the price of the jth asset on the demand for the ith asset. The C matrix will be $w \times MJ$, where w denotes the number of restrictions on the coefficients. A row of the C matrix will contain zeros, a one, and a minus one as elements. Each row will then select the appropriate coefficients in the β vector and impose the equality restriction.

For testing the linear hypothesis, (3.17), we utilize the following F-statistic described by S. N. Roy:[1]

(3.19)
$$F_{w,(n-m)} = \frac{n-m}{w} \frac{y'\Sigma^{-1}X(X'\Sigma^{-1}X)^{-1}C'[C(X'\Sigma^{-1}X)^{-1}C']^{-1}C(X'\Sigma^{-1}X)^{-1}X'\Sigma^{-1}y}{y'\Sigma^{-1}y - y'\Sigma^{-1}X(X'\Sigma^{-1}X)^{-1}X'\Sigma^{-1}y}$$

with $n = MS$, the number of observations, $m = MJ$, the number of independent variables in the entire set of equations, and w = number of restrictions implied by the hypothesis. As Σ is generally unknown, it is replaced by an estimate of the disturbance variance-covariance matrix formed from the single equation least squares residuals.

The test was applied to each equation set in the eleven years, with the result that for all years it was not possible to reject the hypothesis that the "Hotelling conditions" were satisfied. This test lends much credence to the belief that the traditional theory of consumer behavior can be applied to the theory of the demand for financial assets.

Theil and Goldberger have demonstrated the desirability of including relevant a priori information in the estimation procedure.[2] It is possible to estimate (3.9) in light of the "Hotelling condition" restrictions (3.17). In order to include the "Hotelling conditions" in the estimation procedure, it is necessary to minimize

(3.20)　　　$(y - X\beta)' \Sigma^{-1} (y - X\beta) - \mu'(R\beta - r)$

with respect to the elements of β, where y, X, and β are as defined in Eq. (3.9), μ' is a vector of Lagrange multipliers, R is a matrix, and r is a vector, together defining the restrictions. The estimation obtained from this minimization will satisfy the condition that

(3.21)　　　　　　　$R\hat{\beta} = r.$

---

[1] S. N. Roy, *Some Aspects of Multivariate Analysis* (New York: John Wiley & Sons, Inc., 1957).

[2] H. Theil and A. S. Goldberger, "On Pure and Mixed Statistical Estimation in Economics," *International Economic Review*, II (1960).

Given the particular restrictions implied by (3.17), R is simply equal to the C matrix defined in (3.18), and r is a zero vector.

The restricted efficient estimates of the coefficients of the demand functions for demand deposits, time deposits, and savings and loan association shares are listed in Tables 14, 15, and 16 respectively. The restricted efficient estimates differ from the efficient and single equation least squares estimates owing to the gain in efficiency resulting from the addition of restrictions on the coefficient estimates. A summary of own price and cross substitution coefficients is listed in Table 17, and a summary of income, own price, and cross elasticities is included in Table 18.

The results of the restricted efficient cross-section regressions may be summarized as follows:

1. The income coefficients for all the assets are significantly positive, implying that each of the assets is a "superior" asset.[1] The income elasticity for demand deposits is approximately unity in all years. The income elasticity of time deposits is greater than the income elasticity of demand deposits in the early years; the time deposit income elasticity, however, falls sharply in the later years of the analysis. The savings and loan association shares have an income elasticity which is lower than that of demand deposits and time deposits.

2. The own price coefficients of demand deposits and time deposits are highly significant; the demand for savings and loan association shares, however, seems to be quite insensitive to changes in the rate of return on these shares.

3. Demand deposits and time deposits appear to be very weak substitutes in the early years of the analysis. In nine out of the eleven cross sections, the cross substitution effect between demand deposits and time deposits implies independence in demand.

4. The liabilities of savings and loan associations and demand deposits in commercial banks appear to be independent in demand. The cross substitution coefficient between demand deposits and savings and loan association shares does not significantly differ from zero in any of the eleven years. The relatively high standard errors of the cross substitution terms cannot be explained by

---

[1] The traditional tests of significance employed in this section must be regarded with some caution since they do not take explicit account of pre-testing.

arguing that the interest rates are highly collinear. Indeed, the simple correlations among interest rates are very small. Moreover, if multicollinearity was a serious problem, one would not expect to find significant coefficients for the own price terms. The significance of the own price terms, in addition to the low degree of multicollinearity as measured by the simple correlation coefficients among interest rates, lends support to the interpretation that the liabilities of the non-bank financial intermediaries under study are not close substitutes for demand deposits.

5. Demand deposits and mutual savings bank deposits appear to be short-run complements and long-run substitutes. The complementary relationship lends support to the Tobin-Brainard hypothesis that complementarity relationships may exist whenever the public and financial intermediaries hold the same assets.

6. The substitution coefficients between time deposits and savings and loan association shares do not significantly differ from zero in any of the eleven cross-section regressions. The implication of this finding is that time deposits and savings and loan association shares are independent in demand.

7. Time deposits and mutual savings bank deposits appear to be short-run substitutes. The substitution relationship is, however, quite weak in the later-year regressions. The coefficients of the mutual savings bank dummy variable are positive in the early years of the analysis, implying a long-run complementarity relationship between the two assets. In the later years, both the coefficients of the dummy variable and the substitution coefficients imply that time deposits and mutual savings deposits are independent in demand.

8. Savings and loan association shares appear to be weak substitutes for mutual savings bank deposits in the short run. The coefficients of the mutual savings bank dummy variable imply a weak long-run complementarity relationship.

It was shown in Chapter 2 that the substitution relationships between money, as it is narrowly defined, and other liquid assets play a crucial role in determining the effectiveness of monetary policy. One of the necessary conditions for a loss in the effectiveness of monetary policy due to financial intermediation is a strong substitution relationship between money and other financial assets. The results of the restricted efficient estimation procedure tend to reject the hypothesis that time deposits, savings and loan association shares, and mutual savings bank deposits are close substitutes for demand deposits.

Testing the Stability of the Demand Functions Over Time

The discussion of the effectiveness of monetary policy underscored the importance of the stability of the demand function for money as a key determinant of the potential effectiveness of any monetary action. The tests of the stability hypothesis based on the single equation least squares estimates indicated that it was not possible to reject the hypothesis that the demand functions for demand deposits, time deposits, and savings and loan association shares were stable over the time period 1949–59.

It was not possible to compute a pooled regression for the restricted efficient estimates over the entire time period, nor was it possible to test the stability hypothesis directly from the restricted efficient estimates owing to capacity limitations on the computer program. Pooled regressions of the restricted efficient estimates were, however, computed for the periods 1949–53 and 1954–58. These pooled regressions are listed in Table 19 and a matrix of own price, cross, and income elasticities for each of the pooled regressions is listed in Table 2.

TABLE 2. MATRIX OF OWN PRICE, CROSS, AND INCOME ELASTICITIES

Pooled Restricted Efficient Estimates

Dependent variable	Elasticity Estimates at the Mean				
	η_{xd}	η_{xt}	η_{xs}	η_{xm}	η_{xy}
1949–53					
Demand deposits	−.32	.21	−.01	−.13	.98
Time deposits	.12	−.54	.05	.61	.95
Savings and loan association shares	−.01	.02	−.01	.18	.63
1954–58					
Demand deposits	−.38	−.06	.19	−.17	.94
Time deposits	−.03	−.81	−.11	.39	.49
Savings and loan association shares	.06	−.09	−.12	.22	.59

Although it was not possible to reject the stability hypothesis, a review of the coefficients in the demand functions for individual years suggests that these coefficients have been changing in a remarkably regular fashion. This observation is confirmed by the pooled regression estimates. One observes, for example, a gradual decline in the income coefficients of both demand deposits and time deposits, and a corresponding increase in the income coefficient of savings and loan association shares. Moreover, the own price and cross price terms reflect similar regular patterns of change. This is particularly true of the savings and loan association shares own price coefficient and of the cross substitution coefficients between demand deposits and time deposits, demand deposits and savings and loan association shares, and time deposits and savings and loan association shares. Demand deposits and time deposits appear to have become poorer substitutes in the postwar period, whereas demand deposits and savings and loan association shares seem to have become better substitutes.

The theory of consumer behavior described in Chapter 2 suggested that the coefficients of the demand functions for any asset could in principle be affected by changes in the quality of other assets. There is evidence that there were quality changes in the characteristics of the liabilities of savings and loan associations. The 1950 revision of the Federal Savings and Loan Insurance Corporation insurance regulations, which increased insurance coverage on savings and loan association shares to $10,000, presumably changed the quality of these assets in the direction of making savings and loan association shares more comparable to demand deposits and time deposits.

It is interesting to note that in 1951 and 1952 the cross substitution coefficients between demand deposits and savings and loan association shares, and time deposits and savings and loan association shares changed signs. In the period before the change in insurance provisions, the cross substitution terms implied a non-significant complementary relationship between demand deposits and savings and loan association shares and time deposits and savings and loan association shares. In the period following the change in insurance provisions, the signs of the cross substitution terms imply substitution relationships. Whether quality changes caused the observed changes in the estimated coefficients cannot be unambiguously determined. What is clear, however, is that the observed changes in the coefficients are not statistically significant and therefore one must reject the hypothesis that quality changes have had substantial effects on the stability of the parameters of the demand functions.

As a final test of the stability hypothesis, the parameter estimates of the demand functions during periods of "easy" monetary policy were compared with estimates of the demand function parameters during periods of "tight" monetary policy.

Gurley and Shaw have suggested that periods of monetary stringency could induce financial innovations which would have the effect of reducing the stability of the demand for money. This hypothesis can be investigated by comparing pooled regressions for years of monetary ease with pooled regressions for years of monetary stringency. The years 1954 and 1958 were selected to represent years of relative monetary ease and the years 1956, 1957, and 1959 were selected to represent years of relative monetary stringency. The estimated coefficients and their standard errors are listed in Table 3.

TABLE 3. MATRIX OF OWN PRICE, CROSS AND INCOME COEFFICIENTS

Pooled Restricted Efficient Estimates

Dependent variable	Independent Variables				
	P_d	P_t	P_s	P_m	Y
"Easy" Money Period 1954, 1958					
Demand deposits	−498	−9	33	−78	.364
	(105)	(28)	(28)	(42)	(.044)
Time deposits	−9	−93	10	81	.084
	(28)	(18)	(11)	(35)	(.036)
Savings and loan association shares	33	10	−24	22	.069
	(28)	(11)	(15)	(18)	(.020)
"Tight" Money Period 1956, 1957, 1959					
Demand deposits	−494	1	31	−93	.345
	(80)	(23)	(25)	(34)	(.033)
Time deposits	1	−101	4	67	.092
	(23)	(18)	(12)	(31)	(.029)
Savings and loan association shares	31	4	−28	52	.078
	(25)	(12)	(17)	(17)	(.017)

42   *Estimation of Demand Functions for Financial Assets*

Inspection of Table 3 reveals that the coefficients of the demand functions estimated during periods of relative monetary ease do not significantly differ from the corresponding coefficients estimated during periods of monetary stringency. The results of this test are consistent with the following alternative hypotheses:

1. That monetary stringency does not induce financial innovation.
2. That induced financial innovation has no significant effect on the parameters of the demand functions for liquid assets.

Regardless of which hypothesis is correct, the results clearly indicate that the demand functions for demand deposits, time deposits, and savings and loan association shares have exhibited remarkable stability over periods of monetary ease and periods of monetary stringency, implying that monetary policy effectiveness has not been reduced as a result of an unstable demand function for money.

Conclusions

The results summarized in this study have implications for monetary theory, the conduct and effectiveness of monetary policy, and the general question of monetary controls.

Recent monetary theory has placed much emphasis on the role of financial intermediaries in the monetary process. The attention focused on these intermediaries is based on the belief that the liabilities of financial intermediaries are close substitutes for money. The empirical results presented in this study cast substantial doubt on this widely held assumption. Indeed, during the postwar period, when financial intermediary liabilities grew at an extraordinary rate, it was impossible to reject the hypothesis that the demand for money was independent of changes in the yields on the liabilities of financial intermediaries. In particular, the evidence supports the view that the demand for demand deposits was not significantly affected by changes in the yields on time deposits, savings and loan association shares, and mutual savings bank deposits. Since data limitations precluded the explicit estimation of demand functions for currency holdings, one cannot rule out the possibility that the liabilities of financial intermediaries are substitutes for currency. There is, however, no independent evidence to support this hypothesis and it deserves further investigation.

Since demand deposits do not appear to be close substitutes for other liquid assets, the investigation undertaken here suggests that a narrow definition of money be employed in further empirical studies. Utilizing the narrow definition of money avoids many of the conceptual problems of interpreting interest rate and income effects which will vary according to the definition of money adopted. The variety of definitions of

43

44   *Conclusions*

money employed in previous empirical studies has unfortunately confounded the economist's knowledge of the relevant parameters of the demand function, and this confusion can be avoided by a stricter adherence to a single definition. Adoption of a narrow definition of money need not preclude an analysis of the effects of other liquid assets on the monetary mechanism; these assets, however, should be introduced into a monetary model by means other than defining money more broadly.

The findings of the study cast doubt on the assertion that the growth of financial intermediaries has substantially reduced the effectiveness of monetary policy. The evidence does not support the view that the demand function for money has become less stable, nor does the evidence support the view that the demand for money and the supply of money are interdependent as a result of induced financial innovation. The results do, however, suggest that changes in the quality of financial assets may affect the parameters of the demand function for money. Although the evidence does not establish the proposition that quality changes have had substantial effects, the question deserves further investigation at both the theoretical and empirical level.

The suggestion of extending monetary controls to non-bank financial intermediaries has already provoked a host of criticisms. The evidence presented in this paper strongly suggests that further extension of monetary controls be held in abeyance until such time when there exists more empirical support for the necessity of such controls. The implication of the analysis is that the effectiveness of monetary policy has not been impaired as a result of financial intermediation, and the findings lend no support to the proposed policies which seek to extend monetary controls to non-bank financial intermediaries.

APPENDIX A

Demand Function Estimates

*Demand Deposits, Time Deposits,
Savings and Loan Association Shares*

TABLE 4. DEMAND DEPOSITS—DEMAND FUNCTIONS

Single Equation Least Squares Estimates

1949-59

Year	Y	r_d	r_t	r_s	r_m	D_m	I	Cal	DC	Ill	NY	W	S	C	NE	R^2
1949	.475	642	−147	23	144	−319	464	50	150	200	751	66	−20	85	57	.902
	(.095)	(204)	(84)	(39)	(80)	(138)	(233)	(274)	(264)	(238)	(217)	(217)	(205)	(216)	(238)	
1950	.483	641	−154	53	203	−425	452	−5	136	141	705	12	−84	20	−16	.902
	(.096)	(225)	(85)	(45)	(106)	(187)	(249)	(304)	(296)	(250)	(225)	(240)	(222)	(232)	(251)	
1951	.476	628	−65	72	181	−414	441	−148	79	20	613	−122	−220	−111	−170	.906
	(.079)	(217)	(79)	(51)	(106)	(195)	(250)	(305)	(292)	(240)	(219)	(235)	(221)	(224)	(242)	
1952	.454	660	−19	47	97	−281	415	−107	124	65	628	−91	−181	−65	−144	.887
	(.094)	(231)	(64)	(49)	(86)	(172)	(257)	(314)	(300)	(259)	(239)	(252)	(225)	(237)	(253)	
1953	.411	629	−28	46	154	−411	454	−85	166	103	638	−72	−156	−25	−121	.883
	(.095)	(202)	(64)	(58)	(81)	(170)	(250)	(363)	(337)	(301)	(278)	(294)	(268)	(278)	(292)	
1954	.399	639	3	26	145	−379	480	11	260	140	644	−18	−124	−10	−109	.882
	(.086)	(188)	(71)	(58)	(82)	(176)	(256)	(362)	(343)	(299)	(279)	(300)	(274)	(278)	(290)	
1955	.407	703	3	23	186	−466	568	8	249	124	593	−36	−128	−29	−134	.880
	(.082)	(184)	(73)	(61)	(87)	(192)	(259)	(371)	(351)	(304)	(286)	(311)	(285)	(289)	(299)	
1956	.364	559	−34	44	150	−413	468	31	296	158	651	16	−85	16	−82	.877
	(.075)	(177)	(80)	(79)	(79)	(184)	(256)	(443)	(411)	(369)	(362)	(378)	(356)	(351)	(372)	
1957	.338	594	59	37	146	−430	371	−76	249	53	536	−64	−188	−58	−166	.889
	(.069)	(175)	(70)	(69)	(74)	(191)	(246)	(387)	(343)	(305)	(306)	(314)	(300)	(290)	(306)	
1958	.302	566	36	−42	156	−478	272	417	735	452	900	354	221	327	218	.878
	(.075)	(175)	(73)	(62)	(76)	(206)	(266)	(412)	(366)	(332)	(330)	(343)	(320)	(315)	(330)	
1959	.331	581	72	14	105	−354	271	40	386	74	543	26	−94	−8	−88	.897
	(.067)	(154)	(71)	(79)	(63)	(180)	(234)	(420)	(385)	(349)	(344)	(361)	(344)	(338)	(345)	

TABLE 5. TIME DEPOSITS—DEMAND FUNCTIONS

Single Equation Least Squares Estimates

1949-59

Year	Y	r_d	r_t	r_s	r_m	D_m	Cal	DC	Ill	NY	W	S	C	NE	R^2
1949	.208 (.058)	-127 (125)	194 (51)	11 (24)	-224 (50)	444 (85)	-81 (162)	-287 (158)	-158 (144)	-240 (130)	-292 (126)	-316 (118)	-287 (124)	-284 (138)	.842
1950	.232 (.055)	-111 (129)	216 (48)	9 (25)	-271 (61)	527 (107)	-160 (170)	-355 (167)	-220 (142)	-293 (126)	-362 (132)	-366 (121)	-339 (126)	-326 (137)	.843
1951	.195 (.051)	-65 (140)	124 (50)	-20 (32)	-290 (69)	575 (126)	68 (188)	-162 (182)	-26 (150)	-139 (136)	-157 (141)	-169 (131)	-144 (133)	-67 (144)	.820
1952	.191 (.062)	-227 (153)	92 (42)	-42 (32)	-194 (57)	436 (115)	120 (202)	-112 (195)	44 (169)	-47 (154)	-114 (159)	-109 (140)	-92 (148)	-41 (158)	.792
1953	.187 (.064)	-158 (136)	86 (43)	-50 (39)	-188 (54)	436 (114)	176 (236)	-57 (219)	95 (198)	-19 (181)	-56 (188)	-72 (169)	-41 (176)	1 (184)	.788
1954	.156 (.060)	-158 (132)	79 (50)	-52 (41)	-173 (58)	417 (124)	241 (245)	2 (232)	165 (204)	55 (190)	5 (200)	-30 (180)	8 (183)	55 (190)	.764
1955	.147 (.059)	-136 (132)	89 (52)	-43 (44)	-161 (62)	405 (137)	225 (253)	2 (240)	144 (210)	44 (197)	-20 (209)	-55 (189)	-14 (192)	25 (197)	.746
1956	.133 (.056)	-118 (133)	122 (59)	-76 (59)	-140 (59)	380 (138)	279 (313)	83 (291)	207 (264)	73 (258)	28 (264)	-17 (246)	43 (242)	57 (255)	.738
1957	.137 (.060)	-61 (154)	139 (61)	-15 (61)	-54 (65)	199 (168)	-32 (317)	-177 (280)	-22 (254)	-200 (253)	-231 (252)	-279 (238)	-170 (30)	-242 (240)	.692
1958	.121 (.069)	-5 (165)	201 (68)	-50 (58)	-46 (72)	183 (194)	56 (348)	-73 (308)	43 (287)	-164 (283)	-191 (283)	-269 (258)	-143 (255)	-212 (264)	.676
1959	.112 (.080)	-89 (186)	134 (85)	-49 (95)	-66 (77)	230 (219)	184 (467)	-8 (429)	122 (396)	-8 (388)	-62 (396)	-143 (376)	-35 (367)	-77 (371)	.592

TABLE 6. SAVINGS AND LOAN ASSOCIATION SHARES—DEMAND FUNCTIONS

Single Equation Least Squares Estimates

1949–59

Year	Y	r_d	r_t	r_s	r_m	A	D_m	Cal	DC	Ill	NY	W	S	C	NE	R^2
1949	.042 (.021)	1 (45)	−8 (19)	−1 (10)	−33 (18)	.499 (.084)	75 (31)	−37 (63)	118 (67)	−32 (56)	−41 (47)	−24 (48)	3 (45)	−13 (46)	−16 (51)	.915
1950	.042 (.020)	−35 (48)	−4 (18)	5 (11)	−47 (23)	.557 (.082)	99 (39)	−97 (74)	73 (80)	−79 (63)	−62 (49)	−62 (55)	−34 (50)	−45 (52)	−45 (55)	.928
1951	.045 (.019)	−71 (54)	−8 (19)	8 (14)	−61 (26)	.501 (.070)	128 (47)	−115 (80)	125 (84)	−81 (65)	−71 (53)	−75 (57)	−46 (54)	−59 (54)	−55 (57)	.934
1952	.053 (.024)	−86 (59)	0 (16)	11 (13)	−55 (22)	.499 (.063)	126 (44)	−161 (86)	97 (89)	−122 (73)	0 (61)	−1 (64)	−0 (58)	0 (61)	0 (63)	.933
1953	.057 (.030)	−77 (65)	−11 (20)	22 (20)	−46 (26)	.469 (.064)	116 (54)	−166 (119)	57 (120)	−149 (103)	−105 (88)	−124 (92)	−94 (84)	−104 (87)	−109 (90)	.913
1954	.042 (.027)	−90 (58)	−37 (22)	9 (18)	−33 (26)	.548 (.058)	102 (55)	−104 (110)	123 (110)	−95 (94)	−17 (84)	−33 (89)	−6 (80)	−27 (81)	−29 (84)	.937
1955	.068 (.030)	−106 (64)	−17 (21)	52 (16)	−65 (31)	.513 (.052)	186 (69)	−330 (100)	−6 (96)	−246 (81)	−189 (70)	−245 (75)	−190 (61)	−218 (66)	−223 (69)	.972
1956	.075 (.033)	−137 (77)	−30 (35)	−30 (35)	−82 (35)	.452 (.049)	237 (80)	−279 (184)	142 (173)	−171 (156)	−118 (150)	−164 (153)	−110 (143)	−160 (141)	−150 (148)	.924
1957	.068 (.031)	−101 (77)	−25 (31)	13 (30)	−80 (32)	.478 (.048)	253 (84)	−230 (157)	148 (141)	−122 (126)	−60 (128)	−100 (126)	−47 (119)	−99 (114)	−93 (121)	.945
1958	.084 (.037)	−116 (85)	−25 (35)	51 (30)	−75 (37)	.441 (.049)	250 (99)	−334 (178)	121 (161)	−232 (148)	−195 (145)	−254 (145)	−181 (133)	−220 (130)	−236 (136)	.939
1959	.103 (.042)	−81 (98)	2 (43)	47 (49)	−77 (40)	.420 (.049)	269 (112)	−423 (238)	148 (221)	−289 (203)	−299 (198)	−328 (202)	−248 (192)	−286 (187)	−309 (190)	.937

TABLE 7. MATRIX OF OWN PRICE AND CROSS SUBSTITUTION TERMS

Single Equation Least Squares Estimates

1949–59

Year	Dependent Variable	Independent Variables			
		P_d	P_t	P_s	P_m
1949	D	−642 (204)	147 (84)	−23 (39)	−144 (80)
	T	127 (125)	−194 (51)	−11 (24)	224 (50)
	S	−1 (45)	8 (19)	1 (10)	33 (18)
1950	D	−641 (225)	154 (85)	−53 (45)	−203 (106)
	T	111 (129)	−216 (48)	−9 (25)	271 (61)
	S	35 (48)	4 (18)	−5 (11)	47 (23)
1951	D	−628 (217)	65 (79)	−72 (51)	−181 (106)
	T	65 (140)	−124 (50)	20 (32)	290 (69)
	S	71 (54)	8 (19)	−8 (14)	61 (26)
1952	D	−660 (231)	19 (64)	−47 (49)	−97 (86)
	T	227 (153)	−92 (42)	42 (32)	194 (57)
	S	86 (59)	0 (16)	−11 (13)	55 (22)
1953	D	−629 (202)	28 (64)	−46 (58)	−154 (81)
	T	158 (136)	−86 (43)	50 (39)	188 (54)
	S	77 (65)	11 (20)	−22 (20)	46 (26)
1954	D	−639 (188)	−3 (71)	−26 (58)	−145 (82)
	T	158 (132)	−79 (50)	52 (41)	173 (58)
	S	90 (58)	37 (22)	−9 (18)	33 (26)

Demand Function Estimates

TABLE 7. MATRIX OF OWN PRICE AND CROSS SUBSTITUTION TERMS—*(cont.)*

Single Equation Least Squares Estimates

1949–59

Year	Dependent Variable	Independent Variables			
		P_d	P_t	P_s	P_m
1955	D	−703 (184)	−3 (73)	−23 (61)	−186 (87)
	T	136 (132)	−89 (52)	43 (44)	161 (62)
	S	106 (64)	17 (21)	−52 (16)	65 (31)
1956	D	−559 (177)	34 (80)	−44 (79)	−150 (79)
	T	118 (133)	−122 (59)	76 (59)	140 (59)
	S	137 (77)	30 (35)	−30 (35)	82 (35)
1957	D	−594 (175)	−59 (70)	−37 (69)	−146 (74)
	T	61 (154)	−139 (61)	15 (61)	54 (65)
	S	101 (77)	25 (31)	−13 (30)	80 (32)
1958	D	−566 (175)	−36 (73)	−42 (62)	−156 (76)
	T	−5 (165)	−201 (68)	50 (58)	46 (72)
	S	116 (85)	25 (35)	−51 (30)	75 (37)
1959	D	−581 (154)	−72 (71)	−14 (79)	−105 (63)
	T	89 (186)	−134 (85)	49 (95)	66 (77)
	S	81 (98)	2 (43)	−47 (49)	77 (40)

Demand Function Estimates   **51**

TABLE 8. MATRIX OF OWN PRICE, CROSS, AND INCOME ELASTICITIES

Single Equation Least Squares Estimates

1949–59

Year	Dependent Variable	Elasticity Estimates at the Mean				
		η_{xd}	η_{xt}	η_{xs}	η_{xm}	η_{xy}
1949	D	−.32	.31	−.13	−.19	1.08
	T	.15	−.96	−.15	.70	1.13
	S	.00	.12	.03	.30	.66
1950	D	−.31	.31	−.28	−.26	1.07
	T	.14	−1.12	−.12	.90	1.34
	S	.11	.06	−.19	.40	.63
1951	D	−.29	.13	−.36	−.23	1.08
	T	.08	−.66	.27	.97	1.16
	S	.20	.10	−.26	.48	.63
1952	D	−.28	.15	−.37	−.25	1.13
	T	.26	−.52	.55	.68	1.14
	S	.21	.00	−.30	.41	.67
1953	D	−.32	.07	−.25	−.22	1.03
	T	.19	−.51	.65	.66	1.11
	S	.17	.12	−.54	.31	.64
1954	D	−.35	−.01	−.14	−.22	1.00
	T	.20	−.48	.66	.60	.90
	S	.19	.38	−.18	.19	.41
1955	D	−.39	−.01	−.12	−.28	1.03
	T	.18	−.55	.54	.57	.86
	S	.14	.17	−1.01	.30	.52
1956	D	−.34	.10	−.24	−.24	.95
	T	.16	−.82	.94	.51	.79
	S	.25	.27	−.47	.40	.60
1957	L	−.43	−.23	−.22	−.26	.94
	T	.09	−1.09	.18	.19	.77
	S	.19	.26	−.21	.38	.51
1958	D	−.42	−.14	.25	−.28	.84
	T	−.01	−1.53	.57	.16	.63
	S	.21	.25	−.76	.33	.58
1959	D	−.46	−.31	−.09	−.20	.96
	T	.13	−1.04	.56	.22	.59
	S	.14	−.02	−.65	.32	.66

TABLE 9. DEMAND DEPOSITS—DEMAND FUNCTIONS

Efficient Estimates

1949–59

Year	Y	r_d	r_t	r_s	r_m	D_m	I	Cal	DC	Ill	NY	W	S	C	NE
1949	.476 (.095)	644 (204)	-146 (84)	22 (39)	144 (80)	-318 (138)	483 (222)	43 (272)	144 (263)	196 (238)	746 (216)	59 (216)	-27 (204)	78 (214)	50 (237)
1950	.482 (.096)	638 (225)	-155 (85)	55 (45)	204 (106)	-429 (187)	401 (236)	9 (303)	148 (296)	151 (250)	714 (224)	26 (239)	-70 (221)	35 (231)	-1 (250)
1951	.475 (.079)	625 (217)	-67 (79)	73 (51)	181 (106)	-416 (195)	401 (240)	-133 (304)	91 (291)	30 (239)	623 (218)	-108 (234)	-206 (219)	-97 (223)	-155 (241)
1952	.453 (.094)	657 (231)	-21 (64)	48 (49)	96 (86)	-282 (172)	387 (241)	-98 (313)	131 (300)	71 (259)	634 (238)	-82 (250)	-172 (223)	-56 (236)	-134 (251)
1953	.411 (.095)	629 (202)	-28 (64)	46 (58)	154 (81)	-411 (170)	461 (244)	-88 (363)	163 (336)	101 (301)	636 (278)	-74 (293)	-159 (268)	-28 (277)	-124 (291)
1954	.399 (.086)	639 (188)	3 (71)	26 (58)	145 (82)	-379 (176)	492 (249)	7 (362)	256 (342)	137 (298)	641 (279)	-23 (299)	-128 (273)	-15 (277)	-113 (289)
1955	.411 (.082)	714 (184)	13 (72)	32 (61)	183 (87)	-458 (192)	592 (253)	-50 (369)	193 (349)	76 (302)	545 (284)	-89 (309)	-180 (283)	-80 (287)	-186 (296)
1956	.367 (.075)	558 (177)	-31 (80)	46 (79)	151 (79)	-414 (184)	538 (249)	-11 (442)	258 (410)	127 (368)	619 (361)	-23 (376)	-124 (355)	-22 (350)	-124 (370)
1957	.344 (.069)	591 (175)	64 (70)	37 (69)	147 (74)	-430 (191)	490 (234)	-147 (385)	185 (341)	3 (303)	484 (304)	-128 (311)	-252 (297)	-121 (288)	-234 (303)
1958	.311 (.075)	559 (175)	43 (73)	-39 (62)	157 (76)	-476 (206)	428 (255)	310 (408)	639 (362)	374 (330)	820 (327)	257 (339)	126 (316)	233 (311)	117 (326)
1959	.336 (.067)	576 (154)	77 (70)	17 (79)	106 (63)	-353 (180)	370 (229)	-32 (418)	321 (383)	21 (348)	488 (343)	-40 (359)	-159 (342)	-72 (336)	-156 (343)

TABLE 10. TIME DEPOSITS—DEMAND FUNCTIONS

Efficient Estimates

1949–59

Year	Y	r_d	r_t	r_s	r_m	D_m	Cal	DC	Ill	NY	W	S	C	NE
1949	.208 (.058)	−127 (126)	194 (51)	11 (24)	−224 (50)	444 (85)	−81 (162)	−287 (158)	−158 (144)	−240 (130)	−292 (126)	−316 (118)	−287 (124)	−284 (138)
1950	.232 (.055)	−111 (129)	216 (48)	9 (25)	−271 (61)	527 (107)	−160 (170)	−355 (167)	−220 (142)	−293 (126)	−362 (132)	−366 (121)	−339 (126)	−326 (137)
1951	.195 (.051)	−65 (140)	124 (50)	−20 (32)	−290 (69)	575 (126)	68 (188)	−162 (182)	−26 (150)	−139 (136)	−157 (140)	−169 (131)	−144 (133)	−67 (144)
1952	.190 (.062)	227 (153)	92 (42)	−42 (32)	−194 (57)	436 (115)	120 (202)	−121 (195)	44 (169)	−47 (154)	−114 (159)	−109 (140)	−92 (148)	−41 (158)
1953	.187 (.064)	−158 (136)	86 (43)	−50 (39)	−188 (54)	436 (114)	176 (236)	−57 (219)	95 (198)	−19 (181)	−56 (188)	−72 (169)	−41 (176)	1 (184)
1954	.156 (.060)	−158 (132)	79 (50)	−52 (41)	−173 (58)	417 (124)	241 (245)	7 (232)	165 (204)	55 (190)	5 (200)	−30 (180)	8 (183)	55 (190)
1955	.141 (.058)	−154 (131)	74 (51)	−57 (43)	−156 (62)	392 (137)	298 (248)	78 (235)	206 (206)	106 (193)	46 (205)	−1 (184)	48 (187)	88 (192)
1956	.133 (.056)	−118 (133)	122 (59)	−76 (59)	−140 (59)	380 (138)	279 (313)	83 (291)	207 (264)	73 (258)	28 (264)	−17 (246)	43 (242)	57 (255)
1957	.137 (.060)	−61 (154)	139 (61)	−15 (61)	−54 (65)	199 (168)	−32 (317)	−177 (280)	−22 (254)	−200 (253)	−231 (252)	−279 (238)	−170 (230)	−242 (240)
1958	.121 (.069)	−5 (165)	201 (68)	−50 (58)	−46 (72)	183 (194)	56 (348)	−73 (308)	43 (287)	−164 (283)	−191 (283)	−269 (260)	−143 (255)	−212 (264)
1959	.112 (.080)	−89 (186)	134 (85)	−49 (95)	−66 (77)	230 (219)	184 (467)	−8 (429)	122 (396)	−8 (388)	−62 (396)	−142 (376)	−35 (367)	−77 (371)

TABLE 11. SAVINGS AND LOAN ASSOCIATION SHARES—DEMAND FUNCTIONS

Efficient Estimates

1949–59

Year	Y	r_d	r_t	r_s	r_m	A	D_m	Cal	DC	Ill	NY	W	S	C	NE
1949	.043 (.021)	1 (45)	−8 (19)	−2 (10)	−33 (18)	.479 (.078)	76 (31)	−31 (62)	126 (65)	−27 (56)	−39 (47)	−20 (47)	1 (45)	−10 (46)	−13 (51)
1950	.042 (.020)	−34 (48)	−4 (18)	5 (11)	−47 (23)	.553 (.079)	99 (39)	−95 (73)	76 (78)	−78 (62)	−61 (49)	−61 (54)	−33 (50)	−43 (51)	−44 (54)
1951	.045 (.019)	−67 (53)	−8 (19)	6 (13)	−61 (26)	.478 (.065)	130 (47)	−102 (79)	141 (82)	−70 (64)	−66 (52)	−68 (57)	−38 (53)	−52 (53)	−49 (56)
1952	.054 (.024)	−83 (59)	1 (16)	9 (13)	−55 (22)	.475 (.059)	128 (44)	−147 (85)	115 (87)	−109 (72)	−74 (61)	−98 (64)	−64 (57)	−81 (60)	−78 (63)
1953	.058 (.030)	−76 (65)	−10 (20)	20 (19)	−45 (26)	.449 (.060)	118 (54)	−154 (119)	75 (118)	−136 (102)	−100 (88)	−117 (92)	−86 (84)	−97 (87)	−104 (89)
1954	.044 (.027)	−90 (58)	−36 (22)	8 (18)	−34 (26)	.533 (.054)	103 (55)	−99 (110)	134 (109)	−88 (93)	−18 (84)	−32 (89)	−4 (80)	−25 (81)	−29 (84)
1955	.070 (.030)	−104 (64)	−15 (21)	51 (16)	−66 (31)	.493 (.050)	189 (69)	−322 (99)	8 (96)	−238 (81)	−190 (70)	−242 (75)	−188 (61)	−216 (66)	−222 (69)
1956	.077 (.033)	−138 (77)	−29 (35)	28 (35)	−81 (35)	.435 (.047)	237 (80)	−269 (184)	155 (173)	−162 (156)	−113 (150)	−162 (153)	−108 (143)	−157 (141)	−151 (148)
1957	.072 (.031)	−104 (77)	−22 (31)	13 (30)	−81 (32)	.459 (.046)	255 (84)	−229 (157)	157 (141)	−119 (126)	−70 (128)	−108 (126)	−53 (119)	−103 (114)	−102 (121)
1958	.088 (.037)	−122 (85)	−24 (35)	50 (30)	−75 (37)	.422 (.048)	252 (99)	−330 (178)	134 (161)	−224 (148)	−201 (145)	−258 (145)	−183 (133)	−222 (130)	−242 (136)
1959	.107 (.042)	−90 (98)	3 (43)	47 (49)	−78 (40)	.400 (.048)	274 (112)	−418 (238)	160 (220)	−283 (202)	−305 (198)	−335 (202)	−252 (192)	−290 (187)	−317 (190)

TABLE 12. MATRIX OF OWN PRICE AND CROSS SUBSTITUTION TERMS

Efficient Estimates

1949–59

Year	Dependent Variable	Independent Variables			
		P_d	P_t	P_s	P_m
1949	D	−644 (204)	146 (84)	−22 (39)	−144 (80)
	T	127 (126)	−194 (51)	−11 (24)	224 (50)
	S	−1 (45)	8 (19)	2 (10)	33 (18)
1950	D	−638 (225)	155 (85)	−55 (45)	−204 (106)
	T	111 (129)	−216 (48)	9 (25)	271 (61)
	S	34 (48)	4 (18)	−5 (11)	47 (23)
1951	D	−625 (217)	67 (79)	−73 (51)	−181 (106)
	T	65 (140)	−124 (50)	20 (32)	290 (69)
	S	67 (53)	8 (19)	−6 (13)	61 (26)
1952	D	−657 (231)	21 (64)	−48 (49)	−96 (86)
	T	227 (153)	−92 (42)	42 (32)	194 (57)
	S	83 (59)	−1 (16)	−9 (13)	55 (22)
1953	D	−629 (202)	28 (64)	−46 (58)	−154 (81)
	T	158 (136)	−86 (43)	50 (39)	188 (54)
	S	76 (65)	10 (20)	20 (19)	45 (26)
1954	D	−639 (188)	−3 (71)	−26 (58)	−145 (82)
	T	158 (132)	−79 (50)	−52 (41)	173 (58)
	S	90 (58)	36 (22)	8 (18)	34 (26)

Demand Function Estimates

TABLE 12. MATRIX OF OWN PRICE AND CROSS SUBSTITUTION TERMS—*(cont.)*

Efficient Estimates

1949–59

Year	Dependent Variable	Independent Variables			
		P_d	P_t	P_s	P_m
1955	D	−714 (184)	−13 (72)	−32 (61)	−183 (87)
	T	154 (131)	−74 (51)	57 (43)	156 (62)
	S	104 (64)	15 (21)	−51 (16)	66 (31)
1956	D	−558 (177)	31 (80)	−46 (79)	−151 (79)
	T	118 (133)	−122 (59)	76 (59)	140 (59)
	S	138 (77)	29 (35)	−28 (35)	81 (35)
1957	D	−591 (175)	−64 (70)	−37 (69)	−147 (74)
	T	61 (154)	−139 (61)	15 (61)	54 (65)
	S	104 (77)	22 (31)	−13 (30)	81 (32)
1958	D	−559 (175)	−43 (73)	39 (62)	−157 (76)
	T	−5 (165)	−201 (68)	50 (58)	46 (72)
	S	122 (85)	24 (35)	−50 (30)	75 (37)
1959	D	−576 (154)	−77 (70)	−17 (79)	−106 (63)
	T	89 (186)	−134 (85)	49 (95)	66 (77)
	S	90 (98)	3 (43)	−47 (49)	78 (40)

Demand Function Estimates   57

TABLE 13. MATRIX OF OWN PRICE, CROSS, AND INCOME ELASTICITIES

Efficient Estimates

1949–59

Year	Dependent Variable	Elasticity Estimates at the Mean				
		η_{xd}	η_{xt}	η_{xs}	η_{xm}	$\eta_{x\,i}$
1949	D	−.32	.30	−.12	−.19	1.09
	T	.15	−.96	−.15	.70	1.13
	S	−.01	.12	.07	.30	.68
1950	D	−.31	.31	−.29	−.26	1.07
	T	.14	−1.12	−.12	.90	1.34
	S	.11	.06	−.18	.40	.63
1951	D	−.29	.14	−.37	−.23	1.07
	T	.08	−.66	.27	.97	1.16
	S	.19	.09	−.19	.48	.63
1952	D	−.30	.05	−.25	−.13	1.07
	T	.26	−.52	.55	.68	1.13
	S	.20	−.01	−.22	.41	.68
1953	D	−.32	.07	−.25	−.22	1.03
	T	.19	−.51	.65	.66	1.11
	S	.17	.11	−.49	.30	.65
1954	D	−.35	−.01	−.14	−.22	1.00
	T	.20	−.48	.66	.60	.90
	S	.19	.37	−.16	.20	.43
1955	D	−.40	−.03	−.17	−.28	1.04
	T	.20	−.46	.72	.55	.83
	S	.14	.15	−.99	.31	.54
1956	D	−.34	.09	−.25	−.24	.96
	T	.16	−.82	.94	.51	.79
	S	.25	.26	−.44	.39	.61
1957	D	−.43	−.25	−.22	−.26	.96
	T	.09	−1.09	−.18	−.19	.77
	S	.20	.23	−.21	.38	.54
1958	D	−.42	−.17	.23	−.28	.86
	T	−.01	−1.53	.57	.16	.63
	S	.22	.24	−.74	.33	.60
1959	D	−.46	−.33	−.11	.20	.97
	T	.13	−1.04	.56	.22	.59
	S	.16	−.03	−.64	.32	.68

TABLE 14. DEMAND DEPOSITS—DEMAND FUNCTIONS

Restricted Efficient Estimates

1949–59

Year	Y	r_d	r_t	r_s	r_m	D_m	I	Cal	DC	Ill	NY	W	S	C	NE
1949	.477 (.094)	673 (181)	−133 (64)	17 (28)	148 (76)	−324 (131)	497 (220)	46 (240)	150 (236)	196 (211)	744 (196)	59 (187)	−26 (171)	77 (185)	49 (204)
1950	.472 (.095)	720 (205)	−151 (67)	17 (32)	242 (100)	−492 (176)	447 (234)	144 (273)	279 (270)	256 (226)	798 (206)	133 (213)	40 (190)	139 (205)	112 (220)
1951	.462 (.079)	693 (197)	−83 (65)	2 (35)	229 (104)	−501 (190)	432 (238)	147 (267)	351 (260)	243 (212)	810 (194)	112 (204)	27 (183)	121 (192)	75 (209)
1952	.439 (.094)	617 (210)	−71 (57)	−24 (36)	122 (85)	−333 (171)	413 (239)	202 (289)	391 (278)	322 (240)	869 (220)	174 (230)	92 (198)	192 (215)	132 (229)
1953	.367 (.093)	634 (189)	−70 (56)	−26 (41)	191 (79)	−482 (167)	463 (243)	293 (309)	499 (290)	415 (259)	924 (241)	247 (247)	151 (220)	277 (234)	193 (246)
1954	.361 (.084)	641 (175)	−51 (60)	−47 (39)	171 (81)	−427 (174)	500 (249)	397 (300)	632 (285)	464 (249)	950 (234)	326 (242)	205 (214)	308 (225)	218 (236)
1955	.376 (.081)	698 (171)	−48 (61)	−45 (42)	218 (85)	−529 (189)	589 (253)	374 (306)	596 (292)	423 (253)	875 (240)	287 (251)	178 (225)	270 (233)	167 (244)
1956	.335 (.073)	571 (164)	−78 (65)	−66 (52)	165 (79)	−434 (184)	498 (248)	546 (338)	773 (310)	590 (279)	1064 (275)	466 (278)	349 (256)	433 (258)	348 (277)
1957	.339 (.069)	589 (152)	50 (59)	−28 (48)	150 (74)	−435 (190)	472 (233)	163 (322)	453 (291)	246 (257)	720 (262)	130 (258)	9 (242)	122 (237)	15 (254)
1958	.302 (.074)	573 (153)	36 (62)	−76 (46)	165 (76)	−494 (205)	409 (254)	511 (357)	813 (320)	539 (288)	969 (293)	429 (294)	293 (272)	392 (270)	275 (288)
1959	.330 (.067)	567 (141)	59 (63)	−37 (58)	111 (63)	−368 (180)	343 (228)	251 (358)	583 (330)	263 (299)	722 (302)	213 (305)	92 (288)	168 (286)	82 (296)

TABLE 15. TIME DEPOSITS—DEMAND FUNCTIONS

Restricted Efficient Estimates

1949-59

Year	Y	r_d	r_t	r_s	r_m	D_m	Cal	DC	Ill	NY	W	S	C	NE
1949	.205 (.057)	-133 (64)	182 (46)	2 (13)	-216 (45)	428 (78)	-39 (125)	-250 (124)	-122 (118)	-208 (112)	-256 (95)	-278 (83)	-250 (92)	-243 (104)
1950	.237 (.042)	-151 (67)	206 (44)	7 (14)	-269 (55)	520 (98)	-162 (129)	-361 (128)	-218 (114)	-291 (106)	-361 (98)	-361 (84)	-337 (93)	-323 (101)
1951	.199 (.049)	-83 (65)	129 (45)	-1 (15)	-303 (66)	598 (121)	-9 (138)	-232 (133)	-84 (116)	-190 (108)	-218 (100)	-233 (82)	-204 (90)	-131 (101)
1952	.174 (.060)	-72 (57)	119 (39)	-6 (13)	-195 (55)	445 (112)	50 (152)	-167 (146)	-28 (136)	-127 (128)	-181 (116)	-198 (90)	-164 (105)	-122 (113)
1953	.190 (.060)	-70 (56)	107 (39)	-16 (17)	-201 (52)	468 (110)	57 (158)	-161 (150)	-13 (143)	-125 (138)	-161 (123)	-184 (101)	-146 (114)	-107 (120)
1954	.148 (.057)	-51 (60)	101 (46)	-37 (19)	-171 (57)	422 (122)	223 (168)	-24 (168)	131 (150)	7 (148)	-26 (133)	-72 (111)	-27 (122)	19 (127)
1955	.143 (.057)	-48 (61)	105 (47)	-18 (19)	-163 (60)	414 (134)	161 (177)	-63 (176)	77 (157)	-31 (154)	-84 (143)	-138 (121)	-81 (130)	-42 (136)
1956	.139 (.054)	-78 (65)	144 (53)	-31 (28)	-140 (58)	381 (137)	91 (199)	-98 (191)	41 (177)	-95 (182)	-141 (164)	-187 (145)	-118 (148)	-111 (163)
1957	.127 (.059)	50 (59)	167 (49)	-8 (25)	-44 (64)	185 (168)	-43 (228)	-203 (213)	-47 (188)	-257 (201)	-246 (176)	-317 (159)	-193 (155)	-275 (172)
1958	.120 (.067)	36 (62)	211 (55)	-22 (26)	-49 (71)	194 (193)	-55 (268)	-175 (246)	-61 (225)	-266 (242)	-289 (214)	-375 (192)	-240 (193)	-307 (210)
1959	.097 (.079)	59 (63)	170 (69)	5 (35)	-60 (77)	229 (219)	1 (327)	-199 (308)	-76 (284)	-228 (303)	-236 (268)	-348 (243)	-225 (250)	-261 (263)

TABLE 16. SAVINGS AND LOAN ASSOCIATION SHARES—DEMAND FUNCTIONS

Restricted Efficient Estimates

1949-59

Year	Y	r_d	r_t	r_s	r_m	A	D_m	Cal	DC	Ill	NY	W	S	C	NE
1949	.044 (.020)	17 (28)	2 (13)	-2 (9)	-33 (17)	.478 (.078)	77 (30)	-38 (52)	122 (57)	-35 (48)	-47 (41)	-27 (38)	-7 (36)	-17 (37)	-22 (41)
1950	.036 (.019)	17 (32)	7 (14)	2 (10)	-44 (22)	.544 (.078)	96 (38)	-68 (64)	106 (70)	-60 (56)	-49 (44)	-42 (46)	-18 (43)	-27 (44)	-27 (47)
1951	.036 (.018)	2 (35)	-1 (15)	-2 (13)	-55 (25)	.458 (.064)	123 (47)	-40 (69)	208 (74)	-26 (58)	-33 (47)	-22 (49)	3 (46)	-9 (46)	-5 (49)
1952	.040 (.023)	-24 (36)	-6 (14)	-2 (12)	-46 (21)	.466 (.059)	114 (44)	-59 (74)	197 (77)	-42 (65)	-19 (55)	-26 (55)	-1 (49)	-15 (52)	-10 (54)
1953	.041 (.029)	-26 (41)	-16 (17)	9 (18)	-37 (25)	.448 (.060)	105 (54)	-56 (103)	162 (106)	-61 (92)	-35 (78)	-37 (79)	-15 (73)	-24 (75)	-27 (77)
1954	.033 (.026)	-47 (39)	-37 (19)	-1 (17)	-28 (25)	.535 (.054)	96 (54)	-30 (94)	193 (97)	-39 (83)	24 (74)	24 (74)	44 (67)	24 (69)	22 (71)
1955	.059 (.029)	-45 (42)	-18 (19)	44 (13)	-58 (30)	.500 (.049)	175 (68)	-249 (80)	68 (82)	-190 (71)	-150 (64)	-181 (58)	-138 (46)	-164 (52)	-170 (56)
1956	.062 (.032)	-66 (52)	-31 (28)	11 (33)	-71 (34)	.439 (.047)	222 (80)	-140 (163)	264 (155)	-69 (140)	-35 (132)	-55 (133)	-15 (125)	-63 (124)	-56 (130)
1957	.063 (.030)	-28 (48)	-8 (25)	1 (29)	-73 (32)	.464 (.046)	244 (83)	-158 (146)	205 (134)	-74 (120)	-45 (121)	-50 (116)	-10 (111)	-56 (106)	-57 (113)
1958	.078 (.035)	-76 (46)	-22 (26)	42 (28)	-70 (36)	.430 (.048)	245 (99)	-259 (163)	186 (152)	-177 (140)	161 (136)	-197 (131)	-134 (123)	-173 (120)	-191 (125)
1959	.097 (.041)	-37 (58)	5 (35)	32 (46)	-72 (39)	.411 (.047)	262 (118)	-318 (223)	241 (210)	-211 (194)	-241 (189)	-244 (188)	-174 (180)	-214 (176)	-238 (179)

TABLE 17. MATRIX OF OWN PRICE AND CROSS SUBSTITUTION TERMS

Restricted Efficient Estimates

1949–59

Year	Dependent Variable	Independent Variables			
		P_d	P_t	P_s	P_m
1949	D	−673 (181)	133 (64)	−17 (28)	−148 (76)
	T	133 (64)	−182 (46)	−2 (13)	216 (45)
	S	−17 (28)	−2 (13)	2 (9)	33 (17)
1950	D	−720 (205)	151 (67)	−17 (32)	−242 (100)
	T	151 (67)	−206 (44)	7 (14)	269 (55)
	S	−17 (32)	7 (14)	2 (10)	44 (22)
1951	D	−693 (197)	83 (65)	−2 (35)	−229 (104)
	T	83 (65)	−129 (45)	1 (15)	303 (66)
	S	−2 (35)	1 (15)	2 (13)	55 (25)
1952	D	−617 (210)	71 (57)	24 (36)	−122 (85)
	T	72 (57)	−119 (39)	6 (13)	195 (55)
	S	24 (36)	6 (14)	2 (12)	46 (21)
1953	D	−634 (189)	70 (56)	26 (41)	−191 (79)
	T	70 (56)	−107 (39)	16 (17)	201 (52)
	S	26 (41)	16 (17)	−9 (18)	37 (25)
1954	D	−641 (175)	51 (60)	47 (39)	−171 (81)
	T	51 (60)	−101 (46)	37 (19)	171 (57)
	S	47 (39)	37 (19)	1 (17)	28 (25)

TABLE 17. MATRIX OF OWN PRICE AND CROSS SUBSTITUTION TERMS—*(cont.)*

Restricted Efficient Estimates

1949–59

Year	Dependent Variable	Independent Variables			
		P_d	P_t	P_s	P_m
1955	D	−698 (171)	48 (61)	45 (42)	−218 (85)
	T	48 (61)	−105 (47)	18 (19)	163 (60)
	S	45 (42)	18 (19)	−44 (13)	58 (30)
1956	D	−571 (164)	78 (65)	66 (52)	−165 (79)
	T	78 (65)	−144 (53)	31 (28)	140 (58)
	S	66 (52)	31 (28)	−11 (33)	71 (34)
1957	D	−589 (152)	−50 (59)	28 (48)	−150 (74)
	T	−50 (59)	−167 (49)	8 (25)	44 (64)
	S	28 (48)	8 (25)	1 (29)	73 (32)
1958	D	−573 (153)	−36 (62)	76 (46)	−165 (76)
	T	−36 (62)	−211 (55)	22 (26)	49 (71)
	S	76 (46)	22 (26)	−42 (28)	70 (36)
1959	D	−567 (141)	−59 (63)	37 (58)	−111 (63)
	T	−59 (63)	−170 (69)	−5 (35)	60 (77)
	S	37 (58)	−5 (35)	−32 (46)	72 (39)

Demand Function Estimates   63

TABLE 18. MATRIX OF OWN PRICE, CROSS, AND INCOME ELASTICITIES

Restricted Efficient Estimates

1949–59

Year	Dependent Variable	\multicolumn{5}{c}{Elasticity Estimates at the Mean}
		η_{xd}	η_{xt}	η_{xs}	η_{xm}	η_{xy}
1949	D	−.34	.28	−.10	−.19	1.09
	T	.16	−.90	−.02	.67	1.12
	S	−.06	−.02	.07	.30	.69
1950	D	−.35	.30	−.09	−.31	1.05
	T	.19	−1.07	−.09	.89	1.37
	S	−.06	−.09	−.07	.38	.54
1951	D	−.32	.17	−.01	−.29	1.05
	T	.10	−.69	.02	1.01	1.18
	S	−.01	.02	.07	.43	.50
1952	D	−.28	.16	.12	−.17	1.04
	T	.08	−.67	.08	.68	1.04
	S	.06	.07	.04	.34	.50
1953	D	−.32	.17	.14	−.28	.92
	T	.08	−.63	.21	.71	1.13
	S	.06	.18	−.21	.25	.46
1954	D	−.35	.13	.26	−.26	.91
	T	.06	−.61	.47	.59	.86
	S	.10	.38	.01	.16	.32
1955	D	−.39	.13	.24	−.33	.95
	T	.06	−.65	.23	.58	.84
	S	.06	.18	−.85	.27	.45
1956	D	−.35	.23	.36	−.26	.88
	T	.11	−.96	.39	.51	.82
	S	.12	.28	−.17	.34	.49
1957	D	−.42	−.20	.17	−.27	.95
	T	−.07	−1.31	.09	.16	.71
	S	.05	.08	.01	.35	.47
1958	D	−.43	−.14	.46	−.29	.84
	T	−.05	−1.61	.25	.17	.63
	S	.14	.22	−.62	.31	.53
1959	D	−.45	−.25	.23	−.21	.96
	T	−.08	−1.32	−.05	.20	.51
	S	.06	−.05	−.44	.30	.62

TABLE 19. DEMAND DEPOSITS—TIME DEPOSITS—SAVINGS AND LOAN ASSOCIATION SHARES DEMAND FUNCTIONS

Pooled Restricted Efficient Estimates

Eq.	Y	r_d	r_t	r_s	r_m	D_m	I	A	Cal	DC	Ill	NY	W	S	C	NE
								1949–53								
D	.420 (.030)	674 (78)	−98 (21)	2 (13)	97 (30)	−261 (57)	431 (96)		192 (93)	366 (91)	310 (78)	870 (71)	169 (71)	68 (65)	171 (68)	151 (74)
T	.163 (.019)	−98 (21)	100 (14)	−2 (5)	−181 (19)	397 (36)			93 (46)	−135 (47)	5 (43)	−107 (40)	−143 (33)	−172 (28)	−129 (31)	−99 (33)
S	.047 (.008)	2 (13)	−2 (5)	0 (5)	−24 (8)	66 (14)		.490 (.023)	66 (14)	−67 (22)	139 (24)	−61 (19)	−52 (18)	−42 (16)	−15 (15)	−26 (16)
								1954–58								
D	.355 (.027)	600 (63)	20 (17)	−33 (18)	103 (28)	−301 (66)	448 (101)		255 (98)	519 (91)	332 (82)	823 (76)	202 (76)	93 (71)	184 (73)	110 (76)
T	.090 (.022)	20 (17)	120 (10)	9 (6)	−114 (23)	342 (56)			136 (56)	−57 (57)	72 (54)	−69 (52)	−112 (38)	−196 (30)	−100 (35)	−102 (39)
S	.074 (.011)	−33 (18)	9 (6)	7 (9)	−44 (11)	158 (28)		.448 (.019)	−185 (40)	169 (39)	−124 (35)	−122 (33)	−118 (30)	−70 (29)	−105 (29)	−124 (30)

64

[2]

The Theory and Its Implementation

THIS CHAPTER presents the model of bank behavior to be tested in later chapters. It will be shown that a bank's demand for cash assets can be regarded as an application of the static theory of profit maximizing inventory policy under conditions of uncertainty.[1]

In the existing formal theory of banking,[2] the basic assumptions are: (a) banks maximize expected profits (or minimize expected losses),[3] (b) banks construct probability distributions of gains and losses from investment in assets, and (c) following the lead of Edgeworth,[4] profit maximization takes place subject to a specified distribution of cash drains during the planning period.[5]

The salient features of the static theory of banking can be illustrated by means of the following elementary model. Assume that a bank can hold two types of assets—non-interest bearing cash and fixed-interest bearing loans—and can issue three types of liabilities—non-interest bearing deposits repayable in cash on demand, short-term interest bearing debt, and equity securities. Suppose the bank attempts to minimize its expected losses during the planning period by appropriate allocation of its assets between cash and loans. Assume further that the return per

---

[1] K. Arrow, T. Harris, and J. Marschak, "Optimal Inventory Policy," *Econometrica*, XIX (1951), 250–72. A. Dvoretsky, J. Kiefer, and J. Wolfowitz, "The Inventory Problem: I. Cases of Known Distribution of Demand," *Econometrica*, XX (1952), 187–222.

[2] S. Karlin, "One Stage Inventory Models with Uncertainty," in K. Arrow, S. Karlin, and H. Scarf (eds.), *Studies in the Mathematical Theory of Inventory and Production* (Stanford, Calif.: Stanford University Press, 1958), pp. 109–34; R. C. Porter, "A Model of Bank Portfolio Selection," *Yale Economic Essays*, I (1961), 322–59; D. Orr and W. G. Mellon, "Stochastic Reserve Losses and Expansion of Bank Credit," *American Economic Review*, LI (September, 1961), 614–23.

[3] An expected utility maximization model of banking, assuming risk aversion, is presented in E. J. Kane and B. G. Malkiel, "Bank Portfolio Allocation, Deposit Variability and the Availability Doctrine," *Quarterly Journal of Economics*, LXXIX (1965), 113–34.

[4] F. Y. Edgeworth, "The Mathematical Theory of Banking," *Journal of the Royal Statistical Society*, LI (1888), 113–27.

[5] For a multiperiod programing model of bank portfolio behavior, see D. Chambers and A. Charnes, "Inter-temporal Analysis and Optimization of Bank Portfolios," *Management Science*, VII (July, 1961), 393–410.

The Theory and Its Implementation   9

dollar of loans over the planning period is composed of an interest component, y, known with certainty at the beginning of the period, and an expected capital gain or loss component, g, whose probability density is $\phi(g)$, where g is distributed over the range $-1 \leq g < \infty$. The bank is also faced with the prospect that there will be a cash drain or inflow. This expected change in cash will be expressed as a proportion, v, of initial deposits.[6] Let us suppose that the probability density of v is $f(v)$, where v is uniformly distributed over the interval $c \leq v \leq b$, and $c \geq -1$.[7] For simplicity, assume that the cash drain or inflow always occurs at the end of the period after all returns have been accrued on loans but before any of the loans are repaid. Finally, let us suppose that all cash deficiencies (i.e., all cash drains over and above the amount that can be covered by drawing down initial cash assets to zero) must be met by borrowing at short term or by sale of loans, and that the penalty per dollar of cash deficiency is n, a cost that is known with certainty at the beginning of the period. This penalty cost is equivalent to the interest rate on borrowed funds, or to the transactions cost on forced sale of loans, which might be interpreted as a brokerage fee or as the spread between the bid and the asked price on securities. The bank is assumed to operate in perfectly competitive markets so that y, n, and g are independent of the bank's own decisions.

Defining ρ to be cash as a ratio to initial deposits, the expected loss function $E[L(\rho)]$ can then be written as follows:

$$E[L(\rho)] = y\rho + \rho \int_{-1}^{\infty} g\phi(g)dg + \int_{c}^{-\rho} n(-v-\rho)f(v)dv, \quad (2.1)$$

where the first two terms taken together represent the expected alternative cost of holding cash instead of loans, and the third term represents the expected penalty cost of cash drains exceeding ρ. It is assumed that only \$1 of loans can be created by the individual bank, per dollar of excess reserves, because of a loss of all deposits created in the process of making loans. This is the simplest, but not necessarily the most descriptively accurate, assumption about the loan-deposit loss function.

[6] In this model it is taken for granted that all deposits created by lending are drawn down by the borrowers simultaneously with the granting of loans at the beginning of the period. Thus "initial deposits" refers to deposits remaining after loan-created deposits have been removed. Thus the model follows the usual textbook exposition of the deposit expansion multiplier process.

[7] Also note that we assume the bank is not subject to legal reserve requirements. A reserve requirement defined as a fraction, ρr, of deposits can be easily handled by redefinition of v as a cash drain or inflow over the interval $-1 + \rho r \leq c \leq v \leq b - \rho r$. The term "cash" then refers to bank reserves and vault currency in excess of legal reserve requirements.

10   *The Theory and Its Implementation*

Substituting $f(v) = 1/(b - c)$ in (2.1) and evaluating the integrals in the expression gives

$$E[L(\rho)] = y\rho + \bar{g}\rho - \frac{n\rho^2}{2(b-c)} + \frac{nc^2}{2(b-c)} + \frac{n\rho^2}{b-c} + \frac{n\rho c}{b-c}, \quad (2.2)$$

where $\bar{g}$ is the mean of g.

The first- and second-order conditions for a minimum are found by successive differentiation of (2.2) with respect to ρ.

$$\frac{\partial E}{\partial \rho} = y + \bar{g} + \frac{n\rho + nc}{b - c} \quad (2.3)$$

$$= 0 \text{ at a minimum or maximum .}$$

$$\frac{\partial^2 E}{\partial \rho^2} = \frac{n}{b - c} > 0, \text{ since } n > 0, \text{ by assumption.}$$

The demand for cash by the bank is derived from the minimized expression (2.3).

$$\rho = \frac{(c - b)(y + \bar{g})}{n} - c . \quad (2.4)$$

If we set $b = c + k$, where $k > 0$, (2.4) can be rewritten as

$$\rho = \frac{-k(y + \bar{g})}{n} - c . \quad (2.5)$$

Since the mean of the uniform distribution over the range $c \leq v \leq b$ is

$$\bar{v} = \int_c^b \frac{v}{b - c} \, dv = \frac{b + c}{2}, \quad \text{and} \quad b = c + k , \quad \text{we have} \quad \bar{v} = c + \frac{k}{2}.$$

Thus an expression for c in terms of $\bar{v}$ can be derived:

$$c = \bar{v} - \frac{k}{2} . \quad (2.6)$$

Substituting (2.6) in (2.5), yields a demand equation in terms of y, $\bar{g}$, n, $\bar{v}$, and k:

$$\rho = k\left[\tfrac{1}{2} - \frac{(y + \bar{g})}{n}\right] - \bar{v} .^{8} \quad (2.7)$$

---

[8] If $k = 0$, $\rho = -\bar{v}$. But negative values of ρ are not possible in this simple model without reserve requirements. If there were reserve requirements and ρ were defined to be excess cash reserves, ρ could be negative. There arises the problem of defining a penalty for not meeting reserve requirements. We can neglect this complication in the simpler model.

The Theory and Its Implementation   11

Differentiating with respect to the parameters y, $\bar{g}$, n, $\bar{v}$, and k gives:

$$\frac{\partial \rho}{\partial y} = -\frac{k}{n} < 0 \qquad \frac{\partial \rho}{\partial \bar{v}} = -1 < 0 \qquad \frac{\partial \rho}{\partial \bar{g}} = -\frac{k}{n} < 0$$

$$\frac{\partial \rho}{\partial k} = \tfrac{1}{2} - \frac{(y+\bar{g})}{n} \qquad \frac{\partial \rho}{\partial n} = \frac{k(y+\bar{g})}{n^2} \geq 0.\quad[9]$$

The demand for cash varies directly with the penalty cost of a cash deficiency and inversely with the interest rate on loans, the expected capital gain on loans, and the expected cash inflow. The sign of the change in cash with respect to a small increase in k, the range of the distribution of expected cash flows, cannot be determined without more precise knowledge of the values of y, $\bar{g}$, and n. The demand for cash varies directly with k if $n \geq 2(y+\bar{g})$, and inversely if $n < 2(y+\bar{g})$. This may appear to be a strange result, but its reasonableness can be shown on an intuitive level· Suppose, to begin with, that $k = 0$, so that the amount of cash drain, v, is certain to be equal to $\bar{v}$. In this event, the optimal cash ratio will be exactly equal to $-\bar{v}$. This much is clear from (2.7). Now suppose that we hold the expected cash drain, $\bar{v}$, constant while increasing k slightly. Should the bank hold a higher or lower cash ratio now that the exact amount of the cash drain, v, is not known with certainty? Surely the answer will depend on the costs of erring by holding a higher or lower cash ratio than the actual cash drain outcome would require. The unit cost of holding too much cash will be the foregone expected return on loans $(y+\bar{g})$. The unit cost of holding too little cash will be the penalty incurred in borrowing or forced liquidation of assets (n). The higher the expected return on loans relative to the penalty the more likely it is that an increase in k will encourage a bank to take a large risk of holding too little cash, by reducing its cash ratio below $-\bar{v}$. Conversely, if the return on loans is low relative to the penalty, an increase in k will lead the bank to avoid the risk of being short of cash by increasing its cash ratio. This ambiguity in the effect of a change in the dispersion of expected cash drains should therefore cause no surprise; it is a consequence of attempting to minimize expected losses by balancing the opposing earnings risks of having too much or too little cash.

It is important to bear in mind the various simplifications underlying this model of individual bank behavior, some of which have already been mentioned. Perhaps the most fundamental simplification lies in the ex-

---

[9] By assumption, $k > 0$ and $n > 0$, and if $(y + \bar{g}) > 0$, it follows that $\partial \rho / \partial n > 0$. Also it follows from (2.5) that $-\rho = c + k(y + \bar{g})/n \geq c$. If $-\rho < c$, the penalty effect on ρ is no longer operative since no penalty need be incurred. But only if $y + \bar{g} \leq 0$ would there be a reason for banks to hold cash in excess of any conceivable drain. It may be concluded that $\partial \rho / \partial n$ can never be negative.

12   *The Theory and Its Implementation*

tremely aggregative view that is taken of the bank's balance sheet. On the liability side the principal abstractions are that deposits and borrowings can be regarded as homogeneous entities, i.e., that distinctions between time deposits and demand deposits, or among personal, business, government, and interbank deposits, and distinctions between borrowings from the Federal Reserve and from other banks can all be neglected as being of secondary importance to the bank in making decisions as to the amount of cash it wishes to hold. If, for example, the expected cash drain or inflow depended on the proportion of time deposits to total deposits and the bank could control this proportion by varying the relative interest rates paid on time and demand deposits, the demand for cash would be a function of the proportion of time to total deposits and of the relative interest rates on demand and time deposits. Similarly, if there are several different kinds of penalty rates and if these penalty rates vary with the amount of funds to be acquired, the demand for cash will be a function of the several penalty rates.[10] In this study, however, the penalty rate will be interpreted typically to mean merely the discount rate on borrowing from the Federal Reserve, symbolized by d.

The model makes no pretense of being a full theory of bank asset portfolio behavior. Its sole objective is to provide a framework for the analysis of factors influencing the bank's demand for cash. In the context of the usual[11] fourfold division of bank assets into required reserves, primary reserves, secondary reserves, and risk assets, our focus is on primary reserves—those bank assets that can be converted into currency or deposits at essentially zero transactions costs. They include vault cash, excess reserves, and, possibly, deposits with other banks.[12] Lumping together these

[10] If there were more than one borrowing rate and if one of them were below the expected rate of return on loans, the bank would borrow an infinite amount of funds to make loans, quite apart from any need to meet cash deficiencies. The existence of finite borrowings must be attributable, in this model, to an excess of the penalty rate over the expected rate of return on loans. In this study my objective is to examine only the demand for cash and not borrowings.

[11] R. I. Robinson, *The Management of Bank Funds* (New York: McGraw-Hill Book Co., 1962), especially pp. 13–18. W. Steiner, E. Shapiro, and E. Solomon, *Money and Banking* (4th ed.; New York: Henry Holt & Co., 1958), pp. 123–52.

[12] Cash items in process of collection are not included in this concept of primary reserves on the grounds that, in the normal course of bank operations, an amount of deposits approximately equal to the total amount of cash items will be lost through the check clearing process, so that cash items in process do not ordinarily constitute a net addition to the available cash reserves of banks. We shall also want to subtract from deposits an amount equal to reported cash items as is done in calculating "net demand deposits subject to reserves." The Federal Reserve System's practice of granting "float" reserve credit to member banks on a schedule of "deferred availability" involves a concomitant reduction of cash items in process as reported by member banks and an increase in deposits subject to reserves.

The Theory and Its Implementation   13

three assets for the purpose of demand analysis can be justified if the alternative costs of holding these assets fluctuate in a strictly proportional manner[13] or if they are either perfect substitutes or perfect complements for each other. Probably the first of these grounds constitutes the best reason for treating these asset items as a unit, but it is recognized that none of the conditions is fulfilled except approximately. For the particular problems to be investigated in this study, it would not matter greatly if only excess reserves were considered to be cash, or if, on the other hand, the collection were broadened to include certain other highly liquid assets.

A more complete model might include demand and supply equations for each of the principal asset categories, and the demand for cash might be made a function of the expected return on each category of asset. An expanded model could throw light on such portfolio behavior problems as whether cash and risk assets[14] are substitutes or complements, as judged by cross elasticity of demand. Our model sidesteps these refinements by assuming that the earning assets of a bank can be viewed as a uniform class of assets under the general rubric "loans." The expected return on earning assets will be represented by the yield to maturity on short-term secondary reserve assets[15] denoted by the symbol r. It is assumed that the short-term yields to maturity are equal to the expected yields from holding longer-term secondary reserve assets for the same length of time, i.e., that short-term yields are unbiased estimates of expected yields on longer-term securities.[16] The only adjustment of this estimate of the yield on earning assets will be to allow for changes in the risk of loss from default of principal or interest on earning assets. If secondary reserve assets, from which the yield estimate is selected, were entirely free of variations in their default risk, this adjustment would be unnecessary, since in our model the return on secondary reserve assets can be assumed always to equal the expected return on other earning assets. Variations in the default risk of the entire spectrum of earning assets including secondary

[13] H. Wold and L. Jureen, *Demand Analysis* (New York: Wiley & Sons, 1953), pp. 108–9.

[14] Risk assets either lack marketability (i.e., have a high cost of quick conversion into cash) or have a relatively high risk of default. The two characteristics frequently go together.

[15] "Secondary reserves" include assets with low but non-zero transactions costs of quick conversion into cash, and which have only a moderate degree of uncertainty as to the amount that will be realized from their sale.

[16] This assumption has been the subject of much dispute. See D. Meiselman, *The Term Structure of Interest Rates* (Englewood Cliffs, N.J.: Prentice-Hall, Inc., 1962), and R. Kessel, "The Cyclical Behavior of the Term Structure of Interest Rates," Occasional Paper No. 91, National Bureau of Economic Research, 1965.

14   *The Theory and Its Implementation*

reserves is a different matter, however, and must be controlled statistically. This will be done by introducing the market yield spread between corporate bonds of different grade symbolized by P, as a variable in the statistical demand equation.

The tradition that incorporates the cash ratio of banks among the factors determining the money supply (see Chapter I) also lends support to our concentration on the cash position of banks to the exclusion of other items in the bank's portfolio. As a rule, emphasis on the crucial importance of the money supply in influencing the expenditure decisions of the public carries with it, implicitly or explicitly, the notion that credit effects, and specifically, those changes in the structure of the non-cash assets of the banking system that are not accompanied by changes in the money supply, play a distinctly secondary role in the determination of expenditures. The only structural changes in bank portfolio composition that really matter are those that cause changes in deposits or the money supply, and since these changes will necessarily affect the cash ratio of banks, they can be taken care of in an analysis of the determinants of the cash ratio.

With respect to the stochastic properties of the model, the main simplification is the assumption that v, the cash drain or inflow, is uniformly distributed. The assumption is defended only as an expository device, and not as a hypothesis to be tested. It is not unlikely that different probability distributions would yield similar predictions, but this possibility will be neither demonstrated nor explored in this study.

An empirical question of greater interest is the nature of the factors influencing banks in forming their expectations about v, and more particularly, about $\bar{v}$, the mean value of the probability distribution of cash drains and inflows. The fundamental distinction is between those factors determining cash flows that may be regarded as subject to relatively close control by the individual bank and those that are regarded as exogenously determined. For example, it may be reasonable to suppose that the individual bank knows the proportion of "derivative" deposits[17] that will be removed from the bank in consequence of lending. In this event, the bank can control the cash drain arising from its loan operations if it can control the volume of its loans. Again, if the bank can control the planned

---

[17] C. A. Phillips, *Bank Credit* (New York: Macmillan & Co., 1920), p. 40, differentiates between a primary deposit (". . . one that arises from the actual lodgement in a bank of cash or its readily convertible equivalent . . .") and a derivative deposit (". . . one which arises directly from a loan or which is accumulated by a borrower in anticipation of repayment of a loan"). In our model, primary deposits are the same as "initial deposits" owing to our special assumption about the relation between loans and derivative deposits.

The Theory and Its Implementation   15

volume if its outstanding borrowings, no uncertainty with respect to cash flows will arise from this source.[18] The same is true of equity capital.

Under these conditions, the main sources of uncontrolled disturbance to the bank's cash position would be uncontrolled variations in the volume of "primary" deposits.[19] Whatever the source of these uncontrolled variations, a basic hypothesis of this study is that the individual bank at any moment of time has a subjective probability distribution of expected cash inflows or drains during some subsequent interval and that $\bar{v}$, the mean of this probability distribution, tends to be high when the current level of cash is low relative to the amount the bank expects to possess on a permanent basis and conversely. One common-sense illustration of this is as follows: suppose the bank has experienced a recent sharp inflow of primary deposits that has raised total cash above the level the bank expects to maintain over the long run. Then the bank will expect a larger cash drain (or a smaller cash inflow) to occur in the near future than it would have expected in the absence of the inflow, i.e., the bank will expect a relatively low value of $\bar{v}$. Consequently, by our earlier argument, the bank would plan to hold a higher cash ratio than heretofore as a precaution against the increased likelihood of a cash drain.

It is apparent that the testing of this hypothesis about how expectations of cash drains are formed hinges on a specification of the process by which banks form their estimates of the permanent level of cash. This will be taken up in Chapter VII. A few preliminary comments on the nature of permanent cash are in order, however. First, our statistical tests will use observations on selected *groups* of banks or on all member banks of the Federal Reserve System. The assumption that total cash for the banking system is autonomously determined is undoubtedly more nearly valid than that an individual bank's cash is autonomously determined. Nevertheless, the ability of banks to borrow from the Federal Reserve and to set

[18] In our model, the planned level of borrowings is always zero, but this assumption can be modified.

[19] These distinctions between types of controlled and uncontrolled disturbances of the cash position are, of course, extreme. Preservation of "good will" often dictates that a bank permit its borrowers to exercise some control over the volume of its loans. And the volume of primary deposits, far from being exogenously determined, might be regarded as one of the bank's inputs which it seeks to acquire in optimal amounts, i.e., in competitive markets, up to the point where factor cost equals the value of marginal product. Unexpected divergences, however, between the market price for primary deposits and the price offered by the bank would lead to unexpected and possibly very wide fluctuations in its primary deposits. Therefore, even though the banker may attempt to adjust his service charges or rates of interest on time and demand deposits, occasions are likely to arise when his attempts are to some degree unsuccessful and he experiences a cash drain or a cash inflow.

the alternative cost to the public of holding currency versus deposits, enables banks to exercise some control over the nominal volume of their reserves.[20] But short-run variations in the cash reserves of the banking system may be regarded as largely beyond the control of banks as a group.

Second, in a banking system in which legal reserve requirements can be altered, or where differential reserve requirements exist among different classes of banks or types of deposits, changes in the average required reserve ratio, ρ_r, for a group of banks may exert disturbing influences on the group's cash in excess of legal requirements, quite apart from changes in the total volume of cash (including required cash reserves). The importance of the Federal Reserve in determining both total cash reserves and the average level of reserve requirements is overwhelming (in the short run, at least) and there is a high degree of interdependence between the two, as a consequence of conscious Federal Reserve policy. In view of this mutual determinacy, it would be reasonable for banks to form joint expectations about the permanent level of reserve requirements and total reserves. A variable combining both total reserves and the average reserve ratio in a manner appropriate to a policy by the monetary authorities of controlling the maximum deposit creation power of the banking system is R/ρ_r, where R denotes total reserves and ρ_r is the average required reserve ratio for the banking system, or for a selected group of banks. This variable is dubbed "potential deposits"; the difference between current potential deposits and permanent potential deposits will be designated "transitory potential deposits," symbolized by q. The specific hypothesis to be tested is that ρ varies *directly* with transitory potential deposits, q. In other words, q is the empirical counterpart of the theoretical construct $\bar{v}$. Whenever q is large, $\bar{v}$ is small, and conversely. In other words, if transitory potential deposits are high, this implies that banks anticipate an imminent large decline in cash, so that $\bar{v}$ would be small.

The variable k, representing the expected dispersion of the distribution of cash drains or inflows, will enter into the empirical work of later chapters in only a very minor way. In Chapter IV, a test of the effect of deposit instability on the demand for cash is presented, with inconclusive results. No other attempt is made to give empirical content to k. Nor is

---

[20] Of course, in the process of determining their desired ratio of cash to deposits, banks exercise control over their total reserves (for a given total of high-powered money and a given currency-deposit ratio). But this is not likely to be a significant qualification to our analysis in a banking system composed of more than a handful of independent units.

The Theory and Its Implementation 17

there much reason to suppose, from our model, that a clear test of its effect can be devised with the materials at hand.

Still another simplification is that the rate of turnover of deposits has no place in the banking model set forth previously. This follows from the timelessness of the model. All cash drains or inflows occur at one instant of time. A different approach, similar to the Tobin-Baumol models of the transactions demand for cash,[21] would handle cash drains as transactions of known unit size occurring with a known frequency per period of time. If transactions costs are positive, the amount of cash banks desire to hold might be expected to vary directly with the frequency of transactions, i.e., with the rate of deposit turnover. This proposition, however, is not tested in this study.

The demand for total cash will, of course, be greatly influenced by legal reserve requirements if these exist.[22] The first order effect of legal reserve requirements on the bank's total demand for cash can be eliminated from consideration by the expedient of defining the bank's balance sheet as net of required reserves—that is, by subtracting an amount equal to required reserves from both total cash and total deposits[23] This redefined deposit total will be designated "revised deposits."

[21] J. Tobin, "The Interest-Elasticity of Transactions Demand for Cash," *Review of Economics and Statistics*, XXXVIII (August, 1956), 241–47, and W. Baumol, "The Transactions Demand for Cash: An Inventory-Theoretic Approach," *Quarterly Journal of Economics*, LXVI (November, 1952), 545–56. Neither Tobin nor Baumol extend their analyses to take uncertainty into account.

[22] One technicality of some importance in a banking system with legal reserve requirements is the stringency with which the reserve requirement is applied. At one extreme, national banks before the Federal Reserve System began operation were required to maintain reserves up to the full legal minimum at all times. The principal penalty for failure to meet reserve requirements was that no new loans could be made except by purchase of sight bills of exchange. The Federal Reserve has evolved a system based on allowing a bank to meet reserve requirements on the average for a "reserve computation period" (semimonthly for country banks before December 31, 1959; one week, ending with Wednesday for central reserve and reserve city banks). The penalty for failure to meet requirements is an interest charge at 2 per cent per annum above the discount rate. A 2 per cent deficiency of reserves incurred in one reserve period, however, can be made up in the following period without penalty.

At the other extreme, Canadian chartered bank required reserves are determined each month based on deposits for selected preceding Wednesdays. Reserve requirements may be met on the average for the month and till money held on the selected Wednesdays counts as reserves.

[23] Assets and liabilities associated with national bank note circulation (note liabilities, the required lawful money redemption fund, and the required reserve of Treasury bonds bearing the circulation privilege) can be excluded from the balance sheet on essentially the same grounds. Such miscellaneous minor items as customer's liability on acceptances, bank real estate, income collected but not yet earned, and acceptances outstanding can also be thought of as netted against total capital accounts.

18   *The Theory and Its Implementation*

The model is also specialized insofar as there is no role assigned to bank size as an influence on the desired cash ratio. The relevance of such a variable may be seen if we start by writing a demand function for bank cash in the more general functional form:

$$R = F(r, d, P, q, D, O) , \tag{2.8}$$

where

R = nominal amount of bank cash desired
D = nominal amount of revised deposits
O = an index of prices relevant to bank operations (clerical wage rates and the like)
r = yield to maturity on short-term secondary reserve assets
P = spread between yields on bonds of different grades
q = transitory potential deposits .

If R can be supposed to be homogeneous of degree one in D and O, i.e., if

$$\lambda R = F(r, d, P, q, \lambda D, \lambda O) ,$$

by letting $\lambda = 1/D$, we obtain

$$\rho = \frac{R}{D} = G\left(r, d, P, q, \frac{D}{O}\right). \tag{2.9}$$

From the formal point of view, this demand function for cash is implied by a modern quantity theory framework for the demand for money per unit of permanent income or wealth.[24] Alternatively, it would be possible to set $\lambda = 1/O$ and express the demand for cash in real terms.[25] Inasmuch as this procedure departs both from the traditional banking theory emphasis on the cash ratio and from the profit maximization model presented earlier, it will not be pursued. Moreover, empirical fitting of a real cash balance demand function by banks is inexpedient owing to lack of any usable and relevant monthly indexes of prices extending over the eight decades we shall later investigate. The same is true a fortiori for D/O which in (2.9) may be interpreted as a bank size variable.

Therefore, any attempt to test this bank size variable will be aban-

[24] M. Friedman, "The Quantity Theory of Money—a Restatement," in M. Friedman (ed.), *Studies in the Quantity Theory of Money* (Chicago: University of Chicago Press, 1956), pp. 3–24. In Friedman's framework, q would be regarded as a taste or utility determining variable, while r, d, and P would represent asset yield variables affecting the cost of holding cash.

[25] This appears to be the choice made in J. Gurley and E. Shaw, *Money in a Theory of Finance* (Washington: Brookings Institution, 1960), p. 258.

The Theory and Its Implementation   19

doned at the outset, no matter how serious the consequences in terms of specification error. The basic functional relation to be fitted, may be viewed as an incomplete version either of the inventory profit maximization model or of the modern quantity theory as applied to bank demand for cash. It may be written as follows:

$$\rho = H(r, d, P, q) .\qquad(2.10)$$

The desired cash ratio of banks (ρ) is a function of the yield on secondary reserve assets (r), the Federal Reserve discount rate, the spread between yields on bonds of different grade (P), and last but not least, transitory deposit potential (q).

The approach outlined is purely static; time has not been introduced in a way that is essential to the analysis. One is free to interpret this model of banking as simply a bank management game in which the banker-player makes his investment decisions and receives his payoff instantaneously.[26]

One step toward a dynamic model of bank behavior is to introduce lags in adjustment of the bank's expectations with regard to the permanent values assigned to variables affecting its demand for cash. Later we shall do just this in connection with developing a measurement of transitory deposit potential. But there is another type of lag, namely, lag in the adjustment of actual to desired cash positions. The two lags are conceptually different but troublesome to distinguish statistically in models involving both lags. Provided that a separation can be effected empirically, the introduction of lags in response of actual to desired cash involves the introduction of a new variable into the demand equation—the rate of change in cash, symbolized by $\dot{\rho}$. The equation becomes

$$\rho = M(r, d, P, q, \dot{\rho}) .\qquad(2.11)$$

[26] Edgeworth, *loc. cit.*, did, in fact, think of banking as a game of chance. Edgeworth's approach differs from the treatment presented here in that he conceived of a game in which a "disaster" (or bankruptcy) element was also involved. Setting a penalty value on this "disaster," the banker proceeds to minimize his losses or maximize his gains. Apparently Edgeworth was not optimistic about the possibilities for finding precise optimal solutions to the banker's portfolio problem and, instead, proposed to investigate the portfolio behavior of banks by "operational gaming," which nowadays goes under the name "simulation." If one were prepared to assign a penalty cost to bank failure as well as a criterion for the point at which failure occurs, the disaster problem could be integrated into our model, at least in principle. Finding appropriate empirical counterparts for these concepts is not likely to prove an easy task and is not attempted here. The penalty on forced liquidation of assets is not quite the same thing as a bankruptcy penalty. In still another respect, then, our model is rather specialized. An alternative technique for handling disaster, based on choosing the course of action that would produce maximum gain for a given probability of disaster has come to be known as "safety first." See A. D. Roy, "Safety First and the Holding of Assets," *Econometrica*, XX (July, 1952), 431–49, and L. Telser, "Safety First and Hedging," *Review of Economic Studies*, XXIII (October, 1955), 1–16.

20   *The Theory and Its Implementation*

The empirical results presented in Appendix D do not suggest that $\dot{\rho}$ is a useful addition to the model. Therefore, to avoid misunderstanding of its relative importance in the study, further discussion of the disequilibrium variant of our model of stock demand for bank cash is relegated to Appendix A.

One final disclaimer is in order. In this study the aggregation question will, for the most part, be swept under the rug. To be sure, inasmuch as the principal empirical effort is directed at data for New York banks, one might hope for considerable similarity among individual bank elasticities or marginal propensities. But even so, the aggregation procedure does not satisfy the requirements for minimal aggregation bias,[27] so that such bias, with unknown characteristics, is undoubtedly present in our results.

[27] H. Theil, *Linear Aggregation of Economic Relations* (Amsterdam: North-Holland Publishing Co., 1954); R. G. D. Allen, *Mathematical Economics* (2d ed.; London: Macmillan & Co., 1960), p. 700.

[3]

ENTRY IN COMMERCIAL BANKING*

SAM PELTZMAN
University of California, Los Angeles

I. INTRODUCTION

ENTRY occupies a prominent place in economic theory. Yet just as prominent is the almost complete lack of empirical investigation of the subject.[1] This article attempts to identify empirically the determinants of entry in one industry—commercial banking in the United States—in the hope that it may throw light on the determinants of entry in general. The choice of commercial banking for this study does not rest entirely on the ready availability of the relevant data for this industry. It also affords the chance to investigate another topic lightly treated in the empirical literature—the effects of economic regulation on economic performance.

Entry into banking is today closely regulated; the formation of a new bank requires a license, denial of which is non-reviewable, from an appropriate government agency. This article will attempt to measure the extent to which actual entry in banking has been affected by the legal restrictions upon it.

The historical development of the legal restrictions on entry in banking can be summarized briefly. The century prior to 1935 may fairly be described as an era of "free banking," though the history books apply the term only to the part of this period up to the National Bank Act of 1863. Such legal restrictions as were placed on the formation of new banks by both Congress and state legislatures in 1863 and thereafter were largely ineffective. The reason for this was that the state and Federal chartering authorities operated independently of one another—neither had any check on the other within a given state. This legal framework encouraged competition between state and

* This article is drawn from my unpublished doctoral dissertation of the same title, March, 1965 (University of Chicago Library). I wish to express my deep gratitude to George Stigler, Milton Friedman and Lester Telser for their valuable advice, guidance and criticism. The study was financed by the Ford Foundation and the Federal Reserve Bank of Chicago. Computations were performed on the IBM-7094 computer at the University of Chicago Center for Computer Research.

[1] I can find only one recent published article on the subject: E. Mansfield, Entry, Gibrat's Law, Innovation, and the Growth of Firms, 52 Am. Econ. Rev. 1023 (1962). Mansfield in turn claims that previous to his article "there has been no systematic attempt to estimate the quantitative effect of various factors." One subsequent attempt to do this is Hause, New Firm Entry in Manufacturing Industries, August 1962 (unpublished dissertation in University of Chicago Library).

national authorities in the issuance of charters; where an application for a national bank charter was rejected, the state authorities were frequently more than willing to accommodate the spurned applicant, and vice-versa. Competition for charters manifested itself not only in the reluctance of the chartering authorities to use the discretionary powers given them by law, but also in attempts by them to make the law less restrictive. For example, the Comptroller of the Currency, the chartering agent for national banks, responded to low state minimum capital requirements by successfully urging Congress to lower capital requirements for national banks.[2] This competition for charters lasted until the collapse of the banking system in the 1930's. The widely shared belief that this competition, and the consequent "over-chartering" of banks, had contributed to the collapse of the banking system provided the impetus for an end to free banking in the United States.[3]

Termination of free banking required, as we have seen, an end to competition for charters. This was effectively accomplished in the Banking Act of 1935 by its setting up, *inter alia*, of a federally administered "needs" criterion for entry. Specifically the Act requires the Federal Reserve System before admitting a new state bank to membership and the Comptroller of the Currency before chartering a new national bank to pass on

. . . The financial history and condition of the bank, the adequacy of its capital structure, its future earnings prospects, . . . the convenience and needs of the community to be served by the bank . . . .[4]

Most important, however, the Act makes the same requirement of the Federal Deposit Insurance Corporation (the FDIC) before it may insure a new non-member state bank.[5] Administrative decisions (by the FDIC and the other agencies) based on this needs criterion are nonreviewable. Given the relative attractiveness of deposit insurance, the vesting of this discretionary power in the FDIC gives the Federal authorities an effective veto over the chartering policies of the individual states. Today, only state nonmember, noninsured banks can be chartered without Federal approval, and this group is small both from the standpoint of numbers and new entry.[6]

The passage of the Banking Act of 1935 thus ended the *legal* arrangements

---

[2] For a discussion of the effect of charter competition on the ease of entry, see U.S. Board of Governors of the Federal Reserve System, Committee on Branch Group and Chain Banking Materials I at 2, 47, 85, 96, 97, 100, 122 (1932).

[3] Examples of this viewpoint may be found in the works cited in Alhadeff, A Reconsideration of Restrictions on Bank Entry, 76 Q. J. Econ. 246, nn.4 & 6 at 247 (1962).

[4] 12 U.S.C. §§ 1814(a), 1816 64 Stat. 1876 (1950), 12 U.S.C. §§ 1814(a), 1816 (1964).

[5] 12 U.S.C. § 1815 64 Stat. 876 (1950), 12 U.S.C. § 1815 (1964).

[6] Of 13,427 commercial banks in existence on December 31, 1962, 308 were noninsured. 1962 Fed. Res. Bd. Ann. Rep. 166. Of the 2,260 new banks formed from 1936 through 1962, 332 entered as noninsured banks (62 of these entering in 1936-38). 1936-1962 Fed. Res. Bd. Ann. Rep.

permitting free banking by giving the Federal government a veto over the state chartering authorities. There remains the empirical question whether it in *fact* ended free banking. While the Federal authorities themselves quite clearly feel it did,[7] mere citation of the statutes and the opinions of those who administer them can never answer such a question, much less the question of how much or how little the actual level of new entry was affected by the statutory change. These are empirical questions, and this article attempts to answer them.

We will not try to answer these empirical questions with a simple comparison of entry rates before and since 1935. Entry rates can change over time either in response to an effective regulatory policy or in response to independent changes in the economic characteristics of the banking industry. Therefore, we must first isolate those economic characteristics which would importantly affect the rate of entry into banking in the absence of any entry regulation; that is, we need an economic theory of entry into banking. Section II develops such a theory. Once these economic characteristics are identified, we must estimate their independent influence on the rate of entry into banking. This is done in section III. Only when this is done can we go on to estimate the effect of regulation. To make this latter estimate, we will identify the years prior to 1935 as the "pre-regulatory" period and years since 1935 as the "post-regulatory" period. If after accounting for the separate effects of economic forces on the entry rate in both periods, it should happen that the entry rate is still significantly lower after 1935 than it was before, we will attribute that difference to the effect of regulation. If this residual difference is small or insignificant, then we will conclude that regulation has been ineffective: that any observed difference between the rate of entry in the two periods is fully accounted for by changes in the underlying characteristics of the banking industry.[8]

This method eschews the more direct approach of simply investigating the disposition by the regulatory authorities of charter applications which come before them, and simply enumerating the successful applications and those

[7] ". . . Chartering authorities were alert to prevent a repetition of the over-banked situation of the early 1920's. While it may to some persons now seem a desirable situation to have, as in 1921, more than 30,000 banks with 'open doors for borrowers and depositors throughout the United States,' bank supervisors and chartering authorities of the 1930's and 1940's knew that many of those banks closed their doors with great losses and hardships to their depositors and were determined that this should not happen again." 1960 Fed. Dep. Ins. Corp. Ann. Rep. 36.

See also Leonard, Supervision of the Commercial Banking System, in Banking Studies 198 (1941) and the statements of state banking commissioners in the joint Committee on the Economic Report's Monetary Policy and the Management of the Public Debt, S. Doc. No. 123, 82d Cong., 2d Sess., Pt. 2 at 989-995 (1952).

[8] This methodology is similar to that in a recent study of the effects of regulation on electric utility rates. See Stigler and Friedland, What Can Regulators Regulate? The Case of Electricity, 5 J. Law and Econ. 1 (1962).

disapproved. Such an enumeration would be a biased estimate of the relevant measure of regulatory effectiveness—the difference between the number of banks actually entering and the number which would enter without regulation. Moreover, it would at once be biased in two opposite and not necessarily offsetting directions. To illustrate: if several groups apply for a charter in a given area, and all are rejected, but none would apply if a bank were already in the area, counting the number of rejected applications overstates the effect of regulation; in this case regulation has lowered by but one the number of new banks formed. On the other hand, the number of charter applications forthcoming is itself a function of the probability that a given application will be approved. If chartering authorities have been restrictive, or it is believed they will be restrictive, some groups which would otherwise apply will not incur the costs of doing so. Simply counting those applications rejected understates the effect of regulation on this account. There is no obvious way to account for either of these biases inherent in an enumeration of rejected applications—the overstatement of regulatory effectiveness due to "repeat" applications, the understatement due to discouragement of applications. This is why we seek to measure the effect of regulation by comparing the actual behavior of entry in a period subject to regulation with that in a period not subject to regulation.

II. A Theory of New Entry

While the discussion and notation used here pertain to the banking industry, the theory that is developed is meant to apply to any industry. In order to maintain its general applicability, the theory abstracts from the effect of regulation; this is taken up later.

The formation of a new bank is an investment of new capital in the banking industry. New bank entry is therefore part of the more general phenomenon of capital investment in the banking industry. The same statements, of course, apply to any firm or industry. Entry, however, may represent different amounts of capital at different moments in time. This possibility should be accounted for in linking entry and capital investment. To provide such a linkage, express the number of banks in a particular market at a moment in time as,

$$B = \frac{C}{S} \tag{1}$$

where,

B = number of banks;
C = capital invested in the banking industry;
S = average capital size per bank.[9]

---

[9] We mean here capital invested by owners and entrepreneurs; in the banking industry this has historically been almost exclusively equity capital. Equation (1) could, of course,

In logarithmic form, (1) is:

$$\ln B = \ln C - \ln S. \tag{2}$$

Differentiate (2) with respect to time to get,

$$\frac{1}{B}\frac{dB}{dt} = \frac{1}{C}\frac{dC}{dt} - \frac{1}{S}\frac{dS}{dt} \tag{3}$$

This subdivides a change in the number of banks into a change in the stock of capital (that is, the rate of capital investment) and a change in the capital size per bank. The first part of our theory deals with the determinants of capital investment in banking. Later we shall adjust for intended changes in capital size per bank.

Capital Investment in Banking

Since any (positive or negative) flow of capital implies dissatisfaction with the present stock of capital, and vice versa, a primary problem of any theory of capital investment is to link stocks and flows. A convenient theoretical framework which does this is given by Milton Friedman in his *Price Theory*.[10] This framework has recently been exploited successfully by Meigs in his study of the determinants of the free reserve/deposits ratio,[11] and I shall use it here.

In Figure 1(b), let C*C* be a function relating the desired stock of bank capital (C) supplied (or held) by entrepreneurs to the expected rate of return on capital in banking (π). Each abscissa value represents a stock of capital such that, for the given ordinate, entrepreneurs would not wish to add or subtract from it once attained. (We are now abstracting from regulation.) The expected rate of return is assumed to be given autonomously, and the C*C* function is assumed to be positively sloped.[12] This way of defining the C*C* function immediately implies certain intended flow curves. These are illustrated in Figure 1(a), where the vertical axis is the same as for 1(b), and the horizontal axis represents the flow of capital per unit time. For example, if entrepreneurs are satisfied to supply OA at a rate of return OR_1, then the desired flow curve, given a stock of OA,

---

have been expressed as the ratio of any aggregate to its average amount per bank. The use of capital is dictated by the problem at hand—the formation of a new bank is simply a specific form of the investment of capital by owners and entrepreneurs in the banking industry.

[10] Friedman, Price Theory: A Provisional Text 244-246 (1962).

[11] Meigs, Free Reserves and the Money Supply especially ch. iv (1962).

[12] For some industries the elasticity of C*C* will be infinite at the going rate of interest; in order to keep the discussion general, we confine the elasticity to be some positive number. At this level of analysis, the terms "bank capital" and "rate of return on bank capital" are interchangeable with "capital" and "rate of interest."

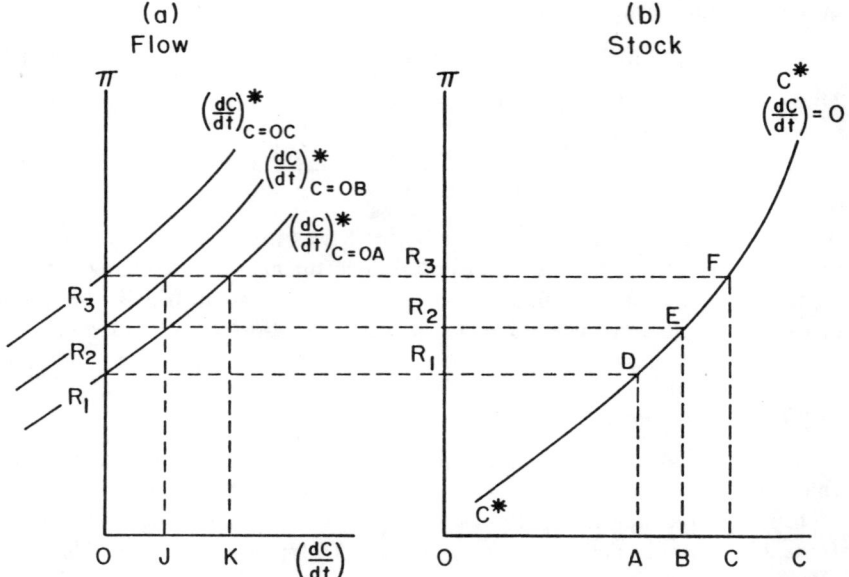

FIGURE 1.—Stock and Flow Supply Curves of Capital

must have a zero abscissa at ordinate OR_1. This is the curve $\left(\dfrac{dC}{dt}\right)^*_{C\,=\,OA}$
(which we assume to be positively sloped).[13] This curve must cut the vertical axis at OR_1, since if entrepreneurs would be satisfied to hold OA at OR_1, and OA is in fact the existing stock, there is no reason for them to add to or subtract from OA at a return OR_1. By the same reasoning, we know that for a stock of OB there is an accompanying intended flow curve, $\left(\dfrac{dC}{dt}\right)^*_{C\,=\,OB}$. Now suppose the anticipated rate of return rises to OR_3, with the desired stock becoming OC as indicated on C*C*. We wish to know how entrepreneurs add to their capital stock over time and move from the existing stock of OA to the new desired stock of OC. Temporarily, after the increase in the rate of return to OR_3, entrepreneurs will be operating on

[13] This assumption is forced on us by the assumed positive slope of C*C* and the assumed autonomous determination of π. This last assumption is another way of saying that the relevant flow demand curves are infinitely elastic. An increase in π away from a previous equilibrium must lead to a positive flow so that the new, higher desired stock is eventually attained. With infinitely elastic flow demand curves, this requires that the flow supply curves slope up: if they slope down and are "forward falling," the system does not have a stable equilibrium; if they slope down and are "backward bending," an increase in π from a previous equilibrium will lead to a negative flow.

the curve $\left(\dfrac{dC}{dt}\right)^{*}_{C\,=\,OA,}$ the flow curve appropriate to the now existing stock. Accordingly, with the rate of return of OR_3, they will wish to invest at the rate OK per unit time. However, as they effect such a positive investment, they simultaneously increase the actual stock of capital. Suppose that they have in fact added OK, and that, in consequence, the actual stock of capital rises to OB. With the stock at OB, entrepreneurs will be operating on the flow curve appropriate to that stock, $\left(\dfrac{dC}{dt}\right)^{*}_{C\,=\,OB.}$ This curve lies to the left[14] of the old flow curve, $\left(\dfrac{dC}{dt}\right)^{*}_{C\,=\,OA,}$ as it cuts the vertical axis at OR_2, the ordinate corresponding to OB on C*C*. On this net flow curve, entrepreneurs will wish to add to capital at a rate of only OJ at the rate of return OR_3. Having effected that addition, they will have once again increased the actual stock and will move to still another flow curve to the left of $\left(\dfrac{dC}{dt}\right)^{*}_{C\,=\,OB,}$ and will now wish to add a correspondingly smaller amount of capital than OJ. This process continues until the actual stock reaches the desired stock of OC. When this happens, entrepreneurs will be operating on the flow curve, $\left(\dfrac{dC}{dt}\right)^{*}_{C\,=\,OC,}$ and they will, as is indicated by the Y-intercept of that curve, desire no further addition to the stock of capital at the rate of return OR_3. The essence of this process is that the flow is largest (OK) when the difference between the desired stock and the actual stock is greatest (AC); as the actual stock approaches the desired stock and the difference narrows (as, for example, when it is at BC), the desired rate of addition to the stock is lowered (to OJ, to continue the example). Finally, when the desired stock is attained, and the difference between the desired and actual stock is consequently zero, the desired rate of flow is also zero. The process works in the same way for a negative discrepancy between the desired and actual stock of capital. The desired rate of disinvestment or capital consumption is greatest when the

[14] That it lies wholly to the left of $\left(\dfrac{dC}{dt}\right)^{*}_{C\,=\,OA}$ follows from the assumed positive slope of the desired stock curve. The flow curves enable us to read off a whole family of desired stock curves, one for each flow; a vertical line drawn at any flow level cuts each flow curve at the level of π which would be needed to maintain the stock for which the flow curve is defined, given that flow level, and the indicated combinations of stock values and π define one of the family of desired stock curves. Only the desired stock curve for a zero flow is illustrated. Were the flow curves to cross, some portion of some of the desired stock curves would bend downward.

excess of the actual stock over the desired stock is greatest. As capital is consumed, however, this discrepancy narrows, and the desired rate of reduction of the stock falls in absolute value. When the actual stock has been cut back to the desired level, the desired rate of change of the stock will be zero. The analysis of adjustment to a negative discrepancy between desired and actual stock is not worked through here, but this may be easily done, using the same apparatus illustrated in Figure 1 and reversing the direction of the posited change in π. The adjustment process may also be illustrated by fixing π and assuming an autonomous change in the stock of capital. This would lead to the same results as fixing C and varying π, as shown here.

The discussion up to now can be summarized by the following equations:

$$C^* = f(\pi, \ldots), \tag{4}$$

which represents the C*C* curve in Figure 1(b). (The ellipses stand for a set of factors other than π which influence the height of the C*C* curve, but which are omitted from the discussion at present.)

$$\left(\frac{dC}{dt}\right)^* = g(C^*, C), \tag{5}$$

which expresses the adjustment process described above. The desired rate of change of the stock of capital depends both on the desired stock of capital and the existing stock of capital.[15] Substituting (4) into (5), we obtain

$$\left(\frac{dC}{dt}\right)^* = h(\pi, C, \ \ldots). \tag{6}$$

The theory imposes the following conditions on these functions:

$$f_\pi > 0. \tag{7}$$

$$g_{C^*} > 0, g_C < 0, \text{ and } g = 0 \text{ for } C^* = C. \tag{8}$$

This says that intended investment is positive when the desired stock of capital exceeds the actual stock and negative when the desired stock is less than the actual stock.

$$h_\pi > 0, h_C < 0. \tag{9}$$

This apparatus enables us to analyze adjustment to a discrepancy between

---

[15] In order to avoid confusion in the later discussion, the reader should distinguish clearly between $\left(\dfrac{dC}{dt}\right)^*$, which is the intended rate of investment, and $\dfrac{dC^*}{dt}$, which is the change in the desired stock of capital with respect to time. The two are not, in general, equal except where adjustment of any discrepancy between desired and actual capital is always continuously complete.

desired and actual capital existing at a moment in time. However, the data we will work with are time series, and their secular behavior will require some modification of the form of adjustment equations like (5) and (6). Specifically, we know that the capital stock in banking, as in many industries, is growing over time (in terms of our model, C*C* is shifting secularly to the right). We must account for this secular growth in the adjustment equations; otherwise the system will not tend to equilibrium over time. This point can be illustrated by applying the model straightforwardly, without any explicit adjustment for the secular trend in C*. For example, we may assume a linear model in which (5) has the form,

$$\left(\frac{dC}{dt}\right)^* = \gamma(C^* - C),\tag{10}$$

where γ is a constant adjustment coefficient which, in general, lies between zero and unity. Now, for simplicity, suppose that C* is a linear function of the rate of return and of time; that is, it has a trend component, deviations from which are a function of the rate of return. This may be written as,

$$C^* = B_1\pi + B_2t.\tag{11}$$

A straightforward application of the model would reduce to combining (10) and (11) as,

$$\left(\frac{dC}{dt}\right)^* = \gamma B_1\pi + \gamma B_2t - \gamma C.\tag{12}$$

Now, suppose we are initially in equilibrium and keep π fixed. This will mean that, assuming equality of intended and actual investment, C will increase by γB_2 per unit time. However, C* will increase by B_2 per unit time, as given by (11). Since B_2 is greater than γB_2, only part of the disequilibrium is made up per unit time, and the gap between C* and C widens over time. Such a system, instead of moving toward an equilibrium is continuously moving away from equilibrium, and this is untenable if we purport to describe how an equilibrium capital stock is in fact attained.

One way to allow the system to attain equilibrium at a moment in time while the desired capital stock is growing secularly is to break the adjustment mechanism into two parts. One part will represent adjustment to disequilibria existing at a moment in time, and this adjustment need not be complete per unit time. This part of the adjustment process may be represented by an equation like (12), where γ is less than unity. The second part of the adjustment process will represent adjustment to the secular increase in the capital stock, and this adjustment should be allowed to be continuously complete, that is, should have an adjustment coefficient of unity. In terms of

20   THE JOURNAL OF LAW AND ECONOMICS

the linear model above, this would amount to letting C increase by B_2 per unit time, to adding B_2 to the right-hand side of (12). More generally, this assumes an adjustment equation where,

$$\left(\frac{dC}{dt}\right)^* = \gamma(C^* - C) + 1 \cdot \frac{\partial C^*}{\partial t}. \tag{13}$$

In this way, an equilibrium capital stock can be attained even if C^* is growing secularly. Further, if variables like π remain unchanged with C^* initially equal to C, the γ term becomes zero, and, as we should expect, yields no investment additional to that deriving from secular growth in the stock of capital. In this analysis, the B_2t term should be thought of as summarizing a set of factors which make the capital stock grow secularly. In principle, any variable which causes C^* to rise secularly should call forth continuously complete adjustment of C to C^*. Hence, if π, for example, were

changing secularly, we would include a term $B_1 \dfrac{d\pi}{dt}$ in the second term on

the right-hand side of (13). In order to simplify, however, we will neglect such terms where their expected values are likely to be negligible due, say, to the absence of any perceptible trend in the variables making them up, or where such variables behave so erratically over time as to make the assumption of continuously complete adjustment untenable.

This last point provides some insight into the economic justification for breaking up the adjustment process in the way we have. One reason why the adjustment process may *not* be continuously complete is that there are specific costs attached to altering plans and to reversing the direction of investment once a course has been set. The organization and planning of investment is a productive factor which is not free, and, where plans and projects must frequently be reversed, a greater amount of this factor will be required. Given this fact, an important determinant of the fraction of any discrepancy between desired and actual capital being made up at a moment in time is likely to be the certainty with which investors estimate any value of the variables in the C^* function. A high rate of return, for example, is likely to call forth less investment if that rate of return is uncertain and later events may thus call for reversal of current plans (with attendant costs), than if it were held with certainty. In the case of stable secular growth in the desired stock of capital, costs imposed by altering plans and the like are absent, and no part of the discrepancy between desired and actual capital caused by such stable growth need be left unadjusted on account of such costs. The assumption of continuously complete adjustment to secular change in the desired stock of capital involves a corollary assumption that the savings induced by the stability of the change causes all costs to be always smaller at the margin than the returns from complete adjustment.

Application of the Theory to Banking

In order to apply this analysis to the secular growth of the capital stock in banking, it will be helpful to specify the reasons for this growth and the role of capital in banking. Basically, capital in banking provides an insurance fund to depositors against the possibility of losses due to a reduction in the value of a bank's assets. Since the sum of deposits and capital differs from a bank's assets by only minor items, the amount of capital is the maximum that the value of a bank's assets can fall before depositors incur losses and the bank becomes insolvent. The more capital a bank has, therefore, the more deposits it may accept and/or the greater risk it may take on its earning assets. Turning this around, we can identify as the most important factor making for secular growth in the stock of capital the secular growth in the level of deposits. Over time, as a bank's deposits increase, it will want to increase its capital to protect its solvency. (Actually, when we speak of deposits we should refer to deposits net of cash assets. Since cash assets cannot decline in value, any increase in deposits matched by an increase in cash assets requires no further insurance in the form of an increase in capital. Hence cash assets may be netted out of both sides of the balance sheet for purposes of this discussion. Unless otherwise specified, therefore, we shall use the terms "deposits" and "deposits net of cash assets" interchangeably.)[16] In order to abstract from the effects of long term growth in deposits on capital, we shall proceed as follows: let

$$C = kD^\alpha, \tag{14}$$

where,

C = capital

D = deposits net of cash assets,

α = some positive constant,

k = ratio of C to D^α.

For present purposes, k may be taken to be a long run constant reflecting the normal fraction of a unit increase in the deposits term of (14) which entrepreneurs wish to match with new capital, so as to maintain their normal level of protection against insolvency. However k will later become a

---

[16] This is, of course, a drastic simplification. Capital's general role of protector of the solvency of a bank means that it must insure against the maximum decline in the value of assets within the time period in which the bank must meet its deposit liabilities. Thus, treasury bills may be considered the same as cash with respect to time deposits; all government bonds, since their prices were pegged, the same as cash for World War II to 1951, etc.

function. Note that I am not restricting the normal elasticity of capital with respect to deposits (α) to be unity. That is, I do not wish to restrict capital to be normally a constant fraction of deposits; α *may* be unity, but for the present I simply assume it to be some positive number.[17] The logarithmic form of (14) is:

$$\ln C = \ln k + \alpha \ln D. \tag{15}$$

Differentiating (15) with respect to time yields,

$$\left(\frac{1}{C} \frac{dC}{dt} \right) = \left(\frac{1}{k} \frac{dk}{dt} \right) + \alpha \left(\frac{1}{D} \frac{dD}{dt} \right) \tag{16}$$

All we have done so far is to break the percentage change in the stock of capital into the percentage change in k and α times the percentage change in D. Similarly any intended change in the capital stock may be broken up into an intended change in k and α times the expected growth in deposits. We will now identify α times the expected growth in deposits as the "secular trend" term in the desired stock of capital. That is, we assume that

$$\frac{\partial C^*}{\partial t} = \alpha \left(\frac{1}{D} \frac{dD}{dt} \right)^{\mathrm{E}} \tag{17}$$

where the E-superscript denotes "expected value." We also assume that entrepreneurs are continuously increasing their capital by this amount in full adjustment to the expected secular growth in deposits. For simplicity, we might assume that the expected secular rate of growth in deposits is a constant per unit time or a constant revised perhaps by past deposit growth;

---

[17] In point of fact, the reason I do not simplify further and restrict α to unity derives from historical evidence against such a procedure. The ratio of capital to deposits net of cash assets has been falling secularly with the secular increase in deposits, and this may indicate that α is less than one. To illustrate, the capital/deposits net of cash ratio for all U.S. Commercial banks has behaved as follows over time:

Year	Deposits-cash assets (billion dollars)	Ratio: Capital/deposits net of cash asset
1900	6.8	.42
1910	14.6	.36
1920	36.7	.20
1930	51.3	.23
1940	60.3	.20
1950	143.8	.10
1960	213.8	.12

Source: U.S. Board of Governors of the Federal Reserve System, All-Bank Statistics [of the] United States, 1896-1955, 36 (1959), and 46 Fed. Reserve Bull. 1359 (1960).

The general tendency seems to be for the ratio to fall fastest when deposits are rising most rapidly, which would, everything else the same, imply an α below unity.

ENTRY IN COMMERCIAL BANKING 23

but whatever it is, it is important that adjustment of the capital stock to it be continuously complete. Identifying $\dfrac{\partial C^*}{\partial t}$ with expected deposit growth is a simplifying assumption, and amounts to saying that any other factors making for secular growth in the stock of capital either have negligible influence or are reflected in the expected growth of deposits. This simplification leaves the remainder of any change in the capital stock to be accounted for by a change in k. Here we may employ in a straightforward fashion the capital theory developed previously. Specifically, let

$$\ln k^* = \phi(\pi, \ldots). \qquad (18)$$

This is analogous to the C*C* function in Figure 1 or equation (4), but instead of making a secularly changing desired stock of capital a function of the rate of return on capital, we make the desired value of a long term constant *ratio* of capital to a power of deposits a function of the rate of return.[18] Similarly, changes in ln k take place in response to the desired value of ln k (ln k*) and the actual value of ln k. However, since changes in ln k involve deviations from a long run constant, we do not assume the adjustment of ln k to ln k* to be continuously complete. In a linear model, this amounts to setting

$$\left(\frac{d \ln k}{dt}\right)^* = \gamma_1(\ln k^* - \ln k), \qquad (19)$$

or,

$$\left(\frac{1}{k}\frac{dk}{dt}\right)^* = \gamma_1(\ln k^* - \ln k)$$

where γ_1 is a positive constant between zero and unity. The intended change in the capital stock, therefore, becomes

$$\left(\frac{1}{C}\frac{dC}{dt}\right)^* = \gamma_1[\ln k^* - \ln k] + 1.\left[\alpha\left(\frac{1}{D}\frac{dD}{dt}\right)^{\mathrm{E}}\right]. \qquad (20)$$

(20) is analogous to the more general equation (13). We can now complete this discussion by substituting (18) into (20) and writing a general function

$$\left(\frac{1}{C}\frac{dC}{dt}\right)^* = \psi\left(\pi,\left[\alpha\left(\frac{1}{D}\frac{dD}{dt}\right)^{\mathrm{E}}\right], \ln k, \ldots\right) \qquad (21)$$

[18] The fact that we measure k in logs does not change the analysis, since the log transformation is monotonically positive. The conclusions of the analysis would not be altered were Figure 1, for example, marked off in units of ln C rather than units of C.

with restrictions

$$\psi_\pi > 0 \tag{22}$$

$$^{\Psi}\!\left[\alpha\left(\frac{1}{D}\frac{dD}{dt}\right)^{E}\right] = +1 \tag{23}$$

$$^{\Psi}\ln k < 0. \tag{24}$$

The Autonomous Determination of The Expected Rate of Return

Up to now, it has been assumed that the expected rate of return is determined independently of capital investment, or that the magnitude of investment we typically encounter is too small to perceptibly affect the rate of return. Violation of this assumption would pose serious problems for the empirical analysis. If capital investment and the rate of return in banking are mutually determined, ordinary least squares regression estimates of the relationship between them would be a mixture of the positive response of investment to the rate of return and the negative response of the rate of return to investment. Conceivably the estimated parameter could be negative, though the "true" parameter of a function like C*C* were positive.

The way in which I shall deal with this problem is to assume a lagged structural relationship. That is, the desired stock of capital (more specifically, the desired value of k) at time t will be assumed to be a function of rates of return prior to t, and similarly for the rate of investment. The necessary corollary, even if obvious, assumption is that prior rates of return are themselves unaffected by current investment.[19] Intuitively, we can visualize a stylized system in which the rate of return is set initially by past investment and "other factors," and investors then respond to this rate of return in the way implied by the theory. This response will in turn affect the current rate of return, which in its turn affects future investment, and so on through time.

Capital Investment in a Theory of Entry

The role of capital investment in explaining variations in entry rates may be derived from equation (3), which we repeat here with asterisks added to denote intended changes:

$$\left(\frac{1}{B}\frac{dB}{dt}\right)^{*} = \left(\frac{1}{C}\frac{dC}{dt}\right)^{*} - \left(\frac{1}{S}\frac{dS}{dt}\right)^{*}. \tag{3$'$}$$

On substituting (21) into (3)$'$, we get:

$$\left(\frac{1}{B}\frac{dB}{dt}\right)^{*} = \psi\left(\pi, \left[\alpha\left(\frac{1}{D}\frac{dD}{dt}\right)^{E}\right], \ln k, \dots\right) - \left(\frac{1}{S}\frac{dS}{dt}\right)^{*}. \tag{25}$$

[19] This is not so obvious an assumption if entrepreneurs base current expected profits on what they expect future investment to be.

ENTRY IN COMMERCIAL BANKING   25

The main focus of this article is on new entry, not net changes in the number of banks. The net rate of change in the number of banks, however, may be broken down into components:

$$\left(\frac{1}{B}\frac{dB}{dt}\right) = E_t - M_t - X_t \qquad (26)$$

or,

$$E_t = \left(\frac{1}{B}\frac{dB}{dt}\right) + M_t + X_t$$

where

  E_t = rate of formation of new banks at time t,
  M_t = rate of merger of banks at time t,
  X_t = rate of bank suspension and liquidation, net of reopenings, at
       time t.

These rates are defined as the number of banks entering, merging or failing per unit time divided by the existing total number of banks. This classification will be convenient in later discussion. (26) may be combined with (25) when we make the model operational by assuming intended changes equal to actual changes:

$$E_t = \psi\left(\pi, \left[\alpha\left(\frac{1}{D}\frac{dD}{dt}\right)^E\right], \ln k, \ldots\right) - \left(\frac{1}{S}\frac{dS}{dt}\right) + M_t + X_t. \qquad (27)$$

We now have to discuss more fully the variables in the ψ — function, both those already in it and those that should replace the ellipses, and we must discuss the determinants of the intended rate of change in capital size per bank. We take up the latter subject first.

Size Changes and Entry

  The problem we have here is basically one of how a given increase in the capital stock is shared between new and old firms. If we assume the existence of a unique, unchanging optimum size of firm, and each firm had already attained that size, the problem would be simple: any percentage change in the capital stock would imply an equal percentage change in the number of firms. However, some recent studies of bank costs present evidence which suggests that it would be wrong to assume that there is a unique optimum size for banks. They indicate that cost curves tend to decline sharply up to some small size and then become relatively flat.[20] The existence of such a

[20] See, *e.g.*, Schweiger and McGee, Chicago Banking, 34 J. of Bus. 203, 325-29 (1961), and Gramley, A Study of Scale Economies in Banking (1962).

long flat segment of the cost curve will make size changes to some extent arbitrary, and this may weaken the relationship between capital investment and entry. If firm size is indeterminate, a given rate of investment could be accompanied by an equal rate of increase in firm size, a less than proportional increase, or even a decline in firm size.

To some extent, we will have to accept this arbitrariness as a limitation on our attempt to link investment with entry. However, even with firm size indeterminate over some range, it is possible to specify factors systematically associated with intended changes in average bank size. Suppose that the size at which the firm cost curve flattens out increases; this means that some previously efficient firms would now be inefficient. Some of these firms will wish to grow more rapidly than the average of all firms in order to attain the new efficient size. Other newly inefficient firms will wish to leave the industry. In any case, the net result of an extension of scale economies is to increase the intended average size of firm.[21] Much the same argument applies to entrants—an extension of scale economies will discourage those firms which had intended to enter at the previous minimum efficient size from doing so; they will increase their entering capital or drop out. For a given amount of capital investment by entrants, extension of scale economies will therefore imply fewer and larger entering firms. Even with an indeterminate average size of bank, if the optimum size of some existing banks increases while the optimum size of the others remains indeterminate, we expect an increase in the average size of bank. One important way in which some firms can grow faster than average is by acquiring other firms; similarly, one way in which a firm may leave the industry is by selling out to another firm. The existence of scale economies, in fact, provides an incentive for such mergers. Firms smaller than the minimum efficient size would find returns to their capital lower than for large firms, and consequently the value of their capital to larger firms would be greater than its value to the smaller firms. Similarly the value to two such smaller firms of their total capital is greater when they merge than the sum of the values of their capital as independent firms. Thus, firms of less than minimum efficient size have an incentive to merge with larger firms or with one another. Increases in scale economies should therefore be positively associated with the rate of merger; the greater are the extensions in possible scale economies, the more should firms be merging to take advantage of them. Since increases in scale economies will cause intended firm size to be larger than the actual average size of firm, we would, in turn, expect the merger rate to be a good proxy for the intended rate of change of firm size.[22]

[21] There is no reason to assume that either the overall stock of capital or rate of investment is affected by an extension of scale economies.

[22] This proposition is, of course, independently testable, but is not meant to imply that all mergers take place solely to take advantage of new scale economies. It does imply

We will now return to the capital investment model in order to clarify some problems left unresolved in the previous discussion. Specifically, we will attempt to give operational meaning to the concept of "expected rate of return," and we will discuss "other factors" that should replace the ellipses in the investment function (21).

Making the Concept "Expected Rate of Return" Operational

In many past investment studies where expected profits played the role of an independent variable, it has been assumed that current profits provide the best observable measure of expected profits. Grunfeld, in his study of the determinants of corporate investment[23] challenged this assumption. He claimed that the good performance of realized profits as an explanatory variable in such studies derives from its acting as a "surrogate variable," that is, one which tends to be highly correlated with a more direct measure of expected profits. Grunfeld identified the "more direct measure" of a firm's expected profits with the *market value of the firm*, the price investors are willing to pay for claims to the future earnings of the firm. His empirical research led him to conclude that this more direct measure of expected profits better explained variation in investment behavior among firms than the current profit measure.

There are good theoretical reasons for anticipating such a result. The acid test of what investors expect future profits to be, after all, is the price they are willing to pay for claims to those profits. To the extent that current profits are subject to nonrecurrent or random influences that do not affect future returns, they should have no effect on either the price investors are willing to pay for claims to future earnings or the investment decisions of entrepreneurs. To the extent that changes in current profits are permanent, this should be reflected in a change in the market's valuation of the firm. The market value of the firm should thus represent a measure of expected profits unbiased by the nonrecurring, temporary factors influencing observed current profits.[24]

---

that one or both partners to a merger is typically a small bank, and that this small bank, on average has higher costs than other banks.

23 Grunfeld, The Determinants of Corporate Investment, in The Demand for Durable Goods 211 (Harberger Ed. 1960).

24 While a firm's market value represents the evaluation of a firm's earning prospects by stockholders and stock market traders, not the managers who make investment decision, there are good reasons to believe that any systematic differences in the two groups' evaluation would not persist (even apart from the obvious observation that sooner or later events will prove one or the other wrong, and either management will change its investment policy or investors will change their evaluation of the firm's future earnings). For example, if management policy indicated that it placed a different evaluation on a firm's prospects than did investors, the firm would become subject to a proxy fight, with the side more closely representing the views of investors standing the better chance of winning. Alternatively, management could buy or sell stock according as the market, in

To make Grunfeld's argument explicit we assume, for simplicity, a firm where the claims to its future earnings are represented by one share of common stock. This share of stock has a market value (V) given by the conventional discount formula,

$$V = \frac{R_1}{1+r} + \frac{R_2}{(1+r)^2} + \cdots + \frac{R_n}{(1+r)^n} + \frac{V_n}{(1+r)^n}, \quad (28)$$

where the R_i are expected dollar earnings of the firm in year i, and r is an appropriate discount rate; V_n is an expected receipt to be realized upon liquidation of the firm n years from now. Without affecting the results of the discussion, we can simplify by making n infinite and choosing an average dollar amount of earnings ($\overline{R}$) such that, when substituted for each of the R_i in an infinite earnings stream, the same discounted value will be obtained. That is, we choose an $\overline{R}$ such that

$$V = \frac{\overline{R}}{r} = \sum_{i=1}^{\infty} \frac{R_i}{(1+r)^i}. \quad (29)$$

We can look at the components of (29) in two ways: we can assume that the values of the R are known and pick an r that equates them to presently observable market values, or we can fix r and pick a set of R and an $\overline{R}$ that are consistent with the observable V. In order to abstract from risk considerations, the latter procedure will be used. In particular, if we choose for r the long-term default-free rate of interest, $\overline{R}$ would be a "certainty equivalent" annual dollar return estimated from (29) as,

$$\overline{R} = rV, \quad (30)$$

where r is now the default-free bond rate, and V is the observable market

---

its opinion, was undervaluing or overvaluing the firm's future earnings. Both types of activity would tend to bring management expectations and market values into closer association. However, the costs of waging proxy fights or the amount of capital required to perceptibly influence the price of a stock might make such activities unlikely, especially for very widely-held firms, and differences in expectations could persist for fairly long periods of time.

A more serious drawback to use of stock market values is that they tell us nothing of the expected time distribution of expected profits. A given increase in today's market value may represent an expected increase of X dollars per year in earnings next year, or some appropriate multiple of X ten years from now. If it represented the latter, and it cost nothing to delay a project, such an increase in market value might be expected to affect investment ten years from now, but not today. Since a stock market value is an estimate only of a sum of future profits discounted to the present, it tells us nothing of the expected distribution of the parts of that sum through time. If current profits more accurately reflect anticipated profits over the near term than do market values, it may be the more appropriate expected profits variable for a study of investment.

value of the share of stock. $\overline{R}$ is not itself directly observable, but is inferred from the observed values of r and V.

In this procedure, the share of stock may be viewed as exchangeable in the market for a default-free bond promising to pay $\overline{R}$ per year for certain indefinitely, with the rate of exchange given by V. To be concrete, if I owned a share of Company X selling in the market at $1,000, and the default-free bond rate was 5 per cent, I could sell my stock and buy $1,000 worth of bonds yielding me $50 per year for certain indefinitely. In this sense, my share of stock is equivalent to a promise to pay $50 per year for certain indefinitely.[25] If investors expected that future earnings of the firm would, after allowance for risk, be the equivalent of something other than $50 per year for certain indefinitely, the value of the stock or the default-free interest rate or both would have to change to maintain equilibrium in the bond market and the stock market.

The expression (30) was employed by Grunfeld as a measure of the expected dollar *amount* of profits per year. To convert this expression to an expected annual profit *rate* (π^*), we must divide rV by an appropriate capital base (C_o). Thus,

$$\pi^* = \frac{\overline{R}}{C_o} = \frac{rV}{C_o} \tag{31}$$

C_o should be a measure of the capital required to duplicate the firm. It should include, therefore, in addition to the replacement cost of its tangible capital, the capitalized value of permanent rents to specialized factors. C_o should, however, be defined to exclude the capitalized value of expected net quasi-rents for capital. We assume that the firm can be duplicated without payment for quasi-rents, and it is in fact this possibility that motivates the investment decision. The ratio of V to C_o then gives the value of a dollar of capital employed in the particular way our hypothetical company is employing it. Multiplying this ratio by the default-free rate of interest gives the certainty equivalent annual rate of return for capital employed by that firm. To continue with our example, suppose it cost $500 to duplicate Company X, and the market valued it at $1,000. With the default-free bond rate at 5 per cent, we infer a certainty equivalent return of $50 per year, or a certainty equivalent rate of return of 10 per cent per year on the $500 investment required to duplicate Company X.[26]

In the empirical work, C_o is represented by invested capital stated at book

---

[25] This is not to say that my stock entitles me to a *legal* claim to $50 per year indefinitely, but only that the market *values* the future earning power of the company as equivalent to that of a consol promising a certain stream of $50 per year indefinitely.

[26] This may be broken down into a "normal" return of $25 or 5 per cent on the $500 plus expected net quasi-rents of $25 or 5 per cent per year.

value, even though this has defects as a measure of the cost of duplicating a firm's assets. Most firms state assets at historical cost rather than replacement cost, and generally do not write them up or down to reflect the value of any rents accruing to the firm. In addition, there are tax incentives to exaggerate depreciation rates on assets, to charge capital expenditures to operating costs, etc. These defects may be less glaring for banks, where capital is invested largely in earning assets with fixed maturity values. Even for banks, however, past interest rate changes not reflected in loan book values, tax incentives to overstate loan loss reserves and depreciation of owned real estate, etc., will introduce distortions. As a practical matter, however, the difficulties involved in adjusting stated book values rule out use of any alternative; and it should be noted that the distortions involved in their use apply both to profit rates deduced from stock market values and to those deduced from current profits, since both measures will be divided by the same capital base.

The empirical work will test two alternative measures of expected profits to see which better fits the model derived here. One such measure, computed from (31), is obtained by multiplying a ratio of market to book value by a default-free interest rate; the other is the ratio of current profits to book value. If Grunfeld's theory has validity for this study, the measure derived from (31) should explain the data better than the current rate of return.

The Influence of Other Factors on Capital Investment and Entry into Banking

A complete specification of all the factors influencing the rate of investment and the rate of entry into banking is obviously impossible. We have so far singled out expected profits, intended size changes, expected growth in deposits, and the stock of capital (deflated by a power of deposits) as affecting the desired rate of change in the number of banks. We list below two additional factors which will be studied in the empirical work, and then proceed to a discussion of the expected effects of regulation on the model.

1. *Risk.*—The use of a "certainty equivalent" rate of return should, theoretically, dispense with the need for an independent estimate of the risk attaching to the stream of future earnings of the firm, at least as regards the returns computed from (31). If investors are risk averse and the expected variance of bank earnings rises, they will place a lower valuation on bank shares, and the certainty equivalent rate of return will fall. However, for measured current profits, some independent estimate of the variance of profit rates is required, since measured profits themselves cannot be regarded as a certainty equivalent return.

There is a more compelling reason, deriving from the nature of the data we shall work with, for adjusting for risk, and it applies both to stock prices and current profits. Profit rates constructed from either stock prices or current profits give more weight to the results of successful firms than to those of firms which fail. In a stock price index, failing banks whose value goes to zero are replaced to preserve continuity of the series; in a current profits series, losses of failing banks are counted only to the date of failure, while ideally the annual rate of their losses (if we measure returns over a one-year period) should be subtracted from the annual rate of return for successful banks. Unless all failing banks failed on December 31, and their losses up to failure were therefore counted for a whole year, current profit figures would not adequately reflect the risk of loss to a new bank, and would overstate expected returns. The amount of overstatement in a particular year would depend on the time distribution of failures over the year. Since the risk that a firm will fail is a relevant magnitude for the decisions of its organizers, and since both stock prices of successful firms and current profits do not fully account for this risk, an independent estimate of this risk is necessary in any empirical estimate of the models derived here. This is likely to be most important for the 1920's and early 1930's when the rate of bank failure was historically high.[27]

The argument may be stated more precisely as follows:[28] suppose an entrepreneur plans to commit his capital to banking for some discrete time period in the expectation of earning a rate of return $(\bar{\pi})$ per that time period. $\bar{\pi}$ can be expressed as

$$\bar{\pi} = P(S) \cdot \bar{\pi}_S + [1 - P(S)] \cdot \bar{\pi}_F \qquad (32)$$

or the probability that the bank will be successful $[P(S)]$ times the expected rate of return if successful $(\bar{\pi}_S)$ plus the probability that the firm will fail while the capital is committed to banking $[1 - P(S)]$ times the rate of return if it fails $(\bar{\pi}_F)$. For simplicity, we assume that failure results in a total loss of capital, so $\bar{\pi}_F$ is equal to -100 per cent per the time unit over which the π are measured. This makes the expected loss for the firm equal to the probability of failure.[29] What we observe in the empirical data is essentially $\bar{\pi}_S$. In order to compute $\bar{\pi}$, therefore, we need an independent estimate of $P(S)$.

[27] In this same period, both new banks and failing banks tended to be small. However, aggregate current profits data and, especially, stock prices will be heavily weighted by the results of large banks. Such figures may, therefore, apart from the reason noted above, not adequately reflect the risk of failure facing new banks. This provides another reason for wanting an independent estimate of the risk of failure.

[28] I am indebted to Lester Telser for pointing out the problem raised here and for suggesting the line of reasoning used here to deal with it.

[29] In point of fact, for the period to which this analysis is most relevant—the 1920's and 1930's—bank stockholders were subject to double liability on the par value of their shares. Thus, they could sometimes expect to lose more than their capital investment in case of a failure.

In the empirical work the probability of failure $[1 - P(S)]$ will be taken to be a function of the actual rate of failure of existing banks. This would appear reasonable on two counts: first, a high rate of failure of existing banks should reflect market conditions making failure more probable for currently established (or establishing) institutions; second, the tendency of bank failures to cause a "run" on existing institutions is stronger the more general are bank failures.

2. Alternative employments for bank capital.—An entrepreneur contemplating the investment of capital in banking must consider not only the expected return on capital in banking, but also that in other industries. An increase in the profitability of capital in banking may coincide with an increase in the profitability of capital in other industries, in which case we might expect investment to increase in all sectors—banking as well as other industries. However, the increase in capital investment in banking should be smaller than if profitability increased only in banking. Thus, the height of the C*C* function should be negatively related to the expected profitability of capital in employments other than banking.

In constructing a variable to reflect profits of capital in alternative uses, we shall want it to be consistent with the variable used for expected profits of bank capital. Where we use stock market data for a bank profits variable, we should use stock market data for other industries; where current profits in banking is used, current profits in other industries should be used as the alternative returns variable. Accordingly, in our test of Grunfeld's hypothesis, a variable following from equation (31) will be constructed for alternative uses for bank capital, and it will be tested against an analogous current profit rate. The operational definition of "alternative uses for bank capital" will be an aggregate of the manufacturing industries.

The Effect on the Model of Introducing Regulatory Limitations on Entry

Up to now we have abstracted completely from the regulatory limitation on new entry in banking. In order to complete the theoretical discussion, we must now consider explicitly the effect of this regulation on our model.

The most important effect of regulation on the model is to cast doubt on the operational significance of functions like C*C* in Figure 1. Quite obviously, a function describing the stock of capital entrepreneurs are willing to hold is operationally meaningless if entrepreneurs are arbitrarily prevented from effecting its acquisition. Such functions must be defined to include the effect of regulation; C*C* should be a function relating the expected rate of return to the desired stock of capital supplied by entrepreneurs and permitted by the regulatory authorities. This, however, calls for some hypotheses about regulation.

1. Effect of Regulation on the Adjustment of Actual to Desired Capital Stock

Regulation may both shift the C*C* function to the left and change its shape. In the first case, we would expect a reduced rate of entry at every level of the expected rate of return—that is, the intercept of an estimate of an equation like (27) should be lowered by the introduction of regulation. This is the most direct test of the impact of regulation on entry, since a significant lowering of the intercept would affirmatively answer the question: everything else the same, was the average level of new entry lower in the post-regulatory period as compared with the pre-regulatory period? Accordingly, the test for a change in intercept will be the primary way in which the effect of regulation will be measured.[30]

2. Effect of Regulation on the Intended Change in Capital Size Per Bank

In addition to (or in place of) restricting the amount of new capital invested in banking, restrictions on entry may increase the normal rate of growth of existing firms. To the extent that size of firm may be expected to grow at some normal rate over time, the previous discussion implied that the merger rate is a proxy variable for intended deviations from this normal rate. Even if this average rate of growth did increase due to restricted entry, there is no clear reason to expect a change in the rate at which entry responds to variations in the merger rate with the introduction of regulation.[31] The most important effect of any increase in the average rate of growth of firm size

---

[30] We might expect an effective regulatory policy, in addition to lowering the level of entry, to change its response to the economic variables in (27). Unfortunately, the direction of any such change is not easy to forecast. For example, an effective regulatory policy might entail a slowing in the rate at which entry *changes* in response to a change, say, in the expected rate of return. Operationally this means a lower coefficient, in a linear estimate of (27), for an expected profits variable post-regulation as compared to pre-regulation. However, this assumes that regulators are not sensitive to the pressures of potential entrants. If they are sensitive to such pressures, an opposite prediction about the coefficient of expected profits would follow. Regulators would find it easier to turn down charter applications when the pressure for obtaining charters is lowest—i.e., when profits are low. However, when profits are high, and the pressures from new entrants are consequently greater, the authorities might permit actual entry to approach free-entry results more closely. Measured over a range of profit rates, then the slope of the response of entry to the profit rate would be *greater* in the post-regulatory period than in the pre-regulatory period, even though the average *level* of new entry would be lower.

[31] There is some evidence that the regulators prefer larger entering banks than do potential entrants. For example, a frequent cause for rejecting applications is insufficient entering capital. Since applicants might hold back committing additional capital until they felt that a larger firm was economically justified, the regulators might find it easier to get groups to commit additional capital when intended growth of firm size (as reflected in the merger rate) is high. On this account, the negative relationship between entry and the merger rate would be lessened by regulation.

34   THE JOURNAL OF LAW AND ECONOMICS

due to regulation, then, should be a lower average level of entry. That is, it should cause the intercept of an entry function to be lower.[32]

There is reason to believe that the degree of association between the rates of entry and merger will be weaker in the post-regulatory period than in the pre-regulatory period, *if* regulation is effective. Effective entry restriction makes merger for monopoly power much more likely of success than otherwise, and we would expect more mergers so motivated to take place in the presence of entry restriction. Since such mergers do not necessarily require unexploited scale economies to make them attractive, the accuracy of the merger rate as a proxy variable for intended size changes due to unexploited scale economies will be reduced by entry restriction.

3. *Other Effects of Regulation*

Since it takes time to process charter applications, regulation of entry might make the response of entry to the factors influencing it operate with a longer *lag* than otherwise. This could occur even if regulation were ineffective in reducing the number of entrants. However, it took some time to process charter applications in the period prior to 1935, so that a longer lag in response after 1935 would be the result only of any time added to the application process by Federal regulation. However, since the empirical work will deal with entry rates measured over one year periods, it may prove difficult to detect such additional lags in response.[33]

To the extent that the regulatory authorities employ their discretionary power in an arbitrary or not easily predictable way, regulation should introduce more variance into the response of entry to economic variables. At one extreme, the authorities might determine the permitted number of new banks on criteria wholly divorced from those motivating entrepreneurs not subject to regulation, for example, by fixing rigid maximum entry levels, by granting charters on the basis of political favoritism, etc. In this situation, entry would

---

[32] It makes no difference to an analysis of the past effects of regulatory restriction on entry whether and in what proportions the restriction was reflected in lower capital investment or greater average growth in firm size. However, it would be important to know this to draw inferences about what would happen were the entry restriction dropped today. If the only effect of entry restriction were an increase in the rate of growth of existing firms, and the rate of capital investment was unaffected, a return to free entry would imply a far smaller increase in the rate of entry than if the size of the capital stock were also materially reduced by past entry restriction.

[33] Indeed, I am told by an officer of a Chicago bank who has assisted most of the recent applicant groups in Illinois that the application procedure typically takes about one year to complete. This covers the period from the decision of the group to organize to the date of approval, rejection or withdrawal of the application before the appropriate Federal authority. If the Illinois experience is typical, the differential lag imposed by Federal regulation should be less than one year.

respond hardly at all to economic variables.[34] At the other extreme, regulatory authorities might permit entry to vary with changes in economic variables in exactly the same manner as prior to regulation, though reducing its average level. In this case, the intercept of an entry function would be lowered, but its other parameters and its overall explanatory power would be left unchanged.[35] The most likely effect of regulation on the predictive power of an entry function would be to reduce it, though relevant economic variables will retain some explanatory power, because of their influence on initial applications.

If nonmeasurable changes in regulatory attitudes persist in their effects over time and tend to be reversed only slowly, one possible result might be the introduction of a greater cyclical component into the rate of entry. That is, we would expect greater than average restriction of entry in one year to persist into the next; similarly for less than average restriction. Operationally, this means that the residuals from an entry estimating function would tend to have a higher degree of positive serial correlation after the onset of regulation than before.

Mathematical Summary

The theory in this section can be summarized by the following equations:

$$B = \frac{C}{S} \tag{1}$$

$$\left(\frac{1}{B} \frac{dB}{dt} \right)^* = \left(\frac{1}{C} \frac{dC}{dt} \right)^* - \left(\frac{1}{S} \frac{dS}{dt} \right)^* \tag{3$'$}$$

$$\left(\frac{1}{B} \frac{dB}{dt} \right) = E_t - M_t - X_t, \text{ or } E_t = \left(\frac{1}{B} \frac{dB}{dt} \right) + M_t + X_t \tag{26}$$

$$\left(\frac{1}{C} \frac{dC}{dt} \right)^* = \psi \left(\pi, \left[\alpha \left(\frac{1}{D} \frac{dD}{dt} \right)^E \right], \ln k, \mu, \pi^0, R, u \right) \tag{21$'$}$$

Here we replace the ellipses in (21) with risk of capital loss (μ), the rate of

---

[34] The phrase "hardly at all" is used rather than "not at all," since the regulatory authorities cannot initiate charter applications, but can only rule on applications initiated by investors. Since such applications would be expected to be related to economic variables, only the most extreme kind of arbitrariness on the part of regulators (for example, a policy of allowing no new banks) would make actual entry totally independent of such variables.

[35] A special case of this would be the totally ineffective regulatory policy, in which case not even the intercept would be reduced.

36 THE JOURNAL OF LAW AND ECONOMICS

return on alternative uses for bank capital (π°), and we introduce regulation (R) and a random error term (u) into the ψ-function.[36]

$$E_t = \psi\left(\pi, \left[\alpha\left(\frac{1}{D}\frac{dD}{dt}\right)^E\right], \ln k, \mu, \pi^\circ, R, u\right) - \left(\frac{1}{S}\frac{dS}{dt}\right) + M_t + X_t \tag{27$'$}$$

In the next section (27)$'$ will be estimated.

III. Empirical Results

In this section, we present empirical estimates of the model developed in the preceding section, and estimate the effect of regulation on entry into banking. In these estimates, aggregate annual data for the United States in the years 1921-62 are used.

The model we wish to estimate, expressed as equation (27)$'$ above, is written in continuous form. Since the data we shall use are measured over annual periods, we introduce the following discrete approximations to the continuous variables in (27)$'$: let

$e_t =$ the number of new commercial banks formed in year t divided by the number of banks existing in year t; this will approximate E_t.

$m_t =$ the number of commercial banks merging in year t divided by the number of banks existing in year t; this will approximate M_t.

$x_t =$ the number of commercial banks failing and liquidating, net of those reopening, in year t divided by the number of banks existing in year t; this will approximate X_t.

$\pi_{t-j} =$ expected annual rate of return on capital in banking in year $t - j$; we introduce a lag to correspond to the recursive model introduced in the preceding section.

$\pi^\circ_{t-j} =$ corresponding expected annual rate of return on capital in other industries in year $t - j$.

[36] This last procedure is for expositional convenience only, since both R and u may be included in either $\left(\frac{1}{C}\frac{dC}{dt}\right)$ or $\left(\frac{1}{S}\frac{dS}{dt}\right)$ or both.

$\ln k_t = \ln \left(\dfrac{C_t}{D_t{}^a} \right)$ = log of the ratio of capital in banking in year t (C_t) to a power (α) of bank deposits, net of cash assets, in year t (D_t); this will approximate $\ln k$.

$g_t{}^E = \alpha$ times the expected percentage increase in deposits, net of cash assets, in year t; this will approximate $\left[\alpha \left(\dfrac{1}{D} \dfrac{dD}{dt} \right)^E \right]$, and we will assume it to be a constant every year.

μ_t = risk of capital loss in year t.

$\left(\dfrac{\Delta S}{S} \right)_t$ = intended change in capital size per bank in year t divided by actual capital size per bank in year t; this corresponds to $\left(\dfrac{1}{S} \dfrac{dS}{dt} \right)$.

R_t = "regulation."

u_t = a random error term.

In order to estimate (27)′, we combine these discrete approximations in a linear model of the following form:

$$e_t = A_1 + B_1 \ln \pi_{t-j} + B_2 g_t{}^E + B_3 \ln k_t + B_4 \mu_t$$
$$+ B_5 \ln \pi^o{}_{t-j} + B_6 R_t + B_7 \left(\dfrac{\Delta S}{S} \right)_t + m_t + x_t + u_t. \quad (33)$$

Since

$$\ln k_t = \ln \left(\dfrac{C_t}{D_t{}^a} \right) = \ln C_t - \alpha \ln D_t, \text{ the } \ln k_t \text{ term in } (33)$$

may be written,

$$B_3 \ln C_t - \alpha B_3 \ln D_t.$$

Breaking the $\ln k_t$ term up in this way will enable us to estimate α. In the theoretical discussion μ_t was held to be a function of x_t; in particular we let

$$\mu_t = A_2 + B_8 x_t; \quad (34)$$

Similarly $\left(\dfrac{\Delta S}{S} \right)_t$ was held to be a function of m_t; we express this relationship by

$$\left(\dfrac{\Delta S}{S} \right)_t = A_3 + B_9 m_t. \quad (35)$$

Since we wish to estimate the effect of regulation on the average level of new entry, and since we date the onset of Federal regulation at the Banking Act of 1935, R_t is expressed as a dummy variable taking the value zero for all years 1921-35 and unity for all years 1936-62. We then substitute the two parts of $\ln k_t$ and equations (34) and (35) into (33) to get

$$e_t = A_1 + B_1 \ln \pi_{t-j} + B_2 g_t^E + B_3 \ln C_t - \alpha B_3 \ln D_t$$
$$+ B_4 (A_2 + B_8 x_t) + B_5 \ln \pi^o{}_{t-j} + B_6 R_t + B_7 (A_3 + B_9 m_t)$$
$$+ m_t + x_t + u_t \qquad (36)$$

Regrouping and combining terms, this becomes

$$e_t = (A_1 + B_2 g_t^E + B_4 A_2 + B_7 A_3) + B_1 \ln \pi_{t-j}$$
$$+ B_3 \ln C_t - \alpha B_3 \ln D_t + (1 + B_4 B_8) x_t + B_5 \ln \pi^o{}_{t-j}$$
$$+ B_6 R_t + (1 + B_7 B_9) m_t + u_t.$$

The combination of terms in the parentheses is constant for every year; we can predict the value of B_2 (it should be unity, since g_t^E is assumed to be fully adjusted to every year) as well as the signs of B_4 and B_7 (see below), but this is not enough information to predict the sign of the combined constant term. The expected values of the other coefficients are as follows:

$B_1 > 0$
$B_3 < 0$
$\alpha > 0$, so $(-\alpha B_3) > 0$
$B_4 < 0$
$B_5 < 0$
$B_6 \leqslant 0$
$B_7 = -1$
$B_8 > 0$, so $B_4 B_8 < 0$, or $(1 + B_4 B_8) < 1$
$B_9 > 0$, so $B_7 B_9 < 0$, or $(1 + B_7 B_9) < 1$.

Equation (36) was estimated by method of least squares using aggregate annual data for the United States for 1921-62. In order to test the Grunfeld hypothesis, two alternative expressions were used for the π. One was the rate of interest times the ratio of market to book value computed from a bank stock price index and from a manufacturing stock price index (henceforth referred to as the "market" rate of return and indicated by the superscript "m" before the π); the other was the current rate of return on capital in banking and in manufacturing (indicated by the "c" superscript before the π).[37] Since the model depends on past values of the π, both one and two-year

---

[37] Both banking profits variables, as well as the D and C variables exclude results of New York City Central Reserve City banks. Preliminary tests indicated that such an exclusion improved the results obtained.

lagged values of the π were used, singly and in combination. Table 1 presents the regression estimates.[38]

The most important conclusions yielded by the regressions are:

(1) they provide striking confirmation of the Grunfeld hypothesis, and

(2) they indicate that Federal regulation of new entry has had a large impact on actual new entry by almost any standard for the term "large." These conclusions are discussed in turn.

Entry and Rates of Return

As between the two alternative definitions of the rate of return variable, regression estimates employing the market rate of return variable consistently yield a better fit to the data than those using current rates of return. In Table 1, regressions T1, T2 and T3 are estimates of the basic model using market and current rates of return alternatively. Of this triplet, regression T1, using the market rate of return lagged one year, best fits the data; it yields the highest coefficient of determination and lowest standard error of estimate. The best fit to the data found by using a single lagged value of the current rate of return is regression T2 where the lag is two years. Neither it nor T3, which uses two lagged values of the current rate of return, fit the data better than T1.

The presence of high collinearity between the banking and manufacturing market rate of return variables[39] makes it difficult to assess the separate effects of the market rate of return in manufacturing. This is reflected in the insignificant coefficient, with the "wrong" sign, of log $^m\pi^0_{t-1}$ in T1. Regression T4 drops that variable, with no reduction in goodness of fit. T4 also reveals clearly the source of the superiority of estimates using the market rate of return. The partial correlation coefficient of log $^m\pi_{t-1}$ with the dependent variable is greater than that for any current rate of return in T2 or T3. Further when, in T5, the best performing current rate of return, $^c\pi_{t-2}$, is added to T4, its coefficient is not significantly positive at the $2\frac{1}{2}$ per cent level, and the overall fit of T5 is virtually identical to that of T4. The market rate of return appears to explain all of that part of the variation of the dependent variable explainable by any rate of return.

Thus, these results strongly confirm Grunfeld's hypothesis that the good fit of current profits variables in estimates of capital investment models (and the fit is "good" here too—banking current rate of return variables do have significantly positive coefficients) reflects their surrogate relationship to mar-

---

[38] A more extensive set of regression estimates and a more detailed discussion of their significance may be found in my dissertation, *supra* note * p. 11. Where a conclusion is asserted here without supporting data, the relevant data may be found in the dissertation.

[39] The simple correlation coefficient of log $^m\pi_{t-1}$ with log $^m\pi^0_{t-1}$ is .837.

TABLE 1

REGRESSION ESTIMATES—DETERMINANTS OF ENTRY RATE, 1921-62 (41 OBSERVATIONS)

Equation	Constant Term	Rates of Return on Capital						Merger Rate	Net Failure Rate	Deposits (logs)	Capital (logs)	Regu-lation	R^2	$S_{y \cdot (x)}$
		From Stock Prices (logs)		From Current Profits										
		Banking	Manu-facturing	Banking		Manu-facturing								
		log $_m\pi_{t-1}$	log $_m\pi^0_{t-1}$	$_c\pi_{t-1}$	$_c\pi_{t-2}$	$_c\pi^0_{t-1}$	$_c\pi^0_{t-2}$	m_t	x_t	log D_t	log C_t	R_t		
T1														
a. Coefficient	.231	1.863	.006					−.232	−.047	.621	−1.100	−.580	.871	.155
b. Standard error		.400	.403					.073	.022	.329	.526	.130		
c. T-ratio		4.656	.015					−3.173	−2.164	1.889	−2.090	−4.472		
d. Partial r		.630	.003					−.483	−.353	.312	−.342	−.614		
T2														
a. Coefficient	−.498				.126		−.040	−.082	−.015	1.212	−1.425	−.720	.789	.199
b. Standard error					.027		.019	.095	.024	.416	.729	.149		
c. T-ratio					4.681		−2.017	−.862	−.601	2.915	−1.954	−4.843		
d. Partial r					.632		−.344	−.148	−.104	.452	−.322	−.645		
T3														
a. Coefficient	−.898			.077	.105	.017	−.063	.007	−.009	1.436	−2.264	−.551	.834	.182
b. Standard error				.030	.027	.018	.020	.092	.022	.398	.745	.148		
c. T-ratio				2.617	3.868	.956	−3.143	.075	−.402	3.606	−3.041	−3.715		
d. Partial r				.425	.571	.169	−.492	.014	−.072	.544	−.479	−.555		

TABLE 1 (Continued)

Equation	Constant Term	Rates of Return on Capital						Merger Rate m_t	Net Failure Rate x_t	Deposits (logs) $\log D_t$	Capital (logs) $\log C_t$	Regulation R_t	R^2	$Sy \cdot (x)$
		From Stock Prices (logs)		From Current Profits										
		Banking log $_m r_{t-1}$	Manufacturing log $_m r^o_{t-1}$	Banking $_c r_{t-2}$	$_c r_{t-1}$	Manufacturing $_c r^o_{t-1}$	$_c r^o_{t-2}$							
T4														
a. Coefficient	.234	1.868						−.231	−.047	.619	−1.097	−.579	.871	.153
b. Standard error		.241						.064	.017	.267	.487	.117		
c. T-ratio		7.735						−3.596	−2.750	2.315	−2.253	−4.968		
d. Partial r		.799						−.525	−.427	.369	−.360	−.649		
T5														
a. Coefficient	.057	1.642			.032			−.178	−.051	.683	−1.327	−.540	.878	.151
b. Standard error		.290			.024			.074	.017	.268	.509	.118		
c. T-ratio		5.660			1.369			−2.399	−2.990	2.547	−2.605	−4.560		
d. Partial r		.702			.232			−.385	−.462	.405	−.413	−.622		

Note: R^2 = coefficient of determination
$Sy \cdot (x)$ = Standard error of estimate
The dependent variable (e_t) and all other ratios are expressed in percentage points (1.00 = 1 per cent)

ket rates of return.[40] This is seen most readily in T4. Both its overall fit and the partial correlation coefficient of the market rate of return variable with the entry rate are superior to any alternative using current profits.

The Effect of Regulatory Limitation of New Entry

The most important test we made to detect the presence of any impact of legal limitation of new entry on actual new entry was for a significant change in the average level of the entry rate from the pre- to the post-regulatory period. This test is summarized by the coefficient of the dummy variable, R_t, in the regressions.

In every one of the regressions in Table 1, the coefficient of R_t is significantly negative. In regression T4, which we have taken as the best estimate of the basic model, this coefficient is nearly five times its standard error, and neither its significance level nor its value is much different in the other regressions. The coefficient of R_t is not only consistently negative and significant, but also represents an effect which is certainly nontrivial relative to the magnitudes we are working with. The coefficient of R_t in T4 is —.579, and it has a standard error of .117. The dependent variable is measured in percentage points, so this coefficient yields the average percentage point reduction in the annual rate of entry, *ceteris paribus,* for 1936-62 as compared to 1921-35. Over the whole 1921-62 period, the rate of entry averaged .766 per cent per year. For 1936-62 it averaged .605 per cent per year. The coefficient of R_t is nearly equal to this last amount. If we may legitimately attribute the effect caught by R_t to regulation (see below), our "best guess" based on this comparison is that the annual rate of entry would, on average, have been nearly double what it actually was in the absence of the limitations on new entry imposed by the Banking Act of 1935. Even if we are willing to accept no more than a $2\frac{1}{2}$ per cent risk of error, we would accept the hypothesis that the "true" value of the coefficient is no greater algebraically than —.579 + 2(.117), or —.345. This is still more than half the average rate of entry actually observed since 1935. A similar lower bound estimate of the coefficient of R_t is —.813, or about $1\frac{1}{2}$ times the observed average rate of entry. These limits, then, yield an order of magnitude for the effect of regulation of between 50 and over 100 per cent of the actual rate of entry since 1935.

The significantly negative and numerically large relation between the entry rate and the dummy variable may, of course, be a misleading measure of the effect of regulation. One problem is collinearity of the dummy variable with other independent variables. Such collinearity might cause the effect attribu-

---

[40] The simple correlation coefficient of log $^m\pi_{t-1}$ with $^c\pi_{t-1}$ is .660. The better results obtained with two-year lagged current profits than with a one-year lag may reflect the closer relationship of $^c\pi_{t-2}$ with log $^m\pi_{t-1}$; the simple correlation coefficient between the two is .729.

table to one independent variable to be "spread" between that variable and the dummy variable, thus biasing the coefficient of the dummy variable as a measure of the effect of regulation. Since we are most concerned about the possibility that the coefficient of the dummy variable may be biased downward—may be an overestimate of the actual effect of regulation—before we conclude that regulation has been effective, let us concentrate on those cases in which collinearity will bias the coefficient downward. There are essentially two cases in which this is a possibility: if the coefficient of a variable other than R_t is *positive*, and there is a permanent negative shift in the average level of that variable after 1935; that is, *negative* collinearity with R_t, then the coefficient of R_t may be "catching" part of the effect of this shift, which would be to lower entry; if the coefficient of a variable other than R_t is negative, and that variable is positively related to R_t, then the coefficient of R_t might be catching the entry depressing effect of the permanent increase in that variable.[41]

A related case concerns the presence of several independent variables, each with secular trend, but with coefficients of different signs. Any variable with secular trend will be collinear with the dummy variable, but if more of the effect attributable to the variables with negative coefficients is caught by the dummy variable than is the effect of variables with positive coefficients, the coefficient of the dummy variable will be biased downward as a measure of the effect of regulation.

In checking these possibilities we shall confine the discussion to equation T4. Since the coefficient of R_t in T4 is in line with the results obtained in the other regressions, any biases due to collinearity should be deducible from variables already in T4.

The first possibility we consider is that the dummy variable is picking up the effects properly attributable to variables with secular trend. There are two variables in T4 with pronounced secular trends—log deposits and log capital. If the coefficient of the dummy variable is biased downward by multicollinearity of R_t with log D_t and log C_t, the coefficient of log D_t in T4 must be greater than its true value and/or that of log C_t lower in absolute value than its true value. R_t would then be picking up the effects of the overweighting of deposits and/or the underweighting of capital which would then be implicit in T4. One way to check on this is to delete both deposits and capital from T4, while leaving the dummy variable in. If multicollinearity of R_t with log D_t and log C_t biases the coefficient of R_t, removal of log D_t and log C_t should significantly change the coefficient of R_t. When log D_t and log C_t are removed from T4, the coefficient of the dummy variable turns out

---

[41] I am indebted to Lester Telser for pointing this out, and for suggesting the approach to be used in dealing with the problem.

to be —.576 with a standard error of .071. Since this is almost identical to the coefficient of R_t in T4, multicollinearity of R_t with log D_t and log C_t in no way biases the coefficient of R_t.

The next problem we deal with derives from the negative (—.423) correlation of the market rate of return in banking variable (log $^m\pi_{t-1}$) with R_t. Given the highly positive correlation of log $^m\pi_{t-1}$ with the entry rate, this raises the possibility that the dummy variable is picking up part of the effects of a permanent decline in the rate of return on bank capital.

Before we admit this possibility, we want to be sure there has in fact been a decline in the expected rate of return in banking. It should be remembered in this connection that the profit rate variable we use is the mean of a truncated distribution of profit rates, where returns of unsuccessful firms are cut off. In order to conclude that the expected rate of return relevant to potential investors has declined, we need to compare means of the full distribution of profit rates; distributions which include the losses of failing firms. One way to generate a mean profit rate which includes the results of unsuccessful firms is by a direct application of equation (32) to annual data where $[1 - P(S)]$ is taken to equal the actual rate of failure and $\bar{\pi}_S$ is set equal to $^m\pi_t$. A time series so constructed averaged 3.017 per cent per year for 1921-35 and 3.614 per cent per year for 1936-62.[42] Therefore, if anything, the true rate of return in banking appears to have risen; the decline in the measured rate of return has been more than offset by a decline in the risk of failure. This goes against an interpretation of the dummy variable as a proxy for a decline in the rate of return in banking. In fact when the "true" rate of return, constructed as described above, was substituted into T4 for log $^m\pi_{t-1}$ the coefficient of R_t remained significantly negative and became larger absolutely. So, we might suspect that the coefficient of the dummy variable is biased *toward* zero, in that it may be picking up part of the effect of a permanent increase in the expected rate of return in banking.

This leaves us to consider only one more variable in T4, the merger rate. There is substantial (—.664) negative correlation between the merger rate and the dummy variable, thus indicating a drop in the intended rate of increase in capital size per bank since 1935. This is not surprising, since most of the communication improvements, like construction of the road network, which enabled banks to extend their market areas were introduced most rapidly in the 1920s. The 1920s, in fact, witnessed the most rapid increase in concentration of bank assets over the whole period of this study.[43] But all

---

[42] The whole series and a detailed description of its construction may be found in my dissertation, *supra* note *, p. 11. It is argued there that this series in fact underestimates the risk of failure prior to 1935, and so yields a mean for 1921-35 which is biased upward.

[43] *Cf.* U.S. Board of Governors of the Federal Reserve System, Recent Developments in the Structure of Banking 18 (1962).

of this would indicate that the coefficient of the dummy variable is biased toward zero, since it may be picking up part of the effect of a permanent decline in the rate of growth of firm capital size. This adds to our confidence that the coefficient of the dummy variable is not overestimating the impact of regulation.

Since the size of the coefficient of the dummy variable is unaffected by intercorrelation with the deposits and capital series and is, if anything, biased toward zero by its association with a permanent increase in the "true" expected rate of return on bank capital and its association with a permanent drop in the merger rate, it appears safe to conclude then that the coefficient of the dummy variable does not overestimate the effect of regulation on entry.[44]

1. Other Effects of Regulation. Regulatory limitation of entry may have effects apart from lowering the average level of the entry rate. It may, as pointed out in the preceding section, increase the lag with which entry responds to other variables and introduce more variance and a larger cyclical component into that response. These possibilities were examined by dividing the data into two subperiods, 1921-35 and 1936-62, and computing regression estimates for each subperiod.

When regression T4 of Table 1 is recomputed for each of the subperiods, the results are,
for 1921-35 data:

$$e_t = 2.849 + 1.897 \; \log {}^m\pi_{t-1} + .175 \; m_t - .040 \; x_t$$
$$\quad\quad\quad\quad (.180) \quad\quad\quad\quad\quad (.098) \quad\quad (.010)$$
$$\quad\quad\quad\quad .966 \quad\quad\quad\quad\quad\quad .536 \quad - \; .811$$

$$+ \; 5.241 \; \log D_t - 14.305 \; \log C_t$$
$$\quad (.951) \quad\quad\quad\quad (2.348)$$
$$\quad .890 \quad\quad - \quad .907$$
$$R^2 = .978 \quad Sy \cdot (x) = .075; \quad\quad\quad\quad\quad\quad\quad (N4)$$

[44] No systematic attempt was (or can be) made to check the possibility that the dummy variable is a proxy for variables, excluded from the regressions, which are not associated with regulation, but which would have caused entry to decline after 1935. However, two such variables were investigated: (1) *deposit growth*. The model assumes constant annual expected deposit growth. A decline in the expected rate of growth of bank deposits subsequent to 1935 would cause entry to decline also. (2) *branch banking*. The formation of new bank branch offices has risen sharply since 1935, both absolutely and relative to the total number of bank offices. New branches may be a substitute for new banks. To the extent that their recent growth is independent of limits on new entry, this growth, and not regulation, may explain the negative coefficient of R_t.

The actual rate of deposit growth and the formation of new branch offices relative to total banking offices were entered in the regressions. However, the coefficients of both were insignificant and the coefficient of R_t remained significantly negative with their inclusion. A fuller discussion may be found in my dissertation, *supra* note *, p. 11.

for 1936-62 data:

$$e_t = -.191 + 2.278 \ \log {}^m\pi_{t-1} - .025 \ m_t - .135 \ x_t$$
$$ (.435) \phantom{\ \log {}^m\pi_{t-1}} (.107) (.335)$$
$$ .753 \phantom{\ \log {}^m\pi_{t-1}} - .052 - .088$$

$$+ .709 \ \log D_t - 1.843 \ \log C_t$$
$$ (.516) (.545)$$
$$ .287 - .594$$
$$R^2 = .830 \quad Sy \cdot (x) = .131.^{45} \tag{R4}$$

These data are consistent with the hypothesis that regulation introduces more variance into the response of entry to economic variables. Regression N4 explains nearly all of the variance in the dependent variable, and its standard error of estimate is nearly half that of the comparable regression, R4, for the period in which entry was subject to regulation.[46] While regulation thus appears to introduce more variability into the overall response of entry to economic variables, the effect of these variables remains generally significant and in the direction indicated by our model. All of the coefficients of R4 have the "right" sign and, with the exception of the coefficient of log deposits, all are significant at 2½ per cent.

The two period analysis was not able to uncover the presence of either additional lags in response or a greater cyclical component in the entry rate. The latter effect—the tendency of a given regulatory policy to persist from one year to the next—should reveal itself in greater positive serial correlation of the residuals of R4 than of those of N4. The von Neumann ratios for these regressions were 2.784 for N4 and 1.508 for R4. Neither of these are significant at 5 per cent.[47] The presence of added lags in response was tested by substituting a two-year lagged expected profit rate for the one-year lag in R4. Regression N4 yielded the best fit to the 1921-35 data, as did T4 for the whole 1921-62 period.[48] If regulation makes entry respond to profits with

[45] The symbols are those of Table 1. Standard errors (in parentheses) and partial correlation coefficients are shown below the regression coefficients. The 1921-35 data contain 14 observations; the 1936-62 data contain 27 observations.

[46] Since the dependent variable is already a percentage, it is not necessary to adjust the standard error of estimate for a change in the mean value of the dependent variable between periods. Even if this were done, however, it would make the difference in residual variance between periods more striking, since the mean of the dependent variable is higher for 1921-35 than for 1936-62.

[47] Significance points for von Neumann's ratio are taken from Ezekiel and Fox, Methods of Correlation and Regression Analysis 341 (1959).

[48] A fuller two period analysis may be found in my dissertation *op. cit. supra* note * p. 11. An important result of that analysis was that it provided added confirmation for the Grunfeld hypothesis. In both of the subperiods, the best fit to the data was yielded by regressions using market rates of return (specifically, by regressions N4 and

a longer lag, substitution of a longer lagged profit rate for the 1936-62 sub-period should improve on the fit of R4. However, the substitution yielded a lower R^2 (.694), so the presence of additional, regulation imposed, lags in response is not detectable in these data.

2. *Effect of Other Variables in the Model.* The regressions in Table 1, and in particular T4, indicate that in addition to the rate of return on capital, all of the other economic variables in our basic model—mergers, failures, deposits and capital—are associated with the entry rate in the expected way; this appears to justify our treatment of new entry as a specific form of capital investment. In interpreting the regression results, it should be kept in mind that the appropriate significance tests for the coefficients of both the failure rate (x_t) as a risk of loss variable and the merger rate (m_t) as a size change variable are for a significant (negative) difference from unity.[49] Both of these coefficients are significantly less than unity.[50] Similarly, the coefficients of log deposits and log capital are significant and of the correct sign. From equation (33), it is possible to estimate the value of α, the elasticity of capital with respect to deposits, by dividing the coefficient of log deposits by the absolute value of the coefficient of log capital. Performing this operation on these coefficients in T4 yields an estimate of .564 for α. This supports the crude data in the preceding section which indicated that α is less than unity.[51]

IV. CONCLUSIONS

The empirical evidence presented in section III yields the following important conclusions:

(1) While there is a significantly positive relationship between entry and both of the alternative measures of the expected rate of return on capital in banking used in this paper, one of these alternatives yields consistently superior results. This is the rate of interest times a ratio of stock market value to book value. Thus Grunfeld's hypothesis that the current rate of return is a surrogate for the direct measure of expected profits provided by security market values is confirmed by this study.

R4 shown here). The best fitting current profits model for the 1921-35 period, employing a one-year lagged profit rate, had a standard error of estimate of .177; that for the 1936-62 period, employing a two-year lagged profit rate, had a standard error of estimate of .160.

[49] See equation (36).

[50] Our presumption that the relationship between entry and mergers would be weakened by effective limitation of entry is supported by comparing the behavior of m_t in N4 and R4; its partial correlation coefficient is smaller in the latter as compared to the former (—.052 as compared to .536).

[51] *Supra* note 17, p. 22. In fact this estimate of α is surprisingly close to the simple slope coefficient of log deposits regressed on log capital, which turns out to be .533.

48   THE JOURNAL OF LAW AND ECONOMICS

(2) All other variables derived from a model which treats entry as a particular form of capital investment are associated with the entry rate in the predicted way.

(3) The legal restrictions on entry into banking enacted into the Banking Act of 1935 have significantly reduced the entry rate into banking compared to what it would have been without these restrictions. In the period since 1935 the number of new banks formed each year has averaged .6 per cent of the existing number of banks. Had the legal restrictions been absent, we estimate that this annual average would have been twice as high—about 1.2 per cent of the existing number of banks. At a minimum, it would have been .9 per cent, still 50 per cent higher than the rate we have observed. Put simply in terms of the number of new banks, a total of 2,272 new banks were formed in the years 1936 through 1962[52]—an average of 84 new banks per year. Had there been no legal restrictions on entry in this period, we estimate that about twice that number—approximately 4500 new banks—would have been formed. Regulation has thus caused there to be 2200 fewer banks than there would otherwise have been.[53]

The advent of regulation has also made the response of entry to economic forces more variable than it was previously. Changes in, for example, the expected rate of return on capital in banking still produce significant changes in the entry rate, but the magnitude of this response varies more from year to year when entry is regulated than when it was not. Therefore, any attempt to use information on changes in economic factors to predict changes in the entry rate becomes subject to a larger margin of error when entry is regulated.

APPENDIX

DESCRIPTION OF SERIES AND SOURCES:

(1) e_t (entry rate): new bank formations divided by average of banks existing at January 1 and December 31, in per cent.

Source: new bank formations—U.S. Board of Governors of the Federal Reserve

---

[52] Source: see Appendix.

[53] This estimate is made as follows: the coefficient of R_t in equation T4, Table 1 (—.579) is the estimated percentage point reduction in the entry rate on account of regulation. To convert this into an estimate of the reduction in the number of new banks in any year due to regulation, this coefficient must be multiplied by the existing number of banks in that year. This multiplication was performed for every year, 1936-62. The sum of these annual estimates—2196—is the estimated total reduction in the number of new banks on account of regulation for the 1936-62 period. This is, however, a gross figure; undoubtedly some of these new banks would have failed or merged. We can take account of this on the assumption that the new banks would have behaved like established banks. From 1936 through 1962, 30.8 per cent of the average number of banks existing in this period disappeared by failure of merger. Reducing 2196 by 30.8 per cent yields an estimate—1519—of the net number of new banks which would have been formed in the absence of regulation.

System, Banking and Monetary Statistics (1943) and Supplement to Banking and Monetary Statistics (1962); 1960 Fed. Dep. Ins. Corp. Ann. Rep. 48 and 49 Fed. Res. Bull. (1962 and 1963).

Source: number of banks—U.S. Board of Governors of the Federal Reserve System, Banking and Monetary Statistics (1943), and Supplement to Banking and Monetary Statistics (1962); 50 Fed. Res. Bull. (1964).

Datum for 1933 is deleted because the source (Banking and Monetary Statistics) reports it found it impossible to distinguish primary organizations from reopenings of suspended banks and mergers.

(2) $^m\pi$ (expected rate of return in banking): rate of interest times ratio of market to book value, banking, per cent.

Source: interest rate—Moody's Aaa Corporates, December values, in Moody's Industrial Manual (1962).

Source: market value—1941-61 data is the year-end value of Standard and Poor's Outside New York City Banks stock price index, Standard and Poor's Corporation, Security Price Index Record (1964). 1919-40 data was constructed by averaging year-end bid prices of a sample of 16 bank stocks reported in the Commercial and Financial Chronicle, Bank and Quotation Record, and splicing to the later series. 1919-40 series may be found in my dissertation, Entry in Commercial Banking, March 1965 (unpublished dissertation in University of Chicago Library)

book value—linear interpolation of capital accounts series, see, *post* (9), to year-end basis, and converted to an index with the property that market-book value ratio equal 1.729 for 1959-61. 1.729 is the average ratio for a sample of banks outside New York City reported in M. A. Schapiro and Co., Bank Stock Quarterly (June, 1962).

(3) $^m\pi^0$ (expected rate of return in manufacturing): rate of interest times ratio of market to book value, manufacturing, per cent.

Source: interest rate—same as (2)

market value—Standard and Poor's Industrial stock price index, Security Price Index Record (1964).

book value—1929-61 from Security Price Index Record; 1919-28 data from Epstein, Industrial Profits in the United States 627 (1934) and spliced to later series.

(4) $^c\pi$ (current rate of return in banking): operating earnings, net of taxes, for member banks outside the Second Federal Reserve District as per cent of mid-year capital accounts.

Source: earnings—Volumes 5 to 48 Fed. Res. Bull. (1919-62).

Source: capital accounts—U.S. Board of Governors of the Federal Reserve System, Summary Report; Assets and Liabilities of Member Banks (1919-62).

(5) $^c\pi^0$ (current rate of return in manufacturing): rate of return on all assets, manufacturing, per cent.

Source: 1926-58 data in Stigler, Capital and Rates of Return in Manufacturing Industries 203 (1963); 1959-61 from data in U.S. Internal Revenue Service, Statistics of Income, using method of construction described in Stigler, and spliced to his series; 1919-25 data is rate of return on invested capital, Epstein, *op. cit. supra* at 621-627, and spliced to Stigler series.

(6) m_t (merger rate): bank mergers divided by average of banks existing at January 1 and December 31 in per cent.

Source: same as (1).

(7) x_t (net failure rate): bank suspensions and liquidations, net of reopenings, divided by average of banks existing at January 1 and December 31, in per cent.

Source: same as (1).

(8) D_t (deposits, net of cash assets).

Source: U.S. Board of Governors of the Federal Reserve System, All-Bank Statistics [of the] United States, 1896-1955 (1959); Banking and Monetary Statistics; volumes 29-49 *Fed. Res. Bull.* (1943-1963). Data is for all commercial banks except New York City Central Reserve City Banks, in billion dollars, as of June 30.

(9) C_t (capital accounts).

Source: same as (8). Data is for all commercial banks except New York City Central Reserve City banks, in billion dollars, as of June 30.

[4]

Money and Prices in Argentina, 1935–1962

INTRODUCTION

THIS study investigates the behavior of money and prices in Argentina from 1935 to 1962.

The period has been chosen for a variety of reasons. The year 1935 marks the establishment of the central bank. This is also the year of origin for many important economic time series. During this period the Argentine economy was subject to substantial and fluctuating rates of inflation, output showed a time pattern of unstable growth, and there were important changes in the nature of economic policies and in the underlying institutional framework (section 1). Such characteristics of the period suggest overall variability of economic magnitudes and allow one to entertain high expectations about statistical results.

Section 2 deals with the nominal stock of money, its rates of change through time, and the fraction of these changes that can be attributed to changes in each one of its proximate determinants. Among them, the reserve-deposit ratio of commercial banks is further analyzed.

The demand for money in real terms is the subject of section 3. The first part is devoted to the aggregate demand for money and an attempt is made to explain the observed variations in real per capita money holdings, for two definitions of money, in terms of changes in the expected rate of change in prices, real measured and permanent income, and the variance of inflation rates. The second part deals with the demand functions for components of the money stock, also in real terms, and the behavior of the ratio of currency to demand deposits and the ratio of savings and time deposits to demand deposits through time.

This paper is based on my "Money and Prices in Argentina, 1935–1962" (unpublished Ph.D. dissertation, University of Chicago, 1966). I owe a great intellectual debt to Milton Friedman and Arnold Harberger for their encouragement, suggestions, and criticisms at every stage of the work. David Meiselman and Larry Sjaastad also offered useful comments on earlier drafts. This work was made possible by the generous financial support given to me by the University of Tucuman (Argentina) and the Ford Foundation.

In section 4 the attention is turned to the dynamic behavior of prices in the Argentine inflationary process. In this section an attempt is made to estimate both the responses of the rate of change in prices to changes in the rates of change in money and other "policy" variables, and the time structure of those responses when they involve lags.

In the last section the main conclusions of the study are summarized.

1. THE INSTITUTIONAL BACKGROUND

From 1935 on, the central bank charter and the banking law have been the most important legal instruments governing the organization and functioning of monetary and banking institutions in Argentina. Three different versions of these instruments have been enacted and each has drastically transformed the monetary institutional arrangements of the economy.

The central bank charter of 1935. The creation of the Argentine Central Bank in May 1935 was the outcome of a long discussion beginning at the end of the nineteenth century, though the precise timing was largely the consequence of the problems raised for the existing banking structure by the economic crisis of the early 1930s.

The bank had the following main objectives:

a. To concentrate enough foreign exchange and gold reserves to moderate the consequences of export fluctuations and foreign capital movements on money, credit, and commercial activities, in order to maintain the value of money.

b. To regulate the quantity of credit and means of payments, adapting them to the actual volume of business.

c. To promote the liquidity and the appropriate functioning of the commercial banking system.

The principal tools of financial management given to the new institution were rediscounting and the fixing of the rediscount rate, open market operations (subject to certain limits), short-term advances to the commercial banks and to the treasury, regulation of new entry into banking, and control over the structure of banks' assets and liabilities. Differentiated minimum reserve requirements were established for demand, savings, and time deposits at levels fixed by law. Interest payments on these categories of deposits were not forbidden but were limited to maximum rates linked to the rediscount rate.

The bank was required to hold a minimum 25 per cent reserve in gold and foreign exchange against its notes and sight liabilities. The law also provided for convertibility to gold (a minimum of 400 Troy ounces), but this provision was suspended and never became effective.[1]

The 1935 charter and banking law ruled the Argentine monetary system for eleven years. The national and international economic developments during this period were quite different from those that had preceded—and to a certain degree influenced—this legislation. Inflation, not deflation, was the danger and the problem. Successively favorable balances of payments before, and particularly during, the World War II years meant that the bank's reserve requirements did not set very close limits on the quantity of money. The authorities used open market operations extensively but their effectiveness was impaired by the limits imposed on the bank's holdings of securities and concern over "the maintenance of an orderly market for government securities," especially during the last years of the period. Contrary to expectations in 1935, little use was made of rediscounting or the rediscount rate which was set at 3.5 per cent in 1936 and remained constant during ten years, with the exception of eighteen months in 1940–41.

The charter reforms of 1946 and 1949. The nationalization of the bank in 1946 and the technical reforms that complemented this measure were the means by which the institution was to accomplish the new, additional objective of

> promoting, orienting and carrying on adequate economic policies to maintain a high degree of activity in order to obtain the maximum level of employment of disposable human and material resources and the orderly expansion of the economy, so that the growth of the national wealth will allow the raising of the standards of living of the population.[2]

Thus the purpose and functioning of the bank were expanded to encompass control over the general economic policy of the country.

Since bankers "do not use their own but others' capital to obtain profits," it was felt necessary to insure depositors against the "inherent risks" of the banking business; hence, all deposits were transferred to and guaranteed by the central bank, commercial banks acting from then on as mere agents of the former. The law also provided for continuous "rediscounting" apportioned according to the "needs of

1. The preceding enumeration of objectives and tools is a summary of the main provisions of Argentine Laws 12155, 12156, and 12160, and of Executive Decrees 61126 and 65227, all of 1935.

2. Executive Decree 14957/46, enacted by Law 12962, section III, article 3.

business" and the bank's promotional objectives. These operations were implemented by discriminatory quantitative limitations imposed on individual banks and by a complex of rediscount rates to be charged according to the type of loan to which the funds were to be applied. To permit "a more efficient monetary regulation and that of the securities market" the maximum limits for open market operations were enlarged and the bank was allowed to issue its own securities.

The law provided for complete regulation by the bank of all interest rates charged on loans or paid by banks on savings and time deposits. Interest payments on demand deposits were forbidden. All banking expenses incurred in the handling of deposit accounts, including interest payments, were to be paid by the central bank. Minimum reserve requirements in gold and foreign exchange were set at 25 per cent of the bank's notes held by the public plus other sight liabilities, not including the transferred deposits.

The 1946 legislation gave the authorities a "sufficient" set of tools but no rule or guiding principle except, perhaps, that they should "regulate means of payments according to the needs of business in order to maintain the purchasing power of money." Private creation of money through the commercial banking system practically ceased. Rediscounting was an instrument with a different meaning. Open market operations were aimed at regulating the securities market, not the quantity of money. Selective credit controls became widely used in order to offer a "rational" allocation of credit, and to provide some rationing criteria for loans that, given the level of interest rates chosen by the bank and the ongoing inflation, were granted at negative real interest rates.

In 1949 a constitutional amendment brought about an administrative reform by which the bank's broad economic policy functions were transferred to a newly created National Economic Council. The new legislation also suspended indefinitely the minimum gold and foreign exchange reserve requirements for the central bank, because "monetary issues have to be linked to the national income and metallic and foreign exchange reserves to the balance of payments." A few months later the bank could not have met these requirements.

The central bank charter of 1957. The bank charter, as modified in October 1957, together with the 1957 banking law, regulated the banking structure of the country up to February 1969.[3]

3. Toward the end of 1967 the appropriateness of the regulations was under discussion, and a new and more comprehensive banking law was being drafted.

Deposits were returned to commercial banks (about ninety of them), but continued to be guaranteed in the sense that the central bank was ready to advance the funds to pay all deposits in case of any bank's failure.

The objectives of the transformed institution were stated as follows:

a. To regulate the volume of credit and means of payments so as to maintain the purchasing power of money . . . and stimulate the orderly and persistent growth of national income with the maximum employment of productive resources.

b. To concentrate and mobilize gold and foreign exchange reserves so as to moderate the effects of balance of payments fluctuations on the value of money and economic activity.

c. To promote the liquidity and the appropriate functioning of the commercial banking system.[4]

The bank was given "all necessary instruments to conduct the credit and monetary policy" of the country. These included all the original (1935) tools of financial management plus the additional power to establish and modify minimum reserve requirements for commercial banks according to the type of deposit and region of the country, and to impose additional marginal requirements on incremental deposits after given dates. The bank was also allowed to establish penalty rates on shortages of required reserves and to authorize banks to hold these reserves in the form of special kinds of bonds.

The law again provided for minimum gold and foreign exchange reserve requirements for the central bank and convertibility of its own notes, but these provisions have not been enforced.

The period 1957–62 was characterized by the use of variations in reserve requirements and selective credit controls as the major tools of monetary management.

2. THE MONEY SUPPLY MECHANISM

This section presents an analysis of the changes in the stock of money in Argentina during the period 1935–62. First there is a description of the relationship between variations in the monetary "base" and in the

---

According to its proponents the main purpose of such reform would be to correct inadequacies of the existing legislation in the light of developments in the Argentine financial sector during the preceding 10 years, and to extend central bank control to nonbanking financial intermediaries whose growth was considered to be particularly significant. This new law was enacted February 1969.

4. Executive Decree 13126 of 1957, article 1.

quantity of money. Then the statistical behavior of the base multiplier and the quantitative influence of each of its proximate determinants is examined. Finally, one of these determinants, the reserve ratio, is further analyzed. The behavior of the ratio of currency to demand deposits and of savings and time deposits to demand deposits is discussed at the end of section 3.

Changes in the money supply, the monetary base, and the base multiplier. The expression

$$M = mB \qquad (1)$$

expresses the quantity of money, M, as a product of the "base multiplier," m, and the monetary "base" or "high-powered money," B.[5] Chart 1 shows the behavior of these three variables during the period under consideration.[6] Their numerical values are given in tables 21 and 22 in the appendix.

Table 1 shows the average annual percentage rate of change of the annual averages of these three variables for the whole period 1935–62 and for each of three subperiods defined on the basis of their institutional characteristics, as explained in section 1.

These figures give an idea of the relative importance of the components of the total change in the quantity of money. They indicate that the changes in B have been quantitatively the most important but that the observed changes in m are not to be neglected: During 1935–45 the negative average rate of change in m "sterilized" a substantial part of the change that would have occurred in M in view of the average rate of increase in B. During 1958–62 the average expansion of m explains of more than a quarter of the average relative change in M, which thus reaches the highest level for the whole period despite the observed deceleration of B.

5. Where $M = C + D + T$ so that the total quantity of money includes currency, C, demand deposits, D, and savings and time deposits, T, held by the public, and where $B = C + R$ so that the monetary "base" includes the amount of currency held by the public and the banking reserves, R, composed of vault cash and deposits of the commercial banks with the central bank. Dividing one equality by the other and taking B to the right side of the equation,

$$M = \frac{C + D + T}{C + R} B, \qquad (2)$$

which is the expanded version of equation (1).

6. The amount of high-powered money during 1946–57 is not shown in this figure because of the institutional characteristics of the subperiod, as explained in section 1 above.

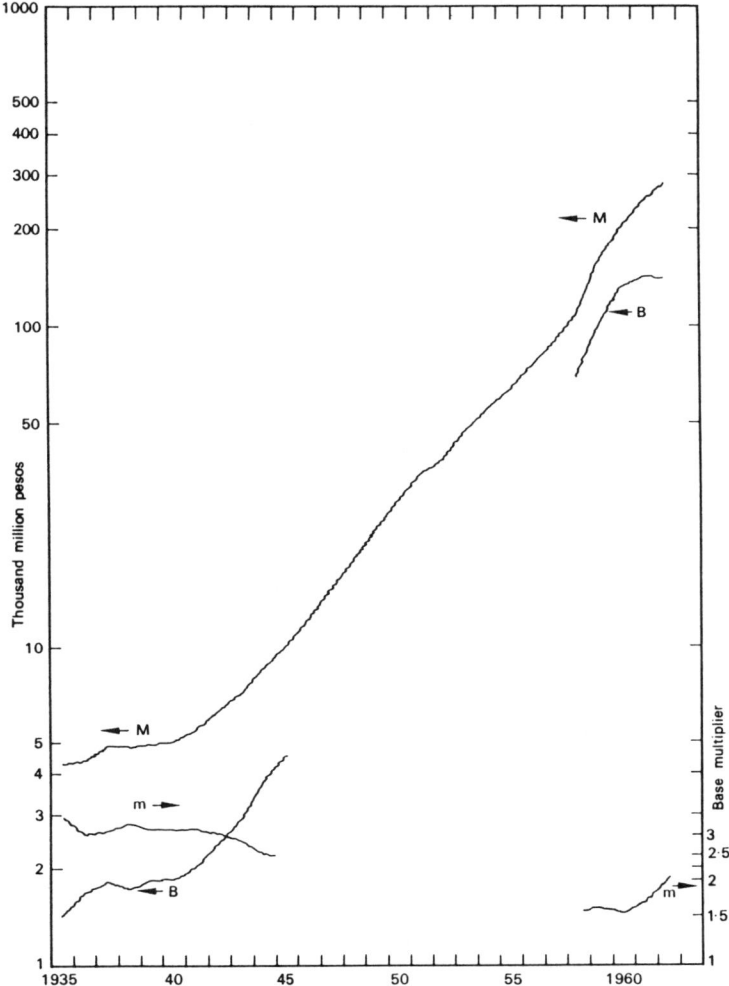

CHART 1. Annual averages of the stock of money, the monetary base, and the
base multiplier, 1935–62.
SOURCES: Tables 21 and 22.

78   *Varieties of Monetary Experience*

TABLE 1

AVERAGE ANNUAL PERCENTAGE RATES OF CHANGES IN THE
STOCK OF MONEY, THE MULTIPLIER, AND THE MONETARY BASE
(RATES OF CHANGE CONTINUOUSLY COMPOUNDED)

PERIOD	ANNUAL PERCENTAGE RATE OF CHANGE OF		
	M	m	B
1935–45........	8.45	−3.09	11.63
		(−.36)	(1.36)
1945–58........	18.45	−2.56	21.01
		(−.14)	(1.14)
1958–62........	24.03	6.21	17.82
		(.26)	(.74)
1935–62......	15.61	−1.45	17.06
		(−.09)	(1.09)

SOURCE: Tables 21 and 22.

NOTE: The average annual rate of change of a given series over a period
of time is the difference between the natural logarithms of the terminal and
initial values of the series divided by the number of years included in the
period.

    The figures in parentheses below the rates corresponding to m and B in-
dicate the fraction of the total relative change in M that each one of them
represents.

For both the initial and the last subperiods the analysis was also
made in terms of the quarterly rates of change corresponding to these
three variables.[7] These quarterly series (given numerically in tables 28
and 29) offer some interesting information which can be summarized by
reference to their averages, the characteristics of their sequence, and
the distribution of their values in absolute terms. The geometric means
of the quarterly rates of change of M, B, and m provide an estimate of
the contributions of the changes in m and B to the growth of the stock
of money which is basically similar to that of the annual series.[8] The
sequence of these quarterly changes show that those corresponding to

    7. When considering discrete intervals of time we must make the analysis of the
total rate of change in money in terms of first differences:

$$\frac{\Delta M}{M} = \frac{\Delta m}{m} + \frac{\Delta B}{B} + \frac{\Delta m}{m} \frac{\Delta B}{B}. \tag{3}$$

The last, additional term represents the interaction of changes in m and in B if
they have taken place simultaneously through the period.

    8. These geometric means are the quarterly rates of change compounded at
quarterly intervals. During 1935–46 the fraction of total relative change in M
accounted for by the relative changes in the multiplier and the monetary base
were −.48 and 1.49, respectively. The interaction term had a value of −.01.
During 1958–62 the corresponding figures were .23, .76, and .01.

B varied widely around a declining trend from 1935 to about 1939–40 and much less widely around an upward trend during the World War II years. During the period 1958–62 these relative changes in *B* showed a markedly negative trend. The relative changes in *m* during 1935–45 showed a weak negative trend after 1937 and were quantitatively less important than those of *B*. Their variability increased during the years 1958–62, but they do not show any definite trend. Table 2 shows the

TABLE 2

NUMBER OF RELATIVE QUARTERLY CHANGES IN THE MULTIPLIER
(CLASSIFIED ACCORDING TO THEIR INTENSITY IN ABSOLUTE VALUE)

$\left\|\frac{\Delta m}{m}\right\|$ %	ABSOLUTE, RELATIVE, AND CUMULATIVE RELATIVE FREQUENCIES						
	1935–45		1958–62		1935–45 and 1958–62		
	Number of Changes	%	Number of Changes	%	Number of Changes	%	Cumulative Upward Frequencies
0–2......	19	42	9	45	28	43	100
2–4......	13	29	5	25	18	28	57
4–6......	7	16	2	10	9	14	29
6–8......	4	9	1	5	5	8	15
8–10.....	—	—	1	5	1	1	7
10+......	2	4	2	10	4	6	6
Total.....	45	100	20	100	65	100	—

SOURCE: Table 30.

frequency distribution of the quarterly rates of changes in the multiplier, in absolute value, during both subperiods. These figures indicate that throughout both subperiods, in approximately one out of three quarters the multiplier has been subject to relative changes of at least 4 per cent.

The next step in this study is an attempt to explain the observed variation in the multiplier and to quantify the contribution of each one of its proximate determinants.

The expression

$$m = \frac{\frac{C}{D} + \frac{T}{D} + 1}{\frac{C}{D} + \frac{R}{D+T}\left(1 + \frac{T}{D}\right)} \tag{4}$$

indicates that the observed changes in the multiplier through time can be explained by changes in the ratios C/D, T/D, and $R/(D + T)$.[9]

The total quantity of money has been roughly about twice the monetary base. This multiplying effect reflects the fractional reserve nature of the Argentine commercial banking institutions. Since, in addition, minimum reserve requirements differentiated by kind of deposits have been established, the size of the multiple depends not only on the distribution of high-powered money between the public and the banks but also on the relative amounts of different kinds of deposits in existence. These are the influences that work through the ratios mentioned above.

If we let the letters c, t, and r represent the corresponding ratios, their individual contribution to the change in m can be approximately measured in the following way:

$$\Delta m = \frac{\partial m}{\partial c} \Delta c + \frac{\partial m}{\partial t} \Delta t + \frac{\partial m}{\partial r} \Delta r + \text{Interaction} \tag{5}$$

where the increments in m, c, t, and r are those actually observed during each quarter, the partial derivatives are evaluated at the beginning of each quarter, and the value of the interaction is obtained as a residual.[10]

TABLE 3

CONTRIBUTION OF EACH RATIO TO THE CHANGES IN THE MULTIPLIER
(AVERAGE QUARTERLY VALUES IN PERCENTAGE)

Subperiod	Δm	$\frac{\partial m}{\partial c} \Delta c$	$\frac{\partial m}{\partial t} \Delta t$	$\frac{\partial m}{\partial r} \Delta r$	Interaction
1935–45.....	−2.85	.48 (.17)	−1.04 (−.36)	−3.03 (−1.06)	.74 (.25)
1958–62.....	2.39	−.89 (−.37)	.12 (.05)	2.52 (1.05)	.64 (.27)

SOURCE: Tables 29 and 33.

NOTE: The figures in parentheses indicate the fraction of the total change in the multiplier accounted for by changes in each of the ratios c, t, and r, and their interaction.

9. Expression (4) is derived from (2) by dividing numerator and denominator of m by D and then multiplying and dividing the last term of the new denominator by $(D + T)$. The new equation thus keeps T/D as a separate variable for analytical purposes but maintains the reserves held by banks as a fraction of total bank deposits.

10. The three partial derivatives are

$$\frac{\partial m}{\partial c} = -\frac{(1 + t)(1 - r)}{[c + r(1 + t)]^2}; \quad \frac{\partial m}{\partial t} = \frac{c(1 - r)}{[c + r(1 + t)]^2}; \text{ and } \frac{\partial m}{\partial r} = -\frac{(1 + t)(c + t + 1)}{[c + r(1 + t)]^2}$$

Table 3 shows, for each subperiod, the average quarterly value of each component of multiplier change. The table shows that the movements in the reserve ratio have been quantitatively the most important during both subperiods. Next in importance were the negative changes in T/D during the first subperiod and the positive changes in C/D (also with negative influence on the multiplier) during the last subperiod.

A. THE RESERVE-DEPOSITS RATIO OF COMMERCIAL BANKS

This section contains a brief summary of the Argentine regulations regarding banks' reserves, a description of the analytical framework used in explaining variations in the reserve ratio, and the empirical results. The C/D and T/D ratios are analyzed at the end of section 3.

Regulations concerning banks' reserves. The banking legislation of 1935 established minimum reserve requirements of 16 per cent for demand and 8 per cent for savings and time deposits for all banks. These requirements were fixed by law. Banks' deposits with the central bank and their holdings of gold and currency could be added to meet legal reserves. For each institution the requirements were computed on the basis of monthly averages of daily balances of aggregate reserves and deposits in all its branches.

The law did not provide for punitive interest to be charged in case of shortages of legal reserves. The central bank was empowered to waive the requirements transitorily for individual banks, but in such cases the bank involved could not pay dividends without the central bank's authorization. If within two years the requirements were not met, or at least a plan to do so in the future was not approved by the central bank, the bank was subject to liquidation.

The 1957 laws gave the central bank the power to use variations in reserve requirements as a tool of monetary management. The possibilities included modifications of basic or average requirements without limitations, the differentiation of requirements for different kinds of deposits, the definition of regions of the country and the differentiation of requirements according to the banks' location, the establishment and modification of additional reserve requirements on incremental deposits

---

where c and $t > 0$, and $1 > r > 0$. For simplicity, the last partial derivative does not take into account that r is itself a function of t. The signs that precede the values of each derivative indicate the direction of the impact on the multiplier of changes in c, t, and r, since all three numerators are positive. The derivatives also show the interdependence between all three ratios.

after a given date with an upper 100 per cent limit, and all their possible combinations. The central bank was also allowed to define the set of assets to be counted as reserves, which could include bonds, in addition to commercial banks' deposits with the central bank and vault cash.

During 1958–62 the authorities did not include bonds in the definition of legal reserves but made intensive use of almost every other possibility open to them for varying legal requirements. Most of those regulations and modifications were coexistent so that a great but unknown number of different legal requirements were in force throughout the country at any point in time.

The 1957 laws gave the central bank the power to establish and modify the penalty rate applicable to shortages of legal reserves and the length of the reserve period. The former was set at 7 per cent in December 1957 and was raised three times before the end of 1962, when it stood at 30 per cent. The length of the reserve period, set at fifteen days in 1957, was also changed to one month in April 1961.

The analytical framework. The main hypothesis of this study is that the observed variation in the reserve ratio of commercial banks can be explained by a simple model which takes institutional and behavioral considerations into account, thus incorporating the policy influences of the monetary authorities as well as the reactions of banks to certain variables which affect their decisions to hold reserves.

A different hypothesis, often made, is that variables other than legal reserve ratios are irrelevant either because it is assumed that banks keep a constant ratio of precautionary reserves to deposits above those requirements, or because the precautionary ratio is assumed to be proportional to the legal ratio, implying a reserve ratio proportional to the legal ratio, or because the precautionary ratio is considered to be a highly volatile and unpredictable magnitude, subject to a large number of influences very difficult to identify. The first two versions of this hypothesis are clearly rejected by the evidence of the first period when, even with constant legal reserve requirements, the reserve ratio showed great variability. This study provides a test for the hypothesis in its third version.

The reserve ratio can be viewed as the sum of the legal reserve ratio plus an excess, precautionary, or usable reserve ratio.[11] A discussion of each of these components and their determinants follows.

11. An alternative approach is to consider the reserve ratio as a weighted average of the ratios of individual banks or groups of banks. This may be an additional and fruitful way of analyzing the Argentine experience, where government-owned commercial banks, foreign banks, and other differentiated groups

Money and Prices in Argentina, 1935–1962   83

When there is statistical information on the amount of legal reserves through time, it is easy to see how variations in this component affect the total reserve ratio. The question of why this component varies may still be interesting, depending on the institutional arrangements and the purposes at hand, but it does not seem to be crucial for the explanation of movements in the total reserve ratio. When this information is not available, as in Argentina, the questions about why and how much this component varies, if at all, become important in trying to explain the behavior of the total reserve ratio.

The sources of variation in the aggregate legal reserve ratio can be easily understood from the following definition:

$$l_t = \sum_{i=1}^{n_t} d_{it} r_{it}^l + \sum_{i=1}^{n_t} \left(\frac{D_{it} - D_{io}}{D_t} \right) m_{it}^l, \qquad (6)$$

where n_t is the total number of legal categories of deposits at each time t, r_{it}^l and m_{it}^l are the average and marginal coefficients applicable to the ith category of deposits at time t, D_{it} and d_{it} are the amount of the ith category of deposits and the fraction of total deposits they represent at time t, D_{io} is the amount of the ith category of deposits at the time $(t = 0)$ when marginal requirements are established, D_t is the total amount of deposits at time t, and $D_{it} > D_{io}$. The first term of expression (6) represents the usual situation, without marginal reserve requirements, in which the aggregate legal reserve ratio is an average of the required coefficients applicable to different kinds of deposits weighted by the fraction of total deposits that each kind represents. The second term represents the additional influence of marginal requirements on incremental deposits after a certain date $(t = 0)$.

Expression (6) shows that the legal ratio can vary through time because of changes in the average and marginal coefficients, the legal classification of deposits and the definition of $t = 0$, which are pure "policy" variables, and also because of changes in the public's preferences for different kinds of deposits which affect their relative importance and their particular rates of growth through time, and which may be independent of any central bank decision.[12]

During 1935–45 the existence of legally fixed but differentiated average requirements for demand and savings and time deposits made

---

operate. The paucity and poor quality of published disaggregated data prevented a full exploration of this alternative.

12. The central bank may influence the desired composition of deposits by controlling interest payments on different kinds of deposits, by varying their operational nature (particularly for savings and time deposits), etc.

changes in d_{it} the only source of variation in the aggregate legal reserve ratio. During the period 1958–62 the sources of variation in the aggregate legal reserve ratio included changes in the "policy" variables as well as in the structure of deposits.

The excess or precautionary reserve ratio is the difference between the actual and the legal reserve ratio. The hypothesis made here is that, given the legal reserve ratio, the value of the excess reserve ratio through time is determined by the commercial banks' demand for precautionary reserves and by the rate at which the central bank injects or withdraws total reserves.[13]

The first part of the hypothesis requires a theory of the banks' demand for excess reserves. The hypothesis is that, given the legal reserve ratio and the total amount of reserves, the banks' desired excess or precautionary reserve ratio is a function of the cost of holding those reserves and the composition of deposits. When banks hold reserves they incur a cost in the form of the foregone yield on earning assets they could substitute for those reserves, so that increases or decreases in those yields can be expected to lower or raise the desired excess reserve ratio. The composition of deposits may be expected to influence banks' expectations about clearing drains and thereby also to affect desired positions. Finally, if those expectations are also subject to other typical intra-year influences, they may introduce seasonal fluctuations in the demand for excess reserves.

The second part of the hypothesis implies that the central bank can interfere with the process by which banks adjust to their desired positions. Given the legal reserve ratio and the composition of deposits, any observed combination of a cost of holding reserves and an excess reserve ratio not on the banks' stock demand curve implies that they are changing the excess reserve ratio toward the desired level. But if the central bank is at the same time injecting or withdrawing reserves, it can offset the banks' intentions by keeping them in a position of secondary equilibrium where the excess reserve ratio remains constant.

When both parts of the hypothesis about the excess reserve ratio are put together they imply the following: If the rate of change in total reserves is constant, either because total reserves are constant or because they are changing at a constant positive or negative rate, changes in the cost of holding money will bring about changes of opposite sign in the ratio. When the rate at which the central bank injects reserves

---

13. This hypothesis was developed by Meigs in his study of free reserves in U.S. banks. See Alexander J. Meigs, *Free Reserves and the Money Supply* (Chicago: Univ. of Chicago Press, 1962).

into the system rises, or the rate at which it withdraws reserves falls, the banks' excess reserve ratio will rise provided the cost of holding reserves does not increase. If it does, the ultimate result will be the sum of two offsetting influences whose net effect on the excess reserve ratio cannot be determined a priori. When the rate of increase in total reserves declines or the withdrawal rate increases, the opposite would be true.

Nothing has been said up to this point about the speed with which banks adjust to desired positions. The hypothesis made here is that banks react not only to contemporaneous changes in the cost of holding reserves or the rate at which the central bank injects or withdraws total reserves, but that they operate with a longer horizon which also takes into account the behavior of these variables in the recent and more distant past.

The preceding discussion about the determinants of variations in the legal and excess reserve ratios leads to the formulation of the following hypothesis for explaining the behavior of the aggregate reserve ratio through time:

$$r = f\left(r^l, d, i, \frac{1}{R}\frac{dR}{dt}, S, u\right), \tag{7}$$

where r^l is a "policy" variable representing the level of legal reserve coefficients, d stands for the amount of demand deposits relative to time deposits, i represents the actual or expected opportunity cost of holding reserves, the fourth variable is the actual or expected flow of total reserves, S is a dummy variable representing seasonal factors working through the legal or the excess reserve components, and u represents other influences on the reserve ratio which have not been considered in the preceding discussion.[14]

14. One such variable is the rediscount rate. The reason for not mentioning borrowing and the rediscount rate in the preceding paragraphs is empirical rather than theoretical. During the first period, as mentioned in section 1, the rediscount rate was constant, and rediscounting or other forms of borrowing were non-existent, except for a period of eighteen months during 1940–41. This exception lacks significance since it was a mere experiment (as it was officially described), or an exercise on the eligibility of paper, rather than a change in central bank policy or in the banks' attitudes toward borrowing. During the second period rediscounting was performed and may have had some influence on the banks' reserve holdings. The reason why no explicit allowance was made for this factor during this period is my belief that nonprice considerations and the use of a great deal of discretion by the central bank have been the most important factors. The rediscount rates' structure was very complicated and unstable through time and some extremely detailed and ad hoc regulations applied to certain operations.

86   *Varieties of Monetary Experience*

The empirical results. The variables in expression (7) are quantitatively defined as follows.

The reserve ratio is the total amount of reserves that banks hold in the form of deposits with the central bank or in the form of vault cash divided by their total deposit liabilities (net of inter-bank deposits). Total deposits include all demand, savings, and time deposits held by the nonbanking public and the government. The values used in the regressions are the end-of-quarter percentages for the periods 1935–45 and 1958–62, without seasonal adjustment, and are graphed in chart 2 (and given numerically in tables 34 and 35).

The index of legal reserve coefficients is used only in the regressions dealing with the period 1958–62. Changes in required reserve coefficients are always announced through central bank circular letters to all commercial banks, and they show that requirements for different classes of deposits tend to move together through time. Under these circumstances the value of only one coefficient applicable to a particular kind of deposit seems to be a good proxy variable to represent changes in the whole spectrum of legal rates. The values of this variable are the end-of-quarter total (average plus marginal) effective percentage rates applicable to demand deposits in Buenos Aires banks, and are given in table 35.

The index of deposit composition is the end-of-quarter ratio of

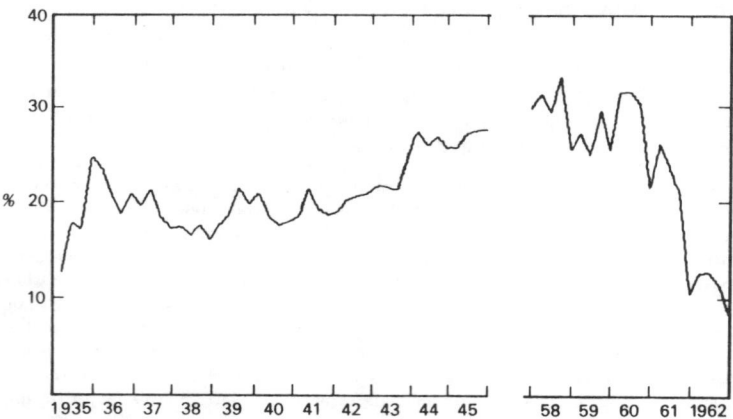

CHART 2. End-of-quarter reserve ratio of commercial banks, 1935–45 and 1958–62.
SOURCES: Tables 34 and 35.

demand to savings and time deposits.[15] During 1935–45 this was the only relevant legal differentiation of deposits, and during 1958–62 it was the most persistent in the sense that it was kept even in the context of other criteria (like region, provincial level of income, etc.). Since the difference between the average legal coefficients for demand and for savings and time deposits was greater during the second than the first period and since, in addition, marginal requirements were imposed only on demand deposits, it was expected that the changes in this variable would have a greater effect on the required reserve ratio during the second period.

The cost of holding reserves is represented by the end-of-quarter interest rates on 90-day certificates of consolidated treasury bonds (1935–45) and on 90-day treasury bills (1958–62). The actual values and several permanent versions of these variables, involving simple moving averages of these rates with an increasing number of terms, are used in different regressions. The results corresponding to the three- and five-term moving averages are reported here; they are approximate measures of the average yields during the semester and the year preceding the observed value of the reserve ratio, respectively. These variables in percentage form and their reciprocals are linearly introduced in the regressions to experiment with alternative forms.

The rate of change in total reserves is the first difference of the natural logarithms of total reserves at the end of quarters t and $t - 1$. This gives the quarterly percentage rate of change, continuously compounded, at which total reserves have been changing during the quarter immediately preceding the observed value of the reserve ratio. Several simple moving averages of these rates of flow with a different number of terms are used in the regression.

Seasonal factors are represented by a set of three dummy variables. An additional dummy variable is introduced in the regressions corresponding to the first period, with a value of unity for all quarters from the end of the second quarter, 1943, to the end of 1945 and zero otherwise. The data on the reserve ratio show a marked upward shift toward the end of 1943, and from then to the end of the period the level of the ratio fluctuates around this new and higher level. In the absence

15. Central bank reserve requirements differentiate only between demand and time deposits. Government deposits in commercial banks should then be subject to either requirement according to their nature. Since no statistical information is available on this subject, the assumption was made that all government deposits were demand deposits and were included, together with privately owned deposits, in the numerator of the index of deposit composition.

of any major changes in banking regulations or central bank policies, it is plausible to think that this shift may have been connected with the June 1943 military revolution which overthrew the existing constitutional government. By causing banks to expect greater economic instability, the new set of circumstances may have led banks to increase their precautionary reserve ratios, other things being equal.[16]

The preceding variables are used in two different sets of regressions corresponding to both subperiods, according to the following:

for 1935–45,

$$r = a + b_1 d + b_2 i_j^* + b_3 \left(\frac{1}{R} \frac{dR}{dt} \right)_k^* + b_4 D + b_5 S_1 + b_6 S_2 + b_7 S_3 + u_1;$$
(8)

for 1958–62,

$$r = a + b_1 d + b_2 i_j^* + b_3 \left(\frac{1}{R} \frac{dR}{dt} \right)_k^* + b_4 r^l + b_5 S_1 + b_6 S_2 + b_7 S_3 + u_2;$$
(9)

where $j = 1, 3, 5$, and $k = 1, 2, 3$. The variables in these equations have the same meaning as in expression (7); D is the shift dummy variable used during the first period, and j and k stand for the number of terms included in the moving averages used in those versions dealing with the cost and flow of total reserves defined as "permanent" magnitudes and denoted by the asterisks. Tables 4 and 5 show the estimated regression coefficients. The seasonal dummy variables were excluded in the regressions reported in these tables because in all cases their coefficients were not significantly different from zero, implying that no unexplained seasonal variation was left after all other variables were introduced in the regressions. The effective numbers of observations are 38 and 16, respectively.

The results in these tables tend to confirm the hypothesis made about the banks' behavior toward reserve holdings. The variables used explain a large fraction (roughly .90) of the observed variability of the reserve ratio and the standard errors of estimate range from about 6 to about 10 per cent of the mean value of the dependent variables, which are equal to 21.13 and 22.05 for the first and second periods, respectively.

16. The shift is not contemporaneous with the occurrence of the revolution but it may very well reflect a lag in response on the part of the banks or the lag involved in the formulation and announcement of the first major economic policies of the new government, which did not begin to take definite shape until several months after the revolution.

Money and Prices in Argentina, *1935–1962*   89

TABLE 4

THE RESERVE RATIO DURING THE PERIOD 1935–45
(ESTIMATED REGRESSION COEFFICIENTS FOR THE RESERVE RATIO WITH
ALTERNATIVE DEFINITIONS OF THE COST OF HOLDING RESERVES AND THE
FLOW OF TOTAL RESERVES)

Version j	k	Constant	d	$1/i^*_j$	$\left(\frac{1}{R}\frac{dR}{dt}\right)^*_k$	D	R^2	$S_{y.x}$
1	1	15.643* (1.372)	4.343 (3.046)	1.729 (1.004)	.0884* (.0277)	2.941* (.974)	.862	1.382
3	1	15.517* (1.298)	4.243 (2.811)	2.138* (1.020)	.0884* (.0269)	2.598* (.998)	.867	1.356
5	1	15.260* (1.227)	4.222 (2.587)	2.766* (1.082)	.0879* (.0260)	2.122* (1.028)	.874	1.319
1	2	16.343* (1.450)	2.954 (3.223)	1.770 (1.006)	.136* (.043)	3.119* (.977)	.862	1.382
3	2	16.609* (1.347)	1.512 (2.993)	2.751* (1.024)	.155* (.041)	2.601* (.963)	.876	1.309
5	2	16.208* (1.258)	1.860 (2.720)	3.311* (1.072)	.152* (.040)	2.103* (.992)	.883	1.273
1	3	16.715* (1.471)	2.535 (3.214)	1.468 (.974)	.185* (.055)	3.284* (.970)	.865	1.364
3	3	17.541* (1.352)	−.616 (3.022)	3.056* (.983)	.233* (.053)	2.617* (.912)	.889	1.240
5	3	17.215* (1.234)	−.620 (2.713)	3.836* (1.016)	.238* (.050)	2.014* (.918)	.899	1.178
Means:			.655	.877 .845 .801	3.150 2.938 2.811			

SOURCE: Tables 27, 29, and 34.

NOTE: The figures in parentheses under the regression coefficients are their standard errors of estimate, and the asterisks indicate that the corresponding coefficients are significantly different from zero at the 5 per cent level.

For the period 1935–45 (table 4) the reciprocal of the cost variable has the expected positive sign implying that, other things being equal, an increase in the yield on certificates of consolidated treasury bonds has tended to reduce the reserve ratio.[17] Changes in the contemporaneous yields do not significantly affect reserve holdings but when successively more comprehensive moving averages of the interest rates are introduced, the explanatory power of this variable improves up to the point where an annual or five-term average is used, implying an average length of six months for the weighting pattern. The coefficients of the actual and expected rate of change in total reserves also shows the

17. The results for the first period are considerably improved when the hypothesis of linearity in the reciprocal of the interest rate is used.

90   *Varieties of Monetary Experience*

expected positive sign and are significantly different from zero in all cases. When alternative definitions of the expected variable are successively introduced, their explanatory power is increased up to the point where a three-term moving average is used, with an implicit average length of the weighting pattern of four and one-half months. The coefficients of the index of deposit composition show the expected signs but they are not significant in any of the regressions in table 4.

For the period 1958–62 (table 5) the coefficients of the variables representing the opportunity cost of holding reserves have the expected signs and are significant in all the regressions. The five-term moving average of current and past interest rates is, again, the one that best explains variations in the reserve ratio. The coefficients of the

TABLE 5

THE RESERVE RATIO DURING THE PERIOD 1958–62
(ESTIMATED REGRESSION COEFFICIENTS FOR THE RESERVE RATIO WITH
ALTERNATIVE DEFINITIONS OF THE COST OF HOLDING RESERVES AND THE
FLOW OF TOTAL RESERVES)

Version j k	Constant	d	i_j^*	$\left(\frac{1}{R}\frac{dR}{dt}\right)_k^*$	r^l	R^2	$S_{y.x}$
1 1	−36.754* (9.235)	25.056* (6.265)	−1.183* (.470)	.0764* (.032)	.508 (.365)	.906	2.909
3 1	−37.924* (7.426)	23.273* (4.941)	−1.397* (.356)	.0675* (.026)	.639* (.294)	.938	2.358
5 1	−34.121* (6.675)	22.859* (4.360)	−1.490* (.313)	.0584* (.023)	.563* (.260)	.952	2.087
1 2	−35.349* (13.801)	24.446* (7.396)	−1.257* (.561)	.0827 (.0772)	.510 (.476)	.870	3.429
3 2	−39.880* (11.900)	22.671* (6.155)	−1.511* (.459)	.0475 (.0684)	.730 (.411)	.904	2.938
5 2	−37.516* (10.485)	22.403* (5.436)	−1.670* (.407)	.0215 (.0622)	.690 (.363)	.925	2.603
1 3	−19.635 (11.250)	24.442* (5.640)	−1.035* (.431)	.259* (.082)	.084 (.382)	.924	2.618
3 3	−25.748* (10.574)	22.703* (5.024)	−1.179* (.394)	.203* (.081)	.329 (.360)	.936	2.399
5 3	−24.374* (9.375)	22.443* (4.495)	−1.319* (.356)	.173* (.075)	.315 (.321)	.949	2.153
Means:		1.819	5.661 5.370 5.079	−2.535 −1.940 −1.016	39.594		

SOURCE: Tables 27, 29, and 35.

NOTE: The figures in parentheses under the regression coefficients are their standard errors of estimate and the asterisks indicate that the corresponding coefficients are significantly different from zero at the 5 per cent level.

variables representing the actual and expected flow of total reserves also have the expected positive sign and significant values, except for the two-term moving average. The ratio of demand to time deposits has significant coefficients of the expected positive sign in all the regressions. The differential behavior of this variable during both periods can be found in the central bank practice toward differential reserve requirements mentioned above and, perhaps, in a different response of the banks' holdings of precautionary reserves to changes in this variable in a period of relatively low and falling excess reserves.

The index of legal reserve coefficients has the expected positive sign in all the regressions but fails to achieve significance in some of them. The variable has significant coefficients in the regressions including expected cost and current rate of change in total reserves, but this significance is lost as lagged flows of total reserves are taken into account. The statistical reason for this result is the existence of positive correlation between the current value of this "policy" variable and the lagged values of the flow of total reserves. One economic interpretation of these results can be that the central bank during this period has tended to move reserve requirements in such a way as to offset changes in total reserves and that it has done so with certain lag. When only the current flow of total reserves is considered, the index of legal coefficients is significant because it is a good proxy variable for past changes in total reserves. But when those changes are in turn taken into account, the current variations in legal reserve requirements tend to lose their significance because, in a way, they have already been expected by the banks. During this period a serious attempt was made to stabilize the level of prices, and the average of the rate of change in total reserves shows a negative value. If the preceding interpretation is correct, then it suggests that the central bank was altering reserve requirements in such a way as to offset part of its previous actions; it provides an explanation for the large number of changes in reserve requirements that the bank felt necessary to introduce during the period and shows that, by these actions, the policy variable was rendered largely ineffective to explain the observed variation in the reserve ratio.

3. THE DEMAND FOR MONEY

From 1935 to 1962 the annual average nominal stock of money in Argentina was growing at an annual rate of either 15.5 or 17.8 per cent depending on whether "money" is defined inclusive or exclusive of savings and time deposits, respectively. During the same period population was increasing at about 1.9 per cent per year and the average annual rates of increase of the different series of price indexes available (GNP deflator, "cost of living," wholesale prices, and "cost of living" exclusive of the housing component) ranged from 15.3 to 16.1 per cent. Consequently, the rate of change of the real per capita money supply ranged from −2.5 to .6 per cent per year, depending on the definition of money chosen and the price index used for deflation.[18]

The composition of the stock of money shows important changes. As table 6 shows, currency doubled from 1935 to 1962 as a fraction of the more inclusive money stock, while savings and time deposits fell from nearly three-fifths of the total to only about one-fifth. As a fraction of income currency rose a trifle, demand deposits fell a trifle, and savings and time deposits fell drastically.

The movements of these series through time has not been smooth or even monotonic. On the contrary, they generally exhibit high variability.

TABLE 6

COMPONENTS OF MONEY EXPRESSED AS FRACTION OF NET NATIONAL
INCOME AND OF TOTAL MONEY SUPPLY

	1935			1962		
COMPONENT	As Fraction of			As Fraction of		
	NNI	M_1	M_2	NNI	M_1	M_2
C—Currency outside banks.....	.1210	.50	.21	.1312	.57	.44
D—Demand deposits..........	.1202	.50	.21	.0994	.43	.34
T—Savings and time deposits ..	.3282	—	.58	.0667	—	.22
$M_1 = C + D$.............	.2412	1.00	—	.2306	1.00	—
$M_2 = C + D + T$...........	.5694	—	1.00	.2974	—	1.00

SOURCE: Tables 20 and 24.

This section analyzes the observed variation in the per capita real quantity of money and its composition in Argentina, during the period 1935–62, in terms of the theory of the demand for money. The first part deals with the aggregate demand for money, and the second part with the composition of the money stock.

A. THE AGGREGATE DEMAND FOR MONEY

During the period under study the Argentine economy was subject to substantial and fluctuating rates of inflation, important variations in real per capita income, and drastic changes in its monetary institutions.

Under such a set of generally unstable circumstances it is only

18. All rates of change used in this section assume continuous compounding.

Money and Prices in Argentina, 1935–1962   93

natural that many will be led to think that monetary velocity or the amount of real cash balances in the hands of the public may have been responding passively to numerous influences difficult to isolate and identify, or that their variations showed mainly changes in tastes or even erratic behavior. An alternative hypothesis—and the one that is pursued in this analysis—is that even in such an environment a sizable fraction of the observed variability of real per capita money holdings can be explained by a few variables that have played a strategic role in people's behavior. Phillip Cagan's[19] study of relatively short hyperinflations in several European countries, and John Deaver's[20] of the Chilean "intermediate" case of less severe though still substantial inflation over a longer period of time and with fluctuating income, have among others provided strong evidence in support of this hypothesis under similar and even more abnormal circumstances.

The particular version of the demand for money hypothesis used in this study is that the real quantity of money demanded is a function of real per capita income, population, and the cost of holding money, and that this function is homogeneous of first degree in population.

Two quantitative definitions of "money" are used in this study. The first, M_1, consists of currency outside banks and demand deposits in commercial banks (net of inter-bank deposits, government deposits, and items in process of collection). The second, M_2, adds savings and time deposits in commercial banks to M_1. The behavior of these deposits during 1935–62 implies differential behavior of the two monetary totals through time. A decision was made to use both definitions in this study and to analyze them separately. The corresponding annual series are graphed in chart 3 and given numerically in table 21.

The cost of holding money in an inflationary environment is equal to the real rate of return on alternative forms of holding wealth plus the rate at which money holdings depreciate in purchasing power, that is, the rate of change in prices minus any interest paid on money. Unfortunately, there are no data on relevant interest rates in Argentina covering the whole period under consideration. However, the level and variability of the rate of inflation have been so high that this component probably dominates changes in the total cost of holding money. Hence, it has been used as an index of this cost.

19. Phillip Cagan, "The Monetary Dynamics of Hyperinflation," in *Studies in the Quantity Theory of Money*, ed. Milton Friedman (Chicago: Univ. of Chicago Press, 1956).

20. John V. Deaver, "The Chilean Inflation and the Demand for Money," above.

94   *Varieties of Monetary Experience*

A further hypothesis is that people react not to the actual or measured rate of inflation but to some concept of the anticipated rate of change in prices. The particular model of expected rates of inflation used is similar to the one developed by Cagan and also used by Deaver. This model postulates the following basic relation:

$$\frac{dE(t)}{dt} = \delta[I(t) - E(t)] \quad \delta > 0 \tag{10}$$

Expectations of price changes are modified through time in proportion to the divergence between the observed inflation, $I(t)$, and the inflation that was expected, $E(t)$.

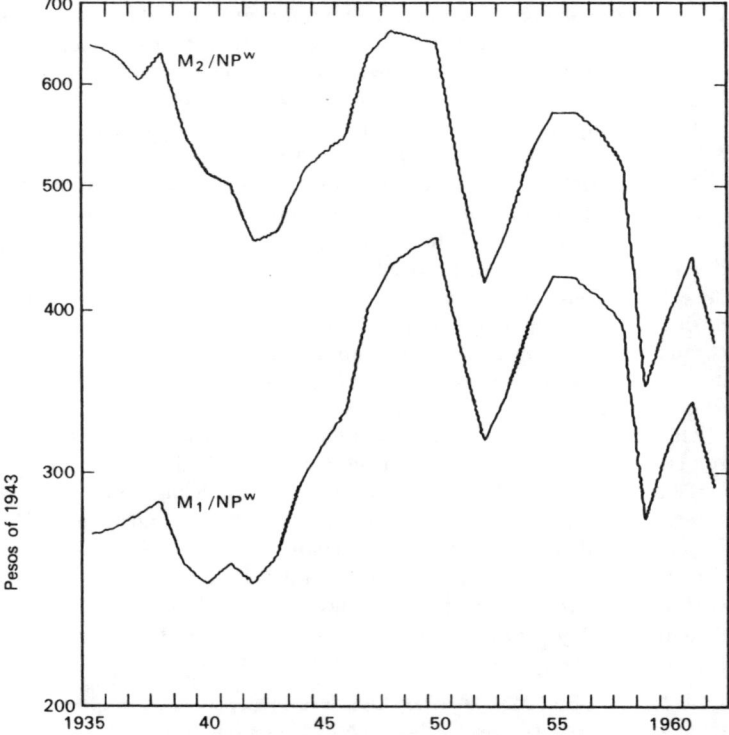

CHART 3. Annual averages of real per capita M_1 and M_2, 1935–62 (annual average wholesale price indexes used as deflators).
SOURCES: Tables 21, 23, and 24.

Money and Prices in Argentina, 1935–1962 95

For discrete time intervals it is possible to approximate (10) by the following:

$$E_{t+1/2} - E_{t-1/2} = \delta\left[I_t - \frac{E_{t+1/2} + E_{t-1/2}}{2}\right]. \tag{11}$$

Lagging half a period and rearranging terms,

$$E_t = \left(\frac{2\delta}{2+\delta}\right)I_{t-1/2} + \left(\frac{2-\delta}{2+\delta}\right)E_{t-1},$$

or

$$E_t = \delta' I_{t-1/2} + (1-\delta')E_{t-1} \quad \text{by making} \quad \delta' = \frac{2\delta}{2+\delta}.$$

This, in turn, yields the following expression:

$$E_t = \sum_{i=0}^{\infty} \delta'(1-\delta')^i I_{t-i-1/2}, \tag{12}$$

where $I_{t-1/2}$ represents the annual rate of inflation centered at the beginning of year t and is approximated by the natural logarithm of the ratio of the annual averages of the wholesale price index for the years t and $t-1$. Expression (12) yields different weighted averages of past rates of inflation with weights declining geometrically toward the past and varying according to the particular coefficient of price expectations, δ, used.[21]

Real per capita net national income is the income variable used in the regressions. The corresponding series appear in table 24. As for the cost of holding money, several versions of a "permanent" concept of income are also introduced in different experiments. This variable is defined in terms of a geometrically declining weighted average of contemporaneous and past measured real per capita levels of income, and yields different series according to the value of the coefficient of income expectations, ϵ, used in the weighting procedure.

Next, the estimated coefficients of the following demand for money function are presented and discussed:[22]

$$\log\left(\frac{M_i}{NP^w}\right)_t = \alpha + \beta E_t^{(\delta)} + \gamma \log\left(\frac{Y}{NP^d}\right)_t^{(\epsilon)} + u_t, \tag{13}$$

21. The number of terms included in these averages, for a given δ, was truncated on the basis of a sum of original weights equal to or greater than .95. A subsequent proportional adjustment of these original weights made their sum equal to unity.

22. In the early stages of the work some experimentation was performed with 25 different values of δ, ranging from .05 to 1, and 6 values of ϵ, ranging from .02

where

$$i = 1, 2$$
$$\delta = .2 \ (.1) \ .7, \text{ and } 1$$
$$\epsilon = .2 \ (.1) \ .4, \text{ and } 1$$
$$t = 1938(1)1962$$

and where

M_i = Annual average nominal stock of two definitions of "money,"
$\quad i = 1, 2$
N_t = Population at the middle of year t
P_t^w = Annual average wholesale price index
$E_t^{(\delta)}$ = Actual ($\delta = 1$) or expected ($\delta \neq 1$) annual rate of change in wholesale prices for the year ending at the middle of year t
Y_t = Nominal net national income
P_t^d = GNP deflator in year t
δ = Coefficient of price expectations
ϵ = Coefficient of income expectations

and where $\beta < 0$ and $\gamma > 0$ on theoretical grounds.

This function was estimated on the basis of twenty-five annual observations for the period 1938–62.[23]

Tables 7 and 8 show the results of the regressions for M_1 and M_2, respectively. In each table the regression coefficients are reported for alternative values of the coefficient of expectations for prices (rows) and income (columns). In general the results tend to confirm the hypothesis

---

to 1. In this chapter the results for several values of δ and ϵ are shown, in addition to those that maximize the coefficient of correlation, and including δ and $\epsilon = 1$, but they have been collapsed to a much smaller and more manageable subset.

23. Even when all the necessary data were available since 1935, the computational requirements of the expected income variable forced 1938 as the initial date. In order to use expected series of similar length without losing much valuable information on the other series, a value for the expected per capita real income for the year 1934 [$y_{34}^{(e)}$] was estimated on the basis of linear extrapolations of several corresponding series computed with all the available data, and was used as the initial value in the equation

$$y_t^{(e)} = \epsilon y_t + (1 - \epsilon) y_{t-1}^{(e)}, \quad \text{where} \quad y_0^{(e)} = y_{34}^{(e)}.$$

defined for several ϵ coefficients. Finally, the first three values estimated with these equations were dropped to lessen the influence of possible errors in the estimated initial value. No similar problem arose in connection with the expected rate of change in prices because the data on prices went back as far as necessary.

that the demand for per capita real money balances in Argentina, during 1935–62, was a stable function of the cost of holding money and real per capita income, and that these two variables alone explain a high fraction of the observed variability of those balances. The signs of the coefficients coincide with those expected on theoretical grounds. The tables also show that the expectational variables for changes in prices and in real income tend to improve the results relatively to those obtained with immediately past inflation and current measured income. The tables also show that the two definitions of money behave somewhat differently in these and some other connections.

Table 7 shows that holdings of real M_1 per capita do not respond significantly (at the 5 per cent significance level) to changes in the current or expected cost of holding money when current measured income is used in the regressions, but that both variables have highly significant coefficients when a "permanent" concept of income is used in the regressions.[24]

The table also shows that for a given coefficient of income expectation, the R^2's show little response to changes in the coefficient of price expectations, so that not much confidence can be put on any particular value of δ as representing the "true" implicit speed of adjustment for price expectations. The R^2's vary much more in general, as the coefficient of income expectation changes. The particular values of the expectations coefficients which maximize R^2 are δ and $\epsilon = .3$.

The results of table 8 show that when savings and time deposits in commercial banks are included in the definition of money, the cost of holding money in terms of immediately past inflation and current measured real income per capita are both statistically significant at the 5 per cent level but can only explain less than half of the observed variability in per capita money holdings. The introduction of permanent versions of these variables significantly improves the results. The values of R^2 are responsive to changes in the coefficients of expectations and reach absolute maxima at $\delta = .2$ and $\epsilon = .3$.[25]

The results in tables 7 and 8, using comparable values of δ and ϵ, show that the estimated equations for M_2 consistently have higher cost coefficients (in absolute terms) and lower income coefficients than those

24. Actually, the estimated response to cost changes is close to the critical region and when all 28 observations are used the coefficients of actual and expected cost of holding money achieve significance even with measured income in the regressions.

25. The values of R^2 for $\delta = .1$ (not shown in table 8) show a marked decline as compared with those that correspond to $\delta = .2$.

TABLE 7

THE DEMAND FOR M_1

(ESTIMATED COEFFICIENTS OF THE COST OF HOLDING MONEY AND REAL INCOME PER CAPITA FOR DIFFERENT COEFFICIENTS OF PRICE AND INCOME EXPECTATIONS)

COEFFICIENT OF PRICE EXPECTATIONS δ	COEFFICIENT OF INCOME EXPECTATIONS ϵ											
	1.0			.4			.3			.2		
	Cost	Income	R^2 / $S_{y.x}$	Cost	Income	R^2 / $S_{y.x}$	Cost	Income	R^2 / $S_{y.x}$	Cost	Income	R^2 / $S_{y.x}$
1.0	−.195 (.113)	1.708* (.162)	.836 / .086									
.7	−.264 (.142)	1.713* (.161)	.838 / .085	−.679* (.092)	2.034* (.111)	.939 / .053	−.745* (.114)	2.039* (.137)	.910 / .064	−.823* (.170)	2.058* (.212)	.812 / .092
.6	−.302 (.156)	1.718* (.160)	.840 / .085	−.783* (.091)	2.064* (.100)	.951 / .047	−.881* (.111)	2.091* (.121)	.932 / .056	−1.000* (.173)	2.147* (.196)	.845 / .084
.5	−.340 (.174)	1.725* (.160)	.841* / .085*	−.901* (.096)	2.097* (.093)	.958 / .044	−1.044* (.108)	2.150* (.106)	.949 / .048	−1.223* (.177)	2.253* (.180)	.877 / .075
.4	−.377 (.198)	1.737* (.162)	.840 / .085	−1.036* (.110)	2.136* (.095)	.958* / .043*	−1.245* (.109)	2.226* (.095)	.962 / .042	−1.520* (.181)	2.396* (.163)	.907 / .065
.3	−.398 (.238)	1.754* (.168)	.834 / .087	−1.215* (.148)	2.205* (.111)	.948 / .048	−1.537* (.131)	2.351* (.098)	.964** / .041**	−2.008* (.196)	2.642* (.152)	.932 / .055
.2	−.364 (.281)	1.763* (.177)	.826 / .089	−1.305* (.216)	2.258* (.145)	.920 / .060	−1.779* (.196)	2.477* (.131)	.944 / .050	−2.591* (.230)	2.972* (.161)	.942* / .051*

NOTE: The figures in parentheses under each coefficient correspond to its estimated standard deviation. An asterisk in the coefficients indicates significance at the 5 per cent level. An asterisk in the coefficient of determination (R^2) and in the standard error of estimate ($S_{y.x}$) indicates maximum and minimum column values, respectively, and a double asterisk indicates maximum and minimum column *and* row values, respectively.

TABLE 8

THE DEMAND FOR M_2

(ESTIMATED COEFFICIENTS OF THE COST OF HOLDING MONEY AND REAL INCOME PER CAPITA FOR DIFFERENT COEFFICIENTS OF PRICE AND INCOME EXPECTATIONS)

COEFFICIENT OF PRICE EXPECTATIONS δ	COEFFICIENT OF INCOME EXPECTATIONS ϵ											
	1.0			.4			.3			.2		
	Cost	Income	R^2 / $S_{y \cdot x}$	Cost	Income	R^2 / $S_{y \cdot x}$	Cost	Income	R^2 / $S_{y \cdot x}$	Cost	Income	R^2 / $S_{y \cdot x}$
1.0	-.602* (.171)	.635* (.245)	.445 / .130									
.7	-.914* (.189)	.663* (.213)	.580 / .113	-1.060* (.201)	.735* (.241)	.575 / .114	-1.049* (.216)	.624* (.260)	.521 / .121	-1.009* (.238)	.444 (.298)	.451 / .130
.6	-1.090* (.188)	.687* (.193)	.656 / .103	-1.275* (.196)	.802* (.214)	.669 / .101	-1.276* (.216)	.713* (.236)	.618 / .108	-1.247* (.244)	.565 (.277)	.544 / .118
.5	-1.300* (.187)	.722* (.173)	.728 / .091	-1.536* (.189)	.880* (.184)	.760 / .086	-1.558* (.212)	.819* (.207)	.714 / .094	-1.552* (.249)	.712* (.254)	.640 / .105
.4	-1.560* (.184)	.782* (.150)	.797 / .079	-1.868* (.173)	.985* (.150)	.847 / .068	-1.928* (.199)	.961* (.173)	.811 / .076	-1.970* (.249)	.913* (.225)	.741 / .089
.3	-1.914* (.187)	.900* (.131)	.849 / .068	-2.359* (.151)	1.172* (.113)	.920 / .050	-2.497* (.180)	1.204* (.135)	.898 / .056	-2.661* (.248)	1.263* (.193)	.840 / .070
.2	-2.233* (.201)	1.051* (.127)	.869* / .063*	-2.827* (.148)	1.385* (.099)	.945* / .041*	-3.098* (.159)	1.500* (.107)	.945*** / .041***	-3.547* (.219)	1.759* (.153)	.923* / .049*

NOTE: See Table 7, n.

of M_1. This, in turn, implies that savings and time deposit holdings in Argentina have been more responsive to cost and less responsive to income variations than either or both currency and demand deposit holdings.[26]

The values of δ which maximize R^2 in the regressions using both definitions of money, namely, $\delta = .3$ and .2, imply an average length of the weighting pattern of about two and one-half and four years, respectively.[27] This seems to be a rather extended horizon in the case of a country subject to substantial and prolonged inflation.

The particular distributed lag model used imposes a single δ for the whole period. However, it seems conceivable that the actual coefficient might have increased through time either according to the length or duration of the inflationary period, or according to the level of the inflation itself. To test these further hypotheses about δ, the data were divided into two subperiods of approximately equal length (1938–50 and 1951–62), and separate demand for money functions were estimated for each subperiod.[28] The results of these regressions (not reported here) were puzzling because, if anything, they showed a tendency for the "best" values of δ to be *lower* during the second than during the first subperiod. These results led to further analysis of the data and it was found that, since the variability of the rates of inflation was also greater during the second subperiod, they were consistent with a third hypothesis, namely, that the value of δ may inversely respond to changes

26. At the time this study was being completed both the National Development Council (CONADE) and the central bank made available a revised set of product and income series for Argentina. Unfortunately the new series had several characteristics which diminished their potential usefulness and made a decision to substitute them for the old series used in this study extremely difficult. First, they only covered the period since 1950 and thus created the problem of appropriate grafting with the figures of the old series for the earlier years. Second, the two sets of new figures showed divergences between themselves raising the additional problem of choice in the face of no information about the nature of their discrepancies. Finally, the plotting of the relative rates of change of the annual real per capita income figures corresponding to each of the new series showed a very high degree of correlation with those of the old series and corresponding regression coefficients not significantly different from one, a result which tended to make the effort of substitution and the dangers of grafting less worthwhile incurring than would have otherwise been the case.

27. An explanation is provided, in the second part of this section, for the lower value of δ when savings and time deposits are included in the definition of money.

28. The trouble with the Argentine experience, however, is that the rates of inflation show a rising trend in the period 1935–62, so that a problem of identification of hypothesis was bound to arise.

in the variance of inflation, since a greater variability may lead people to trust recently observed rates less and to look for more extensive evidence on which to base their expectations.

A different approach was then taken to analyze the influence of the variance of the rate of inflation upon the demand for money. A new variable, representing the variance of inflation, was introduced in the demand function together with the expected cost and real per capita income. This new function was defined as follows:

$$\log \left(\frac{M_t}{NP^w}\right)_t = \alpha + \beta E_t^{(\delta)} + \gamma \log \left(\frac{Y}{NP^d}\right)_t^{(\epsilon)} + \lambda V_t^{(\delta)} + v_t \quad (14)$$

where

$$V_t^{(\delta)} = \sum_{i=0}^{\infty} \delta(1-\delta)^i [I_{t-i-1/2} - E_{t-i}^{(\epsilon)}]^2 \quad (15)$$

and where E_t was defined according to expression (12). The value of λ was expected to be positive on the assumption that an increase in uncertainty—as measured by the degree to which expectations have been frustrated in the past—would lead people to hold more real cash balances than otherwise.

TABLE 9

THE DEMAND FOR MONEY
(ESTIMATED COEFFICIENTS OF REGRESSIONS INCLUDING THE VARIANCE OF
THE RATE OF INFLATION AS AN ADDITIONAL EXPLANATORY VARIABLE)

MONEY DEFINITION	COEFFICIENT OF EXPECTATIONS		EXPLANATORY VARIABLE			R^2 $S_{y.x}$
	Price δ	Income ϵ	Cost	Income	Variance†	
M_1	.4	.4	−1.284* (.179)	2.198* (.098)	1.950 (1.143)	.964* .0416*
	.3	.3	−1.928* (.228)	2.456* (.105)	2.163 (1.066)	.970** .0380**
M_2	.2	.4	−3.555* (.279)	1.592* (.111)	3.499* (1.195)	.961* .0353*
	.2	.3	−4.050* (.276)	1.784* (.112)	4.292* (1.112)	.968** .0320**

NOTE: See note to Table 7.
† Variance of the rate of inflation.

The results of these regressions are reported in table 9 only for those values of δ which maximize R^2, and they show that the coefficients of the new variable have the expected signs and are clearly significant (at the 5 per cent level) for M_2, but that they do not quite reach significance in the case of M_1.

Table 10 provides a comparison of the results of this study with those of Cagan [29] and Deaver [30] for Austria and Chile, respectively.

The values of δ imply an average length for the weighting pattern of price expectations of about eleven quarters for Chile, ten quarters for Argentina,[31] and seven quarters for Austria.

The values of ϵ for Chile and Argentina cannot be properly compared because Deaver did not attempt to estimate the "best" income expectations coefficient.

The results for Chile show lower cost elasticities than those for Argentina and Austria. The results for Chile also show that when savings and time deposits are excluded from the definition of money the cost elasticity decreases and the income elasticity increases, as in the Argentine case.

B. DEMAND FUNCTIONS FOR COMPONENTS OF THE QUANTITY OF MONEY

The study of demand functions for components of the money stock is important because it provides additional information on the behavior of the latter and because it allows some useful inferences in connection with the differential behavior of alternative definitions of "money" through time. In addition, by increasing our knowledge about the manner in which those components behave, they help us to understand the movements of certain relationships which play some role in the observed variations in the money supply, given differentiated fractional reserves for different kinds of deposits.

A good starting point is provided by the same demand function used to explain the observed variability of the aggregate money concepts; that is, by considering the per capita real amounts of currency, demand deposits adjusted, and savings and time deposits to be a function of the cost of holding money and the expected real per capita income. The results of these regressions, using a logarithmic transformation for the

29. Cagan, "Monetary Dynamics," p. 43. The Austrian demand function was chosen for this comparison because this was the mildest hyperinflation Cagan studied.

30. Deaver, "Chilean Inflation," above, pp. 34, 38, and 40.

31. The Argentine average takes $\delta = .3$ as the "best" value, for reasons explained in the next section.

TABLE 10

ESTIMATED COEFFICIENTS OF THE DEMAND FOR MONEY FUNCTION IN ARGENTINA, CHILE AND AUSTRIA

Money Definition	Country	Period	Number and Frequency of Observations	Coefficients of Expectations		Explanatory Variable		R^2
				δ Price	ϵ Income	Cost	Income	
M_1	Chile	1932–55	92 Quarterly	.10	1	−1.476 (.33) [−.050]	.937 (.04)	.863
	Argentina	1938–62	25 Annual	.075	.3	−1.537 (.131) [−.23]	2.351 (.098)	.964
M_2	Chile	1932–55	92 Quarterly	.10	1	−4.888 (.339) [−.155]	.627 (.028)	.852
	Chile	1932–55	92 Quarterly	.10	.3	−5.219 (.472) [−.169]	.617 (.039)	.741
	Argentina	1938–62	25 Annual	.05	.3	−3.098 (.159) [−.43]	1.500 (.107)	.945
	Austria	1921–22	20 Monthly	.15	—	−8.55 [−.35]	—	.989

SOURCE: Phillip Cagan, "The Monetary Dynamics of Hyperinflation," in *Studies in the Quantity Theory of Money*, ed. Milton Friedman (Chicago: Univ. of Chicago Press, 1956), p. 43; John Deaver, "The Chilean Inflation and the Demand for Money," above pp. 34, 38, and 40; my tables 7 and 8.

NOTE: The figures in parentheses under the regression coefficients are their standard error of estimate. The figures in brackets indicate the cost elasticities and are equal to $\beta\epsilon$. The δ's are all converted to a quarterly basis.

TABLE 11

DEMAND FUNCTIONS FOR COMPONENTS OF AGGREGATE MONEY SUPPLY
(ESTIMATED COEFFICIENTS OF THE COST OF HOLDING MONEY AND EXPECTED
REAL PER CAPITA INCOME ($\epsilon = .3$) FOR THREE ALTERNATIVE VALUES OF
THE PRICE EXPECTATIONS COEFFICIENT)

MONEY SUPPLY COMPONENTS AND AGGREGATES	COEFFICIENT OF PRICE EXPECTATION δ	EXPLANATORY VARIABLE		R^2 $S_{y.x}$
		Cost	Expected Income	
Using M_1 value of δ				
Currency.................	.3	−.954*	2.913*	.856
		(.366)	(.274)	.1135
Demand deposits..........	.3	−2.111*	1.804*	.673
		(.383)	(.286)	.1189
M_1.....................	.3	−1.537*	2.351*	.964
		(.131)	(.098)	.0406
Using M_2 value of δ				
Currency.................	.2	−.892	2.899*	.838
		(.469)	(.315)	.1204
Demand deposits..........	.2	−2.674*	2.077*	.717
		(.431)	(.289)	.1107
Savings and time deposits...	.2	−6.013*	.117	.961
		(.334)	(.224)	.0856
M_2.....................	.2	−3.098*	1.500*	.945
		(.159)	(.107)	.0409
Values of δ free				
Currency.................	.6	−.680*	2.810*	.870
		(.214)	(.234)	.1076
Demand deposits..........	.1	−3.423*	2.245*	.753
		(.497)	(.282)	.1033
Savings and time deposits...	.1	−7.538*	.433*	.978
		(.311)	(.177)	.0646

NOTE: The first two sets of estimated coefficients correspond to the values of δ which maximize R^2 in the aggregate demand equations corresponding to M_1 and M_2 (reproduced here to facilitate comparisons). The last set shows the coefficients of the demand for each component for those values of δ which *individually* maximize R^2. The figures in parentheses and the starred coefficients have the same meaning as before (see note to table 7).

dependent variable and for the expected ($\epsilon = .3$) income variable and covering the period 1938–62, are presented in table 11. The annual series of components of the money stock are given in table 20 and the per capita real amounts are graphed in chart 4.

The estimates in the first two sets of equations in table 11 show that in both cases the currency reaction to changes in the expected rate of change in prices is lower (and even nonsignificant) than the reaction of deposits and that savings and time deposits show a much greater reaction than demand deposits. The regressions also show a relatively

Money and Prices in Argentina, 1935–1962   105

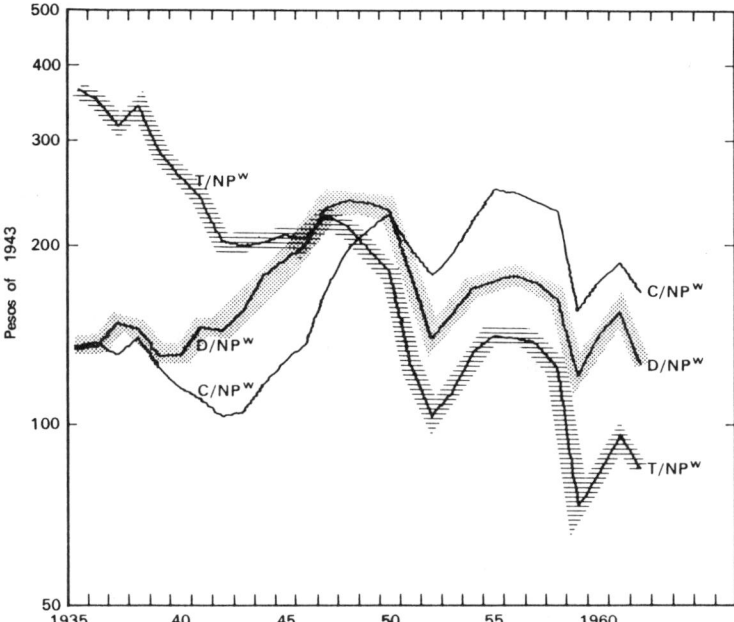

CHART 4. Annual averages of real per capita currency, demand deposits, and savings and time deposits, 1935–62 (wholesale price index used as deflator).
SOURCES: Tables 20, 23, 24.

high expected income elasticity for currency as compared to that of demand deposits and a nonsignificant expected income elasticity for savings and time deposits. In the light of this additional information about the behavior of components, it is easier to explain the differences between the coefficients corresponding to the two aggregate money concepts. The estimates in the third set of equations show that the demand for currency seems to imply a faster reaction to past inflation than the demand for either demand or savings and time deposits.

Finally, the results show that the simple expected inflation and real income model explains a sizable fraction of the observed variations in the real amounts of per capita components of money holdings, but they also suggest that there is still ample room for improvement, particularly in connection with the currency and demand deposits equation. For this purpose several additional variables were considered. A brief discussion of each one of them follows.

When one considers the demand for particular components of money, it is necessary to take into consideration their money returns, because the cost of holding any component with respect to each of the alternative components is the difference between the money return on the former and the money return on each one of the alternative components. The money return on currency is typically zero. The money return on demand deposits is positive if interest is paid and negative if there are service charges or other money costs involved. For the period 1935–62 it is possible to treat demand deposits as if their money rates of return have been constant and to exclude any explanatory variable in this connection.[32] Savings and time deposits yield a money return in the form of interest paid on them by the commercial banks. These rates have been subject to strict maximum regulations during 1935–62 and there are no data on the amounts of actual interest payments. However, actual payments have been generally close to maximum limits and both maximum rates have moved together. Hence the maximum rate of interest on savings deposits is a good approximation to the actual average money returns on these deposits.

Changes in the distribution of income may affect the demands for money components if individuals within different income groups have differential preferences for these components.[33] During the period 1935–62 the fraction of total income going to the labor sector had marked variations in Argentina. If low income groups derive their incomes mainly from labor, then the fraction of total income going to labor can be used as an index of distribution of income.

The spread of banking facilities and the accessibility to banking services might explain some changes in the amounts of desired currency and deposit holdings. The number of persons per bank office was

---

32. Interest payments on demand deposits were forbidden in Argentina in May 1946. During 1935–46 commercial banks were allowed to pay interest on these deposits up to a maximum of one-half of one percentage point, but no data are available on the amount of interest payments, if any. Service charges have been forbidden in Argentina, but a nominal tax has been applied to each check.

33. For instance, if income levels are related to educational levels and they in turn condition money holding practices, then a change in the income distribution may affect the demands for components. Also a redistribution of income may affect the composition of aggregate consumption expenditures and if there are differences in the amounts of currency used per unit of consumption expenditures for different categories of expenditures then the redistribution may affect the partial demands for money. For certain low income groups, currency hoarding may be the only financial means of holding wealth, etc.

the variable used in the regressions in an attempt to capture these effects.[34]

The preceding variables (whose numerical values are given in table 26) were introduced as additional explanatory variables in the demand functions for components of money, after a logarithmic transformation, with the last variable mentioned not being included in the savings and time deposits equation. The results of the new regressions are shown in tables 12, 13, and 14.

TABLE 12

THE DEMAND FOR CURRENCY
(ESTIMATED COEFFICIENTS OF THE COST OF HOLDING CURRENCY, EXPECTED PER CAPITA REAL INCOME ($\epsilon = .3$) AND OTHER VARIABLES FOR THOSE VALUES OF THE PRICE EXPECTATIONS COEFFICIENT WHICH MAXIMIZE R^2)

Coefficient of Price Expectations δ	Cost	Expected Income	Interest on Savings	Income Distribution	Persons Per Bank	R^2 $S_{y.x}$
.6	−.680* (.214)	2.810* (.234)				.870 .1076
.3	−1.820* (.354)	3.137* (.218)	.239* (.059)			.918 .0873
.3	−1.616* (.305)	2.208* (.349)	.215* (.050)	.875* (.280)		.945 .0733
.3	−1.607* (.302)	2.432* (.398)	.269* (.069)	.691* (.321)	.409 (.359)	.949 .0728

NOTE: The estimates in the first row are the same as those in the last set of results in table 11 and are reproduced here to facilitate comparisons. In each row only the results for those values of δ which maximize R^2 are presented.

In general, the results of these tables tend to confirm the a priori expectations as to the direction in which these additional variables would operate in the demand functions for components of money and the increased explanatory power of a more elaborate model. The results, however, also show some puzzling findings difficult to explain.

The currency equations show significant and consistently positive coefficients for the variable representing interest rates paid on savings

34. In some earlier versions of this work the fraction of aggregate national income represented by the revenue from direct taxes (income, capital gains, extraordinary benefits, etc.) and a dummy variable representing the existence of generalized price controls in the economy were also introduced as explanatory variables, but their coefficients turned out to be consistently nonsignificant and the variables were excluded in the regressions reported here.

TABLE 13

THE DEMAND FOR DEMAND DEPOSITS
(ESTIMATED COEFFICIENTS OF THE COST OF HOLDING DEMAND DEPOSITS,
EXPECTED REAL PER CAPITA INCOME (ϵ = .3) AND OTHER VARIABLES, FOR
THOSE VALUES OF THE PRICE EXPECTATION COEFFICIENT WHICH MAXIMIZE
R^2)

Coefficient of Price Expectations δ	Cost	Expected Income	Interest on Savings	Income Distribution	Persons Per Bank	R^2 $S_{y.x}$
.1	-3.423^* (.497)	2.245* (.282)				.753 . .1033
.3	-1.347^* (.410)	1.607* (.252)	$-.210^*$ (.069)			.774 .1012
.3	-1.653^* (.289)	2.998* (.331)	$-.175^*$ (.048)	-1.311^* (.266)		.898 .0696
.3	-1.660^* (.289)	2.805* (.380)	$-.222^*$ (.066)	-1.152^* (.307)	$-.353$ (.343)	.903 .0695

NOTE: See table 12, note.

TABLE 14

THE DEMAND FOR SAVINGS AND TIME DEPOSITS
(ESTIMATED COEFFICIENTS OF THE COST OF HOLDING SAVINGS AND TIME
DEPOSITS, EXPECTED REAL INCOME PER CAPITA (ϵ = .3) AND OTHER
VARIABLES FOR THOSE VALUES OF THE PRICE EXPECTATIONS COEFFICIENTS
WHICH MAXIMIZE R^2)

Coefficient of Price Expectations δ	Cost	Expected Income	Own Interest	Income Distribution	Trend	R^2 $S_{y.x}$
.1	-7.538^* (.311)	.433* (.177)				.978 .0646
.1	-8.672^* (.567)	.787* (.223)	.147* (.064)			.982 .0591
.1	-8.815^* (.562)	1.141* (.328)	.162* (.063)	$-.314$ (.218)		.984 .0576
.3	-3.043^* (.246)	1.880* (.460)	.195 (.094)	$-.689^*$ (.223)	$-.047^*$ (.0075)	.985 .0571

NOTE: See table 12, note.

and time deposits. These results are contrary to expectations, since they would indicate that, other things being equal, an increase in the rates paid on savings deposits would tend to increase the amount of real currency holdings. The results are even more puzzling because the variable operates with the appropriate and significant signs in both deposits equations. The income distribution index is significant in the currency and demand deposits equations and operates with the expected signs. The coefficient of this variable is not significant in the savings and time deposits equations. The introduction of this variable also changes the point estimates of the expected income elasticities in all three regressions, lowering that corresponding to currency and increasing those corresponding to both deposits. The average number of persons per bank shows coefficients with the appropriate positive sign for currency and negative sign for deposits, but the variable does not reach statistical significance.

Finally, these results provide some additional information on the behavior of the price expectation coefficient. When the additional variables are introduced in the demand functions for components, the values of the δ coefficients maximizing R^2 for currency and demand deposits are the same in both cases and the difference noticed in the third set of regression results of table 11 disappears. Yet, the corresponding value of δ in the savings and time deposits equations remains the same, namely, $\delta = .1$. Since a lower value of δ implies a smoother time series for the expected rate of change in prices, a plausible statistical explanation for this disparity may be that the variable is picking up the effect of the noticeable declining trend in the real per capita holdings of savings and time deposits. In order to test this hypothesis, I introduced an additional trend variable in the equations dealing with these deposits. The results, reported in the last row of table 14, show that when the trend is included, the value of δ maximizing R^2 becomes .3, as in the equations for currency and demand deposits, and the cost response is drastically reduced.

The behavior of the C/D and T/D ratios. The preceding analysis of the demand for components of the stock of money provides the basis for an explanation of the behavior of the C/D and the T/D ratios, during 1935–62. The corresponding annual series are graphed in chart 5 and given numerically in table 25.

The C/D ratio shows a declining trend from 1935 to around the end of World War II, followed by a long upward trend which levels off around 1955. From this date to the end of the period, the ratio shows

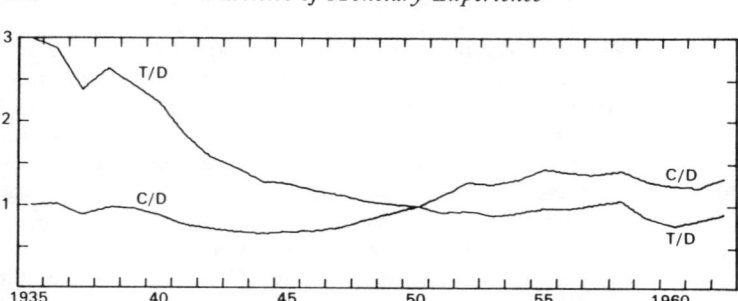

CHART 5. Annual averages of the ratio of currency to demand deposits and the ratio of savings and time deposits to demand deposits, 1935–62.
SOURCE: Table 25.

a slow decline. The estimated coefficients of the demand functions for C and D (tables 12 and 13) imply that the C/D ratio can be expected to react negatively to income changes and positively to changes in the share of income going to labor and interest rates paid on savings deposits. Changes in the expected rate of inflation cannot be expected to affect the ratio because the individual responses are very similar. On the basis of this and the movements observed in the explanatory variables, it is possible to say that the increase in permanent income seems to be the main factor behind the initial decline in the ratio. The sharp increase after the Second World War seems to have been mainly a response to the important increases in the share of income going to labor which took place during those years. The slow decline after 1955 seems to reflect the influence of two forces operating with opposite signs on the ratio, namely, a decline in permanent income and also a decline in the share of income going to labor.

The T/D ratio shows a long and sharp decline from 1935 to about 1952. From this date to 1958 the series shows a slow increase in the ratio. During the last four years the ratio first declines to an absolute low level in 1960 and then rises toward 1962. The coefficients of the partial demands for T and D (tables 13 and 14) show that the ratio would respond negatively to changes in the expected rate of change in prices and in real per capita permanent income, and positively to changes in interest rates paid on savings deposits and changes in the share of income going to labor. Combining this with the observed movements in the explanatory variables, it is possible for me to explain the initial decline mainly in terms of the increase in the expected rate of change in prices and in permanent income. The share of income going to labor also increased toward the end of this first subperiod but its influence was not very important when compared with that of the other two variables. The small rising trend of the ratio during most of the 1950s can be explained by a deceleration and even a decline of the expected rate of change in prices, and of the permanent real per capita income. The increase in the maximum rates of interest allowed to be paid on savings deposits during this period also explains part of the observed increase in the ratio. The increase in the expected rate of change in prices and the decline in the share of income going to labor seem to be the most important influences explaining the fall in the level of the ratio from 1958 to 1960. The subsequent increase seems to have been induced by declining expectations of inflation and permanent real income and by an important increase in the maximum rate of interest that the central bank allowed banks to pay on savings and time deposits.

4. THE DYNAMICS OF INFLATION

The magnitude of the Argentine inflationary process together with the failure of repeated anti-inflationary efforts have produced heated and prolonged debate on the causes of inflation, the role of some important economic variables, and the alleged effects of alternative measures aimed at decelerating the trend of prices. Unfortunately, a corresponding amount of energy and resourcefulness has not been applied to a careful and systematic analysis of the available evidence in Argentina or in other Latin American countries under similar conditions, except for the work done for Chile by Professor Arnold C. Harberger.[35]

This section presents an analysis of the dynamic responses of prices to changes in some of the variables considered to be important in order to estimate their individual contributions to the rate of change in prices. This analysis follows the line of Harberger's study of the Chilean inflation and covers the years 1935–62, with the empirical results for the whole period and for the subperiod 1946–62 being reported separately.

The starting point is a relationship that links the relative rate of change in prices during a given period to the contemporaneous and past rates of change in the quantity of money, under the assumption that

35. Arnold C. Harberger, "The Dynamics of Inflation in Chile" in *Measurement in Economics: Studies in Mathematical Economics and Econometrics in Memory of Yehuda Grunfeld*, ed. Carl F. Christ (Stanford, Calif.; Stanford Univ. Press, 1963). Also Carlos F. Diaz Alejandro, *Exchange Rate Devaluation in a Semi-industrialized Country: The Experience of Argentina, 1955–61* (Cambridge: M.I.T. Press, 1965).

they affect the level of prices through a process of adjustment that involves time.

$$\Delta \log P_t = a_1 \Delta \log M_t + a_2 \Delta \log M_{t-1} + a_3 \Delta \log M_{t-2} + \cdots. \quad (16)$$

Several comments are in order about this relationship.[36] First, on theoretical grounds, one should expect that, other things being equal, an upward and sustained shift in the rate of monetary expansion would, after a while, bring about a similar increase in the rate of price changes. This implies that the sum of the a coefficients should be expected to add up to unity when all the relevant lags are taken into consideration. Second, according to the theory of the demand for money, and the empirical results reported in the preceding section, one should expect a lower level of real cash balances to be consistent with the new and higher rate of change in prices after the above shift has fully worked its effects in the economy. This, in turn, implies that some overshooting will occur in the path of the rate of change in prices during the adjustment period, in order for real cash balances to decline to their lower desired level. Under these circumstances it may be possible to observe some partial sums of the a coefficients to be greater than unity and some of them to be negative, while the total sum approaches unity as the whole adjustment process comes to an end. Third, nothing definite can be said on theoretical grounds about the number of the a coefficients or their individual values, since they depend on the speed of adjustment and on the particular periods chosen for the analysis.[37]

From an empirical point of view the above relationship presents some difficult problems, particularly for choosing the appropriate number of lagged changes in money. The stepwise inclusion of lagged values of the independent variable cannot be terminated on the basis of a sum of the coefficients equal to one, or the lack of statistical significance of the last estimated coefficient, because the overshooting of prices might produce both effects before all relevant lags are included. In addition, multicollinearity will almost surely become a

36. The logarithmic first differences in expression (16) indicate relative rates of change, continuously compounded, for the price level, the contemporaneous and the lagged values of the stock of money, provided e is the base of these logarithms.

37. These two characteristics have, however, an enormous importance from a policy point of view, since they may imply, for instance, that even a cessation of a monetary expansion that has been taking place at a certain rate may not work its full effects on prices until several quarters, or semesters, or even years have elapsed.

problem in an estimation which may include many values of the same variable at successive points in time, if the adjustment is not a rapid one. All this does not mean that some valuable information cannot be obtained from a relationship of this kind. It provides a test for the assumption of lagged response in prices; it allows comparisons of response patterns between different price indexes and alternative definitions of money; and even when it may prove to be impossible to obtain a good idea of the whole pattern of the lags involved, it may still give useful information about the structure of the reaction of prices to money changes for a given number of lags.

The study attempts to explain the relative rates of change in the quarterly averages of the wholesale and the cost-of-living indexes of prices. The money variables used were the semiannual relative rates of change for two definitions of money, with the first term including the change in the average stock of money from quarter $t - 2$ to quarter t, and so on.[38] The use of quarterly and semiannual rates of change for the dependent and independent variables, respectively, also means that the sum of the coefficients should approach one-half rather than one, as the adjustment process comes to an end.

Table 15 shows the estimated coefficients of expression (16) for the period 1935–62 and 1946–62, using both price indexes and M_1 and M_2 as alternative definitions of money. These results tend to confirm the basic hypothesis of the existence of lagged response in prices to changes in money.[39] They also reveal initial overshooting and a later significant deceleration of prices which takes place approximately during the third semester following the acceleration of money. The sum of the coefficients generally falls short of the expected norm of .5 except in those regressions involving the cost-of-living index and the whole period. This seems to provide some evidence that the total adjustment period may take longer than the two years included in these regressions.

The second step in the analysis involves the consideration of further variables which may also affect the behavior of prices. In particular, it seems necessary to consider the role of expectations, real income,

38. This may tend to increase the degree of multicollinearity for a given number of lagged money terms, but it allows the length of the reaction period analyzed to be doubled for a given number of terms.

39. The R^2's are still relatively low but they indicate a remarkable improvement over those corresponding to a set of simple regressions (not reported here), involving the same dependent variables and the contemporaneous quarterly rates of change in money, that ranges from .09 to .19 for the four different combinations of prices and money definitions.

TABLE 15

REACTION OF PRICES TO MONEY CHANGES
(ESTIMATED COEFFICIENTS OF REGRESSIONS OF QUARTERLY RATES OF
INFLATION ON LAGGED SEMESTERLY RATES OF CHANGE IN MONEY)

Price Index	Definition of Money	$\dot{M}_t$	$\dot{M}_{t-2}$	$\dot{M}_{t-4}$	$\dot{M}_{t-6}$	R^2 $S_{y.x}$
Period 1935–62 (N = 101)						
Wholesale........	M_1	.594*	.060	−.336*	.011	.414
		(.078)	(.076)	(.076)	(.077)	.042
	M_2	.739*	.044	−.480*	.032	.380
		(.102)	(.103)	(.103)	(.101)	.043
Cost of living.....	M_1	.420*	.184*	−.078	−.008	.288
		(.084)	(.082)	(.082)	(.083)	.046
	M_2	.541*	.211*	−.168	−.018	.311
		(.105)	(.106)	(.106)	(.104)	.045
Subperiod 1946–62 (N = 63)						
Wholesale........	M_1	.629*	.088	−.445*	−.043	.443
		(.110)	(.103)	(.104)	(.114)	.045
	M_2	.701*	.054	−.546*	−.051	.400
		(.136)	(.126)	(.128)	(.140)	.047
Cost of living.....	M_1	.500*	.224*	−.252*	−.126	.343
		(.117)	(.109)	(.111)	(.122)	.048
	M_2	.563*	.214	−.317*	−.139	.299
		(.145)	(.134)	(.136)	(.149)	.050

NOTE: The figures in parentheses under each coefficient denote their standard errors, and the asterisks, significance at the 5 per cent level. R^2 and $S_{y.x}$ indicate the estimated values of the coefficient of multiple determination and the standard errors of estimate, respectively. N indicates the effective sample size.

other policy variables like the exchange rate and wages, and the possibility of seasonal factors affecting the quarterly rates of inflation.

It has been shown in the preceding section how people's expectations as to the degree of inflation prevailing in the economy influence their desire to hold money. A transformation of the logarithmic stock demand for money allows one to express the relative rate of change in prices in terms of the relative rate of change in money and in real income and the change in expectations. There thus seem to be good grounds for including the changes in expectations in a relationship which attempts to explain the rate of inflation, although some important practical problems must be solved before doing so.

This expectational variable is defined in terms of past rates of change in prices and, according to expression (16), incorporates some influences of past rates of change in money. This problem was solved through a two-stage estimating procedure. First, a multiple regression was run, in which the dependent variable was the change in the expected rate of change in prices from quarter $t-2$ to quarter $t-1$ and where the independent variables were the four corresponding semi-annual rates of change in the stock of money and the quarterly rates of change in the official rate of exchange. The residuals of this regression provided an estimate of the exogenous changes in expectations which could not be accounted for by changes in previous policy variables used in the final regression. Secondly, these residuals were introduced as an explanatory variable in the final regressions under the assumption that they represented exogenous changes in expectations and also served as a proxy variable for still more lagged values of the rate of change in money.[40]

The role that changes in real income play in explaining the variations of the rate of inflation seems clear and needs no further elaboration. The difficulties here arise out of the lack of quarterly data and the inadequacy of some other quarterly series which could have been used as good proxy variables for these changes. A quarterly series was constructed by linearly interpolating the values of real income corresponding to each quarter, subject to the constraint that their sum will add up to the true annual figure. The series appear in table 32.

I also explored the role that devaluations and a centralized (governmental or unionized) wage policy may have played in the Argentine inflationary process, by introducing the rates of change in the official rate of exchange and an index of nominal wages. The basic series appear in table 36.

All these variables were linearly introduced in a relationship of the following type.

$$\Delta \log P_{i,t} = a_1 \Delta \log M_{j,t} + a_2 \Delta \log M_{j,t-2}$$
$$+ a_3 \Delta \log M_{j,t-4} + a_4 \Delta \log M_{j,t-6} + b \Delta RE_{i,t-1}^{(\delta)}$$
$$+ c \Delta \log Y_t + d \Delta \log X_t + e \Delta \log W_t + f S_t + u_t, \quad (17)$$

where

$\Delta \log P_{i,t}$ = Quarterly rate of change of average price index i from quarter $t-1$ to quarter t.

$\Delta \log M_{j,t-k}$ = Semiannual rate of change of average stock of money j from quarter $t-k-2$ to quarter $t-k$, for $k = 0$, 2, 4, and 6.

40. For the period 1946–62 this two-stage procedure also incorporated the current and lagged value of the rate of change of an index of nominal wages in the first regression.

$\Delta RE_{i,t-1}^{(\delta)} =$ "Exogenous" changes in price expectations from quarter $t-2$ to quarter $t-1$. The basic expected rate of change in prices is defined on the basis of price index i, with a quarterly price adjustment coefficient δ. The values of this variable are the residuals of multiple regressions of $\Delta E_{i,t-1}^{(\delta)}$ on all the other variables included in the final regressions (except for the change in real income and seasonal dummy), lagged one quarter.

$\Delta \log Y_t =$ Quarterly rate of change of average real income from quarter $t-1$ to quarter t.

$\Delta \log X_t =$ Quarterly rate of change of official exchange rate for the U.S. dollar from the middle of quarter $t-1$ to the middle of quarter t.

$\Delta \log W_t =$ Quarterly rate of change of an index of nominal wages from the middle of quarter $t-1$ to the middle of quarter t.

$S_t =$ A set of three seasonal dummy variables.

and where i indicates either the wholesale or the cost-of-living price indexes; j indicates M_1 or M_2; and the values of δ are .1, .2, and .3. All the rates of change assume continuous compounding.[41] The results for the period 1935–62 are presented in table 16, where the wholesale price index is used, and table 17, where a cost-of-living index is used. Results for the period 1946–62 are found in tables 18 and 19.

The results show that, in general, the introduction of the additional explanatory variables significantly increases the fraction of total variation in the rates of inflation being explained. The coefficients of the successively lagged changes in money supply reveal approximately the same structure of price responses as mentioned before, with some interesting differences between price indexes and money definitions.[42]

41. The variable $\Delta \log W$ was not included in the regressions dealing with the whole period 1935–62 because the available wage series starts in 1946.

42. For the regressions covering the whole period wholesale prices seem to have a faster initial adjustment (and even overshooting), within the first semester, than those implicit in the cost-of-living index, while there seem not to exist substantial differences between their sums toward the end of the first year. During the second year wholesale prices also seem to decelerate more rapidly so that the total sum of their coefficients is lower than that corresponding to the cost-of-living index which approaches the theoretical norm of one-half after four lagged changes in money are included. In both cases the initial acceleration and subsequent deceleration seems to be more marked for the more inclusive definition of money.

TABLE 16

Estimated Coefficients of Multiple Regressions for the Rate of Change of the Wholesale Price Index
(Period 1935–62)

Money Definition	Coefficient of Price Expectations δ	$\dot{M}_t$	$\dot{M}_{t-2}$	$\dot{M}_{t-4}$	$\dot{M}_{t-6}$	RE	$\dot{Y}$	$\dot{X}$	S_1	S_2	S_3	R^2 / $S_{y.x}$
M_1......	.1	.487* (.074)	.062 (.079)	−.298* (.078)	.043 (.068)	3.194* (.938)	−.550* (.173)	.101* (.023)	.027 (.015)	.024 (.012)	.027* (.009)	.685 / .032
	.2	.495* (.076)	.058 (.080)	−.299* (.079)	.045 (.069)	1.387* (.475)	−.580* (.174)	.100* (.023)	.025 (.015)	.023 (.013)	.027* (.010)	.675 / .032
	.3	.499* (.076)	.055 (.082)	−.299* (.080)	.046 (.070)	.778* (.318)	−.609* (.176)	.100* (.023)	.024 (.015)	.022 (.013)	.026* (.010)	.667 / .033
M_2......	.1	.548* (.093)	.080 (.097)	−.420* (.097)	.073 (.085)	3.879* (.933)	−.445* (.175)	.106* (.023)	.034* (.014)	.028* (.012)	.026* (.010)	.661 / .033
	.2	.559* (.095)	.073 (.099)	−.422* (.099)	.076 (.087)	1.715* (.472)	−.480* (.177)	.105* (.024)	.032* (.014)	.027* (.013)	.025* (.010)	.648 / .034
	.3	.564* (.096)	.069 (.101)	−.423* (.101)	.078 (.088)	.994* (.318)	−.511* (.179)	.105* (.024)	.031* (.014)	.026* (.013)	.025* (.010)	.636 / .034

Note: See table 15, note.

TABLE 17

ESTIMATED COEFFICIENTS OF MULTIPLE REGRESSIONS FOR THE RATE OF CHANGE OF THE COST-OF-LIVING PRICE INDEX
(PERIOD 1935–62)

Money Definition	Coefficient of Price Expectation δ	$\dot{M}_t$	$\dot{M}_{t-2}$	$\dot{M}_{t-4}$	$\dot{M}_{t-6}$	RE	$\dot{Y}$	$\dot{X}$	S_1	S_2	S_3	R^2 $S_{y\cdot x}$
M_1	.1	.321* (.080)	.185* (.086)	-.056 (.084)	.039 (.074)	3.127* (.924)	-.748* (.184)	.091* (.025)	.005 (.016)	.029* (.013)	.001 (.010)	.616 .035
	.2	.332* (.081)	.178* (.086)	-.054 (.085)	.039 (.074)	1.483* (.471)	-.747* (.186)	.090* (.025)	.003 (.016)	.028* (.014)	.001 (.010)	.610 .035
	.3	.339* (.082)	.173* (.087)	-.054 (.086)	.041 (.075)	.897* (.318)	-.759 (.188)	.091* (.025)	.002 (.016)	.027 (.014)	.002 (.010)	.602 .035
M_2	.1	.398* (.095)	.207* (.098)	-.107 (.100)	.032 (.087)	3.430* (.906)	-.716* (.178)	.087* (.024)	.004 (.014)	.028* (.013)	-.0003 (.010)	.631 .034
	.2	.411* (.096)	.198 (.101)	-.109 (.101)	.034 (.088)	1.598* (.464)	-.720* (.181)	.087* (.024)	.003 (.014)	.027* (.013)	-.0002 (.010)	.622 .034
	.3	.417* (.098)	.195 (.103)	-.111 (.102)	.037 (.089)	.947* (.315)	-.735* (.183)	.088* (.014)	.002 (.014)	.026* (.013)	.0002 (.010)	.611 .035

NOTE: See table 15, note.

TABLE 18

ESTIMATED COEFFICIENTS OF MULTIPLE REGRESSIONS FOR THE WHOLESALE PRICE INDEX
(SUBPERIOD 1946–62)

Money Definition	Coefficient of Price Expectations δ	$\dot{M}_t$	$\dot{M}_{t-2}$	$\dot{M}_{t-4}$	$\dot{M}_{t-6}$	RE	$\dot{Y}$	$\dot{X}$	$\dot{W}$	S_1	S_2	S_3	R_2 $S_{y \cdot x}$
M_1	.1	.462* (.105)	-.022 (.108)	-.217* (.103)	-.079 (.092)	4.536* (1.196)	-.514* (.234)	.097* (.024)	.033 (.043)	.006 (.022)	.017 (.019)	.045* (.012)	.760 .031
	.2	.474* (.109)	-.032 (.112)	-.219* (.107)	-.071 (.095)	1.999* (.623)	-.580* (.239)	.093* (.025)	.038 (.044)	.004 (.023)	.015 (.020)	.044* (.013)	.744 .033
	.3	.479* (.112)	-.037 (.115)	-.220* (.110)	-.064 (.097)	1.159* (.427)	-.643* (.242)	.091* (.025)	.039 (.046)	.002 (.023)	.015 (.020)	.043* (.013)	.731 .033
M_2	.1	.539* (.129)	-.085 (.131)	-.260* (.126)	-.091 (.110)	4.792* (1.238)	-.535* (.240)	.099* (.024)	.026 (.044)	.004 (.023)	.012 (.020)	.045* (.012)	.745 .032
	.2	.550* (.133)	-.094 (.135)	-.261* (.130)	-.080 (.114)	2.117* (.640)	-.613* (.244)	.094* (.026)	.032 (.046)	.002 (.023)	.012 (.021)	.043* (.013)	.728 .033
	.3	.546* (.136)	-.095 (.138)	-.261 (.133)	-.071 (.116)	1.224* (.435)	-.682* (.246)	.093* (.026)	.035 (.047)	.001 (.024)	.012 (.022)	.042* (.013)	.715 .034

NOTE: See table 15, note.

TABLE 19

ESTIMATED COEFFICIENTS OF MULTIPLE REGRESSIONS FOR THE COST-OF-LIVING PRICE INDEX
(SUBPERIOD 1946–62)

Money Definition	Coefficient of Price Expectations δ	$\dot{M}_t$	$\dot{M}_{t-2}$	$\dot{M}_{t-4}$	$\dot{M}_{t-6}$	RE	$\dot{Y}$	$\dot{X}$	$\dot{w}$	S_1	S_2	S_3	R^2 $S_{y\cdot x}$
M_1	.1	.307* (.120)	.153 (.123)	−.090 (.118)	−.109 (.105)	3.398* (1.229)	−.731* (.264)	.076* (.027)	.074 (.049)	−.014 (.025)	.043 (.022)	.011 (.014)	.679 .036
	.2	.319* (.120)	.145 (.124)	−.091 (.118)	−.103 (.105)	1.624* (.617)	−.753* (.264)	.075* (.027)	.079 (.049)	−.015 (.025)	.042 (.022)	.011 (.014)	.675 .036
	.3	.323* (.122)	.140 (.125)	−.091 (.119)	−.098 (.106)	.997* (.413)	−.789* (.265)	.074* (.028)	.082 (.050)	−.016 (.025)	.042 (.022)	.011 (.014)	.669 .036
M_2	.1	.371* (.145)	.117 (.147)	−.096 (.141)	−.121 (.124)	3.654* (1.252)	−.771* (.269)	.077* (.027)	.066 (.050)	−.018 (.025)	.038 (.023)	.011 (.014)	.667 .036
	.2	.384* (.146)	.108 (.148)	−.098 (.142)	−.113 (.124)	1.736* (.626)	−.803* (.269)	.075* (.027)	.072 (.050)	−.019 (.025)	.038 (.023)	.011 (.014)	.662 .037
	.3	.384* (.148)	.106 (.150)	−.098 (.144)	−.105 (.126)	1.055* (.417)	−.845* (.267)	.074* (.028)	.076 (.051)	−.020 (.026)	.038 (.023)	.011 (.014)	.654 .037

NOTE: See table 15, note.

Money and Prices in Argentina, 1935–1962 121

These coefficients lend some support to the idea that the adjustment process may be about two years for the cost-of-living index and somewhat longer for wholesale prices, when the exchange rate is held constant.

The variable representing exogenous changes in expectations has the expected positive and significant coefficients in all regressions, and the value of δ which maximizes R^2, namely, $\delta = .1$, is compatible with the value of $\delta = .3$ found as the most appropriate for the stock demand equation using annual observations.[43]

The changes in real income also show significant coefficients of the expected negative sign. These results seem to be quite good when account is taken of the quality of the original quarterly series.[44]

The coefficients of the exchange rate variable show a positive value of about .10, indicating that the direct effect of a 10 per cent devaluation will be about 1 per cent on the wholesale and about .9 per cent on the cost-of-living indexes. This is a surprising result in the light—or, should I say, the heat—of the discussion on the inflationary effects of devaluations in Argentina.[45] Lagged values of this variable have tended to be nonsignificant and to have negative signs in a different set of regressions not reported here.

The regressions corresponding to the subperiod 1946–62 tell basically the same story with some differences in the money coefficients and additional information given by the presence of the wage variable.

The wage variable has a nonsignificant coefficient which ranges from about .03 to about .07 in the regressions for the wholesale and the cost-of-living price indexes, respectively. This, again, is a remarkable figure in connection with the debate on the role of wages in the Argentine inflation, particularly when the period covered by the data is the one most frequently mentioned in the discussion of the alleged wage-push inflation.[46] As in the case of exchange rates the lagged value of

43. These coefficients are compatible in the sense that $\delta = .3$ with annual data and $\delta = .1$ with quarterly data imply an average length of the weighting pattern of approximately 2.5 years and 11 quarters, respectively.

44. The results should not be taken with much enthusiasm, however, because errors in measuring prices would introduce spurious negative correlation between changes in prices and in nominal income deflated by an index of prices and may thus account for some fraction of the explanatory power of this variable.

45. There is no doubt that this is a lower limit for the true potential effect, given the fact that most big devaluations have been accompanied by an elaborate scheme of witholding taxes on exports but, at any rate, it is a smaller number than the figure implicit or explicit in most discussions.

46. It can be granted that these coefficients measure only the current direct

this variable was also introduced in some experiments not explicitly reported here. In the case of the wholesale prices the lagged change in the wage rate was consistently nonsignificant. The coefficients showed some significant values in those regressions dealing with the cost-of-living index with a sum of both coefficients never greater than .17.

Conclusions

From 1935 to 1962 the Argentine stock of money, inclusive of savings and time deposits in commercial banks, increased at an average rate of about 15 per cent per year. Most of this increase can be attributed to increases in the monetary base (high-powered money), but the contribution of the changes in the base multiplier to variations in the stock of money around its growth trend has been substantial. The observed variations in the base multiplier can, in turn, be attributed to changes in the ratio of banks' reserves to deposits (quantitatively the most important of its proximate determinants), to changes in the ratio of currency to demand deposits, and to changes in the ratio of savings and time deposits to demand deposits.

The behavior of the reserve ratio of commercial banks in Argentina during the periods 1935–45 and 1958–62 can be explained mainly in terms of variations in the expected flow of total reserves and in the expected opportunity cost of holding reserves. The effects of changes in the composition of deposits on the reserve ratio are significant only during the second period. Changes in reserve requirements during 1958–62 do not seem to have affected the reserve ratio significantly, mainly because those changes seem to have been passive responses to previous central bank actions affecting the flow of total reserves.

The behavior of the currency-demand deposits ratio from 1935 to 1962 can be explained mainly in terms of variations in permanent income and in the fraction of income going to labor. In particular, the increase of this ratio during the late 1940s and early 1950s appears to have been mainly induced by changes in the distribution of income.

The behavior of the ratio of savings and time deposits to demand deposits in the period 1935–62 can be explained in terms of variations

---

impact of an increase in wages and that the indirect effects may be hidden in the money and perhaps the exchange rate coefficients (if the authorities have, for instance, increased money as a consequence of the potential unemployment that might have arisen because of the increase in wages, or have devalued because of the "loss of competitive position in the world markets" also as a consequence of the wage increase), but even then, the magnitude of the direct effect appears much smaller than that implied by those discussions.

Money and Prices in Argentina, 1935–1962   123

in the expected rate of change in prices, the level of permanent income, and the rate of interest paid on savings and time deposits. In particular the long and marked decline in this ratio from 1935 to about 1952 can be explained by a combination of increasing expectations of inflation and virtually constant rates of interest paid on savings and time deposits.

The study of the demand for money in Argentina during the period 1935–62 reveals that variations in the expected rate of change in prices and in the expected per capita real income explain a very high fraction of the observed variation in per capita real money holdings. This conclusion is independent of the inclusion or exclusion of savings and time deposits in the definition of money. The values of the estimated coefficients show that the cost elasticity increases and the income elasticity decreases when savings and time deposits in commercial banks are included in the definition of money. The results also show that an increase in uncertainty—as measured by the degree to which inflationary expectations have been frustrated in the past—tends to increase desired money holdings, and that this effect is more significant for the more inclusive definition of money.

The analysis of the demand functions for components of the stock of money shows that, in addition to those variables mentioned in the preceding paragraph, variations in the share of income going to labor and in the rate of interest paid on savings and time deposits significantly affect the desired real per capita holdings of currency, demand, and savings and time deposits. The coefficients of these variables are significant in all equations, and, with one exception, they have the expected signs. The exception is the positive coefficient of the rate of interest paid on savings deposits in the currency demand function, which implies significant complementarity rather than substitutability between these two financial assets.

From 1935 to 1962 the changes in the rate of change in money significantly affected the behavior of the rate of inflation, through a process of adjustment which involved considerable time. The results indicate that the adjustment of prices to an acceleration of money seemed to require no less than two years and that it involved initial overshooting and later deceleration of prices. Changes in the expected rate of change in prices and real income also affected significantly the rate of inflation. The role of devaluations and wage increases in the Argentine inflationary process was also analyzed, but the results show that their influence on the rate of inflation failed to achieve the levels and significance usually attributed to them.

APPENDIX
SOURCES AND DESCRIPTION OF THE DATA

The annual and quarterly series appearing in the tables at the end of this appendix can be classified as follows: Money data, price data, income data, and other data.

THE MONEY DATA

The annual and quarterly monetary data consist of a set of basic series (currency outside banks, different kinds of deposits at commercial banks, and banks' reserves), and another set of series derived from them (quantity of money, monetary base, base multiplier, reserve ratio, etc.). The basic series consist of annual averages or end-of-quarter figures derived from end-of-month series based on central bank publications. The description of those monthly series and the way in which published figures were used for the periods before and after June 1940 follows.

The period June 1940 to December 1962. In April 1963, the central bank published a revision of the principal end-of-month monetary series, covering the period from June 1940 to December 1960, in a supplement to its *Boletín Estadístico* of June 1962. The revised data for the years 1961 and 1962 were published in the regular monthly issues of the *Boletín Estadístico* after December 1961. These two sets of data were used, without modification, as the monthly data for the period after May 1940.

The annual basic series appearing in table 20 and in the first column of table 22 are annual averages centered on June 30 of each year. These averages were computed by adding the twelve monthly values of each year plus the value of the previous December and dividing the resulting sum by thirteen. The end-of-quarter series, which appear in table 27 and the first column of table 29, reproduce the end-of-month figures for March, June, September, and December of each year. A description of each basic series follows.

Currency (Amount of currency outside banks). This is a residual series obtained by subtracting commercial banks' holdings of central

Money and Prices in Argentina, 1935–1962   125

bank notes and coin from the total amounts issued. Before 1946, when the issue of treasury currency (five- and one-peso bills plus all coins) was discontinued, the figures include the amount of treasury currency outside the central bank and commercial banks. The figures in this series include currency held by the government and semi-fiscal agencies. For many purposes this is undesirable but there are no data from which these holdings can be derived.

Demand deposits (Amount of commercial banks' demand deposits held by the nonbanking public). This series excludes inter-bank deposits, government deposits, and items in process of collection.

Savings deposits (Amount of commercial banks' savings deposits held by the nonbanking public).

Other deposits (Amount of "other deposits of little mobility" [as they are officially described] held by the nonbanking public). The figures include deposits held in commercial banks in connection with judicial processes, some international trade operations, etc. They also include deposits in foreign currencies during the few and short subperiods in which they were allowed by the central bank.

Government deposits (Amount of commercial banks' demand and time deposits held by the national, provincial, and local governments; and by semi-fiscal agencies).

Bank reserves (Amount of reserves held by commercial banks in the form of gold, currency, and deposits with the central bank). Before 1946 the series also includes the amount of treasury currency held by commercial banks.

The period December 1934 to May 1940. From 1935 to 1948 the central bank published end-of-month figures for the basic series described above. These series were published in the bank's *Revista Económica* (until July 1937), the *Suplemento Estadístico de la Revista Económica* (from August 1937 to April 1946), and the *Boletín Estadístico* (from May 1946 to April 1948). The figures in these series were the aggregates obtained from twenty-three reporting banks whose deposits and reserves represented, in 1935, approximately "ninety-three per cent of all deposits and reserves of the commercial banking system."

Since the banks in the sample remained the same throughout the period, the increase in the number of banks and the probable change in the distribution of deposits between banks made the sample aggregates a declining but unknown fraction of total deposits and reserves through time. It follows that some correction was needed in order to link these old series with the new series, corresponding to the period after May 1940, which were based on information from all the existing banks.

During the period 1940 to 1948 the new and the old series overlapped so that, for each of the basic series, they provided pairs of observations on the same phenomena. Separate regressions of the values of the new series on the values of the old series were run for each of the basic series. These regressions provided estimates of the parameters of lineal functions that were then used to extrapolate the values of the new series for the period 1935–40 on the basis of the information provided by the old series.[47]

The resulting end-of-month corrected figures were then used to construct the annual averages and the end-of-quarter basic series by the same procedure used with the monthly data for the period after June 1940.

47. The estimated functions were the following:

$$C^n = 96.43 + .9943 \, C^o \qquad\qquad r^2$$
$$\qquad\qquad (6.07)\ \ (.0027) \qquad\qquad .9993$$

$$s^n = -243.19 + 1.2671 \, s^o \qquad .9984$$
$$\qquad\quad (15.00)\qquad (.0053)$$

$$t^n = -3.07 + 1.1305 \, t^o \qquad .9739$$
$$\qquad\ (5.63)\qquad (.0194)$$

$$O^n = -21.35 + 1.0835 \, O^o \qquad .9527$$
$$\qquad\quad (12.51)\qquad (.0253)$$

where C^n, s^n, t^n, and O^n indicate the values of currency, savings deposits, time deposits and other deposits in the new series; C^o, s^o, t^o, and O^o indicate the corresponding values in the old series; and r^2 is the coefficient of determination. The number of observations was 93. Since the series corresponding to demand deposits in the old series (D^o) included government deposits (G^o), the following procedure was followed:

$$D^n = -141.43 + .9179 \, D^o \qquad .9981$$
$$\qquad\quad (15.67)\ \ (.0042)$$

$$(D + G)^n = -201.44 + 1.0837 \, D^o \qquad .9986$$
$$\qquad\qquad\ (16.09)\qquad (.0043)$$

and subtracting the first from the second

$$G^n = -60.01 + .1658 \, D^o.$$

Finally, the function for the stock of reserves

$$R^n = -57.65 + 1.1120 \, R^o \qquad .9974$$
$$\qquad\ (10.28)\qquad (.0069)$$

was estimated on the basis of 70 overlapping observations for the period June 1940 to April 1946.

Money and Prices in Argentina, 1935–1962   127

The way in which the remaining monetary series were derived from the basic series is explained in the corresponding tables.

THE PRICE DATA

Two annual and two quarterly series of price indexes are shown in this appendix. The annual series (table 23) correspond to wholesale prices and the GNP deflator; the quarter series (table 31) to the wholesale prices and the cost-of-living index of prices. A description of the sources and procedures followed to construct these series follows.

Wholesale prices. The basic information for the construction of the annual and quarterly series for the period 1935–62 was taken from four monthly series: first, a wholesale price index (1926 = 100) compiled by the *Banco de la Nación Argentina* and the central bank from 1926 to 1948 and published by the central bank in the monthly issues of the *Suplemento Estadístico de la Revista Económica* and the *Boletín Estadístico* from 1937 to 1948; second, two wholesale price indexes compiled by the central bank and covering the periods 1939–53 (1939 = 100) and 1953–56 (1953 = 100). These two series were not published by the central bank until September 1962, when they appeared in its *Boletín Estadístico*. The last is a wholesale price index (1956 = 100) compiled by the *Dirección Nacional de Estadística y Censos* and published in its *Boletín Mensual de Estadística*. All these were linked by the regression method using the overlapping monthly observations, and were then converted to a common base, 1943 = 100.

The figures for the period 1913–25 in table 23 correspond to those of a wholesale price index compiled by the *Banco de la Nación Argentina*, covering the period 1913–27 (1913 = 100) and published in the monthly issues of the *Revista de Economía Argentina*. The figures for the period 1907–12 in table 23 are based on a wholesale price index compiled by the *Sociedad Rural Argentina*, covering the period 1907–27, also published in the *Revista de Economía Argentina*. These two series were linked by the ratio method to the previously mentioned series (1935–62) by using the overlapping information corresponding to 1926–27 and 1913–27, respectively.

Cost-of-Living Index. The figures for the period 1943–62 on table 31 are the quarterly averages of the monthly series published by the *Dirección Nacional de Estadística y Censos* in its *Boletín Mensual de Estadística*. The figures for the period 1935–42 are based on a previous cost-of-living index compiled by the *Dirección Nacional del Trabajo*, covering the period 1933 to 1948, and published in the *Revista de*

Economía Argentina. The overlapping information of the two series was then used to link them by the ratio method.

GNP Deflator. The annual series from 1935 to 1952 was published by the *Secretaría de Asuntos Económicos* in its *Producto e Ingreso de la República Argentina.* The figures from 1953 to 1962 are based on the series of nominal GNP and GNP at constant prices published by the central bank in its *Boletín Estadístico.*

THE INCOME DATA

The annual figures for the net national income at current prices which appear in table 24 are taken from *Producto e Ingreso de la República Argentina* (1935 to 1952), *Boletín Mensual de Estadística* (1953 to 1955), and the central bank's *Boletín Estadístico* (1956 to 1962).

The quarterly series for real net national income in table 32 was derived from the annual series deflated by the GNP implicit price index. The quarterly figures, expressed in annual rates, are the result of linear interpolation of the annual series, subject to the condition that their sum for each year should add up to four times the corresponding annual value.[48]

OTHER DATA

Several additional annual and quarterly series are presented in this appendix. A brief description of their sources follows.

Population. The population series, table 24, is taken from the *Boletín Mensual de Estadística.* In those cases in which the basic information was available only for end-of-year dates, the figures for June 30 were obtained by linear interpolation.

Interest Rates. The maximum rates of interest paid on savings deposits (table 26) from 1935 to 1945 are derived from the rediscount

48. Let y_t denote real income in year t and $q_{i,t}$ the corresponding value for quarter i of year t. The quarterly figures were obtained as follows:

$$q_1 = \frac{4y_t}{\sum q_i} \left[y_{t-1} + \frac{7.5}{12} (y_t - y_{t-1}) \right]$$

$$q_2 = \frac{4y_t}{\sum q_i} \left[y_{t-1} + \frac{10.5}{12} (y_t - y_{t-1}) \right]$$

$$q_3 = \frac{4y_t}{\sum q_i} \left[y_t + \frac{1.5}{12} (y_{t+1} - y_t) \right]$$

$$q_4 = \frac{4y_t}{\sum q_i} \left[y_t + \frac{4.5}{12} (y_{t+1} - y_t) \right].$$

rate (3.5 per cent) and the existing regulations which did not allow them to be greater than the rediscount rate minus one percentage point. For the period after 1945 the rate is taken from information published in the *Suplemento Estadístico de la Revista Económica* (until 1948) and unpublished information obtained from the central bank's statistical office.

The interest rates on consolidated treasury bonds, table 34, are taken from the central bank's annual report and the *Suplemento Estadístico de la Revista Económica.*

The interest rates on treasury bills, table 35, are taken from the central bank's *Boletín Estadístico.*

Labor Income. The series on the share of income going to labor, table 26, are taken from *Producto e Ingreso de la República Argentina* (for the years 1935–52), the *Boletín Mensual de Estadística* (1953 to 1955) and the central bank's *Boletín Estadístico* (1956 to 1962).

Number of Banking Offices. This series (table 26) was obtained from the central bank's *Guía Bancaria* by the following procedure. The *Guía* listed all existing banking offices in Argentina in 1962. Additional information was obtained from the central bank about the date at which each of the existing banking offices started operations. A time series of new banking offices was then constructed and from this a cumulative series of existing banking offices through time. Since bank failures have been negligible in Argentina the figures of this series did not differ significantly from information available in the central bank about banking offices in the last years of the period under consideration.

Index of legal reserve requirements. The series (table 35) was constructed on the basis of average and marginal reserve requirements on demand deposits for Buenos Aires banks according to the central bank's circular letters, the recorded amounts of demand deposits in Buenos Aires' banks, and their increases after the dates of application of marginal requirements.

Exchange rates. The figures in table 36 represents the monthly averages of the official rates of exchange for the United States dollar in the months of February, May, August, and November of each year. This gives the monthly average rates at the middle of each quarter. The figures correspond to the rates applied to imports. During the periods in which multiple rates were in effect the rate applicable to the widest range of imports was chosen. From 1959 on, the figures correspond to the average selling rates published by the central bank in its *Boletín Estadístico.*

Wage index. Since 1946 the *Dirección Nacional de Estadística y*

Censos has published in its *Boletín Mensual de Estadística* monthly series of three indexes corresponding to (*a*) number of workers; (*b*) number of hours worked per worker; and (*c*) total amount of wages paid. The figures in table 36 are the ratios of the values of series (*c*) to the product of series (*a*) and (*b*). The three basic series were published with two different bases (1943 and 1952). These two series were linked by a proportional adjustment on the basis of the overlapping information for the years 1952 and 1953 and expressed on a 1943 basis.

Annual Series

Money and Prices in Argentina, 1935–1962   *133*

TABLE 20

CURRENCY OUTSIDE BANKS AND DEPOSITS OF COMMERCIAL BANKS, 1935–62
(ANNUAL AVERAGE STOCKS IN MILLIONS OF PESOS)

| YEAR | CURRENCY OUTSIDE BANKS (1) | DEPOSITS OF COMMERCIAL BANKS, ADJUSTED | | | | |
		Demand (2)	Savings (3)	Time (4)	Others (5)	Government (6)
1935....	861.0	855.1	1,763.5	571.1	226.5	119.9
1936....	911.6	897.9	1,794.6	554.8	232.5	127.6
1937....	1,017.8	1,149.5	1,970.2	505.7	264.0	173.1
1938....	1,030.5	1,062.4	2,046.7	488.6	265.7	157.4
1939....	1,083.4	1,132.8	2,045.8	452.8	266.1	170.1
1940....	1,084.1	1,231.0	2,044.2	402.2	296.1	190.4
1941....	1,154.2	1,525.1	2,119.6	405.6	299.6	237.7
1942....	1,379.4	1,918.5	2,315.3	400.1	321.9	285.9
1943....	1,567.4	2,301.8	2,610.4	375.4	347.7	418.3
1944....	1,914.1	2,896.4	2,988.9	337.9	395.6	540.5
1945....	2,318.5	3,425.3	3,482.7	309.7	511.1	572.5
1946....	2,932.4	4,265.3	4,178.1	219.6	643.0	612.6
1947....	3,817.4	5,236.6	4,996.4	67.2	836.8	939.3
1948....	5,231.4	6,361.4	5,733.6	41.7	928.2	1,559.1
1949....	7,152.1	7,950.3	6,586.8	32.0	1,441.4	3,383.3
1950....	9,375.6	9,534.7	7,514.0	27.2	1,904.6	3,460.2
1951....	12,578.3	11,380.6	7,977.2	42.9	2,305.1	4,293.0
1952....	15,167.6	11,935.7	8,807.1	48.8	2,191.6	5,021.1
1953....	18,675.3	14,897.2	10,905.4	45.3	2,025.9	5,825.7
1954....	22,339.7	17,099.0	13,248.5	69.4	2,192.9	7,718.4
1955....	27,016.0	18,864.7	15,198.2	31.1	2,796.4	10,143.1
1956....	31,455.7	22,706.0	17,849.3	9.9	3,941.3	14,000.4
1957....	36,616.4	26,802.2	21,168.0	10.5	5,889.8	16,801.1
1958....	45,031.7	31,965.8	24,513.2	140.2	8,925.0	19,785.7
1959....	66,251.3	51,619.5	30,639.9	522.0	12,153.0	26,329.1
1960....	86,273.5	70,211.2	39,514.8	1,879.4	11,335.4	37,422.4
1961....	101,748.9	84,143.4	47,181.7	5,345.5	15,666.3	45,061.3
1962....	118,808.3	90,056.2	52,972.1	7,473.3	19,848.5	37,224.4

TABLE 21

STOCK OF MONEY, 1935–62, FOR THREE DEFINITIONS OF MONEY
(ANNUAL AVERAGE STOCKS IN MILLIONS OF PESOS)

Year	M_1 (1)	M_2 (2)	M_3 (3)
1935.....	1,716.1	4,050.7	4,277.2
1936.....	1,809.5	4,158.9	4,391.4
1937.....	2,167.3	4,643.2	4,907.2
1938.....	2,092.9	4,628.2	4,893.9
1939.....	2,216.2	4,714.8	4,980.9
1940.....	2,315.1	4,761.5	5,057.6
1941.....	2,679.3	5,204.5	5,504.1
1942.....	3,297.9	6,013.2	6,335.2
1943.....	3,869.3	6,855.1	7,202.9
1944.....	4,810.5	8,137.4	8,533.0
1945.....	5,743.7	9,536.2	10,047.3
1946.....	7,197.7	11,595.5	12,238.5
1947.....	9,054.0	14,117.6	14,954.4
1948.....	11,592.8	17,368.1	18,296.3
1949.....	15,102.4	21,721.3	23,162.6
1950.....	18,910.3	26,451.5	28,356.1
1951.....	23,958.9	31,979.0	34,284.1
1952.....	27,103.4	35,959.2	38,150.8
1953.....	33,572.6	44,523.2	46,549.2
1954.....	39,438.7	52,756.7	54,949.5
1955.....	45,880.6	61,109.9	63,906.3
1956.....	54,161.7	72,020.8	75,962.2
1957.....	63,418.6	84,597.1	90,486.9
1958.....	76,997.5	101,650.9	110,575.9
1959.....	117,870.8	149,032.7	161,185.7
1960.....	156,484.7	197,878.9	209.214.3
1961.....	185,892.3	238,419.6	254,085.9
1962.....	208,864.5	269,309.9	289,158.4

NOTE: M_1 includes currency outside banks and demand
deposits of commercial banks (col. [1] plus col. [2] of table
20); M_2 includes M_1 plus savings and time deposits of
commercial banks (M_1 plus cols. [3] and [4] of table 20);
and M_3 includes M_2 plus "other" deposits of commercial
banks (M_2 plus col. [5] of table 20).

Money and Prices in Argentina, 1935–1962 135

TABLE 22

BANK RESERVES, MONETARY BASE AND BASE MULTIPLIER, 1935–45
AND 1958–62
(ANNUAL AVERAGES)

Year	Bank Reserves (Millions of Pesos) (1)	Monetary Base† (Millions of Pesos) (2)	Base Multiplier‡ (3)
1935.....	576.0	1,437.0	2.976
1936.....	780.9	1,692.5	2.595
1937.....	806.0	1,823.8	2.691
1938.....	709.7	1,740.2	2.812
1939.....	774.9	1,858.3	2.680
1940.....	788.0	1,872.1	2.702
1941.....	892.2	2,046.4	2.690
1942.....	1,054.4	2,433.8	2.603
1943.....	1,352.8	2,920.2	2.467
1944.....	1,886.4	3,800.5	2.245
1945.....	2,227.6	4,596.1	2.186
. . .	. . .	. . .	. . .
1958.....	25,556.0	70,587.7	1.567
1959.....	34,641.9	100,893.2	1.598
1960.....	48,041.4	134,314.9	1.558
1961.....	43,711.7	145,460.6	1.747
1962.....	25,157.6	143,965.9	2.009

† The monetary base is defined as the amount of currency outside banks plus the amount of bank reserves (col. [1], table 20, plus col. [1], table 22).

‡ The base multiplier is equal to the money supply, M_3, divided by the monetary base (col. [3], table 21, divided by col. [2], table 22).

TABLE 23

PRICE INDEXES
(ANNUAL AVERAGES, 1943 = 100)

Year	Wholesale Prices (1)	Year	Wholesale Prices (1)	GNP Deflator (2)
1907........	31.6	1935......	48.6	74.6
1908........	31.6	1936......	49.9	75.8
1909........	35.1	1937......	57.4	77.6
1910........	35.1	1938......	53.4	80.3
1911........	34.1	1939......	61.9	82.1
1912........	35.4	1940......	66.0	83.6
1913........	37.8	1941......	72.3	86.0
1914........	38.3	1942......	90.8	94.9
1915........	41.1	1943......	100.0	100.0
1916........	46.4	1944......	108.2	102.1
1917........	57.4	1945......	117.9	117.3
1918........	63.2	1946......	136.5	141.5
1919........	64.9	1947......	141.3	169.9
1920........	68.0	1948......	163.2	198.2
1921........	54.2	1949......	200.8	249.9
1922........	49.4	1950......	241.3	298.5
1923........	51.0	1951......	359.9	407.8
1924........	54.9	1952......	472.2	500.9
1925........	55.6	1953......	526.9	530.4
1926........	50.3	1954......	536.2	572.8
1927........	49.2	1955......	564.3	640.3
1928........	49.5	1956......	652.9	793.7
1929........	48.2	1957......	775.3	981.2
1930........	45.8	1958......	968.5	1,319.7
1931........	44.0	1959......	2,065.0	2,629.3
1932........	44.4	1960......	2,362.2	3,258.8
1933........	42.1	1961......	2,544.5	3,629.3
1934........	49.3	1962......	3,271.8	4,584.2

Money and Prices in Argentina, *1935–1962*   *137*

TABLE 24

POPULATION AND NATIONAL INCOME, 1935–62

Year	Population (Thousands) (1)	Net National Income (Million Pesos) (2)	Real Income Per Capita (1943 Pesos) (3)
1935.......	13,043.8	7,114	731.1
1936.......	13,259.8	7,699	766.0
1937.......	13,490.0	8,870	847.3
1938.......	13,724.5	8,750	794.0
1939.......	13,947.6	8,937	780.5
1940.......	14,169.2	9,190	775.8
1941.......	14,401.5	10,006	807.9
1942.......	14,637.5	11,489	827.1
1943.......	14,877.4	12,298	826.6
1944.......	15,129.5	14,012	907.1
1945.......	15,390.0	15,669	868.0
1946.......	15,653.6	21,330	963.0
1947.......	15,943.8	30,027	1,108.5
1948.......	16,309.8	37,762	1,168.2
1949.......	16,740.3	44,483	1,063.3
1950.......	17,191.8	51,939	1,012.1
1951.......	17,638.8	72,310	1,005.3
1952.......	18,042.7	82,811	916.3
1953.......	18,399.3	94,597	969.3
1954.......	18,748.8	106,306	989.9
1955.......	19,118.6	125,581	1,025.9
1956.......	19,497.6	150,909	975.2
1957.......	19,876.7	190,163	975.0
1958.......	20,252.5	271,162	1,014.6
1959.......	20,605.8	492,309	908.7
1960.......	20,955.4	626,006	916.7
1961.......	21,318.6	745,552	963.6
1962.......	21,684.6	905,563	911.0

TABLE 25

THE RATIOS OF CURRENCY TO DEMAND DEPOSITS, SAVINGS AND TIME DEPOSITS TO DEMAND DEPOSITS, AND RESERVES TO DEPOSITS, 1935–62
(RATIOS OF ANNUAL AVERAGES)

Year	$\dfrac{C}{D}$ † (1)	$\dfrac{T}{D}$ ‡ (2)	$\dfrac{R}{D+T}$ § (3)
1935	1.0069	2.9952	.1686
1936	1.0153	2.8755	.2244
1937	.8854	2.3836	.2072
1938	.9700	2.6365	.1837
1939	.9564	2.4406	.1988
1940	.8807	2.2279	.1983
1941	.7568	1.8522	.2051
1942	.7190	1.5832	.2128
1943	.6809	1.4483	.2401
1944	.6609	1.2852	.2850
1945	.6769	1.2564	.2947
1946	.6875	1.1818	. . . ‖
1947	.7290	1.1268	. . .
1948	.8224	1.0538	. . .
1949	.8996	1.0138	. . .
1950	.9833	.9907	. . .
1951	1.1052	.9073	. . .
1952	1.2708	.9256	. . .
1953	1.2536	.8711	. . .
1954	1.3065	.9071	. . .
1955	1.4321	.9555	. . .
1956	1.3853	.9601	. . .
1957	1.3662	1.0099	. . .
1958	1.4087	1.0504	.3899
1959	1.2835	.8391	.3649
1960	1.2288	.7510	.3908
1961	1.2092	.8104	.2869
1962	1.3193	.8916	.1477

† The values of the ratio of currency to demand deposits are obtained from table 20 by dividing column (1) by column (2).

‡ The values of the ratio of savings and time deposits to demand deposits are obtained from table 20 by dividing the sum of columns (3) to (5) by column (2).

§ The values of the reserve-deposits ratio are obtained by dividing column (1) of table 22 by the sum of columns (2) to (5) of table 20.

‖ The figures for the period 1946–57 are omitted because of the institutional characteristics of the period.

TABLE 26

ADDITIONAL EXPLANATORY VARIABLES IN THE DEMAND FUNCTIONS FOR
COMPONENTS OF MONEY SUPPLY

Year	Rate of Interest on Savings Deposits (Percentage) (1)	Share of Income Going to Labor (Percentage) (2)	Number of Banking Offices (3)
1935.....	2.50	46.1	638
1936.....	2.50	46.0	650
1937.....	2.50	43.9	663
1938.....	2.50	46.2	675
1939.....	2.50	46.3	687
1940.....	2.50	46.4	698
1941.....	2.50	45.7	711
1942.....	2.50	43.5	726
1943.....	2.50	44.4	743
1944.....	2.50	45.2	764
1945.....	2.50	46.7	793
1946.....	2.00	46.8	821
1947.....	1.91	47.9	838
1948.....	1.98	52.4	850
1949.....	1.91	59.4	860
1950.....	2.19	60.9	872
1951.....	2.03	56.7	890
1952.....	2.88	61.0	909
1953.....	2.88	59.2	927
1954.....	2.85	60.7	952
1955.....	2.87	57.9	975
1956.....	2.78	57.0	991
1957.....	5.00	55.8	1,013
1958.....	5.00	56.9	1,058
1959.....	5.00	50.6	1,128
1960.....	5.00	50.3	1,216
1961.....	5.00	52.5	1,327
1962.....	8.00.	52.5	1,433

Quarterly Series

Money and Prices in Argentina, 1935–1962   *143*

TABLE 27

CURRENCY OUTSIDE BANKS AND DEPOSITS AT COMMERCIAL BANKS, 1935–62
(END-OF-QUARTER FIGURES IN MILLIONS OF PESOS)

YEAR	QUARTER	CURRENCY OUTSIDE BANKS (1)	DEPOSITS OF COMMERCIAL BANKS, ADJUSTED				
			Demand (2)	Savings (3)	Time (4)	Others (5)	Government (6)
1934...	IV	852.5	878.5	1770.0	566.2	220.4	124.1
1935...	I	837.8	927.9	1775.4	583.9	228.4	133.0
	II	861.8	837.6	1774.8	585.2	229.7	116.8
	III	858.5	843.8	1751.0	560.1	223.9	117.9
	IV	912.1	836.2	1759.1	556.3	213.5	116.5
1936...	I	901.3	866.8	1784.4	578.7	233.5	122.1
	II	890.8	887.6	1794.6	546.1	239.7	125.8
	III	919.6	901.6	1807.9	544.6	237.1	128.4
	IV	1005.0	1041.3	1853.4	557.6	228.0	153.6
1937...	I	1004.5	1182.9	1955.5	506.3	268.3	179.1
	II	1020.8	1189.1	1961.1	512.0	268.8	180.3
	III	1035.5	1160.9	2010.7	484.1	277.3	175.2
	IV	1080.7	1145.4	2050.0	473.3	246.9	172.4
1938...	I	1036.3	1099.2	2062.2	502.5	266.8	164.0
	II	1011.5	1032.6	2059.8	499.4	266.9	152.0
	III	1022.2	1035.1	2033.4	486.9	264.8	152.4
	IV	1075.6	1063.2	2042.0	472.2	254.2	157.5
1939...	I	1091.5	1107.1	2028.2	460.9	262.4	165.4
	II	1077.1	1131.9	2054.0	456.8	271.1	170.0
	III	1076.6	1169.0	2047.5	450.0	272.0	176.6
	IV	1101.6	1218.6	2035.1	418.9	260.1	185.6
1940...	I	1080.3	1242.9	2039.6	416.7	268.9	189.9
	II	1071.3	1292.5	2055.3	390.3	297.5	192.5
	III	1037.5	1218.8	2058.2	396.6	312.4	189.4
	IV	1127.6	1303.9	2053.5	372.0	334.6	192.5
1941...	I	1108.8	1467.7	2081.7	397.0	311.1	215.8
	II	1125.7	1559.1	2123.8	421.8	289.4	250.9
	III	1168.1	1586.0	2159.9	430.2	287.7	262.4
	IV	1327.8	1771.1	2185.0	382.3	287.5	238.4
1942...	I	1348.1	1872.9	2252.8	401.3	316.7	241.2
	II	1360.9	1956.6	2337.0	399.7	331.4	301.1
	III	1393.9	1932.8	2365.8	407.2	340.0	313.8
	IV	1510.6	2120.4	2440.4	399.2	328.0	345.5
1943...	I	1470.0	2267.5	2541.3	403.8	348.6	385.1
	II	1548.1	2330.6	2642.5	387.0	354.9	449.9
	III	1613.6	2266.5	2650.1	352.8	355.1	417.2
	IV	1770.0	2578.5	2761.1	339.0	346.9	457.1

TABLE 27—*Continued*

| YEAR | QUARTER | CURRENCY OUTSIDE BANKS (1) | DEPOSITS OF COMMERCIAL BANKS, ADJUSTED | | | | |
			Demand (2)	Savings (3)	Time (4)	Others (5)	Govern-Ment (6)
1944...	I	1813.3	2830.4	2879.6	341.5	364.2	584.4
	II	1902.5	2940.0	3001.4	341.3	407.3	563.1
	III	1991.9	3026.0	3102.5	334.5	411.8	535.7
	IV	2197.5	3180.0	3242.5	327:9	449.3	549.9
1945...	I	2218.4	3190.4	3345.8	318.3	491.0	590.0
	II	2307.3	3422.7	3481.4	312.3	514.0	594.0
	III	2384.7	3541.8	3608.4	296.6	547.4	574.0
	IV	2639.9	3831.6	3743.0	293.1	518.4	505.6
1946...	I	2712.1	3852.8	3878.4	286.0	557.9	615.6
	II	2906.4	4150.3	4012.0	267.1	625.2	500.2
	III	3041.9	4602.0	4516.4	139.8	753.4	575.8
	IV	3581.6	4879.0	4700.9	103.2	720.6	770.0
1947...	I	3476.5	5291.4	4920.3	79.6	779.5	951.8
	II	3778.3	5211.2	4982.0	60.9	885.4	998.5
	III	3966.7	5231.3	5088.0	51.5	884.5	832.0
	IV	4771.9	5475.1	5244.7	47.1	856.0	1168.5
1948...	I	4684.2	6171.8	5618.3	44.7	857.9	1052.0
	II	5137.0	6405.9	5729.6	41.7	950.5	1058.0
	III	5501.8	6730.5	5897.3	41.1	994.4	1699.8
	IV	6736.6	7034.8	6093.6	36.4	974.7	3064.7
1949...	I	6561.4	7821.7	6406.0	32.5	1024.7	3354.1
	II	6943.1	8053.1	6565.6	32.8	1753.4	3450.3
	III	7399.7	8005.0	6787.3	29.1	1848.2	3804.9
	IV	9066.4	8511.1	6992.2	25.8	1800.8	3285.3
1950...	I	8710.2	9274.4	7425.8	27.7	1852.2	3423.8
	II	9044.6	9544.3	7647.6	26.7	1846.2	3435.7
	III	9698.9	9931.0	7633.6	28.7	1964.8	3373.6
	IV	11912.1	10136.6	7664.4	26.1	2071.1	3480.1
1951...	I	11649.7	11736.3	8019.8	28.2	2135.8	3737.0
	II	12493.2	11325.1	7968.5	34.5	2341.9	4587.2
	III	12997.9	11633.2	8027.9	59.9	2566.4	4870.1
	IV	15363.0	11381.6	8014.7	63.8	2466.3	4283.1
1952...	I	14263.4	12237.3	8489.0	50.3	2385.0	4663.6
	II	14779.7	11907.4	8723.7	41.1	2215.9	5293.7
	III	15227.6	11986.5	9145.0	31.1	2006.2	5475.1
	IV	18258.2	12157.5	9604.1	52.3	1960.4	4516.7
1953...	I	17752.7	15230.3	10547.2	43.5	2031.3	5080.6
	II	18415.3	14972.3	10911.8	41.2	2017.7	6439.1
	III	18922.4	15684.0	11357.0	39.5	2071.8	6429.8
	IV	22065.2	15666.8	11912.9	70.3	2055.2	6035.2
1954...	I	21228.9	17538.9	12981.1	77.3	2155.8	6903.0
	II	21607.0	17294.0	13292.1	66.0	2194.7	7892.2
	III	22665.5	17350.1	13633.5	66.4	2258.0	8440.4
	IV	26744.2	17135.1	14199.2	74.1	2372.8	8828.9

Money and Prices in Argentina, 1935–1962   *145*

TABLE 27—*Continued*

1955...	I	25916.5	19575.6	15230.1	47.7	2568.0	9038.1
	II	26344.5	18747.7	15190.6	9.6	2884.9	10452.4
	III	27694.0	18461.7	15225.0	16.8	3029.6	10711.2
	IV	31825.6	19786.9	15844.3	16.4	3135.0	10675.5
1956...	I	30597.7	23144.5	17311.4	10.6	3786.3	11714.9
	II	30881.8	22397.1	17802.5	9.5	3962.2	12496.3
	III	31851.1	22857.9	18430.8	7.8	4263.2	16503.2
	IV	36143.4	24094.5	19524.7	7.9	4692.8	16163.1
1957...	I	35963.2	28072.1	21042.0	7.9	5496.5	15638.4
	II	36460.8	27271.4	21394.1	7.3	6082.3	16790.9
	III	36517.1	27079.7	21506.6	6.9	6727.8	17334.1
	IV	41813.0	25770.5	22080.7	49.0	6437.7	17555.3
1958...	I	40712.7	31220.5	22726.8	79.0	8551.1	18363.2
	II	42254.3	30214.7	24113.5	117.3	7645.2	18599.7
	III	46343.6	33842.2	25580.4	195.6	10537.8	20593.3
	IV	60278.4	38548.8	27122.4	262.3	12774.7	23553.7
1959...	I	61327.6	47724.7	29876.7	223.2	11546.1	22485.2
	II	61909.1	61081.5	29074.9	279.4	16719.3	21825.0
	III	68735.1	52717.7	31604.1	686.6	11715.5	29189.5
	IV	84414.6	57742.2	34586.7	1105.1	8947.5	30452.3
1960...	I	82637.1	67602.6	38128.5	1147.6	10208.1	30773.3
	II	84269.8	73644.3	39814.8	1781.1	11461.7	36658.0
	III	87298.2	75049.9	41158.3	2212.6	12096.1	42066.0
	IV	105361.5	73278.4	43166.9	3572.1	13102.9	43528.2
1961...	I	99440.8	84682.2	46452.8	4448.5	14759.8	42719.2
	II	99333.2	86894.0	47146.8	5580.6	15599.8	45473.8
	III	101385.7	85932.5	47919.9	6387.0	16420.1	48437.5
	IV	121684.8	83759.9	50469.2	6354.4	17755.9	41036.1
1962...	I	119466.2	90124.8	52652.2	5585.2	22414.8	38238.3
	II	115840.8	94756.3	51529.6	6434.8	19633.0	37220.7
	III	119162.9	89571.0	53799.7	9111.8	20460.4	36066.0
	IV	135379.0	84284.3	56951.8	10531.6	17456.0	34761.9

146   Varieties of Monetary Experience

TABLE 28

STOCK·OF MONEY, 1935–62, FOR THREE DEFINITIONS OF MONEY
(END-OF-QUARTER FIGURES, IN MILLIONS OF PESOS)

Year	Quarter	M_1 (1)	M_2 (2)	M_3 (3)
1934.......	IV	1,731.0	4,067.2	4,287.6
1935.......	I	1,765.7	4,125.0	4,353.4
	II	1,699.4	4,059.4	4,289.1
	III	1,702.3	4,013.4	4,237.3
	IV	1,748.3	4,063.7	4,277.2
1936.......	I	1,768.1	4,131.2	4,364.7
	II	1,778.3	4,119.0	4,358.7
	III	1,821.2	4,173.7	4,410.8
	IV	2,046.3	4,457.3	4,685.3
1937.......	I	2,187.4	4,649.2	4,917.5
	II	2,209.9	4,683.0	4,951.8
	III	2,196.4	4,691.2	4,968.5
	IV	2,226.1	4,749.4	4,996.3
1938.......	I	2,135.5	4,700.2	4,967.0
	II	2,044.1	4,603.3	4,870.2
	III	2,057.3	4,577.6	4,842.4
	IV	2,138.8	4,653.0	4,907.2
1939.......	I	2,198.6	4,687.7	4,950.1
	II	2,209.0	4,719.8	4,990.9
	III	2,245.6	4,743.1	5,015.1
	IV	2,320.2	4,774.2	5,034.3
1940.......	I	2,323.2	4,779.5	5,048.4
	II	2,363.8	4,809.4	5,106.9
	III	2,256.3	4,711.9	5,023.5
	IV	2,431.5	4,857.0	5,191.6
1941.......	I	2,576.5	5,055.2	5,366.3
	II	2,684.8	5,230.4	5,519.8
	III	2,754.1	5,344.2	5,631.9
	IV	3,098.9	5,666.2	5,953.7
1942.......	I	3,221.0	5,875.1	6,191.8
	II	3,317.5	6,054.2	6,385.6
	III	3,326.7	6,099.7	6,439.7
	IV	3,631.0	6,470.6	6,798.6
1943.......	I	3,737.5	6,682.6	7,031.2
	II	3,878.7	6,908.2	7,263.1
	III	3,880.1	6,883.0	7,238.1
	IV	4,348.5	7,448.6	7,795.5

NOTE: M_1 includes currency outside banks and demand deposits of commercial banks (col. [1] and col. [2] of table 27); M_2 includes M_1 plus savings and time deposits of commercial banks (M_1 plus cols. [3] and [4] of table 27); and M_3 includes M_2 plus "other" deposits of commercial banks (M_2 plus col. [5] of table 27).

Money and Prices in Argentina, 1935–1962   *147*

TABLE 28—*Continued*

1944.......	I	4,643.7	7,864.8	8,229.0
	II	4,842.5	8,185.2	8,592.5
	III	5,017.9	8,454.9	8,866.7
	IV	5,377.5	8,947.9	9,397.2
1945.......	I	5,408.8	9,072.9	9,563.9
	II	5,730.0	9,523.7	10,037.7
	III	5,926.5	9,831.5	10,378.9
	IV	6,471.5	10,507.6	11,026.0
1946.......	I	6,564.9	10,729.3	11,287.2
	II	7,056.7	11,335.8	11,961.0
	III	7,643.9	12,300.1	13,053.5
	IV	8,460.6	13,264.7	13,985.3
1947.......	I	8,767.9	13,767.8	14,547.3
	II	8,989.5	14,032.4	14,917.8
	III	9,198.0	14,337.5	15,222.0
	IV	10,247.0	15,538.8	16,394.8
1948.......	I	10,856.0	16,519.0	17,376.9
	II	11,542.9	17,314.2	18,264.7
	III	12,232.3	18,170.7	19,165.1
	IV	13,771.4	19,901.4	20,876.1
1949.......	I	14,383.1	20,821.6	21,846.3
	II	14,996.2	21,594.6	23,348.0
	III	15,404.7	22,221.1	24,069.3
	IV	17,577.5	24,595.5	26,396.3
1950.......	I	17,984.6	25,438.1	27,290.3
	II	18,588.9	26,263.2	28,109.4
	III	19,629.9	27,292.2	29,257.0
	IV	22,048.7	29,739.2	31,810.3
1951.......	I	23,386.0	31,434.0	33,569.8
	II	23,818.3	31,821.3	34,163.2
	III	24,631.1	32,718.9	35,285.3
	IV	26,744.6	34,823.1	37,289.4
1952.......	I	26,500.7	35,040.0	37,425.0
	II	26,687.1	35,451.9	37,667.8
	III	27,214.1	36,390.2	38,396.4
	IV	30,415.7	40,072.1	42,032.5
1953.......	I	32,983.0	43,573.7	45,605.0
	II	33,387.6	44,340.6	46,358.3
	III	34,606.4	46,002.9	48,074.4
	IV	37,732.0	49,715.2	51,770.4
1954.......	I	38,767.8	51,826.2	53,982.0
	II	38,901.0	52,259.1	54,453.8
	III	40,015.6	53,715.5	55,973.5
	IV	43,879.3	58,152.6	60,525.4
1955.......	I	45,492.1	60,769.9	63,337.9
	II	45,092.2	60,292.4	63,177.3
	III	46,155.7	61,397.5	64,427.1
	IV	51,612.5	67,473.2	70,608.2

TABLE 28—*Continued*

Year	Quarter	M_1 (1)	M_2 (2)	M_3 (3)
1956.......	I	53,742.2	71,064.2	74,850.5
	II	53,278.9	71,090.9	75,053.1
	III	54,709.0	73,147.6	77,410.8
	IV	60,237.9	79,770.5	84,463.3
1957.......	I	64,035.3	85,085.2	90,581.7
	II	63,732.2	85,133.6	91,215.9
	III	63,596.8	85,110.3	91,838.1
	IV	67,583.5	89,713.2	96,150.9
1958.......	I	71,933.2	94,739.0	103,290.1
	II	72,469.0	96,699.8	104,345.0
	III	80,185.8	105,961.8	116,499.6
	IV	98,827.2	126,211.9	138,986.6
1959.......	I	109,052.3	139,152.2	150,698.3
	II	122,990.6	152,344.9	169,064.2
	III	121,452.8	153,743.5	165,459.0
	IV	142,156.8	177,848.6	186,796.1
1960.......	I	150,239.7	189,515.8	199,723.9
	II	157,914.1	199,510.0	210,971.7
	III	162,348.1	205.719.0	217,815.1
	IV	178,639.9	225,378.9	238,481.8
1961.......	I	184,123.0	235,024.3	249,784.1
	II	186,227.2	238,954.6	254,554.4
	III	187,318.2	241,625.1	258,045.2
	IV	205,444.7	262,268.3	280,024.2
1962.......	I	209,591.0	267,828.4	290,243.2
	II	210,597.1	268,561.5	288,194.5
	III	208,733.9	271,645.4	292,105.8
	IV	219,663.3	287,146.7	304,602.7

NOTE: M_1 includes currency outside banks and demand deposits of commercial banks (col. [1] and col. [2] of table 27); M_2 includes M_1 plus savings and time deposits of commercial banks (M_1 plus cols. [3] and [4] of table 27); and M_3 includes M_2 plus "other" deposits of commercial banks (M_2 plus col. [5] of table 27).

Money and Prices in Argentina, 1935–1962   *149*

TABLE 29

BANK RESERVES, MONETARY BASE, AND BASE MULTIPLIER, 1935–45
AND 1958–62
(END-OF-QUARTER FIGURES)

Year	Quarter	Bank Reserves (Millions of Pesos) (1)	Monetary Base† (Millions of Pesos) (2)	Base Multiplier‡ (3)
1934.......	IV	402.5	1,255.0	3.416
1935.......	I	464.4	1,302.2	3.343
	II	635.2	1,497.0	2.865
	III	602.4	1,460.9	2.900
	IV	862.5	1,774.6	2.410
1936.......	I	846.3	1,747.6	2.498
	II	746.2	1,637.0	2.663
	III	675.6	1,595.2	2.765
	IV	801.0	1,806.0	2.594
1937.......	I	801.4	1,805.9	2.723
	II	876.5	1,897.3	2.610
	III	762.0	1,797.5	2.764
	IV	709.3	1,790.0	2.791
1938.......	I	722.3	1,758.6	2.824
	II	666.3	1,677.8	2.903
	III	701.5	1,723.7	2.809
	IV	643.9	1,719.5	2.854
1939.......	I	712.4	1,803.9	2.744
	II	769.4	1,846.5	2.703
	III	889.7	1,966.3	2.551
	IV	816.1	1,917.7	2.625
1940.......	I	877.7	1,958.0	2.578
	II	783.8	1,855.1	2.753
	III	736.2	1,773.7	2.832
	IV	771.3	1,898.9	2,734
1941.......	I	835.5	1,944.3	2.760
	II	1,001.8	2,127.5	2.595
	III	918.8	2,086.9	2.699
	IV	911.5	2,239.3	2.659
1942.......	I	971.8	2,319.9	2.669
	II	1,088.4	2,449.3	2.607
	III	1,115.0	2,508.9	2.567
	IV	1,186.8	2,697.4	2.520
1943.......	I	1,299.9	2,769.9	2.538
	II	1,338.4	2,886.5	2.516
	III	1,294.9	2,908.5	2.489
	IV	1,613.4	3,383.4	2.304

TABLE 29—Continued

Year	Quarter	Bank Reserves (Millions of Pesos) (1)	Monetary Base† (Millions of Pesos) (2)	Base Multiplier‡ (3)
1944.......	I	1,929.3	3,742.6	2.199
	II	1,894.2	3,796.7	2.263
	III	2,010.2	4,002.1	2.216
	IV	2,006.5	4,204.0	2.235
1945.......	I	2,052.5	4,270.9	2.239
	II	2,278.4	4,585.7	2.189
	III	2,383.6	4,768.3	2.177
	IV	2,470.5	5,110.4	2.158
1946.......	I	2,576.4	5,288.5	2.134
...	...	...	...	...
1957.......	IV	21,706.3	63,519.3	2.514
1958.......	I	25,723.3	66,436.0	1.555
	II	23,966.8	66,221.1	1.576
	III	30,322.5	76,666.1	1.520
	IV	26,257.5	86,535.9	1.606
1959.......	I	30,738.4	92,066.6	1.637
	II	32,535.5	94,444.6	1.790
	III	37,393.7	106,128.8	1.559
	IV	34,090.3	118,504.9	1.576
1960.......	I	47,281.2	129,918.3	1.537
	II	52,339.3	136.609.1	1.544
	III	53,044.8	140,343.0	1.552
	IV	38,090.6	143,452.1	1.662
1961.......	I	51,077.8	150,518.6	1.659
	II	47,950.3	147,283.5	1.728
	III	43,515.8	144,901.5	1.781
	IV	21,022.4	142,707.2	1.962
1962.......	I	26,990.3	146,456.5	1.982
	II	27,383.5	143,224.3	2.012
	III	24,449.7	143,612.6	2.034
	IV	17,503.3	152,882.3	1.992

† The monetary base is defined as the amount of currency outside banks plus the amount of bank reserves (col. [1], table 27, plus col. [1], table 29).

‡ The base multiplier is equal to the money supply, M_3, divided by the monetary base (col. [3], table 28, divided by col. [2], table 29).

Money and Prices in Argentina, 1935–1962   151

TABLE 30

CHANGES IN THE STOCK OF MONEY, THE MONETARY BASE, AND THE
BASE MULTIPLIER, 1935–45 and 1958–62
(PERCENTAGE RELATIVE RATES OF CHANGE WITHIN QUARTERS)

Year	Quarter	$\frac{\Delta M_3\dagger}{M_3}$ (1)	$\frac{\Delta m\ddagger}{m}$ (2)	$\frac{\Delta B\S}{B}$ (3)	Interaction‖ (4)
1935.......	I	1.53	−2.14	3.76	−.08
	II	−1.48	−14.30	14.96	−2.14
	III	−1.21	1.22	−2.41	−.03
	IV	.94	−16.90	21.46	−3.63
1936.......	I	2.04	3.65	−1.52	−.06
	II	−.14	6.60	−6.33	−.42
	III	1.20	3.83	−2.55	−.10
	IV	6.22	−6.18	13.21	−.82
1937.......	I	4.96	4.97	.00	.00
	II	.70	−4.15	5.06	.00
	III	.34	5.90	−5.26	−.31
	IV	.56	.98	−.42	.00
1938.......	I	−.59	1.18	−1.75	−.02
	II	−1.95	2.80	−4.59	−.13
	III	−.57	−3.24	2.74	−.09
	IV	1.34	1.60	−.24	.00
1939.......	I	.87	−3.85	4.91	−.19
	II	.82	−1.49	2.36	−.04
	III	.48	−5.62	6.49	−.36
	IV	.38	2.90	−2.47	−.07
1940.......	I	.28	−1.79	2.10	−.04
	II	1.16	6.79	−5.26	−.36
	III	−1.63	2.87	−4.39	−.13
	IV	3.35	−3.46	7.06	−.24
1941.......	I	3.36	.95	2.39	.02
	II	2.86	−5.98	9.42	−.56
	III	2.03	4.01	−1.91	−.08
	IV	5.71	−1.48	7.30	−.11
1942.......	I	4.00	.38	3.60	.01
	II	3.13	−2.32	5.58	−.13
	III	.85	−1.53	2.43	−.04
	IV	5.57	−1.83	7.51	−.14
1943.......	I	3.42	.71	2.69	.02
	II	3.30	−.87	4.21	−.04
	III	−.34	−1.07	.76	−.01
	IV	7.70	−7.43	16.33	−1.21
1944.......	I	5.56	−4.56	10.62	−.48
	II	4.42	2.91	1.44	.04
	III	3.19	−2.08	5.41	−.11
	IV	5.98	.86	5.04	.04

TABLE 30—*Continued*

Year	Quarter	$\dfrac{\Delta M_3\dagger}{M_3}$ (1)	$\dfrac{\Delta m\ddagger}{m}$ (2)	$\dfrac{\Delta B\S}{B}$ (3)	Interaction‖ (4)
1945.......	I	1.77	.18	1.59	.00
	II	4.95	−2.23	7.37	−.16
	III	3.40	−.55	3.98	−.02
	IV	6.23	−.87	7.17	−.06
1946.......	I	2.37	−1.11	3.48	−.04
...	...	...	...	...	...
1958.......	I	7.42	2.71	4.59	.12
	II	1.02	1.35	−.32	.00
	III	11.65	−3.55	15.77	−.56
	IV	19.30	5.66	12.87	.73
1959.......	I	8.43	1.93	6.39	.12
	II	12.19	9.35	2.58	.24
	III	2.13	−12.90	12.37	−1.60
	IV	12.90	1.09	11.66	.13
1960.......	I	6.92	−2.47	9.63	−.24
	II	5.63	.46	5.15	.02
	III	3.24	.52	2.73	.01
	IV	9.49	7.09	2.22	.16
1961.......	I	4.74	−.18	4.93	.00
	II	1.91	4.16	−2.15	−.10
	III	1.37	3.07	−1.62	−.05
	IV	8.52	10.16	−1.51	−.15
1962.......	I	3.65	1.02	2.63	.03
	II	−.70	1.51	−2.21	−.03
	III	1.36	1.09	.27	.00
	IV	4.28	−2.06	6.45	−.13

† From table 28, column (3).
‡ From table 29, column (3).
§ From table 29, column (2).
‖ Product of columns (2) and (3).

Money and Prices in Argentina, 1935–1962   *153*

TABLE 31

PRICE INDEXES
(QUARTERLY AVERAGES, 1943 = 100)

Year	Quarter	Wholesale Prices (1)	Cost of Living (2)	Year	Quarter	Wholesale Prices (1)	Cost of Living (2)
1935....	I	48.7	75.2	1945....	I	114.3	113.6
	II	48.2	77.7		II	117.1	120.2
	III	48.0	80.1		III	118.4	121.3
	IV	49.5	84.6		IV	121.8	122.5
1936....	I	49.4	84.1	1946....	I	129.8	134.5
	II	49.0	86.3		II	137.9	140.2
	III	50.2	87.8		III	139.9	141.3
	IV	50.8	86.2		IV	138.5	145.8
1937....	I	54.5	86.4	1947....	I	138.7	150.1
	II	58.3	89.5		II	140.2	159.1
	III	59.1	88.6		III	142.1	163.3
	IV	57.9	89.1		IV	144.3	165.7
1938....	I	56.5	87.5	1948....	I	150.6	167.7
	II	53.8	88.4		II	158.9	175.0
	III	51.7	87.6		III	168.1	184.3
	IV	51.5	87.9		IV	175.1	194.8
1939....	I	59.7	87.7	1949....	I	186.5	207.1
	II	59.7	89.0		II	195.6	231.9
	III	61.7	89.1		III	205.8	244.3
	IV	66.6	91.0		IV	215.3	262.6
1940....	I	67.4	91.8	1950....	I	222.2	269.4
	II	67.5	92.3		II	230.1	289.3
	III	66.2	91.3		III	244.7	303.7
	IV	63.0	89.3		IV	268.1	325.2
1941....	I	64.3	89.2	1951....	I	305.2	332.7
	II	69.5	91.6		II	343.9	389.6
	III	76.6	95.1		III	383.9	433.1
	IV	78.9	98.5		IV	406.4	467.7
1942....	I	83.9	98.2	1952....	I	439.2	521.4
	II	90.9	99.5		II	461.9	575.9
	III	93.2	98.7		III	485.8	567.5
	IV	95.4	99.3		IV	501.8	586.9
1943....	I	97.1	101.9	1953....	I	521.2	602.8
	II	100.3	102.9		II	528.2	579.7
	III	101.6	97.3		III	528.2	579.4
	IV	101.0	97.9		IV	530.1	579.2
1944....	I	103.7	98.7	1954....	I	526.4	572.5
	II	108.2	98.4		II	529.7	586.8
	III	109.1	100.3		III	524.8	613.6
	IV	111.6	101.4		IV	546.0	656.9

Varieties of Monetary Experience

TABLE 31—*Continued*

Year	Quarter	Wholesale Prices (1)	Cost of Living (2)	Year	Quarter	Wholesale Prices (1)	Cost of Living (2)
1955....	I	552.0	664.3	1959....	I	1,659.4	2,062.0
	II	559.0	676.7		II	2,009.7	2,627.3
	III	566.3	685.8		III	2,277.6	3,002.7
	IV	579.8	702.5		IV	2,313.2	3,165.1
1956....	I	612.3	715.4	1960....	I	2,366.1	3,362.3
	II	647.1	766.7		II	2,339.4	3,443.9
	III	671.4	790.7		III	2,373.5	3,475.9
	IV	680.8	822.6		IV	2,369.9	3,535.4
1957....	I	704.4	855.6	1961....	I	2,405.2	3,580.6
	II	752.4	930.5		II	2,459.7	3,838.2
	III	813.0	1,014.8		III	2,617.3	4,053.2
	IV	831.3	1,059.3		IV	2,695.7	4,212.1
1958....	I	823.6	1,055.5	1962....	I	2,747.6	4,348.2
	II	887.8	1,183.8		II	3,088.1	4,800.9
	III	1,007.9	1,336.5		III	3,537.5	5,355.7
	IV	1,154.9	1,503.8		IV	3,714.0	5,579.9

TABLE 32

QUARTERLY REAL NET NATIONAL INCOME
(ANNUAL RATES IN TENS OF MILLIONS OF PESOS AT 1950
PRICES)

Year	Quarter	Real Income	Year	Quarter	Real Income
1935....	I	2,822.6	1945....	I	3,951.1
	II	2,822.6		II	3,924.1
	III	2,845.6		III	3,973.5
	IV	2,891.6		IV	4,099.3
1936....	I	2,937.9	1946....	I	4,276.2
	II	2,983.9		II	4,403.6
	III	3,054.1		III	4,563.7
	IV	3,148.5		IV	4,756.5
1937....	I	3,334.7	1947....	I	5,029.6
	II	3,431.8		II	5,225.5
	III	3,460.0		III	5,375.2
	IV	3,419.5		IV	5,478.6
1938....	I	3,292.6	1948....	I	5,630.1
	II	3,253.1		II	5,734.4
	III	3,233.1		III	5,739.1
	IV	3,232.4		IV	5,644.4
1939....	I	3,246.5	1949....	I	5,422.1
	II	3,245.8		II	5,329.7
	III	3,249.4		III	5,268.3
	IV	3,257.5		IV	5,238.3
1940....	I	3,250.2	1950....	I	5,211.5
	II	3,258.2		II	5,181.5
	III	3,286.1		III	5,178.9
	IV	3,333.9		IV	5,203.7
1941....	I	3,408.8	1951....	I	5,313.7
	II	3,457.0		II	5,338.9
	III	3,498.3		III	5,306.2
	IV	3,533.1		IV	5,215.6
1942....	I	3,570.8	1952....	I	4,975.4
	II	3,605.6		II	4,887.5
	III	3,630.4		III	4,891.1
	IV	3,644.8		IV	4,986.4
1943....	I	3,604.0	1953....	I	5,198.8
	II	3,618.4		II	5,296.3
	III	3,678.2		III	5,372.1
	IV	3,783.4		IV	5,426.4
1944....	I	4,002.8	1954....	I	5,446.5
	II	4,111.1		II	5,500.4
	III	4,151.2		III	5,566.7
	IV	4,123.3		IV	5,645.2

Varieties of Monetary Experience

TABLE 32—*Continued*

Year	Quarter	Real Income	Year	Quarter	Real Income
1955....	I	5,797.7	1959....	I	5,705.5
	II	5,877.2		II	5,571.5
	III	5,894.4		III	5,522.3
	IV	5,849.1		IV	5,558.0
1956....	I	5,706.3	1960....	I	5,648.7
	II	5,661.8		II	5,684.7
	III	5,653.1		III	5,752.3
	IV	5,680.4		IV	5,851.1
1957....	I	5,714.7	1961....	I	6,061.3
	II	5,742.0		II	6,162.0
	III	5,798.9		III	6,182.6
	IV	5,885.6		IV	6,123.0
1958....	I	6,114.1	1962....	I	5,955.3
	II	6,202.8		II	5,896.7
	III	6,177.9		III	5,867.4
	IV	6,039,2		IV	5,867.4

Money and Prices in Argentina, 1935–1962   *157*

TABLE 33

RATIOS OF CURRENCY TO DEMAND DEPOSITS AND SAVINGS AND TIME
DEPOSITS TO DEMAND DEPOSITS
(End-of-Quarter Figures)

Year	Quarter	C/D† (1)	T/D‡ (2)
1934........	IV	.9704	2.9102
1935........	I	.9029	2.7888
	II	1.0289	3.0918
	III	1.0174	3.0043
	IV	1.0908	3.0243
1936........	I	1.0398	2.9956
	II	1.0037	2.9075
	III	1.0200	2.8722
	IV	.9651	2.5343
1937........	I	.8492	2.3080
	II	.8585	2.3059
	III	.8920	2.3879
	IV	.9435	2.4185
1938........	I	.9428	2.5760
	II	.9796	2.7369
	III	.9875	2.6907
	IV	1.0117	2.6038
1939........	I	.9859	2.4853
	II	.9516	2.4577
	III	.9210	2.3691
	IV	.9040	2.2272
1940........	I	.8692	2.1926
	II	.8289	2.1223
	III	.8512	2.2704
	IV	.8648	2.1168
1941........	I	.7555	1.9008
	II	.7220	1.8184
	III	.7365	1.8145
	IV	.7497	1.6119
1942........	I	.7198	1.5862
	II	.6955	1.5681
	III	.7212	1.6106
	IV	.7124	1.4939
1943........	I	.6483	1.4526
	II	.6642	1.4522
	III	.7119	1.4816
	IV	.6864	1.3368
1944........	I	.6407	1.2667
	II	.6471	1.2755
	III	.6583	1.2719
	IV	.6910	1.2641

TABLE 33—Continued

Year	Quarter	C/D† (1)	T/D‡ (2)
1945.........	I	.6953	1.3024
	II	.6741	1.2586
	III	.6733	1.2571
	IV	.6890	1.1887
1946........	I	.7039	1.2257
. . .	. . .	. . .	. . .
1957........	IV	1.6225	1.1085
1958........	I	1.3040	1.0044
	II	1.3985	1.0550
	III	1.3694	1.0730
	IV	1.5637	1.0418
1959........	I	1.2850	.8726
	II	1.0135	.7543
	III	1.3038	.8348
	IV	1.4619	.7731
1960........	I	1.2224	.7320
	II	1.1443	.7205
	III	1.1632	.7391
	IV	1.4378	.8166
1961........	I	1.1743	.7754
	II	1.1432	.7863
	III	1.1798	.8231
	IV	1.4528	.8904
1962........	I	1.3256	.8949
	II	1.2225	.8189
	III	1.3304	.9308
	IV	1.6062	1.0078

† From table 27, column (1) divided by column (2).
‡ From table 27, sum of columns (3) to (5) divided by column (2).

Money and Prices in Argentina, 1935–1962   *159*

TABLE 34

RESERVE RATIO AND INTEREST RATES ON CONSOLIDATED
TREASURY BONDS, 1935–45
(END-OF-QUARTER PERCENTAGES)

Year	Quarter	Reserve Ratio† (1)	Interest Rate (2)	Year	Quarter	Reserve Ratio† (1)	Interest Rate (2)
1935....	I	12.73		1941...	I	18.68	2.38
	II	17.92	2.88		II	21.57	2.38
	III	17.23	2.75		III	19.44	1.25
	IV	24.77	2.75		IV	18.74	1.17
1936....	I	23.60	2.57	1942...	I	19.11	1.15
	II	20.76	2.02		II	20.44	1.00
	III	18.67	1.99		III	20.80	.97
	IV	20.89	1.97		IV	21.07	.95
1937....	I	19.58	1.88	1943...	I	21.86	.95
	II	21.32	1.89		II	21.71	.95
	III	18.55	1.85		III	21.43	.98
	IV	17.35	1.72		IV	24.89	.85
1938....	I	17.64	2.02	1944...	I	27.56	.64
	II	16.61	2.25		II	26.12	.48
	III	17.66	2.37		III	27.13	.45
	IV	16.14	2.38		IV	25.89	.47
1939....	I	17.70	2.38	1945...	I	25.87	.53
	II	18.84	2.38		II	27.37	.57
	III	21.62	2.38		III	27.82	.71
	IV	19.82	2.38		IV	27.78	.85
1940....	I	21.11	2.38	...	...	...	...
	II	18.54	2.38	...	...	...	...
	III	17.63	2.38	...	...	...	...
	IV	18.12	2.38	...	...	...	...

† The values of the reserve ratio are obtained by dividing the values of column (1), table 29, by the sum of those of columns (2) to (6), table 27.

TABLE 35

THE RESERVE RATIO AND RELATED VARIABLES, 1958–62
(END-OF-QUARTER PERCENTAGES)

Year	Quarter	Reserve Ratio† (1)	Treasury Bill Rate (2)	Index of Reserve Requirement (3)
1957.......	IV	30.19	1.49	17.9
1958.......	I	31.78	1.49	22.7
	II	29.70	1.49	20.0
	III	33.41	1.49	20.0
	IV	25.68	1.49	22.1
1959.......	I	27.48	1.49	38.4
	II	25.23	1.49	41.1
	III	29.70	5.47	39.3
	IV	25.66	7.58	41.1
1960.......	I	31.98	7.08	43.5
	II	32.04	6.27	45.6
	III	30.74	6.10	46.2
	IV	21.56	6.10	41.5
1961.......	I	26.46	6.02	40.4
	II	23.89	6.10	40.4
	III	21.22	6.15	37.0
	IV	10.54	6.15	33.0
1962.......	I	12.91	6.15	35.0
	II	13.07	6.14	37.0
	III	11.70	6.14	37.0
	IV	8.58	6.15	37.0

† See table 34, note.

TABLE 36

EXCHANGE RATE AND WAGE INDEX
(MONTHLY AVERAGES CORRESPONDING TO THE MONTH IN THE
MIDDLE OF EACH QUARTER)

Year	Quarter	Exchange Rate (Pesos/ U.S. Dollars) (1)	Wage Index (1943 = 100) (2)	Year	Quarter	Exchange Rate (Pesos/ U.S. Dollars) (1)	Wage Index (1943 = 100) (2)
1935...	I	3.47		1945...	I	4.23	
	II	3.47			II	4.23	
	III	3.42			III	4.23	
	IV	3.45			IV	4.23	
1936...	I	3.40		1946...	I	4.23	139.6
	II	3.42			II	4.23	124.9
	III	3.39			III	4.23	126.0
	IV	3.47			IV	4.23	143.1
1937...	I	3.26		1947...	I	4.23	184.3
	II	3.24			II	4.23	198.9
	III	3.21			III	4.23	278.8
	IV	3.20			IV	4.23	291.8
1938...	I	3.19		1948...	I	4.23	215.7
	II	3.22			II	4.23	219.0
	III	3.28			II	4.23	212.1
	IV	3.57			IV	4.23	243.9
1939...	I	3.63		1949...	I	4.23	299.1
	II	3.63			II	4.23	292.7
	III	3.69			III	4.23	301.5
	IV	4.23			IV	6.09	333.1
1940...	I	4.23		1950...	I	6.09	397.7
	II	4.23			II	6.09	345.2
	III	4.23			III	6.09	368.5
	IV	4.23			IV	7.50	414.5
1941...	I	4.23		1951...	I	7.50	475.4
	II	4.23			II	7.50	470.6
	III	4.23			III	7.50	484.9
	IV	4.23			IV	7.50	525.0
1942...	I	4.23		1952...	I	7.50	572.4
	II	4.23			II	7.50	605.1
	III	4.23			III	7.50	597.6
	IV	4.23			IV	7.50	681.5
1943...	I	4.23		1953...	I	7.50	757.3
	II	4.23			II	7.50	693.7
	III	4.23			III	7.50	667.9
	IV	4.23			IV	7.50	702.7
1944...	I	4.23		1954...	I	7.50	796.0
	II	4.23			II	7.50	690.9
	III	4.23			III	7.50	858.5
	IV	4.23			IV	7.50	817.3

TABLE 36—Continued

Year	Quarter	Exchange Rate (Pesos/ U.S. Dollars) (1)	Wage Index (1943 = (100 (2)	Year	Quarter	Exchange Rate (Pesos/ U.S. Dollars) (1)	Wage Index (1943 = 100) (2)
1955...	I	7.50	984.9	1959...	I	65.96	3,123.4
	II	7.50	826.3		II	85.42	3,050.6
	III	7.50	779.9		III	84.02	3,294.2
	IV	18.00	841.8		IV	82.83	3,699.7
1956...	I	18.00	963.6	1960...	I	82.92	4,611.7
	II	18.00	932.6		II	83.09	4,338.4
	III	18.00	910.1		III	82.79	4,749.6
	IV	18.00	1,086.0		IV	82.92	5,019.7
1957...	I	18.00	1,443.8	1961...	I	82.70	5,762.2
	II	18.00	1,304.5		II	82.93	5,774.4
	III	18.00	1,236.2		III	82.74	6,322.9
	IV	18.00	1,261.4		IV	83.04	6,911.4
1958...	I	18.00	1,449.6	1962...	I	83.04	7,775.1
	II	18.00	1,776.4		II	105.44	7,176.9
	III	18.00	1,969.1		III	123.60	7,786.7
	IV	18.00	2,061.2		IV	146.93	8,817.3

[5]

Monetary Policy and the Business Cycle
in Postwar Japan

1. INTRODUCTION

THE postwar growth of Japan is an authentic economic miracle. Since recovering her prewar levels of per capita production and income in 1953, Japan has had a growth rate which in real terms has averaged close to 10 per cent a year. This performance is by far the most impressive of any of the major industrial countries in the world. Even the Japanese business cycle has been relatively mild, reflecting mainly variations in a positive growth rate. Optimists have speculated that the Japanese-type business cycle is what may be in store for many industrial countries in the future because the economic policy tools necessary to prevent major economic declines have been developed.

The object of this study is to analyze the postwar cyclical experience of Japan which has taken place, within the context of rapid secular growth in real income. I will do this by developing a business-cycle model which uses as one of its assumptions the modern quantity theory of money. This will not be a monetary business-cycle theory in the usual sense because disturbances from sources other than money can trigger the cycle.

Modern business-cycle models have typically been constructed on the basis of assumptions about interaction among various components of the national income accounts. The Keynesian income-expenditure framework is usually the static equilibrium limit.[1] Most of the initial work in this area was concentrated on specifying alternative lags and analyzing their effects on the cycle. Lloyd Metzler (1948) postulated that there are "three lags in the circular flow of income." The major segments of the circular flow and the possible sources of lags suggested by Metzler are as follows:

$$\text{Production} \xrightarrow{(1)} \text{Income} \xrightarrow{(2)} \text{Consumption (sales)} \xrightarrow{(3)} \text{Production.}$$

1. Some business-cycle model building has been based on the assumption that the economy was in unstable equilibrium. The best known of these is perhaps the Hicks-Domar growth model, with its knife's edge equilibrium growth path.

The first lag between production and income was not considered important because the largest component of income, wages and salaries, is paid with a very short lag, usually weekly or biweekly. The second lag between income and consumption was incorporated in Samuelson's (1939) "Interactions between Multiplier Analysis and Principle of Acceleration." The third lag between sales and production was used by Metzler (1941) in his "The Nature and Stability of Inventory Cycles."[2]

Such lagged endogenous business-cycle models (given realistic values of the parameters) are analogous to the operation of a defective thermostat. If the thermostat is working properly, it can keep the actual temperature in a room very close to the desired temperature. However, if the thermostat is defective in the sense that it transmits signals to the furnace with a lag, then the actual temperature will fluctuate around the desired temperature. The reason is fairly obvious. If the actual temperature rises above the desired temperature, the defective thermostat will not signal the furnace to turn off immediately. Conversely, if the actual temperature falls below the desired temperature, the defective thermostat will not signal the furnace to turn on immediately. In business-cycle models the lags in behavioral responses lead to similar deviations between desired and actual income.

The business-cycle model developed in this study follows in the footsteps of these earlier models. Its cyclical properties are based on highly simplified assumptions about lagged behavior of decision-making units in the economy.

Eight variables are considered in this model: real and nominal variables for income, money, international reserves, and imports. All are measured as quarterly rates of change:[3]

2. The earliest work incorporating dynamic properties into the Keynesian system was contemporaneous with the publication of the *General Theory*. D. H. Robertson considered the second type of lag in "Some Notes on Mr. Keynes' General Theory of Employment," *Quarterly Journal of Economics* 51 (1936): 168–91. Erik Landberg considered the third type of lag in *Studies in the Theory of Economic Expansion* (London, 1937), chap. 9.

3. Because of the impressive growth Japan has enjoyed over the period of this study, virtually all of the economic series considered here have a strong upward time trend. To estimate meaningful behavioral relations under this circumstance requires recognition of this time trend. Various techniques are possible, such as scaling, deviation from trends, or first differences. In this study, scaling was not considered feasible and deviations from trends were not reliable. Thus, first differences in the form of rates of change were employed.

The general convention for computing rates of change at period t is to base it on the difference between period $t - 1$ and t:

Monetary Policy and Business Cycle in Postwar Japan   *167*

$\dot{Y}$ = Nominal gross national product.

$\dot{X}$ = Index of industrial production.

$\dot{M}$ = Nominal money stock. Currency in the hands of the nonbank public plus designated monetary deposits of the banking system.

$\dot{M}*$ = Real money stock. The nominal money stock divided by the GNP implicit price deflator.

$\dot{R}$ = Nominal international reserves. The foreign exchange special account of the ministry of finance, government of Japan. (This series is exclusive of changes in reserves which arise from transactions with foreign central banks or international organizations.)

$\dot{R}*$ = Real international reserves. Nominal international reserves divided by the import price index.

$I\dot{m}$ = Nominal imports on a customs clearance basis.

$I\dot{m}*$ = Real imports. Nominal imports divided by the import price index.

The first assumption of this model is that the modern version of the quantity theory of money provides an accurate determination in the short run of the level of national income. Given a predictable and quantifiable link between the money stock and money income, there will also be a predictable and quantifiable link between changes in the money stock, $\dot{M}$, and changes in money income, $\dot{Y}$. Therefore,

$$\dot{Y}_t = \alpha_0 + \alpha_1 \dot{M}_{t-m} + v_1. \tag{1}$$

The second assumption of this model is that variations in the money supply represent a discretionary policy tool in the hands of the monetary

---

$$\dot{Y}_t = \frac{Y_t - Y_{t-1}}{Y_{t-1}}.$$

However, it would be equally reasonable to compute the change at t as the difference between t and $t + 1$:

$$\dot{Y}_t = \frac{Y_{t+1} - Y_t}{Y_t}.$$

Either alternative would be the rate of change *between* periods and not the rate of change *for* a period. To more closely approximate a smooth rate of change at a point of time, this paper employs a modified form of the central difference theorem used by John Kareken and Robert Solow in "Research Study One, Lags in Monetary Policy" *Stabilization Policies* (Englewood Cliffs, N.J.: Prentice-Hall, 1963), p. 18. The rate of change for any period t equals:

$$\dot{Y}_t = \frac{\dfrac{Y_t - Y_{t-1}}{Y_{t-1}} + \dfrac{Y_{t+1} - Y_t}{Y_t}}{2}.$$

authorities. As such, the money stock can be manipulated in such a way as to achieve some target policy goal. In the case of Japan, this goal is postulated to be attainment of "external stability"; that is, reducing variations in the growth of international reserves, $\dot{R}$. When $\dot{R}$ declines, monetary policy becomes "tighter," and when $\dot{R}$ increases, monetary policy becomes "easier." This is a statement about the behavior of the policy authorities and, as such, is capable of theoretical analysis and statistical verification in the same way as statements about behavior of other elemental decision-making units in the economy. In this sense money stock is an endogenous variable.

$$\dot{M}_t = \beta_0 + \beta_1 \dot{R}_{t-n} + v_2. \qquad (2)$$

The third assumption is that variations in international reserves, $\dot{R}$, are largely dependent upon variations in imports rather than upon variations in exports or capital movements.

$$\dot{R}_t = \rho_0 + \rho_1 I\dot{m}_{t-p} + v_3. \qquad (3)$$

This unusual assumption about the behavior of international reserves will be considered in some detail in section 4C.

The final assumption in this model is that variations in imports are dependent upon variations in income.

$$I\dot{m}_t = \gamma_0 + \gamma_1 \dot{Y}_t + v_4. \qquad (4)$$

The dynamic process of adjustment implied by these statements about behavior can be described as follows: [4] Assume an initial condition of equilibrium growth in income, money, international reserves, and imports. Some exogenous event occurs which causes a deceleration in international reserves. The authorities react with a restrictive monetary policy. $\dot{M}$ decreases, causing money income and imports to decelerate. The decline in $\dot{Y}$ and $I\dot{m}$ will lead to a reversal of the deceleration in international reserves. An increase in $\dot{R}$ will allow the authorities to ease monetary policy and $\dot{M}$ will increase. The resulting rise in $\dot{Y}$ and $I\dot{m}$ will eventually lead to a decline in $\dot{R}$ and the whole process will be repeated again.

4. Previous work linking money, income, and the balance of payments was done by J. J. Polak (1957, 1960). He makes roughly the same set of behavioral assumptions as in this paper. However, the Polak study differs from this one in several important respects. The statistical testing in that study compared average values and ratios of important time series with the underlying theoretical relationship to determine the long-run effect of money on the balance of payments. The present study utilizes regression techniques and difference equations to measure the short-term effect of money on international reserves and income.

It can be observed that increases in income in one period will lead to decreases in income in a future period. The transmission mechanism can be illustrated as follows:

$$\uparrow \dot{Y} \rightarrow \uparrow I\dot{m} \rightarrow \downarrow \dot{R} \rightarrow \downarrow \dot{M} \rightarrow \downarrow \dot{Y}.$$

The implications can be seen more formally by a simple process of algebraic substitution. The four equations (1) through (4) can be reduced to one equation of the following form:

$$\dot{Y}_t = A_0 + A_1(\dot{Y})_{t-z} \tag{5}$$

where

$$A_0 = \alpha_0 + \alpha_1\beta_0 + \alpha_1\beta_1\rho_0 + \alpha_1\beta_1\rho_1\gamma_0,$$
$$A_1 = \alpha_1\beta_1\rho_1\gamma_1,$$

and

$$z = m + n + p.$$

The change of income in period $t - z$ will lead to a predictable change in income in period t. The direction and degree of the change will depend upon the size and sign of A_1.

In section 2, a brief summary of postwar Japanese economic history is presented, including a description of the Japanese financial structure and of the four business cycles from 1953 to 1966. Section 3 discusses the mechanism by which central bank actions affect the money stock. In section 4, the behavioral relations which link income, money, international reserves, and imports are considered. Finally, in section 5, the underlying difference equation is analyzed and the effects of alternative monetary policy actions on the business cycle are considered. The study is closed with a summary and suggestions for future research.

2. The Japanese Economy, 1946–66

The postwar economic history of Japan can be separated into two periods: (1) an immediate postwar period of reconstruction and attainment of prewar levels of per capita output (1946–52), and (2) a later period of rapid but fluctuating growth in output and income (1953–66). In order to set the stage for a description of Japanese financial institutions and the business cycles which emerged in the latter period, it would be useful to review briefly the early postwar years.

A. ECONOMIC RECONSTRUCTION, 1946–52

From 1946 until 1952 Japan was in a period of reconstruction from the devastation suffered during World War II. At the beginning of 1946

Japan was a broken nation, with over 20 per cent of its capital stock destroyed, its people dispersed to the countryside, and its business organization in chaos.

A sudden termination of the war in August 1945 led to a drastic decline in industrial production to one-third of the 1944 level. As this reflected a termination of war production, it had little effect on the civilian population which had already experienced a sharp reduction in consumption in the last year of the war. The average level of production in 1946 was only about one-half of the 1945 level, as the effects of terminating war production continued to unwind and civilian production did not grow. Only a relatively good agricultural harvest in the summer of 1946 plus the massive infusion of food aid from the United States maintained consumption above starvation levels.

During 1947 industrial production hit its postwar trough and started to rise: by 22 per cent in that year, by 46 per cent in 1948, and by 30 per cent in 1949. In spite of these growth rates, however, industrial production in 1949 was only 71 per cent of the 1934–36 average. In this context economic recovery had not been impressive.

The decline in production in 1946 and the relatively slow recovery through 1949 can be attributed in part to the disorganized state of Japanese business and its inability to adjust to the new conditions of civilian production. A major factor in this disorganization was the maldistribution of resources due to a price inflation which averaged 247 per cent per year from 1945 to 1948. These increases were partially due to the elimination of price controls and thus reflected de jure the inflationary pressure built up in the last years of the war. The price increase from 1945 to 1946 was 365 per cent.

The price increases in 1946–48, which averaged 180 per cent per year, were due largely to the very easy monetary policy pursued by the early postwar government. On top of a tripling of the money stock in 1945,[5] the money stock grew at an average annual rate of 90 per cent in 1946

---

5. A major factor in the rise of the money stock in 1945 was the action of the Japanese government at the very end of the war. They paid off all of the long-term government debt in cash, doubling the money stock in one stroke. This is a very curious and perhaps unique experience in modern monetary history and would be worth further detailed investigation. It is curious in that the government thought that it was doing the bond holder a favor by substituting a non–interest-bearing note for an interest-bearing bond. Perhaps the government was afraid that the occupation authorities would repudiate the war debt and thus leave the bond holders with worthless pieces of paper. But even if this action protected the bond holders, it hurt the rest of the Japanese people by adding to price inflation and thereby leaving everyone with less valuable financial assets.

Monetary Policy and Business Cycle in Postwar Japan   171

through 1948. The expansionary policy, which received the support and encouragement of the United States occupation authorities, was designed to channel resources into what the government considered high-priority basic industries necessary for reconstruction.[6]

In the latter part of 1948, increasing concern was expressed regarding the effects of rising prices on the distribution of resources and the possible adverse effect this was having on industrial recovery. This concern led to a major shift in monetary policy. Growth in the money stock was virtually stopped in 1949 largely because the government sector shifted from substantial deficit in 1948 to a moderate surplus in 1949. Rather surprisingly, this sudden shift in policy seems to have had only a moderately depressing effect on the growth in industrial production in 1949. Although prices increased by 60 per cent in 1949, the rate was only one-third of the two previous years. In 1950 the price rise slowed to 18 per cent.

Japan was fortunate in picking this time to put her financial house in order, because she was then able to take effective advantage of the great increase in export demand stemming from the Korean War which started in June 1950. By the middle of 1951 Japan was a major workshop and arsenal in direct support of United Nations troops in Korea. This favorable status resulted in substantial increases in exports. By 1952 this source was almost two-thirds the size of all other forms of exports combined. From the end of 1950 to the end of 1952 foreign exchange reserves increased 100 per cent, from $560 million to $1,138 million.

At the end of 1952 a formal peace treaty with Japan had been signed and the allied occupation was about to terminate (April 19, 1953). Industrial production was 126 per cent of the 1934–36 level, and per capita income was approaching its prewar peak. Traditional foreign markets were again opening up, prices had been stabilized, and some sense of confidence had been restored to the Japanese people.

With the end of the allied occupation, full control of the levers of economic policy-making was returned to Japanese hands. This is the most appropriate point at which to begin the analysis of Japanese business cycles.

The remainder of this section will consider briefly the institutional structure in which monetary policy operated, and will describe the four business cycles Japan experienced between 1953 and 1966.

---

6. Economic Stabilization Board, annual *Economic Survey of Japan*, 1951–52 (July 1952).

B. THE FINANCIAL STRUCTURE OF JAPAN

The institutional underpinning of Japan's financial structure is different from that of the United States and Western European countries. This difference is even deeper than can be presented in a simple quantitative framework. Japan is strongly influenced by the Oriental culture in which the role of the individual is subordinated to the role of the group in the decision-making process. Therefore, business transactions in Japan are substantially different than in the West. These quantitative and qualitative differences would seem to imply that the transmission mechanism by which changes in the financial sector lead to changes in the real sector would be different, and yet this does not seem to be the case. A major implication of this study is that the highly generalized statement of economic behavior embedded in the quantity theory of money is a useful tool of analyzing short-term fluctuations in income in a wide variety of institutional environments.

There are two important features to consider in the institutional structure of Japanese finance: (1) the dependence of the corporate business sector on the banking system for external financing, and (2) the dependence of the banking system on the central bank for reserves. Neither of these conditions is, of course, unique to Japan. What is unique is their extent and how they operate.

Corporate dependence on the banking system. The dependence of corporations on the banking system for a large share of their financing is due to the very rapid rate of growth in corporate investment which has outstripped the rate of growth in corporate profits and retained earnings. This forced corporations to rely heavily on external rather than internal sources of financing. The banking system is the major financial intermediary through which corporations borrow because of the underdeveloped structure of alternative markets.

By the standards of other industrialized nations (or Japan before World War II), the share of internal financing by Japanese business is quite small. Net worth is only one-third of total liabilities plus net worth. In the United States and Western Europe and in prewar Japan, net worth was about two-thirds of liabilities plus net worth.[7] Most of this external financing is done through the banking system.

7. Hugh T. Patrick, *Monetary Policy and Central Banking in Contemporary Japan* (Bombay: University of Bombay Press, 1962), p. 28. The description of Japanese financial institutions in this study draws heavily on Professor Patrick's work.

Monetary Policy and Business Cycle in Postwar Japan   *173*

The immediate postwar chaos in the Japanese economy, combined with the allied occupation policy of destroying the prewar economic power centers which were believed to have contributed to the expansionist military policy, led to the destruction of the equity structure of the major segments of Japanese business. The inflation of the middle and late 1940s also wiped out most of the bonded debt of Japanese corporations.[8]

As a result, the corporate cash flow in the form of retained earnings and depreciation allowances was small relative to the need to finance corporate investment and meet liquidity needs. Corporations were forced to rely heavily on external sources of funds.

TABLE 1

SOURCES OF FUNDS FOR NONFINANCIAL CORPORATIONS
(Share of Total)

	1953	1955	1957	1959	1961	1963
External sources......	.68	.61	.66	.66	.65	.68
Internal sources......	.32	.39	.34	.34	.35	.32
Retained profit.....	(.18)	(.18)	(.14)	(.15)	(.16)	(.12)
Dep. allowance.....	(.14)	(.21)	(.20)	(.19)	(.19)	(.20)

SOURCE: Economic Planning Agency, Government of Japan.

NOTE: As demonstrated by Meiselman (1967), there are serious conceptual problems in the uses of flow of funds data in economic analysis because of the difficulty of arriving at meaningful gross flow data. Thus, tables 1 and 2 should be interpreted as only a very rough measure of the financing conditions of Japanese nonfinancial corporations.

Institutionally, domestic loans from commercial banks were the most important external source of financing. Alternative sources had not developed to sufficient size or flexibility to meet the financing needs of business. The bond market provided an insignificant 3 to 6 per cent of total external financing. It was badly hit by the early postwar inflation, and attempts at recovery were handicapped by government policy of pegging interest rates at a relatively low level. No effective device seems to have been developed to increase the real interest rate sufficiently to make bonds attractive to the investing public. Of the modest amount

8. When serious recovery started in 1948–49, many corporations had no real financial ties with the past, The only continuity was personal ties and a strong sense of identity with the organization. It is interesting to note that although many firms were forced to change their names as a part of the general occupation policy of breaking up the Zaibatsu structure, they reverted to something closely approximating their prewar names only a few months after the effective date of the Peace Treaty in April 1953.

issued, 80 to 90 per cent were purchased by the banking system.[9]

The stock market has grown rapidly since it was reopened in 1949, but it is a relatively expensive source of funds. Traditionally, new stock issues are offered at par value to old stockholders. As the market price is generally several times the par value, corporations consider that the effective annual interest cost of acquiring funds through stock issues is about 25 per cent. In addition, there are substantial tax advantages to acquiring funds by issuing debt rather than equity instruments. Thus, the incentives are great for corporations not to raise funds through the stock market.[10]

In the years just after the war, governmental financial institutions provided an important source of external funds to private corporations. However, over the period considered in this study there has been a steady decline in the importance of this source. Foreign borrowing is also a marginal source of funds. The banking system, on the average, provides two-thirds of the external funds to nonfinancial corporations. (See table 2.)

Dependence of the banking system on the central bank. In general, the loan policy of the banking system can be strongly influenced by central bank actions which affect bank reserves. This influence is enhanced in the case of Japan by the substantial and continuous debt of the banking system with the central bank. The natural sources of reserves for the banking system are from government deficits financed by the central bank and balance of payments surpluses. The banking system uses reserves to meet the demand for currency by the nonbanking public. In Japan, the natural sources of reserves have not been sufficient to meet this demand. The central bank had to meet this deficiency through extensions of central bank credit. From 1953 to 1966 the cumulative increase in central bank credit to the banking system was ¥1,969 billion ($5.5 billion). During the same period the cumulative

9. Since 1962, bonds of the largest corporations held by commercial banks have been eligible for discounting with the Bank of Japan.

10. In the late 1950s and early 1960s there was great interest on the part of the small investor in the stock market. The peak was reached in 1961 when investment trusts, which are purchased exclusively by small investors, received over $1.5 billion in new funds. In September 1961, the market broke and the price fell by more than one-third in less than a year. This collapse in stock prices brought to light the most flagrant form of market manipulations practiced by the security companies, which dominate the market and which are virtually free of supervision. There followed a massive decline in small-investor participation in the market, and investment trusts received only $140 million in new funds by 1963 and no new funds in 1964

TABLE 2

EXTERNAL SOURCES OF FUNDS FOR NONFINANCIAL CORPORATIONS
(Share of Total)

	TOTAL (Billions of Yen)	PRIVATE DOMESTIC SOURCES			GOVERNMENT SOURCES	FOREIGN SOURCES
		Banking System	Stock Market	Bond Market		
1953....	966	66	17	4	13	—
1954....	637	57	19	2	19	2
1955....	844	65	10	4	12	9
1956....	1,805	70	13	4	6	6
1957....	1,612	75	15	2	10	−2
1958....	1,729	71	12	5	9	4
1959....	2,418	65	14	6	8	7
1960....	3,631	64	14	9	6	7
1961....	4,236	61	22	4	6	6
1962....	5,090	73	14	2	6	4
1963....	5,831	71	11	3	6	8
*1964...	5,274	70	12	3	9	6

SOURCE: Economic Planning Agency, Government of Japan.
* Estimated.

increase in the reserves of the banking system was ¥525 billion ($1.4 billion).

The major device for extending Bank of Japan credit is through loans and discounts on commercial paper held by the banks. Starting in the fall of 1962, central bank credit was expanded to include what the Bank of Japan calls open-market operations. These operations do not differ substantially from loans and discounting of commercial paper except that the eligible instruments are long-term bonds rather than short-term bills and notes. In each open-market transaction the seller must agree to repurchase the bond at the option of the Bank of Japan. This option can be exercised only on certain stipulated dates, usually three months apart, and has substantially the same impact on commercial banks as discounting regular commercial paper with a ninety-day due date.

Because central bank loans and discounts and open-market operations are essentially identical instruments, they are treated here as one instrument and called central bank credit. Tools other than central bank credit are unimportant. Official reserve requirements have been applied since 1959, but they average only one-half of one per cent of deposits.[11]

11. The use of a single policy variable makes appraisal of central bank policy easier than if a variety of tools were utilized. With more than one central bank tool, one is faced with the important methodological difficulty which is generally referred to as the index number problem. For instance, how does one determine

The Bank of Japan did not regulate its credit extension to the banking system through the price mechanism. The discount rate plus penalty charges were the cheapest marginal sources of funds. Thus, a nonprice rationing technique called *madoguchi shido*, or window guidance, was used. The operational mechanism of window guidance has evolved over the years. Each commercial bank is given a ceiling beyond which it may not borrow from the central bank. The exact formula for determining the height of this ceiling is a well-kept secret of the Bank of Japan. However, according to Patrick (1962) who has closely investigated the institutional structure of Japanese monetary policy, it is generally geared to the amount of deposits held by each bank. There are only twelve major "city" banks which, under normal conditions, are allowed to borrow from the Bank of Japan.[12]

In the early years of window guidance, central bank credit in excess of ceiling amounts was made available to individual banks at a special penalty rate, and then only on the promise of the affected bank that it would restrict the growth of the loans outstanding. However, as these penalty rates were lower than the cost of alternative marginal sources of funds, the banking system was not discouraged from borrowing, and many of the promised reductions in bank loans were not realized. As the Bank of Japan seemed unwilling to make the penalty rate high enough to discourage borrowing, this technique was gradually reduced in importance and finally abolished in 1962. It was replaced by a system in which banks which requested central bank credit in excess of their ceiling allotment were told to meet their needs in the inter-bank call market. This market, which was quite small prior to 1955, grew to substantial proportions by 1961. Interest rates in the call market are highly sensitive to changes in demand. Peak interest rates in the call market reached 20 per cent per annum in 1957 and 1961 and 13 per cent

the relative importance of a 1 per cent change in the discount rate versus ¥100 billion change in open-market operations ? When this problem arises, it is frequently necessary to construct an indirect test of central bank policy before appraising monetary actions. See Kareken and Solow, "Lags in Monetary Policy," p. 78.

12. Each of the "city" banks has a nation-wide system of branches, and all but two are headquartered in Tokyo. The fastest growing corporations are also headquartered in Tokyo and acquire most of their external financing from the city banks. There are 64 local banks which are restricted by law to doing business only with corporations in their prefectures. Thus, city banks have greater demand than supply of funds from deposits, while the local banks are in the opposite position. This creates the condition where city banks are not only the dominant borrowers from the Bank of Japan, but also major borrowers from the local bank through the call market.

in 1963. This expensive marginal source of funds put a more effective profit squeeze on the banking system than the central bank penalty interest rates, which never were more than 9.5 per cent.

Under this revised system, window guidance procedures also changed. Not only were commercial banks given a ceiling beyond which they could not borrow from the central bank; they were also given a ceiling beyond which they were asked not to extend loans, which was usually stated in the form of a fixed per cent increase in loans outstanding over some base period, for example, a 10 per cent increase over the same quarter in the previous year. Those banks which succeeded in maintaining their outstanding loans close to the target figures established by the Bank of Japan were allowed to replenish their reserve deficiencies from the relatively low-cost central bank credit. Those banks which exceeded their ceiling loan target were denied central bank credit and forced to meet their reserve needs from the high-cost call market.[13]

One of the costs of nonprice rationing of central bank credit was that the commercial banks which were more expansionist and innovating were unable to increase their share of the market. These banks were the first to approach their central bank borrowing ceilings and the first to exceed the central bank's suggested ceiling on new loan commitments to the public. Banks which were less expansionary and less innovating were less likely to exhaust their borrowing ceilings from the central bank and were less likely to exceed their suggested loan ceilings.

The Bank of Japan's window guidance techniques tended to keep the growth rates of the member banks relatively even with one another, irrespective of differences in management or efficiency. Table 3 illustrates this result. The twelve major city banks are listed in order of the size of their deposits as of March 31, 1956. The same ordering of banks was also true as of March 31, 1961, and March 31, 1965, the only exception being that bank number eight moved temporarily ahead of bank number seven in the March 31, 1961, observation. This stability in the ordering of Japan's major banks is probably a necessary condition for their acceptance of nonprice rationing of central bank credit. Whatever its inherent logic it is generally accepted that a fair rule for accepting nonprice rationing is that each participant maintains his same relative position in the group.

13. Many banks attempted to hide the fact that their loans exceeded the recommended ceiling. This was typically done by repayment of the loan on the statement day at the end of the month and re-loaning on the next day. These hidden loans were estimated to be over $500 million in early 1962.

TABLE 3

DEPOSITS OF JAPAN'S MAJOR CITY BANKS
(Billions of Yen)

	March 31, 1956		March 31, 1961		March 31, 1965	
Fuji............	319	(1)	745	(1)	1,354	(1)
Miysubishi......	302	(2)	712	(2)	1,311	(2)
Sanwa..........	286	(3)	686	(3)	1,288	(3)
Sumitomo.......	280	(4)	674	(4)	1,274	(4)
Tokai..........	203	(5)	486	(5)	1,029	(5)
Dai-Ichi........	187	(6)	457	(6)	914	(6)
Mitsui.........	184	(7)	433	(8)	846	(7)
Kangyo.........	181	(8)	435	(7)	829	(8)
Kyowa.........	156	(9)	318	(9)	592	(9)
Daiwa..........	130	(10)	308	(10)	555	(10)
Kobe...........	102	(11)	228	(11)	479	(11)
Hokhaido.......	91	(12)	187	(12)	353	(12)

SOURCE: *Economic Statistics of Japan*, 1965, Bank of Japan.

NOTE: Numbers in parentheses refer to cardinal ordering of banks in each period according to value of deposits.

C. CYCLICAL EXPERIENCE, 1953–66

Each of Japan's four cyclical declines in production was induced by restrictive government policy to correct a decline in international reserves. The Japanese authorities initially experimented with a variety of techniques for implementing this restrictive policy. In the first cycle they employed a wide range of small restrictions, hoping to prevent the effects from being concentrated in any one segment of the economy. Government spending was to be reduced by stretching out some programs and terminating others; special credit facilities to importers were eliminated, and the Bank of Japan initiated a form of rationing central bank credit to the banking system.

It soon became clear that planned restrictions in government spending could not be realized because of the intense political pressures for increased spending from inside the coalition of special interest groups which made up the party in power. For example, in the first restrictive period although government spending was planned to be reduced by 2 per cent, spending actually increased 17 per cent. In succeeding periods when restrictive actions were called for, no serious effort was made to restrict the increase in government spending or to increase taxes.

With most of the weight for restrictive actions imposed on monetary policy, the authorities gradually moved from emphasis on particular credit restrictions to generalized credit restrictions. In the early stages it was believed that if restrictions were needed to correct a deterioration in the balance of payments, then a policy which directly discouraged imports and encouraged exports would be the most useful. However, experience with such policies convinced the authorities that the only effective way to reduce imports and encourage exports was to impose generalized restrictions.[14]

Japan has not employed the orthodox monetary measures to achieve generalized credit restrictions. Reserve requirements did not exist in law or custom until 1959, and since then they have only been used moderately; open-market operations were unfeasible because the appropriate market structure did not exist, and the basic central bank discount rate was either not raised at all or not raised sufficiently to discourage the borrowing demands of the banking system.

The emergence of tight money occurred in substantially the same way in all four cycles. In the late boom phase of the cyclical upswing, the government's cash debt to the Bank of Japan was reduced as tax and other receipts exceeded government spending. At the same time, imports accelerated, causing international reserves to decline. Both of these actions tended to reduce the reserves of the banking system, causing them to increase their borrowings from the central bank. Precisely at the time when the central bank was considering the need to impose restrictive monetary policy because of a decline in international reserves, the amount of central bank credit was growing faster than at times when restrictive monetary policy was not being considered. Tight money policy consisted of insuring that the increase in central bank credit was not sufficient to offset completely the reserve losses of the banking system from government surpluses and balance-of-payments deficits.

This set of circumstances made it politically easier for the authorities to implement a restrictive monetary policy. The initial loss of reserves of the banking system did not come from any overt action of the monetary authorities. As a matter of fact, the authorities permitted a substantial increase in central bank credit to ease the reserve loss. This kept the monetary authorities in a strong position to implement

---

14. The commitment to general rather than particular credit restrictions did not prevent the authorities from attempting to shield certain preferred industries from the effects of the credit restrictions. Basic industries, such as iron and steel whose long-term growth was considered an important national goal, were supposed to receive sufficient funds to insure that their investment plans were not curtailed. There is, however, little evidence to indicate that the preferred industries were any less adversely affected by tight money than was industry as a whole.

effective restrictions through the window guidance technique, while at the same time appearing to be quite generous in providing credit to the banking system. Therefore the monetary authorities were able to follow a restrictive policy even when the political authorities were not completely in favor of it.

First cycle, 1953–56.[15] Japan entered 1953 with abundant foreign exchange reserves and an optimistic business community eager to modernize its plant and equipment. Investment in fixed capital was 21 per cent larger in 1953 than in 1952, which had also been a year of rapid growth in investment. In addition, consumer spending increased 20 per cent as the fruits of the first postwar wave of prosperity were enjoyed by the individual Japanese household. Although the overall increase in nominal demand was 15 per cent, the increase in output was less than 8 per cent. Consequently, prices increased 7.5 per cent, and imports increased 21 per cent. Because of the termination of the Korean War, exports showed no increase. The current account of the balance of payments deteriorated $500 million and, because capital movements were insignificant, there was a similar deterioration in international reserves.

In this first postwar balance-of-payments problem the authorities planned moderately restrictive fiscal and monetary policies. The general account budget expenditures for 1954 were planned to be 2.5 per cent below 1953. But, because of pressures from within the Liberal Democratic Party, which was in power throughout this period, spending actually increased 17 per cent over 1953. The result was a relatively large cash deficit.

With respect to monetary policy, there was no increase in the central bank discount rate because of fear that higher interest costs would weaken the competitive position of Japanese exporters.[16] Other monetary actions were taken. The special credit facilities available to importers since the Korean War period were terminated; in addition, importers were required to make advance deposits with commercial

15. Most business cycle analysts date turning points on the basis of the peaks and troughs in the *level* of business activity. However, because this study concentrates on rates of change, the timing of each cycle is based on peaks and troughs in the rate of change of business activity. As would be expected, turning points in the level of business activity generally occur after turning points in the rate of change in business activity because a deceleration generally occurs before a decline.

16. Patrick, *Monetary Policy and Central Banking*, p. 270.

banks at the time the import contracts were signed. Finally, the Bank of Japan initiated window guidance (*madoguchi shido*), a form of credit rationing discussed above.

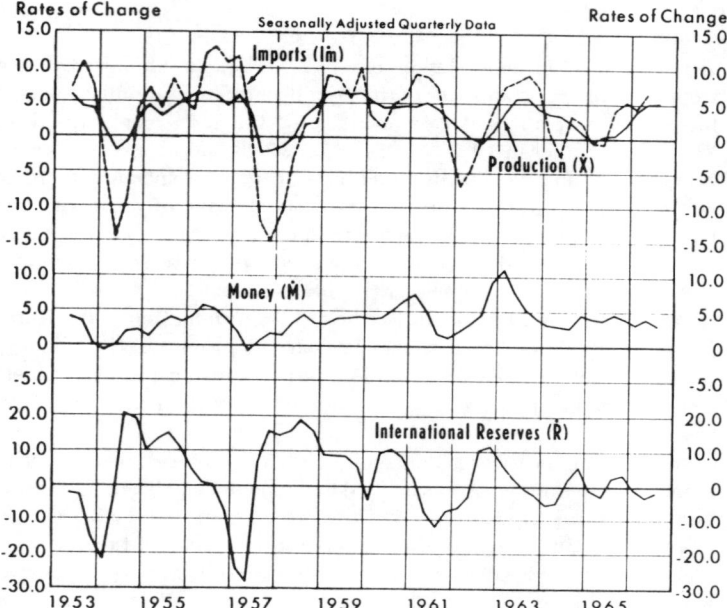

CHART 1. Japan: International reserves, money, production, and imports
SOURCE: Bank of Japan.

These money and credit restrictions were initially imposed in September 1953, and gradually tightened and expanded until they were fully in effect by April 1954. The effects of this policy were felt quickly as the money stock stopped growing in the fourth quarter of 1953 and declined slightly in the first and second quarters of 1954. This had a prompt effect on industrial production and imports; they both stopped growing in the first quarter of 1954 and declined in the second and third quarters. Exports in 1954, responding to a cyclical upswing in the United States and to some dismantling of import controls in Europe, increased at an 8 per cent rate. The sharp decline in imports and the resumption of normal growth in exports permitted international reserves to recover rapidly from the second half of 1954. This improvement continued through the end of 1955.

Second cycle, 1956–58. Starting in the second quarter of 1956, the quarterly growth in imports more than doubled from the average of the previous six quarters because continued growth in industrial production in excess of 5 per cent per quarter required an accelerated use of imported materials. The acceleration in imports caused international reserves to decelerate in the first three quarters of 1956 and to decline sharply in the fourth quarter.

The decline in international reserves triggered a debate within the Japanese government as to whether policy should become restrictive. One group in the ministry of finance insisted that a tight policy was not necessary.[17] It considered that the increase in imports was mainly due to speculative materials imports and that foreign exchange was simply being turned into industrial materials inventories. Their policy prescription was to wait out the speculators, and import demand would soon decline to a more normal level.

Another group in the Bank of Japan contended that the increase in imports was induced by the high level of domestic demand and would continue as long as demand was not curtailed.[18]

In public, the politically more powerful ministry of finance group had apparently won the debate, as no official monetary restrictions were introduced in late 1956 or early 1957. Moreover, a government budget calling for a large increase in spending passed the Diet (parliament) in early 1957. But later events did not support the contentions of the winning group. During the first half of 1957 international reserves declined 55 per cent because of a continued sharp rise in imports. By early May, it was obvious that corrective steps had to be taken immediately.

The discount rate was increased on May 8 from 7.67 to 8.40, and window-guidance procedures originally developed in the first cycle were again applied. No selective credit controls were used, and there was no increase in tariffs or other particular restrictions on imports. However,

17. See Osamu Shimomura, "Tomen no Keizai Kyokumen o Tsuranuku Kihon Dōkō." (The Fundamental Tendencies of the Immediate Economic Situation), *Kinyū Zaisei Jijō*, vol. 8 (February 11 and 18, 1957.)

18. See Yonosuke Goto, "Keiki Dōkō to Junkan Kyokumen no Rikai no tame ni" (Understanding the Tendency of Economic Activity and the Business Cycle), *Kinyū Zaisei Jijō*, vol. 8 (February 25, March 4, 1957).

Monetary Policy and Business Cycle in Postwar Japan   *183*

more preferential treatment was given to exporters with a reduction in the central bank rate on export bills.

Although the Bank of Japan seemed to have lost the policy fight, in fact the money stock had started to decelerate three quarters before the public announcement of tight money and had reached its trough in the second quarter of 1957, when the tight money policy was officially announced. Government cash surpluses and balance-of-payments deficits had drained reserves out of the banking system. The Bank of Japan had been able to take appropriate monetary action even in the face of a publicly stated rejection of tight money policy.

The effects of the monetary restraints were felt promptly. The rate of growth in industrial production and imports reached its cyclical peak in the first quarter of 1957, decelerated moderately in the second quarter, and fell in absolute amount in the third and fourth quarters. An impressive turnaround in international reserves followed, from a 28 per cent decline in the second quarter of 1957 to an 8 per cent increase in the third quarter, and to a 15 per cent increase in the fourth quarter. The growth in international reserves continued at a very rapid rate through 1958 and at a decelerated rate into 1960.

Third cycle, 1958–62. In the period from 1958 to 1961 Japan enjoyed the most rapid growth in her history, perhaps the most rapid growth any country had ever experienced. Real output increased at an average annual rate of 14 per cent, while prices increased at a rate of only 3 per cent. This experience affected the outlook of the Japanese businessmen, who became very optimistic about the future.

The policy authorities were also caught up in this optimistic mood. Some believed that their major contribution to stimulating growth was to provide an easy monetary and fiscal environment. The political leader most thoroughly committed to this point of view was Mr. Hayato Ikeda, who had been finance minister during the 1957–58 cycle. The Ikeda group was brought into power in July 1960 because of a political incident. In the summer of 1960 there were massive student riots against the Japanese–United States Military Security Treaty and the visit of President Eisenhower to Japan. Because the government of Prime Minister Kishi could not control the rioters or guarantee the safety of the president, the visit was cancelled, resulting in the downfall of the Kishi government.

Because Prime Minister Kishi's main mistakes were considered to have been an overly aggressive foreign policy and a domestic policy of riding roughshod over the opposition Socialist Party, it was deemed advisable to bring in a new face who would take a "low posture" on these sensitive political issues.[19] Ikeda was made prime minister in July 1960 on this basis. His interests were largely economic; indeed, he considered himself an economist, and took an active interest in the implementation of monetary policy. In the spring of 1961 he presented a plan to the public which was designed to double national income in one decade, 1960–70.

To implement this plan, Ikeda intended to follow an expansionist monetary policy. As indicated in table 4, during the four-year period

TABLE 4

COMPARISON OF IKEDA AND PRE-IKEDA PERIODS

Per Cent Change in	1956-III to 1960-III	1960-III to 1964-III
Money	60	120
Industrial Production	70	70
Consumer price index	5	26
Import value	37	65
Export value	66	63
International reserves	72	−10
Employment	6	5

NOTE: The beginning and terminal dates for each period were all in the late boom phase of the business cycle.

of the Ikeda administration the money stock increased at a rate twice as fast as in the previous four-year period. On the other hand, industrial production and employment increased at the same rate, while prices rose five times faster and imports rose almost twice as fast. Exports increased at the same rate in both periods. The expansionary Ikeda policies did not increase the rate of real growth but only added to price inflation and balance of payments problems.

Ikeda initiated an expansionary policy as soon as he came into office. The rate of growth of the money stock, which had been at an average quarterly rate of about 4 per cent from the middle of 1958 to the middle of 1960, increased to 5.5 per cent in the third quarter of 1960, 7 per cent in the fourth quarter, and 7.5 per cent in the first quarter of 1961. The acceleration in the money stock led to an increase in aggregate demand, causing imports to accelerate and breaking the price stability which had characterized the Japanese economy since 1954.

19. "Low posture" is a direct translation of the Japanese phrase which conveyed the intention not to take political actions which would trigger strong opposition.

International reserves decelerated in the first quarter of 1961 and fell during the next five quarters. As in the previous cycle, a public debate ensued between the Bank of Japan which proposed a policy of restraint, and the ministry of finance which proposed a policy of continued expansion. Publicly the issue was again settled in favor of the ministry of finance.

The stated policy of the Bank of Japan remained expansionary. The discount rate, which was acknowledged as the official expression of policy, was reduced in August 1960 and again in January 1961. Only towards the end of July 1961, when international reserves had declined by nearly 20 per cent in six months in spite of a large short-term capital inflow, did the Ikeda administration introduce a tight monetary policy.

On July 22 the discount rate was raised from 6.57 to 6.94, and window-guidance procedures reinstituted. On September 29 the discount rate was raised again to 7.30 and the window-guidance procedures tightened. However, as in the 1957–58 downturn, the deceleration in the money stock actually started earlier. Growth in the money stock reached a peak in the first quarter of 1961 and decelerated rapidly through the fourth quarter of 1961.

The deceleration in the money stock was followed by a deceleration in production and imports starting in the third quarter of 1961. However, the rate of deceleration in production was slower than in the two previous downturns. The business community was aware that the tight-money policy was in response to balance-of-payments considerations and would be eased when international reserves started to recover. Past experience had taught them that if they maintained their investment projects through the period of tight money, they would be in better position to take advantage of new and profitable sales opportunities when monetary policy was eased. Thus, a great deal of private effort was put into reducing imports rather than production.

International reserves showed gradual improvement from late 1961; the money stock accelerated moderately during the first three quarters of 1962 and accelerated rapidly in late 1962 and early 1963.

Fourth cycle, 1962–66. The deceleration in production which took place in 1962 was moderate compared with previous downturns. As a result, the margin of unused capacity created was also smaller than in previous downturns. When the growth in production was resumed in the fourth quarter of 1962, the margin of unused capacity was quickly eliminated. This led to the emergence of domestic bottlenecks in certain sectors of the Japanese economy and caused a sharper acceleration in imports in

1963 than had taken place in previous periods of early cyclical upswing. The acceleration in imports pushed the current account into deficit in 1963, even with strong growth in exports. A large short-term capital inflow was not sufficient to prevent international reserves from declining moderately in the last half of 1963.

In reaction to this deceleration in international reserves, the money stock was gradually decelerated from the high levels reached in the first half of 1963 to a growth rate of about 3.5 per cent in the middle of 1964. By previous cyclical standards, such a growth in the money stock would have been consistent with moderately expansionary monetary policy. However, rising prices had induced an increase in the transactions demand for money which absorbed the 3.5 per cent rate of growth in nominal cash balances. Thus production also decelerated slowly through early 1965.

Given the large growth in exports which was taking place in 1963 and 1964, it was apparently the hope of the government that only a moderately restrictive monetary policy would correct the decline in international reserves. This expectation proved correct. By the third quarter of 1964 international reserves started to increase. As in previous cycles, this was the signal to end tight money.

In November 1964, Ikeda resigned as prime minister for health reasons. He left the Japanese business community in what was generally referred to as a "recession mood." It was called a mood because the aggregate economic data indicated that this downturn had been much smaller and more gradual than previous cyclical downturns. And yet the optimism of the business community about the future had been impaired, as reflected in the statistics on new investment which did not show the prompt recovery that had been true of previous periods of monetary ease.

Prior to the fourth cycle, Japanese businessmen had enjoyed three to four years of prosperous growth in sales and profits between periods of tight money. Such a spacing of cyclical downturns allowed businesses to pass through a period of tight money with no impairment of their view of real long-term growth prospects. The Japanese business practice of increasing capacity in excess of short-term expectations of increase in sales had paid off handsomely in these cycles. Even though the fourth cyclical decline in production was relatively moderate, profits had not recovered and inventories had not been worked down from the third cycle just two years before.[20]

20. There were two reasons for the rise in inventories. First, the optimism of businessmen that the rise in inventories would only be temporary, as was the

The new prime minister, Mr. Eisaku Sato, was faced with a serious economic policy dilemma. Should the government take drastic and immediate monetary and fiscal actions which would be necessary to turn the economy around quickly in the face of the "recession mood," or should the government follow a less expansionary policy which might provide a more stable growth in production. The Sato administration chose the latter policy, holding the average quarterly growth in the money stock to around 4 per cent during 1965 and 1966.[21]

Although the recovery in production was somewhat slower than in previous cyclical upswings, problems with the balance of payments were avoided, permitting growth in production to be sustained for a longer period.

3. CENTRAL BANK ACTIONS AND MONETARY POLICY

This section will consider two questions. First, the link between the monetary policy variable (money stock) and the monetary target variable (international reserves), and second, how central bank actions affect the money stock. The latter can be broken down into two subsidiary questions. How does central bank action affect high-powered money, and how does high-powered money affect the money stock?

A. MONETARY POLICY AND MONETARY TARGETS

In the late nineteenth century, most advanced monetary systems were on a gold standard. This meant that gold coins and warehouse receipts for gold bars circulated freely with domestically issued paper to form the basis for the money stock. Because gold was also the international medium of exchange, the money stock was automatically

---

case in previous cycles. Second, given the lifetime employment tradition in Japan, the permanent production workers are not laid off unless there is a permanent reduction in the work force.

21. The major factor in the moderate monetary response was to avoid the expansionist excesses of the previous administration. However, a secondary factor was that international reserves showed no consistent growth in 1965 and 1966. Although the current account registered a large surplus because of a moderate growth in imports and very rapid growth in exports, there was a large capital outflow. The easing of monetary policy and the weakness in business investment pushed Japanese interest rates down just at a time when rates were rising to new historic highs in the United States and money was generally tight in Europe. This caused a substantial shift in trade financing from foreign to domestic sources and made Euro-dollars a less attractive source of funds to Japanese banks. At the same time, the U.S. interest equalization tax (July 1963) and the president's "voluntary" program to support the United States balance of payments (February 1965) reduced the long-term capital in flow.

linked to the balance of payments and to the level and rate of change in international reserves. A balance-of-payments deficit meant a decline in international reserves, an outflow of gold, and a decline in the domestic money stock. A balance-of-payments surplus meant an increase in international reserves, an inflow of gold, and an increase in the domestic money stock.

This automatic link between money and international reserves is now considered broken because gold is no longer a component of the domestic money stock.[22] The monetary authorities have the ability to achieve any desired money stock through expansion and contraction of central bank credit. With the automatic link between international reserves and money broken, the monetary authorities can direct monetary policy toward achieving any monetary target variable they desire, such as a target level of prices, unemployment, or international reserves.

The most generalized method of presenting the link between a target variable and a policy variable is in a stock adjustment mechanism. It is generally recognized that Japanese monetary policy is sensitive to changes in international reserves.[23] If the target level of international reserves is different from the actual level of international reserves, then monetary policy will be adjusted accordingly. If the actual level is less than the target level, policy will be restrictive. If the actual level is greater than the target level, policy will be easy. The stock adjustment mechanism is consistent with a wide range of observed behavior. For example, an acceleration in international reserves could be associated with a restrictive policy if the level of reserves is below the target, while a deceleration in international reserves could be associated with an expansionary policy if the level of reserves is above the target.

The observed behavior of the Japanese monetary authorities is that when international reserves decline, monetary policy in the form of

22. Domestic gold stocks may affect the supply of money even if they are not directly measured in the stock of money. If the central bank must hold a certain stock of gold as a reserve against central bank notes or deposits outstanding, an outflow of gold could theoretically affect the domestic money supply. However, in Japan, central bank notes are backed by full faith and credit of the government and not by gold or any other internationally liquid assets. Only Belgium, The Netherlands, and Switzerland have a legal requirement for gold backing to control central bank note issue. The United States ceased its gold backing on March 15, 1968.

23. See Hugh T. Patrick, *Monetary Policy and Central Banking*, p. 24; Miyoshi Shinohara, *Growth and Cycles in the Japanese Economy* (Tokyo: Kenkyusha Printing Co., 1962); *Money and Banking in Japan* (Research Department, Bank of Japan, 1964), p. 51.

changes in the money stock is restrictive, and when international reserves increase, monetary policy is expansionary. This behavior is consistent with a specific form of the international reserve target which says that if international reserves are falling, the target level is greater than the actual level of reserves. If international reserves are rising, the target level is equal to the actual level of reserves.

The monetary authorities are sensitive to changes in international reserves because of the relatively low level of international reserves held by Japan and the rapidity with which these reserves can be drawn down during periods of balance-of-payments difficulties. The ratio of international reserves (gold plus convertible currencies) to imports has fallen from one-third in 1954 to one-fourth in 1964 and to one-fifth in 1966. The ratio of international reserves to imports of the European Economic Community (Common Market) countries, which Japan resembles in terms of industrial development and absence of reserve currency status, has increased from 41 per cent in 1954 to 44 per cent in 1966. The rate of growth in Japanese reserves from 1954 to 1964 has been about 60 per cent of the rate of growth in imports. For common market countries the rate of growth in reserves has been close to 110 per cent of the rate of growth in imports.[24]

The cost of this slow growth in international reserves is the large potential decline in reserves in a short period of time. In the first two periods of balance-of-payments weakness, Japan's reserves declined 40 per cent and 55 per cent in six months. In the last two periods reserves declined 35 per cent and 15 per cent in nine months.[25]

The observed policy relations between changes in the money stock and changes in international reserves can be stated as follows:

$$\dot{M}_t = \beta_0 + \beta_1 \dot{R}_{t-n}. \tag{6}$$

An increase in $\dot{R}$ will lead to an increase in $\dot{M}$, and conversely a decrease in $\dot{R}$ will lead to a decrease in $\dot{M}$. The only difference between this

24. See *International Financial Statistics*, February 1967, published by the International Monetary Fund.

25. Japan had a relatively modest decline in reserves during the last two periods because she was able to tap the international short-term capital market to a significant extent. The absolute size of Japan's current account deficit was actually much larger in 1964 than in 1954. Although the inflow of short-term capital had increased the apparent stability of the official international reserves position in the third and fourth cycle, it had also increased claims against these reserves. For example, Euro-dollar deposits in Japanese commercial banks (which have an average maturity of 45 days) were about $150 million at the end of 1960 and about $1,250 million at the end of 1964.

hypothesis and others which attempt to explain economic behavior is that there is only one decision-making unit in this case, which is generally and vaguely referred to as the "monetary authorities."

Although the monetary authorities are sensitive to changes in international reserves, the degree of sensitivity varies, depending upon the importance which they attach to other goals. Japanese monetary policy can be divided into two subperiods on the basis of differing sensitivity to changes in international reserves; the first period from 1953 to the middle of 1960, and the second period from 1960 to the end of 1964.

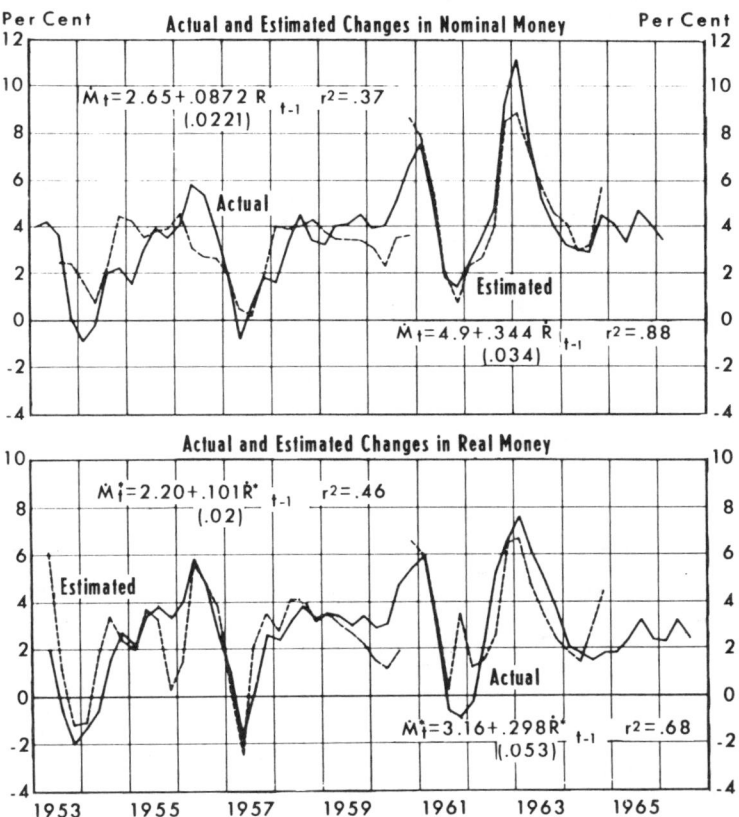

CHART 2. Japan: Actual and estimated changes in nominal money; actual and estimated changes in real money.

Monetary policy in 1965 and 1966 was essentially a reversion to the first period.

There were three prime ministers during the first period: Mr. Yoshida, Mr. Ishibashi, and Mr. Kishi. None of these men had any immediate interest in the day-to-day operation of monetary policy, leaving most decisions to the finance minister, the planning agency director, and the central bank governor. Thus, policy during most of this period was conducted by a committee with no strong personality dominating the decision-making process. Although individual members of this ad hoc committee changed during the period, the collective nature of the decision-making process kept policy relatively uniform in terms of the international reserve constraint.

In July 1960, Mr. Kishi was forced to resign and Mr. Ikeda (finance minister on two former occasions) was made prime minister. Ikeda took over the day-to-day direction of economic policy and the committee approach to policy formulations was abandoned.[26] In an attempt to accelerate the growth in the Japanese economy, Mr. Ikeda initiated a substantially more expansionist monetary policy than did his predecessors. This policy continued over four years until Mr. Ikeda resigned in November 1964.

The increased emphasis on growth during the Ikeda period did not mean that the international reserve constraint was ignored. It meant that the policy coefficients relating changes in international reserves to changes in the money stock were different in these two subperiods. To determine the value of the coefficients, regressions were run on the money and international reserve time series for each subperiod:[27]

---

26. There are no parliamentary obstacles to the prime minister's controlling the levers of monetary policy if he wishes. The Japanese cabinet is structurally similar to the United Kingdom parliamentary ministerial system. The prime minister appoints the minister of finance and the director of the Economic Planning Agency. The governor of the Bank of Japan is accountable to the minister of finance and can be removed at the discretion of the finance minister. Although this has never been done, it is a powerful potential threat.

27. A statistical test of the relationship between two variables where only one decision-making unit is involved may have greater systematic variation between observed and estimated values of the dependent variable than when a large number of decision-making units are involved. For example, the estimated movement in $\dot{M}$ was greater than the observed movement in late 1954 and early 1955, and less than the observed movement in late 1956. These discrepancies between observed and actual movements in $\dot{M}$ are not as apparent when the decision-making unit looks at real rather than nominal variables.

Subperiod 1953-II to 1960-IV [28]

$$\dot{M}_t = 2.65 + .087\dot{R}_{t-1}, \qquad r^2 = .37. \tag{7}$$
$$(.022)$$

Subperiod 1960-IV to 1964-IV:

$$\dot{M}_t = 4.9 + .344\dot{R}_{t-1}, \qquad r^2 = .88. \tag{8}$$
$$(.034)$$

These two equations illustrate the wide range of discretionary monetary policies which can be accommodated within an international reserves constraint in the short run.[29] With no change in the reserve level, monetary policy in the second period was almost twice as expansionary as in the first period (4.9 per cent per quarter versus 2.6 per cent per quarter). For every 10 per cent acceleration in international reserves, there was a 3.4 per cent acceleration in the money stock during the expansionary subperiod and a .9 per cent acceleration in the money stock in the nonexpansionary subperiod. Conversely, deceleration in international reserves led to a sharper deceleration in the money stock in the expansionary subperiod than in the nonexpansionary subperiod. Given Japan's slim foreign exchange reserves, this pattern of behavior is reasonable. A monetary policy which, on the average, is more expansionist must also be more sensitive to declines in international reserves. Whether an expansionary policy with such implications for $\dot{M}$ is desirable will be considered explicitly in section 5.

This study considers real as well as nominal business-cycle move-

28. The lags reported here and in the rest of this study are of the single non-distributed type. Alternative lags were tested and the one with the lowest standard error and highest r^2 was used. This procedure was used whenever lagged relationships were tested statistically.

29. During the last half of 1960 and the first half of 1961, neither equation (7) nor (8) provides an accurate estimate of the actual changes in money. This period can be considered a transition from a less to a more expansionary monetary policy. As a result, (7), my policy equation for pre-Ikeda years, underestimates the growth in this period, while (8), the policy equation for the Ikeda period, overestimates changes in money in this period. This pattern is quite reasonable and reminds us that great caution must be used in applying policy equations in the early period of any new political administration. The Sato administration, which came into power in November 1964, abandoned the expansionist monetary policies of its predecessor. In the first five full quarters of the Sato administration the actual stock of money increased 20 per cent, while the growth in the money stock using the Ikeda policy equation would have been 27 per cent. The growth in money, using the pre-Ikeda policy equation, would have been 13 per cent. Before a realistic policy equation can be established for this new administration, it will probably be necessary to observe one cyclical decline in reserves.

ments; therefore, a structural equation relating real money stock to real reserves was also estimated. The money series was deflated by the implicit price deflator, and international reserves by the import price index:

Subperiod 1953-II to 1960-IV:

$$\dot{M}_t^* = 2.20 + .101\dot{R}_{t-1}^*, \qquad r^2 = .46.$$
$$(.020)$$

Subperiod 1960-IV to 1964-IV:

$$\dot{M}_t^* = 3.16 + .298\dot{R}_{t+1}^*, \qquad r^2 = .68.$$
$$(.053)$$

These results are substantially the same as above. The results are statistically significant and the values of the coefficients are larger in the expansionary subperiod than in the nonexpansionary subperiod.

B. CENTRAL BANK ACTIONS AND MONETARY POLICY VARIABLES

The central bank does not have direct control of the money stock; it can only vary the volume or price at which it extends credit to the banking system. The central bank is in a position similar to that of a monopolist because it can control the price and allow the quantity to vary, or it can control the quantity and allow the price to vary. The comparison is not exact, of course, because a monopolist is a profit maximizer and a central bank is not.

If the central bank wants to control the amount of credit it extends to the banking system, it has essentially two choices: (1) it can price its credit facilities at the rate which will keep commercial bank demand for this credit at the level desired by the central bank; or (2) it can allow the price of central bank credit to remain unchanged and ration the quantity directly. The advantage of the first approach is that rationing is done by market forces like most other commodities and keeps the central bank out of a difficult administrative process. The advantage of the second approach is that if the short-run demand for central bank credit is price inelastic, then a very high interest rate to ration credit by the price mechanism is avoided.

Traditionally, central banks have been unwilling to suffer the public criticism associated with high rates and have chosen nonprice rationing of their credit. Thus, the best measure of central bank action is the volume of credit extended rather than the price at which it is extended.

This generalization applies to Japan. The Bank of Japan has a penalty rate on top of its basic discount rate which is applied to those commercial banks which exceed their designated borrowing ceilings. Because most banks are above the ceiling during periods of tight money, the penalty rate is the operational rate. When the penalty rate is compared with the closest alternative market rate of interest, it is always lower. This differential widens during periods of tight money. Interest rates for call money have gone as high as 20 per cent, while the highest central bank penalty rate has been 9.5 per cent. Nonprice rationing of credit is the major monetary tool of the Bank of Japan.

To understand the effect of changes in central bank credit on the money stock requires consideration of the links which connect these two variables. One can do this by utilizing the analytical technique developed by Friedman and Schwartz.[30]

The money stock is defined as:

$$M = C + D, \tag{9}$$

where

M = Money stock,

D = Designated monetary deposits of the banking system,[31]

and

C = Currency in the hands of the public.

High-powered money is defined in two ways. The uses of high-powered money are:

$$H = C + BR, \tag{10}$$

where

H = High-powered money,

and

BR = Reserves of the banking system.

30. Milton Friedman and Anna Schwartz, *A Monetary History of the United States, 1867–1960* (National Bureau of Economic Research, 1964), Appendix B, pp. 776–808.

31. This is drawn from the money supply statistics of the Bank of Japan. Throughout this study references are made to the banking system when in fact other financial intermediaries such as agricultural cooperatives, mutual loan and savings banks, and credit associations also hold monetary deposits. This is done for simplicity in explanation and because commercial banks hold 80–85 per cent of all monetary deposits. These deposits include current deposits, ordinary deposits, deposits at notice, and special deposits. The only one against which checks can be drawn is current deposits. Other deposits pay interest and are similar to passbook savings in the United States. What the Bank of Japan calls time and savings deposits are excluded from the money supply. These are fixed maturity deposits similar to certificates of deposits (CD's) in the United States. Thus, the Japanese money stock concept is closer to M_2 than M_1. See *Money and Banking in Japan*, pp. 52–53.

Monetary Policy and Business Cycle in Postwar Japan   195

The sources of high-powered money are:

$$H = B + R + G, \tag{11}$$

where

      B = Central bank credit to the banking system,

      R = International reserves,

and

      G = Government debt to the central bank.[32]

The money identity can be written in terms of high-powered money and a money multiplier based on the deposit-currency ratio, D/C, and the deposit-reserve ratio, D/BR:

$$M = H\left(\frac{D}{BR}\right)\left[\frac{1 + \dfrac{D}{C}}{\dfrac{D}{BR} + \dfrac{D}{C}}\right]. \tag{12}$$

Alternatively, the money identity can be written in terms of the sources of high-powered money, including central bank credit, and the money multiplier:

$$M = (B + R + G)\left(\frac{D}{BR}\right)\left[\frac{1 + \dfrac{D}{C}}{\dfrac{D}{BR} + \dfrac{D}{C}}\right]. \tag{13}$$

The central bank can only control B directly. The other influences on the money stock are determined by other decision-making units: R largely depends upon the decision of exporters and importers; G depends upon the fiscal policy decisions of the ministry of finance and the government; the deposit-currency ratio, D/C, depends upon the decision of the nonbank public with respect to the desired composition of their money holdings; the deposit-reserve ratio, D/BR, depends upon the desire of the banking system for excess reserves. It is useful to analyze the linkages between B and M in two stages: first, the link between B and H, and second, the link between H and M.

32. The Bank of Japan is the sole custodian of central government cash and supplier of credit to the government. Government receipts, including receipts for sales of bonds and notes to the public, less government payments to the public, are disposed of by changes in the government's current account with the Bank of Japan. An increase in this account is an increase in high-powered money, and a decrease in this account is a decrease in high-powered money. These transactions between the government and the Bank of Japan are in addition to those related to purchases and sales of international reserves. See *Money and Banking in Japan*, pp. 56–57.

The relation between B and H. The amount of high-powered money in circulation can be found in the balance sheet of the central bank. The uses are central bank notes and deposits of the banking system which are liabilities of the Bank of Japan.[33] The sources are found on the asset side of the balance sheet: central bank credit to the banking system, central bank credit to the government, and central bank holdings of foreign exchange.[34]

High-powered money in the form of currency reaches the nonbank public through the banking system. This is accomplished through the public's drawdown of deposits with the banking system. The banks maintain working balances of vault cash to meet the expected demands of the nonbank public for currency. These working balances must be restored continuously by acquisitions of additional central bank notes from the Bank of Japan. For the banking system as a whole, central bank notes can be acquired in only three ways: (1) selling foreign exchange to the central bank, which can only be generated by a surplus in the balance of payments;[35] (2) presenting a draft on the government's account with the Bank of Japan, which can be generated only by a government cash deficit; (3) borrowing from the Bank of Japan.

All increases in high-powered money, whether it stays in the banks or in the hands of the nonbank public, affect the balance sheet of the banking system. The first two sources of high-powered money reduce other assets of the banking system because foreign exchange assets and claims on the government are converted into high-powered money assets; the third source of high-powered money increases the banking system's liabilities by increasing the debt to the Bank of Japan.

An important institutional question with respect to the operation of monetary policy is whether the banking system responds differently to

33. Deposits of the banking system with the Bank of Japan are an insignificant use of high-powered money. Reserve requirements have existed in law since 1957 and have only been applied to banks since 1959. The range is from 0.25 per cent for banks with deposits of less than ¥20 billion, to 1.5 per cent for banks with deposits in excess of ¥100 billion. Total deposits of the banking system with the Bank of Japan were ¥89 billion as of December 31, 1966. On that same date central bank note issue was ¥2,914 billion, of which ¥477 billion was in the vaults of the banking system.

34. Another source of high-powered money is subsidiary coins issued by the treasury. However, the amount is trivial, adding less than 2 per cent to the value of central bank notes. Subsidiary coins are included with central bank notes in this study.

35. This assumes that commercial banks do not change their working balances of foreign exchange.

an increase in its liabilities than it does to a decrease in its other assets. This same issue arises in international financial discussions about the characteristics of a new international reserve asset; should it be in the form of borrowed reserves through the IMF which must theoretically be repaid, or in the form of owned reserves for which repayment is not even theoretically required? This issue also arises in financial discussions in the United States about whether federal reserve credit extended through the discount window is less expansionary than when extended through open market purchases of government securities. Some authors consider that United States commercial banks prefer to build their reserves on the sale of assets rather than on the basis of debt to the federal reserve system. It is postulated that American banks will reduce loans and take other restrictive actions to clear themselves of debt to the federal reserve as soon as possible.

In the case of Japan, virtually all central bank credit is in the form of direct increases in the debt of the banking system.[36] If Japanese banks treat such debt in the same way as American banks are postulated to treat borrowings from the federal reserve, it is quite possible that central bank credit would be a less expansionary source of high-powered money than, for example, sales of international reserves. However, the institutional factors surrounding central bank borrowing in Japan are different from those in the United States. The Bank of Japan, as a long-term policy, must increase the amount of credit provided to the banking system, because alternative sources of high-

TABLE 5

SOURCES OF HIGH-POWERED MONEY, 1953–66
(Billions of Yen)

	Cumulative Increase
High-powered money..............	2,455
International reserves..............	432
Government debt to central bank.....	700
Other*............................	−646
Central bank credit to banking system .	1,969

SOURCE: Bank of Japan, *Economic Statistics*, 1966.
* Mostly profits of the Bank of Japan.

36. It is interesting to note, however, that small prefectural banks in Japan do have a traditional reluctance to borrow from the central bank. This is because small banks as a whole are not subject to the same intense reserve pressures as the large city banks. Those small prefectural banks which do attempt to borrow are considered to have poor management policies.

powered money are not sufficient to meet demand, as illustrated in table 5. Only half of the growth in high-powered money between 1953 and 1966 was from international and government sources. The remainder was in the form of Bank of Japan credit to the private banking system.

Open-market transactions as a technique to extend central bank credit have not been used in Japan because the appropriate short-term financial markets have not been developed. As a result, the large commercial banks are constantly in direct and substantial debt to the central bank. The reluctance of the American commercial banker to be in debt to the federal reserve is not found among the managers of large Japanese commercial banks.[37] Central bank credit extended through the discount window is as expansionary a source of high-powered money as any other source. This is an important consideration, because it allows one to treat high-powered money as a homogeneous product which does not change in quality because of a change in the composition of its sources.

Although fluctuations in international reserves, the government debt with the central bank, and the level of central bank credit to the banking system do not change the quality of high-powered money, they quite obviously change the quantity of high-powered money. Because all sources of high-powered money are on its balance sheet, the Bank of Japan knows from day to day not only the amount of high-powered money in circulation, but also the changes in the various sources of high-powered money creation. As indicated in chart 3, there have been substantial variations in the sources of high-powered money creation. The "natural" sources of high-powered money fluctuated because of domestic economic conditions.

During periods of economic boom, tax receipts accelerate and the government tends to reduce its debt with the central bank; also imports accelerate, and international reserves of the central bank are reduced. The sharp decline in high-powered money that could result is prevented by an expansion of central bank credit to the banking system. Periods of domestic boom and inflation are associated with periods of the largest Bank of Japan credit extensions.

The same results apply during periods of slowdown in domestic activity. Imports decline and foreign exchange holdings of the central bank increase; tax receipts decline and the government's cash debt to the central bank increases. Both actions tend to increase the supply

37. *Money and Banking in Japan*, p. 123.

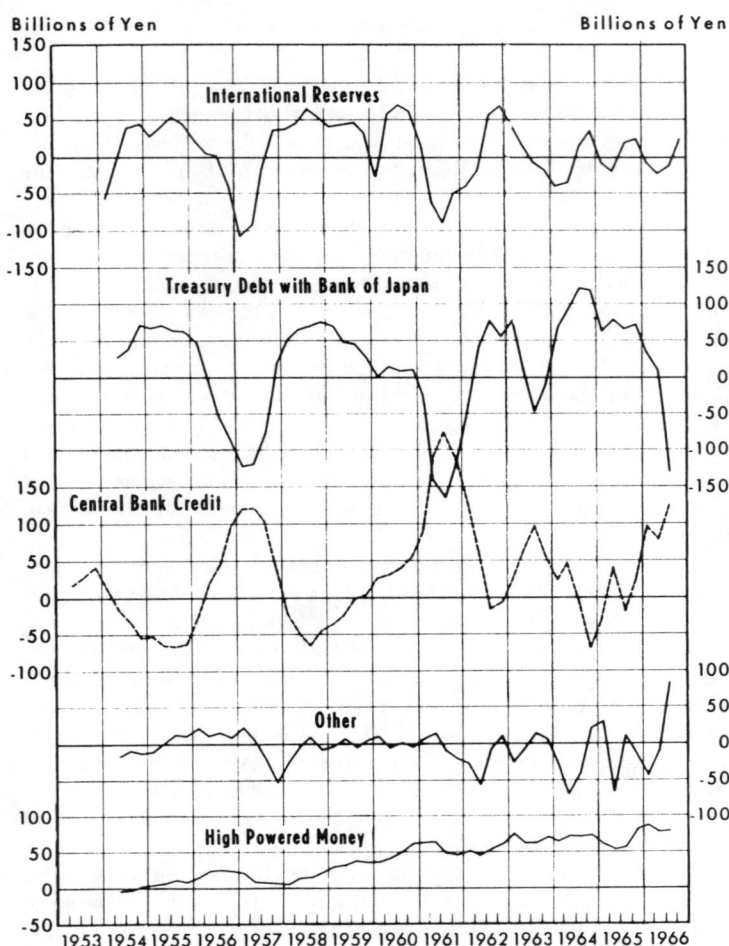

Billions of Yen

Billions of Yen

CHART 3. Japan: Changes in the sources of high-powered money
SOURCE: Bank of Japan.

of high-powered money. To prevent the full amount of the increase, the Bank of Japan reduces its credit to the banking system.

In order to have expansions and contractions in high-powered money consistent with monetary policy objectives, the central bank must take substantial action to break the "natural" expansions and contractions in high-powered money from international and government transactions.

High-powered money is a homogeneous financial asset which the Bank of Japan can control to any degree of accuracy it wishes. This is because it can know the level of high-powered money at any time by striking a balance sheet and because it can change the level at any time by changing central bank credit. Thus, the observed level of high-powered money and the target level of high-powered money are assumed to be the same at all times.

The relationship between H and M. High-powered money can be viewed as a pool banks dip into to meet reserve needs and the public draws on to meet currency needs. The banks and public are, in a sense, competing for use of the high-powered money which the central bank supplies. By definition $(H = BR + C)$, the entire pool is always claimed. If the relation desired by the banking system for deposits to reserves, D/BR, and the relation desired by the public of deposits to currency, D/C, are known, then the money stock, M, can be determined given the amount of high-powered money, H.

The relationship between high-powered money and the total money stock can be seen by recalling equation (12):

$$M = \left(\frac{D}{BR}\right)\left[\frac{1 + \dfrac{D}{C}}{\dfrac{D}{BR} + \dfrac{D}{C}}\right]H.$$

The information needed to compute these ratios comes from the consolidated balance sheet of the banking system and is available only once a month with a four-week time lag. In contrast with H, which can be controlled quite closely, the monetary authorities could miss the money stock target by a substantial margin from month to month because of this information lag. If the time period for determining the target money stock is lengthened, this error will decline because of the decline in the relative importance of the information lag. In this study the time period for determining the money stock target is one quarter, which reduces the error from the information lag to moderate proportions. It is assumed that the observed quarterly money stock is a close approximation of the target money stock.

The deposit-currency ratio, D/C, and the deposit-reserve ratio, D/BR, jointly determine the value of the money multiplier. If these ratios are constant, the money multiplier will be constant and the link between high-powered money and the total money stock will also be constant. If these ratios vary over the cycle, the money multiplier will not be constant and the relationship between high-powered money and the total money stock will fluctuate.[38]

38. The reserves of the banking system are equal to required reserves established by the Bank of Japan and excess reserves of the banking system. There were no required reserves from 1953 to September 1959. During that period the deposit-reserve ratio remained relatively constant and exhibited no significant fluctuations over the cycle. After reserve requirements were imposed, there were sharp changes in the deposit-reserve ratio every time reserve requirements were changed. The ratio fell in the quarter reserve requirements increased, and rose in the quarter reserve requirements decreased. Each time the requirements were changed, finer distinctions were made with respect to the size and source of deposits and the type of bank. By April 1963, there were ten categories of reserve requirements. As requirements were changed for different categories of deposits at different times, variations in the deposit-reserve ratio had a strongly random character from 1959 to 1966.

To eliminate these random fluctuations in the deposit-reserve ratio, changes in reserves due to changes in requirements were eliminated. Only desired reserves of the banking system were used in computing the deposit-reserve ratio, which made the ratio consistent before and after September 1959. The ideal method of making this adjustment in reserves would be to compute the value of required reserves for each time period by multiplying the reserve requirement by the size of deposits by category. Unfortunately, the appropriate deposit data are not available to make this computation.

There is, however, another method of estimating required reserves. The law states that required reserves must be held as deposits with the Bank of Japan. Such deposits had existed prior to September 1959, when required reserves were enforced, but the amounts were small—between ¥2 billion and ¥6 billion. Rough estimates of required reserves in 1965 and 1966 indicate that amounts in excess of those required were about the same as in the 1953–59 period. As deposits in excess of required are less than 1 per cent of other reserves of the banking system, i.e., vault cash, a rough but reasonably accurate adjustment of total bank reserves could be achieved by subtracting all deposits of the banking system with the Bank of Japan from reserves.

This adjustment in reserves of the banking system means that the total uses of high-powered money have been reduced by an equal amount requiring that the sources of high-powered money also be reduced. Typically, the banking system has met increased needs for required reserves by increasing borrowings from the Bank of Japan. Thus, it seems reasonable to make the adjustment on the sources side in central bank credit.

202   *Varieties of Monetary Experience*

The regression between rates of change in H and rates of change in M is:

$$\dot{M}_t = .60 + 1.01\dot{H}_t, \qquad r^2 = .51.$$
$$(.15)$$

For every 1 per cent change in H, there is a 1 per cent change in M. These results are statistically significant, but examination of the residuals in chart 4 indicates that there is a systematic cyclical discrepancy between actual and estimated $\dot{M}$. The residuals fall in periods of tight money and rise in periods of easy money. In a purely definitional sense, this residual is explained by changes in the money multiplier and, underlying that, changes in the deposit-currency ratio and in the deposit-reserve ratio.

The deposit-reserve ratio, D/BR, is dependent on the level of desired reserves of the banking system as described in note 38. This ratio has a relatively stable value with no significant cyclical variations.

The deposit-currency ratio, on the other hand, showed substantial deviations from trend with a cyclical pattern which followed closely

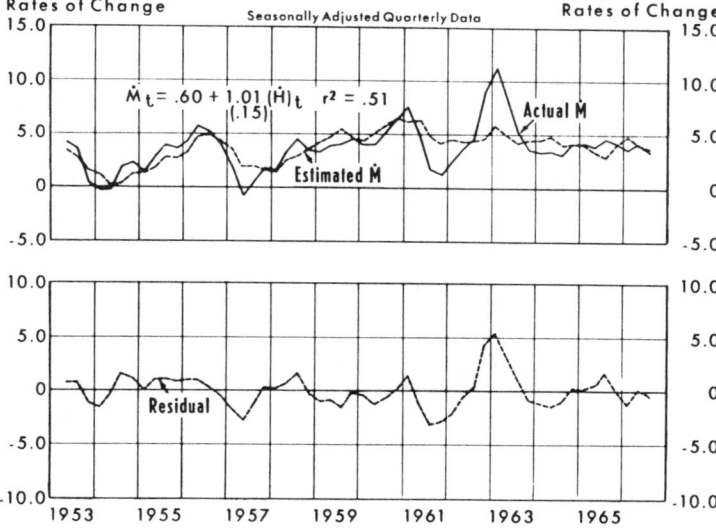

CHART 4. Japan: Estimated value of $\dot{M}$ due to changes in high-powered money.
SOURCE: Bank of Japan.

the acceleration and deceleration of the money stock. During periods of tight money, deposits decrease sharply relative to currency, pushing the ratio down. During periods of easy money, deposits increase sharply relative to currency, pushing the ratio up. Regressing the rate of change of (D/C) and $\dot{H}$ on $\dot{M}$ yields the following results:

$$\dot{M}_t = -.169 + 1.02\dot{H}_t + .737(D/C)_t, \qquad r^2 = .94.$$
$$\quad\quad\quad (.05) \quad\quad (.037)$$

This means that cyclical movements in high-powered money are reinforced by cyclical movements in the deposit-currency ratio. In some periods, movement in the deposit-currency ratio plays a more important role in changing the total money stock than does the rate of change in high-powered money.[39]

The aggregate deposit-currency ratio is a weighted average of the deposit-currency ratios of the subsectors of the economy, of which the household and business sectors are the most important. The cyclical fluctuations in the aggregate deposit-currency ratio can be explained by two factors: first, the deposit-currency ratio of the corporate business sector is much higher than that of the household sector; and second, the effects of tight money policy fall more heavily on the corporate business sector than on the household sector.[40]

---

39. Cagan observed the same results in his study of U.S. money stock.

High-powered money was the major determinant of the secular movement in the money stock, but the deposit-currency ratio was the major determinant of the cyclical movement in the money stock. See *Determinants and Effects of Changes in the U.S. Money Stock, 1875 to 1960.*

40. If the deposit-currency ratios maintained by each sector are constant but differ between themselves, then the aggregate ratio will vary if there is a change in the currency holdings between sectors.

The aggregate deposit-currency ratio can be expressed as follows:

$$(D/C)_a \equiv (D/C)_h(C_h/C_a) + (D/C)_b(C_b/C_a)$$
$$\equiv (D/C)_h(C_h/C_a) + (D/C)_b\frac{C_a - C_h}{C_a}$$
$$\equiv [(D/C)_h - (D/C)_b](C_h/C_b) + (D/C)_b$$

where subscript h stands for household sector, b for business sector, and a for aggregate ratio. Hence, if the sector deposit-currency ratio remains constant, the aggregate ratio can vary as follows:

$$\frac{d(D/C)_a}{dt} = [(D/C)_h - (D/C)_b]\frac{d(C_h/C_b)}{dt}.$$

If monetary policy primarily affects the business sector, there will be a proportionately larger decline in C_b than in C_h and the ratio C_h/C_b will rise. Because $[(D/C)_h - (D/C)_b]$ is negative, the value of $(D/C)_a$ will decline.

The business sector holds its money primarily as monetary deposits, while the household sector holds money primarily in the form of currency.[41] This phenomenon can be observed in the flow-of-funds data.[42] In the household sector, which includes nonincorporated business, for every ¥100 held in the form of currency, only ¥6 are held as deposits on the average. This ratio has been quite stable, ranging between 5 per cent and 7 per cent. In the case of the nonfinancial corporate business sector, for every ¥100 held in the form of currency, there has been about ¥340 held in the form of deposits. The deposit-currency ratios are strongly divergent between the household and business sectors.

The business sector is more affected by changes in monetary policy than is the household sector. The loans of the banking system are largely concentrated in loans to business, with virtually no loans to households. Household debt is not significant even in the mortgage market for single-family residences. Thus, a deceleration in bank loans has its initial effect on business. In attempting to adjust to the resulting liquidity squeeze, there is a strong incentive to economize on money stocks. Because business has a much higher deposit-currency ratio than households, a deceleration in money stocks of business will have a greater effect on deposits than on currency, with the result that the aggregate deposit-currency ratio will fall in periods of tight money and tend to rise in periods of easy money.

The Bank of Japan can come quite close to achieving its money stock target within a quarter time period because it can achieve its high-powered money target exactly and can estimate with a relatively short time lag the predictable cyclical movement in the deposit-currency ratio.

4. THE BEHAVIORAL LINK BETWEEN MONEY, INCOME, IMPORTS, AND INTERNATIONAL RESERVES

The model which ties this study together was presented in section 1. It can be summarized as follows: an acceleration in the money stock

41. The strongly divergent ratios in the personal sector and the corporate sector are due to the fact that individual household checking accounts are almost nonexistent in Japan. Only corporations which do extensive and continuous business with each other find settlement of bills through exchange of monetary deposits a convenient procedure. It is virtually impossible for private persons to transfer funds by check because, legally, a bad check is considered only a breach of contract, not a theft. Thus, the procedure for collecting on a bad check is more expensive and complicated in Japan than in countries where writing a bad check is a criminal offense.

42. Bank of Japan, *Economic Statistics of Japan*, 1966.

leads to an acceleration in income and imports which causes international reserves to decelerate. The policy response is to decelerate the money stock, which will decelerate income and imports and reverse the decline in international reserves. Monetary policy is then eased, which leads to a new acceleration in income and imports. In section 3, the behavior of the policy authorities, the determinants of the money stock, and the relation of the money stock to international reserves were considered. In this section the hypothesized behavior of the decision-making units which provide the other links in the model is investigated. There are three such links: the relation between money and income, between income and imports, and between imports and international reserves.

A. THE RELATION OF MONEY TO INCOME

The relationship hypothesized between money and income is derived from the quantity theory of money. It states that the level of income, Y, is dependently related to the stock of money, M; also, that variations in income, $\dot{Y}$, are dependently related to variations in money, $\dot{M}$. The existence of such a functional relationship does not imply that velocity, V, is constant. However, it does imply that it is functionally stable. This has been the case in Japan. Velocity has not been constant over time, but has exhibited two stable and independent characteristics.

The first was the secular tendency of velocity to rise in the first decade after the war and to decline in the second decade. The second was the cyclical tendency for velocity to rise during periods of tight money and fall during periods of easy money. The secular pattern of velocity may be attributed to the postwar price experience of Japan. Table 6 provides three indexes of prices: wholesale, consumer, and the GNP price deflator. Although the average rate of change in prices

TABLE 6

PRICE CHANGES

	AVERAGE ANNUAL PER CENT CHANGE IN:		
	Wholesale Prices	Consumer Prices	GNP Price Deflator
1946–48.....	180.0	93.6	
1948–53.....	22.5	8.6	
1953–60.....	0.0	1.9	2.0
1960–66.....	1.0	6.0	4.8

SOURCE: Bank of Japan, *Economic Statistics*, 1967.

206   *Varieties of Monetary Experience*

measured by each of these indexes varies, they all show the same inflationary direction.

In the early postwar period, 1946 to 1948, the inflation was substantial. In the period 1948 to 1953 the inflation was sharply reduced, and in the period 1953 to 1960 there was virtually no inflation. The period 1960 to 1966 brought an emergence of new price increases.

According to Cagan (1956), desired real cash balances of money holders in periods of hyperinflation are inversely related to the expected rate of change in prices. An expectation of rapid price increases creates an incentive to reduce the value of real cash balances. When the expected rate of change in prices is small, the desire for real cash balances is unchanged or rising. Cagan's study dealt with relatively short time periods and with high average monthly rates of price increases.

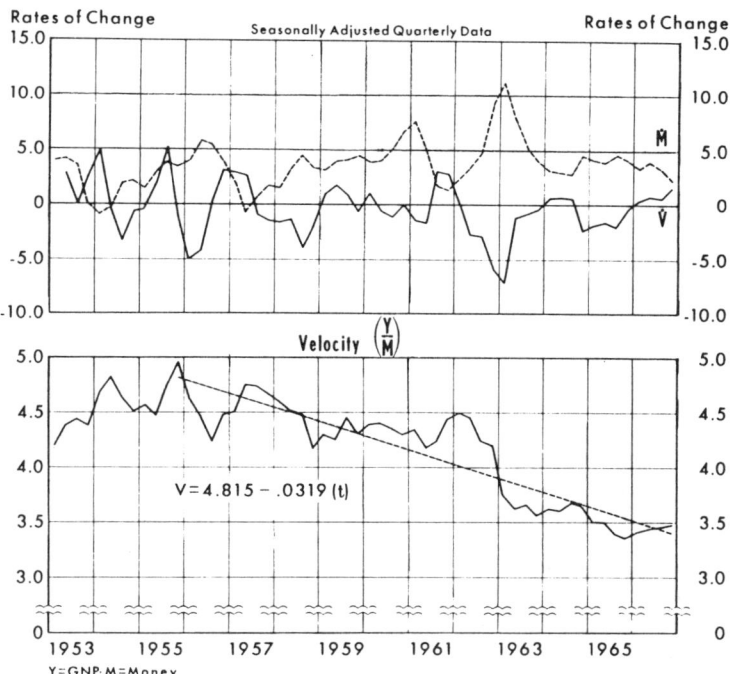

CHART 5. Japan: Money and velocity; velocity (Y/M)
SOURCES: Bank of Japan; Economic Planning Agency, Government of Japan.

When the analysis of real cash balances is conducted in a longer time period with lower price increases, changes in real income also affect the results. Deaver, in a companion study, considers this issue using Chilean data. His results indicate that as inflation becomes less intense, money holders become less sensitive to the rate of inflation. Because they have less at stake, their reactions to price changes are not as prompt. It seems to take several years for money holders to adjust their expectations to relatively moderate changes in inflation.

Deaver's results with respect to Chile seem to be supported by the Japanese case. The rise in velocity (the reciprocal of real cash balances), in the period 1946 to 1955, was in response to the rapid but decelerating inflation of the period 1946 to 1953. There was a gradual decline in velocity from 1955 to 1962, a sharp decline in velocity in 1963, and a continued gradual decline in velocity through 1965.

The decline in velocity from the middle of the 1950s until the early 1960s is consistent with the expectations of continued price stability which followed from 1953–60 price experience. Because the price rise from 1960 through 1966 was largely in consumer goods, it is not surprising that the response in the form of a rise in velocity was lagged. This is especially true considering that real income during this period was rising at a substantial rate. (See latter part of this section for further discussions of this issue.)

The cyclical tendency for velocity to rise during the early period of tight money and fall during the early period of easy money is consistent with rational behavior on the part of money holders. The deceleration in the money stock tends to create an excess demand for money, which pushes up short-term interest rates. The incentive of households and firms is to economize on cash balances, increasing velocity. At the same time reduced spending commitments affect inventories and later production and income. The deceleration in income slows the rise in velocity and in time reverses it.

The opposite process takes place when the stock of money accelerates. The temporary excess supply of money leads to a sharp decline in short-term interest rates, easing the incentive of money holders to economize on cash balances, causing velocity to decline. Associated increase in spending commitments reduces inventories and, after some time lag, leads to increased production and income, slowing the decline in velocity.[43]

43. In the United States, the cyclical pattern of velocity is similar to that of Japan, in spite of the fact that the secular trend of velocity has been just the opposite of Japan from 1955 to 1965.

In spite of this cyclical flexibility in the relationship between money and income, the fluctuations in velocity were not sufficiently large or long-lasting to prevent changes in money from dominating changes in income.

Comparing quarterly rates of change in money with quarterly rates of change in nominal GNP gave the following result:

$$\dot{Y}_t = 1.27 + .51 \dot{M}_{t-2}, \qquad r^2 = .27. \qquad (14)$$
$$(.13)$$

The two-quarter lag in $\dot{M}$ gives the best statistical results, with a one-quarter lag being almost as good. The r^2's with alternative lags in $\dot{M}$ were as follows:

$$\dot{M}_t = .10,$$
$$\dot{M}_{t-1} = .26,$$
$$\dot{M}_{t-3} = .15.$$
$$\dot{M}_{t-4} = .03.$$

Even the best correlation of determination (r^2) is not especially high. One reason for this is that quarterly national income accounts in Japan are still in an experimental stage. And there are frequent changes in accounting practices, coverage, and reporting techniques. Thus, there is some uncertainty about the degree to which the sample is representative of the universe. Large sampling fluctuations result in a substantial amount of random variation in the GNP series.[44] When quarterly rates of change are taken, this random element is magnified, as can be seen in chart 6. A five-term moving average of the GNP series improves the relationship between $\dot{M}$ and $\dot{Y}$, which implies that measurement errors rather than specification errors were the source of irregularity. However imperfect the data, the only information available on nominal GNP is from the quarterly national income accounts.

This study is interested in considering the effects of alternative monetary policies on the business cycle measured not only in terms of nominal income, but also in terms of real income. There are several choices open for measuring the relationship between money and real income.

Consider a money–real-income relation expressed in log linear terms.

$$\log Y = \log \alpha_0 + \log \alpha_1 M_{t-2} \qquad (15)$$

where

$$\log Y = \log y + \log P,$$

44. See Adelman and Adelman, *Readings in Business Cycles* (Homewood, Ill.: Richard D. Irwin, 1965), pp. 290–91.

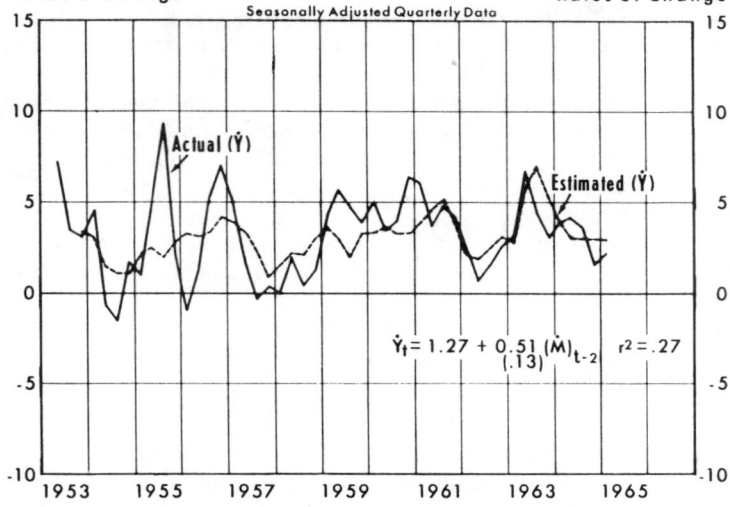

CHART 6. Japan: Actual and estimated changes in nominal GNP
SOURCE: Bank of Japan.

and

$$Y = \text{nominal GNP},$$
$$y = \text{real GNP},$$
$$P = \text{price index}.$$

So

$$\log y = \log \alpha_0 + \log \alpha_1 M_{t-2} - \log P_t. \tag{16}$$

In first differences:

$$\Delta \log y_t = \Delta \log \alpha_1 M_{t-2} - \Delta \log P_t. \tag{17}$$

Fitted to the statistical time series of real GNP, money and the price deflator measured as quarterly rates of change gives:

$$\dot{y}_t = 1.00 + .40\dot{M}_{t-2} - .18\dot{P}_t, \qquad r^2 = .19.$$
$$\quad\quad\;\; (.13) \qquad\quad (.38)$$

The signs are as expected for both the money and the price variables. However, the analysis implies a price coefficient homogeneous to the first degree and an insignificant constant term. In fact, the constant term is large, and the price coefficient is closer to zero than to (-1.0). The fact that the price coefficient is not statistically significant is reassuring. In addition, the coefficient of determination is low. The reason has already been suggested. Nominal income as reported in the national income accounts has a large random element. Dividing through by the implicit price deflator to get real GNP does not reduce the random element. A meaningful statistical test of the underlying behavioral relation is therefore difficult using real GNP.

Fortunately, there is an alternative measure of real output—industrial production.[45] Movements in industrial production and real GNP are quite close when the random element in the real GNP series is accounted for by smoothing with a five-term moving average. The correlation coefficient between rates of change in industrial production and rates of change in real GNP is .78. The industrial production series has been collected for many years, is easily understood, and is relatively straightforward to calculate. Thus, random errors are reduced. In addition, because the quarterly figures are the average of three monthly figures, random variations are reduced further. Thus, industrial production exhibited relatively stable rates of change over time.

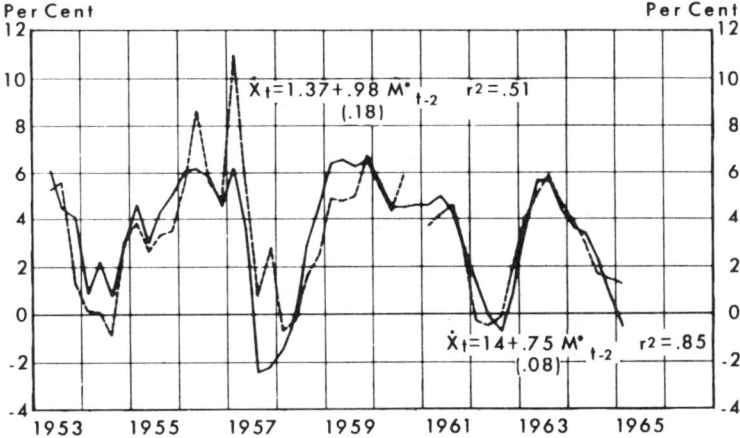

CHART 7. Japan: Actual and estimated changes in real product

45. The relation between industrial production, money, and consumer prices has a closer fit than when real GNP is used:

$$\dot{X}_t = .97 + .75\dot{M}_{t-2} - .46\dot{P}_t, \qquad r^2 = .39.$$
$$(.15) (.39)$$

However, the same statistical problems are evident: a large constant term and an absolute value of the price coefficient less this minus one (−1.0) which is statistically insignificant.

This study is concerned with the differing effects of monetary policy on real and nominal income, and not directly concerned with effects on prices. To handle the real output–money relation without the added complication of explicitly introducing prices into the model, two techniques were tried. First, coefficients relating observed changes in the nominal money stock to changes in industrial production were estimated separately for periods with different rates of change in prices. Second, the money series was deflated by the GNP price deflator and changes in real money compared with changes in industrial production.

With the first technique, the subperiod 1953 to 1960 (when prices increased at a moderate 2 per cent per year) was separated from the subperiod 1960 to 1964 (when prices rose 5 per cent per year). The coefficients estimated separately for each subperiod were:

Subperiod 1953-II to 1960-IV:

$$\dot{X}_t = -.07 + 1.21\dot{M}_{t-2}, \qquad r^2 = .59.$$
$$(.19)$$

Subperiod 1960-IV to 1964-IV:

$$\dot{X}_t = -.54 + .66\dot{M}_{t-2}, \qquad r^2 = .83.$$
$$(.08)$$

This split in the series corresponds to the one in section 3 relating changes in money, $\dot{M}$, to changes in international reserves, $\dot{R}$. The reasons for splitting this series in 1960 are substantially the same in both cases. The monetary policy followed from 1960 to 1964 by Prime Minister Ikeda was more expansionary than that of his predecessors in the years 1953–60.

It should be noted that the coefficient relating $\dot{M}$ to $\dot{X}$ in the period 1953 to 1960 is almost twice as large as the value of that coefficient during the period 1960 to 1964 (1.21 versus .66). Put another way, a 1 per cent increase in the money stock in the earlier period had almost twice as big an effect on real output as a 1 per cent increase in the money stock in the latter period. These results are reasonable under the circumstances. The average growth in real output over the long run is a function of the growth in real inputs of labor, capital, and technology. The average secular growth in the stock of money will not necessarily affect the secular growth in real output. Variations in the growth in the stock of money will, of course, have a major effect on the short-term growth in real output. If the secular growth in the stock of money increases, the coefficient relating the quarterly values of $\dot{M}$ to $\dot{X}$ would be expected to decrease roughly in proportion to the change in the average growth in nominal money stock. This is what happened in the case of Japan. The average quarterly value of $\dot{M}$ moved from 3.1 per cent per quarter in 1953–60 to 4.8 per cent per quarter in 1960–64 (an increase of 55 per cent), while the coefficient relating $\dot{M}$ to $\dot{X}$ moved from 1.21 to .66 in the same period (a decrease of 45 per cent).

The second method of adjusting for changes in prices was to compute coefficients relating changes in the real stock of money to changes in industrial production. The values of the coefficients were estimated for the whole period and also estimated separately for each of the policy subperiods:

Period 1953-II to 1964-IV:

$$\dot{X}_t = 1.23 + .77 \dot{M}^*_{t-2}, \qquad r^2 = .47.$$
$$(.12)$$

Subperiod 1953-II to 1960-IV:

$$\dot{X}_t = 1.37 + .98 \dot{M}^*_{t-2}, \qquad r^2 = .51.$$
$$(.18)$$

Subperiod 1960-IV to 1964-IV:

$$\dot{X}_t = .14 + .75 \dot{M}^*_{t-2}, \qquad r^2 = .85.$$
$$(.08)$$

As with other measures of the money-income relation, the best fit was with a two-quarter time lag in money. The difference in the value of the coefficients between the two policy subperiods was just barely significant. The differences were smaller but in the same direction as in the nominal money–real output relationship. This implies that the amount of real money which households and firms were willing to hold increased in the 1960–64 period relative to the 1953–60 period. How was this possible in the face of an increase in inflationary pressure in 1960–64?

The reasons were suggested earlier in this section. The inflationary pressures in the early and middle 1960s were relatively moderate compared to the early postwar years and compared to the contemporaneous growth in real income. Under such circumstances money holders may not reduce their desired real cash balances.

The reasoning is analogous to substitution and income effects in price theory. An increase in the expected price level will cause the demand for real cash balances to decline,[46] while a rise in real income will cause the

46. A complete measure of the substitution effect would require taking account of the cost of holding money relative to the cost of holding alternative assets. One or more interest rate variables would be needed to measure the demand for

demand for real cash balances to increase. If, as some evidence suggests, the income elasticity of demand for real cash balances is greater than one,[47] then the simultaneous rapid increase in real income and moderate increase in prices could lead to an increase in observed real cash balances and a decline in velocity. Given Japan's rapid growth in real income and relatively mild price increases, the decline in velocity from 1961 to 1965 is not unreasonable.

B. THE RELATION OF INCOME TO IMPORTS

A popular saying is that "Japan must export to live." The truth in this phrase lies in the fact that Japan must *import* to live. Although the ratio of imports to income in Japan is lower than for many industrial nations, she lacks significant quantities of most raw materials required for industrial development. In 1964 she imported 96 per cent of her iron ore, 100 per cent of her raw cotton and wool, 60 per cent of her copper, 99 per cent of her petroleum, and 49 per cent of her industrial coal. With the third largest steel industry in the world, she must import 24 per cent of her steel scrap. In recent years there has also been a significant increase in food imports, as the Japanese diet has shifted towards Western eating patterns more rapidly than has Japanese food production.[48] Finally, Japan imports a wide range of sophisticated machinery and, with the recent trend towards import liberalization, a small but increasing amount of finished consumer goods.

The relationship between income and imports in Japan is substantially different when viewed in secular terms than when viewed in cyclical terms. The elasticity of nominal imports with respect to nominal GNP for the period 1953 to 1965 was not significantly different from 1.0. The elasticity of real imports with respect to industrial production was also not significantly different from 1.0. However, when the relationship between imports and income is computed on a quarter-to-quarter basis, the elasticity varied widely, with most observations in

---

money balances. The sharp quarter-to-quarter movements in short-term interest rates have affected the cyclical movement in velocity. But the long-term trend in interest rates has been stable, after adjustment for price expectations, and therefore probably played little role in the trend of velocity. Because most interest rate data for Japan are misleading, it is not possible to quantify this observation.

47. Milton Friedman, "The Demand for Money," *Journal of Political Economy* 67 (1959): 328–29.

48. The government's price support program for rice discourages shifting to production of other crops.

the range of -1 to $+4$ and some much larger in absolute value. This variation in elasticity is implicit in the following equations:

Nominal imports $(I\dot{m})$ to nominal GNP $(\dot{Y})$:

$$I\dot{m}_t = -3.16 + 1.91(\dot{Y})_t, \qquad r^2 = .39.$$
$$(.36)$$

Real imports $(I\dot{m}^*)$ to industrial production $(\dot{X})$:

$$I\dot{m}_t^* = -3.26 + 2.04(\dot{X})_t, \qquad r^2 = .76.$$
$$(.17)$$

The higher income elasticity of imports observed in the cyclical measure than in the secular measure is due to sharp cyclical movements in the imports of some commodities.

Table 7 illustrates the problem. The average experience during the

TABLE 7

RELATIONSHIP OF PRODUCTION AND IMPORTS TO CONSUMPTION
AND INVENTORIES OF SEMIPROCESSED MATERIALS
(Percentage Change in Four Quarters before and after Peak)

	Industrial Production	Consumption of Semiprocessed Materials	Consumption of Imported Semiprocessed Materials	Inventories of Imported Semiprocessed Materials	Total Imports
1st cycle peak 1954-I					
Before peak	22	20	60	59	32
After peak	1	6	−20	−13	−20
2d cycle peak 1957-II					
Before peak	26	18	48	49	58
After peak	−8	−10	−33	−28	39
3d cycle peak 1961-IV					
Before peak	19	16	53	25	33
After peak	1	−3	−41	−28	−12
4th cycle peak 1964-I					
Before peak	21	24	97	99	34
After peak	8	5	−11	−22	−1
Four cycle averages					
Before peak	22	20	65	58	39
After peak	0	1	−26	−23	−18

SOURCE: Bank of Japan, "Basic Data for Economic Analysis, 1965."

NOTE: Data for the table were available only through 1964-IV. As a result, the timing of the fourth cycle peak is only approximate.

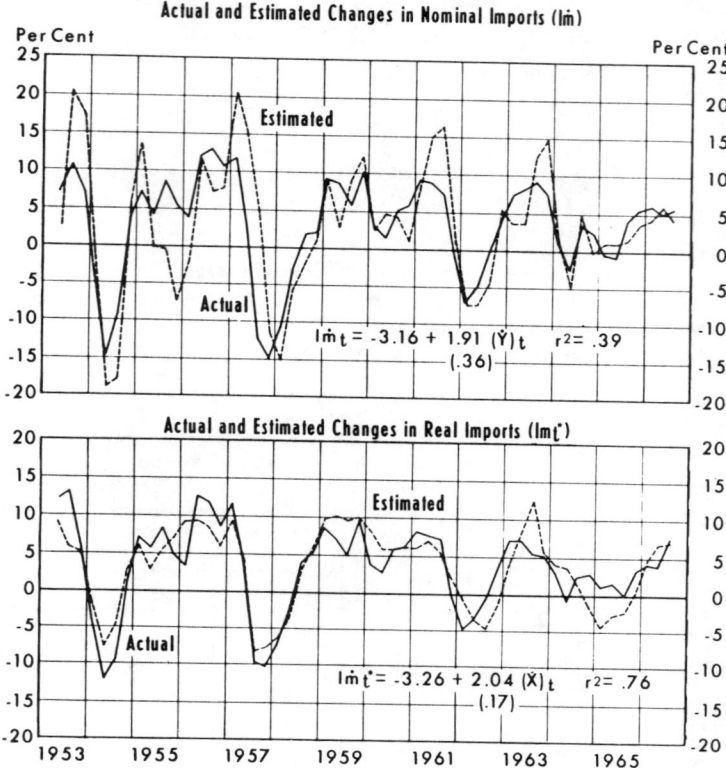

CHART 8. Japan: Actual and estimated changes in nominal imports; actual and estimated changes in real imports.

four business cycles was that the industrial consumption of all semi-processed materials rose and fell proportionately with the rise and fall in industrial production. However, the consumption of imported semi-processed materials tended in the last year of the upswing to rise three and one-fourth times as rapidly as total consumption of semiprocessed materials. In the downswing (four quarters following the peak), the consumption of imported semiprocessed materials declined on the average by 26 per cent, while total consumption was virtually un-changed. This pattern implies a strong cyclical shift between foreign and domestic sources of supply.

This dependence on imports as a marginal source of supply makes Japanese businessmen sensitive to their needs for inventories of such materials. A rise in the consumption of imported semiprocessed materials is associated with a correspondingly sharp rise in the stock of inventories of these materials. Conversely, a decline in the consumption of imported semiprocessed materials is associated with a decline in inventories. As a result, imported inventories have typically increased 58 per cent in the four quarters before the peak of the cycle when their consumption was rising 65 per cent. In the four quarters after the peak in the cycle, inventories of imported semiprocessed materials declined 23 per cent, while their consumption declined 26 per cent.

The dual impact of sharp changes in consumption and inventories of imported semiprocessed materials over the cycle plays a key role in the cyclical pattern of total imports.[49]

The observed cyclical shift between foreign and domestic sources of supply for these important industrial inputs is due to shifts in the relative cost of domestic versus foreign sources of supply. Although the market price of these domestic products does not exhibit a strong cyclical pattern, its nonmarket price does. The nonmarket price of a commodity may be defined as the indirect cost to the consumer of a given purchase. These indirect costs consist of such things as queuing, delays in delivery, and decline in quality of product or services. These nonmarket prices increase substantially during periods of acceleration in domestic demand and decline sharply in periods of deceleration in domestic demand. This creates the incentive to shift from domestic to foreign sources of supply during the late phase of the boom, and to shift from foreign to domestic sources of supply during the period of business decline.

C. THE RELATION OF IMPORTS TO INTERNATIONAL RESERVES

The change in international reserves for any time period can be defined as equal to the surplus or deficit in the balance of payments for that time period. For Japan this procedure presents no serious problems because its currency is not held as an international reserve asset

---

49. It is interesting to note that raw materials, which represent 60 per cent of Japan's total imports, make a relatively small contribution to the deviation of imports from its trend. The relatively modest cyclical pattern in the movement of raw material imports is due to Japan's almost complete dependence on foreign sources of supply. Therefore, shifts between domestic and foreign sources of supply do not play an important role in the quarter-to-quarter fluctuations in imports.

by other countries. The accounting definition of changes in international reserves is as follows:

$$\Delta R_t \equiv BP_t \equiv E_t - Im_t + K_t,$$
$$\Delta R = \text{change in international reserves,}$$
$$BP = \text{balance of payments,} \qquad\qquad (18)$$
$$E = \text{exports of goods and services,}$$
$$Im = \text{imports of goods and services,}$$
$$K = \text{net capital receipts.}[50]$$

The relation hypothesized in the model is that the rate of change in international reserves is predictably related to the rate of change in imports.

$$\dot{R}_t = \rho_0 + \rho_1 I\dot{m}_{t-\rho}. \qquad (19)$$

This relation is derived from the following transformation:

$$R_t \equiv R_{t-1} + K_t + E_t - Im_t. \qquad (20)$$

Differentiating with respect to time,

$$\frac{dR_t}{dt} \equiv \frac{dR_{t-1}}{d(t-1)}\left(\frac{d(t-1)}{dt}\right) + \frac{dK_t}{dt} + \frac{dE_t}{dt} - \frac{dIm_t}{dt}. \qquad (21)$$

Find the per cent change in reserves by dividing by R_{t-1} and restating other terms so they can be written in rate of change form.

$$\dot{R}_t \equiv \frac{1}{R_{t-1}}\left(\frac{dR_{t-1}}{dt}\right) + \frac{K_{t-1}}{R_{t-1}}\cdot\frac{1}{K_{t-1}}\left(\frac{dK_t}{dt}\right) + \frac{E_{t-1}}{R_{t-1}}\cdot\frac{1}{E_{t-1}}\left(\frac{dE_t}{dt}\right)$$
$$- \frac{Im_{t-1}}{R_{t-1}}\cdot\frac{1}{Im_{t-1}}\left(\frac{dIm_t}{dt}\right). \qquad (22)$$

Replace t with $t-1$ in (21) and substitute into (22).

$$\dot{R}_t \equiv \frac{1}{R_{t-1}}\left[\frac{dR_{t-2}}{dt} + \frac{dK_{t-1}}{dt} + \frac{dE_{t-1}}{dt} - \frac{dIm_{t-1}}{dt}\right]$$
$$+ \frac{K_{t-1}}{R_{t-1}}(\dot{K}_t) + \frac{E_{t-1}}{R_{t-1}}(\dot{E}_t) - \frac{Im_{t-1}}{R_{t-1}}(I\dot{m}_t). \qquad (23)$$

50. All international capital transfers are handled in either dollars or pounds sterling. The domestic currency is converted into one of the international currencies at a domestic bank which is authorized to deal in foreign exchange. These banks will match their international receipts and payments daily or weekly and make up the balance with either a purchase or a sale of foreign exchange from the Bank of Japan, which acts as an agent for the foreign exchange special account of the ministry of finance.

By repeated substitution of (21) into (22) until such point that dR_{t-n}/dt equals zero we get the following identity:

$$\dot{R}_t \equiv \frac{1}{R_{t-1}} \cdot \frac{dR_{t-n}}{dt} + \frac{1}{R_{t-1}} \left[\sum_{i=0}^{n-1} (K_{t-i-1})(\dot{K}_{t-i}) \right]$$
$$+ \frac{1}{R_{t-1}} \left[\sum_{i=0}^{n-1} (E_{t-i-1})(\dot{E}_{t-i}) \right] - \frac{1}{R_{t-1}} \left[\sum_{i=0}^{n-1} (Im_{t-i-1})(I\dot{m}_{t-i}) \right]. \tag{24}$$

The identity shows that the per cent change in reserves is a weighted sum of the per cent rate of change of past imports, exports, and capital back to some point in time when the rate of change in reserves was zero. To assert that this identity can be approximated solely by the lagged rate of change in imports, one must show that exports and net capital flows have grown at a relatively stable rate.

The identity (24) can be rewritten factoring out one lagged value of the rate of change of imports.

$$\dot{R}_t \equiv \frac{1}{R_{t-1}} \cdot \frac{dR_{t-n}}{dt} + \frac{1}{R_{t-1}} \left[\sum_{i=0}^{n-1} (K_{t-i-1})(\dot{K}_{t-i}) \right]$$
$$+ \frac{1}{R_{t-1}} \left[\sum_{i=0}^{n-1} (E_{t-i-1})(\dot{E}_{t-i}) \right] - \frac{1}{R_{t-1}} \left[\sum_{i=0\, i \neq p}^{n-1} (Im_{t-i-1})(I\dot{m}_{t-i}) \right]$$
$$- \frac{Im_{t-p-1}}{R_{t-1}} (I\dot{m}_{t-p}). \tag{25}$$

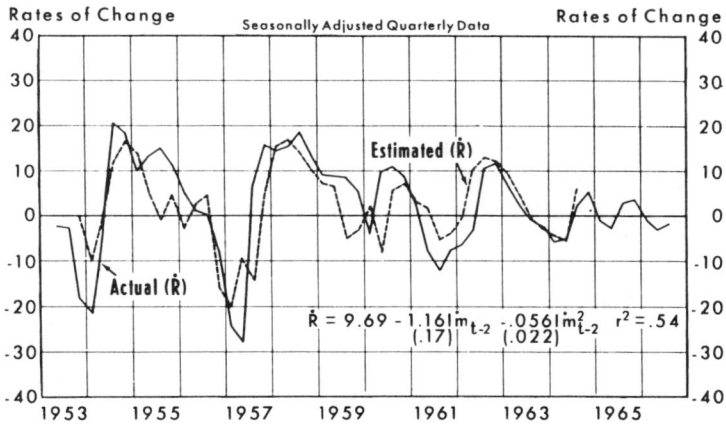

CHART 9. Japan: Actual and estimated changes in nominal international reserves.

SOURCE: Bank of Japan.

The best linear approximation of this identity is specified as follows: the term factored out of the import summation is the "active" term, since it is approximated by $\rho_1 I\dot{m}_{t-p}$ in the regression equation $\dot{R}_t = \rho_0 + \rho_1 I\dot{m}_{t-p}$. The sum of the other terms on the right-hand side is approximated by the constant term ρ_0. The lagged time index p is selected so as to minimize the variation in the terms represented by ρ_0. Conceptually, p should be the time lag that most closely synchronizes turning points in the rate of change of reserves to the negative of the turning points in the rate of change of imports.[51] A polynomial of the form $\dot{R}_t = \rho_0 - \rho_1 I\dot{m}_{t-p} - \rho_2 I\dot{m}_{t-p}^2 - \cdots - \rho_n I\dot{m}_{t-p}^n$ can be used to simulate the cyclical movements of the coefficient $-Im_{t-p-1}/R_{t-1}$ in the identity. In fact, the polynomial form gives the best regression fit and was incorporated into this model as a result.

The evidence presented to justify this form of the identity is of two types. First, exports and net capital flows exhibit a stable growth relative to imports and, second, regressions between rates of change in imports and reserves have reasonably good statistical fits. As the regression evidence is the most straightforward, it is given first.

A second-degree polynomial regression gave the best results.

Nominal imports and nominal reserves:

$$\dot{R}_t = 9.69 - 1.16 I\dot{m}_{t-2} - .056 I\dot{m}_{t-2}^2, \qquad r^2 = .54.$$
$$\phantom{\dot{R}_t = 9.69 -} (.17) \qquad\;\; (.022)$$

Real imports and real reserves:

$$\dot{R}_t^* = 10.1 - 1.23 I\dot{m}_{t-2}^* - .056 I\dot{m}_{t-2}^{*2}, \qquad r^2 = .54.$$
$$\phantom{\dot{R}_t^* = 10.1 -} (.10) \qquad\;\; (.027)$$

With respect to the first type of evidence, it can be noted that Japan has benefited substantially from the stable and prosperous international economic environment which has existed in the postwar period.[52] Of course, the fact that Japan's export growth has been two

51. The assumption would be that the two time series would be out of phase by approximately one-quarter of a cycle. As analyzed in section 5, the cycle is ten quarters long. Therefore, the estimated lags between rates of change of imports and reserves of two quarters are quite consistent.

52. This raises some interesting questions about the international transmission of business cycles. This analysis implies that Japan has been relatively little affected by fluctuations from abroad in the postwar period. Thus, the popular saying that when the U.S. sneezes Europe catches cold and Japan is confined to its bed doesn't seem to hold. Of course, these observations are based on a quite mild business cycle pattern. If the fluctuations were more severe, the international transmission of cycles would probably be more apparent, as was the case in the 1930s.

220   *Varieties of Monetary Experience*

to three times the growth in world trade is largely due to domestic considerations, such as a growing and sophisticated capital plant and well-trained and motivated work force, and an imaginative application of technology to the needs of world trade. None of these domestic factors is strongly influenced by the short-run Japanese business cycle.

As can be seen in chart 10, none of the four periods of decline in reserves can be attributed primarily to export considerations.[53] During

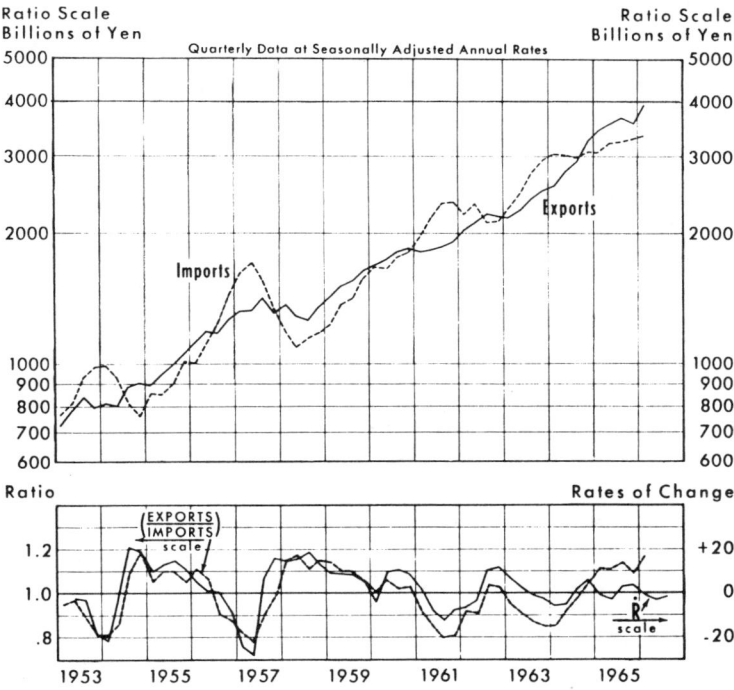

CHART 10. Japan: Current account of balance of payments

SOURCE: Government of Japan Economic Planning Agency.

NOTE: National income accounts basis.

53. Cyclical movements in the current account have been the major cause of fluctuations in foreign exchange reserves, with net capital movements playing a growing but secondary role. Since the mean import-reserve ratio has been close to one (.92), it is possible to illustrate the relative importance of current account

two periods, 1957 and 1963, Japanese exports were rising at a rate faster than average, and in the other two periods, 1953–54 and 1961, exports were rising at a rate slower than average. Each of the four decelerations in international reserves was associated with a rapid increase in imports; the acceleration in reserves was associated in the first two periods with a rapid decrease in imports, and the last two periods with a moderate decrease in imports.

Fluctuations in imports have played a major role not only in the timing of changes in international reserves, but also in the size of their deterioration and subsequent improvement. Notice in chart 10 that variations in imports in the first two cycles were larger than in the last two cycles, and also that fluctuations in international reserves were larger in the first two cycles than in the last two.

From 1953 to the middle of 1960, the ratio of exports to imports moved in a pattern and amplitude almost identical to that of the rate of change in international reserves. This implies not only that imports dominated the current account but also that capital movements were relatively unimportant in the Japanese balance of payments during this period. However, from the middle of 1960 until the end of 1964, the rate of change in international reserves was at a much higher average level than the ratio of exports to imports. This implies a heavy capital inflow during the period.[54]

The emergence of a heavy capital inflow from 1960 to 1964 is consistent with the previous analysis of monetary policy. It will be recalled that Prime Minister Ikeda (July 1960–November 1964) wished to push

---

and capital flows to the rates of change of reserves by superimposing the export-import ratio graph on the rate of change of reserves graph. Algebraically, the procedure is justified as follows:

$$\dot{R}_t = \frac{\Delta R_t}{R_{t-1}} = \frac{K_t + E_t - Im_t}{R_{t-1}} \equiv \frac{K_t}{R_{t-1}} + \frac{Im_t}{R_{t-1}}\left[\frac{E_t}{Im_t} - 1\right].$$

The mean import-reserve ratio is the factor of proportionality between the scale for the rate of change of reserves and the export-import ratio scale. In effect, the export-import ratio is used as a proxy for the measure of the rate of change of reserves due to net quantity flows of current account. The export-import ratio somewhat exaggerates rates of change in reserves due to current account flows, whenever the import reserve ratio is below the mean. The opposite case holds when the import reserve ratio is above the mean.

54. Consistent data on the Japanese capital account are not available during this whole period because of changes in the method of presentation. However, what data are available confirm this result. The sum of long- and short-term capital receipts between 1956 and 1959 was −$126 million; the sum of long- and short-term capital receipts between 1960 and 1964 was +$2.3 billion.

an expansionary monetary policy. Hoping to prevent such a policy from causing the balance of payments to deteriorate, the Ikeda administration substantially reduced restrictions on short-term capital imports and moderately liberalized long-term capital imports.[55] Because controls on export of capital by European countries were also being relaxed, and because the Japanese growth rate and domestic interest rates were considerably higher than in other industrial countries, the reductions of controls on capital led to an immediate and heavy inflow of foreign funds.

In spite of this capital inflow from 1960 to 1964, Japan's balance of payments was still dominated by fluctuations in imports. The capital inflow could only reduce the magnitude of the international reserve loss.[56]

55. A partial listing of the capital liberalization moves taken by the Ikeda administration include:

a. In July 1960 nonresidents of Japan were permitted to purchase yen accounts with foreign currency which were automatically reconvertible into foreign exchange. This permitted Japanese banks with branches in Europe to take advantage of the Euro-dollar market. Within less than three years Euro-dollar deposits in Japanese banks increased more than $1 billion.

b. In the fall of 1960, domestic Japanese banks were given increased freedom to refinance import trade credits with foreign banks. This permitted a substantial expansion in the amount of short-term credit which was available to Japan from foreign sources.

c. From 1960 to 1962, the Japanese government gradually eased restrictions on domestic business organizations' floating bonds abroad, permitted foreign purchasers of Japanese stocks to repatriate their income with only a minimum waiting period, and generally eased the government's administrative restrictions of Japanese corporations assuming foreign liabilities.

The purpose of these liberalization moves was to increase the amount of capital inflow, but because of the Japanese native suspicion of foreign influences, there was relatively little improvement in the attitude of the Japanese government regarding foreign direct investment. Such investment was, and still is, restricted to minority participation to insure that Japanese nationals control the decision-making process.

56. The relative stagnation in international reserves in the face of a strong current account surplus since the end of 1964 is mainly due to the cyclical decline in Japanese interest rates relative to those in the rest of the world. To a lesser extent, it is due to the "voluntary program" of the United States to correct its balance of payments problem, which was initiated on February 10, 1965. The decline in interest rates has hit short-term capital flows, while the voluntary program has primarily affected long-term capital flows. In 1965–66 there was net capital outflow of $1.3 billion from Japan.

The reemergence of boom conditions towards the end of 1965 took longer than usual to affect interest rates. But when rates started to rise toward the end of

5. MONETARY POLICY AND THE BUSINESS CYCLE

The four-equation model of the Japanese business cycle which was presented briefly in section 1 and considered in detail in sections 3–4 can be analyzed formally with the help of difference equations. The unique advantage of difference equations is that in its application to economics, the solution traces out a path over time. In this way the dynamic properties of the model can be analyzed.

A. THE SIMPLEST EXAMPLE

The structural equations which underlie this difference equation in their simplest form are as follows:

$$\dot{Y}_t = \alpha_0 + \alpha_1 \dot{M}_{t-2}, \tag{26}$$

$$\dot{M}_t = \beta_0 + \beta_1 \dot{R}_{t-1}, \tag{27}$$

$$\dot{R}_t = \rho_0 + \rho_1 I\dot{m}_{t-2}, \tag{28}$$

$$I\dot{m}_t = \gamma_0 + \gamma_1 \dot{Y}_t. \tag{29}$$

The lagged values are determined by the statistical results presented in sections 3 and 4.

The reduced form of this system of equations ([26] through [29]) is:

$$\dot{Y}_t = A_0 + A_1 \dot{Y}_{t-5},$$

where

$$A_0 = \alpha_0 + \alpha_1\beta_0 + \alpha_1\beta_1\rho_0 + \alpha_1\beta_1\rho_1\gamma_0, \tag{30}$$
$$A_1 = \alpha_1\beta_1\rho_1\gamma_1.$$

While this equation appears to be of the fifth order, it is in fact a system of five first-order equations, because all equations are of the form:

$$\dot{Y}_t = f(\dot{Y}_{t-h}).$$

Because h is a constant time interval, the equation can be handled as if it were of the first order. For example, instead of saying $t - 5$ (quarters), we can say $t - 1$ (5-quarter interval). To illustrate this, consider the following initial conditions,

$$\dot{Y}_{-4} = 9, \quad \dot{Y}_{-3} = 6, \quad \dot{Y}_{-2} = 1, \quad \dot{Y}_{-1} = 2, \quad \dot{Y}_0 = 5,$$

and the determining equation,

$$\dot{Y}_t = 1 - 2\dot{Y}_{t-5}.$$

1966, the capital outflow was reversed. In the first half of 1967 there was a net capital inflow of $244 million.

The sequence, including the initial conditions, that would be generated is:

$$\begin{cases} 9,\ 6,\ 1,\ 2,\ 5,\ -17,\ -11,\ -1,\ -3,\ -9, \\ 35,\ 23,\ 3,\ 7,\ 19,\ -63,\ -45,\ -5,\ -13,\ -37, \\ 125,\ 89,\ldots \end{cases}.$$

The original sequence can be decomposed into five separate subsequences which have no common elements. Each element of the original sequence with subscript t is placed in the corresponding ith ($i = 1,2,3,4,5$) subsequence when $i_t = (t + 5 - i)/5$ assumes an integral value. Each subsequence can be generated by a first-order difference equation of the form

$$\dot{Y}_{i_t} = 1 - 2\dot{Y}_{i_{t-t}}.$$

1. $\{9,\ -17,\ 35,\ -63,\ 125,\ldots\}$
2. $\{6,\ -11,\ 23,\ -45,\ 89,\ldots\ \}$
3. $\{1,\ -1,\ 3,\ -5,\ldots\ \ \ \ \ \ \ \}$
4. $\{2,\ -3,\ 7,\ -13,\ldots\ \ \ \ \ \ \}$
5. $\{5,\ -9,\ 19,\ -37,\ldots\ \ \ \ \ \ \}$

The elements of each subsequence are uniquely related to the initial condition (first element) of that subsequence. The "behavior" of any one subsequence is mathematically independent of the "behavior" of the other subsequences. However, as the initial conditions are drawn from consecutive observations of the Japanese economy, the subsequences are assumed to be consistently related to one another. Given these nonrandom initial conditions, it is not unreasonable to reassemble the five subsequences (generated from the first-order difference equations) to form the fifth-order difference equation, approximating the cyclical behavior of the Japanese economy.

Specifying the behavior of the first-order equation $\dot{Y}_t = A_0 + A_1\dot{Y}_{t-1}$ also specifies the behavior of the fifth-order equation $\dot{Y}_t = A_0 + A_1\dot{Y}_{t-5}$. For purposes of tracing out the solution of a first-order difference equation, the constant term A_0 can be omitted, as the value A_1 determines the cyclical properties of the model.[57]

If the value of A_1 is positive, then the rate of change in income, $\dot{Y}$, will not have a cyclical pattern. If A_1 is equal to one, income will grow at a constant rate each period and $\dot{Y}$ will be constant. If A_1 is less than one but greater than zero, income will grow at a constantly decreasing rate each period and $\dot{Y}$ will decrease. If A_1 is greater than one, income

57. See Baumol, *Economic Dynamics*, 2d ed. (New York: Macmillan Co., 1959), p. 162.

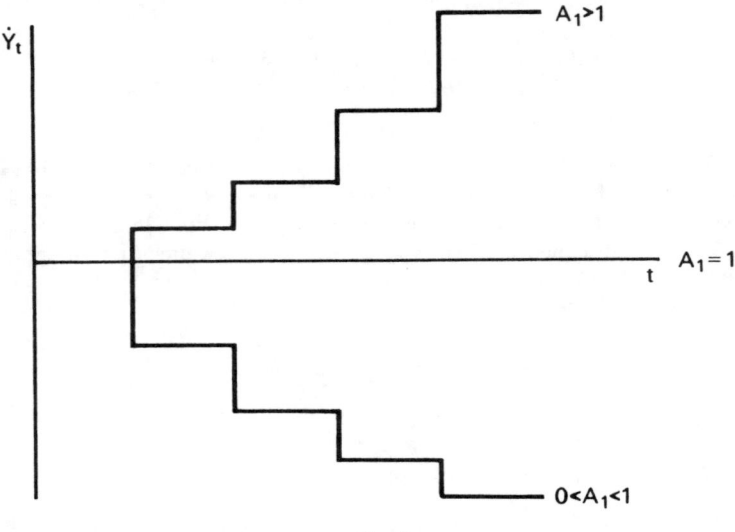

FIG. 1.

will grow at a constantly increasing rate each period and $\dot{Y}$ will increase (see fig. 1).

If, on the other hand, the value of A_1 is negative, the time path of $\dot{Y}$ will oscillate in a regular cyclical pattern. If the value of A_1 is equal to minus one, the cyclical path of $\dot{Y}$ will be of constant amplitude. If the value of A_1 is less than zero but greater than minus one, the cyclical path of $\dot{Y}$ will be damped. If A_1 is less than minus one (its absolute value is greater than one), the cyclical path of $\dot{Y}$ will be explosive (see fig. 2).

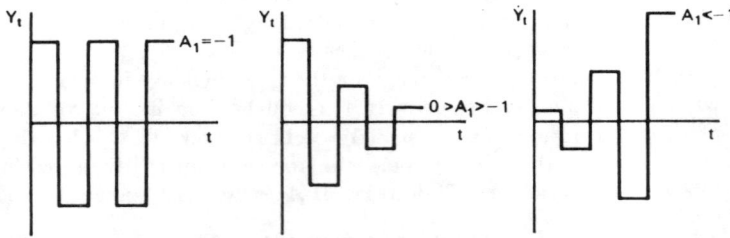

FIG. 2.

On a priori grounds we can postulate that the value of A_1 in this model of the business cycle is negative, because in equation (28) the value ρ_1 is negative; that is, an acceleration in imports will lead to a deceleration in international reserves. As the value of coefficients in the other three equations is positive, the product $A_1 = \alpha_1\beta_1\rho_1\gamma_1$ will be negative. Thus, the model has a built-in cyclical property.

These results can be seen intuitively. Consider the reduced-form equation:

$$\dot{Y}_t = A_0 + A_1\dot{Y}_{t-5}.$$

If A_1 is negative and the value of $\dot{Y}_{t-5}$ is positive, then the product of these two values will be negative. This means that the value of $\dot{Y}_t$ will be smaller than that of $\dot{Y}_{t-5}$. If the value of $\dot{Y}_{t-5}$ is negative and is multiplied by A_1 which is also negative, then the product will be positive and the value of $\dot{Y}_t$ will be larger than $\dot{Y}_{t-5}$. Thus, the value of $\dot{Y}_t$ over time is periodically larger and smaller.[58]

These relations can be viewed schematically.

$$\dot{M}_t \xrightarrow{(+)} \alpha_1\dot{Y}_{t+2} \xrightarrow{(+)} \gamma_1I\dot{m}_{t+2} \xrightarrow{(-)} \rho_1\dot{R}_{t+4} \xrightarrow{(+)} \beta_1\dot{M}_{t+5}.$$

The arrow indicates the hypothesized direction of causality. The sign above the arrow indicates whether the relation is positive or negative. The time subscript indicates the number of quarters between the change in $\dot{M}_t$ and the change in the other variables. The sequence takes five quarters from peak to trough and ten quarters for the entire cycle.

An increase in $\dot{M}$ will increase $\dot{Y}$ and $I\dot{m}$ in about two quarters and reduce $\dot{R}$ in about four quarters. The monetary policy response will lead to a decline in $\dot{M}$ in about five quarters. The cyclical process could be equally well described starting with any of the other variables and would lead to the same results.

There are two major implications of this model. First, the built-in cyclical property is due to monetary policy responding exclusively to changes in international reserves and such changes are due to domestic considerations. Second, the more expansionary the monetary policy, the greater the cyclical fluctuations in income.

The first implication is derived directly from the structure of the model. Coefficient β_1 is a measure of the policy response to changes in

58. The value around which $\dot{Y}_t$ will fluctuate depends strongly on the value of A_0. If A_0 is large, the average value of $\dot{Y}_t$ will be high, and if A_0 is small or negative, the average value of $\dot{Y}_t$ will be low or negative. In one sense, A_0 can be considered as all the unexplained factors in the economy which contribute to its average growth rate, while A_1 represents all of the explicitly considered factors which explain the fluctuations in the growth rate.

international reserves. If monetary policy was not responsive to changes in international reserves, β_1 would be equal to zero. This implies that the product of $\alpha_1\beta_1\rho_1\gamma_1 = A_1 = 0$. In this case, money would grow at a steady rate, β_0, and income would grow at a steady rate $(\beta_0\alpha_1 + \alpha_0)$ subject only to random exogenous influences. Divorcing monetary policy from fluctuations in international reserves would also lead to increased stability in the growth of international reserves. This can be seen by solving the reduced form of the four structural equations for $\dot{R}$ rather than for $\dot{Y}$. The value A_1 would still be equal to the product of $\alpha_1\beta_1\rho_1\gamma_1$.

$$\dot{R}_t = A_{00} + A_1(\dot{R})_{t-5}.$$

If β_1 is zero, then A_1 is also zero and $\dot{R}$ will grow at a steady rate determined by the value A_{00} and random exogenous events.

The economic reasoning behind this is that fluctuations in international reserves are due to domestic factors, namely, variations in imports, and fluctuations in money lead to fluctuations in domestic income. The relationship is, in a sense, a closed loop, with increases in money causing increases in income, and *increases* in income causing *decreases* in money. If the money stock grows at a steady rate, this will lead to a steady rate of growth in income and imports and thereby reduce the variability in international reserves.[59]

The second implication of this model follows easily from the first implication. The more expansionary monetary policy leads to greater fluctuations in income because the more expansionary policy leads to a larger value for the coefficient β_1. As a result, the absolute value of A_1 is larger, which implies larger fluctuations in income.

B. THE ACTUAL DYNAMIC PROPERTIES

The actual set of structural equations used to estimate the behavior postulated in this model is somewhat more complicated than presented in the above example. The statistical estimation of the relation of $I\dot{m}$ to $\dot{R}$ was a second-degree polynomial:

$$\dot{R}_t = \rho_0 + \rho_1 I\dot{m}_{t-2} + \rho_2 I\dot{m}^2_{t-2}.$$

When this is substituted for equation (28) in the example, the reduced form of this system of four equations is as follows:

$$\dot{Y}_t = A_0 + A_1\dot{Y}_{t-5} + A_2\dot{Y}^2_{t-5}, \tag{31}$$

59. Not all target growth rates in the money stock would be sustainable. If the target growth rate is too high, international reserves will decline and a restrictive monetary policy would have to be initiated. Judging by the 1953–66 experience, target growth rate of 3–4 per cent per quarter would be sustainable.

where

$$A_0 = \alpha_0 + \alpha_1\beta_0 + \alpha_1\beta_1\rho_0 + \alpha_1\beta_1\rho_1\gamma_0 + \alpha_1\beta_1\rho_2\gamma_0^2,$$
$$A_1 = \alpha_1\beta_1\rho_1\gamma_1 + 2\alpha_1\beta_1\rho_2\gamma_0\gamma_1,$$

and

$$A_2 = \alpha_1\beta_1\rho_2\gamma_1^2.$$

Equation (31) can be simplified into a first-order difference equation of the second degree by the same process described above. Thus, it can be rewritten as follows:

$$\dot{Y}_t = A_0 + A_1\dot{Y}_{t-1} + A_2\dot{Y}_{t-1}^2.$$

The implications for the time path of $\dot{Y}_t$ in this more complicated reduced form are not as straightforward mathematically or as intuitively understandable as in my previous example. However, in the range of values of A_1 and A_2 which are observed in the case of Japan (between 0 and -1), the results are the same as in the simple case and this can be shown by simulation.

This business-cycle model was tested for both real and nominal values. The values of the nominal coefficients are as follows: [60]

$$\dot{Y}_t = 1.27 + .51\dot{M}_{t-2}, \tag{32}$$

$$\dot{M}_t = 2.65 + .09\dot{R}_{t-1}, \qquad \dot{M}_t = 4.90 + .34\dot{R}_{t-1}, \tag{33), (33a}$$

$$\dot{R}_t = 9.69 - 1.16I\dot{m}_{t-2} - .06I\dot{m}_{t-2}^2, \tag{34}$$

$$I\dot{m}_t = -3.16 + 1.91\dot{Y}_t. \tag{35}$$

Equations (33) and (33a) were estimated for separate periods of monetary policy response to the balance of payments. Therefore, the reduced form has two versions:

$$\dot{Y}_t = 3.19 - .068\dot{Y}_{t-5} - .009\dot{Y}_{t-5}^2, \tag{36}$$

$$\dot{Y}_t = 6.01 - .269\dot{Y}_{t-5} - .035\dot{Y}_{t-5}^2. \tag{37}$$

Equation (36) represents the period of less expansionary monetary policy between 1953 and 1960 and (37) the period of more expansionary monetary policy between 1960 and 1964. The results of simulating this equation over time are presented in chart 11. The initial conditions are the first five observations in 1953 and 1954. This chart confirms the implications of the simple example. A monetary policy which is responsive to changes in international reserves leads to an internally

60. These coefficients are drawn from sections 3 and 4 where each of the behavioral relations was discussed and the statistical results presented.

Monetary Policy and Business Cycle in Postwar Japan   229

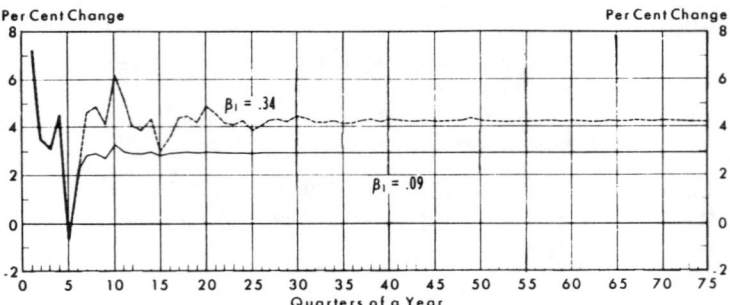

CHART 11. Japan: Simulation of nominal GNP with alternative monetary policies (β_1).

generated cycle in income, and when monetary policy is more expansionary ($\beta_1 = .34$), the fluctuations in nominal income are larger than when monetary policy is less expansionary ($\beta_1 = .09$).

Even though the more expansionary monetary policy leads to larger fluctuations, it also leads to a higher average growth in nominal income. Some fluctuation in the rate of growth of nominal income may seem a small price to pay for increasing the average growth rate. However, this result is illusionary. This we can see by looking at the real variant of the business-cycle model. The values of the real coefficients are given below:[61]

$$\dot{X}_t = 1.37 + .98\dot{M}^*_{t-2}, \qquad \dot{X} = .14 + .75\dot{M}^*_{t-2}, \qquad (38), (38a)$$

$$\dot{M}^*_t = 2.20 + .101\dot{R}^*_{t-1}, \qquad \dot{M}^*_t = 3.16 + .298\dot{R}^*_{t-1}, \qquad (39), (39a)$$

$$\dot{R}^*_t = 10.1 - 1.23Im^*_{t-2} - .056Im^*_{t-2}, \qquad (40)$$

$$I\dot{m}^*_t = -3.26 + 2.04\dot{X}_t. \qquad (41)$$

In the real version of the business-cycle model, there are two monetary policy subperiods as in the nominal version. Thus, in the reduced form, there are also two real variants, one for the period of moderate policy (1953–60) and one for the period of expansionary policy (1960–64):

$$\dot{X}_t = 4.86 - .175\dot{X}_{t-5} - .023\dot{X}^2_{t-5}, \qquad (42)$$

$$\dot{X}_t = 5.53 - .394\dot{X}_{t-5} - .052\dot{X}^2_{t-5}. \qquad (43)$$

When (42) and (43) are simulated in the same manner as in the nominal version, the same results are observed with respect to the effects of monetary policy on the business cycle. A policy responsive to changes

61. Sources of those coefficients are the same as in note 60.

in international reserves leads to cyclical movements in income, and the more expansionary policy ($\beta_1 = .298$) leads to greater fluctuation than the less expansionary policy ($\beta_1 = .101$). However, in this case the average rate of growth of real output is actually somewhat less in the expansionary period than in the nonexpansionary period. These results can be seen in chart 12.

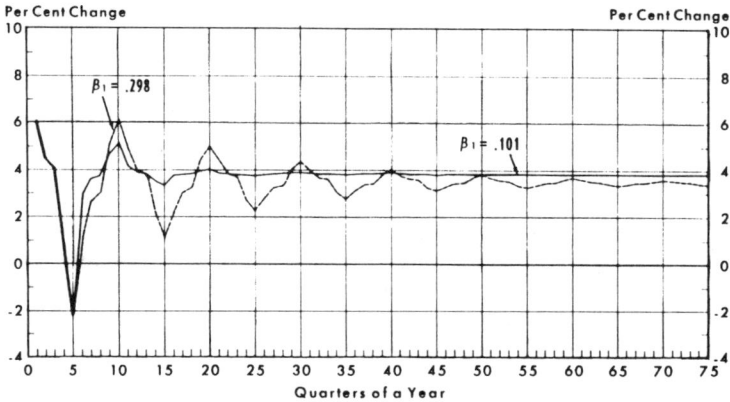

CHART 12. Japan: Simulation of real product with alternative monetary policies (β_1).

The different results in the nominal and in the real business-cycle models are reasonable. In the nominal business-cycle model, the more expansionary period is also one of rising prices, while the less expansionary period is one of relative price stability. Thus, one would expect that a business-cycle model utilizing nominal values would exhibit a higher average growth rate in periods of monetary expansion. One would also expect that a business-cycle model using real values would not necessarily show a higher average growth rate during expansionary periods. These results are consistent with the historic evidence. Nominal income grew more rapidly in the expansionary period (1960–64) than in the less expansionary period (1953–60). But real income grew at about the same rate in both periods.

C. THE SHOCKED DYNAMIC PROPERTIES

So far the cyclical properties of this model have been investigated under a very restrictive set of assumptions. The functional relationships have been treated as if they were exact. But, in fact, random elements are inherent in the statistical estimation of all the equations. By ignoring the random elements I have deliberately sacrificed much of the inherent cyclical properties of the model. As pointed out by Frisch (1933), the random elements alone could induce a cycle.

In spite of the limitation of treating the model as if each of the four equations were exact, the cyclical pattern of the model has been apparent. However, this cyclical pattern is both damped and highly regular in timing. Although the Japanese business cycle has shown some regularity in timing, its pattern has not been damped. Specifically recognizing the random element will eliminate the dampening observed in the simulation of the model.

Because the four structural equations which underlie this model are probabilistic, there is a random error term in each of the equations. These random error terms stem from specification errors, measurement errors, and exogenous factors such as strikes, natural calamities, etc., which temporarily distort the systematic behavioral relation among the variables, and represent sources of irregularity in estimating the original structural equations. The residuals of the four equations in this model can therefore be attributed to a number of different types of errors. Since there appears to be no a priori correlation among the individual sources of error, these residuals or error terms are assumed to be normally distributed.

These error terms have been utilized to introduce realistic random shocks into the model. For each of the structural equations, an additive random error term was specified. Using the same process of algebraic substitution which was used in solving the reduced form of the un-shocked system, a new reduced form equation was constructed. In this equation several error terms appear as parameters analogous to lagged endogenous variables. The size and direction of these shocks are determined by selection of random numbers out of a normally distributed population based on the size of the error terms in each of the structural equations.

The results of simulating this model for both its real and nominal versions are shown in charts 13 and 14. It can be observed that the cyclical pattern of income is no longer damped nor as regular in timing as in the unshocked simulation of the model. It is a more realistic representation of the Japanese business cycle. It is interesting to note that the more expansionary policy leads to larger fluctuations in both nominal GNP and real product than does the less expansionary policy. This is true in spite of the fact that the error terms in the expansionary period are smaller.

It should be kept in mind that contrary to the dynamic properties of

232 *Varieties of Monetary Experience*

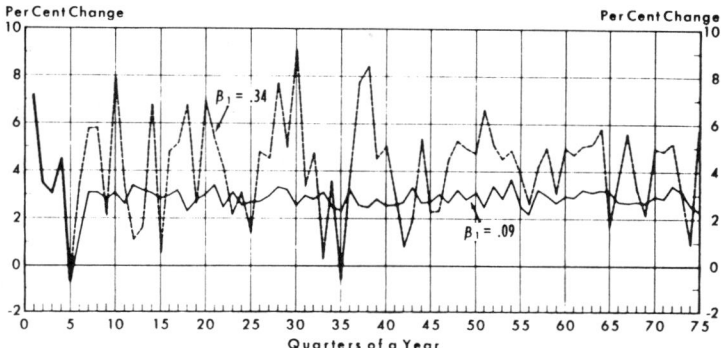

CHART 13. Japan: Shocked simulation of nominal GNP with alternative monetary policies (β_1).

more elaborate economic models which have been tested for the United States and elsewhere,[62] the cyclical fluctuations of this model are inherent in its dynamic properties. The application of random shocks to the system only makes the magnitude and timing of the cycles more in line with real-world observations.

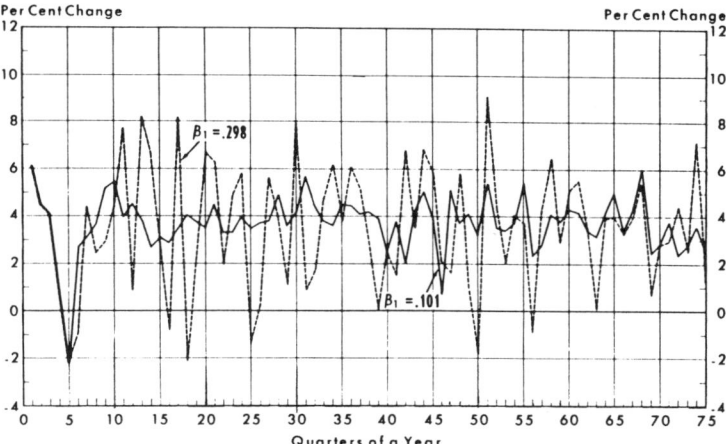

CHART 14. Japan: Shocked simulation of real product with alternative monetary policies (β_1).

62. Adelman and Adelman, *Readings in Business Cycles*, p. 252.

D. CONCLUSION

The Japanese business cycle can be understood reasonably well on the basis of the highly simplified model developed in this study. This model, as with any economic model, is useful only to the extent that its underlying assumptions remain valid. The statements that monetary policy is a function of fluctuations in international reserves and that changes in international reserves are a function of changes in imports are special assumptions which may not be applicable in the future.

The relatively stable international economic environment of post–World War II has led to the dismantling of exchange controls and steady expansion in world trade. In the short run each country's exports are largely a function of the growth and stability of world trade, so it is not unreasonable to attribute fluctuations in Japan's international reserves primarily to domestic factors. A useful direction for future research would be to see whether this same phenomenon can be observed in other countries. If it holds reasonably well, this model may have wider implications for analyzing business-cycle developments in other countries.[63]

The major conclusion of this study is that given the assumptions made, monetary policy directed at reducing fluctuation in international reserves will not only lead to greater fluctuations in income but also to greater fluctuations in international reserves. An important consideration in future research would be to see if alternative monetary policy targets, such as stable prices or reduced unemployment, led to the same results. The basic structural model underlying these alternative policy goals is similar to the one constructed in this study.

Consider the price stability target($\dot{P}_t$). The model could be as follows:

$$\dot{Y}_t = \alpha_0 + \alpha_1 \dot{M}_{t-m},$$

$$\dot{M}_t = \lambda_0 + \lambda_1 \dot{P}_{t-p},$$

$$\dot{P}_t = \delta_0 + \delta_1 \dot{Y}_{t-r}.$$

The reduced form of this series of equations is

$$\dot{Y}_t = A_0' + A_1' \dot{Y}_{t-(m+p+r)},$$

where $\dot{P}$ = rate of change in prices, and where $A_1' = \alpha_1 \lambda_1 \delta_1$.

63. There is some evidence to indicate that a model similar to that developed in this study could explain much of the postwar business cycle experience of the major western European countries. See Federal Reserve Bank of St. Louis, *Review*, November 1967, "Monetary Policy, Balance of Payments, and Business Cycles—The Foreign Experience," by Michael Keran.

A'_1 is negative because λ_1 is negative.

Consider the unemployment target (U_t):

$$\dot{Y}_t = \alpha_0 + \alpha_1 \dot{M}_{t-m},$$

$$\dot{M}_t = \theta_0 + \theta_1 U_{t-s},$$

$$U_t = \phi_0 + \phi_1 \dot{Y}_{t-v}.$$

The reduced form is:

$$\dot{Y}_t = A''_0 + A''_1 \dot{Y}_{t-(m+s+v)},$$

where U is the unemployment rate and $A''_1 = \alpha_1 \theta_1 \phi_1$. A''_1 is negative because ϕ_1 is negative.

The difference equations developed with respect to the price and unemployment targets are mathematically equivalent to the one developed in this study with respect to the international reserve target. And in each case there is a built-in cyclical bias in the application of monetary policy. Whether this bias is significant depends on how sensitive the policy-makers are to these various policy goals. If their response is relatively prompt, that is, the time lags are short, and if the response is relatively moderate, the value A_1 being closer to 0 than to -1, then cyclical bias may not be significant. Further research could usefully explore these issues.

Is it inevitable that monetary policy have a bias toward cyclical instability irrespective of the policy target chosen? There is one policy target which does not have the cyclical bias; that is, a policy of maintaining a steady growth in the stock of money.

APPENDIX

KEY

(Billions of Yen)

		Source
Y	Nominal GNP	(1)
Y^*	Real GNP	(2)
M	Nominal money supply	(2)
M^*	Real money supply	(2)
R	Nominal international reserves	(3)
R^*	Real international reserves	(3)
Im	Nominal imports (millions of U.S. \$)	(2)
Im^*	Real imports (millions of U.S. \$)	(2)
X	Industrial production (1960 = 100)	(2)
$\dot{X}$	Rate of change in series	

SOURCES:

1. *Annual Report on National Income Statistics*, 1967. Economic Planning Agency, Government of Japan.

2. *Basic Data For Economic Analysis, 1966*. Statistics Dept., Bank of Japan.

3. *Economic Statistics Monthly* (various issues). Statistics Dept., Bank of Japan.

TABLE 8

NOMINAL LEVELS
(Billions of Yen)

Year	Quarter	Y	M	R	Im (Millions of U.S. Dollars)
1953.........	I	6,403	1,525	332	521
	II	6,787	1,548	303	566
	III	7,357	1,657	317	640
	IV	7,276	1,661	285	698
1954.........	I	7,817	1,668	202	692
	II	7,943	1,656	173	633
	III	7,700	1,664	188	534
	IV	7,714	1,704	252	519
1955.........	I	7,956	1,735	276	556
	II	7,866	1,768	307	596
	III	8,719	1,845	358	624
	IV	9,400	1,894	411	698
1956.........	I	9,114	1,967	446	672
	II	9,225	2,070	455	752
	III	9,346	2,212	457	856
	IV	10,229	2,275	458	959
1957.........	I	10,701	2,373	382	1,056
	II	11,286	2,382	259	1,196
	III	11,076	2,346	197	1,090
	IV	11,212	2,394	226	914
1958.........	I	11,156	2,421	268	811
	II	11,219	2,488	301	730
	III	11,601	2,593	358	735
	IV	11,298	2,702	427	761
1959.........	I	11,905	2,764	462	789
	II	12,290	2,892	509	895
	III	13,292	2,990	550	912
	IV	13,462	3,124	600	1,003
1960.........	I	14,334	3,266	613	1,109
	II	14,852	3,370	649	1,063
	III	15,364	3,531	729	1,143
	IV	16,047	3,741	788	1,164
1961.........	I	17,311	4,010	851	1,292
	II	18,053	4,296	819	1,405
	III	18,711	4,414	728	1,529
	IV	19,810	4,491	641	1,595
1962.........	I	20,320	4,531	629	1,492
	II	20,867	4,652	562	1,406
	III	20,582	4,852	595	1,367
	IV	21,549	5,160	673	1,374

continued overleaf

Monetary Policy and Business Cycle in Postwar Japan   237

TABLE 8—Continued

1963.........	I	21,616	5,764	730	1,484
	II	22,953	6,305	759	1,622
	III	24,586	6,714	763	1,756
	IV	24,990	7,055	746	1,872
1964.........	I	26,128	7,214	727	1,989
	II	26,982	7,462	666	1,965
	III	28,340	7,716	662	1,929
	IV	28,944	7,980	714	2,044
1965.........	I	29,264	8,367	732	1,993
	II	30,209	8,605	701	2,060
	III	30,537	9,000	693	2,067
	IV	31,699	9,435	737	2,062
1966.........	I	32,738	9,760	738	2,232
	II	34,204	10,091	724	2,285
	III	35,909	10,569	694	2,431
	IV	36,909	10,773	700	2,592

TABLE 9

REAL LEVELS
(Billions of 1960 Yen)

Year	Quarter	Y^*	M^*	R^*	Im^* (Millions of U.S. Dollars)	X (1960 = 100)
1953....	I	7,902	1,960	264.8	415.5	36.3
	II	8,170	1,845	260.7	455.3	39.8
	III	8,534	1,933	256.7	521.6	41.5
	IV	8,464	1,881	214.6	580.7	43.6
1954....	I	9,011	1,986	171.0	585.9	44.2
	II	8,880	1,840	164.7	534.6	44.2
	III	8,700	1,895	199.7	453.7	42.9
	IV	8,558	1,850	235.0	437.2	43.5
1955....	I	9,006	2,034	256.9	465.3	44.8
	II	8,970	1,998	292.9	501.7	45.6
	III	9,818	2,094	333.6	520.4	47.8
	IV	10,544	2,068	375.3	590.0	49.8
1956....	I	10,117	2,264	396.6	571.9	51.9
	II	10,251	2,292	396.5	633.0	55.8
	III	10,226	2,436	399.3	724.2	59.5
	IV	10,964	2,380	357.2	789.3	62.8
1957....	I	11,329	2,591	265.4	854.4	65.0
	II	11,772	2,476	194.4	985.2	70.1
	III	11,556	2,457	185.8	920.6	69.5
	IV	11,724	2,455	224.1	803.2	67.3
1958....	I	11,826	2,634	267.4	742.7	66.7
	II	11,885	2,638	319.7	692.6	64.8
	III	12,313	2,779	383.5	704.7	66.3
	IV	11,908	2,791	443.1	746.1	69.0
1959....	I	12,470	2,947	489.1	782.7	72.6
	II	12,876	3,038	528.0	880.0	77.7
	III	13,726	3,118	574.4	898.5	82.3
	IV	13,781	3,140	595.4	971.0	88.1
1960....	I	14,613	3,370	575.0	1,080.9	92.5
	II	14,823	3,377	639.1	1,048.3	97.8
	III	15,258	3,542	718.7	1,144.1	101.9
	IV	16,245	3,646	786.1	1,174.0	106.9
1961....	I	16,962	3,939	795.0	1,292.0	111.9
	II	17,401	4,139	718.6	1,377.5	116.7
	III	17,706	4,216	631.4	1,499.0	122.7
	IV	18,388	4,124	590.5	1,585.5	127.1
1962....	I	18,613	4,161	557.9	1,502.5	129.8
	II	19,059	4,252	546.8	1,431.8	130.2
	III	18,583	4,435	608.2	1,402.1	129.0
	IV	19,552	4,632	680.0	1,413.6	128.4

continued overleaf

TABLE 9—*Continued*

1963....	I	18,891	5,021	714.7	1,506.6	131.9
	II	19,932	5,473	721.7	1,623.6	138.0
	III	21,242	5,874	704.4	1,730.0	146.1
	IV	21,513	6,014	672.8	1,806.9	153.7
1964....	I	22,471	6,198	632.9	1,916.2	158.9
	II	22,942	6,361	608.8	1,917.1	165.0
	III	23,755	6,572	635.9	1,893.0	168.8
	IV	23,726	6,488	672.2	2,011.8	173.2
1965....	I	23,825	6,769	679.4	2,003.6	174.6
	II	24,269	6,928	656.7	2,062.1	173.5
	III	24,210	7,252	672.7	2,062.9	174.8
	IV	24,498	7,247	697.7	2,064.1	175.5
1966....	I	25,612	7,578	680.8	2,199.0	182.4
	II	26,384	7,823	655.2	2,238.0	189.5
	III	27,402	8,231	642.9	2,378.7	199.1
	IV	27,993	7,945	647.0	2,589.4	209.6

TABLE 10

NOMINAL RATES OF CHANGE

Year	Quarter	$\dot{Y}$	$\dot{M}$	$\dot{R}$	$\dot{i}m$
1953.......	I				
	II	7.2	4.2	−2.4	7.2
	III	3.5	3.6	−2.8	10.8
	IV	3.1	.4	−18.1	7.3
1954.......	I	4.5	−.4	−21.7	−4.3
	II	−.7	−.3	−3.5	−14.5
	III	−1.5	1.9	20.5	−9.2
	IV	1.7	2.3	18.7	4.5
1955.......	I	1.0	1.4	10.0	7.3
	II	4.7	2.9	13.4	4.3
	III	9.3	3.9	14.9	8.4
	IV	2.2	3.6	11.0	5.5
1956.......	I	−.9	4.2	5.0	3.9
	II	1.3	5.7	1.1	12.1
	III	5.3	5.2	.2	12.9
	IV	7.0	3.9	−8.1	10.7
1957.......	I	5.0	2.0	−24.4	11.8
	II	1.7	−.8	−28.0	2.9
	III	−.3	.6	−6.8	−12.3
	IV	.4	1.8	15.9	−14.9
1958.......	I	0	1.6	14.5	−10.7
	II	2.0	3.3	15.4	−2.9
	III	.4	4.5	18.7	1.9
	IV	1.3	3.4	13.0	2.1
1959.......	I	4.3	3.3	9.1	9.1
	II	5.7	3.9	8.9	8.7
	III	4.7	4.0	8.6	5.8
	IV	3.9	4.6	5.5	10.2
1960.......	I	5.0	4.0	−4.1	3.1
	II	3.5	4.0	9.8	1.6
	III	4.0	5.1	10.8	5.1
	IV	6.4	6.5	8.5	6.0
1961.......	I	6.1	7.6	2.1	9.3
	II	3.7	5.0	−7.8	8.9
	III	4.8	1.7	−12.1	7.4
	IV	4.2	1.2	−7.8	−1.1
1962.......	I	2.6	2.4	−6.7	−7.0
	II	.7	3.6	−3.1	−4.6
	III	1.6	4.6	10.4	.2
	IV	2.5	8.9	11.5	4.3
1963.......	I	3.2	11.2	6.5	7.6
	II	6.7	8.0	2.4	8.3
	III	4.4	5.2	−.8	9.2
	IV	3.1	3.6	−2.5	7.5

continued overleaf

Monetary Policy and Business Cycle in Postwar Japan   *241*

TABLE 10—*Continued*

1964.......	I	3.9	3.3	−5.7	1.0
	II	4.2	3.4	−5.0	−2.5
	III	3.6	3.1	2.2	3.4
	IV	1.6	4.1	5.5	2.3
1965.......	I	2.2	4.1	−1.0	−.5
	II	2.2	3.8	−2.9	−.8
	III	2.4	4.6	2.7	4.0
	IV	3.5	4.1	3.4	5.4
1966.......	I	4.0	3.5	− .9	4.4
	II	4.8	4.1	−3.2	6.5
	III	4.0	3.4	−1.8	6.7
	IV				

TABLE 11

REAL RATES OF CHANGE

Year	Quarter	$\dot{Y}\bullet$	$\dot{M}\bullet$	$\dot{R}\bullet$	$\dot{i}m\bullet$	$\dot{X}$
1953....	I					
	II	3.9	2.0	−1.6	12.2	6.1
	III	1.8	.6	−1.5	13.0	4.5
	IV	2.8	−2.0	−16.4	6.0	4.1
1954....	I	2.4	−1.3	−20.3	−4.1	.9
	II	−1.7	−.6	−3.7	−12.0	−2.2
	III	−1.8	1.6	21.3	−9.5	.8
	IV	1.7	2.7	17.7	1.2	2.9
1955....	I	2.4	2.2	9.3	7.2	4.6
	II	4.4	3.4	14.0	5.8	3.0
	III	8.4	3.8	13.9	8.4	4.3
	IV	1.5	3.3	12.5	4.9	5.1
1956....	I	−1.4	4.0	5.7	3.6	6.1
	II	.5	5.8	0	12.5	6.2
	III	3.4	4.7	.7	11.7	5.8
	IV	5.3	2.5	−10.6	8.6	4.6
1957....	I	3.6	1.0	−25.7	11.7	6.2
	II	1.0	−1.7	−26.8	3.9	3.6
	III	−.2	.3	−4.4	−9.7	−2.4
	IV	1.2	2.6	20.6	−10.2	−2.2
1958....	I	.7	2.4	19.3	−7.1	−1.5
	II	2.0	3.2	19.6	−2.6	−.2
	III	.1	3.8	20.0	3.8	2.9
	IV	.6	3.3	15.5	5.4	4.5
1959....	I	4.0	3.5	10.4	8.6	6.4
	II	4.9	3.4	8.0	7.2	6.6
	III	3.5	3.0	8.8	5.0	6.3
	IV	3.2	3.4	3.7	9.7	6.5
1960....	I	3.7	2.9	−3.4	3.9	5.6
	II	2.2	3.1	11.1	2.9	4.5
	III	4.7	4.7	12.5	5.9	4.5
	IV	5.4	5.4	9.4	6.3	4.6
1961....	I	3.5	5.9	1.1	8.3	4.6
	II	2.2	3.3	−9.6	7.7	5.0
	III	2.8	−.6	−12.1	7.3	4.3
	IV	2.5	−.9	−6.5	.1	2.7
1962....	I	1.8	−.3	−5.5	−4.9	1.3
	II	−.1	2.3	−2.0	−3.4	−.1
	III	1.3	5.2	11.2	−.6	−.7
	IV	.8	6.6	11.8	3.7	.9
1963....	I	1.0	7.6	5.1	7.2	3.6
	II	6.0	6.1	1.0	7.2	5.7
	III	3.9	5.0	−2.4	5.5	5.7
	IV	2.9	3.7	−4.5	5.2	4.4

continued overleaf

TABLE 11—*Continued*

1964....	I	3.3	2.1	−5.9	3.0	3.6
	II	2.8	1.8	−3.8	−.6	3.4
	III	1.7	1.5	4.5	2.5	2.3
	IV	.2	1.8	5.7	2.9	.8
1965....	I	1.1	1.8	1.1	1.2	−.5
	II	.8	2.4	−3.4	1.5	.3
	III	.5	3.2	2.4	.1	.5
	IV	2.9	2.4	3.7	3.3	1.9
1966....	I	3.8	2.3	−2.4	4.1	4.0
	II	3.5	3.2	−3.8	4.0	5.0
	III	3.0	2.4	−1.9	7.6	5.1
	IV					

Varieties of Monetary Experience

TABLE 12
RATIOS AND RATES OF CHANGE

Year	Quarter	D/C	(D/̇C)	D/R	(D/̇R)
1954.......	I	2.275		21.8	
	II	2.307	1.3	20.6	−2.1
	III	2.335	2.3	20.9	6.6
	IV	2.414	2.6	23.4	−.2
1955.......	I	2.460	2.4	20.8	−4.6
	II	2.532	2.6	21.3	2.8
	III	2.587	2.1	22.0	2.1
	IV	2.639	2.3	22.2	.5
1956.......	I	2.707	2.8	22.2	1.3
	II	2.789	2.9	22.8	.9
	III	2.864	1.7	22.6	−2.0
	IV	2.887	.2	21.9	−1.6
1957.......	I	2.877	−.6	21.9	−3.2
	II	2.854	−1.3	20.5	−7.3
	III	2.800	−.2	18.8	−5.0
	IV	2.843	1.7	18.5	−1.9
1958.......	I	2.897	1.9	18.1	−1.1
	II	2.953	2.3	18.1	1.1
	III	3.030	2.7	18.5	4.1
	IV	3.117	.7	19.6	−.8
1959.......	I	3.072	0	18.2	−2.8
	II	3.116	.4	18.5	−.8
	III	3.095	−.4	17.9	−1.6
	IV	3.089	.9	17.9	−.3
1960.......	I	3.151	.6	17.8	−2.8
	II	3.125	−.2	16.9	−1.4
	III	3.139	.7	17.3	−.6
	IV	3.170	1.1	16.7	−1.2
1961.......	I	3.211	1.4	16.9	3.5
	II	3.260	−.3	17.9	−1.8
	III	3.194	−2.0	16.3	−4.3
	IV	3.134	−2.8	16.4	−3.4
1962.......	I	3.017	−2.2	15.2	−3.4
	II	2.997	0	15.3	.7
	III	3.016	2.5	15.4	0
	IV	3.148	7.0	15.3	2.9
1963.......	I	3.453	7.8	16.3	4.2
	II	3.659	6.1	16.6	1.2
	III	3.889	3.4	16.7	0
	IV	3.913	−.1	16.6	−2.7

continued overleaf

TABLE 12—*Continued*

1964	I	3.878	−1.4	15.8	−.9
	II	3.807	−1.0	16.3	1.0
	III	3.799	−.1	16.1	−.3
	IV	3.797	−.1	16.2	3.7
1965	I	3.790	.5	17.3	3.0
	II	3.838	1.3	17.2	2.3
	III	3.890	1.8	18.1	5.7
	IV	3.975	.6	19.2	1.1
1966	I	3.934	−.1	18.5	−1.0
	II	3.965	.4	18.8	3.2
	III	3.968	−.1	19.7	1.1
	IV	3.955		19.2	

References

Cagan, P. *Determinants and Effects of Changes in the Stock of Money, 1875–1960*. New York: National Bureau of Economic Research, 1963.

———. "The Economics of Hyperinflation." In *Studies in the Quantity Theory of Money*, ed. Milton Friedman. Chicago: Univ. of Chicago Press, 1956.

Frisch, R. "Propagation Problems and Impulse Problems in Dynamic Economics." In *Economic Essays in Honor of Gustav Cassel*. London, 1933. Reprinted in *Readings in Business Cycles*. Homewood, Ill.: Richard D. Irwin, 1965.

Metzler, Lloyd A. "The Nature and Stability of Inventory Cycles." *Review of Economic Statistics* vol. 23 (1941). Reprinted in *Readings in Business Cycles*. Homewood, Ill.: Richard D. Irwin, 1965.

———. "Three Lags in a Circular Flow of Income," *Income, Employment, and Public Policy: Essays in Honor of Alvin Hansen*. New York: W. H. Norton Co., 1948.

Polak, J. J. "Monetary Analysis of Income Formation and Payments Problems." International Monetary Fund, *Staff Papers* vol. 6, no. 1 (1957).

———. "Monetary Analysis of Income and Imports and Its Statistical Application." International Monetary Fund, *Staff Papers* vol. 7, no. 3 (1960).

Samuelson, P. "Interactions between Multiplier Analysis and Principle of Acceleration." *Review of Economic Statistics* 21 (1939). Reprinted in *Readings in Business Cycle Theory*. American Economic Association, 1944.

[6]

International Differences in Liquid Assets Portfolios

THERE are large differences among countries both in the holdings of liquid assets by the nonbanking sector of the economy and in the allocation among these assets. This study attempts to explain these differences with the use of the tools of monetary theory which have been developed over the last decade or so. In this period monetary theory has tended to move away from an "institutional" approach to a capital theory approach, concentrating more on the holding of money as an asset and less on its function as a medium of exchange;[1] this development increases its usefulness for the present study which by its nature has to deal with diverse institutional structures. The results of the study indicate that the differences among countries in liquid asset portfolios can be explained by the use of those variables entering into a capital theory model of the demand for assets and, what is more striking, that the actual coefficients of the explanatory variables are within a plausible range of those found in national time series studies.

Section 1 of this paper illustrates the magnitude of the differences among forty-seven countries in the holdings of liquid assets by the nonbanking sector of the economy and the allocation of these assets among alternative types. Section 2 presents the theoretical framework used to explain these differences. Sections 3 and 4 present the empirical findings, and Section 5 the summary and conclusions of the study.

1. DIFFERENCES AMONG THE COUNTRIES IN LIQUID ASSET HOLDINGS

The forty-seven countries included in this study represent all the major regions of the world except the communist bloc and Africa (the

This paper is a revised version of my "International Differences in Liquid Assets Portfolios" (unpublished doctoral dissertation, University of Chicago, 1966). I am greatly indebted to Professor Milton Friedman for his helpful suggestions and encouragement during the course of this study.

1. See for example Harry G. Johnson, "Monetary Theory and Policy," *American Economic Review*, vol. 52 (1962).

United Arab Republic is the only African country included, and is classified under "Asia" in the regional classification). The range of social, economic, and institutional characteristics covered by this sample of countries is very great; from a real per capita income of $50 a year in Burma to one of $2,200 a year in the United States; from an average rate of inflation of nearly 70 per cent per year in Korea (1948–56) to a zero rate of inflation in Portugal (1948–56); from a proportion of the population living in cities of over 20,000 people of 70 per cent New Zealand to one of only 8 per cent in Thailand. The number of financial institutions supplying the assets and their characteristics also vary greatly among the countries. In Burma there is approximately one bank office for every half a million people, in Australia one for every two thousand. Besides banks (commercial, savings, cooperatives, and many others) twenty-one countries have widespread post office savings systems and eleven countries have post office giro systems.[2] Table 1 presents the forty-seven countries classified into four regional groups, Europe, Asia, Latin America, and Others, with some of the economic and institutional characteristics of the groups.

Three liquid assets—currency, demand deposits, and time and savings deposits—held by the private nonbanking sector of the economy and the currency-deposits ratio are examined in this study. The quantities of the assets for each of the years 1952–61 were expressed in terms of the number of weeks of income held, and averaged over two five-year periods (1952–56, 1957–61).[3] Expressing the assets in terms of income serves two purposes: it converts the assets into real terms, and it allows an international comparison of quantities. The averaging tends to eliminate short-term cyclical distortions. In final form, the dependent variables are the average number of weeks of income held in the form of a particular asset. There are two observations for all but two countries and one observation for each of these.[4] All deposits except those

---

2. A post office giro system provides facilities for the transfer of accounts among individuals by use of "giro transfer" orders. These differ form checks only in that it is the payer, not the payee, who executes the transfer either with cash or from his giro account (only the payee needs to have an account). See for example John Hein, "A Note on the Giro Transfer System," *Journal of Finance*, vol. 19 (1959).

3. For the sources of the data see appendix B. For some countries data were not available for a full five-year period, so the averaging was done over the number of years for which data were available. Each observation is an average of at least two years.

4. Indonesia and El Salvador.

International Differences in Liquid Assets Portfolios   301

TABLE 1

REGIONAL CLASSIFICATION OF COUNTRIES AND SOME GROUP
CHARACTERISTICS

	Europe	Others**	Asia	Latin America
	Austria Belgium Denmark Finland France Germany Greece Italy Netherlands Norway Portugal Spain Sweden	Australia Canada Ireland Israel Japan New Zealand United Kingdom United States	Burma Ceylon India Indonesia Korea Malaya Pakistan Philippines Taiwan Thailand Turkey U.A.R.	Argentina Brazil Chile Colombia Costa Rica Ecuador El Salvador Guatemala Honduras Mexico Nicaragua Paraguay Peru Venezuela
No. of countries........	13	8	12	14
Av.* per capita income (in dollars).........	768.4	1154.7	109.0	218.8
Av.* Rate of inflation...	4%	5%	7%	10%
Av.* Urbanization......	.373	.531	.153	.242

* For a description of these variables and their derivation see section 4.

** Japan and Israel are included in this group because most of their economic and institutional characteristics are much more similar to those of the countries in this group than to the countries in the Asian group.

tied to a price index or an exchange rate[5] are included, whether held in commercial banks, savings banks, credit cooperatives, or post offices.

One of the problems in comparing differences among the countries in the holdings of deposits is the arbitrary nature of the distinction between demand, time, and savings deposits.[6] In the United States demand deposits are identical to checking deposits, but in many countries all deposits withdrawable on demand are included among

5. The reason for the exclusion of these deposits is that to the holder they are real assets, in terms of the domestic price level, either on a continuous basis for the index-tied deposits or with a lag for the others, depending on the lag between changes in the price level and changes in the exchange rate; as such they are basically different from all the other assets included in this study.

6. In the January 1960 issue of *International Financial Statistics*, the IMF defines deposit money—what I consider as demand deposits—as "deposits unrestrictedly exchangeable on demand into currency at par without penalty." However, in the following paragraph it has this qualification: "It is the way that deposits are regarded by the holders that ultimately determines the boundary between money and quasi money," and presumably the IMF includes among demand deposits what the compiler of the data thinks that the holder regards as money.

The Legacy of Milton Friedman as Teacher II

Varieties of Monetary Experience

demand deposits, whereas in Canada some deposits which are transferable by check are included in time deposits. In the United States time deposits are withdrawable on demand (in practice); in many countries they have to be held for a specific period of time (usually three months to a year) and can only be withdrawn either with prior notice or not at all before the contracted time elapses. Because of the above considerations the same name does not necessarily imply the same asset and total deposits may be a more homogeneous concept for the purpose of international comparisons than the subtotals of the various kinds of deposits.

The four bar charts (1–4) show the distribution of the countries by their holdings of individual assets and by their currency-deposits ratio. Each period average is counted separately so that each country enters twice, except for the two countries for which data for only one period were available. The four regions are combined into two groups: (1) Asia and Latin America, and (2) Europe and Others. The number of observations is measured on the vertical axis, and the quantity of the assets (in weeks of income), or the currency-deposits ratio, on the horizontal axis. The width of each bar is one-half a standard deviation. The vertical line in the center of each chart passes through the mean of each group (the means of the regions within each group are indicated by the lines marked A, E, L, O). In each bar the number of observations from each region is shown. The countries making up some of the extreme observations are also shown.

These charts clearly show the large differences among the countries in liquid asset holdings and in the currency-deposits ratio. The range of currency holdings is over twelve weeks of income, of deposits over fifty weeks, and of currency plus deposits over fifty-two weeks. The highest currency-deposits ratio is nearly thirty times the lowest.[7] The differ-

7. As can be seen from charts 2 and 4, the range is greatly affected by the first-period observations of Greece in the Europe and Others group and Indonesia in the Asia and Latin America group. There is some justification in excluding Greece (1952–56) and Indonesia (1952–56) from the sample. Greece did not attain political stability after World War II until 1950, with the intervening years marked by great instability due to the civil war. Under such conditions the risk associated with the holdings of deposits is very great and it may take some time to restore confidence in this form of holding wealth. Some evidence for this is the change of deposits between the first and second period—a change of over 200 per cent. This is by far the largest change from period to period in the holdings of any asset of any country in the sample. A similar argument applies to Indonesia and Korea. For these reasons the first-period observations of Greece, Korea, and Indonesia were excluded in the regression analysis of section 3.

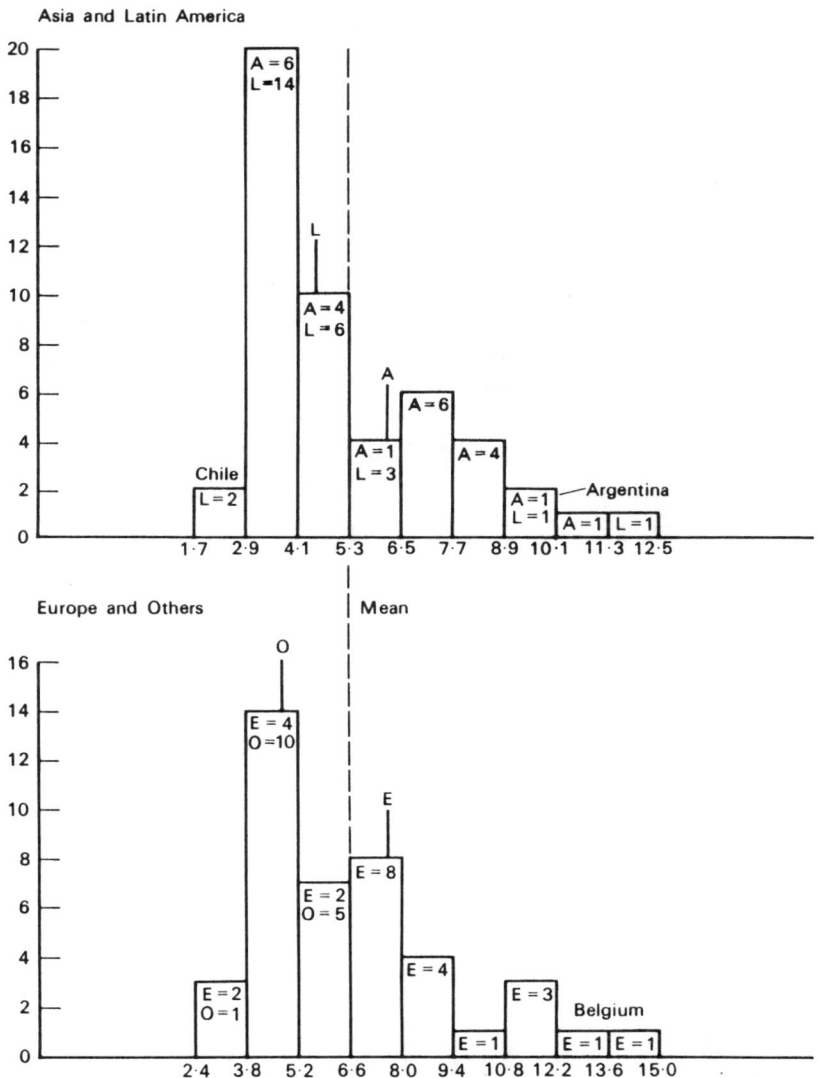

CHART 1. Distribution of countries by holdings of currency

304   *Varieties of Monetary Experience*

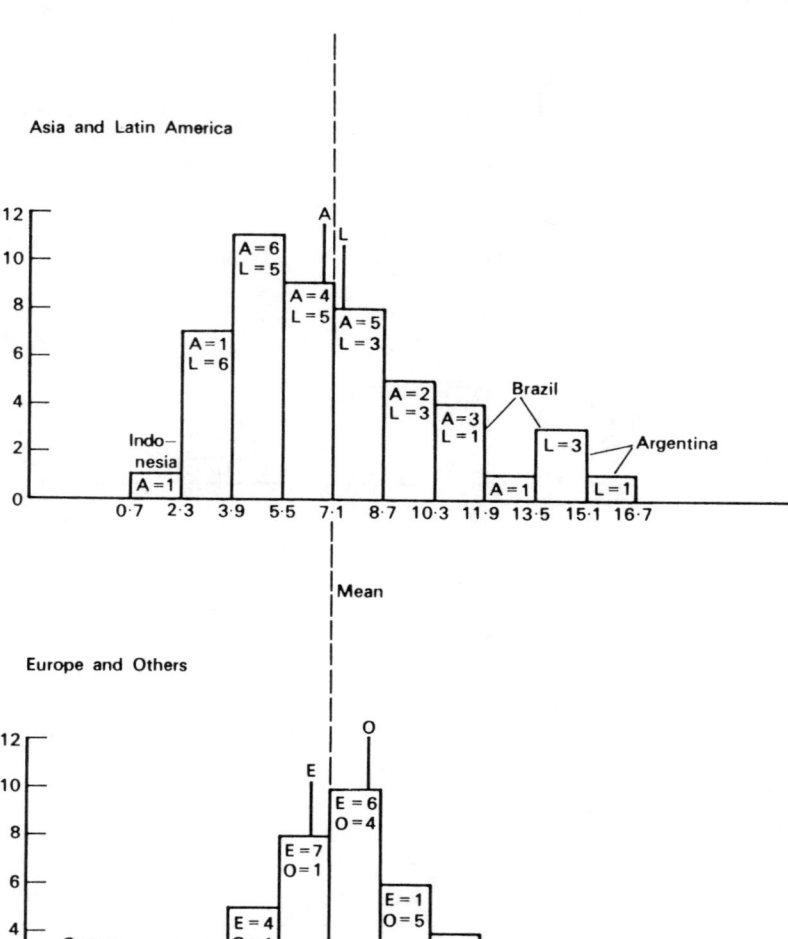

CHART 2. Distribution of countries by holdings of deposits

ences are both intraregional and interregional. Both charts 1 and 4 show a clear dichotomy between Asia and Latin America, and between Europe and Others in currency holdings, and in the currency-deposits ratio. This dichotomy is much more blurred in charts 2 and 3 and no definite regional pattern emerges.

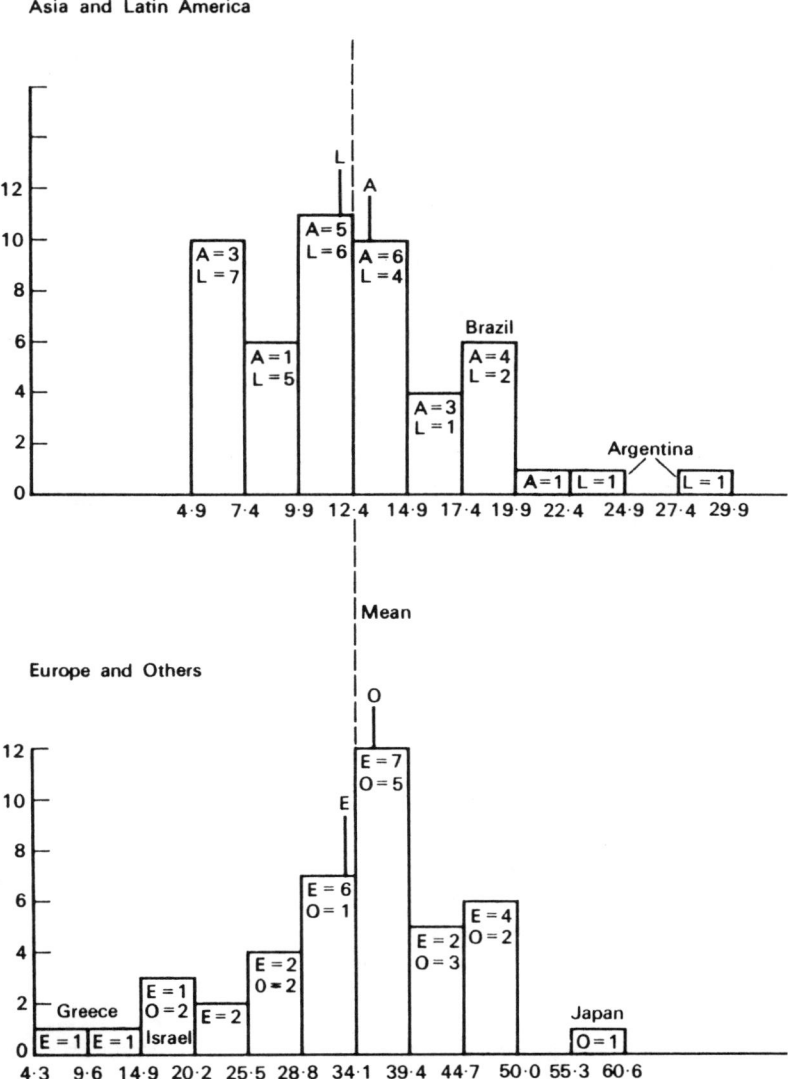

CHART 3. Distribution of countries by holdings of currency and deposits

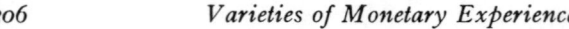

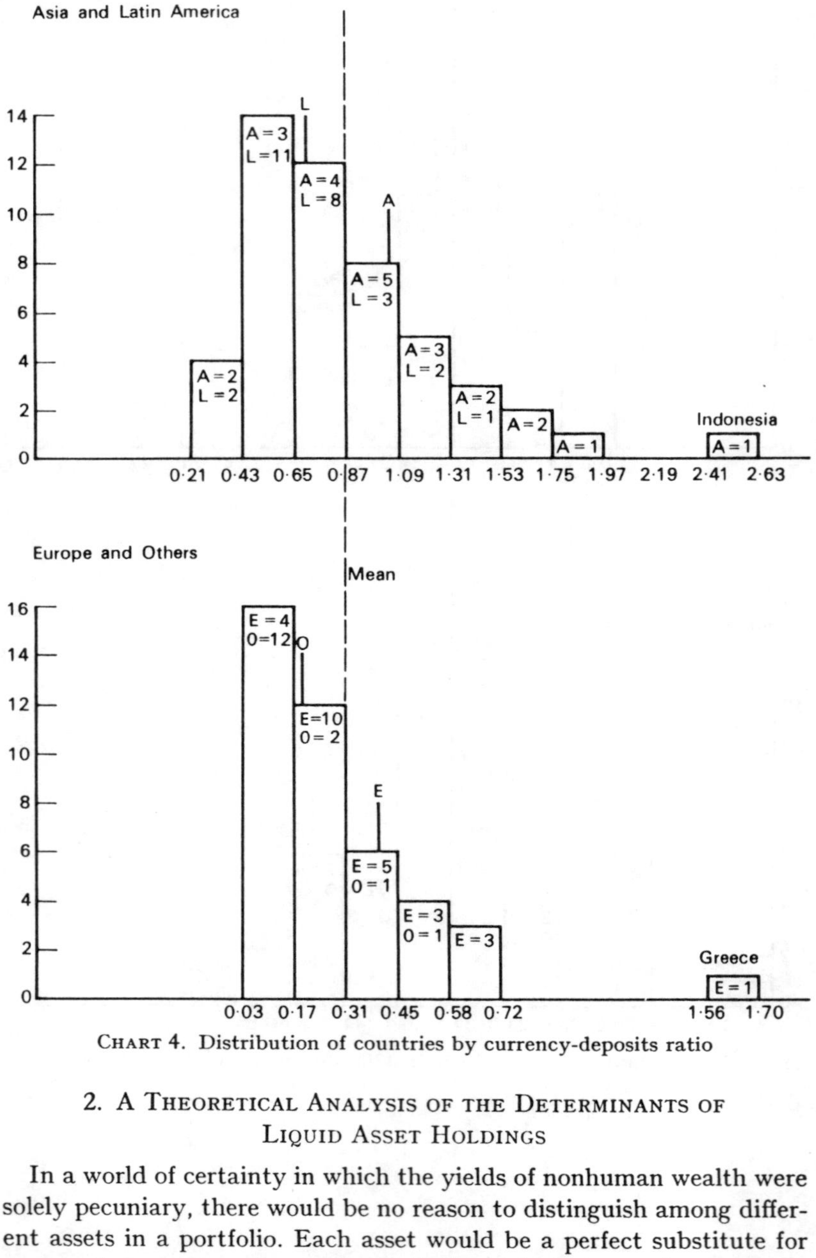

CHART 4. Distribution of countries by currency-deposits ratio

2. A THEORETICAL ANALYSIS OF THE DETERMINANTS OF LIQUID ASSET HOLDINGS

In a world of certainty in which the yields of nonhuman wealth were solely pecuniary, there would be no reason to distinguish among different assets in a portfolio. Each asset would be a perfect substitute for every other asset so the whole portfolio could be treated as a single asset. If the yield of each asset were both pecuniary and nonpecuniary (convenience, security, "liquidity," and other services), there would be a difference between assets producing different combinations of pecuniary and nonpecuniary returns or providing different types of services. As with other services treated in value theory, one would expect diminishing rates of substitution (convex indifference curves) among the services yielded by the assets.

By treating the "liquid" assets as capital goods yielding streams of services, and postulating that people hold these assets for the purpose of acquiring their services, one can describe a very general demand function for an asset,

$$Q_i = f(P_i, P_o, Y, k_i, u)$$

where Q_i is the quantity of the asset measured in real terms, P_i is the price of holding wealth in the form of the ith asset (this price, which would measure the alternative cost of acquiring the services yielded by the asset, would be the difference between the interest yield of this asset and the yield on real capital which does not yield any service stream); P_o is the price or prices of related goods and services, Y represents the budget constraint variables measured in real terms (the exact form these should take is left unspecified for the moment); k_i represents some index of the type and quantity of the services yielded by the asset, to convert the stock of the asset Q_i into the relevant quantity units—the flow of services; and u represents all those variables which may affect the demand for the asset via tastes and preferences, which for the most part will be assumed constant.

If more than one asset is included in Q_i, for example, currency as well as demand deposits, I treat Q_i as a composite good and therefore assume throughout the analysis that the relative prices of the assets within the composite do not change. P_i is now a weighted average of the prices of the assets included in Q_i, and the assumption of proportional price changes among the assets in Q_i is required so that changes in P_i should not result in any substitution among the assets in Q_i. The ratio of two assets (for example, the currency-deposit ratio), each of which has a demand function of the general form described above, will be a function of the variables which enter the individual demand functions; for example,

$$\frac{Q_i}{Q_j} = f(P_i, P_j, P_o, Y, k_i, k_j, u),$$

where P_o now represents the prices of goods and services related to the services yielded by either asset i or j.

Most earlier studies of the demand for assets have used a general function of the above form except that they have not included the set of variables which represents the type or quality of the services yielded by the assets,[8] a set of variables especially relevant to our immediate problem. As most of the earlier studies have used time series, or cross-section data, for subsections of a single country, they have been able to assume that the quality variables, k_i and k_j, are constant; so that changes in the quantity of the assets also measure changes in the quantity of the services of the assets. For the present study, which uses data for countries which vary widely, this assumption is not very appealing and it is pertinent to pay specific attention to variables which reflect differences in the type or quality of the assets. Hence the rest of this section will extend the demand model described above to incorporate specifically the effects of quality variables.

The quality of services yielded by an asset depends both on the specific services provided by the individual suppliers of the assets and on the general economic environment in which the service is used. A quality difference on the supply side would occur, for example, if banks in some countries allowed checks to be written on time deposits or waived the notice requirement on time deposits. An example of an environmental difference would be a difference in the acceptability of checks, which in turn might be the result of such factors as the legal structure of a country or the degree of urbanization. If urbanization involves a greater amount of transactions among strangers, it may lead to checks being less generally acceptable and thus decrease the services provided by a checking account. Another set of variables can be treated as affecting either the quality or the price of the services yielded by an asset. A reduction of the distance between an individual and a bank

---

8. One specific example of such a general function, and the one used as a starting point for this section, is Friedman's demand function for money,

$$\frac{M}{P} = f\left(r_b, \, r_e, \, \frac{1}{p}\frac{dp}{dt}; \, w; \, \frac{Y}{P}; \, u\right),$$

in M. Friedman, "The Quantity Theory of Money: A Restatement," in M. Friedman, ed., *Studies in the Quantity Theory of Money* (Chicago: Univ. of Chicago Press, 1956). In the above function, r_b and r_e are rates of interest on bonds and equities respectively, and $(1/p)(dp/dt)$ is the rate of change of prices. These are the price variables. w is the ratio of human to nonhuman income, which takes human wealth into account. Y/P is real income, the budget constraint variable. u stands for the quantifiable "objective" variables which may be expected to affect the tastes and preferences of individuals, and M/P is the real quantity of money demanded.

office can be viewed as either increasing the quality of a time deposit because it is now easier to use as a medium to exchange and thus yields more "liquidity" services, or as decreasing the price of the service stream yielded by the time deposit because transaction costs have been reduced.

Quality variables of the above kind should be distinguished from variables which reflect or produce changes in the tastes and preferences of individuals. For example, when individuals travel a great deal they may demand more money, not because money as such has changed in quality but because the individual has changed his behavior in the form of his increased desire or necessity to travel. It is the quality variables affecting the service stream of an asset that I want to incorporate into the demand model previously described.

The analysis will use the following symbols:

W = total nonhuman wealth in real terms,

Y_h = human income in real terms,

r_s = real rate of interest (the return to capital which has no service yield),

$Y = r_sW + Y_h$ = total real income,

$\overline{Y}$ = expenditures on all goods and services, other than liquidity services (defined as the services yielded by the assets considered in this study),

$A_i(i = 1, \ldots, n)$ = assets yielding liquidity services,

$Q_i(i = 1, \ldots, n)$ = the quantity of assets, measured in real terms, yielding liquidity services,

$r_i(i = 1, \ldots, n)$ = monetary yield per unit of A_i net of that part of the monetary yield that compensates for the expected rate of inflation,

$k_i(i = 1, \ldots, n)$ = service coefficient of $A_i \cdot k_i$ tells us what flow of services per unit time is yielded by a unit of A_i,

$S_i = k_iQ_i$ = flow of services yielded by Q_i per unit time,

P_i = price per unit of S_i.

On the assumption that the stocks are allocated to maximize the utility of the flows yielded by them, the relevant behavioral variables are the flow of goods and the flow of liquidity services.[9] To get the slope of the relevant price line we have to determine the price per unit of

9. "People have no direct preferences for assets, but only for things consumed." H. Makower and J. Marschak, "Assets, Prices, and Monetary Theory," in G. Stigler and K. E. Boulding, eds., *Readings in Price Theory* (London, 1960), p. 286.

liquidity services. The alternative opportunity cost of holding a unit of wealth in the form of A_l is $(r_s - r_l)\$1$, the difference between the real rate of interest and the rate of return on A_l. However, one unit of A_l yields k_i units of S_i. Therefore P_i, the price per unit of S_i, is $[(r_s - r_i)/k_i]\$1$. The price per unit of other goods is considered to be $\$1$; they are measured in units of income. The utility function to be maximized is $U(S_1 \cdots S_n, \overline{Y})$ subject to the constraint $\sum P_i S_i + \overline{Y} = Y$. Following usual procedures the equilibrium conditions are:

$$U_1 - \lambda \frac{r_s - r_1}{k_1} = 0$$
$$\vdots$$
$$U_n - \lambda \frac{r_s - r_n}{k_n} = 0$$
$$U_{\overline{Y}} - \lambda = 0$$

From the above we can determine the optimum allocation of income among the different types of liquidity services and goods. However, the observable variables are not the services but the assets which yield the services. Therefore we must examine the effect of changes in the independent variables in the model, r_s, r_i, k_i, Y, on the observable dependent variables, $Q_i, i = 1, \ldots$, the stocks, as they operate via the relevant unobservable variables, the flows.

Three cases will be examined: a change in income, a change in r_i, the monetary yield of A_i, and a change in k_i, the service coefficient of A_i.[10] I want to examine the effect of the above changes on the total stock of liquid assets $(\sum Q_i)$ and on the allocation among different assets (Q_i/Q_j). Because of the proportional relationship between the stocks of the assets and the flows of services $(S_i = k_i Q_i)$, any change in Q_i will be proportional to a change in S_i for given k_i. Therefore, when the change in price is due to a change in either the monetary yield of the asset or a change in the real rate of interest, income and price elasticities will be the same for the stocks and for the flows.

If neither goods nor liquidity services are inferior, an increase in income will increase the quantity demanded both of goods and of liquidity services. What happens to the ratio Q_i/Q_j depends on the income elasticities of the liquidity services:

$$d\left(\frac{Q_i}{Q_j}\right) \gtreqless 0 \quad \text{as} \quad \eta_{S_iY} \gtreqless \eta_{S_jY} \quad \text{or} \quad \eta_{Q_iY} \gtreqless \eta_{Q_jY}.$$

10. For example, an improvement in the services offered by banks to deposit holders, an increase in the general acceptability of checks, etc.

International Differences in Liquid Assets Portfolios   311

A change in r_i changes the relative price of liquidity services and other services and the relative price of S_i and S_j. Therefore, both $\sum Q_i$ and Q_i/Q_j will change. The magnitude of these changes will depend on the price elasticities of the various services or assets. Here again, as in the previous case, the elasticities of the assets will be the same as the elasticities of the services.

A change in k_i is more complicated because it involves a change in both relative prices and the quantity of services yielded by the stock of assets. An increase in k_i, implying a fall in the price of S_i which is $[(r_s - r_i)/k_i]\$1$, changes the relative price of liquidity services and other services and of S_i and other liquidity services. The effect of this change on the demand for S_i will depend on $\eta_{S_i P_i}$, the price elasticity of demand for S_i, because $\eta_{S_i k_i} = -\eta_{S_i P_i}$, the elasticity of demand for liquidity services with respect to changes in k, is equal in absolute value but opposite in sign to the price elasticity. However, we want to see what will be the effect of a change in k_i on Q_i, that is, $\eta_{Q_i k_i}$, the elasticity of demand for the asset with respect to a change in quality. Because of the proportional relationship between the stocks of assets and the flows of services ($S_i = k_i Q_i$), $\eta_{Q_i k_i} = \eta_{S_i k_i} - 1$.[11]

However, as the previous discussion has shown,

$$\eta_{S_i k_i} = -\eta_{S_i P_i}$$

and

$$\eta_{S_i P_i} = \eta_{Q_i P_i}.$$

Hence

$$\eta_{Q_i k_i} = -\eta_{Q_i P_i} - 1.$$

From this we see that the effect of a change in k_i on Q_i will depend on the price elasticity of demand for A_i. If it is greater than unity in absolute terms an increase in k_i will increase the demand for the asset.

11.
$$S_i = k_i Q_i,$$

$$\frac{dS_i}{dk_i} = k_i \frac{dQ_i}{dk_i} + Q_i,$$

$$\frac{dQ_i}{dk_i} = \frac{dS_i}{dk_i}\frac{1}{k_i} - \frac{Q_i}{k_i},$$

$$\frac{dQ_i}{dk_i}\frac{k_i}{Q_i} = \frac{dS_i}{dk_i}\frac{1}{Q_i} - 1$$

$$= \frac{dS_i}{dk_i}\frac{k_i}{S_i} - 1 \quad \therefore \quad \eta_{Q_i k_i} = \eta_{S_i k_i} - 1.$$

If it is less than unity, an increase in k_i will decrease the demand for the asset. To see what will happen to the ratio Q_i/Q_j when k_i increases, we can look at

$$\eta_{(Q_i/Q_j)k_i}, \quad \text{which is equal to} \quad \eta_{Q_ik_i} - \eta_{Q_jk_i}.$$

But from the above discussion,

$$\eta_{Q_ik_i} = -\eta_{Q_iP_i} - 1 \quad \text{and} \quad \eta_{Q_jk_i} = -\eta_{Q_jP_i}.$$

Therefore,

$$\eta_{(Q_i/Q_j)k_i} = -\eta_{Q_iP_i} - 1 + \eta_{Q_jP_i},$$

and

$$\eta_{(Q_i/Q_j)k_i} \gtreqless 0 \quad \text{as} \quad (\eta_{Q_jP_i} - \eta_{Q_iP_i}) \gtreqless 1.$$

The three basic assumptions underlying the above argument are:

a. Changes in quality can be considered as changing the stream of services yielded by an asset and thus changing the unit price of the services which are the ultimate "quantity" variables in the demand functions for liquid assets.

b. People react in the same way to a change in the number of units given a fixed money price as to a change in the "money" price per unit.

c. Changes in quality do not change the price elasticity of an asset.[12]

Although a change in quality is considered as actually changing the quantity of services yielded by an asset, some changes may be conceived of as affecting the price of the service rather than its quantity. In this case the effect would be the same as a change in r_i, a straightforward change in the price of the service. However, we can see that these two ways of looking at the effect of a particular variable, for example the average distance from a bank office, do not necessarily yield identical predictions under all circumstances. Let A_1 and A_2 be currency and time deposits respectively and assume that they are substitutes. If a decrease in the average distance from a bank office is considered as a decrease in the price of time deposits, one would predict that the quantity of time deposits demanded would increase, the quantity of currency demanded would decrease, and thus the currency-time deposit ratio would fall, whatever the magnitudes of the various

---

12. This is probably the assumption that is most easily violated, because some changes in quality, especially those induced from the supply side, increase the similarity of two assets (e.g., time and demand deposits) and thus increase the elasticity of demand for each with respect to price.

International Differences in Liquid Assets Portfolios   *313*

price elasticities. The sum of currency and time deposits $(A_1 + A_2)$ would rise if[13]

$$\frac{A_1}{A_2} > \frac{|\eta_{A_2 P_2}|}{|\eta_{A_1 P_2}|}.$$

If the decrease in the average distance from a bank office is considered as an increase in the service yield of time deposits, one would predict that the demand for currency would decrease, the quantity of time deposits demanded would increase if $|\eta_{A_2 P_2}| > 1$, but would decrease if $|\eta_{A_2 P_2}| < 1$; in the former cases, A_1/A_2 would fall, in the latter case A_1/A_2 would fall only if $\eta_{A_2 P_2} + 1 < \eta_{A_1 P_2}$,[14] and the sum $A_1 + A_2$ would rise only if[15]

$$\frac{A_1}{A_2} < \frac{-(\eta_{A_2 P_2} + 1)}{\eta_{A_1 P_2}}.$$

13. Let

$$\beta = \frac{A_1}{A_1 + A_2}; \frac{\beta}{1 - \beta} = \frac{A_1}{A_2};$$

$$\eta_{(A_1 + A_2) P_2} = \eta_{A_1 P_2} \beta + \eta_{A_2 P_2}(1 - \beta).$$

If A_1 and A_2 are substitutes,

$$\eta_{A_1 P_2} > 0,$$

$$\eta_{(A_1 + A_2) P_2} \gtrless 0 \quad \text{as} \quad \frac{\beta}{1 - \beta} \gtrless \frac{|\eta_{A_2 P_2}|}{|\eta_{A_1 P_2}|}$$

or as

$$\frac{A_1}{A_2} \gtrless \frac{|\eta_{A_2 P_2}|}{|\eta_{A_1 P_2}|}.$$

14.

$$\eta_{(A_1/A_2) k_2} = \eta_{A_1 k_2} - \eta_{A_2 k_2}$$

$$= -\eta_{A_1 P_2} - (-\eta_{A_2 P_2} - 1)$$

$$= \eta_{A_2 P_2} - \eta_{A_1 P_2} + 1$$

$$\eta_{(A_1/A_2) k_2} \gtrless 0 \quad \text{as} \quad \eta_{A_2 P_2} + 1 \gtrless \eta_{A_1 P_2}.$$

15. Let

$$\beta = \frac{A_1}{A_1 + A_2}; \frac{\beta}{1 - \beta} = \frac{A_1}{A_2};$$

$$\eta_{(A_1 + A_2) k_2} = \eta_{A_1 k_2} \beta + \eta_{A_2 k_2}(1 - \beta)$$

$$= -\eta_{A_1 P_2} \beta + (-\eta_{A_2 P_2} - 1)(1 - \beta).$$

$$\eta_{(A_1 + A_2) k_2} \lessgtr 0 \quad \text{as} \quad \frac{\beta}{1 - \beta} \lessgtr \frac{-(\eta_{A_2 P_2} + 1)}{\eta_{A_1 P_2}};$$

that is, as

$$\frac{A_1}{A_2} \lessgtr \frac{-(\eta_{A_2 P_2} + 1)}{\eta_{A_1 P_2}}.$$

If we drop the assumption of perfect certainty the holding of any asset involves some risk, and another reason for distinguishing among different assets in a portfolio is introduced. Different assets may have different types or degrees of risk associated with them. For example, the holding of currency involves the risk of theft; the holding of deposits, the risk of a bank failure; and the holding of any fixed coupon rate asset, the risk of a change in the interest rates which would affect its capital value. To incorporate the risk factor into the model of the demand for assets we must introduce some variable(s) that would serve as a proxy for the kind and degree of risk that may affect the holdings of the assets, for example the variance of interest rates.[16]

In summary, my model of the demand for any asset(s) is

$$Q_i = f(P_i, P_o, Y, K, R, u)$$

where Q_i, P_i, P_o, Y, and u are as defined in the first part of this section, K represents the group of variables which characterize the "quality" of the services yielded by the assets, and R represents the risk variables.

3. STATISTICAL ANALYSIS OF ASSET HOLDINGS

A. THE BUDGET CONSTRAINT AND PRICE VARIABLES

In this section[17] I attempt to explain the international differences in the holdings of liquid assets with the use of the budget constraint and own price variables only. It is found that these variables explain a large proportion of the observed differences. Per capita real income in dollars, adjusted for distortions introduced by fixed exchange rate systems, is used as the budget constraint variable. Two variables are used to represent the alternative opportunity cost of holding wealth in the form of the assets studied here: the rate of interest on long-term government bonds, which is available for only twenty-two countries, and the expected rate of inflation, which is approximated by the slope of the logarithmic trend fitted to the cost-of-living index.[18] As it is likely that most interest rates are closely related, the use of the govern-

16. Even though none of the assets studied here is a fixed coupon–rate asset, a change in interest rates may affect them via the substitution from or into fixed coupon–rate assets. See J. Tobin, "Liquidity Preference as Behavior towards Risk," *Review of Economic Studies* (February 1958).

17. For the sources and detailed description of the data, see Appendix B. The data are presented in Appendix C.

18. For the first period average (1952–56) the trend line was fitted to the years 1948–56. For the second period average (1957–61) the trend was fitted to the years 1952–61.

International Differences in Liquid Assets Portfolios   315

ment bond rate as a measure of the alternative opportunity cost of holding liquid assets raises a problem for those assets that have a pecuniary yield. A "high" bond yield may also imply a "high" yield on deposits and vice versa. Thus, two countries may have different bond yields and yet the alternative opportunity cost of holding liquid assets may be the same in both. However, as this is the only interest rate available for a large number of countries it is the only available measure that might indicate the alternative opportunity cost of at least some of the assets. To examine the effects of the rate of interest on liquid assets holdings a subsample of the twenty-two countries for which it is available is also analyzed. The three assets used as dependent variables are: currency (C), deposits (D), and the total of currency and deposits (CD).

TABLE 2

REGRESSION EXPLANATIONS OF ASSET HOLDINGS USING ONLY INCOME AND OWN-PRICE VARIABLES

	Constant	log Y	$\dot{P}$	r	R^2	Standard Error of Estimate
Main Sample						
log C	.751	.011	−.729		.09	.176
		(.042)	(.254)			
log D	−.279	.571	−.932		.61	.222
		(.053)	(.321)			
log CD	.337	.396	−.923		.53	.188
		(.045)	(.272)			
Small Sample						
log C	.956	−.048		−3.504	.11	.170
		(.052)		(1.74)		
log D	.084	.500		−3.07	.71	.164
		(.053)		(1.77)		
log CD	.678	.340		−3.567	.64	.135
		(.044)		(1.46)		

NOTE: The main sample consists of 46 countries with 89 observations; it excludes the first period observations of Greece, Indonesia and Korea (see footnote 7). The small sample consists of 22 countries with 42 observations. The major difference between the two samples is the proportion of observations of Latin American countries included. The proportion of observations from the four regions in the two samples is as follows:

	Europe	Asia	Latin America	Others
Main sample	.28	.24	.30	.18
Subsample	.38	.24	.10	.29

Table 2 presents the three regressions for the two samples, using only real income (Y) and one of the two price variables, $\dot{P}$, the expected rate of inflation, in the main sample, and r, the rate of interest, in the small sample. The logarithmic forms of the functions are used throughout. The standard errors are given in the parentheses.

The regressions presented in table 2 clearly show the importance of income and the price variables in explaining the differences in the holdings of deposits and currency plus deposits. They are significant[19] in all the regressions and explain a major part of the total variation in the holdings of these assets.

What is more striking, however, is the similarity between the price and income elasticities indicated by these results and those obtained in time series studies for the United States, which have been in the range of 1.2 to 1.7 for income elasticities and $-.3$ to $-.7$ for interest rate elasticities. As the assets are measured in terms of income and as $\eta_{XY} = \eta_{(X/Y),Y} + 1$, a zero log coefficient of income implies an income elasticity of demand of unity. (If the coefficient is significantly different from -1, the income elasticity is significantly different from zero.) Thus, the income elasticities of demand are 1.6 and 1.4 for deposits and for the total of currency and deposits respectively in the main sample, and 1.5 and 1.3 in the subsample. The interest elasticities in the subsample are $-.33$ and $-.39$ for deposits and currency plus deposits respectively.[20] In the currency equations even though the price variable is significant, the R^2 is very low and the income and price variables explain very little of the differences in currency holdings.

B. OTHER DETERMINANTS OF LIQUID ASSET HOLDINGS

The other set of variables that may affect liquid asset holdings are the risk variables and the quality variables, variables which are used to distinguish among different types of services yielded by the same asset in different countries because of institutional and environmental differences. Two variables are used to examine the effects of environmental differences: urbanization (U) and the per cent of agriculture in gross national product (Ag).

With respect to urbanization, Cagan in his study of the currency ratio in the United States has mentioned two opposing effects of urbanization on the currency ratio.[21] It "causes people to trade where they are not known which could reduce the use of checks," and it may

19. The 5 per cent level is used throughout when discussing significance levels.

20. The interest rate is measured in $100r$ per cent and the mean value of the interest rate for the sample is .047. The elasticity at the mean is therefore .047 times the coefficient times 2.3 because the dependent variables are in logarithms to the base 10.

21. Phillip Cagan, "The Demand for Currency Relative to the Total Money Supply," *Journal of Political Economy*, 66 (1958): 309ff.

make people more familiar with the use of checks and thus it "encourages the banking habit."

With respect to the ratio of agricultural production to GNP the following argument applies. As one of the functions of money is to bridge the gap between income receipts and expenditures, the length of the pay period may be an important variable in the allocation of assets among cash and interest-yielding assets.[22] Specifically, the longer the pay period, the lower the ratio of cash to income and the lower the currency deposits ratio. It is probably true that the pay period is longer in the agricultural sector than in the commercial or industrial sectors of an economy. Therefore one would expect that the larger the proportion of agriculture in GNP, the longer the pay period and therefore the lower the ratio of cash held to income. In the underdeveloped countries the proportion of agriculture in gross national product and the level of urbanization are so highly correlated that no effort is made to distinguish the two and only the urbanization variable is used. For the developed countries an attempt is made to separate the effects of the two variables by combining a dummy variable for development with the agricultural variable.[23]

The structure of the financial institutions in a country, the number of institutions or offices supplying deposit services, and the type of services supplied may affect the price or the quality of the services yielded by the assets. No reliable data are available for the number of bank offices for the countries examined here.[24] One financial institution that might have important implications for the allocation of assets between currency and demand deposits is the giro post office system. The three major advantages of using checks rather than currency are that the use of checks avoids the risk involved in transmitting payments, the risks of loss or theft; checks provide a record and evidence of payment; and checks allow the transmission of payment without requiring the presence of both parties to the transaction. The existence of a widespread giro system makes it possible for currency to yield many of the

22. See Harry G. Johnson, "Notes on the Theory of Transactions Demand for Cash," *Indian Journal of Economics*, vol. 44 (1963).

23. Any country with a per capita income of over $300 was considered as developed. The construction of this variable makes it partially a development variable.

24. The data for most countries on the number of bank offices are extremely poor. Some give the number of banks without specifying the number of branches; some figures include savings banks, others do not; some countries have post office savings systems so that the number of post offices is relevant, but it is seldom reported.

services provided by checking deposits. It allows payment of currency into the account of the payee and thus makes the transmission of currency via the giro system safer and eliminates the need of having the payee present during the transaction. It also records the transaction. For these reasons a dummy variable for the existence of a post office giro system (G) is included.

To take into account any institutional or other differences for which no specific variable is included, four regional dummies are also included in the regressions.

When the above variables are included as explanatory variables the regressions for deposits and for currency plus deposits for the main sample are:

$$\log D = 1.389 - .407DA - .472DL + .052 \log Y - .615\dot{P}$$
$$ (.089) \quad\;\; (.070) \quad\;\; (.107) \quad\quad\;\; (.305)$$
$$+ .256 \log U,$$
$$(.144)$$

$$R^2 = .64, \quad \text{Std. error} = .21;$$

$$\log CD = 1.457 - .325DA - .006DL + .007 \log Y - .513\dot{P}$$
$$ (.074) \quad\;\; (.061) \quad\;\; (.089) \quad\quad (.252)$$
$$- .078 \log Ag,$$
$$(.073)$$

$$R^2 = .72, \quad \text{Std. error} = .15.$$

DA and DL are the regional dummies for Asia and Latin America respectively.

The most striking aspect of these two regressions, which can be seen by comparing them with those in table 2, is what happens to the income variable when the regional dummies are included.[25] In both the regressions income becomes insignificant (when tested against zero). When the regional dummies are left out income has a positive significant coefficient in both regressions but the R^2's are lower and the standard errors of estimate are greater.[26] Similar results are found in the interest rate subsample. The above results raise the question of whether the significance of income when the regional dummies are excluded is due to its correlation with some unspecified characteristics of the regions or whether the insignificance of income when the dummies are included

25. That this is due to the regional dummies and not to the other variables that are included was seen from the regressions which included the other variables but excluded the regional dummies.

26. For deposits alone $R^2 = .64$ (standard error = .21). For currency plus deposits $R^2 = .58$ (standard error = .18).

is due to the dummies' picking up both the income effects and some other regional effect. This is especially likely to happen when the interregional variations of a particular variable, or worse, a set of variables, are greater than the intraregional variations.[27]

When the observations for deposits and for currency plus deposits were plotted against income, it was found that there is a very marked positive relationship between them and income, except for five countries whose ten observations have a positive relationship with income but seem to lie above the rest of the observations. The five countries are Japan, Ireland, Portugal, Italy, and Spain. Their average holdings of deposits over the two periods are 36.3 weeks of income, their average holdings of currency plus deposits are 43.8 weeks of income, and their average per capita income is $409. (The income range covered by these ten observations is $226–$662.) It is therefore possible that when the dummies for Asia and Latin America are introduced into the regressions, they pick up much of the income effect in the low-income countries, and the presence of the above five countries distorts the income effect on the remaining observations. Two tests were made to see whether this is the case. A dummy variable for the five countries was included as an independent variable, and a sample excluding the five countries was analyzed. It was found that the coefficients of income and most of the other variables in the regressions were nearly identical in the case where all the observations were used with a dummy for the five countries and in the case where the five countries were excluded. In both cases the regional dummies as a group became unimportant and did not affect the coefficients of the income variable and the other variables as significantly as in the regressions presented above.

Table 3 shows the first three steps of a stepwise regression program using deposits as the dependent variable. Case A is the whole sample without a dummy for the five countries discussed above. Case B is the whole sample including a dummy for the five countries (DM), and case C is the sample that excludes the five countries, so that it contains only seventy-nine observations while the other two have eighty-nine. Three points are worth noting in table 3. First, when one compares cases B and C (step 2 of B with step 1 of C, and step 3 of B with step 2 of C) one can see that except for the presence of DM in case B, the coefficients, the standard errors, and the standard errors of estimate of the regressions are nearly identical. Second, in case A the effects of DA on

27. In my sample this is true for both the income variable and the price variable (in the main sample) with Asia and Latin America consisting of the low income, high price countries.

320   *Varieties of Monetary Experience*

TABLE 3

TEST FOR THE USE OF *DM* IN THE WHOLE SAMPLE

	Constant	log Y	DL	DA	DM	R^2	Standard Error
Case A							
Step 1........	−.380	.590 (.055)				.567	.232
Step 2........	−.080	.502 (.051)	−.265 (.049)			.677	.200
Step 3........	.917	.172 (.085)	−.509 (.069)	−.417 (.090)		.740	.180
Case B							
Step 1 (Same as CaseA)							
Step 2........	−.383	.570 (.043)			.462 (.060)	.74	.180
Step 3........	−.156	.507 (.040)	−.199 (.040)		.399	.80	.159
Case C							
Step 1........	−.395	.575 (.045)				.68	.187
Step 2........	−.168	.511 (.042)	−.198 (.041)			.75	.165

both log *Y*, *DL*, and the constant term are very pronounced; and third, the R^2 and the standard errors of estimate after step 3 in case *A* and after step 2 in case *B* are identical.[28] The same pattern occurs when currency plus deposits is used as a dependent variable. This evidence supports the hypothesis that *DA*, especially when combined with *DL*, mainly represents the income effect, which is more significant and enlightening in explaining the dependent variables when used directly, rather than by proxy via the dummies, once the five countries previously discussed are excluded or treated separately via a dummy.

The question remains whether there is any justification for using a dummy for the five countries because they seem to be different. I think, however, that this dummy is no different from the regional dummies. In both cases the use of the dummy signifies ignorance about some variable(s) which affects the holdings of assets. This is true whether one calls this ignorance Asia, Latin America, or "the five countries that are

28. In both case *B* and case *C*, *DA* and the other regional dummies are not significant throughout the regressions.

different." In many ways this dummy is more useful than some of the regional dummies; it seems to represent some unknown effect not revealed by the specified continuous variables, while the other dummies, especially Asia, seem to pick up some of the effects of known and specified variables and therefore do not reveal anything new, but rather becloud what is already known.

Similar results to those presented above are found for the interest rate subsample. They are presented in Appendix A. When the dummy variable for the five countries (DM) is included as an independent variable the three regressions for currency, deposits, and the total of currency plus deposits as dependent variables for the main sample are:

$$\log C = 1.11 + .256DE + .107DA - .079G - .204 \log Y$$
$$ (.051) \quad\;\; (.055) \quad\quad (.060) \quad\;\; (.086)$$
$$- .601\dot{P} - .209 \log Ag,$$
$$(.244) \quad\;\; (.076)$$

$R^2 = .39$,   Std. error $= .15$;

$$\log D = .491 + .419DM - .126DL + .065G + .258 \log Y$$
$$ (.054) \quad\quad (.044) \quad\;\; (.048) \quad\; (.096)$$
$$+ .163 \log U - .165 \log Ag - .696\dot{P},$$
$$(.125) \quad\quad\;\; (.080) \quad\quad\;\; (.281)$$

$R^2 = .83$,   Std. error $= .15$.

(Using only DM and the four continuous variables: $R^2 = .80$; Std. error $= .16$)

$$\log CD = .820 + .333DM - .134DL + .057G + .16 \log Y$$
$$ (.045) \quad\quad (.037) \quad\;\; (.040) \quad\; (.06)$$
$$- .17 \log Ag - .591\dot{P},$$
$$(.06) \quad\quad\;\; (.220)$$

$R^2 = .80$,   Std. error $= .13$.

(Using only DM and the three continuous variables: $R^2 = .76$; Std. error $= .14$)

When these regressions for deposits and for currency plus deposits are compared with those presented earlier which excluded DM, we can see that not only is the standard error of estimate reduced significantly when DM is included; but, what is more significant, when DM is included as the only "regional" dummy, the R^2's are greater and the standard errors are lower than those of the earlier regressions which excluded DM but included the other dummies.

In all the regressions the income and price variables are significant. Currency is the only asset with an income elasticity of less than one (the income coefficient is significantly different from -1). Deposits and currency plus deposits have income elasticities that are greater than one.[29] The proportion of agriculture in GNP is significant in all the regressions; the higher is the degree of agriculture, the lower are the holdings of all liquid assets. Europe and Asia still stand out with respect to their currency holdings; not only are DE and DA significant in the regression for currency but the use of *only* these two dummies results in an R^2 of .32 as compared with .39 when the other variables are also included. The dummy for Latin America is the only significant regional dummy (not counting DM) in the regressions for deposits and currency plus deposits.

For the interest rate subsample the explanatory variables used are the same as those for the main sample, except that the interest rate is used as the price variable,[30] and a "risk" variable, PV, the mean squared deviations around the logarithmic trend line of prices, is also included.[31] This variable is used as a measure of the unexpected changes in the price level and thus as a possible proxy for economic instability. One would expect that the proportion of total wealth held in the form of some or all liquid assets would be positively related to the uncertainty about general economic conditions, because one of the services yielded by liquid assets is that of insurance against the unexpected.[32] The three regressions for currency, deposits, and currency plus deposits are:

$$\log C = 1.521 + .266DM + .244G - .295 \log Y$$
$$(.050) \quad (.042) \quad (.085)$$
$$- .171 \log Ag - 3.501r + 161PV,$$
$$(.085) \quad (1.15) \quad (94)$$

$$R^2 = .66, \qquad \text{Std. Error} = .105;$$

$$\log D = .60 + .363DM + .315 \log Y$$
$$(.040) \quad (.070)$$
$$+ .315 \log U - 3.145r - 131PV,$$
$$(.125) \quad (.99) \quad (79)$$

$$R^2 = .92, \qquad \text{Std. Error} = .087;$$

29. If DM is excluded from the regressions, i.e., the first set of regressions is used, the elasticities of deposits and currency plus deposits are around unity.

30. The expected rate of inflation is too closely correlated with the interest rate (which presumably incorporates it) to separate out their two effects, and is not included in these regressions.

31. An attempt was made to use interest rate variation as a measure of the risk of interest rate changes as an explanatory variable, but it had no effect on the asset holdings.

32. See Milton Friedman and Anna J. Schwartz, *A Monetary History of the United States, 1867–1960* (Princeton: Princeton Univ. Press, 1963).

$$\log CD = 1.299 + .321DM + .099G + .150 \log Y$$
$$(.031) \quad\quad (.027) \quad\ (.055)$$
$$+ .307 \log U - 3.776r - 62PV,$$
$$(.092) \quad\quad\quad (.709) \quad (58)$$
$$R^2 = .92, \quad\quad\quad\quad\quad \text{Std. Error} = .065.$$

As is true with the main sample, the inclusion of DM (or the exclusion of the countries represented by DM—in this subsample Portugal, Ireland, and Italy) makes a significant difference in the regressions. When DM is not included in the regressions, the use of all the continuous variables and the dummies for Asia and Latin America results in a lower R^2 and a higher standard error of estimate for deposits and nearly the same R^2 and standard error for currency plus deposits.[33]

Currency again stands out both because of its relatively low R^2, its high standard error of estimate, and because of the importance of the two dummy variables. Without them the R^2 falls to .48 and the standard error rises to .13.

The results shown by the three regressions presented above are very similar to those obtained in the last section when the whole sample was used. In both cases all the assets show positive income elasticities, with only currency having an elasticity of less than one. In both cases the coefficient of $\log Y$ in the currency equation is significantly different from -1. In both cases all the assets show negative price elasticities, whether measured in terms of an expected rate of change of prices or the rate of interest, with currency having the lowest price elasticity of all the assets.[34] In both cases either $\log Ag$ is significant with a negative coefficient or $\log U$ is significant with a positive coefficient for all the assets. The multicollinearity between $\log Ag$ and $\log U$ makes it very difficult to separate out their two effects. However, both represent some aspect of the difference between an urban and a rural environment, and in both the whole sample and the subsample such a difference clearly appears with respect to all the assets, whether expressed by $\log Ag$ or $\log U$.

33. When DM is excluded the only significant variables are the dummies for Asia and Latin America and $\log Ag$, which by its construction is partially a dummy for development and has a positive coefficient for both deposits and currency plus deposits (which is opposite to that found in the regressions of the main sample).

34. In the interest rate subsample the price elasticity of deposits is probably understated relative to that of currency. Because most interest rates move in the same direction, a specific change in the government bond yield implies a smaller change in the price of deposits, which yield some interest, than in the price of currency, which yields no interest.

The major difference between the whole sample and the subsample is the significance in the former of DL in the regression of deposits and currency plus deposits, and DA in the regression of currency.[35] The negative coefficients of the dummy for Latin America in the whole sample might represent an additional price effect on the assets not picked up by our measure of expected inflation. In the whole sample 30 per cent of the observations are from Latin America. If the price effect of the expected rate of inflation on the assets is underestimated either because of certain extreme observations, for example those of Brazil and Argentina, or because price expectations are affected by what has occurred over a longer period of time than that covered in constructing P, DL might be showing the additional effect of inflation not picked up by $\dot{P}$.[36] The positive coefficient of G in the interest rate subsample can be interpreted either as showing the effect of a giro post office system on currency holdings, as is argued in the next section on the currency deposits ratio, or as showing some other unspecified European effect. PV, although not significant in any of the regressions, has the correct sign in the currency equation but not in the others. If PV does actually represent some measure of economic instability, one would expect that all liquid assets would be positively related to PV.

The results presented in the last section indicate that both the income and the price variables are important determinants of the demand for liquid assets. All the assets have significant positive income elasticities and negative price variable elasticities. If for the moment we exclude the dummy variables, the only other significant determinant of liquid asset holdings is the degree of urbanization. The demand for all liquid assets is greater in urban than in rural areas. There are significant differences among the assets, the most striking being the difference of the income effect on currency and on deposits. Only currency has an income elasticity of less than unity. Using the estimating equations for the interest rate subsample, the estimated income elasticity of currency plus deposits is 1.15 and the price elasticity (using the rate of

35. The positive coefficient of DE and negative coefficient of G in the currency equation of the whole sample do not imply a different result from the positive coefficients of DM and G in the subsample. Except for Greece all the European countries have either a giro system or belong to the DM group and the combinations of G and DE in the whole sample and G and DM in the subsample are very similar.

36. Most of Latin America has a longer history of inflation than other countries and therefore the behavioral adjustment to inflation may be more complete than in other countries. See Phillip Cagan, "The Monetary Dynamics of Hyperinflation" in Friedman, ed., *Studies in Quantity Theory*, p. 63.

interest as the price variable) is $-.42$.[37] For the whole sample the estimated income elasticity is 1.16.

The five countries represented by DM—Japan, Portugal, Spain, Italy, and Ireland—remain a puzzle. What do these countries have in common that makes their demand for liquid assets so high relative to the rest of the world? It seems clear that it is not any characteristics of the structure of their financial institutions, because these differ greatly among the five countries. Spain and Portugal have very few financial institutions and the number of financial institution offices per capita in these two countries is lower than in any other European country with the possible exception of Greece. On the other hand, Italy and Japan have a complex conglomeration of financial institutions serving different sectors of the economy with a large number of offices per capita. The growth rate of real per capita income has also been very different in the five countries. Japan and Italy have had a very high rate of growth over the two periods—41 per cent and 28 per cent respectively; Portugal and Spain a moderate growth rate—18 per cent and 11 per cent respectively; and Ireland a very low rate of 6 per cent. It might of course be true that there is no common factor in the five countries that affects their demand for liquid assets but that different factors in the five countries lead to the same effect, a higher demand for liquid assets.[38]

4. EMPIRICAL ANALYSIS OF THE CURRENCY-DEPOSITS RATIO

In the preceding section we saw that the observed international differences in the holdings of liquid assets could be largely explained by the use of a few economic variables. In this section I want to explore whether the same variables that explain the allocation of wealth between liquid assets and other assets can also explain the allocation of liquid assets among different types. To answer this question the currency-deposits ratio is used as the dependent variable. The samples and the independent variables used in this section are the same as those used in the last section. The problems of the regional dummies discussed there are not as pronounced for the currency-deposits ratios. The dummies for Asia and Latin America have no effect on the regression results. Whether DM is included or not they leave the coefficients, the

37. See note 20.

38. After the work for this study was completed, I learned that Japanese banks require corporations to hold minimum balances when taking out loans and that these balances are held in the form of time deposits yielding interest payments. Thus a large fraction of time deposits in Japan is held by corporations. This may explain the large holdings of deposits in Japan.

standard errors, and the standard errors of estimate unchanged. However, the inclusion of DM, or the exclusion of the countries represented by DM, does reduce the standard error of estimate.

When income alone is used as an explanatory variable, the estimated regression for the main sample is

$$\log \frac{C}{D} = 1.05 - .56 \log Y,$$
$$(.05)$$

$$R^2 = .59, \qquad \text{Std. Error} = .21.$$

When DM is included:

$$\log \frac{C}{D} = .105 - .55 \log Y - .33 \, DM,$$
$$(.04) \qquad\qquad (.06)$$

$$R^2 = .60, \qquad \text{Std. Error} = .19.$$

When the five countries are excluded from the sample:

$$\log \frac{C}{D} = 1.06 - .55 \log Y,$$

$$R^2 = .66, \qquad \text{Std. Error} = .19.$$

When all the variables are used, the only significant variable in addition to $\log Y$ and DM is DO, the dummy for "Others." The estimated equation is

$$\log \frac{C}{D} = .503 - .322 DM - .220 DO$$
$$(.059) \qquad (.067)$$
$$- .082 G - .345 \log Y - .155 \log U,$$
$$(.057) \quad (.087) \qquad\qquad (.151)$$

$$R^2 = .73, \qquad \text{Std. Error} = .18.$$

As can be seen, the reduction in the standard error of estimate due to the addition of the other variable is very small; the use of $\log Y$ and DM alone results in nearly the same standard error of estimate. However, the coefficient of $\log Y$ is affected by the addition of DO and $\log U$.

For the interest rate subsample, the estimated equation using only $\log Y$ as the independent variable is

$$\log \frac{C}{D} = .971 - .542 \log Y,$$

$$R^2 = .66, \qquad \text{Std. Error} = .17.$$

When all the variables are included:

$$\log \frac{C}{D} = 1.104 - .119DM + .209G - .602 \log Y + .46PV - 2.48\dot{P},$$
$$(.065) \quad (.055) \quad (.055) \quad (15) \quad (1.11)$$

$R^2 = .84,$ Std. Error $= .14.$

The one puzzling variable in the above regression is $\dot{P}$. In the analysis of the assets in the preceding section there is no indication that currency has a larger price elasticity than deposits. In fact, when the rate of interest is used as the price variable, currency has a smaller price elasticity. Therefore, it seems doubtful that the negative coefficient of $\dot{P}$ in this equation indicates any difference in price elasticities between currency and deposits. What may be indicated by the coefficient of $\dot{P}$ is that with a higher expected rate of inflation the interest yield on deposits is adjusted to some extent to the expected rate of inflation; and therefore the price effect of inflation is smaller for deposits than for currency, so that the currency deposits ratio is lower.

The two other continuous variables have the expected sign. If PV is actually some measure of economic uncertainty, currency, being a better "cushion against uncertainty" than any other asset, would become a relatively more desirable asset; and thus the currency-deposits ratio would be greater with the greater degree of uncertainty.

Two questions remain to be answered. First, as indicated in the analysis of both the assets and the currency-deposits ratio, why does currency have a lower income elasticity than deposits? Second, is the significance of G in the equations for currency and the currency-deposits ratio due to the institutional peculiarities of the giro post office system or some other unspecified characteristic of Europe? The answer to the latter question cannot be based solely on the significance of G in the regression equations, because the European countries that do not have a giro post office system belong to the DM group. Thus, all the G countries are also all the European countries not included in DM.

In his study of the currency-deposits ratio in the United States, Cagan discusses the relative income effect on currency and deposits.[39]

> The rise in real income per capita would reduce the relative demand for currency if it enhanced the appeal of making payment by check and having a bank account or in technical terms if the income elasticity were less than unity. This may at first seem strange, because we customarily associate such a phenomenon with 'necessities'. With

39. Phillip Cagan, *Determinants and Effects of Change in the Stock of Money, 1875–1960* (New York: National Bureau of Economic Research, 1965), p. 126.

high incomes people switch from them to more expensive items; similarly in their portfolios they might forego income to acquire lower yielding securities that offer nonpecuniary advantages such as liquidity. From this point of view we should not be surprised to find a shift to money balances from higher yielding assets when real income rises. But why a shift from currency to deposits? . . . A shift from currency to deposits cannot be described as providing an asset with greater convenience at the expense of a lower yield.

From this Cagan concludes:

The way out is not to argue that the income elasticity of currency cannot be less than unity but to recognize that income growth is a proxy for a host of other developments which, on balance, may work to increase the demand for deposits relative to currency.[40]

Two points are worth noting in Cagan's discussion. First, the argument in the first sentence is only applicable to the currency–checking-deposits ratio. It is not clear that the fall in the currency-deposits ratio is due solely to the change in the currency–checking-deposits ratio. In fact the other types of deposits (time and savings) have a higher income elasticity than checking deposits.[41] Second, the question of why a shift into assets yielding liquidity should be from currency to deposits is relevant only if liquidity is a single type of service yielded by all liquid assets. If this were true all liquid assets would be perfect substitutes at some price ratio depending on their relative yields. of "liquidity"; and their income elasticities would be the same, irrespective of their monetary returns. However, if one assumes that "liquidity" is not a single service but stands for a variety of different types of services, then different assets which yield different types of liquidity services might very well have different income elasticities. Thus Cagan's statement, "A shift from currency to deposits cannot be described as providing an asset with greater convenience at the expense of a lower yield," is irrelevant to the question of different income elasticities. If deposits provide a service not provided by currency, or provided by currency to a lesser extent, a shift from currency to deposits might show a shift from a service whose income elasticity is less than unity to one whose income elasticity is greater than unity. All that is really required for income to have a negative effect on the currency-deposits ratio is that the income elasticity of currency be less than that of deposits, not necessarily less than unity.

40. *Ibid.*, p. 126.

41. This is also noted by Meltzer for the United States, in Allan H. Meltzer, "The Demand for Money: The Evidence from the Time Series," *Journal of Political Economy*, 71 (1963): 219–46.

Let us separate "liquidity" into two services: (a) a transaction service—the ability at any moment of time now and in the future to make an economic transaction;[42] and (b) an insurance service—the ability to meet unexpected events at any time in the future.[43] Both currency and deposits provide both of these services but not to the same extent. The amount of transaction services provided by a dollar of currency, a dollar of checking deposit and a dollar of time deposit is not the same. Currency allows for instantaneous transactions at any point of time; checking deposits allow this for some types of transactions and in some environmental settings (for example the general acceptability of checks); time deposits require a previous conversion into currency or checking deposits before they can provide the transaction service. All these assets also provide the insurance service as defined above.

If they provided the same amount of insurance service per dollar of assets, then there should be no differential income effect. The allocation among the assets would be determined by relative prices only, which would be determined by the relative yields of transactions services. However, all deposits provide greater insurance services than does currency because of the risks involved in holding currency from theft, loss, fire, and so on. If the insurance service has a greater income elasticity than the transactions services, then as income rises the ratio of currency to all deposits will fall because the demand for the insurance service rises relative to the demand for the transactions service. Therefore, the demand for assets yielding a greater amount of insurance services rises relative to the demand for assets yielding less insurance services but more transactions services. If assets were perfect substitutes with respect to insurance services, the allocation among different types of deposits would be determined by their relative prices and relative yields of transactions services.

Institutional factors affect the quantity of the various types of services yielded by the assets. For example, general acceptability of checks would make checking deposits and currency perfect substitutes with respect to the transactions services. Allowing checks to be written on time deposits and waiving the notice requirement would make checking and time deposits perfect substitutes with respect to the

42. We are interested not only in current transactions services; during a transactions period, liquid assets are a store of wealth which yields the service of the ability to make transactions in the future.

43. This discussion follows the theory presented in section 2 but allows for a liquid asset yielding more than a single liquidity service.

transactions service, and as they are already perfect substitutes with respect to the insurance service they would become perfect substitutes in demand.

This brings us to the question of the giro post office system. This is an institutional arrangement which changes the type of service yielded by currency. It allows currency to yield many of the services provided by checks; and, as currency still yields currency services, one would expect a higher currency-deposits ratio (and a greater holding of currency) when the giro service is provided. I would therefore argue that G does represent the giro post office system as an institution and not some other European effect, especially since there does not seem to be any other obvious general characteristic common to Europe which would increase the demand for currency in Europe relative to the rest of the world.

5. Summary and Conclusions

This study attempted to answer two questions: What determines the absolute amount of liquid assets held by the nonbanking sectors of the economy in various countries? And, what determines the allocation among liquid assets, specifically the currency-deposits ratio? There are at least two ways to evaluate the answers presented in the last two sections. One is by the statistical fit obtained in the regressions and the conformity of the empirical results with those that would be predicted from theoretical considerations. The other is by comparing the results obtained in this study, which has used international cross-section data, with those obtained in other studies of the demand for liquid assets, which have used national data, to determine whether the results obtained in this study are consistent with the others.

The results of this study are impressive on both counts, especially when one considers the wide range of social, cultural, and institutional characteristics represented by the group of forty-seven countries included in the study.

In the interest rate subsample 92 per cent of the variation in the total holdings of currency and deposits was "explained" by the variables used.[44] The three most important determinants of total liquid asset holdings are per capita real income, the rate of interest, and the degree of urbanization. What is more striking, however, is the similarity of the

44. This is a slight overestimate of the explanation achieved, because one of the variables used, DM, is basically an ignorance variable, not an explanatory variable in any real sense of the word.

International Differences in Liquid Assets Portfolios   331

estimated income and interest rate elasticities to those obtained in the time series studies for the United States.

In his study of the demand for money in the United States, Meltzer[45] made an exhaustive analysis for various time periods using various definitions of wealth and income. His estimates of income or wealth elasticities vary according to the particular specification of these variables. It is a moot question whether measured real income used in a cross-section study such as this is more comparable to measured income, permanent income, or wealth. Even though measured income may not be a very good proxy for permanent income or wealth in a time series study, it may be a good proxy for them in an international cross-section study.[46] However, for the purpose of this comparison we are interested in seeing whether the results obtained in this study are within a plausible range of previous findings rather than in pinpointing a particular value. Therefore a complete resolution of the question of income is not necessary.

When Meltzer uses per capita permanent income and the rate of interest as his independent variables and the total of currency, demand deposits, and time deposits as his dependent variable he gets an estimated income elasticity of 1.4 and interest rate elasticity of $-.37$.[47] For other definitions of real wealth and for various subperiods the income elasticities range from about 1.2 to 1.7 and the interest rate elasticities from about $-.30$ to $-.70$. The estimated income and interest rate elasticities of currency and deposits for the interest rate subsample used in this study are 1.15 and $-.42$ respectively.[48] These estimates are close to those obtained by Meltzer, especially when one considers that urbanization is included as an independent variable in my regression for currency and deposits, which, because of its correlation with income, reduces the income coefficient. (When urbanization is excluded, the income elasticity becomes about 1.35.) Conversely,

45. Meltzer, "Demand for Money."

46. It is much more plausible that a 10 per cent difference in measured income between two countries implies about a 10 per cent difference in permanent income or wealth than that a 10 per cent rise in measured income in a country from one year to another implies about a 10 per cent rise in permanent income or wealth.

47. Meltzer, "Demand for Money."

48. Even though currency plus deposits is a broader category than that used by Meltzer (he only includes time deposits in commercial banks in his M_2), I think they are comparable because in most countries the savings deposits that I include are basically time deposits in savings banks rather than commercial banks, which should be an irrelevant consideration.

Meltzer's income variable probably picks up some of the urbanization effects.

The determinants of the holdings of the individual assets, currency, and deposits taken separately, are less clear than those of the sum of currency and deposits. This is indicated both by the higher standard errors of estimate obtained in the regressions and by the very high standard error in the regression for the currency-deposits ratio. The reasons for this are not hard to find. Given that currency and deposits are substitutes to some extent, the variables that would be relevant in determining the allocation of the assets in the portfolio would be, first, relative prices and, second, those institutional, environmental, and other variables, the quality variables, that affect the substitutability among the assets.

Both Cagan and Macesich[49] in their studies of the currency-deposits ratio in the United States and Canada respectively, find that the interest yield of deposits and the tax rate are important determinants of the currency-deposits ratio. Because these two variables are unavailable for the sample of countries used in this study, they were not included among the independent variables. The number of bank offices per capita is probably a more important determinant of the allocation among the assets than of the total asset portfolio. Thus the high standard errors of estimate in the regressions for the individual assets and the currency-deposits ratio may be attributable to the omission of many variables that are relevant to the allocation among the assets in a portfolio of liquid assets but not as relevant to the allocation of wealth among liquid assets and other assets. This also indicates that the portfolio consisting of currency, demand deposits, and time and savings deposits is a behaviorally meaningful and therefore useful subset of all assets because the demand for this subset of assets is stable with respect to a few known variables, in the sense that it is less affected by institutional and other environmental factors than other subsets of assets.

49. Cagan, *Determinants and Effects of Change*; G. Macesich, "Demand for Currency and Taxation in Canada," *Southern Economic Journal*, 29 (1962): 33–38.

APPENDIX A

Table 4 presents the regressions for deposits when only income and the rate of interest are used as dependent variables. Case A is the whole sample when no dummy for Portugal, Ireland, and Italy is included; Case B is the same sample with a dummy (DM) for these three countries; and case C is the sample which excludes the six observations for the three countries.

TABLE 4

TEST FOR THE USE OF DM IN THE INTEREST RATE SAMPLE

Dependent Variable	Constant	log Y	r	DM	R^2	Standard Error
Case A						
log D........	.084	.500 (.053)	−3.07 (1.77)		.71	.164
log CD.......	.678	.340 (.044)	−3.567 (1.457)		.64	.135
Case B						
log D........	.025	.505 (.031)	−3.277 (1.05)	.356 (.043)	.91	.090
log CD.......	.623	.349 (.026)	−3.819 (.860)	.289 (.035)	.87	.080
Case C						
log D........	.046	.507 (.034)	−3.088 (1.17)		.88	.103
log CD.......	.615	.351 (.028)	−3.705 (.964)		.85	.085

APPENDIX B
SOURCES AND ADJUSTMENTS OF DATA

Agriculture—Percentage of GNP

United Nations Statistical Office, *Yearbook of National Accounts Statistics*, 1957–63.

Bruce M. Russett et al., *World Handbook of Political and Social Indicators* (New Haven, 1964).

For three countries (Australia, Sweden, New Zealand) data for only one period were available. An estimate for the second period was made using the growth rate of the percentage of the labor force in agriculture given in Russett et al., *World Handbook*.

Banking and Financial Institutions

H. W. Auburn, ed., *Comparative Banking* (London, 1963).

B. H. Beckhart, *Banking Systems* (New York, 1956).

Bank of Japan Economic Research Department, *Money and Banking in Japan, 1964*.

International Monetary Fund, *International Financial Statistics*, 1962/63 Supplement.

R. S. Sayers, *Banking in Western Europe* (London, 1962).

J. S. G. Wilson, *French Banking Structure and Credit Policy* (London, 1957).

Currency outside Banking System

International Monetary Fund, *International Financial Statistics*, 1963/64 Supplement and other monthly issues.

For two countries adjustment had to be made to the currency data. As Belgium and Luxembourg have a currency union, the currency holdings of Belgium have to be reduced by the currency held in Luxembourg. This was done by assuming that the ratio of currency to income is the same in both countries, and estimating the relative holdings of currency by the relative incomes in the two countries.

All data for the Federation of Malaya exclude Singapore, North Borneo, and Brunei except for the currency outstanding which includes currency held in the above three. As no income data are available for these three, an adjustment by relative income as was done for Belgium and Luxembourg was not possible. The currency was allocated by relative population.

Deposits—Demand, Time, and Savings

Nearly all the data were obtained from the I.M.F. *International Financial Statistics*, 1963/64 Supplement and other monthly issues.

Additional data for the following countries had to be obtained:

Brazil. Deposits at federal and state savings banks are not included in the I.M.F. data. These were obtained from the bulletin of the Superintendecia da Modeda e do Credito, 1965.

United Kingdom. Many deposits in financial institutions other than commercial banks are not reported by the I.M.F. These were obtained from the Bank of England, *Quarterly Bulletin*, 1961, 1962, and 1963.

United States. Deposits at national savings banks and the post office savings system from M. Friedman and Anna J. Schwartz, *The Stock of Money in the United States, 1867–1960*, Appendix A. Deposits at savings and loan associations from the board of governors of the Federal Reserve, *Federal Reserve Bulletin*.

Exchange Rates

The modified exchange rate adjusted for purchasing power parity in United Nations, *Yearbook of National Account Statistics*, 1963, table 3B.

Income

National income data from United Nations, *Yearbook of National Account Statistics*, 1957–63.

Interest Rates

Long-term government bond yield from I.M.F., *International Financial Statistics*, 1963/64 Supplement.

Prices

Cost-of-living index (1958 = 100) in I.M.F., *International Financial Statistics*, 1963/64 Supplement.

Population

Mid-year population estimates from the United Nations, *Statistical Yearbook*, 1952–63.

Urbanization

Percentage of the population living in cities of over 20,000 people from Russett et al., *World Handbook*, p. 49.

APPENDIX C

TABLE 5

DATA FOR THE DEPENDENT VARIABLES, INCOME, AND THE EXPECTED RATE OF CHANGE OF PRICES

Country	C	D	CD	C/D	Y	$\dot{P}$
Argentina	12.5	16.4	28.9	.76	355.8	.182
	9.8	12.7	22.5	.78	366.4	.240
Austria	8.1	15.4	23.5	.53	524.7	.093
	8.1	21.0	29.1	.39	703.0	.018
Brazil	5.4	13.9	19.3	.58	117.5	.144
	4.8	13.6	18.4	.46	115.4	.212
Burma	7.8	5.1	12.9	1.53	50.2	−.015
	10.1	6.4	16.5	1.57	53.0	.010
Chile	2.2	3.8	6.0	.58	340.5	.310
	2.0	4.6	6.6	.43	352.8	.326
Colombia	3.8	8.2	12.0	.46	210.2	.062
	4.1	9.3	13.4	.44	229.5	.078
Ecuador	3.8	4.7	8.5	.81	141.5	.023
	3.7	5.2	8.9	.72	155.4	.005
El Salvador						
	4.9	7.1	12.0	.68	115.7	.014
Finland	3.4	23.1	26.5	.15	514.8	.031
	3.2	26.3	29.5	.12	568.3	.045
Greece	4.4	2.6	7.0	1.68	243.7	.088
	6.1	8.7	14.8	.70	298.2	.042
Guatemala	6.3	4.6	10.9	1.37	132.6	.027
	5.8	6.9	12.7	.84	143.9	.006
Honduras	3.5	3.9	7.4	.91	158.7	.037
	2.9	3.8	6.7	.76	165.8	.013
Indonesia	3.5	1.4	4.9	2.59	93.4	.162
Israel	5.5	9.7	15.2	.57	665.4	.148
	4.6	10.4	15.0	.44	869.5	.063
Japan	5.2	36.2	41.4	.14	250.6	.054
	4.9	52.1	57.0	.09	353.8	.023
Korea	3.6	2.3	5.9	1.54	88.6	.628
	3.8	4.2	8.0	.91	98.4	.188
Malaya	8.6	9.7	18.3	.89	187.0	.023
	8.6	10.2	18.8	.84	185.6	−.011
Mexico	3.6	6.1	9.7	.59	277.0	.075
	3.0	6.4	9.4	.47	323.3	.062
Nicaragua	3.2	2.9	6.1	1.09	194.0	.090
	2.9	2.9	5.8	1.00	186.1	.021
Paraguay	3.8	3.5	7.3	1.08	88.4	.412
	3.8	3.1	6.9	1.21	91.2	.167
Philippines	4.8	5.4	10.2	.89	97.6	−.007
	4.6	7.5	12.1	.62	108.9	.010
Spain	7.0	25.6	32.6	.28	293.5	.038
	7.4	28.9	36.3	.26	324.1	.061

TABLE 5—*Continued*

Country	C	D	CD	C/D	Y	$\dot{P}$
Taiwan	3.0	4.2	7.2	.71	84.6	.146
	3.3	7.7	11.0	.43	91.3	.098
Thailand	7.7	4.1	11.8	1.87	95.3	.061
	7.2	6.2	13.4	1.15	88.1	.035
Venezuela	4.2	7.5	11.7	.57	420.3	.017
	3.8	11.2	15.0	.34	509.4	.012
*Australia	4.5	32.1	36.6	.14	1287.5	.086
	4.0	30.8	34.8	.13	1319.8	.027
Belgium	14.1	21.2	35.3	.67	905.7	.015
	13.2	23.1	36.3	.57	986.3	.014
Canada	3.8	22.4	26.2	.17	1398.1	.024
	3.6	22.2	25.8	.16	1471.7	.014
Ceylon	4.1	11.4	15.5	.36	119.9	.011
	5.4	12.1	17.5	.44	118.6	.006
Costa Rica	4.7	6.4	11.1	.74	224.2	.033
	4.3	7.1	11.4	.61	232.7	.018
Denmark	4.7	27.0	31.7	.17	1019.0	.040
	4.5	28.1	32.6	.16	1165.6	.026
Egypt	10.5	11.2	21.7	.94	117.5	.001
	8.8	11.0	19.8	.80	144.5	.002
France	10.9	16.7	27.6	.65	874.0	.066
	9.7	20.4	30.1	.48	1092.5	.041
Germany	5.3	13.8	19.1	.39	809.2	.010
	5.0	19.3	24.3	.26	1147.1	.014
India	6.8	5.7	12.5	1.20	67.2	.003
	7.2	7.9	15.1	.92	66.8	.026
Ireland	6.3	42.7	49.0	.15	581.2	.042
	5.5	43.3	48.8	.13	616.1	.026
Italy	8.0	31.0	39.0	.26	517.0	.031
	7.9	39.1	47.0	.20	662.9	.020
Netherlands	9.0	27.5	36.1	.33	824.3	.040
	7.8	27.4	35.2	.28	999.5	.026
New Zealand	4.6	34.7	39.3	.13	1581.9	.053
	3.9	32.1	36.0	.12	1587.7	.033
Norway	8.9	31.7	40.7	.28	1090.4	.056
	7.8	31.4	39.2	.25	1194.0	.027
Pakistan	7.0	5.2	12.2	1.35	60.3	.016
	7.2	6.0	13.2	1.20	66.0	.025
Peru	4.0	9.1	13.1	.44	123.5	.079
	4.2	9.1	13.3	.46	132.1	.071
Portugal	11.6	30.3	41.9	.39	226.3	.004
	11.6	33.3	44.9	.35	268.1	.014
Sweden	7.4	39.4	46.8	.19	1284.9	.047
	6.8	41.6	48.4	.16	1442.7	.031
Turkey	5.0	7.4	12.4	.68	196.7	.044
	4.8	7.5	12.3	.63	227.8	.111
United Kingdom	5.9	34.7	40.6	.17	1040.4	.052
	5.5	27.5	33.0	.20	1194.4	.027
United States	4.6	33.6	38.2	.14	2072.0	.019
	3.8	35.6	39.4	.11	2190.1	.014

NOTE: There are two observations for each country except Indonesia and El Salvador. The first observation for each variable is the first period average (1952–56), the second is the second period average (1957–61). For sources and adjustments see Appendix B.

* The following 22 countries are the ones included in the interest rate subsample.

[7]

RATIONAL CHOICE AND PATTERNS OF GROWTH IN A MONETARY ECONOMY*

By Miguel Sidrauski
Massachusetts Institute of Technology

Concluding his excellent survey of recent monetary theory, Harry Johnson [4] suggested that future developments in this field should come from attempts "to break monetary theory loose from the mould of short-run equilibrium analyses, conducted in abstraction from the process of economic growth and accumulation, and to integrate it with the rapidly developing theoretical literature on economic growth."

This paper summarizes an attempt to deal with these issues. Like most theoretical work in rapidly growing fields, it is incomplete and the assumptions on which it is based are relatively crude abstractions. These abstractions, however, allow us to explore certain aspects of the interaction of the real and the monetary phenomena in a model of economic growth in which money, being government noninterest bearing debt, is introduced as an alternative asset to real capital.

Most of the recent work in this field[1] has centered on the analysis of the patterns of growth of a monetary economy by postulating alternative plausible saving functions and demand functions for money. What differentiates this product is the fact that, in line with Patinkin's [6] presentation of the neoclassical theory of money, and with the classical Fisherian theory of saving [2], it is based on an explicit analysis of individuals' saving behavior, viewed as a process of wealth accumulation aimed at maximizing some intertemporal utility function.

The first part of the paper describes the representative economic unit of an idealized economy and it analyzes the constraints imposed on its maximizing behavior. Section II is concerned with the optimizing conditions and presents the derivation of the demand functions for consumption, cash balances, and the stock of capital. The third section introduces an expectations formation hypothesis and presents a simple aggregative macroeconomic model in which the demand functions for assets and consumption are those which were derived from the analysis of the maximizing behavior of individual economic units. The final part of the paper considers the short-run and long-run effects of a change in the rate of monetary expansion as well as the stability of the equilibrium growth path in a monetary economy.

* This paper is a summary of my Ph.D. thesis presented at the University of Chicago. I am very grateful to the members of my committee, H. Uzawa, M. Friedman, and A. Harberger, as well as to my colleagues, M. Teubal and A. Treadway, for their helpful comments and suggestions.
[1] What I have in mind here is the work by Tobin [9], Gurley and Shaw [3], Johnson [5], and Sidrauski [7].

I. *The Model*

The basic economic unit in our model is the representative family. Its welfare at any point in time is measured by a time invariant utility function of the form

$$(1) \qquad U_t = U(c_t, z_t)$$

where c_t stands for the flow of real consumption per unit of time, and z_t for the flow of services per unit of time derived from holdings of real cash balances, both variables being expressed in per capita terms. To simplify, we will assume that the flow of services derived from the holdings of real cash balances is proportional to the stock and, by an appropriate choice of units, we make the factor of proportionality equal to one.

$$(2) \qquad z_t = m_t = M_t/p_t N_t$$

M_t represents the holdings of nominal cash balances by the economic unit, N_t the number of individuals in the economic unit and p_t the money price of the only commodity produced in our model. The instantaneous utility function can then be written

$$(3) \qquad U_t = U(c_t, m_t)$$

It is assumed that the utility function is strictly concave with continuous first and second derivatives[2] and that both commodities are not inferior.[3] We further assume that the total welfare (W) associated with any particular time path (c_t, m_t) can be represented by the utility functional

$$(4) \qquad W = \int_0^\infty [U(c_t, m_t)]e^{-\delta t}dt$$

$\delta > 0$ being the subjective rate of time preference of this family.

At each moment of time the behavior of the economic unit is subject to two constraints, one in terms of stocks and the other one in terms of flows. The stock constraint requires that the total endowment of real nonhuman wealth (a_t), be allocated between capital (k_t) and real cash balances in such a fashion that[4]

$$(5) \qquad a_t = k_t + m_t$$

On the other hand, the flow constraint requires that at any time t disposable income has to be equal to consumption plus saving. Assuming that the production function is linear homogeneous, the capital stock produces an amount $y(k_t)$ of homogeneous output.[5] If we add to this

---

[2] This condition implies that $U_{cc} < 0$, $U_{mm} < 0$, and $J = U_{cc}U_{mm} - U_{mc}^2 > 0$.
[3] This requires: $J_1 = U_{mm} - U_{cm}U_m/U_c < 0$ and $J_2 = U_{cc}U_m/U_c - U_{cm} < 0$.
[4] In what follows all variables are expressed in per capita terms.
[5] We will assume that the production function is "well behaved": namely, $y(0) = 0$, $y(\infty) = \infty$, $y(0 < k < \infty) > 0$, $y'(0) = \infty$, $y'(\infty) = 0$, $y'(0 < k < \infty) > 0$, $y''(k) < 0$.

amount the real value of the net transfers that the economic unit receives from the government (v_t), we obtain the family's gross disposable income, which has to be equal to real consumption (c_t) plus gross real savings (s_t).

$$(6) \qquad y(k_t) + v_t = c_t + s_t$$

Gross real saving is the sum of gross capital accumulation (i_t) plus the gross addition to the holdings of real cash balances (x_t).

$$(7) \qquad s_t = i_t + x_t$$

Gross capital accumulation is equal to the net addition to the capital stock $(\dot{k}_t)$ plus the replacement of the depreciated capital (uk_t) plus the amount of capital accumulation required to provide the newly born members of the economic unit with the same amount of capital as the amount with which the old members are endowed (nk_t); where u is the instantaneous rate of depreciation of capital and n is the instantaneous rate of growth of the number of individuals in the family.

$$(8) \qquad i_t = \dot{k}_t + (u + n)k_t$$

Similarly, the gross accumulation of real cash balances is equal to

$$(9) \qquad x_t = \dot{m}_t + (\pi_t + n)m_t$$

where π_t is the expected rate of change in prices.

Hence the flow constraint for this economic unit can be rewritten

$$(10) \qquad y(k_t) + v_t - (\pi_t + n)m_t - (u + n)k_t - \dot{m}_t - \dot{k}_t - c_t = 0$$

Differentiating equation (5) with respect to time and substituting into (10) we have

$$(11) \qquad \dot{a}_t = y(k_t) + v_t - (\pi_t + n)m_t - (u + n)k_t - c_t$$

Equations (5) and (11) are the stock and flow constraints under which, given the initial condition (a_0) and the values of u, n, π_t and v_t, the rational economic unit will find the time path of consumption and accumulation that maximizes the utility functional (4).

II. *Maximization of the Utility Functional and Derivation of the Demand Functions*

In order to solve this maximization problem we form a new function (I) such that

$$(12) \qquad I = \int_0^\infty \{ U(c_t, m_t) + \lambda_t[y(k_t) + v_t - (\pi_t + n)m_t$$
$$- (u + n)k_t - c_t - \dot{a}_t] + q_t[a_t - k_t - m_t]\} e^{-\delta t} dt$$

where λ_t is the Lagrangian multiplier attached to the flow constraint (11) and q_t the Lagrangian multiplier attached to the stock constraint (5). The conditions for a maximum are given by the Euler equations (13)–(16) together with the transversality condition (17).

(13) $$U_c(c_t, m_t) = \lambda_t$$

(14) $$U_m(c_t, m_t) = \lambda_t(\pi_t + r_t + n)$$

(15) $$y'(k_t) - (u + n) = r_t$$

(16) $$\frac{\dot{\lambda}_t}{\lambda_t} = \delta - r_t$$

(17) $$\lim_{t \to \infty} a_t \lambda_t e^{-\delta t} = 0$$

where r_t is equal to the ratio of the two Lagrangian multipliers q_t/λ_t.

Equations (13)–(16) together with the constraints (5) and (11) form a system of six equations which, given the values of u, n, π_t, and v_t and given the initial stock of real wealth a_0, will describe the time path of the six endogenous variables c_t, m_t, k_t, a_t, λ_t, and r_t. The problem is therefore to find the path of these variables which, satisfying equations (5), (11) and (13)–(16) will also satisfy the transversality condition (17).[6]

From equations (13) and (14) we can solve for the quantities demanded of consumption and real cash as functions of the implicit price of consumption, λ, the implicit interest rate, r, and the expected rate of change in prices, π;

(18) $$c = c^0(\lambda, r, \pi)$$

(19) $$m = m^0(\lambda, r, \pi)$$

and from equation (15) we can solve for the quantity demanded of real capital as a function of the implicit interest rate.

(20) $$k = k^0(r)$$

Considering now the stock constraint (7) we determine the implicit rate of interest as a function of the stock of wealth, the implicit price of consumption and the expected rate of inflation.

(21) $$a = k^0(r) + m^0(\lambda, r, \pi)$$

namely

(22) $$r = r(a, \lambda, \pi)$$

and substituting back into (18), (19) and (20) we can write the demand for consumption, capital and real cash as functions of the stock of real

---

[6] In what follows the time subscripts will be used only where necessary for a better understanding of the text.

nonhuman wealth, the implicit price of consumption and the expected rate of change in prices

$$(23) \qquad\qquad c = c'(a, \lambda, \pi)$$

$$(24) \qquad\qquad m = m'(a, \lambda, \pi)$$

$$(25) \qquad\qquad k = k'(a, \lambda, \pi)$$

Finally, given the expected rate of inflation and government transfer payments, the pair of differential equations (11) and (16) determine the time path of the implicit price of consumption and the stock of wealth. The laws of motion of our system are shown in the phase diagram below. To verify that (λ^*, a^*) is a saddle point we solve the characteristic equation for the linear Taylor approximation to (11) and (16). For the characteristic roots to be real and opposite in sign, guaranteeing that (a^*, λ^*) is a local saddle point the following condition must hold[7]

$$(26) \qquad\qquad (\pi + n)J_1 + J_2 < 0$$

This condition will be satisfied for any expected rate of change in prices which is not smaller than the rate of growth of population. It should be noted that although the slope of the $\dot{a} = 0$ schedule in the phase diagrams may be positive or negative, the solution (a^*, λ^*) is a local saddle point provided that (26) holds.

Therefore, given the initial holdings of assets a_0, there is only one time path of a and λ which will satisfy the Euler conditions (13)–(16), the constraints (5) and (11) and the transversality condition (17). This path

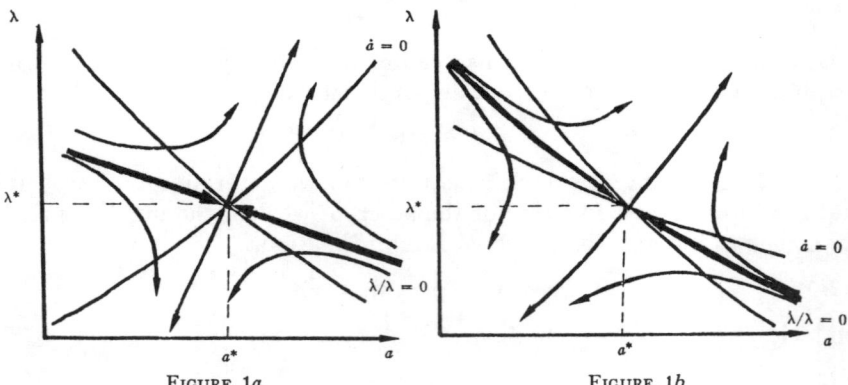

FIGURE 1*a*   FIGURE 1*b*

is indicated by the heavy arrows in Figures 1*a* and 1*b*. All other paths (light arrows) fail to satisfy condition (17). For each total stock of wealth there is one implicit price of consumption λ which will determine

[7] This condition is also derived in [8].

the optimum allocation of the stock of wealth between capital and real money and the optimum allocation of the income flow between consumption and net saving. This implicit price is the value of λ on the heavy arrows that corresponds to the given level of wealth. Clearly, a change in the expected rate of inflation as well as a change in the real value of government transfers will shift the optimum path, hence

$$(27) \qquad\qquad \lambda = \lambda(a, \pi, v)$$

By substituting (27) into (23), (24) and (25) we have shown that the quantities of capital, real money and consumption demanded are functions of total wealth, the expected rate of inflation and the net government transfers to the private sector.

$$(28) \qquad\qquad c = c(a, \pi, v)$$

$$(29) \qquad\qquad m = m(a, \pi, v)$$

$$(30) \qquad\qquad k = k(a, \pi, v)$$

III. *The Expectations Hypothesis and the Macroeconomic Model*

It will be assumed that expectations are induced, i.e., that individuals take past rates of change in prices into account in forming their expectations about a "normal rate of change in prices," on the basis of which they determine the amounts of real cash balances, capital and consumption that they demand at each moment of time. In particular, our hypothesis will imply that when individuals realize that their expectations did not materialize they partially revise what they consider to be the "normal rate of change in prices." This is the so-called "adaptive expectations" model that was originally introduced by Cagan [1] and which can be expressed in terms of the following differential equation

$$(31) \qquad\qquad \dot{\pi} = b(\dot{p}/p - \pi); \quad b > 0$$

From the point of view of the economy as a whole, market equilibrium requires that at each moment of time the demand for money be equal to the total money supply. Thus, given the stock of money M, the equilibrium condition in the money market can be written as follows

$$(32) \qquad\qquad \frac{M}{pN} = m(a, \pi, v)$$

where

$$(33) \qquad\qquad a = \frac{M}{pN} + k$$

The government levies taxes and makes transfer payments to the private sector but it does not undertake any public expenditures. We assume that the excess of transfer payments over taxes is entirely financed by the creation of government noninterest bearing debt which we call money. Therefore, the excess of transfers over taxes is exactly equal to the amount of money issued per unit of time. We also assume that each economic unit in the economy receives the same amount of net transfers; namely, that taxes and transfers are of the per capita type. Hence we can write

$$(34) \qquad\qquad v = \frac{M}{Np} = \theta m$$

where $\theta = \dot{M}/M$. Equations (31)–(34) form a system of four equations in seven unknowns, M, N, k, p, a, v and π. In order to have a complete system that describes the behavior of the economy through time, three additional equations are required. To complete the system we assume that the government maintains a constant rate of monetary expansion and population grows at a constant rate

$$(35) \qquad\qquad M/M = \theta_0$$

$$(36) \qquad\qquad \dot{N}/N = n$$

Finally, since all output that is not consumed is necessarily used for capital accumulation, the rate of change in the capital stock is given by the following expression

$$(37) \qquad\qquad \dot{k} = y(k) - (u + n)k - c(a, \pi, v)$$

We now have a system of seven equations in seven unknowns that describes the time path of our simplified economy. However, before we provide such a description it should be clear from the system of equations that a major difference arises when we go from the analysis of the individual economic unit to the analysis of the economy as a whole. While for the individual economic unit real wealth, the real value of the net government transfers and the expected rate of inflation are the variables that are given at each moment of time, for the economy as a whole these variables are the stock of capital, total population, the nominal quantity of money and the rate at which the government is increasing this quantity. Therefore, considering equations (32)–(34) we can write

$$(38) \qquad\qquad \frac{M}{pN} = \hat{m}\,(k, \theta, \pi)$$

Thus, given M, N, k, θ, and π the price level is determined and therefore the real value of privately held cash is also determined.

Substituting equations (33), (34) and (38) into (37) the rate of change in the capital stock can then be written as

(39) $$\dot{k} = y(k) - (u + n)k - \hat{c}(k, \theta, \pi)$$

where $\hat{c}$ is the consumption level desired for the price level p that equilibrates the money market at each moment of time.

The system of equations that describes the behavior of the economy through time is now given by (31), (35), (36), (38) and (39), the variables of the system being N, M, k, π and p. Differentiating equation (38) with respect to time and making use of (31), (35), (36) and (39) we express the rate of change in the expected rate of inflation as follows

(40) $$\dot{\pi} = \frac{1}{\left[1 + b\,\dfrac{\partial \hat{m}}{\partial \pi}\,\dfrac{1}{\hat{m}}\right]}$$

$$\cdot \left\{\theta - \pi - n - [y(k) - (u + n)k - \hat{c}(k, \theta, \pi)]\right\}$$

Given the rate of monetary expansion the system of differential equations (39), (40) describes the time path of the economy.

By setting $\dot{\pi}$ and $\dot{k}$ equal to zero in equations (39) and (40) it follows that along an equilibrium growth path consumption is equal to net output and the expected rate of inflation is equal to the difference between the rate of monetary expansion and the economy's rate of growth, which along such a path is equal to the rate of population growth. Hence,

(41) $$c^* = y(k^*) - (u + n)k^*$$

(42) $$\pi^* = \theta - n$$

IV. *Short-run and Long-run Effects of a Change in the Rate of Monetary Expansion and the Stability of Equilibrium Growth*

A question that naturally comes to mind is what are the conditions under which the equilibrium growth path characterized by equations (41) and (42) is stable? In what follows we will consider the local stability of our model and for this purpose we have to indicate first how changes in the capital stock, the expected rate of inflation and the rate of monetary expansion affect the demand for consumption and for real cash balances. It can be shown that, in the neighborhood of the equilibrium growth path, consumption and the real value of the stock of money are increasing functions of the stock of capital and of the rate of monetary expansion and decreasing functions of the expected rate of change in prices, namely

(43)
$$\frac{\partial \hat{c}^*}{\partial k^*} > 0 \qquad \frac{\partial \hat{c}^*}{\partial \theta} > 0 \qquad \frac{\partial \hat{c}^*}{\partial \pi^*} < 0$$

(44)
$$\frac{\partial \hat{m}^*}{\partial k^*} > 0 \qquad \frac{\partial \hat{m}^*}{\partial \theta} > 0 \qquad \frac{\partial \hat{m}^*}{\partial \pi^*} < 0$$

An increase in the capital stock raises consumption and the real value of the stock of cash of two accounts. First, because it raises disposable income and, second, because it is associated with an increase in the stock of real wealth. In addition, the increase in the stock of capital lowers its marginal product and therefore results in a decrease of the cost of holding cash, further raising the demand for the alternative asset. Net government transfers to the private sector are assumed to be financed entirely by money creation and therefore an increase in the rate of monetary expansion is equivalent to a rise in private disposable income due to higher government net transfers. The increase in real income raises the demand for both consumption and real cash balances. Finally, an increase in the expected rate of change in prices is equivalent to a rise in the rate of depreciation of one of the assets and it is therefore associated with a decrease in private disposable income which, in turn, lowers the demand for consumption and real money. In addition, the increase in the expected rate of inflation raises the opportunity cost of holding cash, thereby further reducing the demand for this asset.

With this information we now verify what are the conditions under which (k^*, π^*) is a stable solution to the pair of differential equations (39) and (40). For this purpose we solve the characteristic equations for the Taylor approximation to (39) and (40) at (k^*, π^*). From this exercise it follows that the necessary and sufficient conditions for the stability of the equilibrium growth path are

(45)
$$y'(k^*) - (u + n) - \frac{\partial \hat{c}^*}{\partial k^*} < 0$$

(46)
$$\left(1 + \frac{\partial \hat{m}^*}{\partial \pi^*} \frac{1}{\hat{m}^*} b\right) > 0$$

The condition in (45) reflects the fact that an increase in the capital stock has two opposite effects on the rate of capital accumulation. On the one hand, it increases real consumption, thereby lowering the rate of change of the capital stock, and, on the other hand, it raises net output and therefore stimulates capital accumulation. Stability in this model requires the rate of capital accumulation to be a decreasing function of the capital stock.

Since an increase in the expected rate of inflation reduces the demand for cash, it therefore results in a rise in prices. The increase in prices raises people's expected rate of inflation, further reducing the demand for money and causing a new rise in prices. Given that we assume that there is no lag in the adjustment of the actual to the desired stock of cash, the stability of the system depends on the existence as well as the magnitude of the expectations lag, as indicated by the expression in (46).

If the condition in (46) is satisfied, the solution (k^*, π^*) to the pair of differential equations (39) and (40), as indicated by the phase diagram in Figure 2, is a stable node. Provided the system is stable, a constant rate of monetary expansion will therefore guarantee a monotonic approach to the equilibrium growth path.

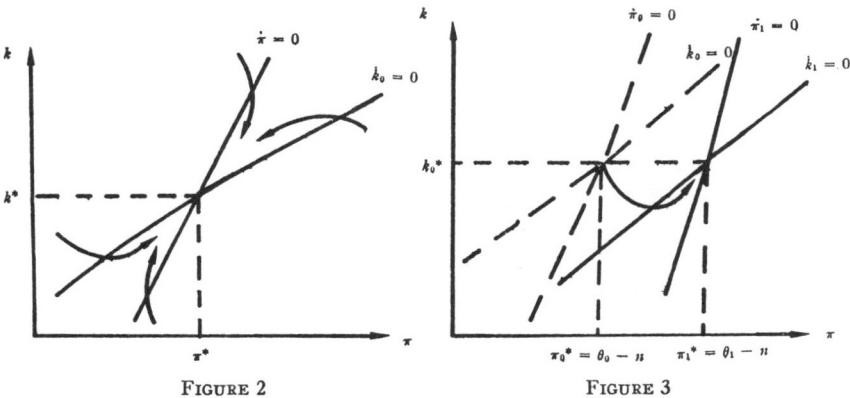

FIGURE 2   FIGURE 3

Consider now a situation in which the economy has reached its equilibrium growth path with $k^* = k_0^*$ and $\pi^* = \pi_0^*$ for $\theta = \theta_0 = \pi_0^* - n$. Suppose now that the government decides to change the rate of monetary expansion from θ_0 to θ_1, where $\theta_1 > \theta_0$. The first impact of this change is an increase in consumption which lowers capital accumulation, as well as an increase in the rate of change in prices which raises the rate of change of the expected rate of inflation. Both the $\dot{k} = 0$ and $\dot{\pi} = 0$ schedules shift to the right (Figure 3). Since we already know that the desired long-run stock of capital is determined only by its rate of depreciation, the rate of population growth and the subjective rate of time preference,[8] and, given that none of these variables are affected by the change in θ, the $\dot{k} = 0$ and the $\dot{\pi} = 0$ schedules will intersect at the same $k^* = k_0^*$ and at π_1^*, where $\pi_1^* = \theta_1 - n > \pi_0^*$. It therefore follows that while a change in the rate of monetary expansion lowers the short-

[8] This can be proved by setting equation (16) equal to zero and substituting into (15). The result of this operation is $y'(k^*) - u = (\delta + n)$.

544   AMERICAN ECONOMIC ASSOCIATION

run rate of capital accumulation, it does not affect the economy's long-run stock of capital.

V. *Conclusion*

Under the assumptions set out in Section I we have proved that in a growth model in which utility maximizing families are the basic economic unit of the system, the long-run capital stock of the economy is independent of the rate of monetary expansion. A rise in the rate of monetary expansion results in an equal absolute increase in the rate of change in prices; it reduces the stock of real cash but it does not affect steady state consumption. It therefore follows that the higher the rate of monetary expansion the lower will be the steady state level of utility. In the short run, an increase in the rate of monetary expansion is equivalent to a rise in government transfers to the private sector. It therefore results in an increase in consumption and a fall in the rate of capital accumulation.

Finally, we have also shown that in the absence of perfect foresight, utility maximization guarantees the fulfillment of only one of the steady state stability conditions; namely, that the rate of capital accumulation be a decreasing function of the capital stock. Since there is no lag in adjustment of the actual to the desired stock of cash, an additional, necessary but not sufficient, condition for the stability of the steady state is the existence of a lag in the formation of expectations.

REFERENCES

1. P. Cagan, "The Monetary Dynamics of Hyperinflation," in *Studies in the Quantity Theory of Money*, ed., M. Friedman (Univ. of Chicago Press, 1956).
2. I. Fisher, *The Theory of Interest* (New York, 1930).
3. John G. Gurley and Edward S. Shaw, *Money in a Theory of Finance*, with a mathematical appendix by A. C. Enthoven (Washington, 1960).
4. Harry G. Johnson, "Monetary Theory and Policy," *A.E.R.*, June, 1962.
5. ———, "The neo-classical One Sector Growth Model, A Geometrical Exposition and Extension to a Monetary Economy," *Economica*, Aug., 1966.
6. D. Patinkin, *Money, Interest and Prices* (Row-Peterson, 1956).
7. M. Sidrauski, "Growth in a Monetary Economy" (Jan., 1966, mimeo.).
8. ———, "Inflation, Optimum Consumption and Real Cash Balances," a paper presented at the meetings of the Econometric Society, New York, Dec., 1965.
9. J. Tobin, "Money and Economic Growth," *Econometrica*, Oct., 1965.

[8]

Interest Rates and Monetary Policy

William E. Gibson

University of California, Los Angeles

I. Introduction

This paper investigates the empirical operation of some recognized theoretical effects of the money stock on market rates of interest. The analysis covers the period since World War II, the period for which extensive quarterly and monthly data are available.

There is a widespread belief among economists that an increase in the money stock lowers interest rates.[1] This conclusion seems to follow from the liquidity-preference relation between the level of interest rates and the quantity of money demanded. As stated by Tobin (1947, p. 126):

> If the demand for cash balances is not completely inelastic with respect to the rate of interest, part of an addition to M will end up in idle balances. The added money will be used to bid down the rate of interest, and the lowering of the rate of interest will make the community willing to hold larger idle balances. So long as either investment or the propensity to consume is favorably affected by a lowering of the interest rate, there will also be an increase in money income. But since there is some increase in idle balances, the increase in money national income cannot be proportional to the increase in M; V cannot be considered a constant.

In Tobin's view interest rates will not return to their original levels as a result of money stock effects alone, but will end up higher than immediately

I am deeply grateful to Milton Friedman and Lester G. Tesler for helpful suggestions and advice on this study. Remaining errors are my own. This research was generously supported by the Federal Reserve Bank of Chicago.
[1] See Ackley (1961); Gramley and Chase (1965, esp. p. 1391); Trieber (1966). See also Federal Open Market Committee, Minutes, 1955 (Allan Sproul, May 10, May 24, and October 25, 1955, pp. 242, 275, 586; W. W. Riefler, August 23, 1955, p. 470; C. E. Earhart, March 2, 1955, p. 103); 1957 (J. L. Robertson, September 10, 1957, p. 553); 1958 (J. L. Robertson, February 11, 1958, p. 119); 1959 (J. L. Robertson, January 6, 1959, p. 16); and 1960 (A. L. Mills, Jr., December 13, 1960, p. 913).

after the money stock increase because of a shift in the liquidity-preference curve in response to an increase in income.

Similarly, monetary authorities tend to take it for granted that an increase in money stock lowers interest rates. From their vantage point, an increase in the money stock by open market purchases tends to lower market rates quickly, since purchasing securities raises their prices and lowers yields. Indeed, they rely on this relation in order to control rates. Accordingly, interest rate movements are frequently viewed as indicators of current monetary policy.

Since the money-interest rate relation is used in implementing monetary policy, it is particularly important that the monetary authorities know how the relation works. If the monetary authorities believed that they lowered interest rates by increasing the money stock, whereas this at first lowered and then later raised rates, the authorities' actions would work first toward and then away from an interest rate goal. Further, if interest rates are viewed as indicators of monetary policy, incorrect conclusions can easily follow if total effects are disregarded in favor of initial effects. The trouble with using interest rates as indicators of monetary policy emerges: If income increases faster than money, interest rates will tend to rise; but if the income increase itself results from increases in the money stock, should monetary policy be called restrictive?

II. Liquidity, Income, and Price Expectations Effects

In order to maintain equality the quantity of money supplied and the quantity demanded, variables in the demand function (and perhaps in the supply function) must change as the stock of money is altered. To trace the effects of changes in the quantity of money on interest rates, we must therefore specify some of the variables in these functions. For the purpose of this section—to present a general and simplified summary of the effects to be expected on theoretical grounds—it will be sufficient to assume that the quantity of money demanded varies inversely with the level of interest rates and the expected rate of price change, and varies directly with the level of nominal income, that is, the demand for money function is of the following form:

$$M^d = M^d\left[i, \left(\frac{1}{P}\frac{dP}{dt}\right)^*, Y\right], \qquad (1)$$

where M^d is the quantity of nominal cash balances demanded, i is the nominal rate of interest or a vector or average of nominal interest rates, $(1/P)(dP/dt)^*$ is the expected rate of price change, and Y is nominal income.

This is a highly simplified demand function. The literature suggests other variables which might also be included, such as wealth, additional interest rates, or the ratio of current to permanent income, and one or more variables measuring the cost of managing a cash balance, since adjusting a stock of cash balances to changes in other variables is not a costless operation.[2]

The effects of money on interest rates can be examined by tracing the movements of the variables in the demand function following change in the money stock.[3] We distinguish three effects: the Fisher (price expectations) effect, the liquidity effect, and the income effect.

A. The Fisher Effect

The Fisher or price expectations effect refers to the relationship between nominal interest rates and the expected rate of change of prices formulated by Fisher:[4]

$$i = r + \left(\frac{1}{P}\frac{dP}{dt}\right)^* + r\left(\frac{1}{P}\frac{dP}{dt}\right)^*, \qquad (2)$$

where r is the rate of interest net of compensation for expected price changes and is here called the "real" rate of interest, and $(1/P)(dP/dt)^*$ is the expected rate of change of prices. As Fisher noted, price inflation during the period of a loan imposes a capital loss on the lender by lowering

---

[2] The managers of cash balances of businesses, for instance, are often regarded as being adept at minimizing the costs of holding cash. They are reputed to be very sophisticated operators in the market for government securities, moving in and out of Treasury bills for short periods and for increasingly smaller amounts. The market transactions costs of such operations have been recognized and taken into account in some studies (see Tobin 1956; and Baumol 1952) but there are also internal costs to a firm engaging in such practices. These include the cost to the firm of managing its cash position. For example, the officer of the firm watching the cash position might be doing something else or, if not, is dispensable. The more of its resources a firm allocates to the management of its money stock, the greater its costs. Similar considerations apply to the costs to households of managing cash positions, although the cost in the form of time consumed might be less obvious. But it takes more time and energy for an individual to handle receipts and payments on a very small working balance than when he has a substantial cushion in his checking account (assuming the same total wealth in each case). Although he may not move frequently in and out of Treasury bills, he may still respond to large enough incentives—costs and returns— in altering his portfolio. The costs of managing cash are therefore measured in wages or the price of leisure, so for the economy as a whole, we can approximate this cost by the level of real wage rates. This also means that, as the cost of managing balances rises, people will be less responsive to changes in transitory income, so that the quantity of money demanded will tend to depend more closely on permanent rather than measured income.

[3] It is assumed that the effects on interest rates are the same no matter how the money stock is increased. Some evidence supporting this assumption may be found in Cagan (1966).

[4] Fisher (1896, 1907, 1930). In what follows the interaction term, $r(1/P)(dP/dt)^*$ which gives the expected rate of depreciation of the interest payments, will be ignored, as it is dwarfed by the other terms.

the real value of his principal and interest. Lenders who expect that prices will rise during the loan term will try to protect themselves. By exchanging money for real capital goods, they could avoid the capital loss, since the nominal value of real capital goods would rise along with prices in general. If such alternatives are open to lenders (and the presence of willing borrowers suggests that they are), they will be willing to exchange money for nominal assets only at a rate sufficiently high to yield the same return after the expected capital loss. Borrowers who use the funds to acquire real assets, on the other hand, will benefit from a price inflation for any given rate of interest, since the nominal values of the real assets they purchase will rise. Hence they will be willing to pay a higher rate when they expect prices to rise. If lenders and borrowers have identical expectations, the market rate of interest will exceed the real rate by the expected rate of price increase times the sum of the principal plus interest, or, in continuous time, times the principal alone. Expected price declines cause similar but opposite effects on real capital values, driving nominal interest rates below real rates by the expected rate of price decline.

The Fisher effect says nothing about the relation between the stock of money and interest rates, only something about the relation between expected price changes and interest rates. But, if all or part of an increase in the money stock is reflected in an increase in prices, then an increase in the quantity of money will set a Fisher effect in motion.

If there is a once-and-for-all increase in the money stock, prices will settle at some new level. A Fisher effect may be generated in the process, but it is unlikely to last, for prices will stop changing once there is full adjustment to the new quantity of money. If there is a price rise and it generates expectations of further rises, interest rates may rise, but they would fall again when prices stop rising and people readjust their expectations. In order for the Fisher effect to raise interest rates more than temporarily, people must expect prices to continue to increase. Empirically, this requires continued price increases, which require continued increases in the quantity of money (see Section IIE, below).

B. The Liquidity Effect

One way in which the quantity of money demanded can adjust to equal a change in the amount supplied is through changes in interest rates, via a liquidity-preference relation: At higher interest rates, *ceteris paribus*, less money will be demanded than at lower rates. The rate of interest is an index of the benefits attainable by shifting one's asset holdings from money to assets yielding monetary returns, and, as such, is the opportunity cost of holding cash balances. When this cost rises, *ceteris paribus*, the quantity of money demanded should fall. Alternatively, the relation implies that a larger quantity of cash balances will be held only at a lower interest rate, *ceteris paribus*. An increase in the money stock can therefore bring about a fall in interest rates. This liquidity effect is so widely recognized, especially by formulators of monetary policy, that it might be called the reigning view on the relation between money and interest rates.[5] As mentioned earlier, there is a basis for this view, particularly from the standpoint of the monetary authorities. When the money stock is increased, the addition must be held by someone. If, before the increase, individuals were holding the amount of money they desired at prevailing interest rates and income, there is no reason to assume that they would wish to hold more money after the increase unless income or interest rates change. The very act of increasing the money stock may tend to lower some interest rates: an open market purchase by the monetary authorities tends to raise security prices and lower their yields; banks seeking to expand their loans to absorb excess reserves can then do so only by offering to lend at lower interest rates. However, an increase produced by purchasing goods and services, or by grants to individuals or others need have no such initial effect.[6] The initial effects on lending and security rates will not spread immediately over the entire term structure of rates. But *some* rates can fall, and further adjustments in other rates will follow in time.

There will also be effects on interest rates beyond those connected with the act of monetary increase. Assume for a moment that the money supply is increased by dropping money from an airplane, and consider the effects in a period not sufficiently long for an income change to take place.[7] Must interest rates fall? On the basis of equation (1) they must, or else $M^s \neq M^d$. If we stop the period an hour after the plane has passed over, however, it may well be that no interest rate has fallen, and in fact $M^s \neq M^d$. But if people are given time to come in from the fields, they should shortly begin to try to draw down their excess balances. Two apparent ways for individuals to do so are to increase spending and to purchase other assets. If nominal income does not increase in the period, people will try to shift into other assets, raising their prices and lowering their yields. Yields will fall until $M^s = M^d$, for otherwise people would be left holding money they did not want. It may be that for very short periods people can be off their demand-for-money schedules, since it may take some time to adjust. In the present context, such excursions off demand schedules will be ignored, and the quantity demanded will be assumed to equal the quantity supplied. This is done, not because people are assumed never to be off demand schedules, but because these departures are assumed to be empirically negligible.

[5] See, for instance, references in footnote 1.

[6] Actually the yields on the stocks of such goods would fall, insofar as they are calculable, but these yields are not normally regarded as market interest rates.

[7] It is possible, on theoretical grounds, that such a period does not exist.

C. The Income Effect

Changes in nominal income can also bring about equilibrium between actual and desired money balances. If income immediately increased following a money stock increase, the quantity of money demanded would increase, perhaps with little change in interest rates. In general, the change in the quantity of money demanded may depend on how the change in nominal income is divided between a change in output and in prices. However, the demand function specified in equation (2) assumes that M^d is a function of *nominal* income only, so that a given increase in nominal income has the same effect on the quantity of money demanded, regardless of how it is divided between prices and output. If, in addition, the demand function for money has a unit income elasticity, it would be necessary, in order for interest rates to be unchanged, that nominal income rise in the same proportion as the money stock.

In this case, if income instantly rises in the same proportion as money, interest rates will remain unchanged, for rates need not move to equate M^d and M^s. The income and liquidity effects will have exactly balanced. But if income does not instantly rise in the same proportion as the money stock, the income change alone will not make desired and actual balances equal, and their equality will require a fall in interest rates. If interest rates fall for this reason and if the money stock is not further increased, income will subsequently increase and raise interest rates toward their former levels. As money holders bid up prices of other assets in response to decreases in interest rates, internal rates of return on these assets will fall. Accordingly, investment and income will increase. Interest rates rise because, at a now-constant M^s, an increase in income would raise desired balances above actual balances unless interest rates rose. Rates will rise when individuals attempt to increase their cash balances by trying to sell assets, lowering their prices and raising their yields. The income effect thus results when an income rise shifts the demand schedule for money outward so that a given stock of money will only be held at higher interest rates.

D. Income and Liquidity Effects Together

Money holders are assumed always to be in short-term equilibrium, although they need not be always in long-run equilibrium. If the money stock changes, interest rates, income, or both are assumed to change to maintain short-run equilibrium. If interest rates fall, the short-run equilibrium position achieved very likely will not be one of long-run equilibrium. After interest rates fall to make $M^s = M^d$, the public will be on a demand curve, but further changes can occur for several reasons. The public may have planned to lower balances by additional spending which could not be completed. Spending and income would then increase in following periods. Alternatively, if investment or consumption spending is negatively responsive to interest rates, income will increase, perhaps with a lag. In both cases interest rates will tend to rise, if the stock of money is not further changed, as the demand schedule for money moves outward.

In the absence of additional changes in the money stock there will be no further liquidity effects, and we can ask how far the income effect will raise interest rates. If we assume there is full employment and abstract from price expectations effects, all income increases therefore take the form of price increases, which increase the demand for nominal balances. If ex ante savings and investment were equal before the increase in the money stock, then at lower interest rates ex ante investment would tend to exceed saving. Increases in the price level will raise interest rates by raising nominal income and hence the quantity of money demanded. Upward pressure on income and prices will continue until the former level of interest rates is restored, the level which equated ex ante saving and investment. This point is reached when prices and income have increased in the same proportion as the money stock.

If, however, the economy is initially below full employment, interest rates may not return to previous levels. A return to old levels requires that the increase in nominal income be the same as with full employment. In terms of *IS-LM* curve analysis, we need to know the slope of the *IS* curve. If the *IS* curve relating interest rates to nominal income is horizontal (as under full employment), interest rates will return to original levels after the money stock is increased. If, perhaps because investment does not depend on income, the *IS* curve is negatively sloped, interest rates will settle below their original levels. Conversely, if the *IS* curve slopes positively, rates will settle above old levels.

Although equation (1) includes measured income, our conclusions require little if any modification if equation (1) instead includes permanent income. In this case, a given increase in measured income will raise permanent income by a smaller amount, raising interest rates by less than if M^d depended on measured income. But the rate of change of measured income need not be the same in both cases; measured income may rise faster when permanent rather than measured income is the variable in the demand function. A given lag in the income effect is consistent with including either income variable in equation (1), but the permanent income formulation allows a cyclical effect which the measured income counterpart does not. If when the income effect just balances the liquidity effect measured income is above permanent income (and it could be far above if permanent income must adjust rapidly), the latter will continue to rise, raising interest rates with it. Later measured income will fall, leading to cyclical approaches of measured and permanent income and interest rates to their new equilibrium levels.

Finally, most of the above discussion has dealt, explicitly or implicitly,

with increases in the money stock. Except for the full-employment constraint, a decrease in the money stock produces similar but opposite effects
on interest rates. Money holders must be induced to desire a smaller stock
of cash, and interest rates will rise if income does not fall immediately. If
permanent income is the appropriate demand variable, there may again be
cyclical adjustments.

E. The Price Expectations Effect Added

Figure 1 shows the final effect on interest rates of an increase in the
money stock. The economy is initially at point E_1, where money stock is
M_1^s and real (and nominal) interest rates are r_1. If income does not rise
immediately following an increase in the money stock to M_2^s, the economy
will move immediately to point P, along the curve L_1, drawn for a given
level of income and expected rate of price change. This fall of interest rates
from r_1 to r_2 is the liquidity effect. As income increases, the L curve will
shift rightward until it reaches the position L_2, which intersects M_2^s at E_2,
where interest rates are again at r_1. We may call the movement from P to
E_2 the income effect, and it obviously just balances the liquidity effect.

If now the expected rate of price change increases, L_2 will shift to the left
to L_3, lowering real interest rates to r_3. Nominal rates will exceed real
rates by the expected rate of price increase. The L curve shifts downward
when $(1/P)(dP/dt)^*$ increases, so that at a given r less money is demanded.

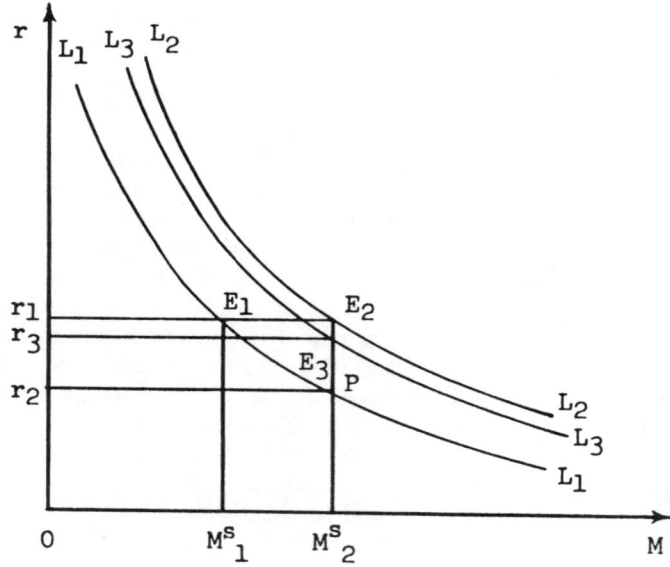

FIG. 1.—Interest rate adjustments to an increase in money stock

At the new equilibrium E_3, real rates are r_3, lower than before the shift in price expectations, because at higher expected rates of price change real assets will be more attractive at the old price ratio than both money and bonds. Asset holders will then try to shift from fixed-price assets to real assets, bidding up the prices and down the yields of the latter.

If the new expected rate of price change is to be maintained, there must be continuing increases in money and prices. Sustained price expectations will then keep nominal rates above real rates and real rates below their original levels.

The effects of expected inflation on nominal and real interest rates can also be seen from a diagram presented by Mundell (1963).[8] He assumes that real investment depends on the real interest rate[9] and real saving depends on real money balances, and that the desired ratio of money to securities depends on the nominal interest rate. Figure 2 shows the two curves, which Mundell calls *IS* and *LM*, which give pairs of interest rates and real cash balances consistent with equilibrium in the goods and money markets, respectively. Equilibrium is at Q when stable prices are expected. Real balances are $(M/P)_0$ and real and nominal interest rates are equal at level i_0. An expected rate of inflation of RT percent per year causes the *LM* curve expressed in terms of the real rate to shift down by RT, and the *IS* curve expressed in terms of the nominal rate rises by RT. When the ordinate is read as the nominal rate, therefore, equilibrium is at R, and the

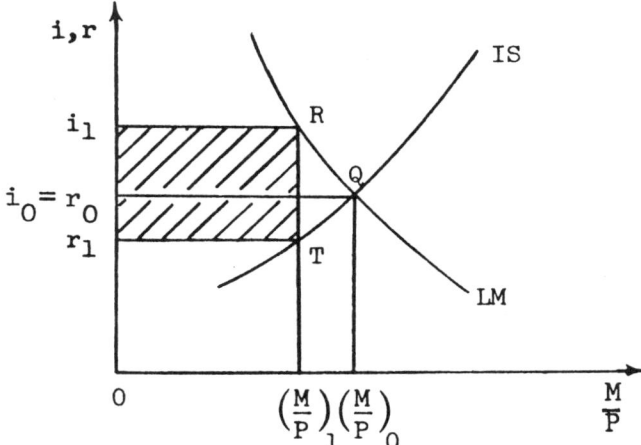

FIG. 2.—Interest rate adjustments to altered price expectations

[8] Mundell's result is derived from Lloyd Metzler's model, which assumes flexible wages and prices and full employment, but Mundell later extended it to the Keynesian unemployment case (Mundell 1965).

[9] Mundell implicitly assumes that the effect of the inflationary tax on the cash balances of businesses is not sufficient to offset the negative relation between the real rate and the level of investment.

nominal rate is i_1. In terms of the real rate, however, equilibrium is at T, with the real rate at r_1. The vertical distance between the two equilibria is the expected rate of inflation ($= RT$), and the shaded area represents the depreciation of real cash balances.

When IS and LM have the slopes shown in figure 2, therefore, expected inflation raises the nominal interest rate, but not by the full expected rate of inflation. The real rate falls because the inflation reduces real cash balances and the resultant decline in wealth stimulates increased saving. Real investment and real saving are higher than in the absence of inflation.

The amount of the fall in the real rate depends on the slopes of IS and LM (as defined here) and on the expected rate of inflation. Figure 2 shows that if the IS curve is horizontal the real rate will not fall, no matter how much inflation is expected. The IS curve will be horizontal if either of two condition holds. First, if investment is perfectly elastic with respect to the real rate, only one real rate will be possible, and the IS curve, drawn on the r, (M/P) plane, will be horizontal. If an increase in the real rate lowers investment, saving must decrease when real balances are increased if larger real balances are to be associated with higher interest rates. Money therefore cannot be neutral if the real rate is to fall; there must be some outside money in the economy. Therefore, in order for anticipated inflation to alter real conditions in the economy, investment must be imperfectly elastic with respect to the real rate, and there must be some outside money in the economy.

The LM curve will normally be negatively sloped if the interest elasticity of demand for real balances is neither zero nor infinite. If the demand were perfectly interest elastic, anticipated inflation would not change nominal rates, and real rates would fall by the anticipated rate of inflation. If the elasticity of demand were zero, real rates would be unchanged, and nominal rates would rise by the anticipated rate of inflation. If (as shown in fig. 2) neither IS nor LM is horizontal or vertical, both real and nominal rates will change when the expected rate of price change increases, but neither will change by the full expected rate.

III. Some Existing Evidence of Money's Effects on Interest Rates

Earlier studies have produced some evidence on each of the three effects on interest rates, although the operation of all three does not appear to have been fully documented. Cagan examined the relationship between changes in the rate of change of money (M_2) and changes in the commercial paper rate, using reference cycle-stage data (Cagan 1966). He found that an increase in the monetary growth rate in stage t has a negative effect on interest rates in stage t, zero net effect in stage $t + 1$, and positive effects thereafter. The initial negative effect is offset by the end of stage $t + 3$, and positive effects were estimated to continue through stage $t + 6$ (Cagan 1966, table 9, p. 389). Since there are nine stages in a cycle, the average duration of a stage is between four and five months. On average, then, positive effects offset negative effects within about a year after the stage in which the monetary growth rate is increased.

Cagan measured the total effects on interest rate changes of an increase in the rate of monetary acceleration for the 1904–61 period (he excluded stages within the 1929–33 contractions and within the World War II years), but he did not consider the relation between the stock of money and the level of interest rates. Other studies have generally not dealt with the total effects of money on interest rates, but some provide evidence on the separate effects.

Tobin's statement, noted earlier, is one of the more straightforward statements of the liquidity effect, for it says that an increase in the money stock lowers interest rates by causing the economy to move down along a liquidity-preference schedule. His evidence for the effect consists of plotting the commercial paper rate against "idle balances," the quantity of money adjusted for transactions needs. He concluded that the resulting negatively sloped curve supports his hypothesis of a liquidity-preference relation. Demand for money studies (Latané 1954; Friedman 1959; Meltzer 1963) now use more complex techniques but give similar evidence on this point: Holding income constant, increased money balances will be held only at lower interest rates. These studies do not, however, chart the effects on interest rates when both money and income are allowed to change.

The income effect has been documented in two parts. First, the positive effect on interest rates of increases in income has been documented, both overall and holding money and the rate of price change constant (Gibson and Kaufman 1968). Second, the relation between money and income has been under consideration in the literature for generations, beginning in a well-organized fashion with the Bullion debates in England at the beginning of the nineteenth century. More recently the Friedman-Meiselman study for the Commission on Money and Credit provides evidence of a close relation between money and income in the United States over a long period, as well as for subperiods (Friedman and Meiselman 1963). The authors found the stock of money more closely related to consumption six months later than at any other date (Friedman and Meiselman 1963, p. 214).

IV. Evidence of the Three Effects

Even for monthly data, the quantity of money and interest rates are positively correlated,[10] indicating that the liquidity-preference relation is

[10] The simple correlation between the ninety-day Treasury bill rate and M_2 monthly is 0.72 for the period 1952–66.

an inadequate description of the overall empirical money-interest rate relation. This positive relation could arise from a positive effect of interest rates on the supply of money or from the operation of income and price expectations effects. Both possibilities are investigated here.

A. Interest Rate Levels and Money Stock Levels

We can use

$$i = f(\ln M_t, \ln M_{t-1}, \ln M_{t-2}, \ldots, \ln M_{t-n}) \tag{3}$$

to measure the total effects of the money stock on interest rates and the distribution of these effects over time.[11] This equation can be interpreted as one of the reduced forms in a system of simultaneous equations, except that it assumes that money is the only exogenous variable. Equation (3) assumes that the primary direction of influence runs from the money stock to interest rates. There are however, reasons for expecting interest rates to influence the money stock: When interest rates rise, banks will be more anxious to acquire earning assets since yields on the latter rise. This will make them willing to operate on a lower reserve-deposit ratio than before, which, given the total amount of reserves available to the banking system, implies a lower excess reserve ratio.[12] For a given rediscount rate, the higher the level of market interest rates, the larger the amount that banks will wish to borrow. If the Federal Reserve does not offset these two effects by open market operations, the money stock will increase. Whether these

---

[11] Seasonal variation in interest rates was apparent from the coefficients of three sets of preliminary regressions using monthly and quarterly interest rates: interest rates on seasonal dummy variables, interest rates on past values of the seasonally adjusted money stock, and seasonally adjusted money on past interest rates. Seasonal coefficients showed a generally rising pattern from March through January; interest rates tend to be below February levels in the months following February, and above February levels in the months preceding February.

In addition, there are seasonal variations in the money stock which do not produce the three effects outlined earlier. These are the changes in the money stock made to accommodate seasonal changes in the demand for money and credit. An aim of the Federal Reserve System is to accommodate seasonal swings in the financial needs of trade, and the System tries to do this by removing seasonal fluctuations from interest rates. The seasonal variation remaining in interest rates suggests that the System is not wholly successful in these efforts, but the fact that it attempts to offset these seasonal fluctuations means that some changes in the money stock (for example, in response to exogenous seasonal movements in income) do not show liquidity effects. While these distortions appear in unadjusted money data, they should be absent from seasonally adjusted money stock data, from which the influence of the System's seasonal actions should be removed.

In order to avoid the seasonal distortions present in the two sets of data, therefore, the analysis which follows uses seasonally adjusted interest rates and money supply series. The data used are described in detail in the Appendix, where sources are listed.

[12] Cagan treated this problem in some detail, using annual data, and concluded that these interest rate effects on money are not sufficient to produce a positive relation (see Cagan 1965).

effects will be as large as the effects of money on interest rates is an empirical question.

The validity of this assumption can be checked by changing the variables in equation (3) to produce

$$\ln M_t = f(i_t, i_{t-1}, i_{t-2}, \ldots i_{t-n}). \tag{4}$$

Estimates of (4) and its first-difference form,

$$\frac{1}{M}\frac{dM}{dt} = f\left[\left(\frac{di}{dt}\right)_t, \left(\frac{di}{dt}\right)_{t-1}, \left(\frac{di}{dt}\right)_{t-2}, \cdots \left(\frac{di}{dt}\right)_{t-n}\right], \tag{5}$$

are presented for monthly data in tables 1 and 2. There is a strong positive relation between current interest rates and the current money stock, even when past interest rates are included in the regression. Except for this positive relation between current variables, however, there seems to be little systematic relation between the current money stock and past interest rates. Nearly all the coefficients of past rates are statistically insignificant. A fairly high fraction of the variation in the money stock is explained by equation (4), but most of this is due to the current interest rate, not to past rates. Although both money and interest rates are seasonally adjusted, there appears to be a slight seasonal pattern present in the coefficients of past interest rates in equations (4) and (5). These coefficients are predominantly negative for lagged levels and changes of interest rates, but coefficients of variables lagged six and twelve months are positive at least as often as they are negative. The seasonal pattern is less pronounced than when equations (4) and (5) were estimated for unadjusted interest rates, but it is puzzling that any seasonal pattern remains, since seasonal variation should be absent from both series. It is not clear why the pattern appears, but it may reflect an imperfection in the adjustment of published money supply series.

If income adjusted instantaneously to make the quantity of money demanded equal to an increased money supply with no other changes, liquidity and income effects would balance, and only price expectations effects would remain. If it takes time for income to adjust to a new level of the money supply, then it should be possible to measure the adjustment path. The assumption that it takes several months for income to adjust therefore implies that either monthly or quarterly data should be useful for this purpose. If liquidity effects can be observed at all, the coefficient of M_t in equation (3) should be negative. A positive coefficient would imply that income effects have balanced liquidity effects and that only positive effects should follow. Since the liquidity effect reflects immediate interest rate movements to equate M^d and M^s, most, if not all, of the negative influence should come in the current period. Following this negative effect, an increase in the money stock should have a positive influence on future interest rates as the income effect operates. In terms of the coefficients of

TABLE 1
RELATION BETWEEN THE MONEY STOCK AND CURRENT AND PAST INTEREST RATES, MONTHLY OBSERVATIONS, 1947–66

$\ln M_1 =$	4.6610* (0.0081)	$+9.5957^*i_t$ (2.2581)	$-2.1764 i_{t-1}$ (3.7972)	$-1.8626 i_{t-2}$ (3.8213)
	$+0.0899 i_{t-8}$ (3.8338)	$-1.5523 i_{t-9}$ (3.8141)	$-2.0591 i_{t-10}$ (3.8171)	$-1.2420 i_{t-1}$ (3.8368)
$\ln M_1 =$	4.4142* (0.0133)	$+15.351^*i_t$ (4.8582)	$-4.8391 i_{t-1}$ (8.3707)	$+2.4377 i_{t-2}$ (8.8956)
	$+0.5720 i_{t-8}$ (8.9113)	$-1.2725 i_{t-9}$ (9.0095)	$+2.1387 i_{t-10}$ (9.0237)	$-4.0239 i_{t-1}$ (8.6185)
$\ln M_1 =$	4.3934* (0.0160)	$+22.653^*i_t$ (6.8401)	$-11.757 i_{t-1}$ (12.813)	$+3.9689 i_{t-2}$ (13.975)
	$-1.5905 i_{t-8}$ (14.686)	$+0.1232 i_{t-9}$ (14.691)	$+1.3677 i_{t-10}$ (14.732)	$-2.9057 i_{t-1}$ (13.666)
$\frac{1}{M}\frac{dM_1}{dt} =$	0.02331* (0.00241)	$+1.1578 Di_t$ (1.6448)	$+0.3567 Di_{t-1}$ (1.7693)	$-0.2804 Di_t$ (1.7630)
	$-0.6892 Di_{t-8}$ (1.7670)	$-0.9224 Di_{t-9}$ (1.7674)	$-1.0009 Di_{t-10}$ (1.7591)	$-1.6115 Di_t$ (1.7718)
$\frac{1}{M}\frac{dM_1}{dt} =$	0.02360* (0.00253)	$+4.0792 Di_t$ (4.0085)	$+6.3755 Di_{t-1}$ (4.2417)	$-1.2714 Di_t$ (4.3079)
	$-1.8517 Di_{t-8}$ (4.3083)	$-2.5457 Di_{t-9}$ (4.3323)	$-7.0717 Di_{t-10}$ (4.3643)	$-5.1044 Di_t$ (4.3572)
$\frac{1}{M}\frac{dM_1}{dt} =$	0.02453* (0.00244)	$+10.490^* Di_t$ (4.7696)	$+3.3061 Di_{t-1}$ (5.4917)	$-5.1707 Di_t$ (5.5944)
	$+4.0887 Di_{t-8}$ (5.8544)	$-2.7537 Di_{t-9}$ (5.8572)	$-7.3692 Di_{t-10}$ (5.9592)	$-0.1337 Di_t$ (5.8664)

NOTE.—For sources and more complete notes see Appendix. $Di = i_t - i_{t-1}$.
* Significant at .05 level.

equation (3), this means that coefficients of past values of M should not be significantly negative and there should be some sufficiently distant values of the money stock for which the coefficients are positive. Nothing in Section II tells how far the liquidity effect must push rates, for this depends on the parameters in equation (1), the time required for income adjustments, the length of the period of observations (weekly vs. monthly, and so on), so that we do not know precisely the values to expect for the coefficient of M_t. However, for a once-and-for-all increase in M with full employment, the cumulative liquidity and income effects should eventually be equal, so that the initial negative coefficient should be matched by a sum of positive coefficients for past Ms, raising interest rates to their initial levels. If the economy initially had unemployed resources, the positive coefficients from the income effect may sum to less or more than the absolute value of the negative coefficient, depending on the shape and shifts of the investment schedule. If permanent income is the appropriate variable in equation (1), cyclical adjustments are possible. Income effects could then cause the positive coefficients to sum to more than the initial negative coefficient even at full employment, but we should then find later negative effects as cyclical adjustment continued.

$-1.6054i_{t-3}$ $+0.0356i_{t-4}$ $+0.7994i_{t-5}$ $+2.5518i_{t-6}$ $+0.6586i_{t-7}$
(3.8022)   (3.8434)   (3.8561)   (3.8705)   (3.8535)
$+7.6332^{*}i_{t-12}$ SE $Y \cdot X = 0.04775$ $R^2 = 0.844$ D-W $= 0.130$
(2.3413) $i = i_b$

$-0.5487i_{t-3}$ $-0.8836i_{t-4}$ $-1.8809i_{t-5}$ $+3.0281i_{t-6}$ $-1.8247i_{t-7}$
(8.9833)   (8.9473)   (8.8854)   (8.8327)   (8.8582)
$+6.7392i_{t-12}$ SE $Y \cdot X = 0.04082$ $R^2 = 0.874$ D-W $= 0.049$
(5.0389) $i = i_{bd}$

$-1.3306i_{t-3}$ $-2.5276i_{t-4}$ $-0.9245i_{t-5}$ $+1.2881i_{t-6}$ $-0.9076i_{t-7}$
(14.219)   (14.586)   (14.649)   (14.624)   (14.657)
$+6.7228i_{t-12}$ SE $Y \cdot X = 0.4752$ $R^2 = 0.845$ D-W $= 0.053$
(7.2912) $i = i_{aaa}$

$-0.6297Di_{t-3}$ $-1.2144Di_{t-4}$ $-0.5111Di_{t-5}$ $-1.3891Di_{t-6}$ $-1.1039Di_{t-7}$
(1.7551)   (1.7787)   (1.7760)   (1.7952)   (1.7658)
$-2.0497Di_{t-12}$ SE $Y \cdot X = 0.03481$ $R^2 = 0.067$ D-W $= 1.451$
(1.7037) $i = i_b$

$+1.9092Di_{t-3}$ $-1.2361Di_{t-4}$ $-6.0238Di_{t-5}$ $-1.1766Di_{t-6}$ $-2.2423Di_{t-7}$
(4.3062)   (4.3047)   (4.2962)   (4.3416)   (4.2845)
$-3.7604Di_{t-12}$ SE $Y \cdot X = 0.03424$ $R^2 = 0.097$ D-W $= 1.478$
(4.1519) $i = i_{bd}$

$+6.8284Di_{t-3}$ $-10.765Di_{t-4}$ $-6.9056Di_{t-5}$ $+4.0632Di_{t-6}$ $-13.967^{*}Di_{t-7}$
(5.7071)   (5.8296)   (5.8315)   (5.8255)   (5.8453)
$-11.783^{*}Di_{t-12}$ SE $Y \cdot X = 0.03298$ $R^2 = 0.162$ D-W $= 1.515$
(5.0853) $i = i_{aaa}$

A once-and-for-all increase in the money stock ought not to produce a sustained change in the expected rate of price change since it will not produce a sustained change in the actual rate. Any price expectations effect produced ought therefore to be offset by opposite effects when the price level settles at a new level. There may, however, be short-run price expectations effects which, although later offset, influence interest rates. In the absence of unemployment and cyclical adjustments, these effects would cause the algebraic sum of the coefficients to exceed zero and then fall back to zero as more past Ms are added. A cyclical effect from permanent income could complicate this sequence, but it ought not to change the final (zero) sum. The entire sequence should change, however, if unemployment exists and real income increases, in which case the sum of the coefficients can be equal to, greater than, or less than zero.

Estimates of equation (3) for monthly and quarterly data on M_1 and M_2 for 1947–66 appear in tables 3–6.

The coefficients in tables 3 and 4 confirm that the negative liquidity effect operates in the same month in which the money stock is changed. While the relation between current money and interest was positive when past interest rates were included in equation (4), the relation is negative

TABLE 2
RELATION BETWEEN THE MONEY STOCK AND CURRENT AND PAST INTEREST RATES, MONTHLY OBSERVATIONS, 1947–66

$$\ln M_2 = +4.8025^* + 18.421^* i_t - 3.7775 i_{t-1} - 3.8638 i_{t-2} - 3.0063 i_{t-3} - 3.3061 i_{t-4}$$
$$(0.0158)\ (4.4020)\ (7.4025)\ (7.4494)\ (7.4123)\ (4.40926)$$
$$+1.5323 i_{t-5} + 4.7483 i_{t-6} + 1.9568 i_{t-7} + 0.1463 i_{t-8} - 2.8540 i_{t-9} - 3.9731 i_{t-10}$$
$$(7.5172)\ (7.5454)\ (7.5123)\ (7.4739)\ (7.4354)\ (7.4412)$$
$$-2.5842 i_{t-11} + 15.164^* i_{t-12} \qquad i = i_b$$
$$(7.4795)\ (4.5642)$$
$$\text{SE } Y\cdot X = 0.09308 \qquad R^2 = 0.848 \qquad \text{D-W} = 0.126$$

$$\ln M_2 = 4.3068^* + 23.928^* i_t - 6.7184 i_{t-1} + 3.0817 i_{t-2} - 0.2571 i_{t-3} - 0.9505 i_{t-4}$$
$$(0.0256)\ (9.3338)\ (16.082)\ (17.091)\ (17.259)\ (17.190)$$
$$-3.8074 i_{t-5} + 5.3238 i_{t-6} - 2.7682 i_{t-7} - 0.5368 i_{t-8} - 1.1694 i_{t-9} + 5.1826 i_{t-10}$$
$$(17.071)\ (16.970)\ (17.019)\ (17.121)\ (17.310)\ (17.337)$$
$$-10.375 i_{t-11} + 19.185 i_{t-12} \qquad i = i_{bd}$$
$$(16.558)\ (9.6811)$$
$$\text{SE } Y\cdot X = 0.08228 \qquad R^2 = 0.881 \qquad \text{D-W} = 0.040$$

$$\ln M_2 = 4.2543^* + 36.420 i_t - 19.535 i_{t-1} + 7.4452 i_{t-2} - 0.7068 i_{t-3} - 5.6655 i_{t-4}$$
$$(0.0302)\ (12.953)\ (24.265)\ (26.464)\ (26.927)\ (27.621)$$
$$-2.6166 i_{t-5} + 2.9964 i_{t-6} - 1.7820 i_{t-7} - 2.9446 i_{t-8} + 0.6803 i_{t-9} + 2.8499 i_{t-10}$$
$$(27.742)\ (27.695)\ (27.755)\ (27.811)\ (27.821)\ (27.897)$$
$$-10.983 i_{t-11} + 22.650 i_{t-12} \qquad i = i_{aaa}$$
$$(25.880)\ (13.807)$$
$$\text{SE } Y\cdot X = 0.08998 \qquad R^2 = 0.858 \qquad \text{D-W} = 0.047$$

$$\frac{1}{M_2}\frac{dM_2}{dt} = 0.04490^* + 0.7048 Di_t - 1.5985 Di_{t-1} - 2.0314 Di_{t-2} - 1.0069 Di_{t-3} - 1.9834 Di_{t-4}$$
$$(0.00248)\ (1.6911)\ (1.8190)\ (1.8126)\ (1.8045)\ (1.8287)$$
$$-0.7501 Di_{t-5} - 2.3066 Di_{t-6} - 1.3599 Di_{t-7} - 0.8786 Di_{t-8} - 0.1554 Di_{t-9} - 1.5484 Di_{t-10}$$
$$(1.8260)\ (1.8457)\ (1.8155)\ (1.8168)\ (1.8171)\ (1.8086)$$
$$-2.1884 Di_{t-11} - 1.6057 Di_{t-12} \qquad i = i_b$$
$$(1.8216)\ (1.7517)$$
$$\text{SE } Y\cdot X = 0.03579 \qquad R^2 = 0.106 \qquad \text{D-W} = 0.794$$

$$\frac{1}{M_2}\frac{dM_2}{dt} = 0.04586^* + 1.2121 Di_t + 3.6758 Di_{t-1} - 4.6851 Di_{t-2} - 2.5582 Di_{t-3} - 4.9604 Di_{t-4}$$
$$(0.00267)\ (4.2323)\ (4.4785)\ (4.5485)\ (4.5466)\ (4.5451)$$
$$-4.9357 Di_{t-5} - 4.6381 Di_{t-6} - 2.6509 Di_{t-7} - 1.2921 Di_{t-8} - 2.7139 Di_{t-9} - 4.6411 Di_{t-10}$$
$$(4.5361)\ (4.5840)\ (4.5237)\ (4.5488)\ (4.5742)\ (4.6080)$$
$$-3.2424 Di_{t-11} - 7.0661 Di_{t-12} \qquad i = i_{bd}$$
$$(4.5361)\ (4.5840)$$
$$\text{SE } Y\cdot X = 0.03615 \qquad R^2 = 0.088 \qquad \text{D-W} = 0.805$$

$$\frac{1}{M_2}\frac{dM_2}{dt} = 0.04631^* + 7.3984 Di_t + 0.7765 Di_{t-1} - 8.4808 Di_{t-2} + 0.1483 Di_{t-3} - 7.1197 Di_{t-4}$$
$$(0.00259)\ (5.0643)\ (5.8310)\ (5.9401)\ (6.0598)\ (6.1899)$$
$$-9.9830 Di_{t-5} + 1.9900 Di_{t-6} - 12.818^* Di_{t-7} + 2.9883 Di_{t-8} - 0.2164 Di_{t-9} - 5.4622 Di_{t-10}$$
$$(6.1919)\ (6.1855)\ (6.2065)\ (6.2162)\ (6.2191)\ (6.3274)$$
$$+1.0029 Di_{t-11} - 12.604^* Di_{t-12} \qquad i = i_{aaa}$$
$$(6.2289)\ (5.3995)$$
$$\text{SE } Y\cdot X = 0.03501 \qquad R^2 = 0.144 \qquad \text{D-W} = 0.786$$

NOTE.—For sources and more complete notes, see Appendix. $Di = i_t - i_{t-1}$, M, i seasonally adjusted.
* Significant at .05 level.

TABLE 3

RELATION BETWEEN INTEREST RATES AND CURRENT AND PAST MONEY STOCKS, MONTHLY OBSERVATIONS, 1947–66

$$
\begin{aligned}
i_b = {}& -0.3737^* -0.3873^* M1_t +0.0754\,M1_{t-1} +0.1483\,M1_{t-2} +0.2103\,M1_{t-3} -0.0209\,M1_{t-4} +0.0550\,M1_{t-5} \\
& (0.0145)\ (0.1393)\ \ (0.2141)\ \ \ (0.2137)\ \ \ (0.2093)\ \ \ (0.2179)\ \ \ (0.2166) \\
& +0.1603\,M1_{t-6} +0.0161\,M1_{t-7} +0.0588\,M1_{t-8} -0.0223\,M1_{t-9} -0.0382\,M1_{t-10} -0.0848\,M1_{t-11} -0.0897\,M1_{t-12} \\
& (0.2242)\ \ \ (0.2298)\ \ \ (0.2324)\ \ \ (0.2387)\ \ \ (0.2453)\ \ \ \ (0.2461)\ \ \ \ (0.1549)
\end{aligned}
$$

$R^2 = 0.815 \quad\quad \text{D-W} = 0.121 \quad\quad SE\ Y\cdot X = 0.00494$

$$
\begin{aligned}
i_{bd} = {}& -0.2687^* -0.1378\,M1_t +0.0355\,M1_{t-1} +0.0960\,M1_{t-2} +0.0613\,M1_{t-3} -0.0138\,M1_{t-4} -0.0154\,M1_{t-5} \\
& (0.0076)\ (0.0729)\ \ (0.1121)\ \ \ (0.1119)\ \ \ (0.1096)\ \ \ (0.1141)\ \ \ (0.1134) \\
& +0.0317\,M1_{t-6} -0.0060\,M1_{t-7} +0.0022\,M1_{t-8} -0.0021\,M1_{t-9} -0.0342\,M1_{t-10} +0.0016\,M1_{t-11} +0.0429\,M1_{t-12} \\
& (0.1174)\ \ \ (0.1204)\ \ \ (0.1217)\ \ \ (0.1250)\ \ \ (0.1285)\ \ \ \ (0.1289)\ \ \ \ (0.0811)
\end{aligned}
$$

$R^2 = 0.887 \quad\quad \text{D-W} = 0.076 \quad\quad SE\ Y\cdot X = 0.00259$

$$
\begin{aligned}
i_{aaa} = {}& -0.2756^* -0.1419\,M1_t +0.0135\,M1_{t-1} +0.0674\,M1_{t-2} +0.0721\,M1_{t-3} +0.0033\,M1_{t-4} -0.0212\,M1_{t-5} \\
& (0.0083)\ (0.0794)\ \ (0.1221)\ \ \ (0.1218)\ \ \ (0.1193)\ \ \ (0.1242)\ \ \ (0.1235) \\
& +0.0431\,M1_{t-6} -0.00273\,M1_{t-7} +0.0374\,M1_{t-8} -0.0118\,M1_{t-9} -0.0623\,M1_{t-10} -0.0126\,M1_{t-11} +0.0798\,M1_{t-12} \\
& (0.1279)\ \ \ (0.1311)\ \ \ \ (0.1325)\ \ \ (0.1361)\ \ \ (0.1399)\ \ \ \ (0.1403)\ \ \ \ (0.0883)
\end{aligned}
$$

$R^2 = 0.874 \quad\quad \text{D-W} = 0.058 \quad\quad SE\ Y\cdot X = 0.00281$

$$
\begin{aligned}
\frac{di_b}{dt} = {}& -0.00027 -0.00389\,DM1_t +0.00140\,DM1_{t-1} +0.00541\,DM1_{t-2} +0.00737\,DM1_{t-3} +0.00048\,DM1_{t-4} +0.00729\,DM1_{t-5} \\
& (0.00016)\ (0.00352)\ \ (0.00356)\ \ \ (0.00369)\ \ \ (0.00379)\ \ \ (0.00383)\ \ \ (0.00382) \\
& +0.00804^*\,DM1_{t-6} +0.00633\,DM1_{t-7} -0.00157\,DM1_{t-8} -0.00426\,DM1_{t-9} -0.00196\,DM1_{t-10} -0.00569\,DM1_{t-11} -0.00266\,DM1_{t-12} \\
& (0.00403)\ \ \ (0.00404)\ \ \ (0.00404)\ \ \ (0.00424)\ \ \ (0.00422)\ \ \ \ (0.00401)\ \ \ \ (0.00391)
\end{aligned}
$$

$R^2 = 0.199 \quad\quad \text{D-W} = 1.435 \quad\quad SE\ Y\cdot X = 0.00149$

$$
\begin{aligned}
\frac{di_{bd}}{dt} = {}& -0.00005 -0.00102\,DM1_t +0.00091\,DM1_{t-1} +0.00394^*\,DM1_{t-2} +0.00368^*\,DM1_{t-3} -0.00127\,DM1_{t-4} -0.00049\,DM1_{t-5} \\
& (0.00006)\ (0.00144)\ \ (0.00146)\ \ \ (0.00151)\ \ \ (0.00151)\ \ \ (0.00157)\ \ \ (0.00157) \\
& +0.00325\,DM1_{t-6} -0.00006\,DM1_{t-7} -0.00034\,DM1_{t-8} -0.00149\,DM1_{t-9} +0.00095\,DM1_{t-10} +0.00189\,DM1_{t-11} -0.00322^*\,DM1_{t-12} \\
& (0.00165)\ \ \ (0.00166)\ \ \ (0.00166)\ \ \ (0.00174)\ \ \ (0.00173)\ \ \ \ (0.00165)\ \ \ \ (0.00160)
\end{aligned}
$$

$R^2 = 0.149 \quad\quad \text{D-W} = 1.442 \quad\quad SE\ Y\cdot X = 0.00061$

$$
\begin{aligned}
\frac{di_{aaa}}{dt} = {}& -0.00005 -0.00096\,DM1_t -0.00051\,DM1_{t-1} +0.00002\,DM1_{t-2} +0.00314^*\,DM1_{t-3} +0.00152\,DM1_{t-4} +0.00007\,DM1_{t-5} \\
& (0.00006)\ (0.00124)\ \ (0.00126)\ \ \ (0.00130)\ \ \ (0.00130)\ \ \ (0.00135)\ \ \ (0.00135) \\
& +0.00098\,DM1_{t-6} +0.00034\,DM1_{t-7} +0.00165\,DM1_{t-8} +0.00028\,DM1_{t-9} -0.00024\,DM1_{t-10} -0.00007\,DM1_{t-11} -0.00079\,DM1_{t-12} \\
& (0.00142)\ \ \ (0.00142)\ \ \ (0.00143)\ \ \ (0.00150)\ \ \ (0.00149)\ \ \ \ (0.00141)\ \ \ \ (0.00138)
\end{aligned}
$$

$R^2 = 0.121 \quad\quad \text{D-W} = 1.117 \quad\quad SE\ Y\cdot X = 0.00053$

NOTE.—For sources and more complete notes, see Appendix. $M1 = \ln M_1$; $DM1 = \dfrac{1}{M_1}\dfrac{dM_1}{dt}$; M, i seasonally adjusted.

* Significant at .05 level.

TABLE 4

RELATION BETWEEN INTEREST RATES AND CURRENT AND PAST MONEY STOCKS, MONTHLY OBSERVATIONS, 1947–66

$$
\begin{aligned}
i_b =\; & -0.2366^* - 0.6237^* M2_t + 0.2417 M2_{t-1} + 0.1475 M2_{t-2} + 0.1239 M2_{t-3} + 0.0284 M2_{t-4} \\
 & (0.0100)\quad (0.1456)\qquad (0.2456)\qquad (0.2478)\qquad (0.2445)\qquad (0.2498) \\
 & + 0.1336 M2_{t-5} + 0.0915 M2_{t-6} - 0.0908 M2_{t-7} + 0.0580 M2_{t-8} + 0.0631 M2_{t-9} + 0.0444 M2_{t-10} \\
 & (0.2485)\qquad (0.2496)\qquad (0.2502)\qquad (0.2517)\qquad (0.2555)\qquad (0.2611) \\
 & - 0.0505 M2_{t-11} - 0.0284 M2_{t-12} \\
 & (0.2623)\qquad (0.1575) \\
 & \text{SE } Y\cdot X = 0.00457 \qquad R^2 = 0.841 \qquad \text{D-W} = 0.161
\end{aligned}
$$

$$
\begin{aligned}
i_{bd} =\; & -0.1469^* - 0.1503 M2_t + 0.0608 M2_{t-1} + 0.0381 M2_{t-2} + 0.0208 M2_{t-3} + 0.0323 M2_{t-4} \\
 & (0.0058)\quad (0.0836)\qquad (0.1411)\qquad (0.1423)\qquad (0.1405)\qquad (0.1435) \\
 & + 0.0238 M2_{t-5} + 0.0126 M2_{t-6} - 0.0419 M2_{t-7} - 0.0048 M2_{t-8} + 0.0348 M2_{t-9} - 0.0186 M2_{t-10} \\
 & (0.1427)\qquad (0.1434)\qquad (0.1437)\qquad (0.1446)\qquad (0.1468)\qquad (0.1500) \\
 & - 0.0150 M2_{t-11} + 0.0419 M2_{t-12} \\
 & (0.1507)\qquad (0.0905) \\
 & \text{SE } Y\cdot X = 0.00263 \qquad R^2 = 0.883 \qquad \text{D-W} = 0.074
\end{aligned}
$$

$$
\begin{aligned}
i_{aaa} =\; & -0.1565^* - 0.1457 M2_t + 0.0459 M2_{t-1} + 0.0270 M2_{t-2} + 0.0113 M2_{t-3} + 0.0330 M2_{t-4} \\
 & (0.0062)\quad (0.0897)\qquad (0.1512)\qquad (0.1526)\qquad (0.1506)\qquad (0.1539) \\
 & + 0.0270 M2_{t-5} + 0.0150 M2_{t-6} - 0.0241 M2_{t-7} + 0.0029 M2_{t-8} + 0.0243 M2_{t-9} - 0.0465 M2_{t-10} \\
 & (0.1530)\qquad (0.1537)\qquad (0.1541)\qquad (0.1550)\qquad (0.1573)\qquad (0.1608) \\
 & - 0.0271 M2_{t-11} + 0.0942 M2_{t-12} \\
 & (0.1615)\qquad (0.0970) \\
 & \text{SE } Y\cdot X = 0.00281 \qquad R^2 = 0.874 \qquad \text{D-W} = 0.056
\end{aligned}
$$

$$
\begin{aligned}
\frac{di_b}{dt} =\; & -0.00027 - 0.01222^* DM2_t + 0.00352 DM2_{t-1} + 0.00285 DM2_{t-2} + 0.00540 DM2_{t-3} + 0.00095 DM2_{t-4} \\
 & (0.00019)\quad (0.00400)\qquad (0.00428)\qquad (0.00441)\qquad (0.00455)\qquad (0.00451) \\
 & + 0.01172^* DM2_{t-5} + 0.00916^* DM2_{t-6} - 0.00141 DM2_{t-7} - 0.00276 DM2_{t-8} - 0.00418 DM2_{t-9} + 0.00408 DM2_{t-10} \\
 & (0.00453)\qquad (0.00454)\qquad (0.00455)\qquad (0.00456)\qquad (0.00475)\qquad (0.00474) \\
 & - 0.00086 DM2_{t-11} - 0.00579 DM2_{t-12} \\
 & (0.00454)\qquad (0.00970) \\
 & \text{SE } Y\cdot X = 0.00151 \qquad R^2 = 0.181 \qquad \text{D-W} = 1.450
\end{aligned}
$$

$$
\begin{aligned}
\frac{di_{bd}}{dt} =\; & -0.000057 - 0.000217 DM2_t + 0.00077 DM2_{t-1} + 0.00107 DM2_{t-2} + 0.00418^* DM2_{t-3} + 0.00128 DM2_{t-4} \\
 & (0.000080)\quad (0.00167)\qquad (0.00178)\qquad (0.00184)\qquad (0.00190)\qquad (0.00188) \\
 & + 0.00084 DM2_{t-5} + 0.00306 DM2_{t-6} - 0.00239 DM2_{t-7} - 0.00129 DM2_{t-8} - 0.00175 DM2_{t-9} + 0.00188 DM2_{t-10} \\
 & (0.00189)\qquad (0.00189)\qquad (0.00190)\qquad (0.00190)\qquad (0.00198)\qquad (0.00198) \\
 & + 0.00206 DM2_{t-11} - 0.00235 DM2_{t-12} \\
 & (0.00189)\qquad (0.00178) \\
 & \text{SE } Y\cdot X = 0.00063 \qquad R^2 = 0.103 \qquad \text{D-W} = 1.429
\end{aligned}
$$

$$
\begin{aligned}
\frac{di_{aaa}}{dt} =\; & -0.000055 + 0.00028 DM2_t - 0.00112 DM2_{t-1} - 0.00179 DM2_{t-2} + 0.00174 DM2_{t-3} + 0.00205 DM2_{t-4} \\
 & (0.000068)\quad (0.00142)\qquad (0.00152)\qquad (0.00157)\qquad (0.00162)\qquad (0.00161) \\
 & + 0.00240 DM2_{t-5} + 0.00181 DM2_{t-6} - 0.00141 DM2_{t-7} - 0.00090 DM2_{t-8} - 0.00026 DM2_{t-9} + 0.00075 DM2_{t-10} \\
 & (0.00161)\qquad (0.00162)\qquad (0.00162)\qquad (0.00162)\qquad (0.00169)\qquad (0.00169) \\
 & + 0.00071 DM2_{t-11} - 0.00032 DM2_{t-12} \\
 & (0.00162)\qquad (0.00152) \\
 & \text{SE } Y\cdot X = 0.00054 \qquad R^2 = 0.085 \qquad \text{D-W} = 1.087
\end{aligned}
$$

NOTE.—For sources and more complete notes, see Appendix. $M2 = \ln M_2$; $DM2 = \frac{1}{M_2}\frac{dM_2}{dt}$; M, i seasonally adjusted.

* Significant at .05 level.

when past values of M are included in equation (3). The most striking result in the estimates is the speed with which the income effects operate. The coefficients show that positive effects offset negative effects by the end of the third month after the month in which M_1 is increased and by the end of the fifth month after M_2 is increased. For quarterly data, the coefficient of the past quarter's money stock is positive and of the same order of magnitude as the current period's negative coefficient. More often than not the first positive coefficient exceeds the negative coefficient in absolute value.

Estimates of coefficients of earlier monetary variables are generally not statistically significant (see also table 7).[13] However, they show a slight cyclical pattern. The positive coefficients sum to more than the initial negative coefficient and are followed by small coefficients of varying signs. The algebraic sums of the coefficients show no marked tendency to exceed zero. The negative coefficients for distant Ms could result from short-lived price expectations effects or from cyclical movements in measured income involved in the adjustments of permanent income.

Since the residuals from equation (3) showed high serial correlation, the first-difference form

$$\frac{di}{dt} = f\left[\left(\frac{1}{M}\frac{dM}{dt}\right)_t, \left(\frac{1}{M}\frac{dM}{dt}\right)_{t-1}, \cdots, \left(\frac{1}{M}\frac{dM}{dt}\right)_{t-n}\right] \qquad (6)$$

was estimated, and the coefficients appear in tables 3–6. The coefficients show the same general patterns found in the level equations. Liquidity effects are quickly overcome by income effects, and cyclical patterns follow. In some cases, however, the algebraic sum of the coefficients tends to remain greater than zero, particularly for the bill rate. If the positive sum resulted from shifts in the investment schedule, the coefficients in equation (3) should also have summed to more than zero. The positive sums for equation (6) may instead reflect price expectations effects, since (6) includes the rate of change of money. But the price expectations effect relates the level of interest rates to the rate of change of money and prices, while equation (6) contains rates of change of both. If, however, the expected rate of price change adjusts slowly to changes in actual rate, we might find money, prices, and interest rates moving together over some ranges. This is essentially the sequence Fisher envisioned to explain the Gibson Paradox, although he did not emphasize the relation between changes in money and changes in prices. If true, the sequence provides an explanation for the positive sum of the coefficients, a result difficult to

[13] Although many of the coefficients in equation (3) and following equations are not statistically significant, it should not be concluded that the positive effects of money on interest rates are not significant. As table 7 shows, for monthly data the combined explanatory influence of M_{t-1} through M_{t-6} is highly significant. Similar significance levels also appear when variables are grouped in other equations below.

TABLE 5

RELATION BETWEEN INTEREST RATES AND CURRENT AND PAST MONEY STOCKS,
QUARTERLY OBSERVATIONS, 1947–66

$$i_b = -0.4000^* \qquad -0.3254^*M1_t \qquad +0.4502M1_{t-1} \qquad +0.1591M1_{t-2}$$
$$\quad\;\; (0.0306) \qquad\quad (0.1484) \qquad\qquad (0.3035) \qquad\qquad\; (0.3378)$$
$$\quad -0.0989M1_{t-7} \quad -0.1789M1_{t-8} \quad +0.0741M1_{t-9} \quad +0.0908M1_{t-10}$$
$$\quad\;\; (0.3296) \qquad\quad (0.3260) \qquad\qquad (0.3132) \qquad\qquad\; (0.1543)$$

$$i_{bd} = -0.2914^* \qquad -0.0897M1_t \qquad +0.1457M1_{t-1} \qquad +0.0091M1_{t-2}$$
$$\quad\;\; (0.0151) \qquad\quad (0.0731) \qquad\qquad (0.1495) \qquad\qquad\; (0.1664)$$
$$\quad -0.0382M1_{t-7} \quad -0.0212M1_{t-8} \quad -0.0741M1_{t-9} \quad +0.1328M1_{t-10}$$
$$\quad\;\; (0.1623) \qquad\quad (0.1605) \qquad\qquad (0.1542) \qquad\qquad\; (0.0760)$$

$$i_{aaa} = -0.2992^* \qquad -0.1088M1_t \qquad +0.1030M1_{t-1} \qquad +0.0896M1_{t-2}$$
$$\quad\;\; (0.0166) \qquad\quad (0.0807) \qquad\qquad (0.1651) \qquad\qquad\; (0.1837)$$
$$\quad -0.0239M1_{t-7} \quad -0.0015M1_{t-8} \quad -0.0832M1_{t-9} \quad +0.1274M1_{t-10}$$
$$\quad\;\; (0.1793) \qquad\quad (0.1773) \qquad\qquad (0.1704) \qquad\qquad\; (0.0839)$$

$$\frac{di_b}{dt} = -0.00090 \qquad -0.03373DM1_t \qquad +0.8177^*DM1_{t-1} \qquad +0.03689DM1_t$$
$$\quad\;\; (0.00073) \qquad\quad (0.02018) \qquad\qquad (0.02642) \qquad\qquad\; (0.02762)$$
$$\quad -0.00697DM1_{t-7} \quad -0.04179DM1_{t-8} \quad +0.02105DM1_{t-9} \quad +0.01138DM1_t$$
$$\quad\;\; (0.0249) \qquad\quad (0.0261) \qquad\qquad (0.0272) \qquad\qquad\; (0.02100)$$

$$\frac{di_{bd}}{dt} = -0.000059 \qquad -0.00771DM1_t \qquad +0.03109^*DM1_{t-1} \qquad -0.00271DM1_t$$
$$\quad\;\; (0.000293) \qquad\quad (0.00816) \qquad\qquad (0.01068) \qquad\qquad\; (0.01116)$$
$$\quad -0.00550DM1_{t-7} \quad -0.00424DM1_{t-8} \quad -0.00348DM1_{t-9} \quad +0.00929DM1_t$$
$$\quad\;\; (0.01005) \qquad\quad (0.01056) \qquad\qquad (0.01100) \qquad\qquad\; (0.00849)$$

$$\frac{di_{aaa}}{dt} = -0.00012 \qquad -0.00829DM1_t \qquad +0.01946DM1_{t-1} \qquad +0.00777DM1_t$$
$$\quad\;\; (0.00028) \qquad\quad (0.00779) \qquad\qquad (0.01019) \qquad\qquad\; (0.01065)$$
$$\quad -0.00236DM1_{t-7} \quad -0.00186DM1_{t-8} \quad -0.00313DM1_{t-9} \quad +0.00915DM1_t$$
$$\quad\;\; (0.00959) \qquad\quad (0.01008) \qquad\qquad (0.01050) \qquad\qquad\; (0.00810)$$

NOTE.—For sources and more complete notes, see Appendix. $M1 = \ln M1$; $DM1 = \frac{1}{M_1}\frac{dM_1}{dt}$; M, i season adjusted.
* Significant at .05 level.

explain on other grounds. The price expectations explanation is made more plausible by the fact that the positive sum is most noticeable for the coefficients for shorter-term interest rates, whose shorter-term expectations should be more sensitive to monthly and quarterly changes in money and prices.[14]

B. *Income and Price Expectations Effects*

These estimates do not permit us to distinguish between income and price expectations effects, since both should be reflected in positive coefficients.[15] Independent evidence on either positive effect does, however,

[14] The low levels of Durbin-Watson statistics for estimates of equation (6) (and for other equations below as well) should not be cause for alarm. For levels and changes in interest rates are surely also determined by nonmonetary factors not included in these equations.

[15] It is similarly not possible to identify the coefficient of M_t in equation (3) with the total liquidity effect, for the latter may be partially offset by income effects within the current month or quarter. If this were the case, both liquidity and income (and perhaps price expectations) effects would be larger than the coefficients reveal. This possibility has received little attention here for two reasons. First, there is some doubt that income can increase fast enough to raise interest rates within the current month or quarter. Second, emphasis here has been on how rapidly the negative effects are offset by positive effects, and for this purpose the composition of current period effects is less important.

$$-0.0257M1_{t-3} \qquad -0.1528M1_{t-4} \qquad +0.0061M1_{t-5} \qquad +0.0878M1_{t-6}$$
$$(0.3507) \qquad\qquad (0.3518) \qquad\qquad (0.3556) \qquad\qquad (0.3495)$$
$$\text{SE } Y \cdot X = 0.00498 \qquad R^2 = 0.821 \qquad \text{D-W} = 0.340$$

$$-0.0056M1_{t-3} \qquad -0.0285M1_{t-4} \qquad -0.0093M1_{t-5} \qquad +0.0456M1_{t-6}$$
$$(0.1727) \qquad\qquad (0.1732) \qquad\qquad (0.1751) \qquad\qquad (0.1721)$$
$$\text{SE } Y \cdot X = 0.00245 \qquad R^2 = 0.900 \qquad \text{D-W} = 0.245$$

$$-0.0389M1_{t-3} \qquad -0.0084M1_{t-4} \qquad -0.0439M1_{t-5} \qquad +0.0577M1_{t-6}$$
$$(0.1907) \qquad\qquad (0.1913) \qquad\qquad (0.1934) \qquad\qquad (0.1901)$$
$$\text{SE } Y \cdot X = 0.00271 \qquad R^2 = 0.889 \qquad \text{D-W} = 0.196$$

$$+0.00105DM1_{t-3} \qquad -0.02977DM1_{t-4} \qquad +0.01475DM1_{t-5} \qquad +0.00278DM1_{t-6}$$
$$(0.0274) \qquad\qquad (0.0271) \qquad\qquad (0.0273) \qquad\qquad (0.0266)$$
$$\text{SE } Y \cdot X = 0.00272 \qquad R^2 = 0.443 \qquad \text{D-W} = 1.116$$

$$+0.00279DM1_{t-3} \qquad -0.00676DM1_{t-4} \qquad -0.00002DM1_{t-5} \qquad +0.00393DM1_{t-6}$$
$$(0.01109) \qquad\qquad (0.01093) \qquad\qquad (0.01105) \qquad\qquad (0.01074)$$
$$\text{SE } Y \cdot X = 0.00110 \qquad R^2 = 0.301 \qquad \text{D-W} = 1.562$$

$$+0.00321DM1_{t-3} \qquad -0.00396DM1_{t-4} \qquad -0.00408DM1_{t-5} \qquad +0.00613DM1_{t-5}$$
$$(0.01058) \qquad\qquad (0.01044) \qquad\qquad (0.01054) \qquad\qquad (0.01025)$$
$$\text{SE } Y \cdot X = 0.00105 \qquad R^2 = 0.244 \qquad \text{D-W} = 1.241$$

allow us to determine that the liquidity effects are offset by income effects alone. A one percentage point increase in the rate of change of prices increases short-term interest rates by only 0.03 percentage points within six months, and there is no increase in long rates within this time.[16] This result seems plausible, for we should expect price expectations to be based on a large range of past price experience so that month-to-month variations would have relatively small effects on predicted price behavior. The dependence of price expectations effects on the lag between money and income makes the absence of such effects even more credible.

Ruling out price expectations effects during the first six months allows us to specify that the initial negative and offsetting positive effects are liquidity and income effects alone. The implicit estimates of the lags between money and income are somewhat shorter than often mentioned in the literature on the lag in the effect of monetary policy (Culbertson 1960, 1961; Friedman 1961). Since the coefficients imply that interest rates return to their former levels three to five months after once-and-for-all change in the money stock, they imply that income changes in about the same proportion as money in three to five months.

[16] See Gibson (1970). For earlier estimates, see references there.

TABLE 6

RELATION BETWEEN INTEREST RATES AND CURRENT AND PAST MONEY STOCKS, QUARTERLY OBSERVATIONS, 1947–66

$$
\begin{aligned}
i_b =\ & -0.2381^* -0.6142^* M2_t +0.7129 M2_{t-1} -0.0934 M2_{t-2} +0.1967 M2_{t-3} -0.2502 M2_{t-4} +0.2072 M2_{t-5} \\
& (0.0239)\ (0.1385)\ \ (0.3053)\ \ (0.3520)\ \ (0.3669)\ \ (0.3845)\ \ (0.4005) \\
& -0.1203 M2_{t-6} +0.1286 M2_{t-7} -0.3506 M2_{t-8} +0.2446 M2_{t-9} -0.0105 M2_{t-10} \\
& (0.3999)\ \ (0.3801)\ \ (0.3601)\ \ (0.3131)\ \ (0.1468) \\
& \text{SE } Y\cdot X = 0.00453 \qquad R^2 = 0.852 \qquad \text{D-W} = 0.383
\end{aligned}
$$

$$
\begin{aligned}
i_{bd} =\ & -0.1772^* -0.1597^* M2_t +0.1638 M2_{t-1} -0.0224 M2_{t-2} +0.0389 M2_{t-3} -0.0193 M2_{t-4} +0.0312 M2_{t-5} \\
& (0.0130)\ (0.0754)\ \ (0.1662)\ \ (0.1915)\ \ (0.1997)\ \ (0.2093)\ \ (0.2179) \\
& -0.0232 M2_{t-6} -0.00001 M2_{t-7} -0.0181 M2_{t-8} -0.0885 M2_{t-9} +0.1383 M2_{t-10} \\
& (0.2176)\ \ (0.2069)\ \ (0.1960)\ \ (0.1704)\ \ (0.0799) \\
& \text{SE } Y\cdot X = 0.00246 \qquad R^2 = 0.899 \qquad \text{D-W} = 0.262
\end{aligned}
$$

$$
\begin{aligned}
i_{aaa} =\ & -0.1972^* -0.1677^* M2_t +0.1280 M2_{t-1} +0.0257 M2_{t-2} +0.0100 M2_{t-3} +0.0022 M2_{t-4} +0.0092 M2_{t-5} \\
& (0.0135)\ (0.0780)\ \ (0.1719)\ \ (0.1982)\ \ (0.2066)\ \ (0.2165)\ \ (0.2255) \\
& -0.0171 M2_{t-6} +0.0113 M2_{t-7} -0.0120 M2_{t-8} -0.0974 M2_{t-9} +0.1535 M2_{t-10} \\
& (0.2252)\ \ (0.2141)\ \ (0.2028)\ \ (0.1763)\ \ (0.0827) \\
& \text{SE } Y\cdot X = 0.00255 \qquad R^2 = 0.902 \qquad \text{D-W} = 0.232
\end{aligned}
$$

$$
\begin{aligned}
\frac{di_b}{dt} =\ & -0.00045 -0.0905^* DM2_t +0.1148^* DM2_{t-1} +0.0078 DM2_{t-2} +0.0218 DM2_{t-3} -0.0391 DM2_{t-4} +0.0264 DM2_{t-5} \\
& (0.00077)\ (0.0203)\ \ (0.0295)\ \ (0.0294)\ \ (0.0301)\ \ (0.0310)\ \ (0.0318) \\
& -0.0042 DM2_{t-6} +0.0072 DM2_{t-7} -0.0601^* DM2_{t-8} +0.0333 DM2_{t-9} +0.0032 DM2_{t-10} \\
& (0.0314)\ \ (0.0301)\ \ (0.0299)\ \ (0.0299)\ \ (0.0210) \\
& \text{SE } Y\cdot X = 0.00262 \qquad R^2 = 0.480 \qquad \text{D-W} = 1.144
\end{aligned}
$$

$$
\begin{aligned}
\frac{di_{bd}}{dt} =\ & 0.00023 -0.0269^* DM2_t +0.0407^* DM2_{t-1} -0.0052 DM2_{t-2} +0.0014 DM2_{t-3} +0.0040 DM2_{t-4} -0.0089 DM2_{t-5} \\
& (0.00032)\ (0.0084)\ \ (0.0122)\ \ (0.0121)\ \ (0.0124)\ \ (0.0128)\ \ (0.0131) \\
& +0.0011 DM2_{t-6} -0.0005 DM2_{t-7} -0.0099 DM2_{t-8} +0.0007 DM2_{t-9} +0.0053 DM2_{t-10} \\
& (0.0130)\ \ (0.0125)\ \ (0.0123)\ \ (0.0123)\ \ (0.0086) \\
& \text{SE } Y\cdot X = 0.00108 \qquad R^2 = 0.322 \qquad \text{D-W} = 1.516
\end{aligned}
$$

$$
\begin{aligned}
\frac{di_{aaa}}{dt} =\ & 0.00018 -0.0249^* DM2_t +0.0259^* DM2_{t-1} +0.0034 DM2_{t-2} +0.0020 DM2_{t-3} +0.0015 DM2_{t-4} -0.0055 DM2_{t-5} \\
& (0.00030)\ (0.0080)\ \ (0.0117)\ \ (0.0116)\ \ (0.0119)\ \ (0.0123)\ \ (0.0126) \\
& +0.0011 DM2_{t-6} +0.0010 DM2_{t-7} -0.0071 DM2_{t-8} -0.0001 DM2_{t-9} +0.0082 DM2_{t-10} \\
& (0.0124)\ \ (0.0119)\ \ (0.0118)\ \ (0.0118)\ \ (0.0083) \\
& \text{SE} = 0.00104 \qquad R^2 = 0.260 \qquad \text{D-W} = 1.369
\end{aligned}
$$

NOTE.—For sources and more complete notes, see Appendix. $M_2 = \ln M_2$; $DM2 = \dfrac{1}{M_2}\dfrac{dM_2}{dt}$; M, i seasonally adjusted.

* Significant at .05 level.

TABLE 7

F-RATIOS OF ANALYSIS OF COVARIANCES OF REGRESSION COEFFICIENTS
OF MONETARY VARIABLES, MONTHLY REGRESSIONS, 1947–66

	$i =$ Treasury Bill Rate		$i =$ Treasury Bond Rate		$i =$ Moody's *Aaa* Bond Rate	
$i = f(M1_t, \ldots, M1_{t-n})$	7.080*	4.394*	6.309*	0.272	9.968*	0.604
$di = f(DM1_t, \ldots, DM1_{t-n})$. . .	6.793*	1.494	4.437*	0.983	3.033**	0.321
$i = f(M2_t, \ldots, M2_{t-n})$	19.803*	0.689	6.374*	0.358	8.729*	1.087
$di = f(DM2_t, \ldots, DM2_{t-n})$. . .	6.692*	1.098	2.804***	1.044	2.569***	0.261

* Significant at 99.9 percent level.
** Significant at 99.0 percent level.
*** Significant at 95 percent level.

V. Summary and Conclusions

The estimates obtained here show that a change in the money stock produces an immediate negative liquidity effect on market interest rates, but also produces (only a little later) positive effects which tend to offset the initial negative influence. Liquidity effects are fully offset by the end of the third month following the month in which M_1 is changed and by the end of the fifth month after M_2 is changed. These positive effects cannot be directly separated into income and price expectations effects, but evidence on total price expectations effects implies that the latter have very little importance over a period as short as three to five months. The longer period required for offsetting the initial negative effects of M_2 suggests that income reacts more slowly to a given percentage change in M_2 than in M_1.

The short periods required for interest rates to return to their previous levels also imply a short lag in the effect of money on income. On the assumption of a unitary income elasticity of demand for money, income increases in roughly the same proportion as money within five months.

Some implications of these findings are clear. Interest rates can be lowered by increasing the money stock, but this act also produces forces which will offset the lowering within several months. This process will produce increases in nominal income (and perhaps in prices), which may be a goal of monetary policy. But the sequence clearly makes it hazardous to view the levels or changes of interest rates as indicators of monetary policy. Since income increases due to money stock increases will be accompanied by higher interest rates, interest rates can as well be regarded as reflecting an easier as a tighter monetary policy. Moreover, to maintain lower interest rates it is necessary to increase money stocks continuously. But this act itself generates expectations of rising prices that tend to raise interest rates.

Appendix

Notes to Tables and Data Sources

All interest rates and rates of change of money are expressed as annual rates. D-W denotes Durbin-Watson statistic. Standard errors are in parentheses.

A. Money

Monthly data, 1947–66 (from which quarterly data were generated) for M_1 and M_2 seasonally adjusted and unadjusted were obtained from the *Federal Reserve Bulletin*, including all revisions through 1966. All money stock data are in billions of dollars.

B. Interest Rates

i_b = the Treasury bill rate. Data was obtained from the *Federal Reserve Bulletin* and *Banking and Monetary Statistics*. Quarterly data were generated from monthly data, which are averages of daily figures for 1947–66.

i_{bd} = Treasury bond rate. Source same as for i_b. Monthly data are averages of daily figures for bonds maturing or callable in ten years or more for 1947–66.

i_{aaa} = Moody's *Aaa* corporate bond yield. Source and years same as for i_{bd}. Monthly data are averages of daily figures.

Interest rates are expressed in percentage terms, that is, a yield of $4.00 per year per $100.00 is expressed as 0.04. Monthly and quarterly interest rates were seasonally adjusted by the ratio-to-moving-average technique at the Federal Reserve Bank of Chicago.

References

Ackley, Gardner. *Macroeconomic Theory*. New York: Macmillan, 1961.

Baumol, William J. "The Transactions Demand for Cash: An Inventory Theoretic Approach." *Q.J.E.* 66 (November 1952):454–56.

Cagan, Phillip. *Determinants and Effects of Changes in the Money Stock in the U.S., 1875–1960*. New York: Columbia Univ. Press, 1965.

———. "The Channels of Monetary Effects on Interest Rates." Mimeographed. Nat. Bur. Econ. Res., 1966.

Culbertson, J. M. "Friedman on the Lag in Effect of Monetary Policy." *J.P.E.* 68 (December 1960):617–21.

———. "Reply." *Ibid.* 69 (October 1961):467–77.

Fisher, Irving. *Appreciation and Interest*. Cambridge, Mass.: American Econ. Assoc., 1896.

———. *The Rate of Interest*. New York: Macmillan, 1907.

———. *The Theory of Interest*. New York: Macmillan, 1930.

Friedman, Milton. "The Demand for Money: Some Theoretical and Empirical Results." *J.P.E.* 68 (August 1959):327–51.

———. "The Lag in Effect of Monetary Policy." *Ibid.* 69 (October 1961): 447–66.

Friedman, Milton, and Meiselman, David. "The Relative Stability of Monetary Velocity and the Investment Multiplier in the United States, 1897–1958." In *Stabilization Policies*, Commission on Money and Credit. Englewood Cliffs, N.J.: Prentice-Hall, 1963.

Gibson, William E. "Price-Expectations Effects on Interest Rates." *J. Finance*, vol. 25 (March 1970).

INTEREST RATES   455

Gibson, William E., and Kaufman, George G. "The Sensitivity of Interest Rates to Changes in Money and Income." *J.P.E.* 76 (June 1968):472–78.

Gramley, Lyle E., and Chase, Samuel B., Jr. "Time Deposits in Monetary Analysis." *Federal Res. Bull.* 51 (October 1965):1380–1406.

Latané, Henry A. "Cash Balances and the Interest Rate: A Pragmatic Approach." *Rev. Econ. and Statis.* 36 (November 1954):456–60.

Meltzer, Allan H. "The Demand for Money: The Evidence from the Time Series." *J.P.E.* 71 (June 1963):231–34.

Mundell, Robert. "Inflation and Real Interest." *J.P.E.* 71 (June 1963):280–83.

———. "A Fallacy in the Interpretation of Macroeconomic Equilibrium." *Ibid.* 73 (February 1965):61–66.

Tobin, James. "Liquidity Preference and Monetary Policy." *Rev. Econ. and Statis.* 29 (May 1947):124–31.

———. "The Interest Elasticity of Transactions Demand for Cash." *Ibid.* 38 (August 1956):241–47.

Trieber, William F. "The Challenge of the Boom." *Federal Res. Bank N.Y. Monthly Review* (June 1966), pp. 123–26.

[9]

English Bank Deposits before 1844[1]

By DOUGLAS K. ADIE

PEEL's Act of 1844 has been a controversial piece of legislation because the Bank of England's authority for discretionary control of the money supply through changes in deposits was based on its provisions for over a century. The features of the Act are as follows: the prohibition of new banks of issue, the limitation of existing country note-issues, the separation of the note-issuing from the banking functions of the Bank of England, the limitation of the Bank of England's fiduciary note-issues, and the 100 per cent reserve requirement for Bank notes issued in excess of this limit. The Act also gave the Bank of England freedom in its management of deposits, since it made no mention of the control of deposits.

Basing discretionary monetary policy on the authority of the Bank Charter Act is ironical, since the Currency School which drafted the Act denied the need for central banking. The Currency School vigorously opposed discretionary control of the money supply, and in their view the 1844 Act replaced discretion with rules. The Banking School, which opposed the Currency School in theory and policy, supported discretion in the control of the money supply.

In espousing the real bills doctrine, the Banking School advocated discretionary control of bank liabilities by the banks themselves. John Fullarton of the Banking School said that money should be provided at all times in proportion to the demands of the community. "So long as a bank issues its notes only in the discount of good bills, at not more than sixty days date, it cannot go wrong in issuing as many as the public will receive from it."[2] The Banking School argued that economic fluctuations would be minimized if the banks regulated the size of their own liabilities by responding to the "needs of trade".[3] James Wilson of the Banking School said that "Banking, above all other professions, is that which under entire freedom and non-interference would soonest be placed in the most perfect position."[4]

For the Currency School, Samson Ricardo said that deviations from fixed rules tended to derange the supply of money (defined by the Currency School as all

[1] The author is indebted to his teachers and colleagues at the University of Chicago and in particular to Milton Friedman, Robert Mundell, and George Stigler for their direction. The author takes blame for errors. Financial assistance from the following is gratefully acknowledged: the William Lyon MacKenzie King Foundation, the Richard M. Weaver Foundation, the Workshop on Money and Banking at the University of Chicago, the Earhart Foundation, and the Ford Foundation. Secretarial assistance was provided by the College of Business Administration, Ohio University. Computer facilities were provided by the University of Chicago and Ohio University.

[2] John Fullarton, *On the Regulation of Currencies* (2nd edn, 1845), pp. 206–7.

[3] Ibid. pp. 152, 226; *First and Second Reports from the Select Committee on Banks of Issue*, Parl. Papers, 1841, v, Q. 957 (J. W. Gilbart); Thomas Tooke, *A History of Prices, and the State of the Circulation, in 1838 and 1839* (6 vols. 1840), III, 185; *Report from the Select Committee on Banks of Issue*, P.P. 1840, IV, Q. 3851 (T. Tooke); *Report from the Select Committee on Bank Acts*, P.P. 1857, 2nd Sess. x, pts i and ii, Q. 2057 (J. S. Mill). Government reports of committees are subsequently called *Committee* and distinguished by dates.

[4] James Wilson, *Capital, Currency and Banking*; being a collection of a series of articles published in the *Economist* in 1845, on the principles of the Bank Act of 1844; and in 1847, on the recent monetarial and commercial crisis; concluding with a plan for a secure and economical currency (1847), p. 29.

notes plus gold held for monetary purposes);[1] Peel and Robert Torrens argued that discretionary control of the money supply endangered convertibility of notes into gold.[2] The public, according to Overstone, blamed the Bank of England for failing to protect sufficiently well the convertibility of notes into gold in 1825, 1837, and 1839.[3] Overstone blamed the Bank's discretionary changes in the money supply for the unstable business climate. He said that the Bank's discretionary decisions caused widespread suffering throughout the entire country;[4] and, later, that the Act of 1844 was the public's attempt to substitute rules for discretion because of the financial crises they had suffered.[5]

Robert Torrens and Samson Ricardo maintained that control of the money supply was too important to be conducted by the Bank of England's managers, since their discretionary decisions affected all Englishmen.[6] George Norman of the Currency School added that the discretionary control of the money supply by the joint-stock and private banks also increased instability and harmed the economy.[7] To eliminate instability in the economy, Overstone advocated the control of the money supply by a fixed rule known to everyone rather than "the private judgment and prudence" of the monetary authority.[8] Peel argued that fixed rules were needed because discretion was not sufficiently safe for regulating the amount of money.[9]

After Peel's Act was passed, Overstone triumphantly claimed, "Never again will one great public body be entrusted with the dangerous power of creating money at its own discretion and extending or contracting the amount of the circulation uncontrolled by any fixed rule."[10] Peel said that the essential feature of the Act of 1844 was the removal of convertible notes entirely from the discretion of any man, body of men, bank, or government.[11]

After 1844, the Bank became conscious of its power to control the activity of other banks, credit conditions, and the money supply through its deposit management, rather than through changes in its notes and deposits. The failure to regulate deposits in Peel's Act permitted this discretionary control of the money

---

[1] Samson Ricardo, *A National Bank. The remedy for the evils attendant upon our present system of paper currency.* Appendix. 'Plan for a national bank by (the late) David Ricardo' (1838), p. 32.

[2] *Debates in the House of Commons on Sir Robert Peel's Bank Bills of 1844 and 1845.* Reprinted verbatim from Hansard, *Parliamentary Debates* (1875), pp. 233–4 (Robert Peel); Robert Torrens, *The Principles and Practical Operation of Sir Robert Peel's Act of 1844, Explained and Defended* (3rd edn, 1858), pp. 146, 150, 154.

[3] *First and Second Reports from the Secret Committee on Commercial Distress,* P.P. 1847–8, VIII, pt i; *Appendix,* ibid. pt ii, QQ. 1406, 1551, 1514 (Samuel Jones Loyd (Lord Overstone)).

[4] Overstone, *Thoughts on the Separation of the Departments of the Bank of England* (1844). Reprinted in *Tracts and Other Publications on Metallic and Paper Currency,* ed. John R. McCulloch (1857), p. 254; *Committee* (1840), QQ. 2764, 2805 (Overstone).

[5] *Committee* (1848), Q. 5207 (Overstone).

[6] Torrens, op. cit. p. 53; S. Ricardo, *Observations on the Recent Pamphlet of J. Horsley Palmer, Esq. on the Causes and Consequences of the Money Market, etc.* (1837), p. 37.

[7] George Norman, *Remarks upon Some Prevalent Errors with Respect to Currency and Banking, and Suggestions to the Legislature and the Public as to the Improvement of the Monetary System* (1838), pp. 87–8.

[8] Overstone, *Thoughts on the Separation* in *Tracts,* ed. McCulloch, p. 254; *Committee* (1840), QQ. 2764, 2805 (Overstone).

[9] Peel, in Overstone, 'Letter to the Editor of *The Times* on the Bank Charter Act of 1844, and on the State of the Currency in 1855–1856', in *Tracts,* ed. McCulloch, p. 349.

[10] Overstone, *Letters of Mercator on the Bank Charter Act of 1844, and the State of the Currency, 1855–1857* (1857), p. 49.

[11] Peel, Hansard, *Parl. Debates,* p. 250.

supply when automatic control was intended. Prof. R. S. Sayers, who supports
the present discretionary monetary policy, has said that Peel's Act

> ...was clutching at a slippery eel when it sought to apply a rule of thumb to the
> monetary situation by regulating the issue of bank notes alone. This was the design
> of the famous Bank Charter Act of 1844; men soon found how to escape its in-
> tentions, though the empty shell long remained, a memorial to those who believed
> that either nature or the law had drawn a sharp line of distinction between what
> was money and what was not money and that an automatic machine could
> sufficiently govern the monetary situation.[1]

The legal framework of the Act remained intact while its underlying principle
—the control of the money supply by rules instead of authority—was denied in
practice because the Act left the Bank free to conduct its banking business as a
central bank. Prof. Hayek, who advocates rules rather than authority in monetary
policy, has suggested that the intentions of the Currency School would have been
implemented by applying the fixed fiduciary issue principle to deposits as well as
to notes. This would have brought deposits under regulation by a fixed rule and
diminished discretion in monetary management.[2]

Against the background of the "rules versus discretion" controversy, the problem of the source of discretionary control of the money supply might be re-
phrased as follows: why did the Currency School omit deposits from regulation
in Peel's Act, 1844?

Several reasons have been suggested why deposits were not controlled by the
Bank Charter Act. First, the Currency School desired the control of notes alone
because earlier financial crises had involved the convertibility of notes but not
deposits.[3] Secondly, the Currency and Banking Schools believed that the limitation on note issues was an ultimate constraint on the creation of deposits. The
Currency School believed further that rigid control of deposits was implicit in the
control of notes. If notes were controlled, there would then be no need to control
deposits explicitly.[4] Thirdly, the Currency School viewed deposit banking as a
commercial enterprise, subject to the minimum regulation consistent with the
shareholder's and creditor's security. No direct interference with deposit banking
appeared justified since the general public could choose whether or not to hold
bank deposits, whereas it had no choice in the matter of notes. Note-issues then
fell within the state's responsibility for the currency while deposits did not.[5] Although the Currency and Banking Schools were generally aware of the importance of deposits in 1844, apart from a few references there was no discussion of
their quantitative importance. Finally, then, deposits were not controlled by the
Bank Charter Act because they were quantitatively insignificant compared to
notes.[6]

---

[1] R. S. Sayers, *Central Banking After Bagehot* (Oxford, 1957), reprinted in Lawrence S. Ritter, ed.
Money and Economic Activity (3rd edn, Boston, 1967), p. 366.
[2] P. Barrett Whale, 'A Retrospective View of the Bank Charter Act', in T. S. Ashton, ed. *Papers in
English Monetary History* (Oxford, 1953), p. 131.
[3] Lionel (Lord) Robbins, *Robert Torrens and the Evolution of Classical Economics* (1958), p. 117.
[4] Ibid. p. 111; Henry Simons, 'Rules versus Authorities in Monetary Policy', reprinted in *Economic
Policy for a Free Society* (Chicago, 1948), p. 162.
[5] Jacob Viner, *Studies in the Theory of International Trade* (1953), p. 250.
[6] Ludwig von Mises and A. E. Feavearyear regarded deposits as quantitatively unimportant before

DOUGLAS K. ADIE

This article examines the last reason suggested above. A little consideration is given to the second reason, but much more work needs to be done. In determining the quantitative importance of English bank deposits, the levels and fluctuations of deposits are considered and compared with notes.[1] Four main questions are posed, two concerning the levels of deposits and two concerning their fluctuations: (1) What were the levels of deposits relative to notes, as measured by their respective means? (2) What were the trends in deposits relative to notes, as measured by their respective percentage rates of increase? (3) Were fluctuations in deposits large relative to the fluctuations in notes, as measured where possible by their respective standard errors of estimate of logs about time trends? (4) Were fluctuations in deposits in the same direction as the fluctuations in notes, as measured where possible by the correlation coefficients between the logs of notes and deposits? The time trend is included for the long-run comparison; excluded for short-run comparisons. The deposits of each of three types of English banks are examined separately: the Bank of England which issued notes and created deposits; London banks, which created deposits; and country banks which issued notes.

I

Gold payments for notes were restricted at the Bank of England in 1797 and resumed in 1821. Peel's Act in 1844 tied Bank note-issues to gold reserves and took steps to eliminate country issues. These dates divide the data into useful periods which will be used throughout this article, except where the availability of data determines otherwise.

Table 1. *Levels of Bank of England Notes and Deposits*

Period	Means (£ million)		Notes/ Deposits	Annual percentage rates of increase*	
	Notes	Deposits		Notes	Deposits
1815–56	20·90	5·40	3·87	−0·42	4·69
1815–21	25·82	1·63	15·84	−3·59	−1·01
1822–44	19·38	4·80	4·03	−0·46	3·96
1845–56	20·94	8·74	2·39	0·49	0·14

Source: Figures for Bank notes are averages of 28 February and 31 August taken from *Report from the Select Committee on Bank Acts*, P.P. (1857), 2nd Sess. x, pts 1 and ii, app. eleven. Figures for Bank deposits are taken from the same source with government deposits and banker's balances at head office subtracted.

* The annual percentage rates of increase are the coefficients β and b expressed as percentages taken from regression equations $\log N = \gamma + \beta T$ and $\log D = a + b T$ where T is the year and N and D are Bank of England notes and deposits respectively. The same kind of calculations are made throughout this article unless otherwise specified.

Peel's Act, 1844. Von Mises argued that the development of deposit banking did not reach significant proportions until Peel's Act itself encouraged it. Feavearyear argued that deposits were a negligible factor in the economic system before the Act because their use in transactions was hindered by the lack of a national cheque-clearing system. See Ludwig von Mises, *The Theory of Money and Credit*, trans. H. E. Batson (New York, 1936), p. 369. See also Albert E. Feavearyear, *The Pound Sterling: A History of English Money* (1931), pp. 289–90.

[1] Notes are used as a criterion for assessing the economic importance of deposits because they were regulated by the Currency School and therefore were considered important. Gold also was regarded as important, but only a few estimates of the gold held by the public are available.

BANK DEPOSITS   289

The means of bank deposits in Table 1 are less than the corresponding means of Bank notes for all periods. With respect to relative levels during the Restriction (1797–1821) when the Bank was released from its obligation to buy its notes with gold, the ratio of notes to deposits rose to its highest level. After the resumption of gold payments in 1821, this ratio fell from 15·84 to 4·03. After Peel's Act, when Bank notes were tied to gold reserves, the ratio fell to 2·39. Except perhaps during the Restriction, the levels of deposits were at no time low enough to be regarded as economically insignificant.

The annual percentage rates of increase in Table 1 indicate that the level of deposits increased after 1821. During 1822–44 deposits increased at 3·9 per cent per annum, while notes decreased. This was the period during which the Currency and Banking Schools tried to influence policy.

Table 2. *Fluctuations of Bank of England Notes and Deposits*

Period	Standard deviations of logs about trend		Correlation coefficients between logs of notes and deposits*			
	Notes	Deposits	$r^2 \cdot T$	$r \cdot T$	r^2	r
1815–56	12	33	4	−0·19	19	−0·43
1815–21	5	45	36	0·60	11	0·33
1822–44	8	30	4	0·19	2	−0·12
1845–56	7	18	24	0·49	23	0·48

Source: Same as source to Table 1.

* $r^2 \cdot T$ is the square of the correlation coefficient between the logs of Bank notes and deposits excluding the trend and expressed as a percentage. r is the correlation coefficient including the trend. The same terminology is used throughout the article.

The standard deviations of logs about trend in Table 2, expressed in percentage terms, indicate that deposits fluctuated more widely than notes throughout the whole period and in each sub-period from 1815 to 1856. The correlation coefficients indicate that during the Restriction and after Peel's Act deposits fluctuated in the same direction as notes. The highest proportion of the variance in deposits "explained" by the contemporaneous variation in notes is only 36 per cent and occurs during the Restriction period. Hence for Bank of England notes and deposits, there is little support for the proposition that fluctuations in notes closely controlled fluctuations in deposits.

II

No private London banks published balance sheets before the 1890's. Consequently, it is difficult to obtain data on London bank deposits. I have been able to get estimates for only nine dates between 1796 and 1857. The periods in Table 3 differ from those in Table 1 in order to make better use of these sparse estimates.

The means and the annual percentage rates of increase for London bank deposits in Table 3 were greater than those for Bank notes over the whole period and in each sub-period, except during the Restriction. The level of London bank deposits surpassed the level of Bank notes and increased at a greater annual rate than Bank notes between 1824 and 1844. This evidence indicates that London bank deposits were a quantitatively significant item in the inventory of financial assets.

DOUGLAS K. ADIE

Table 3. *Levels of Bank of England Notes and London Bank Deposits*

Period	Means (£ million)		Notes/Deposits	Annual percentage rates of increase	
	Notes	Deposits		Notes	Deposits
1796–1857	19·93	38·25	0·52	0·4	1·1
1796–1824	19·85	13·00	1·53	2·6	1·3
1824–44	19·48	22·25	0·88	−0·8	2·4
1844–57	20·97	48·00	0·44	0·3	3·3

Sources: Calculations involving Bank of England notes are based on figures described in source to Table 1. Annual percentage rates of increase for deposits were calculated directly from estimates in Feavearyear, op. cit. p. 304, and my estimates based on Elmer Wood, *English Theories of Central Banking Control, 1819–1858* (Cambridge, Mass., 1939), p. 21n., and the figures for London joint-stock bank deposits in *Report from the Select Committee on Bank Acts*, P.P. 1857–8, v, Q. 1134.

Sufficient data are not available to make direct calculations of fluctuations of London bank deposits. In attempting to measure fluctuations indirectly, I have considered the London joint-stock banks for which information is available. The London and Westminster Bank which began operations in 1834 was the first joint-stock bank in London, apart from the Bank of England. By 1857 there were eight such banks in London with 28 offices. The correlation coefficient between the logs of the number of London joint-stock bank offices and London joint-stock deposits, excluding the time trend for the period 1834–57, is 0·78. This provides some support for using the number of offices as a proxy for deposits.[1]

An indirect comparison of the fluctuation of London bank deposits and country bank deposits is made in Table 4. The availability of data accounts for the periods.

Table 4. *Fluctuations in the Number of London Bank Offices and Issuing Country Bank Offices*

Period	Standard deviation of logs about trends		$r^2 \cdot T$	Correlation coefficients between logs of the number of London bank offices and issuing country bank offices		r
	London bank offices	Country bank offices		$r \cdot T$	r^2	
1809–32	2	8	4	0·21	46	0·68
1809–21	2	9	45	0·67	4	0·22
1822–32	5	5	29	0·54	40	0·63

Sources: The numbers of country bank offices are taken from the licences to issue notes. See Wood, op. cit. p. 14. A licence was required for each office up to a total of four offices. Before 1819, there were few non-issuing banks except in Lancashire. After 1819 these figures understate the number of offices. The number of London bank offices is taken from F. G. H. Price (comp.), *A Handbook of London Bankers* (1890–1). L. S. Pressnell has brought to my attention the fact that these yearly lists inflate the true statistics of bank offices by including merchant bankers and others who were not strictly "bankers" for the public. Probably this does not affect broad trends.

If the number of bank offices is taken as a proxy for deposits, the standard deviations of logs about trends in Table 4 indicate that the fluctuations in London bank deposits were less than those of country banks. This result is supported by

[1] The source of the numbers of London joint-stock bank offices and their deposits is given in the sources to Table 3.

the testimony of Overstone who said that "you will not find the fluctuations in the amount of deposits with London bankers as nearly so great as the fluctuations in the amount of deposits with country banks."[1]

In Table 5, the negative correlation coefficients between the joint-stock deposits and Bank notes or deposits, excluding the time trend, suggest that the short-run fluctuations in London deposits were in the opposite direction from Bank notes or deposits before 1845. The long-run fluctuations in London deposits tended to be in the same direction as Bank notes but the tendency was not strong as measured by the percentage of variation in joint-stock deposits "explained" by the fluctuations of Bank notes.

Table 5. *Correlation Coefficients between Logs of Joint-stock Deposits and Bank Notes or Deposits*

Period	Bank notes				Bank deposits			
	$r^2 \cdot T$	$r \cdot T$	r^2	r	$r^2 \cdot T$	$r \cdot T$	r^2	r
1834–56	1	−0·08	38	0·62	11	−0·34	0	−0·04
1834–44	15	−0·39	13	0·36	16	−0·42	24	−0·46
1845–56	17	0·41	14	0·37	2	0·15	2	0·15

Sources: Same as sources to Tables 1 and 3.

J. H. Palmer, Director of the Bank of England from 1811 to 1857 and Governor in 1830–3, said in 1840 that fluctuations in Bank of England deposits were greater than those of private banks, since as much as one-third of the Bank's deposits might be withdrawn during an unfavourable exchange.[2] Palmer also said that the deposits of London bankers varied, at most, only £3 million to £4 million.[3] I conclude that Bank of England deposits (relative to their size) fluctuated more than London deposits or country deposits.

III

In Table 6 country notes and deposits are compared. The periods differ from those of Table 1 in order to make better use of the sparse estimates.

The levels of the notes–deposits ratio indicate that the level of country deposits exceeded country notes between 1821 and 1844. As early as 1828, Thomas Attwood estimated the total liabilities of all bankers in England and Wales to be £200 million which, while an inflated figure, suggests that country deposits were "important" by this date.[4]

[1] Overstone, 'Extracts from the Evidence of Samuel Jones Loyd Esq. before the Select Committee of the House of Commons on Commercial Distress in 1848', reprinted in *Tracts*, ed. McCulloch, p. 629.

[2] Palmer attributed this difference in the degree of fluctuations between the Bank and other banks to customer relations. Customers of private bankers felt more obliged to maintain a steady level of deposits because their relationship with bankers was personal. Customers of the Bank felt no such obligation.—*Report from the Select Committee on Bank Issue*, P.P. 1840, IV, QQ. 1566–1996.

[3] J. H. Palmer in Tooke, *A History of Prices*, III, 124n.

[4] See Wood, op. cit. p. 21. Robinson said that a large part of the "capital" of every banker in 1825 was deposits.—Ibid. pp. 22–3. Feavearyear supported his low deposit estimates by saying that the development of deposit banking in the country did not begin until after Peel's Act because of the absence of a national cheque-clearing system.—Feavearyear, op. cit. pp. 247–89. This assertion is not consistent with J. W. Gilbart's remark that each country banker was connected with a London bank and so virtually connected with all the country banks for purposes of transmitting money.—J. W. Gilbart, *The History and Principles of Banking* (3rd edn, 1837), p. 151.

DOUGLAS K. ADIE

Table 6. *Levels of Country Notes and Deposits*

Period	Means ($£$ million)		Notes/Deposits	Annual percentage rates of increase	
	Notes	Deposits		Notes	Deposits
1808–50	15·3	45·9	0·33	−4·0	2·3
1808–21	26·8	20·5	1·31	−3·7	2·2
1821–44	10·7	34·1	0·31	−1·9	4·3
1844–50	7·0	59·6	0·12	−5·2	4·9

Sources: Country notes for 1807–32 are crude estimates derived from stamp duties. The reader is warned that these figures should be used only to indicate broad movements. Country notes for 1807–25 are calculated from L. S. Pressnell, *Country Banking in the Industrial Revolution* (Oxford, 1956), p. 188, by taking notes stamped in each year and adding notes stamped in the previous two years. For procedure see Viner, op. cit. pp. 163–5. For 1826–32, the annual figures for country notes are calculated in the same way from *Report from the Committee of Secrecy on the Bank of England Charter*, P.P. 1831–2, VI, app. 99. For 1833–56 the annual figures for country notes are the averages of 28 February and 31 August in *Committee* (1857), app. 15. My estimates for country deposits are based on Pressnell, op. cit. pp. 512–13, 526–31; Wood, op. cit. pp. 21–2; Feavearyear, op. cit. p. 289; *Committee* (1857), apps. 15 and 21.

The annual percentage rates of increase for country deposits in Table 6 exceeded those of notes in all periods. In the period 1821–44, a very large growth took place in country deposits. William Rodwell said that all banks had shared in the joint-stock bank expansion in 1836 which extended the deposit system throughout the country. The large increase in country deposits, he said, accounted for the decrease in country notes from £11·7 million in 1839 to £7·7 million in 1843.[1] William Newmarch, a Wakefield banker and supporter of the Banking School, stated that the aggregate quantity of notes in the United Kingdom increased only £1·5 million from 1834 to 1855, while trade transactions increased five or six times and population increased 30 or 35 per cent.[2] Although Newmarch's estimate of the increase in trade transactions seems to be exaggerated, his argument that deposit banking must have expanded considerably to support the increased trade was not opposed by any contemporary authors known to me.

The distribution of joint-stock banks established in the country between 1837 and 1844 between issuing and non-issuing banks also supports an early development of deposit banking. In 1837–44 only seven issuing banks as against 30 non-issuing banks were established. This indicates that deposits grew substantially compared with notes before 1844.[3]

Since country deposits exceeded country notes in levels and annual percentage rates of increase, and the Currency School regarded country notes as important enough to be eliminated, country deposits were also important enough on quantitative grounds to have deserved consideration in policy-making.

Figures of savings banks deposits, and from Barnard, Leyland, and Gillett, who were country bankers, may be taken to stand for country deposits. The

[1] J. W. Gilbart, *The Logic of Banking* (*Works*, 1856), pp. 541–2.

[2] *Committee* (1857), Q. 174 (W. Newmarch). This evidence does not support Ludwig von Mises's assertion that the country deposit system was in a backward state before 1844.—von Mises, op. cit. p. 369. Deposits increased considerably after the Act of 1844 but this does not imply that deposits were economically insignificant before the Act.

[3] See *Committee* (1857), app. 21.

standard deviations of logs about trend in Table 7 indicate that, except for savings bank deposits in the period 1845–56, all series of country deposits fluctuated at least as much (relative to their size) as Bank notes. This means that the degree of fluctuations of country deposits was quantitatively significant.

Table 7. *Fluctuations in Bank of England Notes and Country Deposit Series*

Standard deviations of logs about trend

Period	Bank notes	Savings bank deposits	Barnard's deposits	Leyland's deposits	Gillett's deposits
1800–45	16		24		
1812–45	10			26	
1817–56	12	61*			
1800–21	10		25		
1812–21	9			9	
1822–45	8		18		
1826–45	9				21
1822–44	8	12			
1845–56	7	6			

Sources: Barnard's, Leyland's, and Gillett's deposits all taken from Pressnell, op. cit. pp. 512–13, 516–17, 518–19. Savings bank deposits are taken from B. R. Mitchell and Phyllis Deane. *Abstract of British Historical Statistics* (Cambridge, 1962), p. 453. Also see source to Table 1.

* This figure is high because savings bank deposits increased at a much higher rate in the first five years than in subsequent years.

Table 8 indicates that except for Barnard's deposits in the period 1807–21 and Leyland's deposits in the period 1822–45, country notes fluctuated more (relative to their size) than the country deposit series. Newmarch said that although country notes and deposits were stable in "quiet times", in periods of unrest country deposits fluctuated more than country notes.[1] This statement is confirmed by the evidence if interpreted in absolute terms, but denied if fluctuations are expressed in percentage terms. Tentatively, it seems that country deposits fluctuated more than Bank of England notes but slightly less than country notes, relative to

Table 8. *Fluctuations in Country Bank Notes and Country Deposit Series*

Standard deviations of logs about trend

Period	Country notes	Savings bank deposits	Barnard's deposits	Leyland's deposits	Gillett's deposits
1807–45	27		23		
1812–45	29			26	
1817–56	26	61*			
1807–21	18		25		
1812–21	17			9	
1822–45	26		18	26	
1826–45	24				21
1822–44	27	12			
1845–56	8	6			

Sources: Same as sources to Tables 1, 6, and 7.

* This figure is high because savings bank deposits increased at a much higher rate in the first five years than in subsequent years.

[1] Ibid. QQ. 1647–9 (Newmarch).

DOUGLAS K. ADIE

their respective sizes. Fluctuations in country deposits were greater than those of London deposits, but not greater than Bank deposits. This indicates that fluctuations in country bank deposits were quantitatively significant.

Thomas Tooke's statement that country bank notes fluctuated more, relative to their size, than Bank notes[1] is supported by the standard deviations of logs about trend in Table 9. Tooke also said that if deposits were added to notes, the fluctuations in country bank liabilities would be still greater (relative to their size) than fluctuations in Bank liabilities, but only if the effects of the East and West India deposits at the Bank were excluded.[2] This suggests that the fluctuations in country deposits were not greater than those of Bank deposits, if the East and West India deposits at the Bank are included. This conclusion is supported by a comparison of the standard deviations of logs about trend for Bank deposits in Table 2 with those of the country deposits series in Table 8.

Table 9. *Fluctuations in Bank of England and Country Bank Notes*

Period*	Standard deviations of logs about trend		Correlation coefficients between logs of Bank of England and country bank notes							
	Bank notes	Country notes	Simultaneous				Country notes lagged one year			
			$r^2 \cdot T$	$r \cdot T$	r^2	r	$r^2 \cdot T$	$r \cdot T$	r^2	r
1807–56	13	26	14	0·37	20	45	6	0·24	14	0·37
1807–21	12	18	53	0·73	0	0·01	36	0·59	6	—0·25
1822–44	8	27	3	—0·18	0	0·01	21	—0·46	1	—0·10
1845–56	7	8	9	0·30	3	0·17	55	0·74	31	0·56

Sources: Same as sources to Tables 1 and 6.

* Periods refer to country notes even when lagged one year.

Table 10 indicates that 38 per cent of the variation in savings bank deposits can be "explained" by the variation in Bank notes in period 1822–44; 28 per cent in period 1845–56. Also 67 per cent of the variation in Leyland's deposits can be "explained" by the variation in Bank notes in period 1800–21. Except for these cases, there is no evidence that country deposit series fluctuated consistently in the same direction as Bank notes. In many cases country deposits fluctuated in the opposite direction from Bank notes. Table 10 offers no evidence that fluctuations in country deposits were closely controlled by fluctuations in Bank notes; so there is no justification on this account, from the Currency School's point of view, for failing to regulate country deposits.

The correlation coefficients between joint-stock deposits and Barnard's, Leyland's, and Gillett's deposits in Table 11 are all positive, suggesting that country deposits fluctuated in the same direction as London deposits. The positive coefficients in Table 5 reinforce this opinion. The negative correlation coefficients between country deposits and Bank notes suggests that country deposits fluctuated in the opposite direction from Bank notes, discrediting the Currency School theory. The percentage of short-run fluctuations in Barnard's and Gillett's deposits "explained" by the fluctuations in joint-stock deposits are 86 and 85 respectively. This suggests that country deposits might have been controlled quite closely by changes in London bank deposits.

[1] Tooke, *A History of Prices*, III, 128.   [2] Ibid.

Table 10. *Fluctuations in Bank of England Notes and Country Deposit Series*

Correlation coefficients between logs of Bank of England notes and logs of

Period	Savings bank deposits				Barnard's deposits				Leyland's deposits				Gillett's deposits			
	$r^2 \cdot T$	$r \cdot T$	r^2	r	$r^2 \cdot T$	$r \cdot T$	r^2	r	$r^2 \cdot T$	$r \cdot T$	r^2	r	$r^2 \cdot T$	$r \cdot T$	r^2	r
1808–45					0	0·05	0	0·02								
1812–45									21	−0·41	55	−0·74				
1817–56	39	−0·63	35	−0·59												
1800–21					0	−0·01	61	0·78								
1812–21									67	0·82	38	0·62				
1822–45					50	−0·71	30	−0·55								
1826–45									13	−0·36	15	−0·39	1	0·12	10	−0·31
1822–44	38	0·62	3	−0·16												
1845–56	28	0·53	30	0·55												

Sources: Same as sources to Tables 1 and 7.

Table 11. *Correlation Coefficients between Logs (1834–45)*

	Savings bank deposits				Barnard's deposits				Leyland's deposits				Gillett's deposits			
	$r^2 \cdot T$	$r \cdot T$	r^2	r	$r^2 \cdot T$	$r \cdot T$	r^2	r	$r^2 \cdot T$	$r \cdot T$	r^2	r	$r^2 \cdot T$	$r \cdot T$	r^2	r
Bank notes	1	0·10	25	0·50	38	−0·62	10	−0·33	64	−0·80	49	−0·70	14	−0·37	53	0·23
Bank deposits	2	−0·13	1	−0·11	62	−0·79	59	−0·77	30	−0·55	1	−0·09	31	−0·56	15	−0·39
Country notes	50	0·71	59	−0·77	49	0·70	36	0·60	52	0·23	66	0·81	69	0·83	17	−0·41
Joint-stock deposits	29	0·54	92	0·96	86	0·93			1	0·09	79	−0·89	85	0·92	90	0·95

Sources: Same as sources to Tables 1, 3, and 7.

Table 12. *Fluctuations in Country Notes and Country Deposit Series*

Correlation coefficients between logs of country notes and logs of

Period	Savings bank deposits				Barnard's deposits				Leyland's deposits				Gillett's deposits			
	$r^2 \cdot T$	$r \cdot T$	r^2	r	$r^2 \cdot T$	$r \cdot T$	r^2	r	$r^2 \cdot T$	$r \cdot T$	r^2	r	$r^2 \cdot T$	$r \cdot T$	r^2	r
1807–45					0	−0·04	69	−0·93								
1812–45									16	−0·40	55	−0·74				
1817–56	17	−0·41	62	−0·79												
1807–21					1	−0·11	32	−0·57								
1812–21									4	0·16	8	−0·28				
1822–45					14	0·37	6	−0·24								
1826–45									3	−0·17	6	−0·25	17	0·41	0	0·06
1822–44	0	0·81	15	−0·39												
1845–56	83	0·91	12	0·35												

Sources: Same as sources to Table 11.

296   DOUGLAS K. ADIE

Table 12, which compares the direction of fluctuations in country notes with those of some country deposit series, indicates that 83 per cent of the variation in savings bank deposits can be "explained" by the variation in country notes in the period 1845–56; 14 per cent of the variation in Barnard's deposits can be "explained" by the variation in country notes in the period 1822–45 and 17 per cent of the variation of Gillett's deposits can be "explained" by the variation in country notes in the period 1826–45. Only 4 per cent of the variation in Leyland's deposits can be "explained" by the variation in country notes. In all other cases country deposit series tended to fluctuate in the opposite direction from country notes. There is no justification here for failing to regulate country deposits in 1844.

The correlation coefficients between the log values of country notes and Bank notes in Table 9 are not great enough to support the proposition that fluctuations in Bank notes controlled country notes. Lagging country notes one year does not alter this conclusion before 1844. Country notes tended to fluctuate in the opposite direction from Bank notes between 1822 and 1844.

IV

A summary of the quantitative conclusions concerning deposits is contained in Table 13 from which a judgement can be made about their importance.

Table 13. *Summary of Quantitative Conclusions Concerning Deposits*

	Bank of England	*London banks*	*Country banks*
1. Level	Bank deposits were lower than Bank notes in all periods, but nevertheless were significant before 1844.	London deposits surpassed Bank notes between 1824 and 1844.	Country deposits exceeded country notes and Bank notes between 1821 and 1844.
2. Trend	Bank deposits increased at a greater rate than Bank notes between 1822 and 1856.	London deposits increased at a greater rate than Bank notes between 1824 and 1844.	From 1808 country deposits increased at a greater rate than Bank notes and country notes.
3. Degree of fluctuation	Bank deposits fluctuated more than Bank notes in all periods.	London deposits fluctuated less than Bank notes.	Country deposits fluctuated more than Bank notes and slightly less than country notes.
4. Direction of fluctuation	Bank deposits fluctuated only slightly in the same direction as Bank notes.	Short-run fluctuations in London deposits were not in the same direction as Bank notes or deposits.	Country deposits fluctuated in the same direction as country notes.

From Table 13, it is clear that deposits were at least as quantitatively important as notes in the period 1822–44 before Peel's Act. If deposits were negligible in amount, decreased, or fluctuated only slightly compared with notes, the suggestion that the Currency School neglected deposits in Peel's Act on quantitative grounds would have been supported by evidence. However, the evidence does not show this and the few casual empirical statements made by members of the Currency and Banking Schools seem to indicate that they were aware of the true magnitudes involved.

The suggestion that the Currency School omitted deposits from regulation because they believed fluctuations in Bank notes caused fluctuations in deposits depends on an examination of the literature. Simple empirical tests suggest that a strong positive relationship did not exist between the fluctuations in Bank notes and deposits. Not finding a positive relationship does not discount this suggestion. Further research comparing the views of the Currency and Banking Schools concerning sources of change in the supply of notes and deposits, and comparing these with the actual sources of change, would clarify some important details surrounding the origin of discretionary monetary policy.

Ohio University

[10]

Competitive Interest Payments on Bank Deposits and the Long-Run Demand for Money

By BENJAMIN KLEIN*

This paper tests two assumptions made in previous demand for money studies. The first assumption concerns the role assigned to "the" interest rate in the demand for money function. Common practice identifies the rate of interest with "the opportunity cost of holding money." In Section I, this formulation is shown to blur an important distinction between "the price of money" and "the price of money substitutes" and to implicitly assume that the relevant price variable is the difference between these two distinct prices.

A second assumption is that the current ban on interest payments on demand deposits is fully effective. In Section II, I operationally define these price variables and estimate perfectly competitive interest payments on commercial bank deposits. This is done by crudely measuring commercial bank marginal costs and assuming that all "excess" profit is passed on to depositors in indirect ways. Section III presents estimates of a more complete long-run demand for money relationship which

explicitly includes an own price and a cross price as separate influences, and assumes that the prohibition of the payment of interest on deposits is totally ineffective. Although no firm conclusion is reached concerning the proper functional specification of the demand function, the results significantly improve upon previous demand for money estimates which assumed that the interest payment prohibition is totally effective. In Section IV, the results are summarized and implications of the analysis for monetary theory are presented. My competitive demand for money formulation leads to a reinterpretation of the existing evidence on what is generally referred to as "the interest elasticity of demand for money." This estimate is shown to be significantly biased downward. It also implies that the demand for and supply of money are more interdependent than is usually assumed.

I. The Own and Cross Prices of Money

Although theoretical work on the microfoundations of monetary exchange is progressing rapidly, money is still commonly considered empirically to be a durable producer and consumer good which yields an unspecified "monetary service" flow. This study, like most previous empirical demand for money studies, ignores the important unanswered theoretical question of what these services consist of. The services are merely assumed to enter a utility function and the demand for money is then implicitly derived from the demand

* University of California, Los Angeles. This paper is based on my unpublished Ph.D. dissertation. I am indebted to Milton Friedman, Levis Kochin, Anna Schwartz, and the managing editor of this *Review* for useful comments and to Irene Abramson, Stephen Ferris, and Charles Lieberman for able research assistance. I am also grateful to Friedman and Schwartz for graciously supplying much of the underlying data employed in this study and to the UCLA Institute of Government and Public Affairs and the National Bureau of Economic Research for providing financial support. This paper is not, however, an official National Bureau publication since it has not undergone the full critical review accorded National Bureau studies.

932   THE AMERICAN ECONOMIC REVIEW   DECEMBER 1974

for these unspecified monetary services.[1] The purpose of the following exercise is not to throw light upon the analytical foundation of the demand for money, but by deriving a demand function, to properly define price of money variables.

Assume that in addition to money there exists one other dollar denominated financial asset which is an alternative source of monetary services. The flow of monetary services yielded an individual can then be represented by:

$$(1) \qquad N = N(M/P, S/P, \beta)$$

where N is the flow of real monetary services yielded per unit time, M/P is the stock of real cash balances held, S/P is the real stock of the monetary substitute asset held, and β is a portmanteau variable representing all other possible N-determining variables which are assumed to remain constant throughout this analysis. Equation (1) can be thought of as the individual's production function for monetary services with both (M/P) and (S/P) assumed to have declining marginal productivities.

For simplicity and to facilitate comparisons between financial assets and commodities, let X represent a scalar measure of a vector of the commodity service flows yielded by the nonfinancial goods and services consumed by the individual. The price level P is then defined as the dollar rental price of a unit rate of commodity services, measured in dollars per unit time per X. The individual's utility function can then be written:

$$(2) \qquad U = U(X, N)$$

where X equals the rate of consumption of commodity services and N equals the rate of consumption of monetary services.

Assume that in addition to yielding

marginal nonpecuniary monetary service returns, money yields a marginal pecuniary interest rate return equal to r_M and the substitute asset yields a marginal pecuniary interest rate return equal to r_s. Assume further that there exists another financial asset called a bond B, which yields no nonpecuniary monetary service returns and marginal pecuniary interest payments equal to i.

Finally, consider the individual's rate of consumption of commodity services. The X flow that can be purchased and consumed per unit time by the individual is a function of the rate of net dollar receipts to the individual.

$$(3) \qquad X = [Py_0 + r_M \cdot M + r_s \cdot S + iB](1/P)$$

where X equals the rate of flow of commodity services; y_0 equals the individual's given real rate of permanent earnings, measured in commodity services; M, S, and B equal the dollar value of the individual's money, substitute asset and bond holdings, measured in dollars; and r_M, r_s and i are the respective rates of return on these financial assets, measured in dollars per dollar per unit time. The term in brackets represents the individual's money income.

Now assume the individual has a given total of real nonhuman wealth W_0 where

$$(4) \qquad W_0 = M/P + S/P + B/P$$

and the individual maximizes utility subject to his given real human and nonhuman wealth (y_0 and W_0) and to the budget constraint that all income is spent. From (2) and (3) form the Lagrangian

$$(5) \qquad V = U(X, N) - \lambda[PX - Py_0 \\ - r_M \cdot M - r_s \cdot S - iB]$$

From (4) note that

$$(4') \qquad B = PW_0 - M - S$$

If we assume that the individual takes the market interest yields and the rental price

---

[1] See for example, Milton Friedman (1956), p. 4 and Gregory Chow, p. 113. For a more complete analysis and an attempt to partially standardize the money stock in terms of its service flow, see the author (1972).

of output services as a constant with respect to his own purchases, then substituting (4') into (5) and differentiating with respect to the individual's decision variables X, M, and S, the necessary conditions for a constrained maximum are:

(6) $\quad \dfrac{\partial V}{\partial X} = U_X - \lambda P = 0$

(7) $\quad \dfrac{\partial V}{\partial M} = U_N N_{(M/P)}(1/P) - \lambda(-r_M + i) = 0$

(8) $\quad \dfrac{\partial V}{\partial S} = U_N N_{(S/P)}(1/P) - \lambda(-r_s + i) = 0$

Assuming the usual second-order conditions hold, the optimum quantities of X, M, and S are then given where

(9) $\quad \lambda = \dfrac{U_X}{P} = \dfrac{U_N N_{(M/P)}(1/P)}{(i - r_M)}$

$\qquad = \dfrac{U_N N_{(S/P)}(1/P)}{(i - r_s)}$

Equation (9) states the usual equilibrium condition that the marginal utility of a dollar of income spent in all directions must be equal; i.e., marginal utility divided by price must be the same for all goods.[2] The rental price of a unit of commodity services is P while $(i - r_M)$ denoted by P_M is the rental price of the monetary service stream from a dollar of money and $(i - r_s)$ denoted by P_S is the rental price paid for the monetary service stream from a dollar of monetary substitutes.[3] The rental price

$(i - r_M)$ can be considered as the marginal pecuniary alternative cost per unit time of holding a dollar of money and in equilibrium will equal the value of the monetary services from a marginal dollar of money.[4] Similarly, $(i - r_s)$ represents the marginal alternative cost of holding the monetary substitute asset and in equilibrium will equal the value of the monetary services from a marginal dollar of substitute asset.

If we assume that permanent income y_p can be considered as the relevant empirical constraint (i.e., proxy for y_0 and W_0), then the conditions of utility maximixation imply that the demand for real cash balances may be written as:

(10) $\qquad (M/P)^d = f(y_p, P_M, P_s)$

where $\partial(M/P)^d/\partial y_P > 0$, $\partial(M/P)^d/\partial P_M < 0$ and, as long as the substitution in production effect dominates any scale of production effect,[5] $\partial(M/P)^d/\partial P_s > 0$. The variable P_M can be considered as the own price and P_s as the cross price of money and both P_M and P_s should be entered as variables in the demand for money function.

Equation (10) does not resemble common formulations of the demand for money which are typically represented by:

(11) $\qquad (M/P)^d = h(y_p, r_s)$

Some sense can be made of formulations such as (11) if we interpret them as im-

---

[2] There may be some confusion with regard to the good "money" since λ is sometimes called "the marginal utility of money." This is incorrect; λ should more properly be called the marginal utility of money income (i.e., the change in an individual's utility from a one dollar change in his income allocated optimally across goods) and distinguished from the marginal utility of money U_M (i.e., the change in an individual's utility from a dollar change in his money holdings). Equation (9) states that in equilibrium U_M and λ are related by the income foregone in holding a dollar of money $(i - r_M) = U_M/\lambda$.

[3] Edgar Feige (1964) defines similar "prices" but in his empirical analysis assumes that the pecuniary rate

of return on the asset yielding no nonpecuniary monetary services remains fixed, leaving alternative r_s measures and r_m as the sole variables in the demand functions.

[4] Alternatively, interest payments plus the value of monetary services equals i. When net pecuniary and nonpecuniary returns are considered, then money and every other asset traded in the economy must in equilibrium yield on the margin *the* interest rate.

[5] An increase in P_s will, *ceteris paribus*, increase the demand for money for a given desired monetary service flow; but an increase in P_s will decrease the monetary service flow demanded and hence decrease the demand for money (see the author (1972)). The first effect is assumed to always dominate and our alternative asset is assumed to be a substitute for money in the sense of a positive cross partial derivative.

934   THE AMERICAN ECONOMIC REVIEW   DECEMBER 1974

plicitly assuming that (a) the relevant price variable in the demand for money function is the difference between the own and cross prices of money, and (b) interest payments on money are zero. Assumption (a) implies that i, the benchmark return on the asset yielding no monetary services, need not be considered in the demand function; and assumption (b) implies that the rate of interest paid on money need not be considered.

Most previous demand for money estimates have made these two assumptions. Assumption (b) is generally recognized as a deficiency in existing demand for money studies. David Laidler (1966b, p. 545, fn. 4) explains this discrepancy between what is recognized to be theoretically correct and existing empirical work on the grounds that reliable data on interest payments on deposits over a substantial time period do not exist. Explicit interest payments were not systematically reported until 1919 and implicit interest payments have never been systematically reported.[6] The latter fact is of particular importance with regard to demand deposits where explicit interest payments have been pro-

nibited since 1933. The two previous demand for money studies that have not assumed that interest payments on money are zero (Richard Selden and Tong Hun Lee (1967)) cover much shorter time periods (1919–51 for Selden and 1951–65 for Lee) and measure interest on demand deposits post-1933 as the negative of bank service charges, thereby assuming that the interest prohibition has been totally effective and ignoring implicit interest payments completely. This study takes account of implicit interest payments on deposits by making the alternative assumption that the interest prohibition is totally ineffective.[7]

On the other hand, assumption (a) has not generally been recognized as a deficiency in existing demand for money studies. Both Selden and Lee, for example, assume that $(P_M - P_s)$ is the correct variable by considering the relevant price variable to be the difference between the yield on money substitutes and the yield on money, $(r_s - r_M)$. This "net interest rate" variable confuses the own and cross price effects and makes it difficult to interpret their empirical results. The separate response of the demand for money to each price cannot be determined, and the specification implicitly assumes that changes in the benchmark rate of return have no effect on the demand for money.[8] If we

---

[6] Implicit interest payments may take many forms. Reduced interest rates on loans to depositors combined with compensating balance requirements may be a major avenue by which implicit payments are made. The compensating balance requirement is then considered not an added constraint to the consumer but merely ties the loan rate explicitly to "working" deposit holdings. This may explain why the arrangement generally exists on business rather than consumer loans (those customers most likely to receive interest payments on their deposits) and why the requirement is always stated in terms of average rather than minimum deposit levels. It may also explain why stated commercial bank lending (say, prime) rates, which are really rates net of implicit interest payments, can be below market borrowing (say CD) rates. (See the author (1970, Appendix 1) for a discussion of the deposit-loan reciprocity arrangement between commercial banks and their customers.) In this paper, however, I am not concerned with how commercial banks may evade maximum deposit interest regulations but solely with whether the assumption of complete evasion explains observable phenomena better than the alternative assumption that these regulations are never evaded.

[7] Michael Darby has recently used a crude version of the r_M series I calculate here in quarterly demand for money regressions for the postwar period with results favorable to my hypothesis. (He, however, uses total reserves rather than the correct concept of reserves held by banks against demand deposits and also fails to make any adjustment for possible returns from the Federal Reserve to commercial banks in deriving his r_{M_1} series.) In addition, Robert Barro and Anthony Santomero have recently used the results of a private survey of commercial banks concerning the reported rate at which service charges are remitted as a function of demand deposit balances on small consumer-type accounts in a household demand for money function. The correlation between their interest on demand deposits series and the one used here for the period 1950–68 is .89.

[8] In a reply to comments on his study, Lee (1969) enters r_s and r_M (i.e., service charges on demand de-

assume that the own price effect is greater in absolute value than the cross price effect on the demand for money, then our demand for money equation (10) implies that $\partial(M/P)^d/\partial i$ will be negative. An increase, for example, in the benchmark rate of return which increases both the price of monetary services from money and the price of monetary services from the substitute asset will then decrease the demand for money.

In the regressions that follow, I estimate equation (10) without making assumptions (a) and (b). The important unanswered question of whether commercial banks evade the current prohibition of interest payments on demand deposits is not begged and the economically meaningful P_M, P_s specification is tested.

II. Estimates of the Prices

I shall operationally measure the "pure" pecuniary marginal rate of return i by the yield on long-term (up to thirty-year) corporate bonds r_L. Our data requirements limit us to the use of highly marketable assets upon which long historical interest rates series exist. Therefore, although long-term corporate bonds represent what in commonly vague terminology is called the least "liquid" asset that fulfills this criterion, they can be assumed to yield significant nonpecuniary monetary service returns. Hence r_L underestimates the true "pure" pecuniary rate of return and is an essentially arbitrary and biased zero monetary service benchmark.[9] The marginal

yield on a monetary substitute r_s will be operationally defined as the short-term (four-six month) commercial paper rate.[10] The rental price of monetary services from a dollar of monetary substitutes P_s is then equal to $(r_L - r_s)$.

The marginal return on money r_M is defined as a weighted average of interest on currency r_C and interest on deposits r_D.

$$(12) \qquad r_M = \left(\frac{C}{M}\right) r_C + \left(\frac{D}{M}\right) r_D$$

The money supply M is defined as currency C plus commercial bank deposits D and is represented by M_1 if bank deposits are defined to include only demand deposits and by M_2 if bank deposits are defined to include demand and time deposits. Interest on currency is assumed to equal zero.[11] Interest on bank deposits is estimated by measuring the marginal costs of producing monetary services yielded by a dollar of deposits MC_D and assuming that perfect competition among banks forces each of them to pass on to their depositors, in an open or covert manner, all marginal profit from their deposit accounts; or equivalently, that the rental price of monetary services from a dollar of deposits is equal to the marginal costs of monetary services from a dollar of deposits.

$$(13) \qquad (i - r_D) = MC_D$$

where r_D represents the "competitive" (or zero marginal profit) rate of interest paid on deposits by commercial banks.[12]

---

posits) as separate variables in demand for money regressions but still does not explicitly consider a benchmark return nor specify own and cross prices.

[9] The return on the much more illiquid asset human capital may be a superior measure of i, but it is extremely difficult to obtain reliable annual estimates of this return. If r_L is a return on a close substitute for money (i.e., a good alternative source of monetary services) rather than a measure of the benchmark rate of return, then $\partial(M/P)^d/\partial r_L$ rather than being indeterminate, will be negative. My particular empirical formulation therefore crucially depends upon how suitable r_L is as a measure of the benchmark rate of return.

[10] I experimented with alternative short-term interest rates in various subperiods and found the price of savings and loan shares to be statistically significant in the postwar period while the price of time deposits was found to be statistically insignificant in demand for M_1 regressions. Given the strong postwar trends in these series, however, any conclusions reached concerning substitutability solely on the basis of this evidence must clearly be tentative.

[11] Although some currency has at times paid interest. See Friedman and Anna Schwartz, p. 644, fn. 3.

[12] Individual commercial banks are assumed to be facing perfectly elastic demand curves. If competitive

936   THE AMERICAN ECONOMIC REVIEW   DECEMBER 1974

The major element of MC_D is the interest foregone by commercial banks on the margin on the assets in their portfolio. Any asset which a bank holds that on the margin yields a rate of return less than i should properly be considered as a marginal cost of producing monetary services. Assume that a commercial bank's portfolio consists of two assets, non-interest bearing reserves (R) and investments (I) which yield a marginal rate of return of r_I, and that $R + I = D$. If (R/D) and (I/D) are the bank's marginal reserve to deposit and investment to deposit ratios, then the foregone interest cost per marginal dollar of deposit is $i(R/D) + (i - r_I)(I/D)$. If we assume that all other commercial bank costs are not marginal costs, then competitive interest payments on deposits are, from (13),[13]

$$(14) \qquad r_D = r_I(1 - [R/D])$$

If (R/D) is also equal to the average reserve to deposit ratio, then from (12)

$$(15) \qquad r_{M_2} = r_I(1 - [H/M_2])$$

where high-powered money (H) equals currency (C) plus total commercial bank reserves (R).

An estimate of r_{M_1} can be obtained from our general relationships, equations (12)–(14), by letting D represent solely demand deposits DD and replacing R with R_{DD}, reserves held by commercial banks against demand deposits.[14]

---

interest payments are not made on deposits then r_D would be less than $(i - MC_D)$ with the bank in disequilibrium earning a marginal rate of pure profit (i.e., marginal revenue is greater than marginal cost). Every firm in the banking industry would therefore want to expand output and new firms would want to enter the industry. We can assume that new entry is restricted by government licensing and that the market is shared among existing firms in nonprice ways (say, randomly). However, if banks are permitted to engage in nonprice competition, then the difference between price and marginal cost will be eliminated. As long as there were *some* type of variable expenditure by a bank which to the consumer was equivalent to an increase in r_D (however small), then each bank's attempt to expand its output would in the process raise MC_D (and to some extent r_D) and thereby eliminate any marginal profit. If individual commercial banks have rising marginal cost schedules, then total profit may remain positive. This represents a rent on the government franchise limiting entry. If individual commercial banks were assumed to face negatively sloped demand curves, then the profit-maximizing price of monetary services from deposits would remain greater than marginal cost. Each banking firm would have some type of specific capital (say, a particular location or brand name) which determines the position of its demand curve and therefore its market share. Some of the profit earned by the firm would then represent a rent on this specific capital and r_D would still be negatively related to MC_D. In operationally defining r_D changes over time in the degree of competitiveness of the banking industry are ignored.

[13] Alternatively, we can derive (14) by defining MC_D less broadly to equal the marginal reserve ratio multiplied by the marginal rate of interest that would be

earned by commercial banks if they could replace the reserves with earning assets $r_I(R/D)$, and then by assuming that r_D will equal the difference between r_I and MC_D. This formulation has the drawback of misleadingly identifying commercial bank costs with reserves. But even if there were no reserve requirements and commercial banks held no reserves, the marginal cost of producing monetary services and the competitive rental price of monetary services from money would not be zero since r_I is generally less than i. Annual commercial bank operating expenditures (which, including taxes and dividends, have recently been about 5 percent of total outstanding deposits) are ignored in measuring MC_D because these expenditures are not generally marginal costs but are related to, for example, the number and type of transactions made. A perfectly competitive banking system would cover these expenditures by correctly pricing transactions. (If, for example, interest were paid via reductions in loan rates, highly active accounts would receive less of a reduction for the same average demand deposit balance than less active accounts). The marginal interest on deposits, defined in equation (14), is what should enter the demand for money, while an average interest on deposits variable, which would include the additional expenditures, would determine the number and type of deposit accounts (i.e., the all-or-none decision). In addition, some of these expenditures may represent for our calculations not costs of producing deposits but implicit interest payments on deposits in the form of "free service" to customers.

[14] Equation (16) would be equivalent in form to equation (15) and $(DD - R_{DD})/M_1$ could be written as $1 - (H/M_1)$ if M_1 were defined consistently to include reserves held by commercial banks against time deposits as part of "currency held by the nonbank public" $(C = H - R_{DD})$. This definition would treat the high-powered money held by commercial banks against time deposits in a way logically equivalent to the present treatment of the cash holdings of nonbank financial intermediaries (for example, savings and loan institutions). However, I use the common, less inclusive but

(16) $r_{M_1} = r_I[(DD - R_{DD})/M_1]$

The marginal return on commercial bank investments r_I is measured by r_s because the *true* r_I is very difficult to obtain. Reported rates of return earned by commercial banks are inadequate because they are gross average rates of return and not a measure of the marginal profit a bank can earn. Such rates are also meaningless if reduced interest rates on loans is the major way in which interest on demand deposits is paid.

It should be emphasized that these estimates of the perfectly competitive marginal return on money assume that the regulations governing the maximum interest rates which banks are permitted to pay on their deposit liabilities, the prohibition of all interest payments on demand deposits, and the ceiling rate set by regulation Q on time deposits, are completely ineffective, i.e., are evaded costlessly. "Indirect" price competition by commercial banks is so efficient that marginal profit

is eliminated entirely by increases in r_D rather than by increases in MC_D. But for these measures to be empirically valid in the regressions that follow, all that is necessary to assume is that the costs of making interest payments on deposits have not changed significantly over time.

The returns on money defined in equations (15) and (16) also assume that commercial bank reserves yield no interest. If however, the Federal Reserve subsidizes member commercial banks in proportion to their reserves, then this subsidy will be passed on to depositors by the same competitive process by which we assume interest is being paid on deposits. Such subsidy payments must therefore be subtracted from MC_D and the r_D estimate revised upward. Our r_D estimates are therefore modified for the subsidies given by the Fed to member commercial banks in the form of credit extended at less than the market interest rate. These include bank float which is extended at a zero interest rate and borrowings by commercial banks at the discount rate.[15] Modifications are also

---

possibly more economically meaningful, definitions of C and M. (Note that any attempt to estimate the demand for the more inclusive M_1 magnitude would have to include legal reserve requirements on commercial bank time deposits as an explanatory variable.) Similarly, M_2 is defined exclusive of large negotiable certificates of deposit for the 1961–70 period and therefore, during this period, R is defined as consistent with the deposit total-in our monetary aggregate and does not include required reserves held on large CDs. These reserves are also not considered as part of C and hence are totally excluded from H. To estimate R_{DD} one must allocate excess commercial bank reserves between demand and time deposits. I construct R_{DD}, and therefore r_{M_1}, by allocating excess reserves between the different deposits in proportion to the relative quantities of the deposits. This may be considered to yield a somewhat low estimate of excess reserves held against demand deposits. Two alternative but somewhat more arbitrary estimates were also made: (a) allocating excess reserves in proportion to required reserves, and (b) allocating all excess reserves to demand deposits. Demand for money regressions comparing the three alternative estimates yield almost identical results except for the period from 1933 to 1942 when excess reserves were significant. And for that period the estimate we have used in constructing r_{M_1} yields slightly superior results.

[15] This credit has at times been significant. Through the 1960's float averaged more than 10 percent of total member bank reserves, and for the first few years after the Federal Reserve was established, borrowings were greater than reserves. This latter phenomenon is analogous to the usual "discounts" new firms often make to obtain a market share. Borrowings were greatest from 1918 to 1921, while the Federal Reserve's share of the deposit market was rising from 45 to 65 percent, and taking account of borrowings helps to explain some of the increase in the demand for money in this period. Float is subtracted from member bank reserves by the Fed. This definition of bank reserves is somewhat misleading. Bank float should be considered as a part of member bank reserves and subtracted out only when making calculations of commercial bank costs. Regressions which include float in reserves, however, yield slightly superior results than the reported regressions which exclude float. The hypothesis that float is an interest-free loan of reserves to member banks from the Fed is therefore rejected. But these results are dominated by the post-1950 period when float becomes significant and exclusion produces poorer results by exacerbating the unexplained postwar decrease in the demand for money. In my 1972 paper, I show that one possible partial explanation for the postwar increase in velocity

938   THE AMERICAN ECONOMIC REVIEW   DECEMBER 1974

made for the subsidy from the Treasury in the form of federal government demand deposits held at commercial banks. If we assume that the federal government does not participate in the evasion of interest prohibition on demand deposits, then the interest earnings from government demand deposits, adjusted for the reserves held against them, are a subsidy to commercial banks.[16]

Finally, estimates of the marginal return on money are further modified by subtracting the service charges that individuals pay on demand deposits and the losses that they expect to incur in holding deposits if the bank fails. These elements can be considered as covering additional commercial bank marginal costs of producing deposits.[17]

---

may be a decrease in the "quality" of money (measured by the predictability of prices).

[16] These deposits averaged $6.4 billion in 1970, or more than 20 percent of total commercial bank reserves. The largest banks generally hold the largest quantities of government deposits and the deposits can be considered as a subsidy given approximately in proportion to reserves held. The large increase of government demand deposits during 1943–46 (when the ratio of government demand deposits to total bank reserves reached a level of nearly one) and the subsequent sharp postwar decrease in these deposits helps to explain movements in the demand for money during this period. The other relatively large increase in government demand deposits occurred in 1918 (when the ratio of government demand deposits to total reserves rose to more than one-half), and, although real cash balances decline sharply, inclusion of this variable improves the fit.

[17] There are, however, a priori reasons to suggest that service charges should not be subtracted out. Service charges face the depositor in per transaction or per unit time and not per dollar deposit terms and therefore do not enter the relevant marginal P_M. If the number of transactions an individual makes per unit time and the average balance he holds are substitutes, the effect on the demand for money of service charges should be in the opposite direction. A rising service charge rate per transaction would decrease the number of transactions and increase the average deposit balance. This may possibly be tested by looking at total bank clearings and average level of demand deposits as service charges change. However, in my work regressions which do not subtract service charges from estimates of r_D yield poorer results than those which do. Service charges monotonically increased from .15 percent of demand

III. Results

Estimates of equation (10) using annually averaged data and the definitions outlined above are presented in Table 1. The time period 1880–1970 is covered for M_2, with subperiods 1880–1918 for M_2 and 1919–70 for M_1 and M_2 reported separately. (The strong unchanging trends in the variables over shorter periods cast serious doubt on the effective number of degrees of freedom present within smaller subperiods.) Money and income are defined in real permanent per capita terms; i.e., the demand function is assumed homogenous of the first degree in permanent prices and measured population.[18]

---

deposits in 1946 to .61 percent of demand deposits in 1967, where they have stabilized. Hence inclusion helps to "explain" some of the postwar rise in velocity. Service charges on deposits may therefore actually enter the demand for money as negative interest payments (or as a reduction in "free" services) as Selden, Lee, Feige (1964), and Phillip Cagan consider them to be. But, as we shall see below, an "actual" interest payment on money variable does not work very well over the 1919–70 period. And when alternative explanations for the changing postwar trend in velocity are considered (see the author (1972)), service charges lose their explanatory power.

[18] Changes in permanent prices and measured population are assumed to cause equal percentage changes in the nominal quantity of money demanded. Some evidence on this proposition with respect to measured prices can be found in Allan Meltzer. Friedman (1959) argues that holders of cash balances are likely to determine the quantity to hold in terms of longer term price movements, and successfully uses a permanent price index deflator. But Friedman's series, which is merely a weighted average of past measured price levels with no adjustment made for trend, cannot be meaningfully extended through the 1960's when a dollar fiduciary standard with a clear positive long-term trend in the price level replaced any remaining semblance of a gold commodity standard with its general presumption of a long-term stable price level (see the author (1974)). (The downward bias is obvious when one considers the level of the ratio of measured to unadjusted permanent prices, which is greater than one every year since 1940, is 1.03 in 1963 before the rapid inflation begins, and reaches a level of 1.08 in 1970.) Any attempt to adjust the permanent price level series must be somewhat arbitrary. I crudely use the accelerating level of the long-term interest rate as a market measure of the postwar acceleration of the long-term trend of prices and measure trend over the 1952–70 period by subtracting the long-term rate of interest from the average long-

TABLE 1—DEMAND FOR MONEY FUNCTIONS, ANNUAL OBSERVATIONS,
1880–1970 AND SUBPERIODS

Time period	$\log M = a_0 + a_1 \log y_p + a_2 P_s + a_3 P_M$				R^2	D.W.	Standard Error
	a_0	a_1	a_2	a_3			
M_2							
1880–1970	−13.92	1.328	.327	−.342	.988	1.05	.0773
	[.6957]	(78.90)	(52.98)	(16.67)	(14.01)		
1880–1918	−15.20	1.515	.214	−.277	.987	1.15	.0523
	[.4413]	(21.21)	(13.83)	(6.09)	(6.18)		
1919–70	−13.82	1.312	.353	−.350	.954	.70	.0762
	[.3432]	(49.18)	(31.29)	(8.86)	(7.08)		
M_1							
1919–70	−15.68	1.562	.416	−.446	.905	.50	.1254
	[.3956]	(32.59)	(21.06)	(11.83)	(9.25)		

Note: All *logs* stand for natural logarithms. The absolute values of the *t*-statistics are given in parentheses beneath the coefficient estimates; *D.W.* represents the Durbin-Watson statistic; R^2 the coefficient of determination. The standard error of the dependent variable for each time period is bracketed beneath each date.

The regressions are not run with the *logs* of P_s and P_M because these variables are sometimes negative. This points up the fact that r_L is an arbitrary base from which to measure monetary services. But some

term rate during 1946–51, smoothing a monotonically increasing series to the nearest quarter of a percentage point. The adjusted permanent price level series remains below measured prices, but the measured to permanent price ratio is only 1.01 in 1963 and rises to only 1.04 in 1970. Surprisingly, the long-term interest elasticity of demand for money is not increased very much over this period when this is done. The demand for real per capita M_1 using Friedman's unadjusted permanent prices for 1953–70 is:

$$\log M_1 = -13.82 + 1.319 \log y_p - 1.474 r_s$$
$$\quad\quad (3.51) \quad\quad (2.22) \quad\quad\quad (3.62)$$

$$-.045 r_L + 2.128 r_{M_1} \quad R^2 = .661$$
$$(1.60) \quad\quad (3.72)$$

while using my adjusted permanent prices it is:

$$\log M_1 = -13.66 + 1.300 \log y_p - 1.509 r_s$$
$$\quad\quad (3.39) \quad\quad (2.13) \quad\quad\quad (3.62)$$

$$-.050 r_L + 2.179 r_{M_1} \quad R^2 = .701$$
$$(1.74) \quad\quad (3.71)$$

With regard to the deflation by measured population, the use of per capita averages of aggregated income and money holdings may not be an appropriate approximation. Some measure of the dispersion of income and money holdings may also be relevant. In addition, since foreign holdings of currency are included in the money estimates, the *U.S.* population figures used are somewhat arbitrary.

zero benchmark must be chosen, and as long as the monetary service yield in the benchmark asset remains constant over time, the only effect on P_M and P_s will be a once and for all decrease in their levels. Elasticity expressions are, however, not invariant under changes of origin and therefore this is one reason for running demand for money regressions in semilog form.[19]

[19] "Since there are no natural zeros from which we measure economic magnitudes, the elasticity expressions can be seen to be essentially arbitrary" (Paul Samuelson, p. 125). Modern portfolio theory does not suggest that interest rates or interest differentials should enter in a logarithmic form and there is some economic reason to expect a one percentage point change in P_M, independent of the level at which it occurs, to represent the same increase in the cost of holding money and to have the same effect on the demand for money. The commonly used logarithmic functional form implies a proportionately greater effect for every percentage point change in interest the lower the rate of interest and an undefined demand for money at a zero rate of interest. But as long as there are some increasing marginal costs associated with holding cash balances, we should expect the demand for money curve to cut the axis and a finite determinant money demand at negative interest rates. In addition, once we introduce risk considerations associated with the future real value of money, even at a zero (or negative) net cost of holding money, an optimum portfolio will not consist entirely of money. If there is a negative covariance between the movements of the price level and the return on physical

TABLE 2—COMPARISON OF TABLE 1 DEMAND FOR MONEY RESULTS WITH
BENCHMARK DEMAND FOR MONEY RESULTS

Dependent Variable and Time Period	Table 1			Benchmark		Table 1 S.E. Benchmark S.E.
	y_p	P_s	P_M	y_p	r_s	
M_2						
1880–1970	1.33	.33	−.34	1.52	−.06	.64
	(53.0)	(16.7)	(14.0)	(47.8)	(8.4)	
1880–1918	1.52	.21	−.28	2.13	−.03	.76
	(13.8)	(6.1)	(6.2)	(38.3)	(2.5)	
1919–70	1.31	.35	−.35	1.27	−.06	.94
	(31.3)	(8.9)	(7.1)	(29.2)	(10.1)	
M_1						
1919–70	1.56	.42	−.45	1.31	−.10	.84
	(21.1)	(11.8)	(9.3)	(16.5)	(9.7)	

All of the estimates of the income elasticity and the logarithmic price slopes of demand for money in Table 1 have the correct sign and are statistically significant at the .99 confidence level. But to interpret these results they must be compared to some standard estimates of the demand for money. As a first step I will use estimates of equation (11) as a benchmark, with *the* interest rate entering in a semilog function. Table 2 compares these benchmark estimates with the estimates of Table 1. At the end of each row is the ratio of the standard error of estimate of the regression

reported in Table 1 to the standard error estimate of the benchmark regression. This number can be thought of as a measure of the reduction in the sum of squares achieved by using the demand for money function we have been estimating, compensating for the sacrifice of a degree of freedom. If it is less than one, it means that the results reported in Table 1 have more explanatory power than the benchmark results. The results reported in Table 1 improve upon the benchmark results in all periods, with the regression over the entire 1880–1970 time period showing the most dramatic improvement. This is possibly the most meaningful regression, since much of the variation that must be explained occurs between the subperiods.[20]

The demand for M_2 estimates of Table 1 also show substantially more stability over time than the benchmark estimates, with

assets, individuals who dislike risk will diversify and hold a fraction of their wealth in common stocks and other real assets, even if the return is lower. The Keynesian analysis often cited to justify a logarithmic demand for money function considers nominally denominated bonds as the alternative to money and ignores the risk associated with unanticipated price level changes. Riskiness consists solely of the capital losses associated with interest rate changes and money is assumed to be a riskless asset. The *log-log* interest rate results were highly erratic and generally much poorer than the results in Table 1. For example, over the 1880–1970 time period:

$$\log M_2 = -\underset{(63.60)}{14.30} + \underset{(44.33)}{1.419 \log y_p} - \underset{(7.19)}{.724 \log r_s}$$

$$-\underset{(1.21)}{.088 \log r_L} + \underset{(6.10)}{.481 \log r_{M_2}}$$

$$R^2 = .983; \ DW = .50; \ SE = .0930$$

[20] Although first differencing may eliminate much of the information (I consider my r_M variable to be a proxy for the general level of interest payments on money and have much less confidence in its year to year movements), the first difference results over the 1880–1970 period are:

$$\Delta \log M_2 = \underset{(1.92)}{.009} + \underset{(7.33)}{1.030 \, \Delta \log y_P} + \underset{(4.25)}{.080 \, \Delta P_s}$$

$$-\underset{(4.03)}{.099 \, \Delta P_{M_2}}$$

the F-statistic for identity of coefficients between the two subperiods falling to 8.1 from 45.8 ($F_{.01} = 3.6$). Much of this improvement is due to the decrease in the estimated income elasticity for 1880–1918, which is produced by the sharp decline that occurred in H/M_2 over this period.[21] The estimated income elasticity for 1880–1918, however, remains greater than the income elasticity estimate for 1919–70. This is expected since money like all goods should have a declining income elasticity of demand as income rises; entering the consumer's budget as a luxury, but eventually becoming a necessity.[22] It is therefore misleading to ask what *the* income elasticity of demand for money is.

$R^2 = .514$; $DW = 1.34$; $SE = .0358$; SE/Benchmark $SE = .94$. This regression is presented so that it can be compared to previously reported results and not to correct for serial correlation. The very low $D.W.$ statistic indicates a high degree of serial correlation in the errors and therefore our OLS estimates do not have minimum variance. But although the precision of our coefficient estimates is less than indicated by the reported standard errors, it should be noted that the reported T-values are extremely high. The GLS estimates, using the Cochrane-Urcutt iterative technique, for the 1880–1970 period are:

$$\log M_2 = -\ 12.330 + 1.063 \log y_P + .072\ P_s$$
$$(16.90)\quad (9.97)\quad\quad (3.89)$$

$$-\ .087\ P_{M_2}$$
$$(3.65)$$

$R^2 = .998$; $DW = 1.37$; $SE = .0343$; $\rho^* = .96$

$$\log M_2 = -\ 12.634 + 1.137 \log y_P - .044\ r_s$$
$$(17.86)\quad (10.89)\quad\quad (2.33)$$

$$= -\ .056\ r_L + .052\ r_{M_2}$$
$$(4.37)\quad\quad (2.12)$$

$R^2 = .998$; $DW = 1.30$; $SE = .0320$; $\rho^* = .96$

[21] See the author (1973) where it is also demonstrated that once H/M_2 is included in a velocity relationship the seemingly inconsistent movements in velocity and the rate of interest emphasized by Friedman and Schwartz are reconciled. The H estimates used in this earlier work mistakenly included bank float for 1968–70 and thereby exacerbated the unexplained discrepancy that remains between velocity and interest rate movements over this recent period.

[22] If income elasticities of luxury goods do not fall, then as income grows we should see individuals specia¹-

The regressions reported in Table 1 are simultaneously testing both hypotheses: the significance of the competitive interest return on money variable and the functional form specification embodying the price of monetary services. I shall now attempt to test each hypothesis separately by running the same regressions in the more general semilogarithmic interest rate form with r_L, r_s, and r_M, in addition to $\log y_P$, entering as separate variables. The results are reported in Table 3. Although the interest on money variable remains significant in all but one of the time periods (1880–1918), the interest rate functional form appears to outperform the price functional form with a lower standard error of estimate for all four regressions. In addition, the estimated demand for M_2 becomes slightly more stable over the two subperiods with the F-statistic falling to 7.0 ($F_{.01} = 3.3$). However, the Durbin-Watson statistic is now lower for all four regressions and it is therefore not unambiguously clear which functional specification is superior.

The much lower magnitude of the r_L coefficient than of the r_s or r_M coefficients for the demand for money regression over the entire 1880–1970 period suggests that it may be appropriate to consider long-term corporate bonds as we have, i.e., as a benchmark asset yielding no monetary services rather than as a close substitute for money. The closeness of the r_L co-

---

izing in the consumption of these goods. But since the weighted sum of the income elasticity of demand for all goods must equal one, in the limit as the luxury goods weights increase, the income elasticities must fall to one. This may partially explain the postwar rise in velocity. The downward trend in the income parameter should produce some additional serial correlation in the residuals in the regressions over the entire period since these regressions use an average income elasticity which underestimates the true income elasticity in the early years and overestimates the true income elasticity in the later years.

TABLE 3—DEMAND FOR MONEY FUNCTIONS, ANNUAL OBSERVATIONS, 1880–1970 AND SUBPERIODS

Time Period	$\log M = a_0 + a_1 \log y_p + a_2 r_s + a_3 r_L + a_4 r_M$					R^2	D.W.	Standard Error
	a_0	a_1	a_2	a_3	a_4			
M_2								
1880–1970	−14.09	1.372	−.285	−.058	.303	.990	.94	.0721
	(82.50)	(52.44)	(13.28)	(4.06)	(12.09)			
1880–1918	−16.87	1.829	−.110	−.130	.131	.991	.74	.0451
	(21.85)	(14.23)	(2.62)	(5.73)	(2.33)			
1919–70	−13.59	1.287	−.208	−.039	.200	.960	.46	.0720
	(48.56)	(31.56)	(3.11)	(1.88)	(2.69)			
M_1								
1919–70	−14.31	1.381	−.165	−.129	.170	.918	.32	.1181
	(20.87)	(14.23)	(1.66)	(3.02)	(1.51)			

efficient to zero also indicates another alternative functional form of the demand for money equation that should be tested. Although the magnitude of the P_M coefficient is generally greater in absolute value than the P_s coefficient (as one would expect), it is not much greater. The sum of a_2 and a_3 is negative in three out of four regressions, but is never greater in absolute value than 0.07. Clearly the two price effects offset one another to a large extent. And it is possible that although each coefficient separately has a high t-value, the sum which is numerically much smaller might not be statistically significant at all. The significance of a_2 and a_3 separately might merely reflect the fact that r_s enters both prices, in one case positively affecting the demand for money and in one case negatively affecting the demand for money. I therefore tested this possibility by running regressions using the difference between the price of money and the price of money substitutes $(P_M - P_s)$ in addition to income as the relevant independent variable. Since $(P_M - P_s)$ is equivalent to $(r_s - r_M)$ I am also testing the Selden-Lee assumption that the relevant price variable is the difference between the rate of return on a substitute asset and the rate of return on money. If the t-ratio of $(a_3 + a_4)$ were less than one then a regression using

only $(r_s - r_M)$ would give better results than the more complete and complicated regressions of Table 1.[23] The results are reported in Table 4. They are generally inferior to those in Table 1 with higher standard errors of estimate for three of four regressions, implying that one should, in general, "pay" the extra degree of freedom to obtain the separate price effects on the demand for money. But the Selden-Lee hypothesis that $a_2 = -a_3$ cannot be rejected using an F-test at the 99 percent confidence level in three of four regressions. The empirical suitability of the Selden-Lee functional form specification (not the particular r_M variables they use) remains an open question.

Finally, to test if the maximum interest payment regulations on deposits are being evaded, we can compare our results for the most recent time period with results obtained assuming that the regulations are effective and that no implicit interest payments are being made by banks. The demand for money over 1919–70 using actual reported interest payments on deposits, modified by expected losses and service charges in constructing an actual interest payments on money variable (r_{MA}) is:

[23] Note that $a_2 P_s + a_3 P_M = (a_2 + a_3) P_s + a_3 (P_M - P_s)$. See Yoel Haitovsky.

TABLE 4—DEMAND FOR MONEY FUNCTIONS, ANNUAL OBSERVATIONS,
1880–1970 AND SUBPERIODS

Time Period	$\log M = a_0 + a_1 \log y_P + a_2 (r_s - r_M)$			R^2	$D.W.$	Standard Error
	a_0	a_1	a_2			
M_2						
1880–1970	−13.96	1.328	−.315	.988	1.12	.0780
	(78.81)	(52.48)	(17.05)			
1880–1918	−17.17	1.815	−.139	.981	.70	.0630
	(26.45)	(18.28)	(3.83)			
1919–70	−13.81	1.312	−.356	.954	.69	.0755
	(50.34)	(31.61)	(11.11)			
M_1						
1919–70	−15.66	1.547	−.399	.902	.54	.1263
	(32.33)	(20.95)	(12.09)			

(17) $\log M_2 = -13.19 + 1.220 \log y_p$
         (37.43) (22.84)

$$-.022 r_s - .046 r_L - .038 r_{M2A}$$
$$(1.50)\quad (2.06)\quad (1.04)$$

$$R^2 = .954;\ DW = .29;\ SE = .0764$$

A comparison of these regressions with the third line in Table 3 demonstrates the superiority of the competitive interest on money variable to the actual interest on money variable.[24] This suggests the conclusion that the complete lack of effectiveness of interest rate regulations is closer to the truth than the commonly accepted assumption that it is a totally effective constraint on bank behavior.[25] But, more

[24] A measure of actual interest payments on money not modified by service charges and expected losses yielded even poorer results. Demand for M_1 regressions using an actual interest payments on money variable cannot be run over the 1919–70 time period because interest payments on demand deposits were not reported separately from interest payments on time deposits until 1927. Actual interest payments on M_1, however, did perform poorly over the 1927–70 period. A composite interest payments on M_2 variable, defined as a weighted average of actual reported interest payments on time deposits and my perfectly competitive interest payments on demand deposits, performed poorest of all over this period.

[25] Since $(1 - [H/M])$ is merely a proxy for r_M/r_s, r_M could actually equal, for example, $(.01)\ r_s(1 - [H/M])$ and yield significant regression results although the interest rate regulation is almost completely effective. This, however, seems highly unlikely given the fact that the magnitude of the P_M and P_s coefficients are nearly the same.

generally, the two alternative hypotheses we compared can be thought of as representing two extremes on a continuum; and some third hypothesis in between the costless evasion and no evasion hypotheses, may work best of all. Direct estimates of the interest paid on deposits, say, via reduced loan rates, would therefore be extremely useful.

IV. Summary and Implications

The significance of the "competitive" r_M variable in the demand for money function, whether entered indirectly as in Tables 1 and 4 or directly as in Table 3, is the primary conclusion of this paper. This represents a substantial advance, since no alternative interest on money series covering as long a time period now exists. The series presented here (and listed in the Appendix) is shown to make a significant improvement over the common assumption that interest on demand deposits equals zero, or the negative of service charges and expected losses on deposits.

My particular demand for money formulation also clarifies, to some extent, the debate which has occurred on whether a short-term or a long-term interest rate is the "proper" variable to use in the demand for money.[26] Most of the discussion has

[26] For example, Martin Bronfenbrenner and Thomas Mayer and Ronald Teigen use a short-term interest

been almost completely devoid of any theoretical argument and the issue has generally been settled in favor of a short-term rate on empirical grounds.[27] The model I have presented suggests a theoretical reason for including both interest rates in the demand for money; a long-term interest rate as a measure of the rate of return on an asset yielding no monetary services and therefore as the opportunity cost of holding an asset yielding monetary services, and a short-term interest rate as a measure of the rate of return on an asset yielding a significant monetary service flow and therefore as the foregone pecuniary return on close substitutes for money.

In addition, my demand for money formulation points up the deficiencies in the usual interpretations of what economists call the interest elasticity of demand for money. Estimates of such a concept are obtained from regressions which do not consider the rental prices of the monetary service stream yielded by assets, but merely the rates of interest paid on assets. And such regressions generally omit from consideration the interest paid on money; therefore measuring a cross rate effect without holding the own rate constant. Because interest payments on money and on money substitutes are highly positively correlated with one another and influence the demand for money in opposite directions, such "observed" interest elasticities will be severely biased downward.[28]

---

rate while Meltzer, Karl Brunner and Meltzer, Robert Eisner, Carl Christ and Henry Latané use a long-term rate.

[27] See, for example, Laidler (1966b), H. R. Heller, and Lee (1967).

[28] Since we use r_s as a measure of r_I, the marginal rate of return earned by commercial banks on their investment portfolio, r_s and r_M must *necessarily* be positively correlated. An alternative measure of r_I would make the proposition an empirical one. To get an idea of the bias, consider, for example, the following stepwise results for the 1919–70 period.

$$log\ M_1 = -14.21 + 1.313\ log\ y_p - .100\ r_s$$
$$(26.70)\quad (16.50)\qquad\quad (9.69)$$

$$R^2 = .866;\ DW = .35;\ SE = .1477$$

But recognition of the fact that the *true* interest elasticity of demand for money, estimated while holding interest payments on money constant, is much greater than what has been estimated by previous studies should not necessarily be considered as a refutation of those who believe *the* interest elasticity of demand for money to be small. These results emphasize that the magnitude of the effect will depend upon what one considers to be held constant when carrying out an experiment. The usefulness of a particular specification of *ceteris paribus* conditions depends upon the purpose the calculation is to be used for. For policy considerations it may be the actual observed interest elasticity which is relevant. Policy makers may only wish to know if changes in the level of interest rates will cause (i.e., be associated with) large changes in velocity. My model supplies a theoretical justification for expecting a small total measured interest rate effect on the demand for money and the results supply an empirical justification for the net effect remaining negative; i.e., for the interest rate on money variable not dominating. An increase, for example, in the anticipated inflation rate unambiguously produces a decrease in the demand for money when the demand function is specified in the price form of Table 1 as long as the P_M coefficient is negative. Since

$$log\ M_1 = -15.63 + 1.542\ log\ y_p - .392\ r_s + .390\ r_{M_1}$$
$$(27.38)\quad (17.57)\qquad\quad (5.60)\qquad (4.20)$$

$$R^2 = .902;\ DW = .54;\ SE = .1276$$

Once we take account of interest payments on money, the short-term interest rate effect on the demand for money is multiplied in magnitude by a factor of nearly four. Note that since the regression is in semilog form, the coefficient on the short-term interest rate does not represent the interest elasticity, but rather an estimate of the logarithmic slope; i.e., a measure of the percentage change in the quantity of money demanded from a percentage *point* change in the interest rate. If $log\ M = br$, then $d\ log\ M/dr = dr/r$. Since $d\ log\ r = dr/r$, the interest elasticity $d\ log\ M/d\ log\ r$ then equals br. Evaluated at the sample means over the entire 1880–1970 period the respective interest elasticities are -1.086 for r_s, $-.224$ for r_L, and $+.821$ for r_{M_1}.

r_L and r_s will increase by the same amount (when interest rates are stated in continuous terms), P_s will be unchanged while r_M will increase by less than r_L (at the sample mean r_{M_2} will rise by the increase in the expected inflation rate multiplied by $\bar{r}_{M_2}/\bar{r}_s$ or .711, which is $(1 - H/M_2)$ in the simplest case), and P_M will therefore rise. Our price results imply that a one percentage point increase in the expected inflation rate will increase the demand for money .099 percent; i.e., $(.342)(.289)$. In terms of the interest rate specification of Table 3, there is no such obvious negative relationship but our results imply that, again evaluated at the sample means for the 1880–1970 period, a one percentage point increase in the expected inflation rate will decrease the demand for money .128 percent; i.e., $.285 + .058 - (.303)(.711)$.[29]

This competitive banking model also implies that policy makers must be concerned with the effects of particular policy changes on commercial bank costs. Changes in bank costs will influence interest payments on money and therefore the demand for real cash balances. An increase, for example, in reserve requirements offset by open market purchases which keeps the money supply constant will raise the costs to banks of producing deposits and by leading to a fall in the rate of interest paid on deposits and therefore in the demand for money will have an expansionary effect on the economy. That is, changes in the composition of money will have nonneutral effects. And, in general, one must know how a particular change in the money supply is brought about to fully determine its effects.[30]

My results also have implications for the definition of money. The proper definition of money has become an essentially empirical issue of finding that particular subgroup of assets which yields a relatively simple and stable demand function. And current debate has narrowed down to the question of whether to include commercial bank time deposits as part of the money supply. Past results on this question have been somewhat ambiguous. For example, Laidler concludes that " . . . the stability of the demand function for money is improved by including time deposits in the definition of money" (1966a, p. 55) while Brunner and Meltzer argue that " . . . our results seem to suggest clearly that currency plus demand deposits is the more appropriate definition" (p. 390).[31] Brunner and Meltzer, however, also argue on theoretical grounds for the narrower definition of money. They say that the inclusion of interest yielding time deposits obscures part of the substitution effect between money and nonmoney, i.e., to " . . . mix the effects of general and relative changes in interest rates and to obscure a part of the wealth adjustment process" (p. 350;

[29] These calculations assume that H/M will be invariant to changes in the expected inflation rate. But since interest on currency is assumed to equal zero, changes in the rate of expected inflation will decrease the relative price of deposits compared to currency, thereby producing a decrease in the desired currency to deposit ratio and a decrease in H/M. The increase in r_M at the sample mean will therefore be somewhat greater and the net effect on the demand for money therefore be somewhat less than indicated by our calculations.

[30] Note that if the same experiment is analyzed in terms of a Patinkin-type model, the implications are reversed. Changes in the "inside" to "outside" (or interest bearing to non-interest bearing) money ratio disturb neutrality via a positive wealth effect on the demand for money. Also note that changes in the discount rate will have some economic impact in addition to any "psychological" or "announcement" effects. An increase in the discount rate increases commercial bank costs (reduces the subsidy from the Fed), raises the competitive price of money and is therefore, ceteris paribus, expansionary.

[31] Some of the disagreement is due to alternative definitions of the other variables in the demand function—a short-term or a long-term interest rate, nonhuman wealth or permanent income. Laidler attempts to compare alternative formulations and concludes that permanent income is superior to nonhuman wealth (1966a) and then using permanent income finds a short-term interest rate and a definition of money that includes time deposits to yield the most stable relationship (1966b).

946 THE AMERICAN ECONOMIC REVIEW DECEMBER 1974

also see Meltzer, p. 225). This is analogous to what I have identified as confusing the own and cross effects of a change in interest rates and a reason why observed interest elasticities of demand for money are under-estimates of "true" interest elasticity. But Brunner and Meltzer's argument justifies a definition of money which excludes time deposits only if interest payments are not also made on demand deposits. This is an empirical hypothesis that is not true pre-1933 and which has been tested for the post-1933 period and found to be unwarranted. If interest is paid on demand deposits then we have the same problem of "obscuring the substitution effect" with respect to demand deposits; and Brunner and Meltzer are left with currency as the sole legitimate component of the money supply. A much better method to isolate a pure interest rate effect is not to eliminate from consideration as money all assets which yield interest but to explicitly introduce the own price of money. Once this is done, no particular definition of money is implied.

All single equation estimates of the demand for money, such as those reported here, run the risk of the "identification problem." I estimate the demand for real cash balances using annually averaged data and therefore am assuming that most, if not all, of the market adjustment takes place within a year, and that individuals are *on* their demand curves. My regressions are therefore estimates of a long-run or "equilibrium" demand for money.[32] But since H/M, the inverse of the money multiplier, now enters on the demand side as well as the supply side, the identification problem is magnified. Increases in R/D or C/D which will cause decreases in the supply of money will now also cause decreases

---

[32] Feige (1967) suggests that " . . . cash balance portfolio adjustments to desired positions are completed within a single year" (p. 471). Also see Lee (1967, p. 1177).

---

by a competitive banking system in interest payments on money and hence a decrease in the demand for money. For example, if H is taken as exogenous, then the nominal supply of money and hence H/M is partially determined by the holders of money along with real cash balances. A more complete simultaneous model would therefore include a demand for money function and a demand for currency relative to deposits function, which partially determines H/M and which therefore feeds back into the demand for money. If a desired commercial bank reserve ratio is introduced, it will partially determine bank costs and hence interest payments on deposits, and therefore will feed into the demand for money and the demand for currency relative to deposits functions. The competitive banking model we are using here emphasizes the necessity of developing a general equilibrium model of the monetary system.

APPENDIX
Construction of the Interest Rate Paid on Money Variables
Competitive Interest Paid on M_2

$$r_{M_2} = r_s[1 - (H_2/M_2)] + (r_s^w - r_d^w)(B/M_2)$$
$$+ r_s[(G_{DD} - R_G)/M_2]$$
$$- l_D^*(D/M_2) - s_{DD}(DD/M_2)$$

Competitive Interest Paid on M_1

$$r_{M_1} = r_s(DD - R_{DD})/M_1$$
$$+ (r_s^w - r_d^w)(B/M_1)(R_{DD}/R_D)$$
$$+ r_s(G_{DD} - R_G)(1/M_1)(R_{DD}/R_D)$$
$$- l_D^*(DD/M_1) - s_{DD}(DD/M_1)$$

where:

$M_2 = C + D$, currency plus commercial bank demand and time deposits, less large negotiable certificates of deposit beginning in 1961 (Friedman and Schwartz, *Fed. Res. Bull.*).

$M_1 = C + DD$, currency plus commercial

bank demand deposits (Friedman and Schwartz, *Fed. Res. Bull.*).

r_s = rate of interest on short-term (four–six month New York City) commercial paper (Friedman and Schwartz).

$H_2 = C + R_D$, currency plus reserves held by commercial banks on deposits; where R_D equals vault cash plus deposits at Federal Reserve banks, excluding commercial bank float and reserves held on large certificates of deposit, assuming since 1966 that all large CD's are issued by banks with more than $5 million of deposits (Friedman and Schwartz, *Fed. Res. Bull.*).

R_{DD} = reserves held by banks on demand deposits; where member bank excess reserves and nonmember bank vault cash are allocated between demand and time deposits in proportion to the relative quantities of demand and time deposits, and member bank required reserves are estimated by subtracting the product of member bank time deposits and the effective required reserve ratio on time deposits from total member bank required reserves (Friedman and Schwartz, *Banking and Monetary Statistics, Fed. Res. Bull.*, *FRB* Surveys of "Time and Savings Deposits," *FDIC Assets and Liabilities of Commercial and Mutual Savings Banks*).

B = member bank borrowings at Federal Reserve banks (*Banking and Monetary Statistics, Fed. Res. Bull.*).

r_d^w = weighted annual average of discount rate at Federal Reserve Bank of New York, where weights are determined by monthly borrowings in the System (*Banking and Monetary Statistics, Fed. Res. Bull.*).

r_s^w = weighted annual average of monthly short-term commercial paper rate, where weights are determined by monthly borrowings in the System (Friedman and Schwartz, *Banking and Monetary Statistics, Fed. Res. Bull.*).

G_{DD} = government demand deposits at commercial banks, adjusted for a 1 percent interest payment by banks, 1909–32 (Friedman and Schwartz, *Fed. Res. Bull.*).

R_G = reserves held by commercial banks against government demand deposits (assumed to be the same as the average for

Competitive Interest Payments on Money 1880–1970

Date	r_{M2}	Date	r_{M2}
1880	2.73	1900	3.05
1881	2.88	1901	3.08
1882	3.14	1902	3.64
1883	3.17	1903	4.07
1884	2.89	1904	3.10
1885	2.24	1905	3.32
1886	2.87	1906	4.32
1887	3.51	1907	4.82
1888	2.94	1908	3.22
1889	3.01	1909	2.98
1890	3.56	1910	3.77
1891	3.37	1911	3.06
1892	2.51	1912	3.66
1893	4.37	1913	4.34
1894	1.80	1914	4.35
1895	2.18	1915	2.71
1896	3.74	1916	2.70
1897	2.15	1917	3.85
1898	2.45	1918	4.89
1899	2.86		

Date	r_{M2}	r_{M1}	Date	r_{M2}	r_{M1}
1919	4.48	4.20	1945	0.51	0.45
1920	5.95	5.53	1946	0.55	0.48
1921	5.25	4.84	1947	0.63	0.54
1922	3.56	3.29	1948	0.90	0.77
1923	4.00	3.68	1949	0.93	0.79
1924	3.11	2.85	1950	0.92	0.79
1925	3.24	2.98	1951	1.42	1.26
1926	3.44	3.16	1952	1.56	1.38
1927	3.27	2.99	1953	1.70	1.49
1928	4.02	3.67	1954	1.01	0.85
1929	4.82	4.42	1955	1.48	1.28
1930	2.80	2.56	1956	2.32	2.04
1931	1.79	1.59	1957	2.69	2.35
1932	1.77	1.54	1958	1.68	1.41
1933	0.52	0.39	1959	2.88	2.49
1934	0.34	0.25	1960	2.79	2.38
1935	0.46	0.36	1961	2.13	1.74
1936	0.45	0.36	1962	2.39	1.94
1937	0.55	0.43	1963	2.64	2.12
1938	0.46	0.33	1964	2.99	2.40
1939	0.32	0.21	1965	3.36	2.68
1940	0.35	0.26	1966	4.31	3.46
1941	0.32	0.24	1967	3.96	3.11
1942	0.34	0.27	1968	4.65	3.70
1943	0.45	0.39	1969	6.28	5.04
1944	0.50	0.43	1970	6.19	4.95

ordinary demand deposits, i.e., $R_G = (R_{DD}/DD)(G_{DD})$, except for the particular years when *U.S.* government demand deposits were exempted from reserve requirements and $R_G = 0$).

l_D^* = expected losses on commercial bank deposits; an exponentially declining weighted average of current and past actual losses on deposits, using Friedman's consumption function weights ($\beta = .33$). When loss rates are not reported annually, but only as an average over five- or twenty-year periods annual estimates are obtained by interpolating by the annual number of bank suspensions (*FDIC Annual Reports, Banking and Monetary Statistics*).

s_{DD} = service charges on demand deposits (Cagan, *FDIC Annual Reports*).

All variables are annual averages centered on June 30. Friedman and Schwartz refer to data supplied by them.

REFERENCES

R. J. Barro and A. J. Santomero, "Household Money Holdings and The Demand Deposit Rate," *J. Money, Credit, Banking*, May 1962, 4, 397–413.

M. Bronfenbrenner and T. Mayer, "Liquidity Functions in the American Economy," *Econometrica*, Oct. 1960, 28, 810–34.

K. Brunner and A. H. Meltzer, "Predicting Velocity: Implications for Theory and Policy," *J. Finance*, May 1963, 18, 319–54.

P. Cagan, *Determinants and Effects of Changes in the Stock of Money, 1875–1960*, New York 1965.

G. C. Chow, "On the Long-Run and Short-Run Demand for Money," *J. Polit Econ.*, Apr. 1966, 74, 111–31.

C. F. Christ, "Interest Rates and Portfolio Selection Among Liquid Assets in the U.S.," in C. Christ et al., *Measurement in Economics*, Stanford 1963.

M. R. Darby, "The Allocation of Transitory Income Among Consumers' Assets," *Amer. Econ. Rev.*, Dec. 1972, 62, 928–41.

R. Eisner, "Another Look at Liquidity Preference," *Econometrica*, July 1963, 31, 531–38.

E. Feige, *The Demand for Liquid Assets: A Temporal Cross-Section Analysis*, New Jersey 1964.

———, "Expectations and Adjustments in the Monetary Sector," *Amer. Econ. Rev. Proc.*, May 1967, 57, 462–73.

M. Friedman, "The Quantity Theory of Money—A Restatement," in his *Studies in the Quantity Theory of Money*, Chicago 1956, 1–21.

———, "The Demand for Money—Some Theoretical and Empirical Results," in his *The Optimum Quantity of Money and Other Essays*, Chicago 1969, 41–134.

——— and A. J. Schwartz, *A Monetary History of the United States 1867–1960*, Princeton, 1963.

Y. Haitovsky, "A Note on the Maximization of $\bar{R}^2$," *Amer. Statist.*, Feb. 1969, 23, 20–21.

H. R. Heller, "The Demand for Money—The Evidence from the Short-Run Data," *Quart. J. Econ.*, June 1963, 79, 219–46.

B. Klein, "The Payment of Interest on Commercial Bank Deposits and the Price of Money: A Study of the Demand for Money," unpublished doctoral dissertation, Univ. Chicago, June 1970.

———, "The Demand for Quality-Adjusted Cash Balances," Nat. Bur. Econ. Res. unpublished paper, 1972.

———, "Income Velocity, Interest Rates and the Money Supply Multiplier: A Reinterpretation of the Long-Term Evidence," *J. Money, Credit, Banking*, May 1973, 5, 656–68.

———, "The Recent Inflation and our New Monetary Standard," disc. pap. no. 48, UCLA, Mar. 1974.

D. Laidler (1966a) "Some Evidence on the Demand for Money," *J. Polit. Econ.*, Feb. 1966, 64, 55–68.

———, (1966b) "The Rate of Interest and the Demand for Money—Some Empirical Evidence," *J. Polit. Econ.*, Dec. 1966, 64, 545–55.

H. A. Latané, "Income Velocity and Interest Rates: A Pragmatic Approach," *Rev. Econ. Statist.*, Nov. 1960, 42, 445–49.

T. H. Lee, "Alternative Interest Rates and the Demand for Money: The Empirical Evidence," *Amer. Econ. Rev.*, Dec. 1967, 57, 1168–81.

———, "Alternative Interest Rates and the Demand for Money: Reply," *Amer. Econ. Rev.*, June 1969, 59, 412–18.

A. H. Meltzer, "The Demand for Money: The Evidence from the Time Series," *J. Polit. Econ.*, June 1963, *17*, 219–46.

P. A. Samuelson, *Foundations of Economic Analysis*, Cambridge 1963.

R. T. Selden, "Monetary Velocity in the United States," in *Studies in the Quantity Theory of Money*, Chicago 1956, 179–257.

R. Teigen, "Demand and Supply Functions for Money in the United States: Some Structural Estimates," *Econometrica*, Oct. 1964, *32*, 476–509.

Board of Governors of the Federal Reserve System, *Fed. Res. Bull.*, various issues, 1961–71.

————, *Banking and Monetary Statistics*, Washington 1943.

————, "Member Bank Reserves and Related Items," *Supplement to Banking and Monetary Statistics, Sec. 10*, Washington 1962.

————, "Changes in Time and Savings Deposits and Commercial Banks," *Fed. Res. Bull.*, various issues, 1968–71.

Federal Deposit Insurance Corporation, (*FDIC*) *Annual Report*, Washington 1940, 1960–71.

————, *Assets and Liabilities of Commercial and Mutual Savings Banks*, June 1969-Dec. 1971.

[11]

The Allocation of Transitory Income Among Consumers' Assets

By Michael R. Darby[*]

This article uses an all-capital model to consider the allocation of transitory income among consumers' assets. All transitory income is assumed to be saved. Two basic hypotheses are stated: 1) A fraction of transitory income flows into transitory cash holdings, and these holdings are converted into durable goods and financial assets at a constant rate. 2) The fraction of transitory income immediately used to accumulate durable goods depends on the households' present holdings of transitory assets. The greater the absolute value of the ratio of such assets to total permanent assets, the smaller will be the fraction of transitory income converted into durable goods, and therefore the larger will be the conventionally defined savings ratio.

An error in the standard method of estimating permanent income is reported in the Data Appendix, and a general class of easily reproducible estimators is presented. The increase in money demand resulting from transitory income is put at .4 or .5 of transitory income, and the estimated rate of adjustment of transitory money holdings was about .2 or a bit higher. Hypothesis 2) is strongly supported by the tests conducted. The maximum fraction of nonmonetary transitory savings going into durable goods is put at around .4.

The first hypothesis offers one reason

why the lags in the effect of monetary policy might appear long and variable. The second hypothesis implies that the marginal propensity to spend out of transitory income is variable and near its minimum at the cyclical peak and trough. This weakens the basis of the multiplier analysis, particularly for countercyclical policy recommendations. The model as a whole provides a transmission mechanism for changes in the quantity of money to directly affect spending.

The importance of distinctions between transitory and permanent stocks and flows receives strong confirmation from this study.

The first section outlines the theoretical framework. The second discusses the estimation of the demand for transitory money holdings and presents the empirical results. The third section presents the remaining empirical results. The final section discusses the implications of these results, with emphasis on macro-economic theory.

I. The All-Capital Model

Definitions

My basic theoretical model is an all-capital world derived from Milton Friedman (1957).[1] The consumer holds his wealth in the forms of money, financial

* Assistant professor of economics, Ohio State University and visiting assistant professor, University of California, Los Angeles. This paper is derived primarily from my dissertation and was supported by a Federal Deposit Insurance Corporation Graduate Fellowship in banking, finance, and economics. I am especially indebted to Milton Friedman, Marc Nerlove, J. Richard Zecher, P. A. V. B. Swamy, and Arnold Zellner.

[1] Most previous work in this framework has been on the consumption function, but some work has been done on the effects of transitory income upon specific assets, most notably by Gregory Chow (1955), (1960), (1966), Brian Motley, Meyer Burstein (1957), (1960), and Paul Smith. The present article is the first to consider the total allocation of transitory income under a portfolio constraint.

assets,[2] durable goods, and human capital. Permanent income flows from these assets at a permanent (or long-run expected) rate r_p.[3] These assets are the integral of the past flows of permanent savings.[4]

The concept of dividing an "appropriately" measured income into permanent and transitory components is by now familiar. Transitory income is not true income but merely a shift of expected income between then and now.[5] The receipt of transitory income is a receipt of assets in the current period offset by a liability of equal net present value consisting of income receipts at a lower level in the past and future.[6] In a perfect capital market, permanent consumption, assets, and savings are based upon long-run expectations; so the assets received (or lost) as transitory income would be accumulated over time. These assets would have a long-run expectation of zero, but would only rarely attain that particular figure.

At this point it is necessary to introduce some notation: The subscripts P, T, and N denote, respectively, the permanent, transitory, and nonmonetary transitory components of the variable which they modify.

A_t = Assets at time t[7]

Y_t = Income at time t

S_t = Savings at time t

M_t = Money holdings at time t

D_t = Durable goods stock at time t

Familiar demand curves exist which determine the allocation to specific assets of the fixed, at any instant of time, total permanent assets. The variables involved are yields on the various assets, permanent income (or assets), expected price changes, and r_p. The inclusion of age and family status captures the insight of the "life cycle" hypotheses while still allowing for long-run saving.[8] In future sections more explicit assumptions will be necessary.

Hypotheses on the Allocation of Y_{Tt}

Transforming one of the usual identities, we have

$$(1) \qquad S_{Tt} = Y_{Tt} - C_{Tt}$$

Transitory consumption, C_{Tt}, is taken as an independent random disturbance with zero mean. Transitory savings, S_{Tt}, is therefore the amount to be allocated.

Money is taken to be currency plus demand deposits. For this money, like a consumers' durable good,[9] the return is mainly in the form of a flow of services. Unlike durable goods, the value of money holdings cannot be changed without changing the service flow.[10] The service flow at the permanent level is optimal by utility maximization, but this does not imply that money will therefore be fixed at the permanent level. The flow of services is based on its use in making transactions or, more generally, as a store of value, and these functions require that the level of money fluctuate around the long-run level in order to yield utility. Thus we are in a dynamic framework in which the

---

[2] In my view, liability choices are essentially part of the portfolio decision; so liabilities of ultimate wealth holders are treated as negative financial assets.

[3] "These assets" properly refers only to (permanent) assets which are viewed as making up wealth as opposed to (transitory) assets which merely offset an expected future receipt of opposite sign.

[4] Thus permanent income is viewed as an effect of rational decisions based on the individual's possibilities and utility surface.

[5] This differentiates transitory income from windfalls, which are fortuitous, instantaneous changes in wealth, and which are discussed later in this section.

[6] The reverse would occur for a receipt of negative transitory income, of course. The reader can make this qualification, where necessary, in the remainder of this paper.

[7] All stocks and flows are in real terms. All flows in this section are at instantaneous annual rates.

[8] In this regard it is important to recall the inclusion of human capital in the individual's portfolio.

[9] On this point, see Chow (1966), pp. 113, 126.

[10] For example, by changing age, durability, or required maintenance.

current desired level depends on past, present, and expected future conditions.

Transitory savings are in the nature of a shock. Taking account of costs of adjustment, it is hypothesized that a large proportion of transitory savings, positive or negative, will first flow into money holdings and then, only gradually, will money holdings be adjusted to the permanent level as the surplus or deficit is eliminated by transfers to or from financial assets or durable goods or transitory savings of opposite sign. This "shock absorber" hypothesis can be written as

$$(2) \qquad \frac{dM_{Tt}}{dt} = \beta_1 S_{Tt} + \beta_2 M_{Tt}$$

where β_1 is the fraction of transitory savings going directly into cash, and $\beta_2 (\beta_2 < 0)$ is the rate at which transitory money holdings are drawn down.[11] Thus, if a level of S_{Tt}, say $S_{Tt}{}^0$, were maintained for long enough, dM_{Tt}/dt would approach zero as M_{Tt} approached $-(\beta_1/\beta_2)S_{Tt}{}^0$.

Define nonmonetary transitory savings as

$$(3) \qquad S_{Nt} = S_{Tt} - \frac{dM_{Tt}}{dt}$$

The remaining problem is to determine the allocation of this amount among durable goods, financial assets, and human capital.

Consumers' durable goods essentially yield income to the consumer as a flow of services. Assuming the market works, durable goods stocks of different values can yield close to the same total cost by variations in the mix of interest, depreciation, maintenance, and other costs. Durable goods have high transaction costs for large changes, but gradual changes in

value can be easily accomplished by altering timing of replacement purchases.

Financial assets yield income primarily in the form of pecuniary returns. I assume that at least for some of these assets a yield close to the permanent interest rate can be obtained with small transactions costs.

Human capital investments yield both service flows directly and rental income in the labor market. Human capital is very illiquid as sale is prohibited and depreciation is generally slow.

Human capital seems a poor candidate for transitory investments[12] for the reasons just outlined; so I assume essentially no transitory investment in human capital occurs. Therefore transitory investment is to be apportioned between durable goods and financial assets. Let the fraction of a marginal transitory investment going into durable goods (1—the fraction going into financial assets) be called δ, and let δ_0 be its value if nonmonetary transitory assets, A_{Nt}, are zero. I hypothesize that δ will monotonically decrease from δ_0 as the absolute value of A_{Nt} increases. This follows directly from the assumed increasing costs as the level of durable goods diverges further from the optimal long-run (permanent) levels due to increasing costs of substitution in consumption and production[13] as well as increasing liquidity problems, and from the observation that financial assets suffer these losses to a much lesser extent, due to the greater importance of their pecuniary yield and their more liquid nature. Low or high levels of $|A_{Nt}|$ must be relative to something. In this case A_{Pt} is the obvious choice, representing the size of the base to which these changes are being made.

---

[11] These β's may vary in response to yet other variables (such as in a hyperinflation), but will be taken as constants for the current problem. Note that contrary to Chow (1966) and Motley, the assumption is made—in order to obtain sensible steady-state results—that changes in desired levels are fully adjusted to, but that only a fraction of the transitory portion is adjusted.

[12] "Investment" is used in a strictly microeconomic sense here and should not be confused with the concept of the same name used in the standard macroeconomic model.

[13] Under the usual curvature assumptions on the utility and production functions.

Thus all S_{Nt} is assumed to be divided between durable goods and financial assets. The hypothesis can be stated as

(4) $$\frac{dD_{Tt}}{dt} = f(A_{Nt}/A_{Pt}) \cdot S_{Nt}$$

(5) $$\frac{df}{d|A_{Nt}/A_{Pt}|} < 0$$

Qualifications to the Model

Part of what we call transitory income consists really of windfalls, and this should be separated out. If people aren't sure at the time of receipt whether or not wealth has increased, a prediction scheme in which a fraction of transitory assets flows into permanent assets is suitable, and this is basically how we in fact estimate permanent income.

Besides the usual aggregation problems, much transitory income is cancelled out in the aggregate data; so that the focus must be on cyclical problems. This could cause difficulties if the distribution of transitory income across families changes markedly within the sample period. On aggregation, however, we have much less need to worry about nonzero values of C_{Tt} and can substitute Y_{Tt} for S_{Tt}.

The model assumes that any asset allocation within the wealth constraint can be accomplished. This is true for the individual, and I must assume that inventories and production are such that it will also hold for the economy as a whole.

The usual care must be taken in applying the constructs in this model to similarly named data or constructs in income-expenditures models.

II. Data Series and Money Demand Results

Data Series and Estimates

The period covered in the empirical study is the 80 quarters from 1947-I to 1966-IV. This was the longest period for which all required data series were complete at the start of estimation.

Brief descriptions of the data series used follow.[14] The basic series are:

$P_t =$ Consumer Price Index (1957–1959 base), middle month of quarter.

$P_{Dt} =$ Implicit Personal Consumption Durable Goods Price Index (1958 base), quarterly.

$Y_t =$ Private Income = disposable income + undistributed corporate profits,[15] at seasonally adjusted quarterly rates ($SAQR$), deflated by P_t.

$M_t =$ Money supply (currency + demand deposits), seasonally adjusted last month of quarter ($SALMQ$), deflated by P_t.

$HM_t =$ High powered money, $SALMQ$, deflated by P_t.

$DX_t =$ Personal consumption durable goods expenditures, $SAQR$.

$RL_t =$ U.S. government long-term bond yield, quarterly average (QA).

$RS_t =$ U.S. Treasury three-month bills, market yield, QA.

The variables Y_t, M_t, and HM_t are in real terms (deflated by P_t) with dimensions of 1958 dollars (per quarter for Y_t). The yield variables are in percentage points which have the dimensions of $1/time$. The price indices have the dimension t dollars/1958 dollars with $1958 = 1.000$.

The stock of durable goods, end of quarter, D_t, is estimated from the quar-

---

[14] Sources for the P_t, P_{Dt}, Y_t, and DX_t are the 1966 and 1967 supplements to the *Survey of Current Business*. The M_t series is from various issues of the *Federal Reserve Bulletin*. The HM_t series is the source base published in the August 1968 *Review* of the Federal Reserve Bank of St. Louis. Both RL_t and RS_t data were taken from the Board of Governors of the Federal Reserve System, *Supplement to Banking and Monetary Statistics, Section 12, Money Rates and Securities Markets* and various issues of the *Federal Reserve Bulletin*. Complete detail is found in the appendix to my dissertation.

[15] Undistributed corporate profits estimate the capital gains that should be included in income. No attempt is made to estimate the service flows direct from assets.

terly durable goods expenditures by application of a perpetual inventory method based on double declining balance depreciation:[16]

(6) $D_t = .95 \cdot D_{t-1} + DX_t / P_{Dt}$

Raymond Goldsmith's estimates are used for the 1946 benchmark.

The estimated yield on money, quarterly average, RM_t, is derived by Benjamin Klein's method:

(7) $RM_t = (1 - HM_t / M_t) RS_t$

This is based on the hypothesis that banks avoid the restriction on payment of interest on demand deposits completely. This hypothesis will be tested in connection with other texts.

The computation of permanent income, Y_{Pt}, and transitory income, Y_{Tt}, from Y_t is explained in the Data Appendix.

Empirical Results for Money Demand

The general problems in aggregation have already been discussed. For the money demand model there is an additional problem. The money stock is held not only by individuals but also by businesses, and no good data exist which estimate the stock held by each. In testing the model, one must view the firms either as holding the cash for their owners or—what is more reasonable—as acting in much the same way as ultimate wealth holders in regard to transitory money balances. I make the latter assumption and apply the model to the available data.

The shock absorber hypothesis of money demand is summarized in equation (2). In order to apply discrete time-series to the continuous time model, it is taken that transitory demand at the end of a quarter will be increased by a fraction of transitory savings in the quarter and that a

fraction of transitory money holdings at the beginning of the period will be worked off over the course of the quarter. Unfortunately there is no series on transitory money stock nor any obvious way to estimate one. However since measured money stock is the sum of its transitory and permanent components, it is possible to test the hypothesis when it is combined with a linear permanent demand function:

$$M_t - M_{t-1} = \beta_1 Y_{Tt} + \beta_2 (M_{t-1} - M_{Pt-1})$$
(8) $$+ M_{Pt} - M_{Pt-1} + \epsilon_t,$$

where ϵ_t is a random term admitted to the transitory demand to allow for shocks and discrepancies and where Y_{Tt} has been substituted for S_{Tt} as previously discussed. Simplifying,

(9) $M_t = \beta_1 Y_{Tt} + (1 + \beta_2) M_{t-1} + M_{Pt}$
            $- (1 + \beta_2) M_{Pt-1}$

I assume that permanent money demand is based on the linear demand function:

(10) $M_{Ft} = \beta_3 + \beta_4 \cdot Y_{Pt} + \beta_5 \cdot RL_t$
            $+ \beta_6 \cdot RS_t + \beta_7 \cdot RM_t$

Substituting equation (10) into equation (9) and simplifying,

(11) $M_t = \beta_3 (1 - \beta_8) + \beta_1 Y_{Tt} + \beta_8 M_{t-1}$
            $+ \beta_4 Y_{Pt}^* + \beta_5 RL_t^* + \beta_6 RS_t^*$
            $+ \beta_7 RM_t^* + \epsilon_t,$

where $\beta_8 = 1 + \beta_2$ and the asterisked variables are computed by substituting for X in

(12) $X_t^* = X_t - \beta_8 X_{t-1}$

By the usual Taylor series justification, this non-linear equation may be estimated by ordinary least squares iterated on the estimated values of β_8.[17] If the equation

---

[16] This assumes a ten-year average life of durable goods. See Laurits Christensen and Dale Jorgenson, pp. 294–97.

[17] The problem is essentially in the multiplicative constraints on the coefficients in equation (9). The differencing of the permanent variables as in equations (11)

TABLE 1—REGRESSION COEFFICIENTS: MONEY DEMAND EQUATION DEPENDENT VARIABLE: M_t

		Constant	Y_{Tt}	M_{t-1}	$Y^*_{p_t}$	RL^*_t	RS^*_t	RM^*_t	R^2	SEE
1	1947-II–	24.901	.3797	.8047	.1938	−1.1075	−36.246	56.745	.94701	1.18927
	1966-IV	(5.6001)	(.09602)	(.04327)	(.0757)	(1.5583)	(9.1490)	(14.413)		
		4.4466	3.9542	18.596	2.5608	−.7107	−3.9618	3.9371		
2	1953-I–	30.118	.5651	.7674	.1599	−.3628	−31.935	49.104	.96619	.84158
	1966-IV	(9.3135)	(.1089)	(.07158)	(.06813)	(1.2513)	(8.7407)	(13.647)		
		3.2338	5.1881	10.721	2.3466	−.2900	−3.6536	3.5981		
3	1947-II–	49.36	.5664	.6040	.2483	−1.505	−21.58	33.41	.86297	2.02406
	1966-IV	(8.714)	(.1118)	(.0690)	(.0064)	(1.189)	(7.992)	(12.63)		
	GLS	5.664	5.068	8.758	3.741	−1.266	−2.700	2.645		

Note: The standard errors are given in parentheses below the coefficients and the *t*-values are given below the standard errors.

iterates, it has the usual properties of a least squares regression. Note however that there are still problems of the lagged dependent variable which implies that the estimates have only large-sample justification and possible problems from autocorrelation of the residuals.

Certain predictions can be made about the size and sign of the values of the regression coefficients. The coefficient β_1 estimates the fraction of transitory income flowing into cash balances and not reinvested during the quarter; so β_1 should be in the range 0 to 1, with the middle more likely than either extreme. The coefficient β_2 is restricted to the range from 0 to −1, but should be no slower than people adjust their expectations (−.1); also $\beta_2 < −.5$ is unlikely since it does not reflect any outflow in the first quarter at a possibly higher rate. Therefore the estimated range of $\beta_8 = 1 + \beta_2$ is from .5 to

.9. The coefficient β_4 should be positive and, under the simplest form of the quantity theory, should equal about four times the fraction of a year's income held as money,[18] around 1.7. The coefficients β_5 and β_6 should be negative, as these interest rates reflect yields on alternatives to money holdings. If the hypothesis that banks avoid the prohibition of payment of interest on demand deposits is true, β_7 should be positive and greater in absolute value than either β_5 or β_6, which are for cross-yields.

Table 1 reports the results of running the regressions for equation (11). Besides the regression for the whole period, there is also an equation for 1953-I through 1966-IV and a generalized least squares (*GLS*) version of regression.

Number 1 is the key regression. The three interest rate coefficients are entirely consistent with Klein's hypothesis.[19] The

and (12) allows the use of a simple iterative method of solution: 1) Choose an initial value, β_8^0 of β_8 (I estimated an unconstrained version of equation (9) for this but the convergence was rapid so that 1.0 would have been as good); 2) compute the asterisked variables in equation (11) using β_8^0 and equation (12); 3) run the *OLS* regression for equation (11) using these variables; and 4) replace the value β_8^0 with the regression coefficient of M_{t-1} in step 3) and repeat steps 2) through 4) until the absolute value of the change in the estimated β_8 is less than some small tolerance (here .0001).

[18] Recall that flows are expressed as quarterly rates.
[19] Converting these coefficients to elasticities of demand for money at the sample mean, the figures are −.01 with respect to RL_t, −.61 for RS_t, and +.60 for RM_t; so proportionate increases in all three interest rates would leave money demand virtually unaffected. I also ran the basic equations deleting the RM^*_t term; there were no significant changes in the noninterest rate coefficients, but the RS_t coefficient went to an insignificant −.31 with the RL_t coefficient virtually unchanged. The elasticities are −.01 for RL_t and −.005 for RS_t. It would appear that earlier studies which found a sig-

estimate of β_1 is in the expected range and significantly different from zero. The estimate of β_8 is in the high end of the predicted range, indicating a fairly slow adjustment of transitory money balances.[20] The estimate of β_4 is much lower than predicted by the simple quantity theory.

The lower than mid-range estimates of β_1 and β_8 might be attributed to the increased moneyness of securities pegged by the Federal Reserve before 1953 relative to the later part of the period.[21] Regression 2 was run to test this possible change in the underlying model. The estimates of β_1 and β_8 move in the expected direction, but the null hypothesis that the 1947-II[22] to 1952-IV sample was drawn from the same population as the 1953-I through 1966-IV sample cannot be rejected at the .95 level of significance.[23] Therefore the 1953-I through 1966-IV regressions cannot be regarded as other than suggestive.

The lower coefficient estimated for permanent income can be attributed to the linearity restriction on the permanent money demand function, to the hypothesis that unitary income elasticity is far from correct, to the hypothesis that a broader definition of money is required, or to the particular period studied.[24] The variable Y^*_{Pt} has very little variation from a trend, so it would be difficult to obtain estimates of the separate effects of changes in permanent income. Hence it is not clear precisely what information is contained in the estimate of β_4.

The shock absorber model is strongly supported by the data. Transitory income increases the demand for money by about 40 percent of the amount of transitory income, and transitory money balances are worked off at a rate of about 20 percent per quarter. There is suggestive evidence that both these percentages have increased since the 1940's. All the estimates were significantly different from both ends of the range permitted within the model.

III. Durable Goods Demand Results

Estimation Procedure

It is desired to construct a test of the hypothesis of equations (4) and (5) on the allocations of S_{Nt} between durable goods and financial assets. In this case also there are data problems. Since there is no D_{Tt} series, I must again assume a permanent demand function in linear form:

$$(13) \quad D_{Pt} = \gamma_1 + \gamma_2 (P_{Dt}/P_t) + \gamma_3 Y_{Pt} + \gamma_4 RL_t$$

This is essentially Chow's (1960) hypothesis, with the interest rate term added because durables are viewed as competing with other assets for a share of the whole.[25]

---

nificant *net* effect of interest rate changes suffered from specification bias, with the interest rate variable serving as a proxy for the omitted variable transitory income.

[20] It is possible that this high value of β_8 may in part be due to autocorrelation in the residuals. E. Malinvaud (p. 472) summarized the evidence and suggests ordinary least squares in this type of model (even without the complication of the non-linear constraints) because of the relatively large errors inherent in estimating the correlation coefficient ρ. The main effect of autocorrelation is to bias the estimated standard errors downward; so somewhat higher standards of significance are advisable in considering the regression coefficients presented here. Nevertheless, I did run a generalized least squares version of regression 1 (using an estimated ρ of .5341). The estimate of β_8 decreased to a bit over .6 and of β_1 increased into the .5 range, but there were no other interesting changes. Little reliance should be put on these estimates, but they are presented as regression number 3.

[21] See Friedman and Anna Schwartz, p. 625.

[22] The first quarter was lost due to lagged variables.

[23] The $F(7, 65)$ statistic of 1.84 is such that the hypothesis would just be rejected at the .90 level of significance.

[24] I am indebted to Friedman for the point that in this period money demand was adjusting slowly to its long-run demand from the high levels caused by the uncertainties and illegal activities of the war prior to, and during, the early part of the period, while alternatives to money, such as time deposits and savings and loan shares, were growing rapidly. Rerunning the regressions for $M_{2t} = M_t +$ time deposits and for 1961-I through 1966-IV increases the estimate of this coefficient, but not enough to solve all the problem.

[25] Although the inclusion of RS_t might also seem to be an improvement, the life of durable goods appears to be too long for this rate to have any effect; the inclusion of RS_t in the regression has essentially no effect.

I chose to represent the variation in the fraction of S_{Nt} going into D_{Tt} by the specific form:

$$(14) \quad \Delta D_{Tt} = \gamma_5 e^{-(\eta A_{Nt}/A_{Pt})^m} \cdot S_{Nt} + \epsilon_t,$$

where $m = 4,$[26] ϵ_t is a random error, and γ_5 and η are parameters to be estimated. The coefficient of S_{Nt} has the desired properties of having a maximum value (γ_5) when $A_{Nt} = 0$ and decreasing with increasing $|A_{Nt}/A_{Pt}|$. Estimation of the η parameter allows for search over a wide range of rapidity of that decrease.

Unfortunately, data series are lacking for the three variables on the right-hand side of equation (14). The replacement of A_{Pt} by Y_{Pt} is straightforward.[27] I use Y_{Tt} as a proxy for S_{Nt},[28] and A_{Tt} for A_{Nt}. The estimate of A_{Tt} is based on the prediction scheme discussed in the last part of Section I:

$$(15) \quad A_{Tt} = (1 - b)A_{Tt-1} + Y_{Tt}$$

The choice of the parameter b is the same as for permanent income, or .1. However an initial value, $A_{T,0}$, is required. Even the sign of $A_{T,0}$ is an open question. Some would argue that people were not yet recovered from paying for the war at the end of 1946; while others would suggest that excess assets were accumulated during the war. Lacking a direct estimate, $A_{T,0}$ will be left as a parameter to be estimated.

Now substituting in equation (14) and

[26] A check of other values of m showed $m = 2$ to display too little variation; the results were substantially the same for $m = 6$ as for $m = 4$.

[27] Since $Y_{Pt} = r_P \cdot A_{Pt}$ for annual rates, this will merely decrease the value of η by a factor of $r_P/4$.

[28] Changes in M_{Tt} including business balances would not be really appropriate for estimating $S_{Nt} = Y_{Tt} - \Delta M_{Tt}$. Nevertheless, I also tried estimates of S_{Nt} as Y_{Tt} less an estimate of ΔM_{Tt} (based on the results of the previous section) and on changes in my estimate of A_{Tt}. However since regression 1 was primarily carried out to test the money demand hypothesis, the ΔM_{Tt} estimates introduced the autocorrelation difficulties discussed in fn. 20, while the ΔA_{Tt} series was dominated by trend components; so neither attempt led to good results.

adding the result to the first difference form of equation (13), the equation to be estimated is:

$$(16) \quad \Delta D_t = \gamma_1^* + \gamma_2 \cdot \Delta(P_{Dt}/P_t) \\ + \gamma_3 \cdot \Delta Y_{Pt} + \gamma_4 \cdot \Delta RL_t \\ + \gamma_5 \cdot e^{-(\eta \cdot A_{Tt}/Y_{Pt})^4} \cdot Y_{Tt} + \epsilon_t,$$

where the constant γ_1^* should be 0, but is included to remove any linear trend. This equation can be estimated by non-linear least squares over an η and $A_{T,0}$ search grid.[29]

Estimated Durable Goods Demand Equations

A nonzero γ_1^* would indicate the presence of a linear trend. By simple price theory, γ_2 and γ_4 should be negative, while γ_3 should be positive. The fraction γ_5 is restricted to the range from 0 to 1. If it is not significantly different from the marginal propensity to consume, say .9, and $\eta = 0$ is accepted, then a simple func-

[29] An approximate test of whether the inclusion of the exponential factor in the γ_5 term is significant can be based on the likelihood ratio. The null hypothesis is that the fraction of transitory income flowing into durable goods is constant regardless of A_{Tt}/Y_{Pt}, or simply $\eta = 0$. The alternative hypothesis is that the fraction is determined as in equation (14), or $\eta \neq 0$. Assuming independent normally distributed disturbances, the likelihood ratio is

$$\lambda = (SS/SS_0)^{T/2}$$

where SS is the sum of the squared residuals of the unconstrained estimate, SS_0 is the sum of squares of the estimate made assuming the null hypothesis to be true, and T is the number of observations. (Here 79; one observation is deleted due to taking first differences.) This is known to be distributed, if the null hypothesis is true and as $T \to \infty$ according to $-2 \cdot log\ \lambda \sim \chi^2(k)$, where k is the number of restrictions, in this case 1 (see Maurice Kendall and A. Stuart, pp. 230–31). Therefore the test of the significance of this alternative hypothesis is based on comparison of the statistic $-T \cdot log(SS/SS_0)$ with the $\chi^2(1)$ distribution. The specification (14) is only one of many possible specifications so that acceptance of the null hypothesis would not be conclusive evidence against the hypothesis of equations (4) and (5), except as this specification is a good approximation for most other specifications of this hypothesis, but rejection of the null hypothesis would offer strong evidence in support of the hypothesis of those equations.

TABLE 2—REGRESSION COEFFICIENTS: DURABLE GOODS DEMAND EQUATION, DEPENDENT VARIABLE: ΔD_t

	Constant	$\Delta\left(\frac{P_{Dt}}{P_t}\right)$	ΔY_{Pt}	ΔRL_t	γ_b	η	$A_{T,0}$	R^2	SEE
4	1.5041	−18.997	1.1807	−1.1489	.4014	6.4	−20	.778	.527
	(.1674)	(6.5799)	(.2133)	(.5538)	(.05182)				
	8.9863	−2.8871	5.5355	−2.1522	7.7455				
5	1.5144	−22.906	1.1872	−1.0710	.3077	[0]	—	.728	.584
	(.1983)	(7.3573)	(.2534)	(.5935)	(.05181)				
	7.6385	−3.1134	4.6841	−1.8046	5.9400				

Note: The standard errors are given in parentheses below the coefficients and the *t*-values are given below the standard errors.

tion with durable goods expenditures as consumption is satisfactory. The search grid was a matrix in which $A_{T,0}$ varies from −$50 billion to $50 billion in steps of $10 billion, and η varies from 0 to 100,[30] ultimately in steps of .1.

The non-linear least squares regression for equation (16) is presented in Table 2 as regression number 4. There is a significant trend,[31] but otherwise the coefficients are as expected. The estimates of η and $A_{T,0}$ are 6.4 and −$20 billion, respectively.

Regression 5 was run under the assumption $\eta = 0$ to test the significance of the exponential part of the γ_b term,[32] and the null hypothesis was easily rejected in favor of the alternative of $\eta \neq 0$.[33] This offers strong support to the hypothesis that a decreasing fraction of transistory income goes into durable good at increasing absolute values of A_{Nt}/A_{Pt}.

These results strongly confirm the im-

portance of taking separate account of durable goods expenditures, as the marginal propensity to spend out of transitory income on durables is at most about .5, and at times less. Paul Smith reported results of a two-stage least squares estimation that indicated that the marginal propensity to spend out of transitory income on nondurable goods and services is about zero. I checked directly on three alternative simple consumption functions, with Y_{Pt} and Y_{Tt} independent variables, and as dependent variables, alternatively:

$C1_t =$ Personal Consumption Expenditures, $SAQR$

$C2_t = C1_t$—Personal Consumption of Durable Goods, $SAQR$

$C3_t = C2_t$—Personal Consumption of Clothing and Shoes, $SAQR$[34]

The regression results are presented in Table 3. Note that regression 6 is misspecified under the hypothesis of this paper, but should provide a reasonable estimate of the average marginal propensity to spend out of transitory income. The other regressions indicate, not surprisingly, that inventory changes are important for clothes and shoes, as for durable goods as

[30] η is basically a scaling factor and sign makes no difference in the value of the expression; so only positive values were considered. A maximum value of 100 appeared to be much more than sufficient.

[31] The significant constant is probably due to trends in tastes, an income elasticity of demand for durable goods greater than unity, or too slow a rate of depreciation, or some combination of these factors.

[32] This means an *OLS* regression on equation (16) with the penultimate term changed to $\gamma_3 Y_{Tt}$.

[33] The χ^2 test statistic (see fn. 29) is equal to 16.1. The .95 point of the $\chi^2(1)$ distribution is 3.84 and the .999 point is 10.8.

[34] All consumption expenditures are in terms of 1958 dollars. The series on seasonally adjusted real expenditures on clothing and shoes was generously provided by the Office of Business Economics, U.S. Department of Commerce.

TABLE 3—SIMPLE CONSUMPTION FUNCTIONS

	Dependent Variable	Constant	Y_{Pt}	Y_{Tt}	R^2	SEE
6	$C1_t$	−1.640 (.3807) −4.308	.9026 (.00456) 198.0	.5005 (.04028) 12.43	.99812	.66649
7	$C2_t$	1.867 (.2677) 6.975	.7318 (.00320) 228.3	.1226 (.02832) 4.328	.99856	.46854
8	$C3_t$	.4280 (.3008) 1.423	.6716 (.00360) 186.5	.04306 (.03183) 1.353	.99783	.52659

Note: The standard errors are given in parentheses below the coefficients and the *t*-values are given below the standard errors.

defined by the Office of Business Economics, and account for most of the remaining effect of Y_{Tt}. The final regression is in almost complete conformity with Friedman's hypothesis, even to the insignificant constant term.

IV. Implications and Conclusions

The results strongly support Friedman's permanent income approach. Both the direct hypothesis of a zero effect for transitory income on consumption, and derived hypotheses on the demand for money and durable goods received confirmation from the analysis of the aggregate data for the postwar period.

The marginal propensity to spend out of private income derived from the results is of particular interest. Permanent income is consumed according to a proportionality factor; so we can take, for purposes of cyclical analysis, this marginal propensity to be this factor of proportionality multiplied by the increase in permanent income due to current income[35] plus the marginal propensity to spend transitory income.[36] It was shown that transitory income is spent, in the usual

sense, only to build up the inventories of durable or semi-durable goods. It was also shown that the fraction of transitory income so spent varies with the absolute value of the ratio of transitory assets to permanent assets. Now this absolute value moves cyclically, with peaks in its value near the peaks and troughs of the business cycle. Thus the marginal propensity to spend also fluctuates and is near minimum at these points.[37] Therefore the standard macro-economic models would be at their weakest near these points, due to the apparent increases in the savings ratio defined in terms of consumption goods expenditures.

It is possible to give more precise numerical values to the quantities involved. Taking the total inventory effect to follow the pattern of the dominant durable goods portion, the maximum value, for zero transitory assets, of the marginal propensity to spend current income would be

[35] That is, about $.9 \times .1 = .09$.

[36] Although changes in consumers' inventories are not consumption, they do provide, in the short run, changes in the aggregate demand for goods and services.

[37] There are eight National Bureau of Economic Research (*NBER*) reference cycle peaks and troughs in the period covered. The average reduction in the marginal propensity to spend on durable goods out of transitory income was to 72 percent of the maximum propensity, but the range was from 8 to 100 percent of the maximum. For 1966-IV the reduction was to 65 percent, although this was not labeled a peak by the *NBER*. Thus, the variation has economic, as well as statistical, significance.

about .74.[38] The reductions due to higher levels of the absolute value of transitory assets are large enough to reduce the average, over time, marginal propensity to spend current income to about .59. At a cyclical peak or trough this figure would typically be about .56,[39] with further decreases in the quarters just past the peak or trough.[40]

The money demand hypothesis provides an explanation for the lag in the effect of monetary policy. Consider a change in monetary policy which leaves the community, through a portfolio shock, with larger cash balances than planned. These extra cash balances are transitory money balances, which will be drawn down only gradually, thus delaying the full effect of the policy change. At the quarterly rate of .2 it would take about three quarters for half of the effect of the policy change to be felt, which is close to Friedman's (1961) results on the lag. There are however two (offsetting) further factors to be considered. Suggestive evidence indicated that the adjustment coefficient is higher than .2, at least in the post-Accord period, and may be in the range from .25 to .4 which would shorten the period for half the effect to be felt to two or even one-and-a-half quarters. On the other hand, the short-run increase in income from the working down of money balances is an increase in transitory income and hence absorbs part of the money balances, thus increasing the lag to some extent.

The previous case was for zero initial transitory money balances. If the Federal Reserve was engaged in a change of mone-tary policy, initial transitory money balances would be of opposite sign and the magnitude of the effect would depend on the relative size of the policy change to the transitory money balances built up under the preceding policy. This factor may explain the observed variability in the initial effect of a policy change of a particular size, since the initial effect will be generally weaker the longer the preceding opposite policy was maintained.

Another related result of interest to monetary theorists is the fact that interest rate changes had generally insignificant net effects, earlier estimates of significant effects apparently being due to failure to take separate account of permanent and transitory income effects.

Macro-economic modelers should have no difficulty in adapting these results to their particular model. Usual care should be taken in going from estimates of stocks to expenditures, and the concept of private income is new to some models, but generally there are no difficulties. Different estimation techniques might be more appropriate in a modeling, as opposed to testing, context, however.

The most general conclusion from the results of this study is that permanent income and transitory income have separate effects on the demands for assets, the precise nature of the effects depending on the nature of the asset. In particular, practically all previous studies have been concerned with the question: "Does permanent or measured income explain best the demand for this asset?" It is now clear that this question is entirely inappropriate. In general, both have effects.[41] An example is the controversy over whether, abstracting from other variables, money demand is a constant fraction of permanent or measured income. Actually it

[38] The ratio of the γ_5 estimates in regressions 4 and 5 (see Table 2) is 1.3, and the coefficient of Y_{Tt} in regression 6 (see Table 3) is .5; so the inventory change response would be put at $1.3 \times .5 = .65$. Adding the .09 permanent income effect yields .74.

[39] Computed as $.65 \times .72 + .09 = .56$.

[40] Since transitory income is still positive (negative) and adding to the absolute value of transitory assets in the period just following a peak (trough).

[41] Although the appropriate concepts are permanent income and transitory income (measured less permanent income).

seems to be a constant times permanent income plus a (different) constant times transitory income.

V. Summary and Concluding Remarks

This article investigated the allocation of the transitory component of income among the various classes of consumers' assets. Particular emphasis was placed on the effects of cyclical variations. The analysis and empirical results led to new and interesting conclusions on the marginal propensity to spend and the question of "long and variable lags" in the effect of monetary policy.

Areas for future study would be to apply the model to panel data, extend the period studied, consider whether housing might better be treated as a consumers' durable good, estimate cash holdings of the personal sector, and study the formation of and adjustments in the expectations of the long-run interest rate.

Data Appendix

Estimation of Permanent Income

Practically all investigators of permanent income have derived their estimates as

$$(A.1) \quad Y_{Pt} = b \cdot Y_t + (1 - b + c) Y_{Pt-1}$$

where b is a parameter to be or previously estimated, and c is the estimate, $\hat{\beta}_2$, of the trend coefficient β_2 in the regression

$$(A.2) \quad log \ Y_t = \beta_1 + \beta_2 \cdot t + \epsilon_t$$

The initial value of Y_{Pt} is $e^{\hat{\beta}_1}$. This estimate is derived from a continuous time adaptive expectations model. In discrete time, however, what is desired is

$$(A.3) \quad Y_{Pt} = b(Y_t - Y_{Pt}^e) + Y_{Pt}^e,$$

where Y_{Pt}^e is the expected value in $t-1$ of permanent income in t. With a linear trend, this is simply $(1+c)Y_{Pt-1}$. So equation (A.3) can be rewritten in this case as

$$(A.4) \quad Y_{Pt} = b \cdot Y_t + (1 - b)(1 + c) Y_{Pt-1},$$

which is the linear adaptive expectations

estimator and differs from the estimator (A.1).[42]

Consider the possibility of a non-linear trend, say due to increasing productivity of capital. That is $\hat{\beta}_3$ is significant in the regression

$$(A.5) \quad log \ Y_t = \beta_1 + \beta_2 \cdot t + \beta_3 \cdot t^2 + \epsilon_t$$

Then differentiation yields

$$(A.6) \quad Y_{Pt}^e = (1 + \hat{\beta}_2 + 2 \cdot \hat{\beta}_3 \cdot t) Y_{Pt-1}$$

The quadratic trended adaptive expectations estimator is

$$(A.7) \quad Y_{Pt} = b \cdot Y_t + (1 - b)(1 + \hat{\beta}_2 + 2 \cdot \hat{\beta}_3 \cdot t) Y_{Pt-1}$$

The extension to any other order trend is straightforward, but for longer periods it might be more appropriate to adjust continuously a linear trend estimated over previous ten or fifteen years.

The $\hat{\beta}_3$ coefficients were highly significant for the postwar private income series; so the quadratic trended estimators were used in this paper.[43] Aggregate Y_{Pt} is computed as

$$(A.8) \quad \begin{aligned} Y_{Pt} = .1 \cdot Y_t + .9(1.006169 \\ + .00006384 \cdot t) Y_{Pt-1} \end{aligned}$$

where in 1947-I t is 1 and where b is taken to be .1.[44] The per capita Y_{Pt} is computed as

[42] The error term bc is unlikely to change any conclusions from previous studies because of its small magnitude and because permanent income series were usually not derived from computing the trend separately; when the weights b and c are estimated simultaneously, the result will be correct though the amount of the trend will be misstated.

[43] The t-value for the t^2 term was 5.0. Experiments with the linear trended estimator confirmed the superior explanatory power of the quadratic trended estimator, but the differences were not such that any major proposition was dependent upon the choice of estimator.

[44] A quarterly b of .1 is approximately equal to an annual b of .35 which is about the middle of the estimates obtained in the various consumption studies. The fact that Y_{Pt} estimates are used in various phases of this study makes it impossible to choose b on the basis of best fit in any one equation. A check on robustness over a reasonable range of bs was made on some of the results; the exact value of b did not appear to be critical and .1 appeared to be a very good estimate of the actual value.

$$\text{(A.9)} \quad \begin{aligned} Y_{Pt} = {} &.1 \cdot Y_t + .9(1.001521 \\ &+ .00007624 \cdot t)\, Y_{Pt-1} \end{aligned}$$

The initial values are 58.52 and 411.3, respectively. In a table of data not printed with this paper,[45] I report the values of Y_{Pt} for aggregate data and also the more customary linear trended estimate Y_{Pt}^A:

$$\text{(A.10)} \quad Y_{Pt}^A = .1 \cdot Y_t + .9078786 \cdot Y_{Pt-1}^A$$

with the initial value of 56.49.

Transitory income series are computed as simply

$$\text{(A.11)} \qquad Y_{Tt} = Y_t - Y_{Pt}$$

Selected Data Series

Besides Y_{Pt} and Y_{Pt}^A, I have also computed aggregate series of Y_t (private income), D_t (durable goods stock), F_t (financial assets), and RM_t (yield on money).[46] Where YN_t is nominal private income, PO_t is the personal outlays series, $SAQR$, ΔMN_t is the change in nominal money supply for the quarter, and PI_t is the Private Investment Price Index (1958 base), quarterly, F_t is computed as

$$\text{(A.12)} \quad \begin{aligned} F_t = {} &F_{t-1} + (YN_t - PO_t \\ &- \Delta MN_t)/PI_t \end{aligned}$$

F_0 at the end of 1946 is estimated from Goldsmith as 978.42. Note that all the money stock is subtracted from F_t and the business portion must be added back for some uses.

REFERENCES

A. Ando and F. Modigliani, "The 'Life Cycle' Hypothesis of Saving: Aggregate Implications and Tests," *Amer. Econ. Rev.*, Mar. 1963, *53*, 55–84.

W. J. Baumol, "The Transactions Demand for Cash: An Inventory Theoretic Ap-

---

[45] The data will be supplied by the author upon request.

[46] Y_t, Y_{Pt}, and Y_{Pt}^A are in billions of 1958 dollars per quarter (multiply by 4 for annual rates); D_t and F_t are in billions of 1958 dollars at the end of quarter; RM_t is in percentage points and a quarterly average. Complete source detail on these series is located in the appendix to my dissertation.

proach," *Quart. J. Econ.*, Nov. 1952, *66*, 545–56.

K. Brunner and A. H. Meltzer, "Comment on the Long-Run and Short-Run Demand for Money," *J. Polit. Econ.*, Nov. 1968, *76*, 1234–40.

M. L. Burstein, "The Demand for Household Refrigeration in the United States," unpublished doctoral dissertation, Univ. Chicago 1957.

——, "The Demand for Household Refrigeration in the United States," in A. C. Harberger, ed., *The Demand for Durable Goods*, Chicago 1960, 97–145.

V. K. Chetty, "On the Long-Run and Short-Run Demand for Money," *J. Polit. Econ.*, Nov. 1969, *77*, 921–31.

G. C. Chow, "The Demand for Automobiles in the United States," unpublished doctoral dissertation, Univ. Chicago 1955.

——, "Long-Run and Short-Run Demand for Money: Reply and Further Note," *J. Polit. Econ.*, Nov./Dec. 1968, *76*, 1240–43.

——, "On the Long-Run and Short-Run Demand for Money," *J. Polit. Econ.*, Apr. 1966, *74*, 111–31.

——, "Reply: A Note on the Estimation of Long-Run Relationships in Stock Adjustment Models," *J. Polit. Econ.*, Nov. 1969, *77*, 932–36.

——, "Statistical Demand Functions for Automobiles and Their Use in Forecasting," in A. C. Harberger, ed., *The Demand for Durable Goods*, Chicago 1960, 147–78.

L. R. Christensen and D. W. Jorgenson, "The Measurement of U.S. Real Capital Input, 1929–1967," *Rev. Income Wealth*, Dec. 1969, *15*, 293-320.

M. R. Darby, "The Dynamics of the Allocation of Transitory Income Among Consumers' Assets," unpublished doctoral dissertation, Univ. Chicago 1970.

M. Friedman, "The Demand for Money: Some Theoretical and Empirical Results," *J. Polit. Econ.*, Aug. 1959, *67*, 327–51.

——, "The Lag in the Effect of Monetary Policy," *J. Polit. Econ.*, Oct. 1961, *69*, 447–66.

——, "Savings and the Balance Sheet," *Bull. Oxford Univ. Inst. Econ. Statist.*, May 1957, *19*, 125–36.

————, *Studies in the Quantity Theory of Money*, Chicago 1956.

————, *A Theory of the Consumption Function*, Princeton 1957.

———— and A. J. Schwartz, *A Monetary History of the United States, 1867–1960*, Nat. Bur. Econ. Res. *Stud. in Business Cycles*, Vol. 12, Princeton 1963.

R. W. Goldsmith, *The National Wealth of the United States in the Postwar Period*, Nat. Bur. Econ. Res. *Stud. in Capital Formation and Financing*, Vol. 10, Princeton, 1962.

M. G. Kendall and A. Stuart, *The Advanced Theory of Statistics*, Vol. II, New York 1961.

B. Klein, "The Payment of Interest on Commercial Bank Deposits and the Price of Money: A Study of the Demand for Money," unpublished doctoral dissertation, Univ. Chicago 1970.

E. Malinvaud, *Statistical Methods of Econometrics*, Chicago 1966.

F. Modigliani and R. Brumberg, "Utility Analysis and the Consumption Function: An Interpretation of Cross-Section Data," in K. E. Kurihara, ed., *Post Keynesian Economics*, New Brunswick 1954, 388–436.

B. Motley, "A Demand-for-Money Function for the Household Sector—Some Preliminary Findings," *J. Finance*, Sept. 1967, *22*, 405–18.

P. E. Smith, "The Demand for Durable Goods: Permanent or Transitory Income?", *J. Polit. Econ.*, Oct. 1962, *70*, 500–04.

J. Tobin, "The Interest Elasticity of Transactions Demand for Cash," *Rev. Econ. Statist.*, Aug. 1956, *38*, 241–47.

Fed. Reserve Bank St. Louis *Rev.*, Aug. 1968.

U.S. Board of Governors of Federal Reserve System, *Fed. Reserve Bull.*, various issues.

————, *Supplement to Banking and Monetary Statistics, Section 12, Money Rates and Securities Markets*.

U.S. Office of Business Economics, *Surv. Curr. Bus.*, supplements, 1966, 1967.

[12]

Inflation and Real Interest Rate:
A Long-Term Analysis

Edi Karni

University of Chicago

Irving Fisher's theoretical analysis of the behavior of the nominal interest rate concluded that the nominal rate of interest is equal to the real interest rate plus the anticipated rate of change in the price level. This proposition is not fully confirmed by empirical evidence. As a result, Fisher made the following conclusion:

> When the cost of living is not stable, the rate of interest takes the appreciation and depreciation into account to some extent, but only slightly, and, in general indirectly. That is, when prices are rising, the rate of interest tends to be high but not so high as it should be to compensate for the rise, and when prices are falling, the rate of interest tends to be low, but not so low as it should be to compensate for the fall. [Fisher 1930, p. 43]

One way to overcome the above difficulty is to assume that the expected rate of change in prices lags behind the actual rate of change in prices. Another solution was suggested by Mundell (1963), who attributes the discrepancy observed by Fisher to changes in the real interest rate. While the two approaches just mentioned are not mutually exclusive, in

This paper was presented in the course "Money and Interest Rates" given by Professor Milton Friedman at the University of Chicago (1970), and I have benefited from comments of the participants. I would like to express special gratitude to Stanley Fischer and Robert J. Gordon for their helpful suggestions. I have also benefited from a discussion of various points with Robert A. Mundell, Rudiger Dornbusch, and Jacob A. Frenkel. Any remaining deficiencies are my sole responsibility.

order to separate and thus clarify the arguments of the second approach, the rest of this paper is based on the assumption that the expected rate of change in the price level is equal to the actual rate of change.

Utilizing the apparatus developed by Metzler (1951) and assuming that real investment depends on real interest while real savings depend on real balances, Mundell (1963) was able to show that the real rate of interest falls during inflation: "The conclusion is based on the fact that inflation reduces real money balances and that the resulting decline in wealth stimulates increased saving" (Mundell 1963, p. 283). This conclusion leads toward a monetary theory of growth. The lower real interest stimulates the investment process and, as a result, accelerates economic growth.

This paper proves that a once-and-for-all increase in the rate of change of the price level has a long-run effect on the real interest rate which differs from the short-run analysis of Mundell. The real interest rate is reduced only temporarily and tends in the long run to rise back to its original level. The original level will be attained exactly if and only if the underlying investment process is "all-inclusive" in the sense of Friedman (1967).

The model which serves as a basis for the analysis is presented in Section I. The properties of the suggested model are investigated in Section II. Section III summarizes the main conclusions.

I. The Model

I employ the following notation: $Y =$ income level (nominal); $\pi =$ profits in real terms; $r =$ real rate of interest; $i =$ nominal rate of interest; $P =$ price level; $M =$ nominal quantity of money; $I =$ investment in nominal terms; $S =$ savings in nominal terms; $w =$ total wealth in real terms; $m = M/P$; and $(\dot{P}/P)^* =$ the expected rate of change in the price level.

At the outset of this section, a modified version of Mundell's model is discussed. The most important improvement introduced here is the definition of saving as a function of total wealth rather than the amount of real balances alone. This modification brings this model closer to the one suggested by Metzler than Mundell's own version. A second change is the allowance for long-run changes in income level in response to variations in investment.[1] It is still assumed with Mundell that profits are a con-

---

[1] This change is introduced into the model simply by allowing income to be determined by (1.1). This way was chosen because it is relatively less complicated. An alternative way of formulating the model under the new assumptions requires an explicit and detailed consideration of the production sector, that is,

$$\frac{Y}{P} = F(K; L), \qquad (1.1')$$

stant fraction of total income; that is, the production function has an
elasticity of substitution equal to unity, as in equation (1.1):

$$\pi = c \cdot \frac{Y}{P} \quad 0 \leqslant c \leqslant 1. \tag{1.1}$$

The rest of the model includes:

$$w = m^s + \frac{\pi}{r}, \tag{1.2}$$

$$\frac{I}{P} = I(r), \quad I'(r) < 0, \tag{1.3}$$

$$\frac{S}{P} = S(w), \quad S'(w) < 0, \tag{1.4}$$

$$I = S, \tag{1.5}$$

$$m^d = \frac{\pi}{r} f(i), \quad f' < 0, \tag{1.6}$$

$$m^s = \frac{M^s}{P}, \tag{1.7}$$

$$m^d = m^s, \tag{1.8}$$

$$i = r + \left(\frac{\dot{P}}{P}\right)^*. \tag{1.9}$$

---

where L = the aggregate amount of labor employed and K = the aggregate amount
of physical capital employed. For the short run, it is assumed that

$$K = K_0 \tag{1.2'}$$

and

$$L = L_0. \tag{1.3'}$$

In the long run, the supply of both factors of production is a variable which must
be determined within the model. Therefore, (1.3') will be substituted by (1.4') and
(1.5'), and (1.2') is dropped:

$$\frac{WR}{P} = F'_L (K; L) \tag{1.4'}$$

and

$$L = j\left(\frac{WR}{P}\right), \tag{1.5'}$$

where WR denotes the nominal wage rate. It seems that the approach mentioned here,
in spite of its appeal to economic intuition, does not yield any substantial changes in
the results for the problem discussed in this paper. The way the model is presented
in the paper was chosen by virtue of its simplicity.

Equations (1.3)–(1.5) determine the equilibrium in the real sector.[2] Equations (1.6)–(1.8) determine the equilibrium in the monetary sector. Equations (1.1)–(1.3) are definitions and assumptions of the model.

It should be noted that equation (1.9) includes an element $(\dot{P}/P)^*$ which is not determined within the above system of equations. In order to close the system, another equation which determines the formation of price anticipation as a function of other past, present, or future variables should be added. Again, in order to avoid complications which do not contribute to the validity of the argument presented here, it is assumed that

$$\left(\frac{\dot{P}}{P}\right)^* = \frac{P}{P}. \tag{1.10}$$

The anticipated rate of change in prices at any point in time is equal to the actual rate of change in prices, which is determined by past changes in real income and the quantity of money.

The above model consists of ten equations with eleven variables: Y, π, w, r, I, S, m^d, m^s, P, i, and $(\dot{P}/P)^*$.

In the short run, it is supposed that Y/P is fixed; therefore, the above model, with equation (1.11),

$$\frac{Y}{P} = Y_F, \tag{1.11}$$

is the short-run model.

The long-run equilibrium for a stationary economy is given by replacing (1.5) and (1.11) by

$$\frac{I}{P} = 0 \tag{1.12}$$

$$\frac{S}{P} = 0. \tag{1.13}$$

We turn now to investigate the implication of the suggested model for long-run behavior of the real interest rate.

---

[2] The way the above model was constructed was intended to make it as close as possible to the one suggested by Mundell. The modifications introduced are those needed for a presentation of the same arguments in the long-run context. However, it should be noted that the same arguments may also be presented in terms of a model constructed by Friedman (1967), in which both saving and investment are functions of wealth and the real rate of interest. For that purpose, (1.3) and (1.4) should be replaced by

$$\frac{I}{P} = I(r; w) \tag{1.6'}$$

and

$$\frac{S}{P} = S(r; w), \tag{1.7'}$$

respectively.

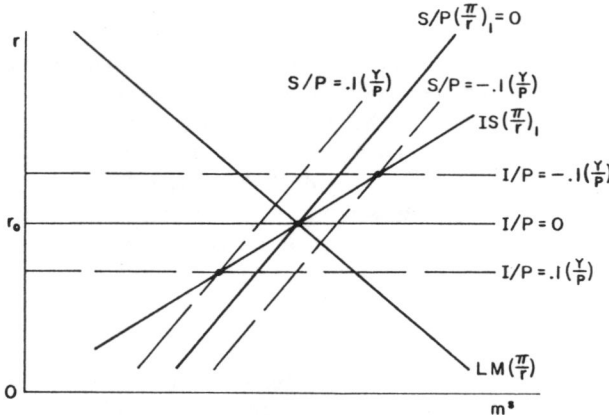

Fig. 1.—Initial situation: long-run equilibrium position

II. Money and Real Interest Rate: Long-Run Relationships

Figure 1 presents a long-run equilibrium situation. The real sector of the economy is described by I, S, and IS curves. The monetary sector is represented by the LM curve. In long-run equilibrium, the IS and LM curves intersect at a point where $I = S = 0$.

By (1.3) above, I/P is a function of the real rate of interest alone; therefore, it is independent of the level of w or any of its components. This is reflected in the horizontal slope of the I/P curve. The long-run equilibrium of real investment is at r_0, where $I/P = 0$. For values of r different from r_0, I/P differs from zero. In particular, $I/P > 0$ for $r < r_0$, and it is larger the lower r is. For $r > r_0$, $I/P < 0$ and is larger in absolute value the higher r is, within the technical constraint. The curve labeled $I/P = 0$ is fundamentally different from the others in the sense that any other curve represents a temporary situation, since the increment (decrement) in capital resulting from positive (negative) investment will cause the economy to move away from this position. No such forces are generated by the investment process when $I/P = 0$. Therefore, this level of investment corresponds to the stationary state.

The way I/P is graphed suggests something about the properties of the investment process itself. Economic rationality on the part of the investor requires that investment decisions are based on the real interest rate as well as on the marginal efficiency of investment; that is, the investment function (1.3) may be written as follows:

$$\frac{I}{P} = I(\rho - r), \quad I' > 0, \tag{2.1}$$

where ρ denotes the marginal efficiency of capital.

The investment function (1.3) assumes that we are dealing with an all-inclusive concept of investment and capital, so that the marginal efficiency of capital is constant at $\rho = r_0$.[3] We also assume that ρ is independent of the amount of real balances. Otherwise, I/P curves would be positively sloped, since an increase in real balances would increase the ratio of monetary to human and nonhuman capital, thus increasing the own rate of return of the latter; so r would have to increase with real balances in order to keep the level of investment constant.

Real saving according to (1.4) is a function of wealth. The corresponding $S'P$ curves are positively sloped, since an increase in the rate of interest reduces the amount of wealth while an increase in real balances increases it. Therefore, a change in the real interest rate must be accompanied by a change in the same direction in real balances in order to keep real savings constant. The savings schedules plotted in the r-m^s plane are defined for a given level of nonmonetary wealth. An increase in the amount of the latter results in a leftward shift of the whole system of curves and a shift in the opposite direction when nonmonetary wealth decreases, since saving is a function of total wealth and not just monetary wealth. As in the case of investment discussed earlier, the curve $S/P = 0$ represents a stationary equilibrium while the other curves represent temporary equilibria.

The IS curve is the locus of points, along which $I = S$. These are points of equilibrium in the real sector, all except the point where $I = S = 0$ are points of a temporary equilibrium. The IS curve is also plotted for a given level of nonmonetary wealth. Any shift in the S/P curves shifts the locus of equilibrium points, thus shifting the IS curve in the same direction.

Each LM curve is the locus of points which correspond to equilibrium in the monetary sector. As m^s increases, the nominal rate of interest must fall to induce an increase in the demand for money. The fall in the interest rate increases the demand for money not only by increasing the amount of nonmonetary wealth, but also by increasing the desired ratio of real balances to other assets. Since this desired ratio depends on the

---

[3] An "all-inclusive" concept of capital refers to a broad definition of capital which includes all sources of productive services. The three main categories of capital included in this concept are: material capital, human capital, and monetary capital. Along the same lines, an all-inclusive concept of investment defines a process of accumulation of stocks of each of the above categories of capital. It follows that the "all-inclusiveness" of investment implies an expanding universe in which all sources of productive services are growing at the same rate. The absence of a "fixed" source of productive services accounts for the constancy of the marginal efficiency of capital. Note, however, that investment in human capital is treated here as an increase in the supply of labor available. The labor input is measured in terms of effective units of work, given by the product of the number of persons engaged in the production process and the average amount of human capital they possess. This rather strong assumption is employed here in order to simplify the argument. Relaxation of this assumption is equivalent to the introduction of a not-all-inclusive concept of investment process. This case is treated later in this paper.

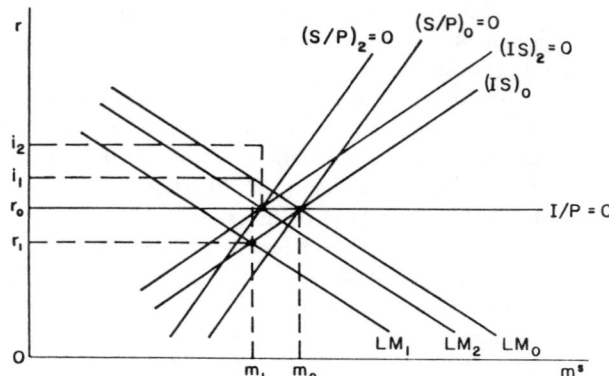

Fɪɢ. 2.—Successive equilibrium positions during an inflationary process

nominal interest rate, and it is the real interest rate which is plotted on
the vertical axis, the *LM* curve shifts as a consequence of any alteration
in the expected rate of change in the price level. The *LM* curve depends
also on the amount of nonmonetary assets. For a given rate of interest, an
increase in nonmonetary assets increases the demand for money and
causes a rightward shift of the *LM* curve.

We now investigate how the equilibrium position is affected by a change
in the anticipated rate of inflation, both in the short run and the long
run.[4] For this purpose, figure 2 reproduces some of the curves in figure 1.
The subscripts to the labels of the curves indicate successive points in
time. The curves with subscript 0 indicate the initial position in which
the rate of anticipated inflation is zero and thus $r_0 = i_0$. The long-run
equilibrium quantity of real balances is m_0.

Suppose that the anticipated rate of change in prices becomes positive.
This reduces the demand for money, causing a leftward shift of the *LM*
curve to LM_1. Equilibrium in both the real and the monetary sectors is
restored at the intersection of IS_0 and LM_1, with a real rate of interest

---

[4] The inflation is produced by an increase in the rate of increase in the money
supply from zero to some positive level θ. Once the rate of inflation becomes fully
anticipated and a new equilibrium path is restored, the nominal quantity of money
and the price level both increase at the same rate. Equation (1.8) then assumes
the form:

$$m^s = \frac{M^s\, e^{\theta t}}{\hat{P}\, e^{\theta t}} = \frac{\pi}{r}\, f(r + \theta) = m^d \qquad (1.8')$$

where t denotes the period of time that elapsed since the change in the rate of
increase in the money supply occurred and $\hat{P}$ denotes the price level that has been
established when the new equilibrium path was initially reached. Equation (1.8')
indicates a decline in the real quantity of money in response to the increase in the
cost of holding it.

r_1 and a nominal rate of interest i_1, $i_1 - r_1$ being the anticipated rate of inflation. The quantity of real balances is reduced to m_1.

To this point, the discussion is the same as Mundell's. However, the equilibrium in the real sector is reached at a point off the $(S/P)_0 = 0$ curve at which $I/P = S/P > 0$. Nonmonetary wealth is accumulated, resulting in a rightward shift of LM and a leftward shift of the S/P and the IS curves, a process which continues as long as positive net investment is taking place. Eventually, the economy will return to its $I/P = 0$ curve, with a real interest rate of r_0 and a nominal interest rate which is higher by the expected rate of inflation. The amount of nonmonetary wealth is higher than the corresponding amount in the initial position, and the amount of real balances is now smaller. Total wealth must be the same in the final equilibrium as it was in the initial situation, since saving has returned to its initial value of zero. The change in the composition of wealth results in an increase in income and a reduction in the flow of money services. The analysis does not indicate whether real balances in the final equilibrium position are larger or smaller than in the short-run equilibrium (m_1). The result depends on whether the scale effect of an increase in nonmonetary wealth dominates the substitution effect resulting from the higher interest rate.

If the increase in capital resulting from the investment process is not all-inclusive, the accumulation of nonmonetary wealth will result in a downward shift of all the investment schedules, since an increase in the ratio of material capital to other forms of capital reduces the internal rate of return on the former (ρ), thus causing the accumulation of capital to stop at a lower interest rate. In this case, the final stationary state will be reached at a real interest rate which is lower than r_0.

A particular case is when real balances are a factor of production. This requires constant returns to total capital, not just nonmonetary capital as before. Thus, the increase in nonmonetary capital that results from the inflation process is not all-inclusive, and a downward shift of the investment schedule during the accumulation process takes place. The stationary-state real interest rate is inversely proportional to the anticipated rate of inflation. (For a different exposition of the same argument, see Mundell [1971, chap. 5].)

The above argument may be summarized as follows. An increase in the expected rate of inflation initially decreases the demand for real balances, thus inducing an increase in saving. The excess supply of saving causes a reduction in the real interest rate to the point at which induced investment eliminates this excess supply. Positive investment causes the stock of nonmonetary capital to grow, which reduces saving and reverses the direction of change of the real interest rate. Whether the latter will reach its initial level depends on whether the increase in capital is all-inclusive or not.

Mundell has already observed that the inflationary process stimulates growth. In his words:

> Foreseeable fluctuation in the rate of interest can thus have very real effects on economic activity. When prices are expected to rise, the money rate of interest rises by less than the rate of inflation giving impetus to an investment boom and acceleration of growth. [Mundell 1963, p. 283]

It should be noted, however, that the acceleration of growth of real income has its cost in terms of reduction in the flow of money services resulting from the reduction in the stock of real balances.

Whether the capital formation process, generated by the lower real interest rate, is all-inclusive or not, the acceleration of growth is a temporary phenomenon. As the real interest rate converges toward its stationary-state level, the inflationary-induced investment is eliminated. The higher rate of inflation produces a new composition of total wealth, that is, a smaller amount of real balances and a larger amount of non-monetary wealth, and as a result income increases while the flow of monetary services decreases. This is not the "trade-off" between a higher rate of inflation and a higher rate of growth, which is implied by Mundell's conclusion.

III. Conclusions

The analysis of the long-term behavior of the real interest rate, within the framework of a macroeconomic model and in terms of capital theory leads to the following conclusions:

a) A once-and-for-all increase (decrease) in the rate of change in the price level temporarily reduces (increases) the real rate of interest.

b) In the long run, the real rate of interest tends to converge back toward its original stationary-state level. Whether it will reach that level or not depends on whether the investment process generated by the lower real interest rate is all-inclusive. If it is not all-inclusive, the real rate of interest will be lower than the one prevailing before the change in the rate of change in prices took place.

c) Fisher's theory of the interest rate is consistent with the model presented in this paper, provided that we are dealing with long-lasting changes in the rate of inflation or deflation and an all-inclusive investment process. The model is also consistent with short-term discrepancies between Fisher's theory and empirical evidence. It is consistent with long-term discrepancies only in the case where the investment process is not all-inclusive.

d) An increase in the rate of inflation due to its effect on the real

interest rate accelerates the rate of growth of the economy only temporarily, and at the cost of a reduction in the flow of monetary services.

e) Contrary to Mundell's conclusions, the trade-off in this model is
between a higher rate of inflation and a higher rate level of nonmonetary
wealth rather than a permanently higher growth rate.

References

Fisher, Irving. *Theory of Interest.* New York: Macmillan, 1930.
Friedman, Milton. *Price Theory.* Chicago: Aldine, 1967.
Metzler, Lloyd. "Wealth, Saving, and the Rate of Interest." *J.P.E.* 59 (April
    1951): 93–116.
Mundell, Robert A. "Inflation and Real Interest." *J.P.E.* 71 (June 1963):
    280–83.
———. *Monetary Theory.* Pacific Palisades. Calif.: Goodyear, 1971.

[13]

Currency in Circulation and the Real Value of Notes

IN RECENT YEARS economists have devoted a great deal of attention to the behavior of various measures of liquid assets. Many such measures include currency in circulation as one of their components. The purpose of this paper is to improve the published figures on currency in circulation by estimating the amount of currency lost.[1] This is done by establishing a relationship between currency losses and the real value of currency notes.

Currency in circulation is defined as the total amount of currency outstanding less currency holdings of the Treasury and Federal Reserve banks. Data on currency outstanding are obtained by subtracting the total quantity of currency redeemed from the total quantity of currency issued. Currency in circulation is thus overstated by the amount of currency lost.[2] This paper will use the evidence from various series and types of currency

---

*This article is an extension of a segment of the author's Ph.D. thesis. The author is grateful to Milton Friedman and Lester Telser for their helpful comments. The author has also benefited greatly from suggestions of an anonymous referee and the comments of a number of present and former colleagues at the Federal Reserve Bank of Chicago, including Gary Alford, Frank Cooper, George Kaufman, Nick Lash, and Larry Mote.

[1] Currency lost includes all currency irretrievably lost, destroyed, in collections, or otherwise so disposed as never to be presented for redemption.

[2] Pursuant to the Old Series Currency Adjustment Act of June 30, 1961, the Treasury has periodically written off quantities of various types of notes no longer issued as irretrievably lost or destroyed. As of June 30, 1971, the Treasury had subtracted $344,436,000 from the amount previously listed in circulation. Since the Treasury made very low loss estimates, and in any case only for currency types no longer issued (currency of types still issued accounts for 98.8 percent of all currency listed in circulation), the currency in circulation figures undoubtedly remain overstated.

ROBERT D. LAURENT *is an economist at the Federal Reserve Bank of Chicago.*

no longer issued to estimate yearly figures for all currency in circulation adjusted for losses.[3]

Estimating Currency Losses

Currency was first issued by the United States government in 1861, and in the years since, eight different types of currency have been issued.[4] If old series notes (the larger sized pre-1930 notes) are distinguished from the current new series notes, then 14 different types of United States currency have been issued. If one selects a denomination of a type of currency which is no longer being issued and which is, moreover, no longer being returned for redemption, then the amount of that currency listed in circulation may be taken as the amount of that currency lost. As an example, $10 old-series Silver Certificates were last issued in 1929. Between June, 1957, and June, 1971, only $1,740 in $10 old-series Silver Certificates was redeemed and only $60 was redeemed in the last year of this period. In such circumstances the $1,460,576 of this type of currency listed as outstanding in June, 1971, may be assumed to be a very close estimate of the amount of currency lost.[5]

The total amount of a certain type and denomination of currency lost may be considered as the cumulative result of a process in which a certain fraction of the currency in circulation held by the public is lost each year.[6] Thus, in the first year (year t) that a type of currency is in circulation, the amount of currency lost may be expressed as[7]

$$L_t = \theta_t \alpha,$$

where θ_t is the amount held by the public at the end of year t and α is the proportion of the currency held by the public which is lost each

[3] For three earlier attempts to gauge the order of magnitude of currency losses see Milton Friedman and Anna Schwartz, *A Monetary History of the United States, 1867-1960* (Princeton: Princeton University Press, 1963), pp. 442-43; George G. Kaufman, *The Demand for Currency*, Staff Economic Studies (Washington: U.S. Board of Governors of the Federal Reserve System, 1965), pp. 17-18; and George Garvy and Martin R. Blyn, *The Velocity of Money* (New York: Federal Reserve Bank of New York, 1969), pp. 98-99.

[4] In chronological order: Old Demand Notes, National Bank Notes, U.S. Notes, Gold Certificates, Silver Certificates, Treasury Notes of 1890, Federal Reserve Notes, and Federal Reserve Bank Notes.

[5] Currency lost may not represent an integral number of notes due to the redemption, at times in the past, of fractional parts of notes.

[6] Currency held by the public is defined as currency in circulation minus currency held as vault cash by commercial banks and mutual savings banks. Currency held by the public was obtained by assuming that the proportion of all coin and currency held as vault cash in each year applies to each particular type and denomination of currency. The use of currency held by the public is equivalent to assuming that there are no currency losses from bank vault cash.

[7] This ignores the minor effects due to the difference between the amount of currency in circulation at the end of year t and the average amount in circulation over year t.

year. The currency lost in year $t + 1$ is α times the amount of currency in circulation held by the public at the end of year $t + 1$ and may be expressed as

$$L_{t+1} = (\theta_{t+1} - \theta_t \alpha)\alpha = \theta_{t+1}\alpha - \theta_t \alpha^2$$

so that the total lost at the end of year $t + 1$ is

$$L_t + L_{t+1} = (\theta_t + \theta_{t+1})\alpha - \theta_t \alpha^2.$$

The same procedure yields the total lost at the end of year $t + 2$:

$$L_t + L_{t+1} + L_{t+2} = (\theta_t + \theta_{t+1} + \theta_{t+2})\alpha - (2\theta_t + \theta_{t+1})\alpha^2 + \theta_t \alpha^3.$$

Generalizing, total currency lost through year $t + n$ is

$$L_t + L_{t+1} + L_{t+2} + \ldots + L_{t+n} = \alpha\left(\sum_{i=0}^{n} \frac{i!}{i!0!} \theta_{t+n-i}\right)$$

$$- \alpha^2\left(\sum_{i=0}^{n-1} \frac{(i+1)!}{i!1!} \theta_{t+n-i-1}\right)$$

$$+ \alpha^3\left(\sum_{i=0}^{n-2} \frac{(i+2)!}{i!2!} \theta_{t+n-i-2}\right) - \ldots$$

$$+ (-1)^{n+1}\alpha^n\left(\sum_{i=0}^{1} \frac{(i+n-1)!}{i!(n-1)!} \theta_{t-i+1}\right)$$

$$+ (-1)^{n+2}\alpha^{n+1}\left(\sum_{i=0}^{0} \frac{(i+n)!}{i!n!} \theta_{t-1}\right).$$

Given the total amount lost in a certain denomination and type of currency and the amounts held by the public for each year, one may obtain the value of α, the loss rate per note held by the public per year.

So that the amount listed in circulation will be a close estimate of the amount lost, estimates were computed only for those denominations and types of currency for which less than $500 was redeemed in the year June 30, 1968, to June 30, 1969. The last year (n) chosen for the sample period was the last year in which more than $500 of that type and denomination of currency was redeemed. Estimates of annual loss rates were computed for 38 types and denominations of currency. Using the

TABLE 1

ESTIMATES OF LOSS RATES FOR NOTES IN CIRCULATION HELD BY THE PUBLIC

Type of Note	Yearly Loss Rate Estimate	Denomination in Dollars	Average Consumer Price Index for Note-Years Held by the Public	Period Covered in the Estimate	Note-Years Held by the Public Used in Deriving Estimates (In Thousands)
United States Note	.00558	1	.86	1863–1963	880,375
National Bank Note	.00574	1	.68	1865–1936	58,920
Treasury Note of 1890	.00509	1	.49	1891–1936	57,401
Federal Reserve Bank Note	.00546	1	1.04	1919–1958	272,582
United States Note	.00487	2	.81	1863–1968	363,145
National Bank Note	.00382	2	.68	1865–1932	21,122
Silver Certificate	.00359	2	.60	1887–1961	391,579
Treasury Note of 1890	.00365	2	.49	1891–1934	24,214
Federal Reserve Bank Note	.00412	2	1.02	1919–1958	41,060
Old Demand Note	.00127	5	.57	1862–1878	3,518
Silver Certificate	.00172	5	.58	1887–1965	685,450
Treasury Note of 1890	.00172	5	.49	1891–1945	37,607
Federal Reserve Bank Note	.00217	5	1.01	1916–1953	18,410
Old Demand Note	.00127	10	.57	1862–1878	1,619
United States Note	.00165	10	.62	1862–1967	395,677
Silver Certificate	.00113	10	.51	1878–1957	129,765
Treasury Note of 1890	.00105	10	.49	1891–1954	21,024
Federal Reserve Bank Note	.00185	10	.96	1916–1947	1,830
Old Demand Note	.00089	20	.57	1862–1877	734
United States Note	.00117	20	.61	1862–1964	103,951
Silver Certificate	.00086	20	.52	1878–1957	37,344
Treasury Note of 1890	.00089	20	.50	1891–1954	3,913
Federal Reserve Bank Note	.00128	20	.97	1916–1966	803
United States Note	.00033	50	.61	1862–1959	11,966
Silver Certificate	.00068	50	.58	1878–1959	4,344
Treasury Note of 1890	.00055	50	.50	1893–1930	47
Federal Reserve Bank Note	.00276	50	.99	1920–1941	12
United States Note	.00042	100	.59	1862–1961	7,713
Silver Certificate	.00070	100	.50	1878–1961	1,298
Treasury Note of 1890	.00084	100	.50	1891–1945	350
United States Note	.00066	500	.62	1862–1967	1,070
National Bank Note	.00221	500	.70	1864–1937	78
Silver Certificate	.00043	500	.51	1878–1947	33
United States Note	.00027	1000	.59	1862–1964	1,177
National Bank Note	.00136	1000	.74	1865–1917	15
Gold Certificate	.00060	1000	.69	1866–1968	1,120
Silver Certificate	.00038	1000	.52	1878–1961	23
Treasury Note of 1890	.00047	1000	.49	1891–1961	53

criteria described above, only old-series notes qualified and only denominations between $1 and $1,000 were considered.[8]

The values of α were determined by using a computer to approximate the values through an iterative procedure. Table 1 presents the loss rate estimates for the various types and denominations of currency and indicates the periods used to compute the estimates. Table 1 also lists the number of note-years held by the public in the sample used for each loss rate estimate. The number of note-years held by the public for any estimate is the sum of the number of notes of currency in circulation held by the public (adjusted for losses) for all the years covered in the sample.

The Role of Real Value

It is clear from Table 1 that as denomination rises the loss rate falls. This relationship seems reasonable, since one would expect greater care to be exercised in the handling and storage of more valuable notes. Relationships between currency loss rates and denominations were estimated and are given by the first two regressions in Table 2. These regressions were estimated by giving to each loss rate estimate in Table 1 a weight proportional to the number of note-years held by the public. This gives each note-year held by the public the same weight in determining the relationship between loss rate and denomination. There are two reasons for adopting this procedure. First, the various loss rate estimates are derived from populations with vastly different amounts of notes held by the public, and it seems reasonable to place more faith in the reliability of estimates based on larger populations. Second, it seems likely that estimates based on small populations might deviate systematically from estimates based on larger populations. It might be expected, for example, that the activities of currency collectors would be concentrated in those notes which are relatively rare, giving those notes a higher loss rate than might otherwise be expected. These estimates based on small populations should be less heavily weighted because the far greater part of total currency losses occur in notes experiencing such wide circulation that the impact of currency collectors on the loss rate is minor. The results of the linear and semi-logarithmic forms at the top of Table 2 confirm that a significant inverse relationship exists between currency loss rates and currency denomination.

The same rationale explaining the inverse relationship between currency loss rates and denomination at any given point in time suggests the currency loss rates might also be affected by price level changes over time. If

---

[8] Denominations greater than $1,000 account for a very small part of currency in circulation and an even smaller part of the total currency lost. Only 39 notes of $5,000 or $10,000 denominations could be lost, as of June 30, 1969, in those types of currency no longer issued. This is despite the issuance up to that date of over 200,000 five-thousand dollar notes and over 450,000 ten-thousand dollar notes in these types of currency.

218 : MONEY, CREDIT, AND BANKING

TABLE 2

RELATIONSHIP BETWEEN LOSS RATE ESTIMATES (LR), DENOMINATION (D)
AND CONSUMER PRICES (P)

*Denomination**

$LR = .001146 + .004591 \, (1/D)$ $R^2 = .915$ $R^2_{adj} = .886$ s.e. $= .00070$
    (7.98)   (17.21)

$LR = .005352 + .001761 \, ln\,(1/D)$ $R^2 = .898$ $R^2_{adj} = .864$ s.e. $= .00077$
    (46.30)   (15.62)

Real Value

$LR = .001565 + .004731 \, (P/D)$ $R^2 = .864$ $R^2_{adj} = .818$ s.e. $= .00088$
    (10.09)   (13.27)

$LR = .005672 + .001535 \, ln\,(P/D)$ $R^2 = .934$ $R^2_{adj} = .911$ s.e. $= .00062$
    (52.84)   (19.75)

Denomination, Price

$LR = .000101 + .001917 \, P + .003968 \, (1/D)$ $R^2 = .927$ $R^2_{adj} = .878$ s.e. $= .00072$
    (.15)   (1.69)   (8.21)

$LR = .005812 + .002336 \, ln\,P + .001391 \, ln\,(1/D)$ $R^2 = .939$ $R^2_{adj} = .898$ s.e. $= .00066$
    (28.17)   (3.37)   (8.89)

*ln represents the natural logarithm. Figures in parentheses are t values.

holders exercise more care in the handling and storage of larger denomination notes because these notes have a higher real value, then they should also exercise more care in the handling and storage of a particular denomination of currency when prices are low relative to when prices are high. Prices are expected to have less effect than denomination on the estimates in Table 1 because denomination changes by a much greater factor than prices over the various estimates. Nevertheless, if currency loss rates depend upon the real value of notes, then prices should have an effect on the currency loss rate estimates. An average consumer price index was computed for each estimate and included in Table 1. This average was computed by weighting an average consumer price index for each year by the number of notes of that particular type held by the public in that year.

The consumer price figures given in Table 1 were used to test the relationship between loss rate estimates and the real value of notes. The results, given in Table 2 for both forms of the regression, indicate that whether the addition of price data improves the explanation of loss rates depends upon the form of the relationship. Nevertheless, the best relationship is one utilizing the real value of notes in a semilogarithmic form. This form of the relationship between loss rate and the natural logarithm of the inverse of the real value of currency notes may be seen in Figure 1. The semilogarithmic relationship is shown by the curve formed of the joined solid and broken curves. Figure 1 also shows the loss rate estimates and the relative weights assigned to each estimate. In addition, loss rates were run on prices and the inverse of denomination taken separately in

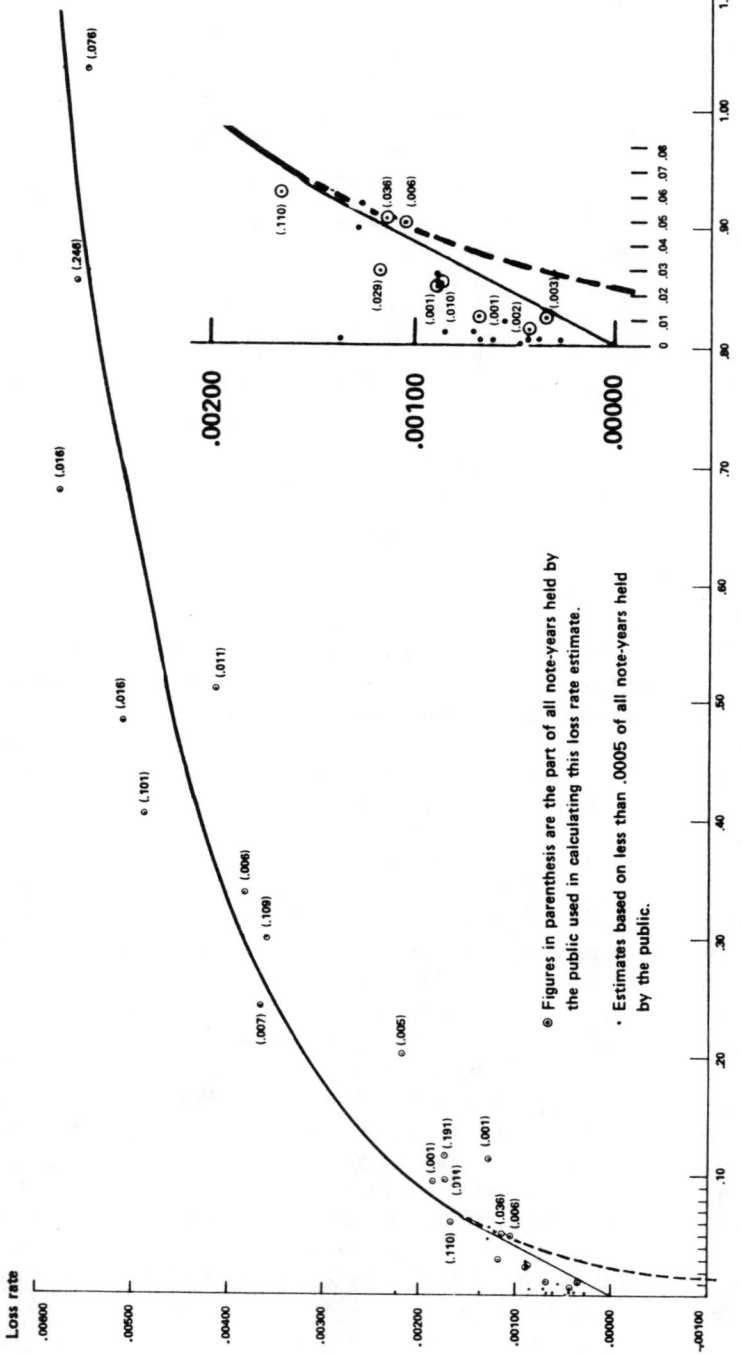

Fig. 1. Relationship between Loss Rates and the Inverse of the Real Value with the Estimates for Each Type of Note

both linear and semilogarithmic forms. These equations are given in the last two regressions in Table 2. The closeness of the coefficients indicates that the effects of price and denomination on loss rates might well be represented by the real value of notes. The semilogarithmic real value equation continues to perform best, even when the results of regressions allowing prices and the inverse of denomination to vary independently are included.

The semilogarithmic relationship plotted in Figure 1, when translated into real value terms, implies that each incremental increase in the real value of currency lowers the loss rate by a smaller amount. The explanation would seem to lie in the relationship between the amount of resources expended in protecting a currency holding and the loss rate for the holding. Through such devices as fireproof storage boxes or safe deposit boxes, it would seem that marginal changes in expenditures on currency protection would change loss rates substantially when a relatively small total amount is spent on currency protection. At higher levels of total expenditures on currency protection, it would seem that marginal changes in expenditures would change loss rates much less even for very large currency holdings.

Total Currency Losses

Currency losses for all notes in circulation over the period 1861-1971 were computed by using the semilogarithmic form of the weighted real value equation in Table 2. An adjustment was made to this equation for purposes of estimating total currency losses. The equation as estimated gives negative loss rates for notes of high real value—an obvious impossibility. Therefore, a straight line through the origin and tangent to the original curve was substituted for a portion of the original curve. The portion of the original curve removed is shown as a broken curve in Figure 1, with the new segment shown as a straight line out of the origin. This relationship was used to compute an annual loss rate for each year and denomination. This rate was then multiplied by the value of that denomination of currency held by the public (adjusted for previous currency losses and adding back any currency removed from circulation as lost by the Treasury) to obtain the amount of currency lost in each denomination and year. By cumulating the losses year by year for each denomination, an adjusted series on currency in circulation is compiled.[9]

Table 3 presents figures on currency listed in circulation and currency in circulation adjusted for losses. It should be reiterated that all figures

[9]An additional advantage of the weighted regression appeared during the calculation of total currency losses. Because of the discontinuance of certain high denomination notes and higher price levels in the last 30 years, the loss rate estimates used in estimating the greater part of total currency losses were from the range of the relationship spanning the most heavily weighted estimates.

TABLE 3
ADJUSTED U.S. GOVERNMENT CURRENCY IN CIRCULATION AS OF JUNE 30
(In Thousands of Dollars, 1861–1971)

Year	Currency listed in Circulation*	Currency in Circulation adjusted for losses	Year	Currency listed in Circulation	Currency in Circulation adjusted for losses	Year	Currency listed in circulation	Currency in Circulation adjusted for losses	Year	Currency listed in Circulation	Currency in Circulation adjusted for losses
1861	0	0	1889	829,010	811,823	1917	2,563,441	2,511,427	1945	25,503,595	25,190,063
1862	123,988	123,876	1890	869,941	852,060	1918	3,424,170	3,367,483	1946	26,916,210	26,564,346
1863	315,883	315,363	1891	906,525	887,907	1919	3,838,678	3,775,937	1947	26,926,410	26,533,977
1864	447,163	445,983	1892	985,756	966,377	1920	4,416,991	4,346,977	1948	26,468,463	26,034,186
1865	525,550	523,618	1893	1,013,039	992,877	1921	3,925,658	3,849,582	1949	26,022,552	25,547,795
1866	606,724	604,071	1894	1,018,085	997,231	1922	3,525,956	3,444,341	1950	25,648,808	25,133,719
1867	611,109	607,767	1895	988,583	967,088	1923	3,778,284	3,690,779	1951	26,220,817	25,662,313
1868	628,055	624,023	1896	919,527	897,385	1924	3,715,263	3,621,857	1952	27,337,623	26,733,223
1869	612,987	608,300	1897	994,536	971,726	1925	3,646,614	3,547,341	1953	28,348,625	27,696,590
1870	620,312	614,946	1898	1,040,633	1,017,092	1926	3,734,740	3,629,408	1954	28,116,700	27,417,769
1871	659,272	653,192	1899	1,079,438	1,055,094	1927	3,720,555	3,609,193	1955	28,360,149	27,613,983
1872	681,097	674,280	1900	1,223,557	1,198,328	1928	3,650,487	3,533,228	1956	28,751,375	27,956,627
1873	695,266	687,705	1901	1,299,806	1,273,616	1929	3,841,494	3,718,071	1957	29,028,161	28,183,411
1874	718,978	710,717	1902	1,357,408	1,330,194	1930	3,646,735	3,517,441	1958	29,059,765	28,164,175
1875	697,099	688,192	1903	1,478,915	1,450,534	1931	3,970,004	3,835,079	1959	29,689,473	28,741,655
1876	655,936	646,448	1904	1,549,972	1,520,393	1932	4,789,228	4,648,677	1960	29,718,400	28,718,113
1877	647,269	637,215	1905	1,603,577	1,572,770	1933	4,989,805	4,843,488	1961	29,935,320	28,882,119
1878	638,635	628,040	1906	1,714,021	1,681,857	1934	4,939,275	4,786,652	1962	31,111,156	30,003,392
1879	622,353	611,250	1907	1,806,483	1,772,819	1935	5,104,831	4,945,661	1963	32,645,149	31,481,028
1880	672,161	660,465	1908	1,979,882	1,944,603	1936	5,732,721	5,566,156	1964	34,582,138	33,357,207
1881	717,620	705,272	1909	2,004,629	1,967,859	1937	5,906,528	5,732,087	1965	36,185,103	34,896,643
1882	730,786	717,745	1910	2,050,245	2,011,874	1938	5,893,478	5,711,323	1966	38,428,060	37,071,749
1883	778,294	764,575	1911	2,115,333	2,075,316	1939	6,445,071	6,254,924	1967	40,358,442	38,930,032
1884	785,642	771,302	1912	2,154,592	2,112,920	1940	7,174,145	6,975,300	1968	42,668,776	41,163,435
1885	803,570	788,673	1913	2,257,815	2,214,292	1941	8,852,232	8,642,167	1969	45,482,094	43,894,424
1886	755,901	740,503	1914	2,279,116	2,233,721	1942	11,563,603	11,337,818	1970	48,559,865	46,881,621
1887	788,039	772,092	1915	2,002,784	1,955,567	1943	16,461,966	16,212,576	1971	52,258,888	50,482,192
1888	817,774	801,217	1916	2,197,030	2,147,713	1944	21,408,918	21,130,404			

*Currency in circulation figures differ from those published because these include only paper currency of denominations of $1 through $1,000 inclusive. In addition, in the years after 1961, currency subtracted from published figures by the Treasury have been added back (see fn. 2). The reader may reconcile the above series with the published currency in circulation figures by subtracting the following amounts from the above series—1962: $1,000,000; 1963-1964: $59,000,000; 1965: $132,100,000; 1966: $144,436,000; 1967: $294,436,000; 1968-1971: $344,436,000.

for currency listed in circulation have Treasury loss corrections added back into the series.[10] The figures in Table 3 indicate that as of 1971, $1,776,696,000, or approximately 3.4 percent of the amount listed in circulation, was irretrievably lost. This is approximately five times the value of currency presently removed from the currency circulation figures as "irretrievably lost." The figures also indicate that currency lost has accounted for between 1.2 percent and 3.6 percent of the currency listed in circulation during the first seventy years of the twentieth century. Loss rates in the year from June 30, 1970, to June 30, 1971, ranged from .006909 for $1 notes to .000051 for $1,000 notes. Total currency lost during this same year was approximately $98 million, or roughly 0.2 percent of the value of currency in circulation. Estimates indicate that over the last 25 years cumulative currency lost as a percentage of currency in circulation has risen from 1.2 percent to 3.4 percent. This was due to a relatively high and rising average annual currency loss rate and, at least until very recently, a slow rate of increase in currency in circulation. The average annual currency loss rate has increased because the effects of increasing prices, which lower the real value of currency and raise the loss rate, have out-weighed a shift in distribution by denomination which has tended to lower the average currency loss rate. Table 4 gives the distribution of currency in circulation and currency lost as of June 30, 1971 by denomination. These figures indicate that more than 60 percent of the value of all currency lost was lost in $10 and $20 notes.

Two experiments were run to determine the likely size of the errors involved in the estimates of currency losses. One source of error is a result of the semilogarithmic real value equation used to estimate currency losses. The standard error for that equation is approximately 17 percent of the weighted average of the loss rate estimates. Two additional calculations of total currency losses were made, one with all loss rates raised 17.3 percent and another with all loss rates lowered by the same percentage. These runs give estimates of total currency lost as of June 1971 of $2,068,351,000 and $1,480,593,000. These estimates are 4.0 and 2.8 percent of the currency listed in circulation as of that date. The pattern of currency losses over the period 1861–1971 is very similar for all the runs. The change made to correct for negative loss rates was also varied to measure the significance of this factor in the total loss estimates. One run for total currency losses was made assuming that all notes whose real value placed them in the dotted portion of the curve in Figure 1 had a loss rate equal to that given at the tangent point between the curve and the straight line out of the origin (.00154), while a second run assumed that all these notes had a zero loss rate. Both assumptions represent extremes regarding loss rates for notes in this range of real values. These assumptions give total

---

[10] For a more complete description of the adjustment see the footnote to Table 3.

TABLE 4

ESTIMATES OF CURRENCY LOST BY DENOMINATIONS THROUGH JUNE 30, 1971
(In Thousands of Dollars)

	$1	$2	$5	$10	$20	$50	$100	$500	$1000	Total
					Denomination					
					Currency Listed in Circulation*					
	2,442,299	142,534	3,181,320	9,178,426	19,173,012	5,081,945	12,604,047	210,078	245,227	52,258,888
					Currency in Circulation Adjusted for Losses					
	2,176,397	123,563	2,901,342	8,628,859	18,636,081	5,022,513	12,539,310	209,420	244,707	50,482,192
					Currency Lost					
	265,902	18,971	279,978	549,567	536,931	59,432	64,737	658	520	1,776,696

*See fn., Table 3.

currency lost figures as of June 1971 of $2,120,993,000 and $1,558,190,000, which are respectively 4.1 percent and 3.0 percent of the currency listed in circulation as of that date. The pattern of losses is somewhat different under these two assumptions with the differences being most pronounced in the period before 1900. But even in the run with higher losses, the largest loss estimate in any year is only 4.4 percent of the amount listed in circulation. The results indicate that substantial changes in the assumptions involved in computing currency losses have minor effects on total currency losses.

Implications of Results

This paper has presented evidence supporting a strong relationship between currency loss rates and the real value of currency. Using this relationship to compute a series for currency in circulation adjusted for losses suggests that the general disregard by economists for currency irretrievably lost has probably not had a significant impact on empirical studies utilizing currency figures. The estimates imply that lost currency presently accounts for about 3.4 percent of all currency listed in circulation, and that the largest error over the 110-year period examined was 3.6 percent—which translates into less than a 1 percent error in narrowly defined money. Even with substantial changes in the assumptions involved in calculating currency losses, losses are confined to a range between 2.5 percent and 4.5 percent. An examination of the time series for currency in circulation adjusted for currency losses reveals that the patterns are not very different from the published series over the period 1860–1971. The mean absolute percentage change for the adjusted currency in circulation series is 8.17 percent and the same figure for the unadjusted series is 8.10 percent. The average absolute difference between the two series for the annual percentage change in currency is 0.12 percent and the maximum difference in any year is 0.64 percent.

The estimates of lost currency presented in this paper are based on evidence obtained from the behavior of old series currency notes. The most recent of these notes were issued shortly before 1920. The application of relationships derived from the behavior of these notes to more recent currency figures assumes that the relationship between currency losses and the real value of notes has remained invariant. The possibility exists that the relationship may have changed significantly due to such factors as changes in the extent to which U.S. currency circulates outside the United States or changes in the activities of currency collectors. As yet, no type of new series notes has reached a stage at which currency losses may be estimated with great accuracy. Some experimentation with new series Silver Certificates indicates that the currency loss estimates given in this paper may err on the low side for this type of currency.[11] However, additional testing must await a time when loss estimates for new series notes may be established more accurately.

APPENDIX: DATA SOURCES

Currency Held by the Public

Currency held by the public is defined as currency in circulation minus vault cash held by commercial banks and mutual savings banks. The figures for currency held by the public are derived by applying estimates for percentage of currency in circulation held as vault cash to figures for currency in circulation broken down by denomination and type.

Currency in Circulation

1860-1928: *U.S. Treasury, Annual Report of the Secretary of the Treasury, 1928.* Washington, D.C.: G.P.O., 1928. Pp. 554–55.

1929-1951: Idem. *Paper Currency of Each Denomination Outstanding* (published monthly).

1952-1965: Idem. *Circulation Statement of United States Money* (published monthly).

1966-1971: Idem. *Statement of United States Currency and Coin* (published monthly).

The breakdown of currency in circulation into denomination and type is available from the author on request.

Percentage of Currency in Circulation Held as Vault Cash

Where figures for December 31 are not available, estimates are interpolated so as to fall at the end of the calendar year. Estimates for the years 1943–1971 also have minor adjustments to take account of vault cash held by mutual savings banks.

1861-1865: Milton Friedman and Anna Jacobson Schwartz. *Monetary Statistics of the United States.* New York: National Bureau of Economic Research, 1970. Table 13, pp. 224–25.

1866-1906: Ibid. Table 20, pp. 340–41.

1907-1942: Ibid. Table 27, pp. 402–13.

1943-1960: Idem. *A Monetary History of the United States, 1867-1960.*

---

[11] Application of the semilogarithmic real value regression in Table 2 to data on new series Silver Certificates gives a total loss estimate of approximately $240 million while currency listed in circulation is approximately $417 million and declining at only about $2.5 million a year. On the basis of the behavior of other notes in the period after their issuance was stopped, these figures would appear to indicate that the regression has under-estimated losses of new series Silver Certificates.

226 : MONEY, CREDIT, AND BANKING

Princeton, N.J.: National Bureau of Economic Research, Princeton University Press, 1963. Table A-1, pp. 717–21 and Table A-2, pp. 743–44.

1961–1971: Board of Governors of the Federal Reserve System. *Federal Reserve Bulletin*. Washington, D.C. (published monthly).

Consumer Price Index (1926 = 1.00)

1860–1957: U.S. Bureau of the Census. *Historical Statistics of the United States, Colonial Times to 1957*. Washington, D.C.: G.P.O., 1960. 1860–1879: *Consumer Price Index* (Hoover), p. 127. 1890–1913: *Cost-of-Living Index* (Rees), p. 127. 1914–1957: *Consumer Price Index* (Bureau of Labor Statistics), pp. 125–26.

1958–1971: Bureau of Labor Statistics. *U.S. Consumer Price Index.*

[14]

THE INCOME EFFECTS OF THE SOURCES OF MONETARY CHANGE: AN HISTORICAL APPROACH*

MICHAEL DAVID BORDO
Carleton University

This paper attempts to answer the question — does the way in which the quantity of money is introduced into the economic system matter or only the amount introduced? The question of the importance of the sources of monetary change has become a key issue between Monetarists and Neo-Keynesians. The approach of the paper is to compare different periods in U.S. monetary history over the time span 1834-1914, which exhibited different sources of monetary change, to see whether the source of monetary change significantly affected the relationship between money and income between these periods, as well as within them. In the majority of cases examined, the income effects of the sources of monetary change were found to be insignificant.

Does the way in which money is introduced into the economic system matter? Or only the amount of money introduced? In other words, do the sources of change in the quantity of money have significant effects on the level of nominal income independent of the effects of changes in the quantity of money?

The quantity of money in any country at any moment of time can be viewed as the sum of high powered money or base money (H) and money created by banks $(B \equiv (M-H))$, i.e., $M^s \equiv H + (M-H) \equiv H + B$. A change in the amount of money can come either from a change in high powered money (H) or from a change in bank created money (B). In turn, a change in high powered money may have different sources such as: changes in the monetary gold stock; the government's budget deficit or surplus; open market operations; government purchases of silver; government accumulation or refunding of its debt and changes in government deposit balances in commercial banks. Finally, a change in B can be produced by the extension of loans to individuals and by the purchase or sale of government or other securities.

The basic question to be answered in this paper is whether a given change in the stock of money consisting of different combinations of high

*This study is derived from my doctoral dissertation at the University of Chicago (1972). I would like to thank the following for their help: Milton Friedman, Robert Fogel, Richard Zecher, Benjamin Klein, Anna J. Schwartz, Ehsan Choudhri, Soo Bin Park and an anonymous referee at Economic Inquiry. I, of course, take full responsibility for any errors. Financial assistance was generously provided by the Canada Council. Earlier versions of this paper were presented at the Econometric Society Meetings in Toronto (Dec. 1972), at the Sixth Annual Cliometrics Conference at Madison, Wisconsin (April 1973) and at Simon Fraser University (October 1973).

powered money and bank created money will lead to the same level of nominal income. In a broader context, when high powered money can be affected in other ways, a similar question is whether the same change in high powered money produced in different ways will lead to the same level of income. Finally, we ask whether a given change in B produced by bank loans will have the same effect as one produced by bank investments.

The approach of the paper is to examine five distinct subperiods in U.S. monetary history over the period 1834-1914, each of which exhibited clearly different sources of monetary change ranging from gold discoveries to greenbacks to bank credit, to determine the extent to which the source of monetary change affected the income money relationship both between the periods as well as within them.

Section I briefly relates the paper to a recent debate in monetary theory. Section II presents the data and briefly describes the historical periods covered in the paper. Section III examines the interperiod evidence. Section IV uses a simple regression to test whether the different sources of monetary change are statistically significant within each of the subperiods as well as within several longer composite periods. Finally, Section V is a brief conclusion.

The results of this study indicate that in the majority of periods examined the effects of the sources of monetary change were insignificant, while in those cases where significant effects were detected they tended to be unimportant.

I. THE DEBATE OVER THE EFFECTS OF THE SOURCES OF MONETARY CHANGE

The question of the importance of the sources of monetary change is ancient, traceable at least to Richard Cantillon (1755). Later it is clearly stated in the works of J. S. Mill.[1] As well, it plays an important role in the monetary theory of the Austrians, especially Menger and Hayek.[2]

---

1. The issues of a Government paper, even when not permanent, will raise prices; because Governments usually issue their paper in purchases for consumption. If issued to pay off a portion of the national debt, we believe they would have no such effect. (Mill, 1844, p. 589).
Later he states that the way in which money is first introduced will have temporary effects on real magnitudes.

> . . . it is of course possible that the influx of money might take place through the medium of some new class of consumers, or in such a manner as to alter the proportions of different classes of consumers to one another, so that a greater share of the national income than before would thenceforth be expended in some articles, and a smaller in others; exactly as if a change had taken place in the tastes and wants of the community. If this were the case, then until production had accommodated itself in this change in the comparative demand for different things, there would be a real alteration in values, and some things would rise in price more than others, while some perhaps would not rise at all. *These effects, however, would evidently proceed, not from the mere increase of money, but from necessary circumstances attending it.* (Emphasis mine.) (Mill, 1917, pp. 491-492).

2. See O. Morgenstern (1972, p. 1184).

Recently it has become a focus of debate between Neo-Keynesians and Modern Quantity theorists. In a recent symposium between M. Friedman and several of his critics, J. Tobin states, "If all kinds of debt matter, then the genesis of new money makes a difference" (Tobin, 1972, p. 862). Friedman in his reply states "it may be that, at least for the Neo-Keynesians, I was mistaken in regarding their treatment of price flexibility as the main issue between them and the monetarists. Perhaps the emphasis on the first round effect is the main issue and their treatment of price flexibility a minor corollary." (Friedman, 1972, p. 917).[3]

For Tobin and the Neo-Keynesians, the source of new money matters because of possible effects on the community's financial portfolio comprising high powered money, long- and short-term government debt, private debt, bank creaated money and physical capital.[4] The composition and magnitude of a change in the community's portfolio is important because of its impact on the supply price of capital *(SPC)*, the rate of return investors require in order to hold equity capital in their portfolios.[5] The change in the *SPC* will generate an excess demand for the existing capital stock and lead to net investment.[6]

Tobin distinguishes three different composition or first round effects accompanying a change in the money supply.

The first is the wealth effect of a change in the stock of net monetary wealth, comprising high powered money and government debt, holding both the composition of net monetary wealth and bank created money constant.[7] If we conceive of a framework where the *SPC* is determined by the intersection of a liquidity preference curve between net monetary wealth and capital and the given stock of net monetary wealth, then e.g. an increase in *H* caused by say a gold discovery would lead to a movement along the liquidity preference curve and a fall in the *SPC*.

Secondly, a change in bank created money holding net monetary wealth constant will shift the liquidity preference curve, e.g. an increase in bank deposits will lower the curve and reduce the *SPC* in the same way that the introduction of a money substitute reduces the demand for money. The extent of the shift in the curve depends on which assets are purchased by banks: reserves, private claims or government securities.

---

3. By the 'first round effect' Friedman means the effects of the sources of monetary change rather than the initial as opposed to the permanent effects of monetary change. In this paper we will use the terms 'first round' and 'sources of monetary change' interchangeably.

4. See Tobin (1961, 1963), Tobin and Brainard (1963, 1968).

5. See Tobin (1961, p. 35).

6. See Witte (1963).

7. It is important to note that Tobin and his colleagues assume prices to be rigid and hence do not distinguish between nominal and real magnitudes in their analysis which is what enables them to compare directly monetary wealth and physical capital; e.g., in (1968, p. 101) Tobin and Brainard take the replacement value of physical assets to be equal to one and use it as the numeraire of the system.

Tobin calls this substitution effect the money effect.

Thirdly, a change in the composition of a given stock of monetary wealth will, ceteris paribus, lead to a shift in the liquidity preference curve, e.g. an open market purchase of short-term government debt with demand debt will shift the curve downward. This also represents a substitution effect.[8]

The impact of the substitution effect on the *SPC* depends on the elasticity of substitution between the assets involved. In general an asset swap involving close substitutes will have less of an effect on their relative yields and hence on the *SPC* than a swap between poor substitutes.

Thus, according to this approach a gold discovery should have a stronger impact on nominal income because of the wealth effect than an open market purchase of existing government securities of similar magnitude, while the extension of bank created money to finance new investment should have a greater impact than the purchase of existing securities.

In Tobin's words:

> You cannot repeat the consequences for employment, income and spending of newly mined gold by purchasing a million dollars of old government securities — even though both operations increase high powered money by a million dollars. (Tobin, 1965, p. 467).

and

> I would expect a) [commercial loans by banks to private borrowers to stimulate more spending on GNP than does] b) [exchange of bank certificates of deposit for Treasury bills previously held by the public.] (brackets mine). If so, the same *M* packs a bigger wallop if it is the counterpart of operations like a) than if it is the results of asset swaps like b). You will never detect the difference if you confine your attention to the liabilities of the banking system. (Tobin, 1965, p. 467).

By contrast the modern quantity theory of money emphasizes a more comprehensive portfolio comprising the stocks of all assets from government securities to human capital. As a result, it downplays the singular importance attached by the Neo-Keynesians to the effects of changes in the portfolio of financial assets. Instead, the substitution process affects the relative prices of all goods and factors rather than just the prices of

---

8. See D. Fand (1969, pp. 556-87).
   Tobin's distinction between the wealth effect of a change in monetary wealth, holding bank money constant and the money or substitution effect of a change in bank money holding monetary wealth constant is identical to the Gurley and Shaw (1960) and Patinkin (1965) distinction between the effects of changes in outside money and inside money.

financial assets and capital.[9] This extensive nature of the capital account implies the relative unimportance of changes in any one type of financial asset relative to any other. Thus, e.g., a change in government short-term debt relative to certificates of deposit should not have a substantially different impact on the level of income than a change in savings and loan shares relative to ordinary time deposits.

In addition to deemphasizing the importance of the particular assets involved in the substitution process, this approach also deemphasizes the importance of the wealth effect because of the difficulty of distinguishing between monetary wealth and other components of the capital account.[10] Moreover, special emphasis is placed on the sum of currency and deposits *(M)* rather than on the larger collection of financial assets because of the more stable relationship between the stock of money and nominal income than between any other combination of financial assets and nominal income.[11]

This approach does not deny that there may be a first round effect— that is an empirical question. It can rationalize its absence but is not contradicted by its presence provided the first round effect is not dominant.

In sum, there appears to be little difference in the theoretical frameworks of the two approaches. Whatever differences exist may be resolved by attempts to answer empirical questions of the sort posed by this study.

As Friedman states:

> . . . on reflection Tobin will undoubtedly agree that the crucial issue is not whether government interest bearing time debt is of any significance but whether it is of enough significance to introduce significant error into a relation between money and income—or, put differently, whether knowledge of the sources of change in money permits an economically and statistically significant improvement in predictions of the future course of income. (Friedman, 1972, p. 922).

II. THE HISTORICAL PERIODS

The five historical periods examined in this study are: 1834-42, 1843-59, 1869-78, 1879-96 and 1897-1914.

---

9. See Friedman and Schwartz (1969), Friedman and Meiselman (1963).

10. In addition, on purely empirical grounds, G. Morrison (1965, pp. 136-146) points out that the wealth effect can only be trivial, since if you assume the interest rate relating permanent income to wealth as 10 per cent, and the marginal propensity to consume from permanent income as .8, then the marginal propensity to consume from a change in wealth is .08 which is not very large.

11. Whether we include demand deposits or demand deposits plus time deposits in our definition of money is an empirical question — that combination which has the closest relationship to nominal income will be the most acceptable. A. Marty (1961, pp. 56-62) points out that although it is true that the government can determine the price level by controlling the nominal quantity of any particular asset, it should operate on assets among which the degree of substitution is high and which are complements relative to other assets; whether monetary wealth serves this function more than currency plus demand deposits, or plus demand and time deposits, is an empirical question.

The first period 1834-42 is made up of two episodes combined for purposes of convenience:[12] 1834-37 an inflation traditionally associated with the expansionary economic policies of Andrew Jackson;[13] 1838-42 a period of deflation and depression associated with widespread bank failures, and general monetary and financial instability.

1843-59 is a period of mild inflation, the first six years represents a recovery from the previous deflation, while the remaining eleven years is the era of the California and Australian gold discoveries, when much of the new money entering the economic system consisted of newly mined gold.

1869-78 is the greenback period when the U.S. had a flexible exchange rate with the rest of the world.[14] This period of deflation is interesting to us because there was virtually no change in the stock of high powered money over the period so that all of the change in the stock of money was produced by and consisted of bank created money.

1879-96 is a period of worldwide deflation. In this period the country was once again part of the international specie standard. Here much of the change in M was caused by changes in the monetary gold stock as well as by government silver purchases.

Finally, 1897-1914 is a period of inflation fueled largely by important gold discoveries in Alaska and South Africa as well as by a rapid expansion of the banking system.

Table 1 presents a number of important features of our five periods as well as the entire period 1834-1914 and two major subperiods: 1834-59 and 1869-1914.

Section A presents for each period the average percentage change per year in the money supply, high powered money, bank created money, the price level, nominal and real income. Section B presents the average level of income velocity of circulation as well as three measures of the composition of the stock of money and its two components H and B: the average ratio of high powered money to money, the average ratio of the monetary gold stock to high powered money and the average ratio of loans to bank earning assets. Sections C through E present the division of a change in the stock of money between its components H and B as well as the sources of change of each of H and B. Finally, Section F presents a measure of

12. Since I later run regressions using yearly data with at least two independent variables, a four year period such as 1834-37 would not have contained enough degrees of freedom so I combined it with 1838-42, thereby increasing the number of observations to nine.

13. Recently, however, a number of economists (Macesich 1960 and Temin 1969) have attributed the inflation to increases in the money supply produced by specie inflows as the U.S. adjusted to external factors required by her adherence to the international specie standard.

14. It is important to note that I omitted the Civil War decade 1860-68 because of the lack of both monetary and physical volume data. This period would have been most interesting to study because it was a period of substantial inflation fueled almost entirely by government paper money issues.

TABLE 1
A Description of the Period 1834-1914

PERIOD	1834-42 (1)	1843-59 (2)	1869-78 (3)	1879-96 (4)	1897-1914 (5)	1834-1914 (6)	1834-59 (7)	1869-1914 (8)
Number of Years	8	16	9	17	17	80	25	45
A. Percentage change per year in:								
(1) Money Supply	1.8	8.1	2.5	5.3	7.5	5.8	5.1	5.6
(2) High Powered Money	8.4	6.2	0.0	3.3	4.8	5.5	7.1	3.3
(3) Bank Created Money	-1.9	10.2	5.4	6.8	8.5	5.9	4.0	7.1
(4) Nominal Income	3.5	6.2	1.1	1.7	5.2	4.2	5.5	3.2
(5) Real Income	2.3	4.9	4.4	2.7	3.2	4.4	4.3	3.5
(6) Prices	1.4 (-1.2)	1.3 (1.5)	-3.3	-1.0	2.0	(0.1)	1.2 (0.2)	-.3
B. Average Level of:								
(7) V (ratio)	6.9	7.6	5.0	3.5	2.3	5.0	7.5	3.4
(8) H/M (ratio)	.35	.45	.48	.40	.34	.36	.43	.33
(9) Gold/H (ratio)	1.0	1.05	.14	.41	.50	.62	1.04	.38
(10) Loans (ratio) Earning Assets	.96	.93	.66 (.86)	.80 (.89)	.78 (.81)	.83 (.89)	.95	.76 (.85)
C. Fraction of the change in the stock of money consisting of a change in:								
(11) High Powered Money	1.69	.39	0	.20	.17	.21	.51	.18
(12) Bank Created Money	-.69	.61	1.00	.80	.83	.79	.49	.82
D. Fraction of change in high powered money (total change = 1.00) consisting of change in:								
(13) Monetary Gold Stock	1.25	.95	2.82	.51	.69	.55	1.02	.52
(14) National Bank Notes			.23	-.15	.26			.15
(15) Silver Purchases			2.90	.71	.02			.19
(16) Other Government Operations	-.25	.05	-4.95	-.07	.03	.45	-.02	.14

512   ECONOMIC INQUIRY

TABLE 1 (Continued)

PERIOD	1834-42 (1)	1843-59 (2)	1869-78 (3)	1879-96 (4)	1897-1914 (5)	1834-1914 (6)	1834-59 (7)	1869-1914 (8)
E. Fraction of Change in Bank Earning Assets (loans plus investments) (total change = 1.00) consisting of a change in:								
(17) Loans	0	.92	1.04 (1.10)	1.25 (1.14)	.77 (.80)	.77 (.81)	.83	.79 (.81)
(18) Investments	1.00	.08	-.04 (-.10)	-.25 (-.14)	.23 (.20)	.23 (.19)	.17	.21 (.19)
F. The Nominal Money Elasticity of Income								
(19)	.576	.741	.459	.248	.781	.666	.956	.591

Sources by line:

(1) 1834-59, M. Friedman and A. Schwartz, (1970), Table 13, p. 216; 1869-1914, M. Friedman and A. Schwartz, (1963), Table A-1, p. 704.

(2) 1834-59, Friedman and Schwartz, (1970), Table 13, p. 216; 1869-1914, Friedman and Schwartz, (1963), Table B-3.

(3) 1834-59, Friedman and Schwartz, (1970), Table 13, p. 216; 1869-1914, Friedman and Schwartz, (1963), Tables A-1 and B-3.

(4) 1834-59, GNP series in 1860 prices from data supplied by R. Gallman from worksheets underlying Gallman (1966) "Gross National Product in the United States 1834-1909." This series was then inflated by the Warren Pearson wholesale price index adjusted to Gallman's underlying implicit price trend. 1869-1914, Gallman NNP Variant III from unpublished data at the National Bureau of Economic Research.

(5) 1834-59, Gallman's GNP series in 1860 prices; 1867-1914, Gallman's NNP Variant III in 1929 prices.

(6) 1834-59, Warren Pearson's wholesale price index adjusted to Gallman trend and in brackets the Warren Pearson wholesale index; 1869-1914, NNP Variant III implicit price deflator.

(1) - (6) Continuously compounded—the change in the natural logarithm of the variable over each period was divided by the number of years and multiplied by 100.

(7) Series underlying (5) divided by (1).

(8) Same as (1) and (2).

(9) 1834-59, total specie stock and high powered money (specie outside the Treasury) from Friedman and Schwartz, (1970), Table 13, p. 216; 1875-1914, from P. Cagan, (1965), Table F-7, p. 340; 1869-74 from data sources underlying Table F-7. For the data used, see M. Bordo (1972) Appendix II, Table 14.

(10) Loans divided by the sum of loans and investments. Items in brackets exclude national bank bonds from investments. Data: a) 1834-59. From Comptroller of the Currency Annual Report, reprinted in *Historical Statistics*, 1961, p. 624, for all banks (state banks, private banks and mutual savings banks). b) 1869-96, national banks only, from Federal Reserve Board, (1944), p. 20. c) 1897-1914, all commercial banks (national banks and state commercial banks) from Federal Reserve Board, 1955, p. 35-36.

TABLE 1 (Continued)

Sources by line (continued):

All commercial bank data which is comparable to Friedman and Schwartz's money supply series is only available beginning in 1896, so I was faced with the dilemma of which series to use for 1869-95. For the period 1834-59 there was no choice open to me. My criteria for using national bank data as a proxy for all commercial bank data rather than the Comptroller's All Bank series was based on a comparison of the loan to investment ratio for national banks, state banks, non national banks, all banks and all commercial banks for the period 1896-1914. It was found that the national bank ratio most clearly approximated the state bank ratio and hence the commercial bank ratio which led me to use that ratio for the early period.

The bracketed entries exclude national bank notes from the bonds backing national bank notes in the post Civil War period because we have been defining high powered money to include national bank notes (see M. Bordo, Appendix II, Table 11) and therefore it would not be consistent with this definition to include the bonds backing a component of H as a component of $(M-H)$. As a proxy for the bonds backing national bank notes I used estimates of national bank notes outstanding *(Historical Statistics,* 1961, Series X61, p. 627), on the assumption that national bank notes were 100 percent government bond backed. This assumption produces too low an estimate for eligible bonds for the period before 1900 when national banks could only issue notes up to 90 percent of the free value of their eligible bonds. Thus to be strictly accurate any excess of the value of eligible bonds over notes outstanding is really not a duplication of H and should not be included.

For the data used in this line and for the comparison of loan investment ratios, see M. Bordo, (1972), Appendix II, Tables 15 and 16, and Figure 5.

(11) - (12) The total change in high powered money and bank credit from beginning to end of the period divided by the total change in the money stock.

(13) - (16) To calculate the sources of change in high powered money I follow the approach used by Cagan (1965) Appendix F-5 and F-6. He defines the sources of change in high powered money before 1914 as equal to the sum of changes in the monetary gold stock, changes in national bank note liabilities, Treasury silver purchases, changes in debt, the budget surplus or deficit, changes in Treasury deposits in commercial banks and miscellaneous accounts. Bordo (1972) Appendix II, Table 21, extends Cagan's original estimates which began in 1875 back to 1869. In addition, Bordo (1972) Appendix II, Table 19, gives the sources of change in high powered money for the period 1834-59 using a very similar approach.

For the pre-Civil War period I isolated two key sources of change in high powered money: changes in the monetary specie stock, and government operations, where high powered money is defined as total specie outside the Treasury.

Changes in the monetary specie stock are caused mainly by a) specie flows to finance deficits or surpluses in the Balance of Payments Accounts, and b) domestic gold production. Bordo (1972) Appendix II, Table 20, gives the breakdown of the monetary specie stock into these components for this period.

Government operations is the aggregation of a) the surplus or deficit, b) changes in debt and c) changes in government deposits in state banks. Before the Civil War, the Treasury had a tendency to run a surplus, since government expenditures were virtually constant while government revenues, derived mainly from land sales and tariffs (payable only in specie), varied with the level of income. This surplus would tend to deflate the economy by reducing the stock of high powered money, ceteris paribus. The resultant fall in the price level would then lead to an offsetting gold flow. This process was mitigated by two forces: a) the government would use the surplus to retire its debt, thus leading to a rise in high powered money and b) it would deposit part of the surplus in its accounts in the state banking system. The latter offset ceased to work after the establishment of the Independent Treasury system in 1846. After that date, a dollar taken from H and deposited in a subtreasury branch meant a dollar reduction in H.

In the post Civil War period, I isolated the effects of changes in national bank notes and Treasury purchases of silver on high powered money, in addition to changes in gold and government. Data: 1834-59, see Bordo, Table 19, Appendix II; 1869-1914, see Bordo, Table 21, Appendix II. The fraction of change is derived by dividing the change of the variable from beginning to end of the period by the change in high powered money.

(17) - (18) The total change in loans is divided by the total change in the sum of loans plus investments (earning assets). Items in brackets exclude national bank bonds from investments.

(19) The coefficient B_1 from the regression: $\log Y = B_0 + B_1 \log M + e$, taken from Table 2. All the coefficients are significant at the five percent level.

the relationship between the nominal quantity of money and nominal income — the money elasticity of income, which is the regression coefficient from a log linear regression of income on money.[15]

Section A speaks for itself. There are considerable differences in the rate of monetary growth across each of the five periods except for the two inflationary episodes: 1843-59 and 1897-1914. At the same time, the growth in the quantity of money parallels growth in nominal income while growth in the two components of money, H and B, differ between every period.

Section B contains a number of interesting features. First, V falls considerably over the five periods with the exception of the second period. The secular fall in V can be explained by the argument of Friedman and Schwartz (1963) that real cash balances can be regarded as a luxury good with an income elasticity greater than one, and also by the rapid expansion of the banking system which raised the return to and lowered the cost of holding money, particularly deposits. The rise in the 1840's reflects a decline in the public's holding of real cash balances following the suspension of specie payments in 1837, the panic of that year and 1839, and the large number of bank failures in that period.

Second, H/M, the inverse of the money supply multiplier, here representing the composition of a dollar, varied considerably across the five periods. It rose between the first and second periods primarily because of the dramatic decline in importance of the Second Bank of the United States between 1834 and 1841 and a large number of bank failures in the early 1840's. This rise was reversed after the Civil War with improved banking conditions commonly associated with the institution of the National Banking System in 1864. As well, over the entire period 1869-1914 there is a close correlation between H/M and V. Klein (1973) argues that this reflects a close positive relationship between the own rate of return on money and the demand for money.

Third, G/H, representing the division of a dollar of H between gold and other sources, varied considerably. It fell sharply after the Civil War, reflecting the U.S. abandonment of the gold standard in favour of greenbacks, while the subsequent increase reflects efforts to restore specie payments. After 1879 the ratio remained relatively stable as the country adjusted to the rules of the gold standard except for the 1890's when a series of adverse balances of payments and gold outflows prompted some sterilizing actions by the Treasury.

Finally, the L/EA ratio, representing the composition of a dollar of B, declined steadily throughout the period, reflecting the increased desirability of government and other securities as the capital market improved.

15. Log refers to natural logarithms throughout the study.

Sections C through E reveal considerable diversity between the sources of change in M across the five subperiods.

In Section C, the fraction of change in M consisting of a change in H is between .2 and .4 in three of the five periods as well as over the entire period. By contrast, the overwhelming importance of change in H in the period 1834-42 can be explained by the difficulties experienced by the commercial banks during the last three years of that period, whereas the negligible influence of changes in H in the period 1869-78 reflects the effects of a deliberate attempt by the then Secretary of the Treasury (McCulloch) to reduce the stock of greenbacks, created to help finance the Civil War, in an attempt to deflate the economy and restore specie payments.

In Section D, changes in the monetary gold stock represent the key source of change in H in both the pre Civil War periods as well as in 1869-78, while silver purchases were most important in 1879-96. In Section E, loans proved to be the largest fraction of change in earning assets with only one exception: 1834-42.[16]

Finally, in Section F, the money elasticity of income varies considerably across the five subperiods with the exception again of the two inflationary episodes. Indeed a Chow test to determine whether the nominal income money regression changed over time, revealed significant differences at the one percent level in seven out of ten pairwise comparisons of the five subperiods.[17]

III. THE INTERPERIOD EVIDENCE

The data presented in Table 1 allows us to conduct a crude interperiod test of the importance of the first round. By comparing the different measures of composition, as well as the sources of monetary change with the money elasticity of income in row (19) we can determine whether differences in the size of the elasticities between periods are related to differences in the size of the ratios between periods.

A comparison of row (19), the money elasticity of income, with row (8), the average ratio of high powered money to money, representing the

---

16. The different result for 1834-42 is evident in a very substantial decline in the loan investment ratio in the period 1838-42. One could argue that either the panic of 1837 and 1838 and widespread financial collapse led to the substitution of cash and government securities for private loans in bank's portfolios, or that the data underlying the extremely high loan investment ratios of 1834-37 are completely unreliable. The significant difference between those four years and the rest of the pre-Civil War period suggests that it is not too unreasonable to put emphasis on the latter explanation.

17. When the comparison is made in real terms, i.e., when I ran the regression:

(2A) $log\ (Y/P) = B_0' + B_1'\ log\ (M/P) + e'$

and tested for the stability of B_1' over time, I found it to be considerably more stable than the nominal equation reported in the text. Indeed there was no significant differences in B_1' between three of the five subperiods: 1843-59, 1869-78 and 1897-1914.

composition of a dollar, reveals virtually no relationship between the size of the elasticities and the composition of money. The most striking thing to notice is that the two periods with most similar ratios, 1834-42 and 1897-1914, have different elasticities. Finally, comparing 1834-42 and 1896-78, both periods with fairly similar elasticities, reveals no similarities in the ratios.

Similarly, if we compare row (19) to row (9), the average ratio of gold to high powered money, and to row (10), the average ratio of loans to earning assets, there appears to be no relationship between elasticities and ratios.

In a different vein, if we examine the direction of changes between successive periods in both the elasticities and the three ratios, somewhat of a pattern emerges. Comparing row (19) to (8) reveals that the average ratio of high powered money to the money stock tends to rise and fall with the money elasticity of income between 1834-42 and 1843-59 and between 1869-78 and 1879-96. When we compare row (19) with row (9), the average ratio of gold to high powered money, we find a positive relationship between every successive period except 1869-78 and 1879-96. Finally, comparing row (19) to row (10), the average ratio of loans to earning assets, rises when the elasticity falls and falls when it rises between every period except 1843-59 and 1869-78.

The rank correlation coefficients between rows (19) and rows (8), (9) and (10), a crude measure of association, are—.50, .60 and .10 respectively, with none being statistically significant at the five percent level.

Finally, a comparison between the money elasticities of income and measures of: the fraction of change in money consisting of a change in high powered money (row (11)); the fraction of change in high powered money consisting of a change in the monetary gold stock (row 13)); and the fraction of change in earning assets consisting of a change in loans (row (17)), reveals even less of an association.

Thus the evidence from Table 1 suggests that movements of the three ratios may conceivably explain the differences in money income elasticities between the periods; however, it is impossible to separate the effects of each of them. The ideal test of the ceteris paribus effects of each of the ratios would be to regress them on the money elasticity of income for different periods. Unfortunately, it is impossible to conduct this test with only five subperiods. To circumvent this problem, in the next section I attempt similar regressions within each of our periods.

IV. THE INTRAPERIOD EVIDENCE

The approach of this section is to estimate a stepwise regression equation to test first for the significance of the composition of the money stock within each period, then for the significance of the composition of high powered money, and finally for the significance of the composition of bank earning assets.

Logically, if the composition of high powered money and the composition of bank created money significantly affect income, then so should the composition of the money stock. This implies that it should be sufficient for us to test only for the significance of the composition of money. However, it is conceivable that the effects of the composition of high powered money and bank created money average out when we compare H and B, making it necessary for us to test for the effects of composition of H and B as well.

Equation (1) represents a simple model to detect possible significant effects of the sources of monetary change:

(1) $log\ Y = B_0 + B_1\ log\ M + B_2\ log\ (H/M) + B_3\ log\ (Gold/H) + B_4\ log\ (Loans/EA) + u.$

The coefficients B_2, B_3 and B_4 represent the ceteris paribus effects of the composition of M, H and B respectively. We test to see whether each of B_2, B_3 and B_4 in turn are significantly different from zero, holding M constant. Initially we take M alone as an independent variable to serve as a benchmark and we run the regression:

(2) $log\ Y = B_0 + B_1\ log\ M + e.$

Next we account for the composition of the money supply in equation:

(3) $log\ Y = B_0 + B_1\ log\ M + B_2\ log\ (H/M) + E.$

If both B_1 and B_2 were significant, then the composition of money would have an effect on income in addition to that of the money stock; if B_2 were insignificant while B_1 were significant, composition would not matter.[18]

If it should turn out that B_2 is significant then we must ask whether this reflects the effects of either the composition of H or the composition of B or both. Moreover, even if B_2 were insignificant, significant composition effects or H and B may be averaged out by this simple test.

Thus I expand (3) into (4) and (1):

(4) $log\ Y = B_0 + B_1\ log\ M + B_2\ log\ (H/M) + B_3\ log\ (Gold/H) + d.$

___

18. In addition, if B_1 were zero yet B_2 were significant and negative, it would indicate that it is the money multiplier alone which is influencing income. If both B_1 and B_2 were significant and of equal magnitude, it would indicate that high powered money alone affects income. Finally, if both B_1 and B_2 were insignificant, then we could conclude that money does not affect income.

These results can be better understood if we perform a series of transformations on our benchmark equation (2) $log\ Y = B_0 + B_1\ log\ M + e.$

This can be broken into (5) $log\ Y = A_0 + A_1\ log\ (M/H) + A_2\ log\ H + E$ where (M/H) represents the money multiplier.

Further, rearranging produces (3) $log\ Y = B_0 + B_1\ log\ M + B_2\ log\ (H/M) + E$ where $B_0 = A_0$, $B_1 = A_2$ and $B_2 = (A_2 - A_1)$.

It can thus be seen e.g. that when $B_2 = 0$, $A_2 = A_1$ and the composition of money does not matter.

(1) $log\ Y = B_0 + B_1\ log\ M + B_2\ log\ (H/M) + B_3\ log\ (Gold/H) + B_4\ log\ (Loans/EA) + u.$

In addition to tests for the statistical significance of composition effects, I ask whether adding another independent variable at each step improves the significance of the regression; whether adding $log\ (H/M)$, $log\ (Gold/H)$ and $log\ (Loans/EA)$ in turn increases the explained variation of the log of nominal income. To answer this question I use the sequential F test based on the Analysis of Variance.

As a rough test of Tobin's framework, a positive and significant B_2 would indicate the presence of the wealth effect of a change in H, ceteris paribus, a negative B_2 the substitution effect of a change in bank created money, ceteris paribus; whereas significant coefficients of B_3 and B_4 would tell us if the portfolio effects of changes in the composition of H and B, respectively, matter.

In this paper I ran the regressions using the levels of logs. A log linear rather than a linear form is used because the linear form does not account for the steady secular decline in velocity over the period 1834-1914 which would produce a steadily decreasing money income multiplier; in addition, the double log specification presents the coefficients as elasticities, allowing us to make comparisons across distant periods. Furthermore, I present the results using levels of the data rather than first differences because of the relatively poor quality of the early national income data which produces poor results when differenced. Nevertheless, although they are less significant, the log difference results (which are available from the author on request) are not substantially different.

An implication of my use of the levels of annual data is that I am testing whether the sources of change in money affect the ultimate equilibrium relationship between money and income. In a sense, the study is concerned with comparative statics rather than dynamics since none of the tests have been designed to determine whether the sources of change in the money supply affect the transmission mechanism between a change in the money supply and the resultant change in income. It is possible that the source of monetary change can affect the transmission mechanism yet have no effect on the final equilibrium level of income.

In addition, the use of annual data, which is all that is available in this period, precludes the detection of significant first round effects occurring in time spans shorter than a year. Finally, the study did not experiment with difficult lag structures, except for a built-in six month lead of money on income produced by the dating of the money and income time series.

As mentioned above, the regressions in this study use historical data which may be less reliable than more recent data. Of special concern is Gallman's national income data, especially before 1880, (see Gallman 1966), and the money supply data before the Civil War (see Rutner 1974). Thus the results reported here should be taken as a rough indication of the presence or absence of composition effects.

Table 2 presents stepwise regressions of equation (1) for each of the five subperiods. For the period 1834-42 we only test for the composition of the stock of money because in that period high powered money was virtually identical to the monetary specie stock and the loan earning asset ratio was very close to unity.

Examining the results of equation (3) for the five periods in Table 2 reveals that in no subperiod does the composition of the money stock matter, but in one period, 1834-42, high powered money alone matters, an understandable result in the light of banking conditions in that period. In addition, the F-test reveals $\log (H/M)$ to add significantly to the regression in only one period, 1834-42.

The results of equation (3) in one sense ends the matter, composition of money effects appear in only one period, 1834-42, the period which was most unstable and with the least reliable data. However, adding the gold high powered money ratio as well as the loan earning asset ratio to the regression should tell us if the tests of equation (6) are too blunt to pick up possible income effects of the composition of high powered money and the composition of bank created money.

Regressions of equation (4) in Table 2 reveal that in none of the four subperiods used for the test did the composition of H matter, nor did it add significantly to the regression.

When the loan earning asset ratio is included in the regression in equation (1), Table 2, the composition of earning assets matter while that of M and H do not in one period: 1879-96; money alone matters in two: 1843-59 and 1897-1914, while neither M, its composition nor the composition of H and earning assets matter in one: 1869-78. Also in 1879-96 the ratio of loans to earning assets adds significantly to the regression.

In brief, with the exception of one period, 1879-96, neither the composition of high powered money nor the composition of earning assets significantly affect the level of income in addition to the effect of the quantity of money.[19]

Next, we combine the five subperiods into four composite periods to see whether the sources of monetary change matter over longer time spans. The periods chosen were: 1834-1914, the entire period; 1843-1914, the entire period omitting 1834-42 because of its unstable nature; 1834-59, the pre-Civil War period; and 1869-1914, the post-Civil War period.[20]

The regression results for these longer periods in Table 3 are in marked contrast to the results for the five subperiods in Table 2.[21] The composi-

19. In addition, I have run the same regressions in real terms, with very similar results. These results are available from the author on request.

20. Because of the special nature of 1834-42 mentioned above I tested only for the effects of the composition of the money stock for the longer periods containing the years 1834-42.

21. The log difference regression results for composite periods are very similar to those using the levels of logs with much of the autocorrelation removed.

TABLE 2

Five Subperiods

A. $LOG\ Y = B_0 + B_1\ LOG\ M + B_2\ LOG\ (H/M) + B_3\ LOG\ (Gold/H) + B_4\ LOG\ (Loans/EA) + u$

Coefficients of Independent Variables (T-Values in Brackets)

PERIOD (SE log Y)	EQUATION	B_0	B_1	B_2	B_3	B_4	$\bar{R}^2$	SEE	DW	F
1834-42 (.1120)	2	4.155 (3.960)*	.5761 (2.896)*				.415	.0857		
	3	5.0407 (6.5924)*	.4792 (3.4749)*	.3631 (3.0625)*			.763	.0578	3.36	9.39*
1843-59 (.3163)	2	3.626 (17.216)*	.7407 (20.531)*				.961	.0624	1.78	
	3	3.6409 (16.991)*	.7473 (17.9254)*	.1453 (.7844)			.962	.0632	1.58	.62
	4	3.3071 (9.2773)*	.8253 (11.4819)*	.1676 (.9107)	-1.0575 (1.1619)		.963	.0624	1.72	.33
	1	3.3265 (9.4531)*	.7884 (10.1638)*	.0616 (.3037)	-.6341 (.6554)	-1.3039 (1.1705)	.964	.0616	2.31	1.34
1869-78 (.0576)	2	5.578 (7.055)*	.4589 (4.256)*				.617	.0356		
	3	6.3526 (1.4443)	.3418 (.5155)	.1236 (.1794)			.608	.0381		1.01
	4	3.2191 (.4578)	.8252 (.7682)	.3526 (.3256)	.0432 (.5909)		.568	.0400		.34
	1	-2.1843 (.3850)	1.2814 (1.5042)	-.4087 (.4737)	-.0960 (1.2169)	-2.9673 (2.4274)	.762	.0297		5.91

continued overleaf

TABLE 2 (Continued)

PERIOD (SE log Y)	EQUATION	B_0	B_1	B_2	B_3	B_4	$\bar{R}^2$	SEE	DW	F
1879-96 (.0878)	2	7.315 (17.965)*	.2477 (4.916)*				.577	.0588	1.47	
	3	6.4404 (6.6390)*	.4023 (2.4591)*	.3982 (.9933)			.576	.0588	1.64	1.00
	4	6.4835 (5.8331)*	.3968 (2.2056)*	.3879 (.9018)	.0091 (.0903)		.546	.0609	1.63	.00
	1	9.8076 (5.6677)*	-.0350 (.1437)	.1704 (.4404)	-.2328 (1.7073)	1.0264 (2.3197)*	.655	.0531	1.29	5.06*
1897-1914	2	2.844 (12.544)*	.7805 (31.600)*				.982	.0395	2.01	
	3	3.030 (5.7751)*	.7445 (7.8858)*	-.1074 (.3958)			.982	.0406	1.92	.15
	4	2.3218 (2.4795)*	.7963 (7.2036)*	-.1302 (.4749)	-.2904 (.9149)		.982	.0408	1.88	.91
	1	2.5205 (2.6677)*	.8306 (7.3022)*	-.0345 (.1213)	-.1336 (.3879)	1.0980 (1.1201)	.982	.0404	1.89	1.26

Notes: a. For data sources and definitions see Appendix to Table 1.

          b. The regression program used did not report *DW* statistics for small periods such as 1834-42 and 1869-78.

          c. $\bar{R}^2$ is the coefficient of determination adjusted for degrees of freedom, *SE log Y* is the standard deviation of the dependent variable, *SEE* is the standard error of estimate, *DW* is the Durbin Watson Statistic.

          d. * signifies statistically significant at the 5 per cent level.

TABLE 3

Composite Periods

A. $LOG\ Y = B_0 + B_1\ LOG\ M + B_2\ LOG\ (H/M) + B_3\ LOG\ (Gold/H) + B_4\ LOG\ (Loans/EA) + u$

Coefficients of Independent Variables (T-Values in Brackets)

PERIOD (SE log Y)	EQUATION	B_0	B_1	B_2	B_3	B_4	$\bar{R}^2$	SEE	DW	F
1834-1914 (.9875)	2	3.935 (44.301)*	.6664 (56.364)*				.978	.1470	.233	
	3	4.0039 (59.3558)*	.7202 (62.6411)*	.4711 (7.446)*			.988	.1109	.448	53.98*
1843-1914 (.7997)	2	4.365 (64.607)*	.6154 (70.819)*				.988	.0910	.492	
	3	4.3057 (61.1276)*	.6436 (42.8640)*	.1625 (2.2701)*			.989	.0880	.524	5.15*
	4	4.3145 (48.7261)*	.6400 (24.0378)*	.1467 (1.2258)	-.0049 (.1651)		.988	.0887	.525	.00
	1	4.3831 (57.7470)*	.5970 (24.8345)*	-.0128 (.1207)	.0817 (2.6846)*	-.7463 (5.007)*	.992	.0748	1.15	25.32*
1834-59 (.4428)	2	2.298 (5.938)*	.9557 (13.452)*				.881	.1527	.49	
	3	3.2927 (10.8586)*	.8789 (18.9790)*	.6627 (5.8403)*			.952	.0990	.787	52.72*
1869-1914 (.4660)	2	4.566 (30.228)*	.5915 (32.909)*				.961	.0923	.42	
	3	3.8421 (6.1434)*	.7267 (6.4454)*	.3861 (1.2510)*			.962	.0918	.478	1.47
	4	3.3207 (4.7234)*	.7917 (6.6645)*	.4719 (1.5275)	-.0638 (1.5367)		.963	.0904	.531	2.37
	1	3.6787 (6.8211)*	.6931 (7.5178)*	.1535 (.6342)	.0253 (.7158)	-.7866 (5.6021)*	.979	.0688	1.38	31.55*

Notes: See Table 2.

tion of money is significant in every case; the composition of high
powered money in one out of two possible cases; and the composition of
earning assets in both possible cases.[22]

In terms of the Tobin framework outlined in Section I, the positive
coefficients for B_2 indicate the presence of a wealth effect accompanying
a change in high powered money, while the significant coefficient for
B_4 detects a substitution effect associated with a change in the composition of bank earning assets.

To which set of results should we attach greater significance? The
subperiods or the composite periods? In general, more weight should be
attached to the longer periods, if they are homogeneous — if they are
made up of subperiods with similar composition effects — because of the
increased degrees of freedom. This suggests that the most important
results for the simple test of the composition of money is the period 1843-
1914, since the other two composite periods when significant composition effects were detected, 1834-59 and 1834-1914, cannot be considered
homogeneous periods because they are a mixture of one period when H
alone matters with others when it does not. Similarly, the most important
results for the test of the composition of high powered money is 1869-
1914, since it is composed of three periods where the composition of H
is insignificant. Furthermore, none of the composite periods where the
composition of earning assets matter can be considered important since
they are not homogeneous periods since each contains one period where
it matters — 1879-96 — and others where it does not.

Finally, in those periods where the source of monetary change matters,
how much does it matter? To answer this question, I compare $\bar{R}^2$ from
the benchmark regression of *log M* on *log Y* with $\bar{R}^2$ from those regressions where the source of monetary change contributed significantly to
the explanation of variation in the dependent variable. In Table 2, first
round effects were sufficiently important to add over five percent to $\bar{R}^2$ in
two cases, 1834-42 and 1879-96. The result for the 1834-42 period, as
mentioned above, rather than demonstrating the importance of the composition of money, reflects the fact that high powered money alone
affected income in that period of monetary instability. In the composite
periods in Table 3, of all the cases with significant F ratios, the inclusion
of the first round effects increased $\bar{R}^2$ by over five percent in one one
period: 1834-59.

V. CONCLUSIONS AND IMPLICATIONS

The results of the regression tests conducted in Section IV suggest that
in at least three out of five independent and economically distinct subperiods in the time span 1834-1914, there do not appear to be any signifi-

22. Again, as in Table 2, when the regressions are run in real terms the results are similar.

cant income effects associated with the sources of change in the money supply. In the other two periods, as well as over several composite periods, significant first round effects were detected but in only three cases could they be considered important enough to increase the explanation of variations in economic activity by over five percent: 1834-42, 1834-59 and 1879-96.

In all three of these periods, the composition of money mattered because of the wealth effect of a change in high powered money, while in the latter period a significant substitution effect from a change in the composition of bank earnings assets was detected.

The intraperiod results in Section IV differ from the interperiod comparisons of Section III which suggest that the sources of monetary change may matter. However, because of the less rigorous nature of the interperiod comparisons, I attach more weight to the latter evidence.

These results for the nineteenth century U.S. experience, though based on less than perfect data, lend support to the case presented by Friedman and Meiselman (1963) and others for the important influence of changes in the money supply in the twentieth century. As well, they complement the findings of Cagan's (1972) study that the first round effects of monetary change on the level of interest rates tend to be unimportant. Finally, the results support those economists who believe that monetary policy should be concerned primarily with changes in the money supply rather than with changes in all of the financial assets in the community's capital account.

REFERENCES

Bordo, Michael, "The Effects of the Sources of Change in the Money Supply on the Level of Economic Activity: An Historical Essay." Unpublished Ph.D. Dissertation, University of Chicago, 1972.

Cagan, P., *Determinants and Effects of Changes in the Stock of Money, 1875-1960*. New York: Columbia University Press, 1965.

_____ , *The Channels of Monetary Effects on Interest Rates*. New York: National Bureau of Economic Research, 1972.

Cantillon, Richard, *Essays on the Nature of Commerce*. London, 1755.

Fand, David, "Keynesian Monetary Theories, Stabilization Policy and the Recent Inflation," *Journal of Money, Credit and Banking*, August 1969, *1*, 556-87.

Friedman, Milton, and Meiselman, David, "The Relative Stability of Monetary Velocity and the Investment Multiplier in the United States." *Commission on Money and Credit, Stabilization Policies*. Englewood Cliffs, N.J.: Prentice Hall, Inc., 1963.

Friedman, Milton, and Schwartz, Anna J., "Money and Business Cycles." *The Optimum Quantity of Money and Other Essays*. Edited by Milton Friedman. Chicago: Aldine Publishing Co., 1969.

_____ , *A Monetary History of the United States, 1867-1960*. Princeton: Princeton University Press, 1963.

_____ , *Monetary Statistics of the United States*. New York: National Bureau of Economic Research, 1970.

_____ , "Comments on the Critics." *Journal of Political Economy*, No. 5, September 1972, *80*, 908-950.

Gallman, Robert, "Gross National Product in the United States, 1834-1909." Studies in Income and Wealth. Vol. XXX: *Output, Employment and Productivity in the United States after 1800.* New York: National Bureau of Economic Research, 1966.

Gurley, John, and Shaw, Edward, *Money in a Theory of Finance.* Washington: Brookings Institution, 1960.

Klein, Benjamin, "Income Velocity, Interest Rates and the Money Supply Multiplier: A Reinterpretation of the Long Term Evidence." *Journal of Money, Credit and Banking,* May 1973, *5,* 656-668.

Macesich, George, "Sources of Monetary Disturbances in the United States, 1834-45," *Journal of Economic History,* September 1960, *20,* 407-34.

Marty, Alvin, "Gurley and Shaw on Money in a Theory of Finance," *Journal of Political Economy,* February 1961, *69,* 56-62.

Mill, John Stuart, "Reviews of Books by Thomas Tooke and R. Torrens," *Westminster Review 41,* June 1844, 579-93.

——————— , *Principles of Political Economy.* London: Longmans Green, 1917.

Morgenstern, O., "Thirteen Critical Points in Contemporary Economic Theory: An Interpretation." *Journal of Economic Literature,* December 1972, *10,* 1163-1189.

Morrison, George. "The Influence of Money on Economic Activity: A Selective Summary of the Evidence," *American Statistical Association,* Proceedings of the Business and Economic Statistics Section, September 1965, 136-46.

Patinkin, Don, *Money, Interest and Prices.* New York: Harper and Row, 1965.

Rutner, Jack L., "Money in the Antebellum Economy: Its Composition, Relation to Income and Its Determinants." Unpublished Ph.D. dissertation, University of Chicago, 1974.

Temin, Peter, *The Jacksonian Economy.* New York: W. W. Norton and Co., Inc., 1969.

Tobin, James, "Money, Capital and Other Sources of Value," *American Economic Review,* March 1961, *51,* 27-37.

——————— , "An Essay on Principles of Debt Management." *Commission on Money and Credit, Fiscal and Debt Management Policies.* Englewood Cliffs, N.J.: Prentice Hall, 1963a.

——————— , "The Monetary Interpretation of History," *American Economic Review,* June 1965, *55,* 26-37.

——————— , "Friedman's Theoretical Framework," *Journal of Political Economy,* September 1972, *80,* 852-863.

Tobin, James, and Brainard, William, "Financial Intermediaries and the Effectiveness of Monetary Control," *American Economic Review,* May 1963, *53,* 383-400.

——————— , "Pitfalls in Financial Model Building," *American Economic Review,* May 1968, *58,* 99-122.

Witte, James, "The Microfoundations of the Social Investment Function," *Journal of Political Economy,* December 1963, *71,* 441-56.

United States Department of Commerce, *Historical Statistics of the United States, Colonial Times to 1957.* Washington, 1961.

[15]

REGULATION D AND THE VAULT CASH GAME

WARREN L. COATS, JR.*

MONEY SUPPLY control and behavior are importantly influenced by the institutional and legal framework in which money is produced. An important change in that framework was activated on September 12, 1968 when drastically revised procedures for calculating and meeting the Federal Reserve's reserve requirement (Regulation D) were put into effect. The implications of these rule changes have been examined elsewhere;[1] it is the more limited objective of this paper to examine the evidence for what I call the vault cash game.

Under the new rules of 1968, reserves eligible for meeting the current week's reserve requirement consist of the current week's average daily deposits at the Fed plus the average daily vault cash held two weeks ago. This provision inadvertently introduces a source of potential reserve adjustment not present under the earlier rules where vault cash was not lagged in the reserve calculation. Although shifting reserves from vault cash to deposits at the Fed does not affect the level of reserves (R), it does affect the volume of reserves eligible for meeting the reserve requirement in the current period (R^a).[2] This occurs because vault cash in the current period is not counted toward the current reserve requirement while deposits at the Fed are.

The purpose of the 1968 changes in Regulation D was to improve the reserve adjustment mechanism, and thereby smooth the behavior of the money markets where reserves are traded, and improve the Federal Reserve's control over the relation between reserves and deposits, and hence over the money supply. The particular contribution of lagging vault cash was that its fairly regular monthly cycle then tended to offset the similar monthly cycle in Federal Reserve Float.[3] The vault cash game, however, tends to weaken the Federal Reserve's control over reserves (R^a), hence over the money mechanism.

I. THE GAME

In terms of the pecuniary rate of return earned on vault cash and deposits at the Fed (zero), the two ways of holding reserves are perfect substitutes.

* Assistant Professor of Economics, University of Virginia. This paper is based on parts of my doctoral dissertation for the University of Chicago. My many debts are enumerated there. I would like particularly to express my gratitude to Milton Friedman, Robert J. Gordon, Richard Zecher and the Federal Reserve Bank of Chicago. None of them has seen this paper. It has also benefitted from the comments of an anonymous referee.

1. Warren L. Coats, Jr., "The September, 1968, Changes in "Regulation D" and Their Implications for Money Supply Control," unpublished doctoral dissertation University of Chicago, June, 1972.

2. It does, however, affect reserves as currently reported. The reserve figure now reported is $R_t^f + V_{t-2}$, where R_t^f is deposits at the Fed in the current week and V_{t-2} is vault cash two weeks ago.

3. New changes in Regulation D originally slated for September, 1972 will change this by changing the behavior of Float.

In fact, under the old rules deposits at the Fed would appear to have no advantages over vault cash as long as some modest amount of reserves is maintained in that form. Volatility in check clearing through the Fed (which can sometimes be rather considerable) gives rise to the need to hold some reserves at the Fed, as does the potential desire to sell Federal funds which is done through that account.

Banks will have a desired level of vault cash as well, which protects them against very short-run, unexpected variations in deposit-to-currency conversions. As required reserves are surely considerably in excess of these various needs,[4] the division of reserves between vault cash and deposits at the Fed is fairly arbitrary within wide limits. The new rules necessitate some potentially important changes in the above analysis. Vault cash now has an additional advantage over deposits at the Fed.

If we contrast two situations, each with the same level of actual reserves but the first with a high level of vault cash and a low level of deposits at the Fed and the second with the opposite mix, the banking system in the first case can meet an increase in required reserves more easily by simply shifting vault cash to deposits at the Fed.

Banks now enjoy a limited control over their own reserves (the reserves that matter in meeting the reserve requirement, i.e., R^a) not previously enjoyed. This enables banks to postpone meeting the current reserve requirement by lowering R^a_{t+2} in order to increase R_t^a. The implied carry-over is limited only by the level of vault cash on hand to be transferred to deposits at the Fed and the minimum vault cash that must be kept on hand for accommodating daily cash flows.

In order to appreciate more fully the uses of this vault cash game in reserve management, consider the following hypothetical example. For individual banks expecting no change in deposits and reserves on average, but experiencing short-term fluctuations about these averages, temporarily surplus reserves (plus or minus) can be adjusted in the usual ways or by adjusting vault cash. If reserves and deposits increase by the same amount, surplus reserves increase by that amount since required reserves will not be affected for two more weeks.[5]

If the higher surplus reserves are sold on the Federal funds market, a like amount of reserves will have to be bought later to offset subsequent reserve losses plus enough to cover the lagged increase in required reserves. On average, about as much Federal funds must be bought as sold. This can be avoided by adding the surplus to vault cash.

These alternatives are examined in Table 1. The example depicts a regular cyclical behavior of deposits and reserves about a constant mean beginning in period —1 and reaching full operation in period 1. If vault cash is held con-

---

4. The validity of this assertion was supported by the results of a study by Lucille Mayne which compared the level of reserves held by Illinois State banks—where there is no reserve requirement—with that of member banks. See *The Effect of Federal Reserve System Membership on the Profitability of Illinois Banks 1961-1963* (University Park: Pennsylvania State University, 1967), pp. 87-96.

5. The most important of the September 1968 changes in Regulation D was the lagging by two weeks of the demand deposit base used in calculating required reserves.

Regulation D and the Vault Cash Game   603

TABLE 1
THE VAULT CASH GAME VERSUS THE FED FUNDS MARKET

Period	Deposits	Reserves	Required Reserves	Deposits at the Fed	S^1	S^2	Vault Cash	Deposits at the Fed	Reserves Allowable Toward Requirement	Reserves Excess
−4	500	100					50	50		
−3	500	100					50	50		
−2	500	100	100	50	0	0	50	50	100	0
−1	550	150	100	50	50	50	100	50	100	0
−0	500	100	100	50	0	0	50	50	100	0
1	450	50	110	60	−60	−10	40	10	110	0
2	500	100	100	50	0	0	50	50	100	0
3	550	150	90	40	60	50	100	50	90	0
4	500	100	100	50	0	0	50	50	100	0
5	450	50	110	60	−60	−10	40	10	110	0
6	500	100	100	50	0	0	50	50	100	0
7	550	150	90	40	60	50	100	50	90	0
8	500	100	100	50	0	0	50	50	100	0
Average for t = 1–8	500	100	100	50	0	10	60	40	100	0

S^1 is the Federal funds sales when surplus reserves are adjusted that way. S^2 is the addition to vault cash when surplus reserves are adjusted that way. All columns to the right of S^2 refer to the vault cash adjustment case.

stant at 50 throughout with deposits at the Fed adjusting as needed to just meet the reserve requirement in each period, then S^1 is simultaneously the level of surplus reserves and Federal funds sales (or purchases where negative). After the appropriate action in the Federal funds market, excess reserves are kept at zero throughout. After the cyclical pattern is established, Federal funds sales are exactly offset by purchases (periods 1–8).

The lagging of the vault cash allowable toward the reserve requirement creates a new possibility for using temporarily surplus reserves. S^2 and subsequent columns refer to this case. Surplus reserves are held as vault cash while deposits at the Fed are always adjusted to just meet the reserve requirement. The table shows how this use of vault cash might work and indicates that banks would be led on average to hold more vault cash and less deposits at the Fed. In one respect Table 1 might appear to overstate the vault cash adjustment capability. Since it is a daily average level of required reserves that must be met and likewise since a dollar of vault cash shipped off to the Fed on the last day of a settlement week (Wednesday) only adds one seventh of that amount to the week's daily average of eligible reserves, the reserve adjustment capability of a vault cash shift is diminished. However this is equally true of any other reserve adjustment technique and therefore does not diminish the importance of the vault cash game.

What a bank chooses to do would depend on the relative transactions costs of the vault cash game and Federal funds transactions and more importantly on the bank's expectations of future levels of the Federal funds rate, the degree of uncertainty with which those expectations are held, and the degree of its aversion to the risk of unexpected changes in that rate. Ceteris paribus, the greater the uncertainty and/or the greater the risk aversion, the more attractive vault cash will appear relative to lending in the Fed funds market. The cost to banks of using vault cash rather than the Fed funds market for reserve adjustments is the interest foregone on the first Fed funds sale (in period −1) less the transactions costs of using that market, plus the possible ill will of the Federal Reserve. The addition of the vault cash game to an individual bank's reserve adjustment options should make reserve adjustment easier. The cost to the Federal Reserve is a weakened control over reserves and money.

II. The Evidence

If the shifting of vault cash to adjust a bank's reserve position has taken place because of the new rules, vault cash should be more volatile than before. There is only slight evidence that this has happened. Between the old and new rule periods tested (January, 1966 through August, 1968 and October, 1968 through March, 1971) the average absolute week-to-week percentage change in vault cash has risen from 3.98 per cent to 4.11 per cent, a difference not statistically significant.

The pressure of reserve adjustment is greatest during periods of changing monetary policy. The vault cash game is most likely to be played during such periods. An examination of the subperiod breakdown given in Table 2 lends

TABLE 2

COMPARISONS OF AGGREGATE VAULT CASH BEHAVIOR BETWEEN NEW AND OLD RULES

Rules	Monetary Policy	Date	Vault Cash		Vault Cash/ Demand Deposits	
			Mean	Average Absolute Percentage Change	Mean	Average Absolute Percentage Change
Old	Firm	1/ 5/66-11/ 2/66	3,850	3.934	28.9	4.17
	Transition	1/ 5/66- 7/ 6/66	3,793	4.050	28.38	4.18
	Stable	7/13/66-11/ 2/66	3,924	3.757	29.67	4.17
New	Firm	12/25/68- 1/14/70	4,727	4.082	30.00	4.33
	Transition	12/25/68- 5/ 7/69	4,660	4.459	29.63	4.74
	Stable	5/14/69- 1/14/70	4,765	3.854	30.21	4.09
Old	Easy	11/ 9/66-11/29/67	4,141	3.912	30.16	3.98
	Transition	11/ 9/66- 4/12/67	4,106	4.137	30.26	4.08
	Stable	4/19/67-11/29/67	4,165	3.736	30.09	3.92
New	Easy	1/21/70- 3/31/71	5,040	4.176	30.83	4.56
	Transition	1/21/70- 9/23/70	4,898	4.323	30.59	4.83
	Stable	9/30/70- 3/31/71	5,230	4.105	31.16	4.34

Data source: Vault cash and demand deposit data were taken from the *Federal Reserve Bulletin.* Vault cash, which is reported there with a two week lag, is used here unlagged.

support to this proposition.[6] Table 2 gives the mean and average absolute percentage change in vault cash and the ratio of vault cash to demand deposits for four subperiods where each subperiod is further divided into the transition and stable components. These measures of volatility are consistently higher in the transition subperiods. However, this pattern is as pronounced under the old rules as under the new, although volatility is consistently higher under the new rules than for the comparable periods under the old.

It may be, however, that a vault cash game of sorts was played under the old rules as well. Under the old rules a situation existed on Wednesdays somewhat comparable to the current week's vault cash under the new rules. "Cash in vault" at the opening of business on Wednesday was counted as reserves while cash delivered to a Federal Reserve Bank before the close of business on Wednesday was also counted as reserves (on deposit at the Fed). Currency shipped on Wednesdays therefore counted twice and to my knowledge almost all banks are within six driving hours of a Federal Reserve Bank. It might also be noted that the *large* monthly currency and coin shipments to and from Federal Reserve Banks are roughly offsetting (with seasonal variations).[7]

Two additional investigations bring less aggregated data to bear on the vault cash question. It is possible that increased vault cash volatility for individual banks is offsetting in the aggregate and thus washes out in those figures. In Table 3 individual bank vault cash figures show no change in aver-

TABLE 3
INDIVIDUAL BANK VAULT CASH VOLATILITY IN THE SEVENTH DISTRICT

	Period	Coef. of Var. Weighted Average	Average Absolute Percentage Change	Mean Level in Thousands	Mean Level Divided By Deposits at Fed
All Banks (142)	Old Rules	0.103	8.8	2,615	0.902
	New Rules	0.103	8.6	2,875	0.951
Weekly Reporting Banks (53)	Old Rules	0.102	6.4	6,522	2.248
	New Rules	0.102	6.4	7,181	2.375

Data source: Detz-Goodman Deposit Data, Federal Reserve Bank of Chicago. Old rules are the 86 weeks from 1967 to the rule change, and the new rules are the 65 weeks from the rule change to the end of 1969. Deposits at Fed are the appropriate averages of monthly figures for Seventh District member banks' deposits at the Chicago Fed as reported in the *Federal Reserve Bulletin*. The weighted average of individual coefficients of variation is obtained by summing the individual bank standard deviations of weekly vault cash figures and then dividing by the sum of the mean values. The data represent a 10 per cent sample (142 banks) of individual Seventh District member banks.

6. The subperiods chosen are the result of a codification of the Federal Open Market Committee directives into an index of monetary policy done originally by Brunner and Meltzer, *The Federal Reserve's Attachment to the Free Reserve Concept* (Washington: House Committee on Banking and Currency, 1964), partially undated by Meltzer, "The Appropriate Indicator of Monetary Policy" (unpublished paper), and further updated by me. They delineate periods of "firmness" and "ease" according to the FOMC directives and further subdivide these periods into an initial period of transition (e.g., during which policy might move from ease to greater and greater firmness) followed by a "stable" period during which the new policy is maintained.

7. See Table 4. I am indebted to Mr. V. A. Hansen, Assistant Vice-President in the Cash Department of the Federal Reserve Bank of Chicago, for the data contained in Tables 4 and 5.

age volatility but do reveal a slight rise in their mean level even when divided by the average level of deposits at the Chicago Fed prevailing over each period.[8] Inventory theory suggests that as the scale of operation for the sample banks increases (the money supply grew over the period tested), the ratio of vault cash to money (or deposits) needed for net currency withdrawals declines. The evidence here seems contradictory. It is not inconsistent, however, with the hypothesis that, although individual banks found vault cash more desirable because of the vault cash game, they played it no more heavily on average for each of the years sampled but in the aggregate under the new rules tended to ship currency in synchronization with other banks because the entire system tended to experience reserve pressures simultaneously.

A final attempt to determine whether there was an increase in the vault cash game is reported in Tables 4 and 5. The ratios of currency shipments in and out of the Chicago Fed to the average level of member bank reserve

TABLE 4
GROSS SHIPMENTS OF CURRENCY AND COIN IN THE SEVENTH DISTRICT

To and From:	1966	1967	1968 Jan.-Aug.	1968 Oct.-Dec.	1969	1970
	Average Monthly Shipments in Dollars					
Chicago Banks	356,597	326,718	337,397	367,314	364,093	367,605
Non-Chicago Banks	232,270	237,680	237,965	277,986	258,860	271,291
All Banks	588,867	564,398	575,362	645,301	622,952	638,895
	Ratio of Above to Average Seventh District Member Bank Deposits at the Chicago Federal Reserve Bank in Thousands					
Chicago Banks	.128	.117	.111	.120	.111	.113
Non-Chicago Banks	.083	.085	.078	.091	.079	.084
All Banks	.211	.201	.189	.211	.191	.197

Data source: Federal Reserve Bank of Chicago, Cash Department and various *Federal Reserve Bulletins*, 1966-1971.

TABLE 5
GROSS SHIPMENTS OF CURRENCY AND COIN IN THE SEVENTH DISTRICT

To and From:	1967	1968	1969	1970
	Average Monthly Shipments for October through December in Dollars			
Chicago Banks	356,273	367,314	393,597	391,918
Non-Chicago Banks	262,539	277,986	299,338	313,210
All Banks	618,812	645,301	692,935	705,128
	Ratio of Above to Average Seventh District Member Bank Deposits at Chicago Federal Reserve for October through December in Thousands			
Chicago Banks	.122	.120	.122	.120
Non-Chicago Banks	.090	.091	.093	.096
All Banks	.211	.211	.214	.216

Data source: Same as Table 4.

8. I am indebted to Roberta Detz and Nancy Goodman of the Federal Reserve Bank of Chicago for making their individual bank data available to me.

Regulation D and the Vault Cash Game   607

deposits in each period (Table 4) reveal no shift in vault cash activity. Even the small increase immediately after the rule change can be seen in Table 5 to reflect an apparent seasonal bulge near the end of each year. It is interesting to note, however, that the October-December average ratios rise steadily, though modestly, while the yearly average ratios do not. The money supply experiences an enormous seasonal spurt during the fourth quarter of each year, which is partially but by no means totally supported by a similarly timed bulge in the monetary base. This may well be a seasonal period of intensified reserve pressure, i.e., a period when the vault cash game is more likely to be played.

The mere possibility of the vault cash game makes it hard to believe that it is not at least occasionally played. It is also true that frequent or heavy utilization of it would be easily detected and disapproved of by the Fed. That kind of disapproval (for such a small return) bank presidents can get along without. The evidence assembled here, although somewhat mixed, suggests that the game has been played only lightly if at all.

[16]

EFFICIENT CAPITAL MARKETS AND THE QUANTITY THEORY OF MONEY

RICHARD V. L. COOPER*

THROUGHOUT the discussion of efficient capital markets, little attention has been given to the apparent contradiction between the quantity theory of money and the efficient markets hypothesis. Yet the relation between the money supply and stock prices found by Sprinkel [1964] seems to refute other findings of capital market efficiency. Using the quantity theory of money, Sprinkel finds that money supply changes can be used to predict stock prices. However, if capital markets are efficient, past information (such as money supply changes) cannot be used to predict stock prices. *The intent of this paper is to provide a plausible framework for estimating the relationship between the money supply and stock market returns and, therefore, to offer another test of the efficient markets hypothesis.*

Although the quantity theory of money and the theory of efficient capital markets appear to be contradictory, the major finding of this paper is that the two theories are in fact complementary. The results presented here offer additional support for the concept of market efficiency, since stock returns lead rather than lag money changes. It seems that Sprinkel's conclusions are based on a misspecification of his model.

The hypothesis developed here (referred to as the SQ-EM model) is a combination of the simple quantity theory (SQ) model and the efficient markets (EM) model. The SQ-EM model suggests that the money supply may be an important factor in determining the market rate of return (consistent with the SQ model) but that returns may actually lead money changes (consistent with the EM model) since all available information, such as anticipations about future money changes, are incorporated into current returns. Cross spectral analysis of money changes and returns reveals that the SQ-EM model provides a plausible interpretation of the relationship between the money supply and stock returns. Money is found to lag returns; most of the correlation is found in the lower frequencies, corresponding to the greater success in predicting longer run movements in money changes than shorter run fluctuations.

Section I presents the background for the quantity theory and efficient capital markets models and the theory behind the combined model. Section II presents the data and the methods of estimating the model. The results from cross spectral estimation are given in Section III. The conclusions, along with a possible second interpretation of the results, are given in Section IV.

* The Rand Corporation, Santa Monica, California. I am indebted to Arnold Zellner, Milton Friedman, Eugene Fama, Marc Nerlove, and Robert J. Gordon for their very helpful comments and suggestions. Of course, any remaining errors are my sole responsibility. I am also thankful to the Federal Reserve Bank of Chicago and to NSF grant GS-2347 for financial support.

I. Money and Stock Returns

A. *Background*

The quantity theory of money has played a large role in determining the relationships between the money supply and various other economic variables. Although it does not explicitly treat the relationship between the money supply and stock returns, the assumptions underlying the quantity theory can be used to derive that relationship, at least in broad terms. Sprinkel [1964] was the first to explicitly test a model incorporating the simple quantity theory (SQ) in a model of asset pricing.

In the SQ model, as the supply of money expands more than normally (more than increased demand due to increased real income, changed tastes, etc.),[1] the public's portfolio of desired versus actual cash holdings is thrown out of balance. Consequently, individuals tend to shift out of money holdings to other financial assets, physical assets, and current consumption. Although the individual can make such a shift, the public cannot—the stock of money must be held. Therefore, the prices of other assets and consumption are bid up until a new equilibrium is reached.

The lag between money supply changes and security prices through the above mechanism may be relatively short. A longer lag resulting from anticipated price changes is also to be expected. As the money supply continues to expand more than normally, prices rise more regularly. The public anticipates these rising prices and attempts to further shift out of cash holdings (because of inflation). Therefore, the prices of current consumption and of assets without fixed nominal returns rise relative to money and bonds.

In pursuing the SQ model, Sprinkel decided on a comparison between stock *prices* and a moving average of *rates of change* of the money supply. By a visual examination of the data, he inferred that money changes lead stock prices by about two months on the upturns and by about 15 months on the downturns. The SQ model ignores the recent developments in the business finance literature. In particular, it does not take account of the theory of efficient capital markets (EM model).

In an efficient market, new information is rapidly incorporated into the prices of assets sold in the market, so that current asset prices reflect all currently available information.[2] Investors need not expend resources searching for additional information.

One form of the EM model is stated in terms of expected returns.

If
$$y_t^j = r_t^j - E(r_t^j \mid I_{t-1}),$$

then
$$E(y_t^j) = 0, \tag{1}$$

where r_t^j represents returns for investor j for time period t, and I_{t-1} represents the vector of information available to all investors at the beginning of time period t. Equation (1) asserts that capital markets present a fair game (in the

---

1. A "normal" change in the money supply is defined as the change resulting in no change in the general price level.

2. For a review of the efficient capital markets literature, see Fama [1970].

statistical sense) to each and every investor. Further, equation (1) suggests that stock returns ought to be temporarily independent.

It is useful to designate strong, intermediate, and weak forms of the EM model. The original statement, where $I = I^s$ represents *all* available information, is the strong form. In the weak form, $I = I^w$ represents only the past history of prices (or returns). Therefore, I^w is a subset of I^s. The intermediate form of the model defines $I = I^m$ as $I^w \subset I^m \subset I^s$. It is impossible to test the strong form of the model.[3] The weak form is the easiest to test, for if investigators could find serial correlation in stock returns, the efficient markets model could be rejected. The results from those tests suggested acceptance of the EM model. The next logical step is to test various specifications of the intermediate form. The present study falls into the intermediate category. Information is defined:

$$I^m = \{r_t, r_{t-1}, \ldots, M_t, M_{t-1}\}.$$

That is, I^m is the set of past returns *and* relevant monetary variables.

Sprinkel suggests that stock market prices are a function of past changes in the money supply. But if the efficient capital markets hypothesis holds, using past information, such as money supply changes, should not result in successful prediction of future rates of return to holding common stock.

B. *Portfolio Model*

In the portfolio model developed here, it is assumed that individuals can hold wealth in two forms: money and common stock.[4] The marginal returns of these assets determine the quantities of assets that individuals will hold. The marginal return of an asset is the sum of its marginal pecuniary return (equals the average return in competitive markets) and the marginal return for the nonpecuniary services provided by that asset.[5] Sprinkel makes a fundamental misspecification in his model by developing it in terms of stock prices rather than stock returns.

A portfolio is said to be balanced when the marginal returns to holding these two assets are equal. Hence, in equilibrium

$$\text{MNPS}_t{}^M - \bar{P}_t = \text{MNPS}_t{}^S + \bar{r}_t{}^s, \tag{2}$$

where the left hand side (l.h.s.) of (2) is the return to money and the right hand side (r.h.s.) is the return to stock and where

$\bar{P}_t =$ anticipated percentage change in the general price level,
$\bar{r}_t{}^s =$ anticipated real pecuniary return of stock (dividends plus the percentage change in stock price, $P_t{}^s$), and
$\text{MNPS}_t{}^j =$ marginal nonpecuniary return to the jth asset (the risk of the jth asset is incorporated into its nonpecuniary returns).

Equation (2) represents the equilibrium situation for both the SQ model

---

3. Note that "all information" includes prices, earnings, mergers, dividends, weather reports, presidential proclamations, world crises, etc.

4. A three asset model—money, stock, and bonds—is developed in Cooper [1971].

5. This model depends heavily upon Friedman's [1969] work.

and the combined quantity theory/efficient capital market (SQ-EM) model. In the SQ model, money supply changes affect the MNPS schedules[6] and P. Therefore, money changes induce portfolio adjustments. The result is that since money supply changes induce portfolio adjustments in the SQ model, money supply changes lead stock returns. However, the SQ model ignores anticipations about $\bar{r}^s$.

On the other hand, anticipations are a primary component of the SQ-EM model. When information relevant to returns becomes available, the EM model predicts that prices will rapidly adjust. Since the SQ model predicts that the market return is, in part, a function of the money supply, information about future money supply changes is of paramount importance. Consequently, if information about money supply changes is available before the actual changes, anticipated returns will be adjusted accordingly. In other words, anticipated returns and observed returns may *lead* money supply changes, even though the causation is from money to returns.

Since it is unlikely that money supply changes can be fully anticipated, one would expect stock returns to be affected by the unanticipated component of money changes as well as by the anticipated component. In particular, the unanticipated component should lead returns in the manner suggested by the simple quantity theory model.[7] As a result, returns will be a function of the anticipated and unanticipated components of changes in the money supply

$$r_t^s = A(L)m_t^a + B(L)m_t^u + e_t,^8 \tag{3}$$

where m_t^a = anticipated (forecast) money change,[9]
      m_t^u = unanticipated money change,
      e_t = error term, and
      $A(L)$ and $B(L)$ are polynomials in L such that $L^j x_t = x_{t-j}$.

Equation (3) represents the combined quantity theory/efficient capital markets model. However, neither the timing nor the magnitude of the effects of the efficient markets portion of the SQ-EM model have been detailed.

The money supply, like many macroeconomic variables, is dominated in its time series behavior by long run trend and cyclical components. This equivalent to the statement that the frequency domain representation of money supply changes (the power spectrum of money changes) is dominated by low fre-

---

6. MNPS$_t^M$ is implicitly a function of everything in the demand for money except for returns on alternative assets. In particular, the quantity theory of money proposes that the MNPS$_t^M$ *schedule* is itself a positive function of income; the MNPS$_t^S$ schedule is likewise a positive function of income. The assumption underlying the proposed model is that the income effects on MNPS$_t^M$ and MNPS$_t^S$ cancel each other out. Therefore, the difference between MNPS$_t^M$ and MNPS$_t^S$ is primarily a function (negatively sloped) of money. For a more complete discussion of the model, see Cooper [1971] and Cooper [1972a].

7. See footnote 8 below.

8. In its strictest version, the EM model suggests that $b_i L^i = 0$ for $i > 0$. However, because of transaction costs, b_i may differ somewhat from zero. Also, see footnote 2, page 888.

9. Some difficulty in notation arises here. Suppose that $m_t^a{}_{,t+i}$ is the currently anticipated money change expected to occur in period $t + i$. Therefore, $m_t = m_t^a{}_{,t-i} + m_t^u$. For generality and notational simplicity I have defined $m_t^u = m_t^u{}_{,t-i}$. The forecast period problem is explicitly faced in Section III.

quency components. Therefore, one would suspect that predictors of money supply changes would be better at predicting the long run and cyclical trends than the more erratic short run fluctuations. That is to say, m_t^a may be a reasonably good predictor of long run and cyclical changes in m_t but a poor predictor of short run changes in m_t.

As a result, returns would be expected to anticipate the longer run movements in m_t, but not the shorter run movements. In the longer run movements of r_t^s, one would expect the anticipations about money changes to dominate. On the other hand, since m_t^a may be a poor predictor of short term movements in m_t, one would expect simple portfolio adjustments to excess money holdings to dominate short term movements in r_t^s. In other words, one would expect returns to *lead* money for *longer* term movements in money changes and possibly *lag* for the *shorter* term movements.[10]

Next, consider the magnitude of these respective effects. Since m_t^a reflects long-term movements in m_t, one would expect m_t^a to have large consequences on portfolio adjustment and, hence, to have a significant impact on the rate of return. Alternatively, it would be expected that short term movements in m_t would not have much impact on r_t^s for two reasons. First, because of transactions costs, it may be too costly to adjust to small day-to-day fluctuations in the portfolio. Second, and perhaps more important, there is apt to be a substantial amount of noise in the short term movements in r_t^s. Therefore, the measured impact of m_t^u upon r_t^s is likely to be small, whereas the impact of m_t^a upon $\bar{r}_t^s$ (and on r_t^s) might be rather large.[11]

Finally, consider the timing. How much might r^s lead m? This question is answered by the time lag between m^a and m. For example, if changes in money can be forecast with reasonable accuracy three months ahead but poorly four months ahead, then the efficient markets model suggests that returns would lead money by something near three months. In any case, the lead of r^s over m should reflect the lead of m^a over m. Two main instruments for measuring m^a were considered for this paper: past values of m_t and the monetary base.

This description of the SQ-EM model suggests that the model may better be evaluated in the frequency domain than in the time domain. This is further supported by the evidence in Sections II and III.[12]

II. DATA AND METHODS OF ESTIMATION

A. *The Data*

The measure of the market rate of return used here is Standard and Poor's Composite 500 (SP500) index. Though not quite as broad as Fisher's (1966) index, the SP500 is broader, for example, than the Dow-Jones industrials and is available for a longer period of time than Fisher's index. Preliminary analysis of these three indexes indicated similarity in their characteristics. For example,

---

10. The strict form of the EM model would suggest simultaneity rather than a lag. See footnote 8 page 890.

11. This suggests that, even if m_t^u leads r_t^x, the magnitude is likely to be so small that this information cannot be used profitably.

12. For a frequency domain description of the model, see Cooper [1971] and Cooper [1972a].

when subjected to cross-spectral analysis, they showed coherences always greater than 0.85, and the phase angles were never statistically significantly different from zero. Moreover, the relationship between the money supply and each of these indexes was approximately the same. Therefore, although the results here are based on the SP500, the basic hypotheses tested seem more general.

The return for period t is the dividend yield for period t plus the percentage change in the price of the index. Returns, as defined above, were compared with the simple percentage price changes. With the exception of the mean of the two definitions, returns are identical to percentage changes in stock prices. Cross spectral analysis showed a coherence greater than 0.99 for each estimated frequency and a phase angle never statistically significantly different from zero.

The results from Section I and above indicate that Sprinkel should have compared percentage changes in money with *percentage changes* in stock prices rather than with stock prices.

The literature contains ample debate over the appropriate time series to use for the money supply. The Federal Reserve Bank refers to the money supply as currency plus demand deposits (M_1); Friedman and Schwartz [1964] find a more useful definition for their purposes to be M_1 plus time deposits (M_2); and Chetty [1969] proposed a weighted average of currency, demand deposits, time deposits, savings and loan shares, and mutual savings bank shares (M_n).[13]

Preliminary work indicated that M_2 and M_n behave in a very similar manner. Further, M_1 was found to be superior to M_2 for the time period analyzed in this study in that returns and percentage changes in M_1 were more highly correlated than returns and percentage changes in M_2. Therefore, the money variable in this paper is defined as percentage changes in the M_1 definition of the money supply.

In addition to the definition of the money supply, the question of whether to use seasonally unadjusted or adjusted data arises. The SQ-EM model does not specify which data to use. If investors base their predictions upon past values of adjusted data, then adjusted data should be used; if predictions are based on unadjusted data, then unadjusted data should be used. Since the theory here is not fully developed, it was decided to use empirical means to select the appropriate money series. Seasonally adjusted data did somewhat better than unadjusted data (although the differences was not substantial).[14]

Finally, the results presented in this paper are based on monthly observations on price changes and money changes for the period 1947 to 1970. In an earlier effort,[15] weekly data were examined. Although the results for the weekly data were much like those for the monthly data, the very short time period of available weekly data (only since 1959) makes resolution of the spectra difficult. Ideally, one would choose the entire length of the data record. However,

13. Lee [1971] suggests that Chetty's results are substantially altered if a different time period is used. However, Lee's findings should not affect the results in this paper.

14. The coherence peak for unadjusted data was as high as for adjusted data, but not quite as broad. Seasonally unadjusted results are found in Cooper [1971].

15. See Cooper [1971] and Cooper [1972a].

the entire data record may not satisfy certain statistical requirements. In particular, spectral analysis requires that the time series are covariance stationary. To determine whether the time series under investigation were covariance stationary, the basic data record (1918-1970) was broken up into several subperiods. The only covariance stationary period appeared to be 1947-1970.[16] This may, in part, be because the methods for reporting money supply data changed considerably in 1947. Therefore, the results in this paper are based on 1947-1970 monthly data.

B. *Methods of Estimation*

Sprinkel used visual examination of the data for examining his hypothesis. Although visual examination gives the analyst more flexibility than most statistical procedures, it has a number of severe drawbacks. Some sort of averaging must be used to make much sense out of the erratic returns and money series. (Sprinkel used a six-month moving average of money supply changes.) Averaging necessarily suppresses some information and often results in spurious correlations.[17] Another serious shortcoming is that the user may subconsciously admit or exclude certain data points on the basis of whether those data fit his particular theory. Therefore, it is usually desirable to have some form of probabilistic test whereby the analyst can base his decision on whether to accept or reject the hypothesis on some well-founded statistical procedures.[18]

The first alternative procedure to be considered is regression analysis. Returns could be regressed on current, lagged, and future values of money supply changes. The SQ model would have returns lagging money supply changes; hence, current and lagged values of money supply changes should be the determinants of returns. The SQ-EM model would have returns both leading and lagging[19] money supply changes—a result of incorporating anticipations about future money supply changes into the model—with *most of the variation in returns attributed to leading values of money supply changes.*

Table 1 provides the regression results for monthly data; Table 2 provides the regression results for quarterly and annual data. The monthly regression results illustrate a very low R^2, a consequence of the large amount of variance explained by frequencies in the high end of the spectrum. When 19 terms are included in the regression, only three are statistically significantly different from zero; when six terms are included in the regression, only one is statistically significantly different from zero. These results would lead one to question whether there is any relation at all between money and returns. On the other hand, the annual regression results in Table 2 show an R^2 of 0.625 (and an adjusted R^2 of 0.524), thus indicating the strength of the relation between money and returns in the long run. However, when the coefficients themselves are examined, the largest of the coefficients for the annual data shows no lead

---

16. For a more thorough treatment of the methodology and the results, see Cooper [1971].

17. The effects of different filtering procedures are given in Jenkins and Watts [1968]. Adelman [1965] illustrates the type of erroneous conditions that can emerge from filtering by considering Kuznets' long swings hypothesis. Fishman [1969] derives Adelman's results in more detail.

18. Of course, these tests are valid only so far as the underlying assumptions are valid.

19. Or, in the strict form, coincident with money changes.

TABLE 1

REGRESSION ESTIMATES FOR MONTHLY DATA:

$$r_t{}^s = \sum_{i=-s_1}^{s_2} a_i m_{t-i}$$

Coefficient	19 Money Terms Included		6 Money Terms Included	
	Estimate	Std. Error	Estimate	Std. Error
R^2	0.169		0.109	
$\overline{R}^2$	0.069		0.079	
a_{-6}	-1.601	1.045		
a_{-5}	-0.431	1.067		
a_{-4}	0.442	1.082		
a_{-3}	1.905^a	1.106	1.136	0.988
a_{-2}	2.141^a	1.116	2.150^a	1.024
a_{-1}	1.418	1.142	1.702	1.059
a_0	1.080	1.126	0.730	1.058
a_1	-1.168	1.127	-1.436	1.030
a_2	0.317	1.116	0.273	0.993
a_3	-0.973	1.115		
a_4	0.160	1.115		
a_5	0.973	1.108		
a_6	0.040	1.102		
a_7	0.573	1.106		
a_8	-1.950^a	1.109		
a_9	0.972	1.113		
a_{10}	-0.544	1.115		
a_{11}	-0.000	1.085		
a_{12}	-1.379	1.051		

[a] Significant at 90 per cent confidence level.

TABLE 2

REGRESSION ESTIMATES FOR QUARTERLY AND ANNUAL DATA:

$$r_t{}^s = \sum_{i=s_1}^{s_2} a_i m_{t-i}$$

Time Period	a_{-2} (Std. Error)	a_{-1}	a_0	a_1	R^2	$\overline{R}^2$
Quarterly	-0.977 (0.942)	2.557 (1.080)	2.302 (1.082)	-0.758 (1.110)	0.204	0.156
Annual		-2.032 (0.879)	3.549 (0.876)	-2.815 (0.852)	0.625	0.524

or lag (versus the two to three month lead for monthly data); and the meaning of the negative coefficients for $t-1$ and $t+1$ is not at all clear. In addition, the cumulative effect of a unit change in money is shown to result in a change of 2.6 in the monthly model and -1.2 in the annual model. Therefore, it is very difficult to assess the validity of either the SQ or the SQ-EM model by regression techniques.

Through spectral analysis, the relationship between money and returns can be examined in the frequency domain. As Cooper [1972b] demonstrates, it is sometimes very useful to state a hypothesis in the frequency domain to take advantage of certain properties of the spectral estimators.

Spectral analysis was chosen as the method of estimation for three reasons. First, the SQ and SQ-EM models developed in the last section are not parametrically specified. That is, there is little a priori information about the precise form of the polynomials in equation (3). Although Hause [1971] notes that it is not appropriate to view the phase spectrum in the framework of a distributed lag model since the phase represents pure delay in the frequency domain, the phase spectrum can be used to distinguish general lead or lag patterns. Since the distinction between the SQ and SQ-EM models is straightforward (i.e., the SQ model proposes that money lags returns), the phase spectrum may be used to differentiate between the two models. Spectral analysis affords the opportunity to distinguish between the two models without parametrically specifying them.

Second, the discussion in the last section indicates that the relationship between the money supply and returns is not expected to be the same across all frequencies, particularly for the SQ-EM model. Since time-domain techniques (such as regression analysis) average the effects among variables across all frequencies, these techniques may not provide an adequate means of estimating the model.

Third, one would expect that the power spectrum of stock returns would be flat. From equation (1) in the last section,

$$E(r_t{}^s\, r_{t-1}{}^s, \dots, r_{t-k}{}^s, \dots) = E(r_t{}^s) \qquad (4)$$

knowledge of the past history of returns does not assist in the prediction of future returns. If the spectrum of returns is other than flat, returns are temporarily dependent, a condition not allowed by (4). A flat spectrum means that each frequency component is equally important in explaining returns. The power spectrum for returns (not shown here) indicates that (4) is indeed valid. However, as developed in the last part of Section I, the coherence between money and returns is expected to be much larger for the low frequencies than for the high frequencies.

Suppose that low frequencies are defined as those frequencies corresponding to cycles of 12 months or more: the low frequency range consists of the lower one-sixth of the spectrum and the high frequency range consists of the upper five-sixths of the spectrum for monthly data (lower 1/26 and upper 25/26 for weekly data). Therefore, for the SQ/EM model in particular, the coherence is expected to be low for five-sixths of the spectrum for monthly data (and low for 25/26 of the spectrum for weekly data!). If regression analysis is used with either weekly or monthly data, the results will indicate little or no relation between money and stock returns, when, in fact, money and returns may be highly correlated for the lower frequencies. On the other hand, the annual regression results presented in Table 2 show substantial correlation between money and returns but do not permit identification of leads and lags. These comments apply not only to regression techniques but to all time-domain techniques (such as the Box-Jenkins [1970] methods). Therefore, spectral

896   *The Journal of Finance*

analysis seems to afford the best opportunity to estimate the relationship between money and stock returns.

III. Estimation of the Model

A. *Cross Spectral Results*

Figures 1-4 provide a description of the frequency domain relation between money and returns for monthly data over 1947 to 1970. The coherence[20] be-

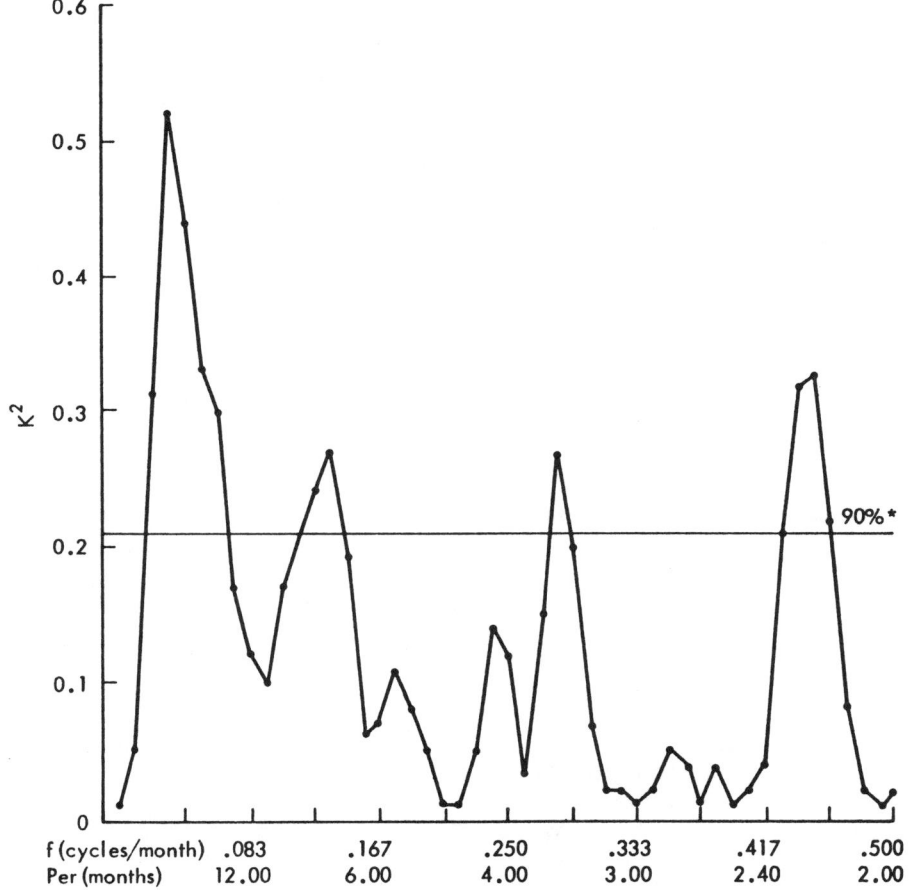

* 90% confidence for non-zero coherence of a single estimate of K^2.
This applies to the remaining figures, as well.

Figure 1a
Coherence of monthly money changes and returns: $M = 48$

20. The regression analog to coherence is the R^2 measure: the coherence ranges in value between zero and one, with a value of one showing perfect correlation.

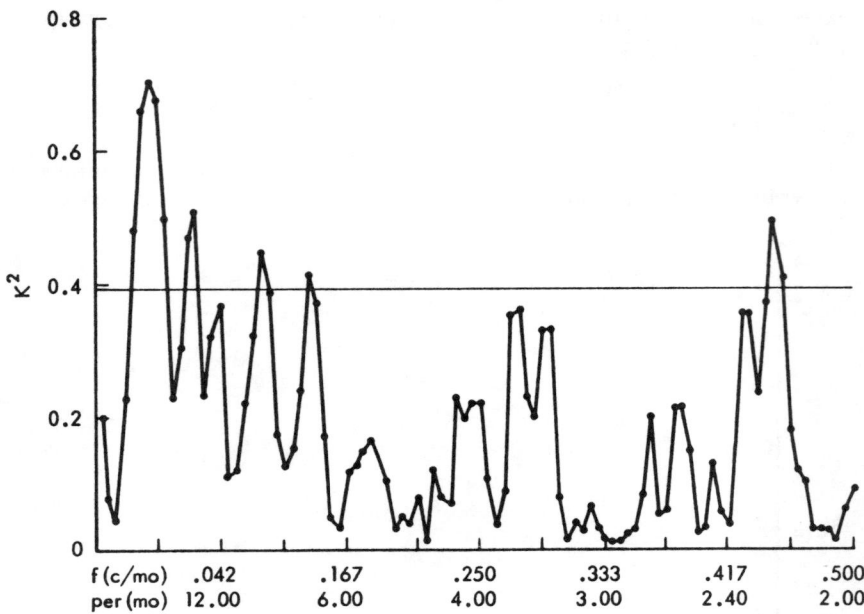

FIGURE 1b
Coherence of monthly money changes and returns: $M = 96$

tween money and returns when 48 lagged terms are used (i.e., $M = 48$) is given in Fig. 1a. The relation between money and returns is strongest in the low end of the frequency domain (or, alternatively, for the longer periods). That is, the peak is the lower one-third of the spectrum. The 90 per cent confidence line indicates that almost two-thirds of the statistically significant (from zero) estimates are in the very low frequency bands.[21] In fact, the relationship between money and returns is significant at the 0.01 confidence level for cycles of six months or more in length.[22] Therefore, whatever correlation exists between money and returns is almost solely in the low frequencies, consistent with the SQ-EM model.

An alternative estimate of the coherence spectrum between money and returns is given in Fig. 1b, where $M = 96$ (i.e., 96 lagged terms are estimated for the auto and cross covariances). These estimates provide finer resolution, but at the cost of greater variance in the estimates. Again, the coherence is much larger for the low frequency end of the spectrum (for cycles about 48 to 8 months in length) than for the high. These estimates show a coherence over the low end of the spectrum between about 0.4 and 0.75. Therefore, the coherence estimates of both Figs. 1a and 1b show money and returns to have a fairly strong relation in the low end of the frequency spectrum and little rela-

21. The 90 per cent confidence test is not a joint test (across frequencies); it is a test of non-zero coherence for a single estimate.

22. For the joint test over frequencies, see Cooper [1971].

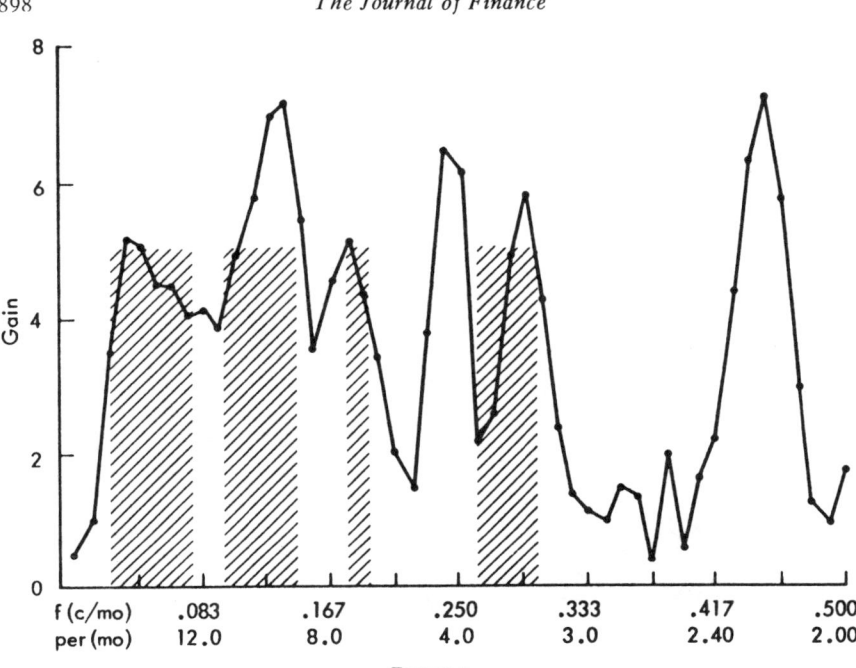

FIGURE 2
Gain for monthly money and returns: $M = 48$

tion in the high end. It is clear from these results why the monthly regression reported in the last section has a small R^2 while the annual regression has a fairly large R^2.

The gain between the money supply and the cross spectrum of money and returns given in Fig. 2 is the frequency-domain analog of the regression coefficient in the time domain. For the peaks in the coherence the gain is generally between 4.0 and 8.0; for the low frequency peak with the highest coherence, the gain is about 5.3. This spectrum indicates that fluctuations in the money supply are amplified several times when translated into fluctuations in returns. Further, these estimates differ considerably from the cumulative effects of changes in the money supply on returns, as measured in the time domain. From the last section, the cumulative effects of a unit change in the money supply were given by the monthly regression model as about 2.6. This points to the errors-in-the-variables nature of the problem as noted by Cooper [1972b]. That is, since the "true" variables (i.e., m" and m") are not included in the regression model, the coefficient of the measured variable (i.e., m) should be biased toward zero.

The other measure of interest is the lead/lag spectrum. The lead or lag for a particular frequency can be found by multiplying the phase shift for that frequency by the length of the period corresponding to that frequency. However, as given in Cooper [1972], there is some difficulty in interpreting the phase spectrum: namely, the phase is only unique in the range 0 to 2π. For

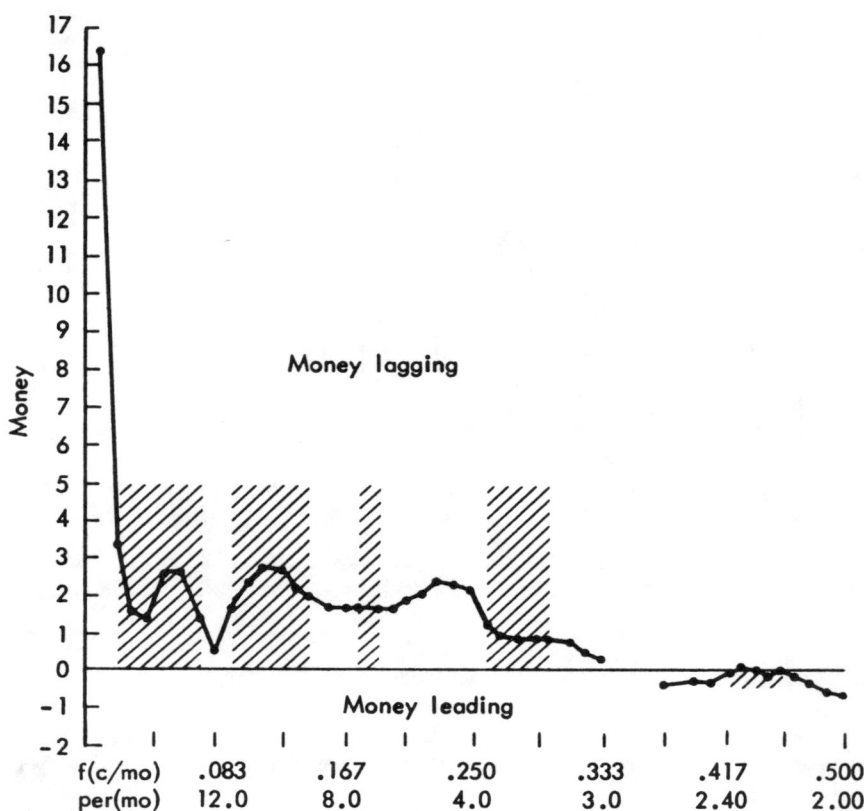

FIGURE 3

Lead/lag for monthly money and returns—SQ-EM interpretation—M = 48

example, for a phase shift of one-quarter cycle for a frequency corresponding to eight months, the phase may be interpreted as money lagging returns by two months, or lagging by ten months (two plus eight), etc., or even leading by six months. Therefore, a priori information must be specified for a unique representation of the lead/lag spectrum.

Two interpretations of the lead/lag spectrum are offered here, one is consistent with the SQ-EM model (Fig. 3), the second with the SQ model (Fig. 4). The SQ-EM model interpretation seems to be the more reasonable interpretation of the two presented, since the SQ version reports money leading anywhere between 80 months to no lead or lag at all. On the other hand, for the low frequencies the SQ-EM interpretation given in Fig. 3 shows a relatively constant lag: money seems to lag returns by about one to three months. For the higher frequencies, the SQ-EM model shows money leading returns by a very short period, though the low coherences in the high frequencies do not permit much confidence in these high frequency results. The shaded areas in these

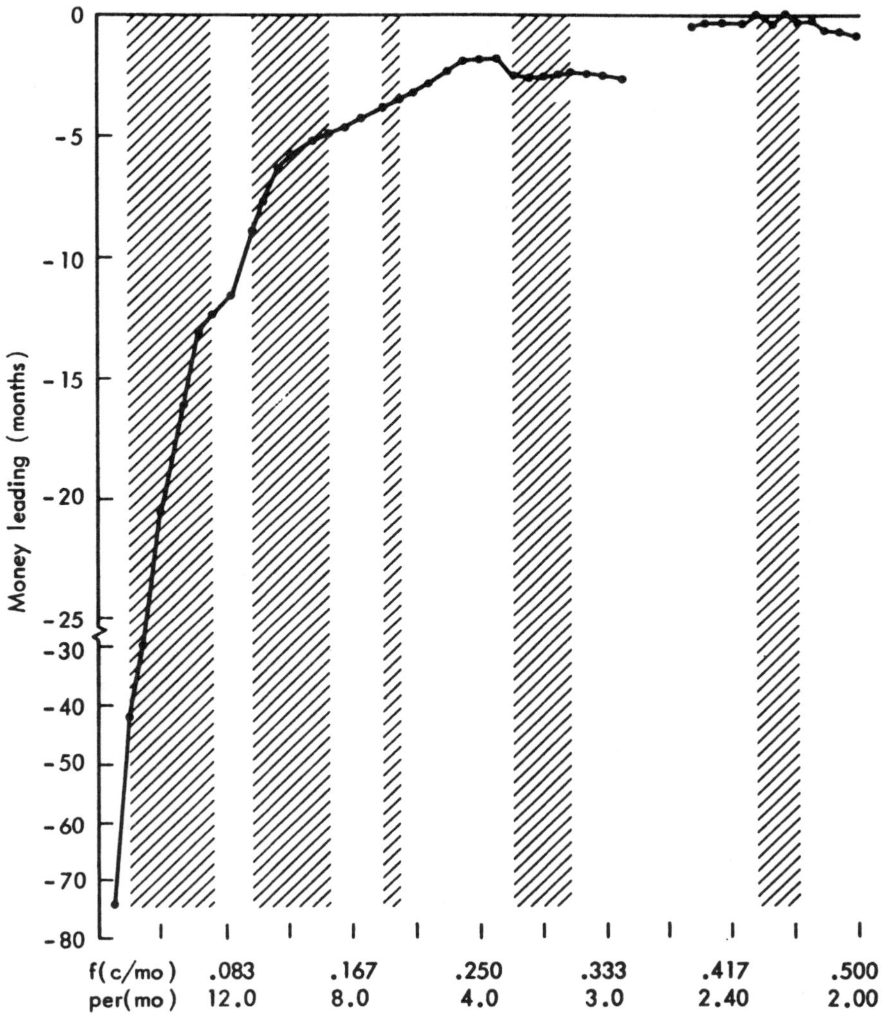

FIGURE 4

Lead/lag for monthly money and returns—SQ interpretation—M = 48

two figures show where the coherence is statistically significantly different from zero. Since the variance of the phase angle estimator is inversely related to the coherence, the phase sentence estimates where coherence is high are more reliable than where coherence is low.

The cross spectral results suggest that the SQ-EM model is preferable to the SQ model in explaining the relationship between money and stock returns. The phase spectrum results would seem to require rejection of the SQ model. In addition, the coherence results suggest that the SQ-EM model may offer a reasonable explanation of the relationship between money and returns. In fact, if the SQ-EM model is compared with the hypothesis that money and returns are unrelated, the cross spectral results (particularly the joint significance test over the low frequencies) seem to favor the SQ-EM interpretation.

B. *Anticipations and the SQ-EM Model*

Although the implications of the SQ-EM model for the *measured* money changes and returns cross spectrum were developed in Section I and estimated earlier in this section, specific estimation of the SQ-EM model (as represented by equation (3)) depends upon identifying the anticipated component of the money supply changes series. Since the anticipated component of money changes is not observed, a proxy variable must be used. Two such variables are considered in this study: forecasts from past money observations and forecasts from current and past monetary base observations.

Since money supply changes do not have a flat power spectrum, money supply changes are not temporally independent. Therefore, past values of money supply changes can be used to predict future values of money supply changes. The forecasts based on current and past realizations of money supply changes were derived by a simplified form of the signal extraction techniques suggested by Nerlove [1967] and Grether [1969]. The anticipated component of money series is then reduced to finding a combined autoregressive and moving average scheme that has the same spectral shape as does the money series to be fitted.

It was found that a third order autoregressive model describes the money spectrum quite well. Since no moving average term is included, least squares can be used to refine the estimates.[23] The results for the three regressions associated with the third order model,

$$m_t = a_1 m_{t-1} + a_2 m_{t-2} + a_3 m_{t-3} + \text{const} + e_t, \tag{5}$$

are given in Table 3. There is little additional information contained in the

TABLE 3
AUTOREGRESSIONS OF MONEY SUPPLY CHANGE
$m_t = a_1 m_{t-1} + a_2 m_{t-2} + a_3 m_{t-3} + \text{const}$

a_1	a_2	a_3	const	R^2		
0.1394	0.2236	0.3122	0.0769	0.2601	(one period	(6a)
(0.0570)	(0.0563)	(0.0579)	(0.0222)		forecast)	
	0.2569	0.3539	0.0916	0.2442	(two period	(6b)
	(0.0551)	(0.0558)	(0.0215)		forecast)	
		0.4365	0.1301	0.1850	(three period	(6c)
		(0.0548)	(0.0206)		forecast)	

money terms lagged four or more periods—indeed, the adjusted R^2 falls after the third lagged variable is included.

The residual vector for each of the estimated equations (6a, b, c) has a

---

23. If a moving average process is included, least squares is not appropriate. In this case the Box-Jenkins [1970] iterative procedure is applicable.

relatively flat power spectrum, per the design of the extraction procedure. Equations (6a, b, c) reveal that money changes may be forecast one, two, *or* three periods ahead with a reasonable degree of accuracy. Of course, the one-period forecasts are better than the two or three period forecasts (since more information is included) and the two-period forecast is better than the three-period forecast. That is,

$$R^2(m^{1a}) > R^2(m^{2a}) > R^2(m^{3a}) \gg R^2(m^{4a}), \text{etc.,}[24]$$

where m^{ja} refers to the j period forecast. However, the R^2 indicates that little additional information is gained in waiting from the two period forecast to the one period forecast.

The multiplicity of good forecasts poses a new problem: Which forecast is incorporated into stock prices? The answer is most probably that current prices reflect some sort of weighted average of these forecasts, with the largest weights assigned to the one, two, and three period forecasts. Because of the lack of a well-defined forecast, it is still difficult to obtain estimates of the SQ-EM model.

However, one very interesting fact comes out of this estimation: the forecast period indicated in Table 3 coincides with the lead of returns over money given by the lead/lag in Fig. 3. That is, the cross spectral results show that money lags returns by about one to three months. Similarly, using past observations on the money supply changes, future money supply changes can be forecast ahead one to three months with a reasonable degree of accuracy. Therefore, the lead of m_t^a over m_t is quite compatible with the lead of returns over money. This evidence lends additional support to the SQ-EM model.

Alternatively, changes in the monetary base could be used as a forecast of changes in the money supply. Again, it is difficult to determine the particular forecast period or the precise formulation of the distributed lag model given by equation (3). Therefore, it was decided that multivariate spectral estimation affords perhaps the best opportunity to determine the relation between the monetary base, the money supply, and returns.

The multiple and partial coherences for the money changes and base changes with returns are given in Fig. 5 for monthly data for 1947 to 1970. The multiple coherence exhibits the same general pattern as the simple coherence between money and returns in Fig. 1a. The partial coherence for money and returns show similar behavior to the simple coherence of money and returns. The partial coherence for the monetary base and returns is not quite as high as for money and returns; yet there are several statistically significant peaks and the highest is in the low frequency range, consistent with the SQ-EM model.

More interesting than the coherence spectra is the partial phase spectrum between money and returns given in Fig. 6. The inclusion of the base into the model appears to account for some of the lead of returns over money. In the very lowest frequencies, money is shown to lead returns; in the other parts of the spectrum the lead to returns over money is reduced (versus the simple

---

24. From $m_t = a_4 m_{t-4} + \text{const} + e_t$, the $R^2 = 0.059$. Therefore, considerably less information about m_t is contained in m_{t-4} than in m_{t-3}.

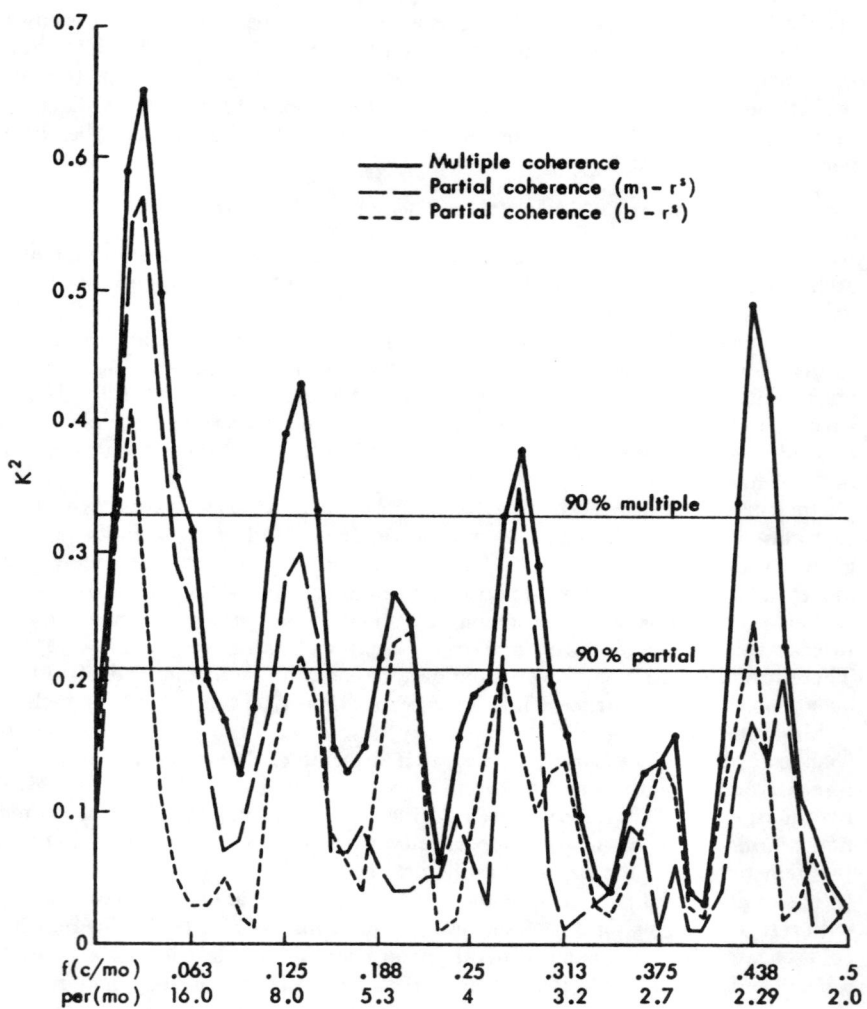

FIGURE 5
Multiple and partial coherences for monthly money and base with returns: $M = 48$

money and returns model). Although the entire lag component is not accounted for (indicating that there are other monetary indicators besides the monetary base), Figs. 5 and 6 lend additional support to the SQ-EM model.

IV. CONCLUSIONS

A. *The Quantity Theory and Efficient Markets*

The quantity theory of money is the basis for the two hypotheses examined in this paper regarding the determination of the market return on stocks. Just

904   The Journal of Finance

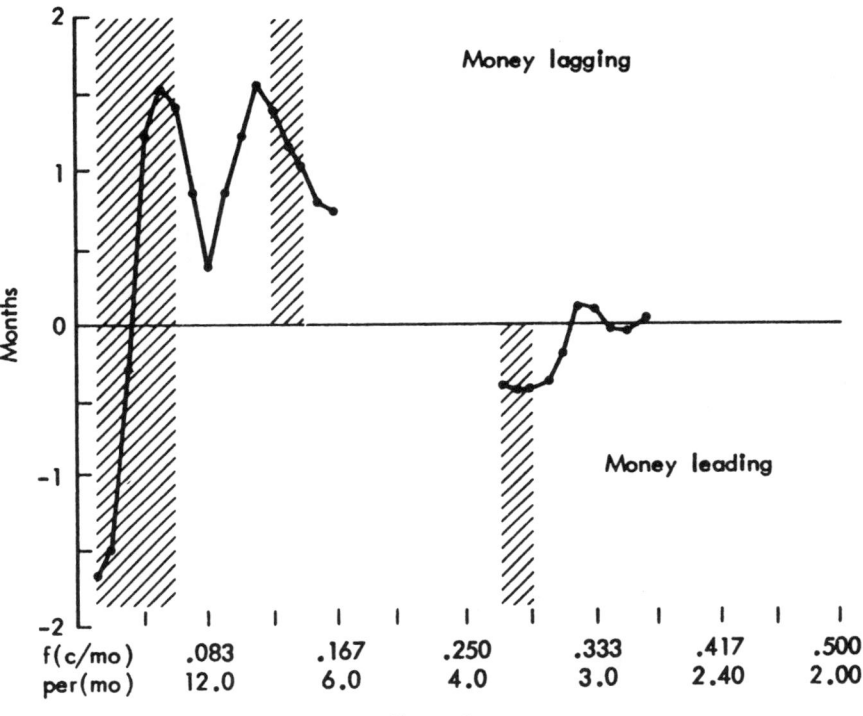

FIGURE 6

Partial lead/lag for monthly money and returns (partial lead/lag for base and returns not given because the phase is too erratic): M = 48

as the quantity theory of money does not postulate that money is the only variable affecting income and prices, the SQ and SQ-EM models developed here do not posit that money is the only variable affecting stock returns. Rather, the models hypothesize that the money supply is an important force affecting the market rate of return on stocks.

The SQ model proposes that money supply changes induce portfolio changes, leading to subsequent changes in stock prices. However, this hypothesis is in direct conflict with the efficient capital markets model, since past information cannot be used to predict future price changes. Therefore, the SQ-EM model suggests that although money supply changes may be an important force affecting stock market returns, returns may actually lead money changes since anticipations about future money supply changes will be included in current prices. In effect, the *SQ-EM model is just an extension of the efficient markets model*, where information includes not only past prices, but also current and past money supply changes. These two hypotheses should then be compared with the weak form of the efficient markets model where information consists only of past prices. Thus, the SQ-EM model becomes a test of two hypotheses: (1) capital markets are efficient, and (2) money supply changes are an important determinant of the market rate of return.

Regression analysis does not seem to provide an adequate means for testing the model. Monthly regressions show an R^2 of approximately 0.05 while annual regressions show an R^2 of 0.50. However, the annual regressions do not permit identification of leads and lags.

Spectral analysis reveals significant coherence for the lower frequencies (longer periods), consistent with the annual regression results.[25] In addition, the spectral results show returns leading money changes for these lower frequencies by one to three months, thus calling for rejection of the SQ model. On the other hand, these estimates are consistent with the SQ-EM model. The SQ-EM model is further supported by evidence showing that the best predictors for the money supply are one to three-month predictors. In fact, a review of Table 3 indicates that little real additional information is gained in going from the two-period forecast to the three-period forecast. That is, the two-period forecast is almost as good as the three-period forecast. Similarly, the lead/lag spectrum shows most of the lead for returns over money to occur in the two to three month range. Therefore, the lead of returns over money is consistent with the information content of past money changes. Finally, incorporation of the monetary base into the estimation (as an indicator of money changes) considerably reduces the lead of returns over money changes.

Given the above findings, why does Sprinkel find evidence to support money changes leading stock prices? First, Sprinkel uses visual examination of the data to test his model. Although visual examination is often a useful preliminary step, conclusions based solely on such evidence are very tenuous. Second, and perhaps more important, Sprinkel misspecifies the model by comparing changes in money with stock prices rather than *changes* in stock prices. It can be shown[26] that prices lag changes in prices by approximately one-quarter of a cycle in the low frequency part of the spectrum. For example, consider the frequency $f = 0.042$, corresponding to a period of 24 months. From Figure 3, returns lead money changes by 1.5 for that frequency. However, prices lag returns (i.e., changes in prices) by 0.225 cycles for $f = 0.042$, which translates into 5.5 months in the time domain. Therefore, money changes *lead* stock *prices* by approximately four months (5.5-1.5) for $f = 0.042$, even though they *lag* stock *returns* by 1.5 months. This shows the importance of considering returns rather than prices in the model.[27] It appears that this misspecification led Sprinkel to erroneously validate the SQ model.

---

25. For the frequency domain representation of the SQ and SQ-EM models, see Cooper [1971] and [1972a].

26. If y_t is defined as $y_t = x_t - x_{t-1}$, the phase angle of the cross spectrum between x and y is given as

$$\theta_{xy}(f) = 0.5 \ (f - 0.5), \ 0 \leqslant f \leqslant 0.5.$$

Therefore, x_t lags y_t by one-quarter cycle at $f = 0$ and the lag decreases linearly until it is zero at $f = 0.5$. (See Jenkins and Watts [1968].)

27. If prices could be predicted with certainty over the entire spectrum, then returns could be predicted with certainty. However, when prices cannot be forecast over the entire spectrum, then the distinction made here between prices and price changes becomes important. For example, in this study the relationship between money and returns is strong only over the very low frequency bands. As a result, whereas money changes are shown to lag returns by one to three months, they actually lead prices. However, since this occurs in only the very low frequencies, this knowledge about prices cannot be turned into an advantage in predicting returns.

B. *Endogenous Money Model*

At a first glance, the results from Section III might suggest another hypothesis regarding the relationship between money and stock returns: the endogenous money model.[28]

In its "strict" form, the endogenous money model proposes that changes in the money supply are solely a function of stock returns and the interest rate. Suppose stock returns and interest rates rise. If the policy of the Fed is the stabilization of interest rates, then the Fed will increase the money supply by an open market purchase of securities. Therefore, stock prices and interest rates will lead money supply changes. Further, the difference between this model and the SQ-EM model is that in this case the causality is from returns to money, the reverse of the SQ-EM model.

Causality between two series cannot be determined by a simple comparison between them. Instead, the choice between a particular hypothesis and several competing hypotheses is the result of a comparison of the implications of each and how well these implications conform to actual events. What, then, are the implications of the endogenous money model? First, since changes in stock prices lead to subsequent changes in the money supply, returns should lead money for the entire spectrum. Second, since the Fed changes the money supply through open market operations, the monetary base is the first variable to be affected. Further, since there is less than perfect correlation between the monetary base and the money supply, the relationship between the base and returns should be stronger than the relationship between the money supply and returns.

The results from the last section can be used to evaluate the endogenous money supply model. The lead lag spectrum in Fig. 3 indicates that the money supply lags returns for the low frequencies (consistent with the endogenous money model) but leads returns for the higher frequencies (not consistent with the endogenous money model). Since the evidence showing money leading for the higher frequencies is not strong, the endogenous money model cannot be rejected on the basis of the lead/lag spectrum alone. However, the evidence on the relation between money and returns versus the base and returns is sufficient to reject the "strict" form of the endogenous money model. Although the cross spectral results for the base and returns were not presented in Section III, it was necessary to compute them to estimate the trivariate model of the base and money with returns. Those results show substantially greater correlation between money and returns than between the base and returns.

The comparison between the SQ-EM model and the endogenous money model given here is analogous to the Friedman-Meiselman comparison of the simple Keynesian and simple quantity theory models. On this basis, the SQ-EM model is selected in favor of the endogenous money model. It is important to note that the endogenous money model does not preclude the existence of the SQ-EM model (and vice versa). In fact, the true model is probably a combination of these two plus other models. However, these results indicate that the SQ-

---

28. This hypothesis was suggested to me separately by Robert J. Gordon and Earl Rolph.

EM model provides a more reasonable interpretation of the data than either the SQ or the endogenous money models.

C. *Summary*

Two important propositions can be established on the basis of the evidence presented in this paper. First, the efficient markets hypothesis cannot be rejected because of Sprinkel's findings. The results presented in Section III show that stock returns lead money supply changes; they do not lag money changes. Second, money supply changes do appear to have an important effect on stock returns. The most plausible explanation of the relation between money supply changes and stock returns seems to be a combination of the efficient markets model and the quantity theory of money. That is, anticipations about future money supply changes are incorporated into current stock returns. Therefore, although the results do not point exclusively toward the SQ-EM model, they are at least consistent with the SQ-EM representation. Further, the SQ-EM model appears to be preferable to the endogenous money model.

BIBLIOGRAPHY

Irma Adelman. "Long Cycles—Fact or Artifact?" *American Economic Review*, LV (June, 1965), 444-463.

G. E. P. Box and Gwilym M. Jenkins. *Time Series Analysis: Forecasting and Control*. San Francisco: Holden-Day, 1970.

V. K. Chetty. "On the Nearness of Near-Moneys," *American Economic Review*, LIX (June, 1969), 270-281.

Richard V. L. Cooper. "Money and Stock Returns." Ph.D. Dissertation, University of Chicago, 1971.

——————. *Efficient Capital Markets and the Quantity Theory of Money*. P-4886, The Rand Corporation, Santa Monica, August, 1972 (1972a).

——————. *The Use of Spectral Analytic Techniques in Economics*. P-4882, The Rand Corporation, Santa Monica, August, 1972 (1972b).

Eugene F. Fama. "The Behavior of Stock Market Prices," *Journal of Business*, XXXVIII (January, 1965), 34-105.

——————. "Risk, Return, and Equilibrium: Some Clarifying Comments," *Journal of Finance*, XXIII (March, 1968), 29-40.

——————. "Efficient Capital Markets: A Review of Theory and Empirical Work," *Journal of Finance*, LV (May, 1970), 383-417.

Lawrence Fisher. "Some New Stock Market Indexes," *Journal of Business*, XXXIX (January, 1966), 191-225.

George Fisher. *Spectral Methods in Econometrics*. Cambridge: Harvard University Press, 1969.

Milton Friedman. "The Optimum Quantity of Money," in Milton Friedman, *The Optimum Quantity of Money and Other Essays*. Chicago: Aldine Publishing Company, 1969.

Milton Friedman and Anna J. Schwartz. *A Monetary History of the United States, 1867-1960*. Princeton: Princeton University Press, 1964.

David M. Grether. "Distributed Lags, Prediction, and Signal Extraction," Cowles Foundation Discussion Paper No. 279. New Haven: Yale University, September, 1969.

J. G. Gurley and E. S. Shaw. *Money in a Theory of Finance*. Washington, D.C.: Brookings Institution, 1960.

John C. Hause. "Spectral Analysis and the Detection of Lead-Lag Relationships," *American Economic Review*, LXI, March 1971, pp. 213-217.

Gwilym M. Jenkins and Donald G. Watts. *Spectral Analysis and Its Applications*. San Francisco: Holden-Day, 1968.

R. C. Jennison. *Fourier Transforms and Convolutions for the Experimentalist*. New York: Pergamon Press, 1961.

Benjamin F. King. "Market and Industry Factors in Stock Price Behavior," *Journal of Business*, XXXIX (January, 1966), 139-190.

Tong Hun Lee. "On Measuring the Nearness of Near-Moneys: Comment," *American Economic Review*, LXII, March, 1972, pp. 217-220.

John Lintner. "The Valuation of Risk Assets and the Selection of Risky Investments in Stock Portfolios and Capital Budgets," *Review of Economics and Statistics*, XLVII (February, 1965), 13-37.

——————. "Security Prices, Risk, and Maximal Gains from Diversification," *Journal of Finance*, X (December, 1965), 587-615.

Helen Makower and Jacob Marschak. "Assets, Prices, and Monetary Theory," *Economica*, New Series 5 (1938), 261-288. Reprinted in George J. Stigler and Kenneth E. Boulding (eds.). *A.E.A. Readings in Price Theory*. VI (Chicago: Richard D. Irwin, Inc., 1952), 283-310.

Harry Markowitz. *Portfolio Selection: Efficient Diversification of Investment*. New York: John Wiley & Sons, 1959.

A. James Meigs. "Monetary Policy and Stock Prices in the 70's—Another Point of View." Mimeographed remarks for Argus Research Conference on "The New, Economics and the Stock Market in the 1970's." Phoenix, Arizona: November 23, 1969.

Marc Nerlove. "Distributed Lags and Unobserved Components in Economic Time Series." Cowles Foundation Discussion Paper No. 221. New Haven: Yale University, March, 1967.

Robert Officer. "The Time Series Behavior of the Market Function on the N.Y.S.E." Ph.D. dissertation, University of Chicago, 1972.

Michael Palmer. "Money Supply and Stock Prices," *Financial Analysts Journal*, XVI (July/August, 1970), 19-27.

William F. Sharpe. "Capital Asset Prices: A Theory of Market Equilibrium Under Conditions of Risk," *Journal of Finance*, XIX (September, 1964), 425-442.

Beryl W. Sprinkel. *Money and Stock Prices*. Homewood Illinois: Richard D. Irwin, Inc., 1964.

[17]

The Honest Government's Guide to the Revenue from the Creation of Money

Leonardo Auernheimer

Texas A & M University

The analysis of the revenue from the creation of fiat money is usually carried out in terms of comparative statics. Given the value of relevant parameters, the rate of inflation which maximizes revenue is characterized as the one yielding the highest stream of revenue once all adjustments have been completed: either some rate of monetary expansion is set, and the results corresponding to the long-run values of the variables are analyzed (Friedman 1971), or the inflation rate is fixed at the outset and adjustments taken to be instantaneous, but assuming away any effect of the once-and-for-all changes in real cash balances on the variable to be maximized (revenues), that is, assuming that those changes are met by once-and-for-all changes in the price level (Bailey 1956). Of course, both procedures amount to the same thing.

This is, indeed, the correct analysis in processes in which the transition period can be assumed away because the long-run value of the variable to be maximized is reached asymptotically from the very beginning, so that the highest stream at any point is also the stream with the highest present value at the initial point. This is not so in the case of the revenue from the creation of money.

The purpose of this paper is to show, first, how explicit consideration of revenues accruing during the adjustment period (or "at" the adjustment, when it occurs instantaneously) is essential for the understanding of the essence of money as a capital good; and second, how for a particular adjustment behavior—instantaneous adjustment—taking due account of once-and-for-all changes produces results very different from those reported in the literature. In general, lower "revenue-maximizing" rates of inflation are called for, and in particular, those rates are indepen-

This paper was written at the University of Chicago, and it is based on a chapter of my dissertation. I am thankful to S. Fischer, R. Gordon, C. A. Rodriguez, L. Sjaastad, and R. Zecher, and in particular to M. Friedman, who asked the right question. A pitiless comment by H. G. Johnson and a set of careful suggestions by an anonymous referee forced me to restate the argument in what I hope is a clearer fashion. After this paper was submitted for publication, an unpublished paper by Charles D. Cathcart was brought to my attention, in which some of the points made here are independently developed by Cathcart.

dent of the rate of growth of the economy. For expository purposes, we first proceed to demonstrate the second point.

I. The Assumptions

The explicit consideration of transitional effects makes it necessary to specify the assumptions very precisely. For the particular case we examine, they are: (a) When some rate of inflation (π) is announced, it is believed by the public and "implemented" immediately by the government. (b) The adjustment of actual to desired cash balances is so quick that it is proper to treat it as being instantaneous. (c) No once-and-for-all changes in the price level are allowed, that is, when a "lower than the preexisting" rate of inflation is announced, the government steps into the market and "sells" the additional real balances desired by the public. Likewise, when the rate of inflation is increased, it is prepared to "repurchase" the excess of existing over desired real balances. This means that no once-and-for-all "subsidies" or "capital levies" are imposed upon the public.

Assumptions (a) and (b) are the same as the ones used, for example, by Bailey (1956). Assumption (c) is critical, and requires some elaboration.

Assumption (c) does not present any difficulty for the case where some lower (than the preexisting) rate of inflation is announced, and the government reaps the once-and-for-all increase in total wealth; there is no reason why it should not do so, interested as it is in maximizing revenue. The question is, Why should government proceed in a symmetric fashion when a higher rate of inflation is announced, that is, to intervene in the market and sell goods so that no once-and-for-all change in the price level occurs?

There are at least two reasons for assuming so. In the first place, a "once-and-for-all" change in the price level is a short-hand expression for a very short period of high inflation; strictly, there is some "cheating" by part of the government in allowing that to happen. Here is where the adjective "honest" applies. The same assumption is used by Foley and Sidrausky (1971) in analyzing the effect of changes in the rate of inflation, in the context of their model.[1] The second reason is that, if the symmetry is not imposed, the model becomes highly unstable when the other two assumptions are maintained. The reasons for this are explained in Section IV below.

---

[1] "The change in the target rate of inflation is reflected by a change in the slope of the p_m (semilogarithmic) line at time T, but there is no jump in p_m at time T. If, when the government announces a change in the rate of inflation, it does not want to disappoint private expectations about the course that p_m will follow, then no jump in p_m can be allowed at $t = T$. Otherwise, the rate of change of p_m at $t = T$ would be infinity" (Foley and Sidrausky 1971, p. 190).

Finally, it is worthwhile to mention that at least assumption (c) acquires full empirical relevance in cases where the preexisting rate of inflation is higher than the "optimum" rate, as described below.

II. The Analysis

In what follows, for simplicity, I will use a Cagan-type function of the demand for money and assume constant income elasticity (not necessarily equal to unity). I also assume, as it is usually done, that government is the only issuer of money.

Total real revenues per (infinitely small) period are defined as

$$R_t = \frac{dM}{dt}\frac{1}{P} = \frac{dM}{dt}\frac{1}{M}\frac{M}{P} = \rho m_t, \tag{1}$$

where ρ is the (proportional) rate of monetary expansion, and m is real cash balances.

By differentiating the identity $m = M/P$,

$$R_t = \rho m_t = m_t \pi_t + \dot{m}_t,$$

where π_t is the rate of inflation and a dot over the variable denotes the time derivative.

If the desired stock of money—identically equal to the actual stock—is

$$m_t = A \cdot e^{\gamma t} \cdot e^{-b(r+\pi)}, \tag{2}$$

where $\gamma = $ a "growth factor" (equal to $n + g\eta$, for $n = $ rate of population growth; $g = $ rate of growth of per capita income; $\eta = $ income elasticity of demand); $r = $ "the" real interest rate; $A, b > 0$, parameters, then $\dot{m}_t = \gamma m_t - b m_t \dot{\pi}$. If adjustments are instantaneous, $\dot{\pi} = 0$ after $t = 0$, so that the flow of revenue after $t = 0$ becomes $R_t = m_t \pi + \dot{m}_t = m_t(\pi + \gamma)$. Assuming that the future is discounted by government at the prevailing rate of interest r, at any time $t = 0$ the present value of the revenue from the creation of money, for some constant rate of inflation, is given by

$$V_{t=0} = \int_{t=0}^{\infty} m_t(\pi + \gamma)e^{-rt}\, dt + (m_{t=0+} - m_{t=0}), \tag{3}$$

where $m_{t=0}$ are cash balances at the preexisting rate of inflation, π_0; and $m_{t=0+}$, cash balances corresponding to the new rate of inflation, π, that is, just after the change.

The first term in expression (3) is the present value of the flow of revenue obtained at each period after $t = 0$; this is the term usually considered in the literature. The second part is the once-and-for-all "sale" (positive or negative, according to whether $m_{t=0+} \gtrless m_{t=0}$, or $\pi \lessgtr \pi_0$) of real cash balances which takes place at $t = 0$.

Given the assumed form of the demand for money, equation (3) becomes

$$V_{t=0} = Ae^{-b(r+\pi)}(\gamma + \pi) \int_{t=0}^{\infty} e^{(\gamma - r)t} \, dt$$

$$+ Ae^{-br}(e^{-b\pi} - e^{-b\pi_0}). \tag{4}$$

Assuming $r > \gamma$, so that the integral converges to some finite value,[2]

$$= \frac{Ae^{-b(r+\pi)}(\gamma + \pi)}{(r - \gamma)} + Ae^{-br}(e^{-b\pi} - e^{-b\pi_0}). \tag{5}$$

Differentiating with respect to the rate of inflation,

$$\frac{\partial V_{t=0}}{\partial \pi} = Ae^{-br} \cdot e^{-b\pi} \left(-\frac{b}{\gamma - r} + \frac{1}{\gamma - r} - \frac{b\pi}{\gamma - r} + b \right),$$

and equating to zero,

$$1 - b\gamma - b\pi + b(\gamma - r) = 0,$$

$$\pi = \frac{1}{b} - r. \tag{6}$$

That is, the revenue-maximizing rate is independent of the rate of growth of the economy.[3]

From expression (6) it follows that, to the extent that the basic assumptions are met, the usual analysis overestimates the "revenue-maximizing" rate (and, consequently, errs also in the calculation of magnitudes such as maximum revenues, ratio of maximum revenues to total income, etc.). The interested reader can easily calculate the extent of the overestimation for particular values of the parameters.

The overestimation is larger the lower the value of the growth factor, γ. This result is consistent with a particular interpretation of the approach taken in this paper. In the usual analysis, the concern is with the revenue derived from keeping the new desired real balances constant, and from providing future "generations" with the same balances,[4] but not from taking charge of the difference in the real stock desired by existing

---

[2] The case when $r < \gamma$ confronts us with the same situation where an individual owns a stream of income which grows at a constant rate, larger than the rate of interest of the economy. Such an individual is infinitely wealthy, provided he can borrow ad infinitum. If he tries to consume ad infinitum, eventually the rate of interest will rise. The relationship between the rate of growth and the rate of interest in the steady state has been ignored here.

[3] An alternative proof, along the lines of the calculus of variations, is immediate.

[4] Unless income per capita does not grow, so that the "growth factor" γ reflects only population growth, the term "generation" has a special meaning in this particular interpretation. It refers to some combination of "new bodies" and "new purchasing power."

people at $t = 0$. In other words, we consider existing people just like future "generations."[5] The larger the growth factor, γ, the smaller the weight of instantaneous "sales" in "total new sales" as a source of revenue —as opposed to the revenue derived from a tax on existing balances.

From expression (5), a geometric interpretation is straightforward. At any instant $t = 0$, the difference between the present value of future total revenue (at the preexisting rate π_0) and the present value of the revenue from some alternative rate, π, can be expressed as

$$(\Delta V)_{t=0} = (m_{t=0+} - m_{t=0}) + \frac{m_{t=0+}(\gamma + \pi)}{r - \gamma}$$
$$- \frac{m_{t=0}(\gamma + \pi_0)}{r - \gamma}. \tag{7}$$

The first term in expression (7) is the once-and-for-all gain (loss) from changing to a lower (higher) rate of inflation; the second and third, the present values of the two alternative streams. This can be reduced, after some transformations, to

$$(\Delta V)_{t=0} = \left(\frac{1}{r - \gamma}\right) [m_{t=0+}(r + \pi) - m_{t=0}(r + \pi_0)],$$
$$= \left(\frac{1}{r - \gamma}\right) [(r + \pi)(\Delta m) + (\Delta \pi)(m_{t=0})], \tag{8}$$

where $(r + \pi)(\Delta m) =$ (area A) + (area B) in figure 1, and $(m_{t=0})(\Delta \pi) =$ (area C). The increment in the total present value will be zero when area $(A + B)$ and area C are equal, independently of the value of γ. The analysis can be carried out at any point in time, that is, for any position of the demand curve $L - L$.

Notice that this can also be expressed as a flow, by multiplying the total marginal present value (8) by the rate of interest; in particular, when $\gamma = 0$, it becomes

$$r(\Delta V)_{t=0} = (r + \pi)(\Delta m) + m_{t=0}(\Delta \pi).$$

Observe also that these results are the same as what would be obtained when revenue per period is taken to be equal to $m(r + \pi)$; the meaning of this will become clear in Section III.

III. A Digression on the Economics of the Supply of Capital Goods

In a recent paper (Friedman 1971), Friedman asks the question:

---

[5] I am indebted to Stanley Fischer for this interpretation.

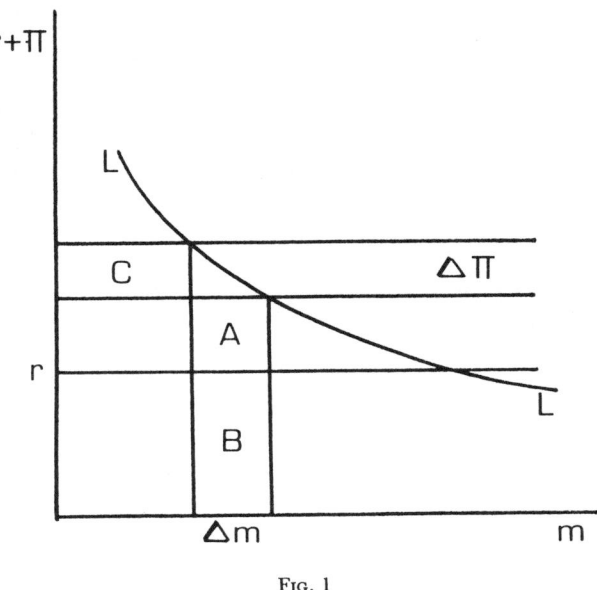

Fig. 1

It has always seemed natural to assimilate a government monopoly of fiat money issue with a private monopoly of a product produced at zero cost—Cournot's mineral spring. Yet we have just demonstrated that this is not correct. The owner of the spring will maximize his proceeds by charging a price at which the price elasticity of demand is unity. And this will be true whether the economy is stationary or growing. . . . Why is this not also true for the government which can issue money at zero marginal cost? Why will it not also maximize its revenue by pricing at the unit-elasticity point on its demand curve, regardless of whether there is growth or not?

The answer is because there are two different prices that are relevant to money issue—one, the goods and services that are given up to acquire a dollar; the other, the number of cents per dollar per year that the money holder must spend to keep his real balances constant. Only the latter is analogous to the price of the mineral water. [Friedman 1971, pp. 854–55]

Then, he suggests an analogy with the "monopolistic producer and servicer of . . . durable equipment who sells the equipment but charges an annual fee for servicing it."

Our analysis points toward a somewhat different interpretation. The correct analogy seems to be with Friedman's producer and servicer of durable equipment, provided that (1) the equipment has a fixed sale price (equal to unity, in our money case); (2) the producer is committed to "repurchase" the equipment at that fixed price. An alternative example, amounting to the same thing, is the case of a monopolist renting a capital good (say, telephones), at an explicit rental per unit per year (π), and charging a fixed and refundable deposit. At any period, total revenues are made up of the explicit rental on the existing stock ($m\pi$ in our money case), and of the net receipts of deposit funds ($\dot{m}$ in our case). The analogy in this case is exact, and we need only to introduce assumption (c) (Section I above) when adjustments are instantaneous. In both cases (telephones and money), what is bought by the public is services, and the total price paid for those services is made up of the "explicit rental," π, plus the "implicit rental," the real interest rate.[6] The correct maximization procedure, then, is with respect to the total paid for the services sold; this yields a result identical to that obtained from the production and sale of any other product, that is, independent of the rate of growth of the economy.[7]

IV. The Consequences of Relaxing Some Assumptions

The analysis of Section II is limited by the extreme restrictiveness of assumptions (a)–(c), discussed in Section II. We proceed now to show the extent to which the relaxation of each of them would modify the results.

1. If assumptions (a) and (b) are maintained, and assumption (c) is not imposed, the model is unstable. Consider a situation where, for each discrete change in the rate of inflation, the government is allowed to bear (reap) or not the once-and-for-all losess (gains). If so, the optimal behavior will be to reap the gains when π is lowered, and let the public bear the losses when π is increased. Take, as an initial position, $\pi = (1/b) - r$ (assuming no growth, for simplicity); now, it will be profitable to switch to the higher rate of inflation $\pi = 1/b$, to which a higher stream is attached, since there will be no once-and-for-all loss to (more than) compensate for the gain in the flow (i.e., only the first term in expression [3] is relevant). If, instead, $\pi = 1/b$ is taken as the initial position, then it is profitable to change to a lower rate, $\pi = (1/b) - r$, as the once-and-for-all gain more than compensates for the loss in the

---

[6] The theory of the optimum quantity of money makes it clear that this last component is a cost for money holders; the literature on the revenue from the creation of money does not, in general, see it as a "revenue" for the money issuer. For an exception, see Johnson (1969*a*, 1969*b*).

[7] The question is somewhat similar to the one arising in the case of a monopolist selling some capital good, where the (exponential) rate of depreciation can be controlled by the producer. In a recent paper (1970), Swan has shown that some erroneous conclusions in the literature were derived precisely because of ignoring once-and-for-all changes in the existing stock—changes which, as a purely mathematical matter, cannot be captured by static maximization procedures when capital goods, and their price—instead of services and rentals—are considered.

present value of the future stream (i.e., now, both terms in expression [3] are relevant). The result is that there will always be incentives for "jumping" from any of the two rates of inflation to the other. Obviously, we cannot expect the other two assumptions to survive under these circumstances.

2. Assumptions (*b*) and (*c*) are twin brothers: if a lag in the adjustment of actual to desired cash balances is allowed for—removal of assumption (*b*)—then assumption (*c*) is no longer necessary, and the analogy with the private monopolist as described in the previous section is exact. It can be easily shown, indeed, that the "instantaneous-adjustment" case is but a particular limiting instance of the more general case.

3. Removal of assumption (*a*) presents different difficulties. The analogy with the private monopolist as described above is preserved in its formal presentation, but no longer can the "control variable" be taken as being the same: while our monopolist can set the explicit rental at every period, the same is not true of the fiat money issuer. But, in any case, statements about the optimum (constant) value of the explicit rental which are valid for any of the two remain valid for the other.

4. If no restrictive assumptions are imposed, then no rule on optimum behavior can be deduced a priori (even if, for example, the rate of monetary expansion is forced to be constant from the very beginning) without knowing the exact form of the adjustment and the expectations equations. Of course, it will be true that for the whole adjustment period total revenues are

$$\int_{t_0}^{t_1} R_t \, dt = \int_{t_0}^{t_1} m_t \pi_t \, dt + \int_{t_0}^{t_1} \dot{m}_t \, dt,$$

where $t_1 - t_0$ is the duration of the adjustment period. For any change in the equilibrium rate of inflation, from the demand for money function we know precisely the sign and magnitude of the second integral. The problem, though, is that nothing can be said regarding the magnitude of the first integral. Furthermore, the problem is complicated when earlier flows carry a larger weight than later ones (in particular, if the problem is analyzed in the context of a model allowing for a lag in the rate of inflation after a stepwise change in the rate of monetary expansion).

V. Conclusions, and Two Implications

We have shown how explicit consideration of changes occurring at the transition allows, in general, for a better understanding of some characteristics common to both money and other capital goods. For a particular adjustment process (instantaneous adjustment), we have deduced a "revenue-maximizing" rule different from the one derived in the literature.

Even though the main point in this note is theoretical, at least two empirical considerations follow. First, that there may be substantial once-and-for-all gains (for both growing and stationary economies) from a reduction in the rate of inflation, gains which may accrue almost immediately, provided that adjustments are fast and government can effectively persuade the public about its intentions; these once-and-for-all gains may be large enough to compensate for a fall in the subsequent permanent stream. This is still more relevant in cases where some time is needed either for decreasing the level of public expenditure or for raising revenues from conventional taxes.

Second, the argument shows how, in principle, the provision of the optimum quantity of money is "self-financed" (in the sense that there is no need to impose conventional taxes for the payment of interest on cash balances) if at every instant (1) the first component of total revenues ($\dot{m}$) is used to purchase real capital and integrate an "investment fund" (presumably in the form of equity) and the second component ($m\pi$) is used to pay interest on real balances; (2) the interest received on the "investment fund" (mr) is used to complete interest payments in real cash balances. Of course, if in the past government has consumed part or all of the "investment fund," and at some point it decides to start paying interest on money, then it would need "outside financing." But if this is the case and the economy is growing, the proportion of interest paid on money which needs to be "outside financed" decreases over time, and eventually becomes negligible after a few years.[8]

References

Auernheimer, Leonardo. "Essays in the Theory of Inflation." Ph.D. dissertation, Univ. Chicago, 1973.

Bailey, Martin J. "The Welfare Cost of Inflationary Finance." *J.P.E.* 64 (April 1956): 93–110.

Foley, D. K., and Sidrausky, M. *Monetary and Fiscal Policy in a Growing Economy.* New York: Macmillan, 1971.

Friedman, Milton. "Government Revenue from Inflation." *J.P.E.* 79 (July/August 1971): 846–56.

Johnson, Harry G. "Inside Money, Outside Money, Income, Wealth, and Welfare in Monetary Theory." *J. Money, Credit, and Banking* 1, no. 1 (February 1969): 30–45. (*a*)

———. "A Note on Seigniorage and the Social Saving from Substituting Credit for Commodity Money." In *Monetary Problems of the International Economy*, edited by R. A. Mundell and A. Swoboda. Chicago: Univ. Chicago Press, 1969. (*b*)

Swan, Peter L. "Durability of Consumption Goods." *A.E.R.* 60 (December 1970): 884–94.

[8] For further elaboration of this point, and some hypothetical calculations, see Auernheimer (1973, chap. 1).

[18]

The Demand for High-Powered Money

By JAMES R. LOTHIAN*

The resurgence of the quantity theory in the past two decades has brought with it a renewal of an often-debated question—how to define money. Though the answers that have been given vary widely, most economists, with little hesitation, would probably settle on a monetary total similar to M_1 or M_2 in the United States as "the" definition of money.

What this paper shows, however, is that the choice is not nearly so simple. Empirical analysis is often circumscribed by lack of data on many of the variables theory suggests can affect the demand for money, such as the interest rates paid on various categories of deposits and the quality or "moneyness" of those deposits. Under some circumstances the omission of these variables can have a serious effect on the stability of conventional deposit-inclusive definitions of money, causing them to be highly imperfect indicators of the effects of money on the overall economy.

The solution that I propose in these situations is to return to a narrower definition of money, high-powered money alone. The rationale is that since high-powered money is of relatively constant quality over time and space, such specification errors are likely to be less important for high-powered money than for deposit-inclusive totals. The demand for high-powered money should be more stable than the demand for other monetary aggregates.

Since differences in deposit quality and deposit interest rates are likely to be particularly great across countries, I test this proposition by analyzing the demand functions for high-powered money and for various other monetary assets estimated across an international time-section sample spanning forty countries in the postwar period. On the whole the results support my hypothesis. I find that high-powered money is unambiguously the most stable total across the countries in my sample, even when it is judged on the basis of the constant velocity model and the other totals are judged on the basis of a more sophisticated model of money demand. Moreover, I find evidence of several sorts that the factors which a priori could be expected to produce this result have actually been operable.

I. Theoretical Considerations

A. *Money Demand Functions*

To be able to make a judgment about which monetary total is most stable in demand, and hence which is the most useful definition of money, we first have to decide which variables we will assume to be the most important determinants of demand and which we will assume to have only a negligible impact and will ignore in the statistical analysis.[1] In discussing the

* Economist, First National City Bank. In preparing this paper and the dissertation upon which it is based, I have benefitted from the comments and assistance of a large number of people. I am particularly indebted to Milton Friedman for key suggestions in the dissertation stage of my work and to Arthur Gandolfi for valuable discussions of various drafts of this paper. I also want to thank W. H. Bruce Brittain, Phillip Cagan, Robert J. Gordon, Wallace Huffman, Dudley D. Johnson, James P. Smith, Richard Zecher, and the managing editor of this *Review*.

[1] Milton Friedman and Anna Schwartz (1970) provide a strong statement of the position that choosing a definition of money is primarily an empirical issue. They argue further that stability in demand is an appropriate criterion for deciding between alternative definitions of money. A related criterion for defining money has been advocated by V. Karuppan Chetty, who has attempted to estimate directly the substitution relationships between various monetary totals.

factors affecting the stability of high-powered money relative to deposit-inclusive definitions of money and in the subsequent statistical analysis, I assume a simple and widely used money demand function that is derivable from the modern quantity theory and has the form:

$$(1) \qquad m = f(y_p, r)$$

where m is the desired ratio of money to income, y_p is permanent real income, and r is "the" nominal rate of interest.

As a first approximation for statistical purposes, I also use a more restrictive formulation based upon the constant velocity model of the earlier quantity theory,

$$(2) \qquad m = k$$

where k—the Cambridge k—is a constant.

Before we actually use these demand functions to evaluate competing definitions of money empirically, I want to discuss in detail some of the other omitted influences on money demand and their likely effects on the various monetary totals. But first, let us briefly outline a more general approach to the demand for money that relaxes some of the restrictive assumptions implicit in equation (1).

A model of money demand like Benjamin Klein's (1970, 1974), which is similar to the formulations used by Edgar Feige (1964) and by Morris Perlman and is in the spirit of the new approaches to consumer theory developed by Gary Becker and Kelvin Lancaster (1966, 1971), is a particularly useful starting point. In his model Klein makes explicit the distinction between the services individuals receive from money and the real stock of money that they hold, and he assumes that the services are what provide utility to money holders. Then by specifying an individual's demand and production functions for monetary services he derives an individual's (stock) demand function for money that we can express as

$$(3) \qquad m = g(y_p, P_M, \beta_M)$$

where P_M is the price of the monetary services from the marginal unit of money, equal to the difference between r and the rate of interest paid on money r_M, and β is an index of the quality of money, a term from the individual's production function for monetary services.[2]

B. Conventional Definitions of Money

The estimation of an equation based on (1) rather than on the more complete formulation (3) can lead to several types of specification error when money is defined conventionally to include deposits.[3] Let us consider the effect of omitting r_M first.

Since r_M is likely to move together with the overall level of interest rates, the coefficient in the auxiliary regression of r_M on r will be positive, which means that the coefficient of r in the regression based on (1) will be biased downwards in absolute value. But if the correlation between r and r_M is high, this type of specification error may have only a small effect on the stability of the demand for conventionally defined money.

Both across countries and within some countries over time this is unlikely to be the case. With no interest paid on currency, r_M will be equal to the product of r_D, the rate paid on deposits, and D/M, the ratio of deposits to money. If the interest rate paid on deposits is competitive (in the sense of reflecting a zero marginal profit), it in turn will equal $r_I(1-R/D)$,

---

[2] Equation (3) is derivable from a demand function for monetary services of the form $S^d = D(R, y_p)$ and from a production function for monetary services of the form $S = \beta_M(M/P)$, where S represents monetary services; M/P is the real stock of money; β_M is a variable coefficient of production; R is the rental price of a unit of monetary services, equal to P_M/β_M; and the superscript d signifies quantity demanded.

[3] See Henri Theil, pp. 504–56, for a discussion of specification analysis. Note that to simplify the discussion throughout, I am only considering one alternative definition of money, the sum of currency and total commercial bank deposits.

where r_I is the interest earned on bank assets and R/D is the ratio of bank reserves to deposits.[4] Hence, even if movements in r and r_I are closely related, differences in R/D due to differences in reserve requirements or in other factors affecting banks' preferences for reserves relative to deposits will be reflected in differences in r_D. The existence of ceilings on either r_I or directly on r_D, which cannot be evaded costlessly, will also reduce the correlation of r and r_M.

What may be an even more serious problem empirically than unaccounted differences in own interest rates on money are differences in the quality of money. These differences can stem from differences in the degree of financial development of different countries or from the method used by banks to circumvent regulatory constraints on the interest they pay on deposits and earn on their assets. This second source of problems would be relevant both across countries that have differing regulations and within countries having high and variable rates of inflation along with regulations.

We can categorize these quality differences under a number of headings, each of which has slightly different implications. One assumption is that quality differences, or differences in the services offered in connection with money, are exactly equivalent to implicit interest payments on deposits. In this case their omission produces the same results as omission of explicit interest payments.

Another assumption is that quality differences are of a factor-augmenting form, involving differences in the β_m of equation (3). In this case their impact is more difficult to assess, since an increase in β_M has

both a negative production and a positive price effect on the derived demand for money, with the net outcome ambiguous. If the net effect is positive this type of quality difference will cause a downward bias in the income coefficient in regression counterparts of (1), since countries that are more financially sophisticated are also likely to be on the whole more developed. It may also cause a downward bias (in absolute value) in the interest rate coefficient if deposit rate ceilings are the rule, since in countries with high rates of inflation banks will make more attempts to circumvent regulations.

When circumvention of interest ceilings provides the impetus, another form of what we have termed "quality changes" may take place. Banks may introduce a new liability that is unregulated as a substitute for the regulated deposits. In some instances, such as with Eurodollar deposits at foreign branches of American banks, these new liabilities may be close substitutes with existing deposits and, in principle, simply could be added to these totals to preserve their homogeneity. In actuality, however, this is unlikely to be an option, since the success of introducing new unregulated liabilities as substitutes for existing deposits depends upon their going unnoticed by the authorities. Hence, to the extent that this is the method of circumvention, the interest coefficient will be biased upwards in absolute value. Countries with high rates of inflation will have recorded deposit totals that are lower than the true totals that include the new goods.

A fourth and perhaps most realistic assumption is that quality differences affect not only the monetary service stream received from deposits, but also their substitutability with other assets. That is, we can view deposits as supplying more than one type of service, bond-type services in addition to monetary services. Some types of regulations and some patterns of finan-

---

[4] This formulation is discussed in Klein (1970, 1974). As he points out, even where entry into banking is regulated, competitive interest rates could still exist if competition is allowed in the provision of nonprice services which are viewed by individuals as equivalent to explicit interest payments.

cial development may lead to a change in the mix of these services. For instance, to circumvent ceilings on deposit rates, banks may offer relatively more bond-type services in connection with deposits, thus increasing their substitutability with bonds and decreasing their substitutability with currency. The end result would be to decrease the stability of the demand for money defined to include deposits.

C. *High-Powered Money*

All of these factors—changes in own interest rates and the various types of quality changes—have direct effects on deposits but not on currency held by the public, making currency a potentially attractive alternative to broader definitions of money.[5] However, if we use currency alone as the definition of money rather than, say, the sum of currency and total commercial bank deposits or M_2, a consistent accounting practice would be to redefine the currency component of M_2 to include all of high-powered money.[6]

The use of high-powered money as the definition of money can also be viewed from a different perspective. When no interest is paid on either the deposits of commercial banks with the monetary authorities or on currency and hence on vault cash, reserve holdings of commercial banks set an upper limit on the extent to which interest can be paid on deposits. Reserves are in effect the portion of deposits which

always yield only monetary services and no interest. The remainder of deposits, equal to the difference between deposits and reserves, is the portion of deposits which, at least potentially, yields interest. A holder of deposits is thus a participant in a tie-in sale, receiving these two components of deposits. The similarities in service flows between the reserve portion of deposits and currency held by the nonbank public and between the excess of deposits over reserves and other interest-bearing assets, such as bonds, may mean that the reserve portion of deposits is a close substitute with currency held by the nonbank public, while the remainder of deposits is a close substitute for the other interest-bearing assets.[7]

The analogy between this approach and Lancaster's is readily perceivable. In the simple case with which we are dealing, we can distinguish three assets and two characteristics: the former are currency, deposits, and bonds; the latter are moneyness (common to currency and deposits) and bondness (common to bonds and deposits). In this formulation, Lancaster's model explains several phenomena relevant to our discussion. In particular, it provides a rationalization for the proposition that changes in the mix of characteristics of deposits towards relatively more bondness make deposits and bonds closer substitutes, since in Lancaster's model " . . . closeness of substitution [is] an intrinsic effect, depending on objective characteristics of goods . . . " (1967, p. 67). Hence it explains why such changes will increase the stability of high-powered money relative to money defined to include deposits. As we approach the polar case in which the only part of deposits that yield monetary services is the high-powered money por-

---

[5] See Friedman and Schwartz (1970, pp. 142–46), for a similar argument.

[6] When deposits of commercial banks are included in the definition of money, vault cash of commercial banks and other high-powered money reserves of commercial banks are excluded to avoid double-counting. However, if commercial bank deposits were excluded a consistent procedure would be to redefine currency held by the public to include the total monetary liabilities of the monetary authorities, or high-powered money. One way to view this is that the public is now expanded to include commercial banks just as the public can be considered to include nonbank financial intermediaries when money is defined as the total of currency and commercial bank deposits.

[7] While this may not hold as a general proposition it will be more nearly the case when variations in deposit quality affect the meaning of deposits to holders, as I explain below using Lancaster's framework.

tion, progressively smaller increases in the cost of holding deposits will lead to progressively larger decreases in deposit holdings. And in the polar case itself, deposits will be a linear combination of the characteristics of the other two goods and any increase in the cost of holding deposits will cause them to be technologically inefficient (in consumption) and hence cease to exist.[8]

II. Empirical Results

A. *The Data and Empirical Model*

To compare the stability of the demand for high-powered money with that of other monetary totals across countries, I have used analysis of variance techniques and their multiple regression analogues. The data used span 40 countries over the period 1952 to 1966. For each country, I have fifteen yearly observations for real per capita net national product (in 1958 dollars), for the rate of increase of the cost of living index, and for four monetary totals: high-powered money, currency held by the public, deposits, and the sum of currency and deposits, which I refer to as M_4 throughout. Deposits are defined broadly to include all private deposits at bank-type financial intermediaries, and high-powered money is defined as the total monetary liabilities of the monetary authorities. It therefore includes total currency outstanding along with bank and, where they exist, other private deposits at the central bank. For 22 of the countries I also have yearly figures for long-term bond yields.[9] Separate analysis is carried out for this 22-country sub-sample.

[8] In this case (which is the case of the tie-in sale) the demand for high-powered money will be unaffected by individual's choices of deposits versus currency and will depend only on their choice of characteristics. This becomes less true as deposits become more efficient, that is, as the production possibilities curve becomes more concave.

[9] The income total for almost all countries was net national product in current prices, taken from the United Nations' (*U.N.*) *Yearbook of National Account*

The regressions are based on the two simple general demand functions presented above and take the following form in the covariance analyses:

$$(4) \quad log\,(M/Y)_{it} = \alpha_i + \delta_t + \beta_1\,log\,(y/L)_{it} + \beta_2 r_{it} + \epsilon_{it}$$

where i denotes the country, t denotes the time period, M/Y is the number of weeks of income held as the particular asset, y is real income, L is population, r is the rate of interest, α_i, δ_t, β_1, and β_2 are parameters to be estimated, and ϵ_{it} is the error term assumed spherical normal.[10] This formulation assumes that: (a) actual and desired money balances are equal; (b) the demand function is homogeneous of degree one in population and of degree zero in prices; (c) the income elasticity is constant; (d) the semilogarithmic interest rate slope term is constant; and (e) measured income is a close approximation for permanent income. The first four assumptions are standard in much money demand analysis. The last assumption is an empirical expedient that may be imperfect within countries over time but appears reasonable

Statistics, 1969. Publications of the *U.N.* principally issues of the *Demographic Yearbook*, provided midyear estimates of population. The bulk of the data for the four monetary totals, the data on interest rates, and the cost of living indices (1958 = 100), used to convert the income figures to constant prices and to compute yearly rates of change of prices, came from the 1966–67 and 1967–68 supplements to the International Monetary Fund's (*IMF*) *International Financial Statistics*, together with various monthly issues of that publication. Exchange rates for 1958, adjusted for changes in purchasing power parity and used to convert real per capita income to dollars, came from the *U.N. Yearbook of National Account Statistics, 1963*, Table 3B. I initially used only a broad definition of deposits because of difficulties in constructing a series for demand deposits at commercial banks, the most important of which was that for some years for some countries separate demand deposit data were not available from the *IMF*. As reported in the conclusion, later work with a demand deposit series obtained in part from other sources alters none of my results.

[10] The corresponding regression for an analysis of variance imposes the constraint that $\beta_1 = \beta_2 = 0$.

TABLE 1—ANALYSES OF VARIANCE AND COVARIANCE[a]

Mean Squares for:	Degrees of Freedom	Variable[b]			
		$log (H/Y)$	$log (C/Y)$	$log (D/Y)$	$log (M_4/Y)$
40-Country Sample					
Analysis of Variance					
Countries	39	1.364	2.156	8.512	5.430
Years	14	.031	.136	.546	.179
Remainder	546	.015	.009	.029	.016
Analysis of Covariance					
Countries	39	1.239	2.086	3.011	2.235
Years	14	.018	.016	.069	.016
Remainder	545	.015	.009	.028	.015
22-Country Sample					
Analysis of Variance					
Countries	21	.801	1.892	6.369	3.777
Years	14	.059	.073	.099	.028
Remainder	294	.011	.009	.015	.008
Analysis of Covariance					
Countries	21	.760	1.828	1.178	.878
Years	14	.012	.002	.009	.004
Remainder	293	.011	.008	.012	.007

[a] The International Monetary Fund (IMF) was the main source of monetary data and the United Nations ($U.N.$) the main source of income data.

[b] High-powered money, currency, broadly defined deposits, and the sum of currency and broadly defined deposits are represented by H, C, D, and M_4, respectively, and nominal income by Y.

across countries, where differences in transitory income seem to be a relatively small proportion of differences in measured income. The next to last assumption, unlike the logarithmic formulation that is also sometimes used, implies a finite demand for money at a zero rate of interest, and is justifiable if there are some increasing marginal costs of holding money.

B. *Stability of Alternative Totals*

Analyses of variance and of covariance of the monetary totals are presented in Table 1 to provide evidence on the relative stability of each of the four totals over time and across countries under both specifications of the demand for money function. The mean squares for countries and years of the analyses of variance are measures of the absolute variation in the frac-

tion of income held in the form of each asset (or in velocity) across countries and over time, while those in the analyses of covariance are measures of the variations in asset holdings across countries and over time after allowance is made for the effects of the independent variables, real per capita income in the full sample, and both real per capita income and the rate of interest in the subsample. Tests of significance of these mean squares are therefore tests for significant departures from the respective models of the demand for money.[11]

[11] The mean square for countries is the regression sum of squares due to the dummy variables used to allow the α_i to differ, the mean square for years is the regression sum of squares due to the dummy variables used to allow the δ_t to differ, and the remainder sum of squares is the sum of squared errors from the regression. A test of the null hypothesis that the α_i are all equal is a test

The results of both types of analyses strongly support the view that narrower totals in general and high-powered money in particular are more homogeneous across countries. In the analyses of variance for the full sample, the country mean square for high-powered money is less than two-thirds that of currency and less than one-third of the other two assets. In the subsample, it is at the most one-half of the mean square of the other three assets. In the analyses of covariance, high-powered money, too, is the least variable across countries in both samples. What is particularly surprising when these results and the analyses of variance results are compared is the minute reductions in the mean square for high-powered money across countries (1.36 to 1.24 in the full sample and .80 to .76 in the subsample) and the lower unadjusted mean square for high-powered money than the adjusted mean squares for either deposits or M_4 (1.36 versus 3.01 and 2.24 in the full sample and .80 versus 1.18 and .88 in the subsample).

Over time the results are more mixed, and appear somewhat different from those obtained across countries. In the analyses of variance, high-powered money proves least variable in the full sample and M_4 in the small sample, while in the analyses of covariance, currency and M_4 prove equally less variable in the full sample and currency proves least variable in the small sample. However, in both sets of covariance analyses, with the exception of deposits in the full sample, these mean squares for years are insignificant at the .05 level.[12]

C. *Estimated Demand Functions*

Summary statistics and coefficients of the independent variables for the regressions underlying the covariance analysis—pooled regressions with individual intercepts for countries and years—together with the results of five other types of regressions are presented in Tables 2 and 3. These results permit comparison with the findings of other demand for money studies and also help illuminate the differences between the cross-country and within-country stabilities of different totals.

The implied income elasticities and the interest rate coefficients are for the most part highly significant and agree closely with estimates obtained in previous money demand studies.[13] The pooled regressions with single intercepts, the pooled regressions with individual yearly intercepts, and the country-mean regressions, all capture primarily cross-country relationships.[14] In these regressions the income elasticities of demand for real balances range from close to 1.0 for currency to close to 1.5 for deposits. The interest elasticities (evaluated at the mean of the interest rate, .054) all indicate an inelastic response of asset holdings to changes in interest rates and range from less than $-.10$ for high-powered money to a little over $-.40$ for money.

---

for no significant variation across countries; a test of the null hypothesis that the δ_j are all equal is a test for no significant variation over time. Rejection of the alternative hypotheses that in each instance they are unequal implies that velocity can be taken as constant and equal to its geometric mean.

[12] All of the mean squares in the analyses of variance, with the exception of the mean square for years for high-powered in the full sample (which is barely significant at .05), are highly significant. Those for countries in the analyses of covariance remain so.

[13] For example, see the time-series studies by Klein, Allan Meltzer, Friedman and Schwartz (forthcoming), A. A. Walters, and the cross-state studies by Feige and Arthur Gandolfi. Note that my estimates of income elasticities (of real cash balances held in the form of each asset) equal one plus the income coefficient. Hence an income coefficient significantly different from minus one implies an income elasticity significantly different from zero. Correspondingly, a coefficient of determination close to zero implies no additional gain in explanatory power from relaxing the assumption of unit income elasticity (or from including interest rates).

[14] Both the yearly intercepts and the averaging inherent in the country-mean regressions dictate this. The primarily cross-country nature of the regressions with single intercepts is peculiar to these data. Such regressions treat within-country and cross-country variation the same, and the latter is a predominant portion of the total variation in holdings.

TABLE 2—SUMMARY STATISTICS FOR REGRESSIONS FOR THE 40-COUNTRY SAMPLE[a]

Dependent Variable	Coefficients of[b]		R^2	Standard Error	Coefficients of[b]	R^2	Standard Error
	$\log (y/L)$	g_p			$\log (y/L)$		
Pooled: Intercepts for Years					**Pooled: Intercepts for Countries**		
$\log (H/Y)$	.090		.08	.310	−.117	.02	.122
	(.013)				(.033)		
$\log (C/Y)$	.070		.03	.384	−.374	.28	.094
	(.016)				(.026)		
$\log (D/Y)$	.497		.62	.477	.745	.32	.170
	(.019)				(.046)		
$\log (M_4/Y)$	.455		.57	.404	.455	.25	.122
	(.016)				(.033)		
Pooled: Single Intercept					**Pooled: Intercepts for Countries and Years**		
$\log (H/Y)$	.085		.07	.309	.009	.00	.122
	(.012)				(.053)		
$\log (C/Y)$	.062		.02	.385	−.217	.05	.093
	(.016)				(.041)		
$\log (D/Y)$	.601		.62	.473	.417	.05	.167
	(.019)				(.074)		
$\log (M_4/Y)$	.456		.57	.400	.332	.06	.122
	(.016)				(.050)		
Country Means					**Pooled: Error Component for Countries**		
$\log (H/Y)$	.086	−.214	.05	.295	.090	.09	.274
	(.048)	(.574)			(.012)		
$\log (C/Y)$	.049	−1.164	.05	.370	.072	.04	.355
	(.060)	(.720)			(.015)		
$\log (D/Y)$	.586	−.587	.63	.457	.599	.65	.427
	(.063)	(.892)			(.018)		
$\log (M_4/Y)$	.438	−.871	.58	.390	.456	.59	.368
	(.062)	(.760)			(.016)		

[a] The *IMF* was the main source of monetary and price data and the *U.N.* of income and exchange rate data.

[b] Real per capita income in 1958 dollars is represented by y/L and the average rate of change of the cost of living index by g_p. Standard errors of the coefficients are beneath them in parentheses.

The pooled regressions with individual country constants and the pooled regressions with individual yearly and country constants both seem to capture primarily time-series relations. They yield estimated elasticities fairly similar to those from the three types of cross-country regressions. The only substantial differences are in the interest elasticities of deposits and money and the income elasticities of high-powered money and currency, all of which are lower in the pooled regressions with individual country constants than in the cross-country regressions.

The standard errors of these regressions provide information similar to though not fully independent of the results of the covariance analyses. Again, high-powered money is the most stable total across countries. Within countries currency appears somewhat more stable than alternative totals, though again the differences among them are slight.

A problem with the within-country comparisons, however, is that for none of the assets are the individual within-country regressions statistically homogeneous.[15] The implication is that from the standpoint of the time-series relations there are

[15] The *F*-ratio to test jointly the homogeneity of both slopes and intercepts in the regressions for the individual countries, showed significant differences at less than the .001 level for all assets in both samples. Tests of individual yearly regressions revealed the opposite—no significant differences at the .10 level.

TABLE 3—SUMMARY STATISTICS FOR REGRESSIONS FOR THE 22-COUNTRY SAMPLE[a]

Dependent Variable	Coefficients of[b]		R^2	Standard Error	Coefficients of[b]		R^2	Standard Error
	$\log(y/L)$	r			$\log(y/L)$	r		
Pooled: Intercepts for Years					**Pooled: Intercepts for Countries**			
$\log(H/Y)$	.044	−1.143	.04	.248	−.206	−3.254	.17	.107
	(.013)	(.734)			(.044)	(.805)		
$\log(C/Y)$	−.016	−3.795	.04	.361	−.336	−3.468	.36	.089
	(.019)	(1.068)			(.037)	(.671)		
$\log(D/Y)$	.523	−8.065	.80	.301	.577	−2.199	.35	.110
	(.016)	(.889)			(.046)	(.828)		
$\log(M_4/Y)$	.379	−7.891	.75	.255	.354	−2.731	.26	.081
	(.013)	(.756)			(.034)	(.614)		
Pooled: Single Intercept					**Pooled: Intercepts for Countries and Years**			
$\log(H/Y)$	.039	−1.745	.05	.248	−.007	−1.769	.01	.106
	(.013)	(.710)			(.073)	(.923)		
$\log(C/Y)$	−.020	−4.214	.05	.355	−.331	−3.488	.13	.090
	(.018)	(1.018)			(.062)	(.784)		
$\log(D/Y)$	.527	−7.568	.79	.297	.495	−2.993	.17	.110
	(.015)	(.851)			(.075)	(.957)		
$\log(M_4/Y)$	.381	−7.568	.75	.251	.296	−3.280	.16	.082
	(.013)	(.721)			(.056)	(.712)		
Country Means					**Pooled: Error Component for Countries**			
$\log(H/Y)$	.045	−1.069	.00	.236	.045	−1.038	.05	.213
	(.048)	(2.900)			(.012)	(.696)		
$\log(C/Y)$	−.014	−3.897	.00	.366	−.014	−4.015	.04	.328
	(.074)	(4.400)			(.018)	(1.072)		
$\log(D/Y)$	.524	−8.747	.82	.291	.524	−8.746	.82	.263
	(.059)	(3.577)			(.014)	(.857)		
$\log(M_4/Y)$	.380	−8.523	.77	.251	.380	−8.543	.23	.226
	(.051)	(4.318)			(.012)	(.739)		

[a] The IMF was the main source of monetary, price, and interest rate data and the $U.N.$ of income and exchange rate data.

[b] Real per capita income in 1958 dollars is represented by y/L and the rate of interest by r. Standard errors of the coefficients are beneath them in parentheses.

some important omitted variables that differ in their impact from one country to the next. An alternative way of dealing with the time-series relations therefore may be in order. One solution is to use an error component model, such as that proposed by Pietro Balestra and Marc Nerlove, which views the error term in the model as being made up of two parts: a cross-country error and a remainder. When this technique is used we get another set of time-series estimates which are also presented in Tables 2 and 3. What they show is, as in the cross-section regressions, the clear superiority of high-powered money.

In both samples the standard errors of estimate for the regressions for high-powered are lower than those for the regressions for the other assets.

One reason for the differences between the relative stabilities of different totals across countries and within countries uncovered in some of the regressions is brought out by examination of the interest rate coefficients. In the regressions in which high-powered money is most stable, its sensitivity to interest rates is much lower than that of deposits and M_4. This is precisely what one would expect if there were specification bias in the deposit and money regressions, caused by either the existence of close substitutes for deposits introduced to circumvent interest rate ceilings, or by a greater degree of substitutability of deposits for bonds than of the high-powered money portion of deposits for bonds.

What may be more important sources of differences between the two sets of results are differences between cross-country and within-country variations in deposit quality. One might plausibly expect the former to be considerably greater since differences in the degree of financial development across countries are probably much greater than those that are likely to exist within countries over the relatively short time span covered by the sample. Omitting this variable, therefore, would decrease the stability of M_4 relative to narrower totals across countries and have little effect within countries.

This second explanation, moreover, is given credence by several additional types of evidence. In the analyses of variance and of covariance, variations in holdings of deposits and of M_4, both absolutely and relative to high-powered money, were much lower in the small sample that is the more homogeneous of the two with respect to degree of financial development. Regressions run with country means and incorporating the ratio of banking offices to population as an index of deposit quality also support this hypothesis.[16] Hence, differing degrees of financial sophistication

[16] The data and their sources are described in my dissertation. The regression for the country means of deposits for 34 countries in the full sample for which data were available was

$$log \ (D/Y) = .413 + .345 \ log \ (y/L)$$
$$(.093)$$
$$+ 1637.8B/L - 1.260g_p$$
$$(563.3) \qquad (.776)$$

$$R^2 = .74; \qquad SE = .382$$

and for the 22 countries in the small sample was

seem to account for at least part of the difference between the performance of M_4 and high-powered money across countries and, therefore, may also account for part of the differences between the cross-country and the time-series results.

III. Summary and Conclusions

The central theoretical proposition of this paper is that substantial variations in the cost of holding deposits relative to the costs of holding currency and other assets and in the quality or "moneyness" of deposits, such as exist across countries and within some countries having high and varying rates of inflation and ceilings on deposit rates, will substantially reduce the stability of the demand for money defined conventionally to include deposits while having only a minor effect on the stability of the demand for money defined more narrowly as high-powered money alone. In these circumstances high-powered money may therefore be a more useful definition of money than deposit-inclusive monetary totals.

The empirical evidence I have presented in the main supports this proposition. I have found that across countries high-powered money is the most stable of the four totals I have examined even when it is judged on the basis of the simple constant

$$log \ (D/Y) = .484 + .425 \ log \ (y/L)$$
$$(.076)$$
$$+ 945.0B/L - 9.174r$$
$$(492.7) \qquad (3.347)$$

$$R^2 = .85; \qquad SE = .274$$

where B/L is the deposit quality variable and where standard errors are beneath the coefficients in parentheses. Higher income coefficients were obtained in similar regressions that omitted B/L (.528 and .524, respectively), which is what one would expect if an increase in deposit quality caused by increased financial development has a positive effect on the demand for deposits and if more financially developed economies are also more developed on the whole. In the above regressions B/L was significant in both instances at the .05 level which it never was when I used high-powered money as the dependent variable.

velocity model and the other totals are judged on the basis of a more sophisticated model of money demand. Moreover, this greater stability of high-powered money appears directly attributable to the factors which theory suggests will have an important destabilizing influence on the demand for deposits. Specification analysis of various types of regressions, the observed differences in the stability of M_4 relative to high-powered money in the two samples, and the results of regressions which use a proxy for the quality of deposits as an independent variable all tend to confirm the importance of variations in deposit quality. The one major piece of evidence which does not support the hypothesis is that high-powered money is if anything less stable than either currency or M_4 within countries. But as already mentioned, this finding is consistent with the other evidence if, as appears reasonable, variations in deposit quality are on average of only minor importance within countries.

Moreover, this greater cross-country stability of narrower totals in general and high-powered money in particular is not just a statistical quirk peculiar to these data. Analysis of other studies indicates that this result still holds when other assets, specifically M_1 and its deposit component, are considered and other samples are used.[17] As an additional check, I compiled an M_1 series for my group of countries. The regressions I ran for both the 40 countries and the 22 countries also indicate that high-powered money is more

[17] Estimates of coefficients of variation of velocity derived from regressions similar to mine contained in studies by Hannan Ezekial and Joseph Adekunle, by Morris Perlman, and by Henry Wallich show that currency is more stable than broader totals (either M_4 or both M_1 and M_4, depending upon the study) and that holdings of both broader totals are more variable than high-powered money is in my full sample. Additional comparisons which I have made with an extended and otherwise revised version of Perlman's data and which I report in my dissertation show high-powered money to be the most stable total.

stable than either M_1 or the deposit component of M_1.[18]

My findings also provide evidence of several sorts bearing on the overall stability of money demand. They show that given the variations in factors which could plausibly be expected to affect the demand for money across countries, it is reasonably stable. Estimates of international variations in money holdings are not radically greater than the intranational estimates.[19] In addition, even though these international variations are both significant and substantial, it is clear that even so simple an hypothesis as constant velocity has considerable merit. For example, from knowledge of high-powered money and of its average velocity, one can account for an overwhelming proportion of the variance in the level of nominal income or in its rate of change—over 95 percent of the variance of the level in 1958 and over 90 percent of the variance of its average annual rate of change. In addition, my estimates of money demand functions on the whole accord fairly well with esti-

[18] The regression for the country means of M_1 holdings for the 40-country sample was

$$log\ (M_1/Y) = .840 + .259\ log\ (y/L) - .276g_p$$
$$\qquad\qquad\quad (.056) \qquad\qquad (.411)$$

$R^2 = .39; \qquad SE = .345$

and for the 22-country sample was

$$log\ (M_1/Y) = 1.337 + .233\ log\ (y/L) - 3.912r$$
$$\qquad\qquad\qquad (.056) \qquad\qquad (3.338)$$

$R^2 = .50; \qquad SE = .278$

where standard errors of the coefficients are beneath them in parentheses. We can compare the standard errors of estimate of these regressions of .345 and .278 with the standard errors of estimate for similar regressions for high-powered money of .295 and .236, respectively.

[19] Friedman and Schwartz (forthcoming) report coefficients of variation of the levels of velocity of M_2 in the United States of .32, and in the United Kingdom of .18 over the years 1880–1968. Estimates for the velocity of total adjusted commercial bank deposits from cross-state data, made available by Gandolfi, range from .17 in 1929 to .20 in 1933.

mates others have obtained from long-term studies of the United States and the United Kingdom and from cross-section studies of the United States.[20] Given the substantial independence of my data from theirs, this close agreement of results provides a strong corroboration of their results. Conversely, it casts considerable doubt on estimates from postwar time-series for those two countries which in general conflict greatly with both long-term time-series and cross-section estimates.[21]

An obvious implication of my findings is that for international studies in which the stability of the demand for money is a key assumption, such as in monetarist models of the balance of payments or of exchange rates, the use of high-powered money as the definition of money may prove extremely fruitful. In studies of that type it also has the added advantage of eliminating the need for separate relationships to explain the conventional money multiplier and conventional money demand. For countries having no income data or data of dubious accuracy there are also direct applications for these findings. By extension they also may prove useful in time-series studies of economic conditions in countries experiencing rapid inflation or substantial changes in their financial structure.

My results also have implications for monetary policy. Since inflation coupled with regulation of banking tends to reduce the homogeneity of deposits, conventional definitions of money may become highly imperfect indicators for monetary policy in such situations. On the one hand, my findings suggest that policy should be such that supply and demand are not made more interdependent. And on the other, they suggest that, having made them so, the monetary authorities should look for a more homogeneous total as an indicator and not deduce from the instability in demand of a nonhomogeneous total that monetary aggregates play only a weak role in the economy.[22]

Perhaps the most interesting implications of these results are for the definition of money. Most of the current debate over how to define money has centered upon whether to include various types of time and savings deposits in the definition of money. My results suggest that the focus of current debate has been too narrow, that the range of plausible alternative definitions of money and the factors influencing the selection of one of these alternatives are both broader than is commonly realized. They indicate that an earlier definition of money as high-powered money alone may be a useful alternative to these conventional definitions of money. And because the differences in the performance of high-powered money and deposit-inclusive definitions of money across countries can be attributed to variations in deposit quality, these results also indicate the importance of asset quality in deciding upon a definition of money.

[22] The United Kingdom currently provides an instructive example. Changes in the regulations surrounding banking appear to be a major cause of the marked divergences over the past several years in the growth rates of the two published deposit-inclusive definitions of money. These changes have undoubtedly decreased the homogeneity of both totals and thus have drastically increased the difficulties in assessing British policy.

[20] In addition to the studies cited in fnn. 13 and 17, see the cross-country study by James Hanson and Robert Vogel.
[21] Estimates of income elasticities obtained from the studies referred to in the previous footnote tend to fall in the range of 1.0 to 1.3. Estimates obtained with postwar data (see Stephen Goldfeld) are usually considerably below 1.0.

REFERENCES

P. Balestra and M. Nerlove, "Pooling Cross Section and Time-Series Data in the Estimation of a Dynamic Model: The Demand for Natural Gas," *Econometrica*, July 1966, *34*, 585–612.

G. S. Becker, *Economic Theory*, New York 1971.

V. K. Chetty, "On Measuring the Nearness of Near-Moneys," *Amer. Econ. Rev.*, June 1969, *59*, 270–81.

H. Ezekial and J. O. Adekunle, "The Secular Behavior of Income Velocity," *Int. Monet. Fund Staff Pap.*, July 1969, *16*, 224–37.

E. Feige, *The Demand for Liquid Assets: A Temporal Cross-Section Analysis*, Englewood Cliffs 1964.

———, "Alternative Temporal Cross-Section Specifications of the Demand for Demand Deposits," in H. G. Johnson and A. R. Nobay, eds., *Issues in Monetary Economics*, London 1974.

M. Friedman and A. J. Schwartz, *Monetary Statistics of the United States, Estimates, Sources and Methods*, New York 1970.

——— and ———, *Monetary Trends in the United States and the United Kingdom*, Nat. Bur. Econ. Res. forthcoming.

A. E. Gandolfi, "The Stability of the Demand for Money During the Great Contraction, 1929–1933," *J. Polit. Econ.*, Oct. 1974, *84*, 969–83.

S. M. Goldfeld, "The Demand for Money Revisited," *Brookings Papers*, Washington 1973, *3*, 577–646.

J. S. Hanson and Robert C. Vogel, "Inflation and Monetary Velocity in Latin America," *Rev. Econ. Statist.*, Aug. 1973, *55*, 365–70.

H. S. Houthakker, "New Evidence on Demand Elasticities," *Econometrica*, Apr. 1965, *33*, 272–88.

B. Klein, "The Payment of Interest on Commercial Bank Deposits and the Price of Money," unpublished doctoral dissertation, Univ. Chicago 1970.

———, "Competitive Interest Payments on Bank Deposits and the Long-Run Demand for Money," *Amer. Econ. Rev.*, Dec. 1974, *64*, 931–49.

K. Lancaster, "A New Approach to Consumer Theory," *J. Polit. Econ.*, Apr. 1966, *77*, 132–57.

———, *Consumer Demand: A New Approach*, New York 1971.

J. R. Lothian, "The Demand for High-Powered Money," unpublished doctoral dissertation, Univ. Chicago 1973.

A. H. Meltzer, "The Demand for Money: The Evidence from the Time-Series," *J. Polit. Econ.*, June 1963, *71*, 129–246.

M. Perlman, "International Differences in Liquid Asset Portfolios," in D. Meiselman, ed., *Varieties of Monetary Experience*, Chicago 1970.

H. Wallich, "Quantity Theory and Quantity Policy," *Ten Economic Studies in The Tradition of Irving Fisher*, New York 1967.

A. A. Walters, *Money in Boom and Slump*, 3d ed., Inst. Econ. Anal., Hobart Paper, *44*, London 1971.

International Monetary Fund, *International Financial Statistics*, 1952–1969.

United Nations, *Demographic Yearbook*, 1965–69.

———, *Statistical Yearbook*, 1961–67.

———, *Yearbook of National Account Statistics*, 1963, 1969.

[19]

On the Specification of the Demand for Money: The Real Rate of Return versus the Rate of Inflation

Benjamin Eden

The Hebrew University, Jerusalem

I

The demand for money is sometimes specified as a function of the anticipated rate of inflation and sometimes as a function of the anticipated real rate of return on money.[1] In the absence of uncertainty, individuals hold point anticipations and it does not matter which specification is used, since the real rate of return and the rate of inflation are monotically related.

When consumers are uncertain about future prices, it makes a difference whether anticipations with respect to the mathematical expectations of the real rate of return on money or anticipations with respect to the expected rate of inflation are used to explain changes in the demand for money. The difference arises from the fact that the rate of inflation is not a linear function of the real rate of return. In this note, we provide evidence that supports the specification of the demand for money as a function of anticipations with respect to the expected real rate of return on money, over the usual specification which uses the expected rate of inflation.

II

Consider a consumer who lives in a world in which money is the only available asset and there is an aggregate consumption good. The consumer anticipates n possible states of the world (i.e., n possible evolutions of the world) which are characterized by the consumer's future income

---

This note is based on the first chapter of my Ph.D. dissertation which was submitted to the University of Chicago. I would like to thank the committee members: W. A. Brock, R. J. Barro, S. Fischer, and M. Friedman. I also benefited from comments provided by J. Frenkel and two anonymous referees.

[1] See, e.g., Friedman (1956) for the first specification. The second specification stems from the portfolio approach to the demand for money (see Tobin 1958).

[*Journal of Political Economy*, 1976, vol. 84, no. 6]

and the future price level. He uses these anticipations to plan his consumption and holdings of real balances for two periods.[2] Let

C_0 = level of consumption in period 0;

C_1^i = level of consumption in period 1 in state of the world i $(i = 1, \ldots, n)$;

M_0 = quantity of nominal balances in period 0;

P_0 = the price level in period 0 (the price of consumption in terms of money);

$m_0 = M_0/P_0$ = quantity of real balances in period 0;

M_1^i = quantity of nominal balances in period 1 in state of the world i $(i = 1, \ldots, n)$;

P_1^i = price level in period 1 in state of the world i $(i = 1, \ldots, n)$;

$m_1^i = M_1^i/P_1^i$ = quantity of real balances in period 1 in state of the world i $(i = 1, \ldots, n)$;

W_0 = initial real wealth;

I_1^i = nominal income in period 1 in state of the world i $(i = 1, \ldots, n)$;

$W_1^i = I_1^i/P_1^i + M_0/P_1^i$ = real wealth in period 1 in state of the world i $(i = 1, \ldots, n)$;

q_i = the consumer's subjective probability that state of the world i will occur $(i = 1, \ldots, n)$

We will also use the following random variables:

$$\tilde{I}_1 = \{I_1^i \text{ with probability } q_i; i = 1, \ldots, n\}$$
$$\tilde{P}_1 = \{P_1^i \text{ with probability } q_i; i = 1, \ldots, n\}.$$

The consumer allocates the available resources in each period between money and the consumption good. His behavior is described by a maximization of a utility function in which consumption and real balances appear as arguments:[3]

$$V(C_0, m_0, C_1^1, \ldots, C_1^n, m_1^1, \ldots, m_1^n).$$

---

[2] See Patinkin (1965) for a detailed framework of period analysis.

[3] The inclusion of real balances as an argument in the utility function is widely used since Samuelson (1947) and Patinkin (1965). This approach assumes that some important aspects of consumers' behavior can be captured without specifying the exact nature of the services which are provided by money.

It is assumed that the utility function is additive and that the consumer maximizes expected utility, thus:

$$V(\cdot) = U(C_0, m_0) + \rho \sum_{i=1}^{n} q_i U(C_1^i, m_1^i),$$

where ρ is a subjective rate of discount. The maximization is done subject to a single budget constraint in period 0 and an anticipated budget constraint for period 1:

$$\max_{C_0, M_0, C_1^i, M_1^i \geq 0} U\left(C_0, \frac{M_0}{P_0}\right) + \rho \sum_{i=1}^{n} q_i U\left(C_1^i, \frac{M_1^i}{P_1^i}\right)$$

$$\text{s.t. } (a) \ C_0 + \frac{M_0}{P_0} = W_0, \tag{1}$$

$$(b) \ C_1^i + \frac{M_1^i}{P_1^i} = W_1^i = \frac{I_1^i}{P_1^i} + \frac{M_0}{P_1^i} \ (i = 1, \ldots, n).$$

Assume that $U(\cdot)$ is strictly quasi-concave to define

$$F(X) = \max_{C,M} U\left(C, \frac{M}{P}\right)$$

$$\text{s.t. } C + \frac{M}{P} = X$$

$$\text{and } C, M \geq 0,$$

where $F(\cdot)$ is the maximum second period's utilities that the consumer can get from an amount of real resources X in the second period.

There are two sources of benefits from holding real balances: (a) "utility" in the present (which might stand for the "transaction motive" for holding money), and (b) uses in the future (the "store of value" function of money). When the consumer holds point anticipations (I_1, P_1), the value of holding M_0 today for future use, measured in period 1's utility units, is:

$$F\left(\frac{M_0 + I_1}{P_1}\right) - F\left(\frac{I_1}{P_1}\right).$$

When future magnitudes are uncertain, the expected value of holding M_0 for future use is:

$$E\left[F\left(\frac{M_0 + \tilde{I}_1}{\tilde{P}_1}\right) - F\left(\frac{\tilde{I}_1}{\tilde{P}_1}\right)\right].$$

The consumer weighs the total benefits from holding money (present plus future use) against the benefits of consumption today. Formally, this decision can be described by:

$$\max_{C_0, M_0 \geq 0} U\left(C_0, \frac{M_0}{P_0}\right) + \rho E\left[F\left(\frac{M_0 + \tilde{I}_1}{\tilde{P}_1}\right)\right] \tag{2}$$

$$\text{s.t. } C_0 + \frac{M_0}{P_0} = W_0.$$

At a solution of (2) the expected marginal utility from holding one dollar as money (present and future uses) equals the marginal utility of a dollar's worth of present consumption. Thus,

$$U_2\left(\bar{C}_0, \frac{\bar{M}_0}{P_0}\right)\frac{1}{P_0} + \rho E\left[F'(\tilde{W}_1)\frac{1}{\tilde{P}_1}\right] = U_1\left(\bar{C}_0, \frac{\bar{M}_0}{P_0}\right)\frac{1}{P_0}. \tag{3}$$

Where $(\bar{C}_0, \bar{M}_0)$ is a solution to (2), $U_i(\cdot\cdot)$ denotes partial derivatives and

$$\tilde{W}_1 = \frac{\bar{M}_0 + \tilde{I}_1}{\tilde{P}_1}.$$

Multiplying (3) by P_0 and substituting yields:

$$A(\bar{m}_0, W_0) = U_1(W_0 - \bar{m}_0, \bar{m}_0) - U_2(W_0 - \bar{m}_0, \bar{m}_0)$$
$$= \rho E\left(F'(\tilde{W}_1)\frac{P_0}{\tilde{P}_1}\right), \tag{4}$$

where $\bar{m}_0 = \bar{M}_0/P_0$ and the first equality defines the function $A(\cdot)$ as the difference between the marginal utility of consumption and the marginal utility of money in the first period.

In what follows we specialize in assuming that the consumer is risk neutral. Thus $F'(\cdot)$ is a constant. Let $k = \rho F'(\cdot)$, where k is the "utility" of a unit of real wealth in the future, and define the real rate of return on money to be

$$\tilde{R} = \frac{M_0/\tilde{P}_1 - M_0/P_0}{M_0/P_0} = P_0/\tilde{P}_1 - 1.$$

Then (4) can be rewritten as

$$A(\bar{m}_0, W_0) = k[1 + (E\tilde{R})]. \tag{5}$$

Reducing consumption in the present by one unit implies having an additional unit of real balance today and having $1 + \tilde{R}$ more units of real wealth in the future. Since (5) implies that the difference in the marginal utility between present consumption and present real balances is equal to the expected utility of $1 + \tilde{R}$ units of real wealth in the future, it insures that at the optimum the above change in allocation will not increase the expected utility.

The partial derivative of $A(\cdot\cdot)$ with respect to real balances is

$$\frac{\partial A(\cdot\cdot)}{\partial \bar{m}_0} = -U_{11}(\cdot\cdot) + 2U_{12}(\cdot\cdot) - U_{22}(\cdot\cdot),$$

which is positive if we assume that the second order conditions of the problems are satisfied. Since $A(\cdot\cdot)$ is increasing in real balances, an increase in the expected real rate of return on money increases the demand for money.

General equilibrium considerations which are developed in the second chapter of Eden (1975) leads to the above result without using the assumption of risk neutrality. Specifically, it is shown that, even if all consumers have aversion to risk, the mean of the distribution of the real rate of return on money is the only moment of the distribution which effects the equilibrium quantity of money.

III

Previous studies attempted to explain changes in the demand for money by using anticipation with respect to the expected rate of inflation rather than the expected real rate of return on money. To appreciate the implications of this misspecification, we turn now to examine the relationship between the real rate of return and the rate of inflation.

The discrete rate of inflation (for the period $0 - t$):[4]

$$\tilde{\pi} = \frac{\tilde{P}_t - P_0}{P_0}$$

is related to the real rate of return by

$$1 + \tilde{R} = \tilde{P}_0/\tilde{P}_t = \frac{1}{1 + \tilde{\pi}}. \tag{6}$$

Since the function $1/(1 + \pi)$ is convex in π, Jensen's inequality combined with (6) implies that the expected real rate of return on money is greater when the rate of inflation is random compared to a nonrandom rate of inflation (holding the mean constant):

$$1 + E\tilde{R} = E\frac{1}{1 + \tilde{\pi}} \geq \frac{1}{1 + E\tilde{\pi}}. \tag{7}$$

To illustrate inequality (7) consider the following example: let $P_0 = 2$ and consider the following alternatives for the price level in period t.

Alternative 1: $P_t = 2$ with probability 1.

Alternative 2: $\tilde{P}_t = \begin{cases} 3 \text{ with probability } 1/2 \\ 1 \text{ with probability } 1/2 \end{cases}$.

---

[4] For a similar discussion on the continuous rate of inflation, see Eden (1975).

1358   JOURNAL OF POLITICAL ECONOMY

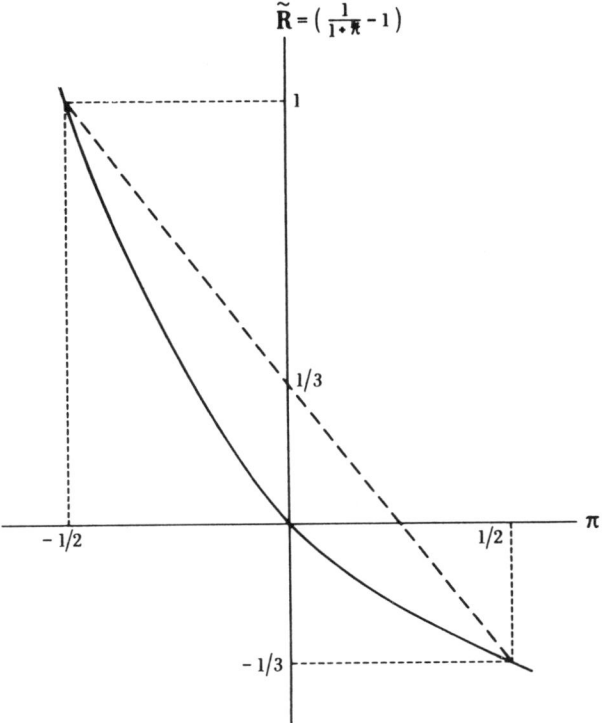

Fig. 1.—The relationship between the expected real rate of return on money and the rate of inflation.

Under both alternatives the expected rate of inflation equals zero. The expected real rate of return under alternative 1 is

$$P_0/P_t - 1 = 2/2 - 1 = 0$$

and under alternative 2

$$E(P_0/P_t - 1) = 1/2(2/3 - 1) + 1/2(2/1 - 1)$$
$$= -1/2\tfrac{1}{3} + 1/2 \cdot 1 = \tfrac{1}{3}.$$

Thus, the expected rate of return is higher for the random rate of inflation. This result is derived graphically in figure 1.

Further, it can be shown that the expected real rate of return increases with the variance of the rate of inflation (holding higher order moments constant). Therefore, if the demand for money is misspecified by using the expected rate of inflation rather than the expected real rate of return, the anticipated variance will show a significant positive effect.[5]

Empirically, the distinction between the real rate of return and the rate of inflation is important only when there are changes in the anticipated variance of the rate of inflation. It is shown in Eden (1975) that during the post–World War I periods of hyperinflations, changes in the variance of the rate of inflation were substantial and therefore the performance of the real rate of return in explaining changes in the demand for money was significantly better than the performance of the rate of inflation (in Cagan's [1956] original study).

References

Cagan, P. "The Monetary Dynamics of Hyperinflation." *Studies in the Quantity Theory of Money*, edited by M. Friedman. Chicago: Univ. Chicago Press, 1956.

Eden, B. "Aspects of Uncertainty in Simple Monetary Models." Ph.D. dissertation, Univ. Chicago, June 1975.

Friedman, M. "The Quantity of Money—a Restatement." *Studies in the Quantity Theory of Money*, edited by M. Friedman. Chicago: Univ. Chicago Press, 1956.

Patinkin, D. *Money, Interest and Prices*. New York: Harper & Row, 1965.

Samuelson, P. A. *The Foundations of Economic Analysis*. Boston: Harvard Univ. Press, 1947.

Tobin, J. "Liquidity Preference as Behavior toward Risk." *Rev. Econ. Studies* 25 (February 1958): 65–86.

[5] It was argued that the distinction between the real rate of return and the rate of inflation will disappear for certain functional forms of the demand for money. Since any monotone function of the expected rate of return will increase with the variance of the rate of inflation, and a function of the expected rate of inflation will not, this assertion is not correct.

[20]

On Indexation and Contract Length

Jo Anna Gray

University of Pennsylvania

This paper examines the joint determination of labor contract length and the degree of wage indexation in a neoclassical model modified to incorporate short-term wage rigidities and uncertainty, both real and monetary. A number of propositions are demonstrated. Optimal indexing may not insulate the real sector from unanticipated monetary shocks. For any given degree of indexing, contract length decreases with the level of uncertainty and increases with the cost of contracting. If indexing is costly, indexing provisions will appear only in longer contracts. The proportion of contracts indexed will increase with the variance of monetary disturbances. Finally, monetary variability may cause resource misallocation among industries. Some related policy implications are noted.

This paper investigates the effects of wage indexation on macroeconomic fluctuations in a model which highlights the joint determination of two contract characteristics: contract length and an indexing parameter. The analysis departs from much of the earlier literature on indexing in its incorporation of real as well as monetary disturbances into the theoretical structure[1] and in its explicit consideration of contract length. Interest in such a framework and analysis has three sources. The first is the issue of the costs of price level uncertainty. One of the conclusions of the paper is

I am indebted to Robert Barro, Milton Friedman, Robert Lucas, Tom Williams, and an anonymous referee for valuable comments on previous drafts of the paper. Financial support was provided by the U.S. Labor Department.

[1] In recent papers dealing with indexing, Barro (1976a) and Fischer (1977) also incorporate aggregate real disturbance into their analyses. The stabilization aspects of the indexing issue were recognized by a variety of earlier writers, including Jevons (1896), Fisher (1922), Marshall (1925), and Pigou (1933), as well as later proponents of indexing such as Friedman (1974). However, with the exception of Pigou (1933, p. 295), these writers confine their discussions to frameworks which, either implicitly or explicitly, admit only monetary disturbances.

[*Journal of Political Economy*, 1978, vol. 86, no. 1]
© 1978 by The University of Chicago. 0022-3808/78/8601-0001$01.51.

that optimal indexing, even if costless, will not completely insulate the real sector of an economy from the effects of unanticipated monetary shocks. It is further demonstrated that the costs of monetary variability may be distributed differentially across industries, thereby imposing an additional cost on the system in the form of resource misallocation among industries.

A second source of interest stems from the potential costs and consequences of government regulation of indexing arrangements. In the absence of externalities or distortions, government regulation of private contracting arrangements presumably imposes social costs; the framework introduced in this paper is useful in identifying the nature of those costs.

In addition to its policy implications, the analysis offers considerable descriptive power. In particular, it provides explanations for the paucity of indexed wage contracts in some countries, for the existence of partial indexation, and for the appearance of cost-of-living clauses predominantly in longer contracts.

The design of the paper is to develop, in the first section, a simple macroeconomic model which is used, in the second section, to derive optimal values for an indexing parameter and the length of contracts. In the third section the analysis is extended to permit contract length to vary by industry, and an indexing cost is introduced. A summary of the conclusions and implications of the paper is contained in the final section.

I. The Model

The continuous time framework described in this section is a simple neoclassical model modified to incorporate short-term wage rigidities and uncertainty.[2] The wage rigidities are produced by a fixed contracting cost and a contracting scheme that calls for the setting of a nominal base wage and an indexing parameter before full information on the economic variables relevant to production decisions is received. Uncertainty is incorporated in the form of stochastic disturbances in the money supply and production functions that generate, respectively, monetary and real shocks to the system. Since the base nominal wage is fixed for the period of the contract, these shocks may cause employment and output fluctuations through changes in the real wage rate (via price level fluctuations) and in the marginal product of labor.

The paper is concerned with the distinction between real and monetary aggregate shocks. Accordingly, relative price and quantity fluctuations are excluded by specifying a one-commodity model. Because indexing is designed to provide protection from unexpected movements in the price level, the model abstracts from anticipated changes and trends by postu-

---

[2] A discrete time variant of this framework is developed in Gray (1976).

ON INDEXATION AND CONTRACT LENGTH 3

lating stochastic disturbances with zero mean.[3] The forecast variances of these terms (conditioned on information available at the time contracts are negotiated) are assumed to be increasing functions of time, indicating greater uncertainty about more distant points of future time. The capital stock is assumed fixed, so aggregate output can be written as a function of total labor input and a stochastic productivity factor, α.

$$\ln Y_t = \delta \ln L_t + \alpha_t. \tag{1}$$

Here δ is the elasticity of real output with respect to labor input, and α_t can be described by the continuous time counterpart of a random walk (a Wiener process) with zero mean and forecast variance $V_{\alpha_t} = tV_a$ conditioned on information available at time $t = 0$. The production process is homogeneous of degree less than one ($0 < \delta < 1$).

The nominal money supply is generated by the stochastic process

$$\ln M_t^S = \bar{M} + \beta_t, \tag{2}$$

where β_t can be described by a Wiener process with zero mean and forecast variance $V_{\beta_t} = tV_b$ conditioned on information available at time $t = 0$. The covariance between α_t and β_t is assumed to be zero. The demand for nominal money balances is assumed, for simplicity, to take the Cambridge form:

$$\ln M_t^D = \ln k + \ln P_t + \ln Y_t, \tag{3}$$

where k, the desired ratio of money to nominal income, is constant. Prices are assumed to adjust instantaneously to insure continuous equilibrium in the money market:

$$\ln M_t^D = \ln M_t^S. \tag{4}$$

The labor market is described by equations (5) and (6). The supply and demand functions take familiar forms, with demand depending on the real wage rate, w_t, and the productivity factor,[4] α_t:

$$\ln L_t^D = -\eta(\ln w_t - \alpha_t) + \eta \ln \delta, \qquad \eta = 1/(1 - \delta), \tag{5}$$

$$\ln L_t^S = \varepsilon \ln w_t + \eta \ln \delta. \tag{6}$$

---

[3] Fully anticipated movements in the price level are taken into consideration during contract negotiations and do not require the kind of ex post adjustment of the nominal wage rate for price level changes which indexing provides. Therefore, in an economy experiencing a perfectly anticipated constant rate of inflation, the analysis of this paper indicates no case for indexation, regardless of the level of that rate. However, the greater the uncertainty associated with any mean rate of inflation, the stronger the case for indexing. Thus the incentive to index is related to the (imperfectly anticipated) variability of the price level, not to its mean rate of change.

[4] The labor demand function is derived by differentiating the production relationship $Y_t = e^{\alpha_t}L_t^{\delta}$ with respect to labor and equating the result (the marginal product of labor) to the real wage rate. This gives a demand function of the form $L_t = (w_t/\delta e^{\alpha_t})^{1/(\delta-1)}$, which in log form is equation (5).

4   JOURNAL OF POLITICAL ECONOMY

The elasticities of supply and demand for labor are given by ε and η, respectively, and are defined nonnegative. The constant in the labor supply function, $\eta \ln \delta$, is chosen so that $\ln w^*$ is equal to zero.[5]

The level of employment is contingent on the nature of contracts as well as the labor market conditions embodied in equations (5) and (6). A contract specifies the values of three parameters: the base nominal wage rate (W^*), an indexing parameter (γ), and a contract length (l).[6] A number of potential complications are sidestepped by assuming that the base wage is set at the level that corresponds to equilibrium in the labor market when the realized values of the disturbance terms are zero.[7] This level is designated by an asterisk and is referred to as the certainty equivalent of the nominal wage rate. Negotiating a contract is assumed to entail a fixed cost (C) while, for the moment, indexing is assumed to be costless. The time at which contracts are negotiated is assigned the value $t = 0$ and the period for which a contract applies runs from $t = 0$ to $t = l$. Once contracts have been negotiated, the level of employment becomes completely demand determined for the period of the contract. Workers are assumed to supply whatever amount of labor is demanded by employers at the negotiated wage rate.

Contract length and the indexing parameter are assumed to be set at those values which minimize the expected costs per period resulting from (i) deviations of the log of actual output ($\ln Y_t$) from the log of its desired

---

[5] As discussed subsequently, an asterisk denotes the "certainty equivalent" of a variable or the value of that variable which corresponds to full equilibrium in all markets when both disturbance terms take on the value zero, i.e., when $\alpha_t = \beta_t = 0$.

[6] While contracting theory is a current and rapidly developing area of research, there does not yet exist a theory of optimal contract form. In the absence of such a theory, I have chosen to appeal to actual contracting practices in selecting a contract form. Accordingly, the contract form specified in this section is intended to capture the more commonly observed features of labor contracts relevant to a study of indexing. It should be noted, however, that a second and possibly superior arrangement is available. The alternative involves setting joint ceiling and floor values on the size of the disturbance terms (α_t and β_t) and agreeing to recontract whenever the size of the disturbances exceeds the ceiling or falls below the floor. The ceiling and floor would then be set at those values for which the costs associated with deviations of actual output from optimal are just equal to the costs of recontracting. This kind of price adjustment model is developed by Barro (1972) in the context of a monopolist faced with stochastic demand for its output. The parallel between Barro's paper and the present framework is, however, incomplete in one crucial aspect. In the case of the monopolist, the "signal" (the level of demand) is exogenously determined. In the present paper, the "signal" (the values of the disturbance terms) may be filtered and distorted by the firm. While the size of monetary shocks is presumably public information, firms may have an advantage over workers in obtaining information on the size of real shocks and therefore the productivity of labor. Since firms have an incentive (at least in the short run) to understate labor productivity, it may be argued that problems of moral hazard make this alternative contract form undesirable.

[7] Formally, the base nominal wage rate can be found by equating equations (5) and (6), subject to the constraint that the disturbance terms are at their means: $\alpha_t = \beta_t = 0$.

level ($\ln Y_t^o$) and (ii) the cost of contracting. Formally, then, l and γ are obtained by minimizing the loss function (Z) given by equation (7):

$$Z = 1/l\left(\lambda \int_o^l \phi_t \, dt + C \right), \tag{7}$$

where $\phi_t = E[(\ln Y_t - \ln Y_t^o)^2]$, and λ is a relative price which converts losses expressed as squared output deviations into losses expressed in the units of the contracting cost.[8] Desired output is defined as that level of output which would prevail in a perfectly frictionless version of the economy postulated in this paper. In such an economy, the log value of output would be given by

$$\ln Y_t^o = \delta \ln L_t^o + \alpha_t, \tag{8}$$

where L_t^o is the level of employment corresponding to the intersection of the labor supply and demand schedules given by equations (5) and (6).

II. Some Implications

The framework developed in Section I will now be used to derive and interpret expressions for the optimal degree of wage indexation and optimal contract length. The interdependence of these two control variables is emphasized in the policy discussion that concludes this section.

The Optimal Degree of Indexing

In this part, an optimal degree of indexing is derived that depends on the underlying stochastic structure of the economy set out in equations (1)–(6). It is shown that in such an economy the optimal degree of indexation will generally lie between zero (no indexing) and one (full indexing). The economic intuition behind this result rests on the distinction between real and monetary disturbances. While indexing insulates the real sector from monetary disturbances, it exacerbates the real effects of real disturbances.[9] Consequently, in a system subject to both types of shocks, full

[8] It would be desirable for the term ϕ_t to approximate the loss in consumers' surplus associated with deviations of actual from optimal output. Consumers' surplus measures are, however, difficult to implement in the present framework: specifically, a form of the loss function that would approximate consumers' surplus losses would not permit closed-form solutions for either the indexing parameter or contract length. Accordingly, the loss function given in equation (7), while not lacking in intuitive appeal, was selected primarily on the grounds of analytical convenience. An analogous loss function is employed by Barro (1976b) as a criterion for evaluating monetary policy.

[9] This result is also obtained by Fischer (1977), while Bernstein (1974) points to the world supply shocks of 1973–74 in arguing for the potentially adverse effects of wage indexation.

indexation will not be desirable. Rather, the analysis suggests an optimal degree of partial indexation.

This optimal degree of indexing (γ^o) can be obtained from equation (7) and the first-order conditions for a minimum. Partial differentiation of the loss function with respect to the indexing parameter results in the following condition:

$$\partial Z/\partial \gamma = 1/l \int_o^l (\partial \phi_t/\partial \gamma)\, dt = 0. \qquad (9)$$

Solving this equation produces the expression for the optimal degree of indexing given by equation (10).[10] Since this result has been developed fully elsewhere (Gray 1976), the details of the analysis have been relegated to Appendix A.

$$\gamma^o = \theta + (1 - \theta)[\varepsilon/(1 + \varepsilon)], \qquad (10)$$

where $\theta = V_b / \left\{ \left[\dfrac{\eta^2(1 + \varepsilon)}{\varepsilon + \eta} \right] V_a + V_b \right\}$, $V_a = (1/t)V_{\alpha_t}$, and $V_b = (1/t)V_{\beta_t}$.

Examination of the terms entering equation (10) reveals that the optimal degree of indexing, γ^o, is a weighted average of the optima corresponding to the extreme cases of an economy subject only to monetary shocks ($V_a = 0$) and an economy subject only to real shocks ($V_b = 0$). In the case of monetary shocks only, γ^o, takes on the value one. The rationale behind a policy of full indexation in such an economy is clear: since indexing can completely insulate the real sector from monetary disturbances and since the only shocks to the system are monetary in this case, full indexation is desirable.

When, on the other hand, V_b is set equal to zero (the case of an economy subject only to real shocks), γ^o assumes the value $\varepsilon/(1 + \varepsilon)$, which is nonnegative and less than one. The rationale behind this result rests on the observation that some response of the real sector to real shocks is to be desired. Consider, for example, the case of a positive real shock. In a perfectly competitive, frictionless economy, such a shock would result in increases in both employment and output (relative to their certainty equivalents). Employment would rise due to the increased marginal product of labor[11] in conjunction with a positive supply elasticity of labor. Output would rise on two counts: increased productivity per worker, and an in-

---

[10] The solution of equation (9) is simplified by the specific form assumed for the distributions of the stochastic terms α_t and β_t. Because the variances of these terms are linearly dependent on time, the solution to the equation $\partial \phi_t/\partial \gamma_t = 0$ is independent of time and consequently provides the general solution to equation (9); i.e., $\gamma_t^o = \gamma^o$ for all t.

[11] Differentiation of the production relationship $Y_t = e^{\alpha_t}L_t^{\delta}$ (which in log form is equation [1]) suffices to show that the marginal product of labor is directly proportional to the real disturbance term, α_t.

crease in the number of workers (or, alternatively, in the number of hours worked). In the less than perfectly frictionless economy postulated in the present paper, the responsiveness of the real wage rate (and, consequently, of the level of employment) to real shocks depends on the value which the indexing parameter assumes. It can be shown that in general the desired levels of output and employment exceed those achieved in a nonindexed economy but fall short of those in a fully indexed economy. Clearly, then, the desired levels can be obtained through some degree of indexing less than one but greater than zero. Within the specific framework of this paper, this optimal degree of indexing, as indicated above, is positively related to the elasticity of supply of labor, ε.

For the general case in which the variances of both disturbance terms are nonzero, γ^o lies between unity and $\varepsilon/(1 + \varepsilon)$. The dependence of γ^o on the relative magnitudes of the two types of disturbances is reflected in the weights, θ and $(1 - \theta)$. As the relative size of monetary disturbances (V_b) increases, θ increases and γ^o approaches unity. Conversely, as the relative size of real shocks (V_a) increases, $(1 - \theta)$ rises and γ^o approaches $\varepsilon/(1 + \varepsilon)$. Much less obvious is the dependence of the optimal degree of indexing on the elasticities of supply and demand for labor. It can be shown, however, that γ^o is positively related to ε and negatively related to η.

Optimal Contract Length

We turn now to the determination of optimal contract length. The economic intuition underlying the results of this part is straightforward: longer contracts have the advantage of amortizing the fixed cost of negotiating a contract over a longer period, thereby minimizing the per period losses due to transactions costs. Shorter contracts, on the other hand, imply smaller (per period) expected losses due to deviations of output and employment from their desired levels. This results from the particular form assumed for the distributions of the disturbance terms, a form which associates greater uncertainty with more distant points of future time. The optimal contract length, then, is determined by a condition that, at the margin, balances the per period savings on transactions costs that could be achieved by lengthening the contract against the concomitant increased losses in the form of larger expected output and employment deviations. It follows that increased uncertainty will bring about a shortening of contract length, while increased contracting costs will lead to a lengthening of contracts.

Formally, the optimal contract length is found in a manner analogous to the optimal degree of indexing. Equation (7), the first-order conditions for a minimum, and a substantial amount of manipulation yield an expression for the cost minimizing contract length, l^o, in a freely adjusting economy (see Appendix B for details):

$$l^o\Big|_{\gamma=\gamma^o} = \left(\frac{\varepsilon + \eta}{\delta\eta^2}\right)\phi, \qquad \text{where } \phi = \left[\frac{(2C/\lambda)(V_a\eta^2 + V_b)}{V_a V_b}\right]^{1/2} > 0. \ (11)$$

Differentiation of equation (11) with respect to V_a and V_b demonstrates the effect on contract length of increased real and monetary variability, respectively,

$$\frac{\partial l^o}{\partial V_a} = \left(\frac{C}{\lambda}\right)\left(\frac{\varepsilon + \eta}{\delta\eta^2 V_a}\phi\right) < 0, \tag{12}$$

$$\frac{\partial l}{\partial V_b} = \left(\frac{C}{\lambda}\right)\left(\frac{\varepsilon + \eta}{\delta V_b^2 \phi}\right) < 0. \tag{13}$$

As expected, increased variability—regardless of source—shortens contract length. Similarly, the effect of increased contracting costs on contract length is positive:

$$\frac{\partial l^o}{\partial C} = \left(\frac{\varepsilon + \eta}{2C\delta\eta^2}\right)\phi > 0. \tag{14}$$

Some Policy Implications

The framework and results developed above can now be used to examine the costs associated with (i) increased monetary variability and (ii) government regulation of contracting arrangements.

The cost associated with an increase in monetary variability has two components. First, the increased variability brings about a shortening of contract length. This reduction means that the fixed cost of contracting is amortized over a shorter interval of time, implying a higher per period cost of contracting. This, then, is the loss associated with the system's adjustment to the increased variability. In addition, there is a loss associated with that part of the effects of the increased variability for which the system is unable to adjust. Specifically, despite compensating changes in contract length and the indexing parameter, there is an increase in the average (per period) losses due to undesired output and unemployment fluctuations over the life of the contract. These results can be formalized by differentiating the loss function (eq. [7]) with respect to V_b (the variance of monetary shocks), an exercise which is left to the interested reader.

The preceding portions of the paper assume an economy in which contract length and the indexing parameter adjust freely and automatically in order to minimize the value of the loss function specified by equation (7). We now consider the possibility of government regulation of contract provisions. In particular, the effect on contract length (assumed still free to adjust) of prohibiting indexing is examined. In figure 1 optimal contract

ON INDEXATION AND CONTRACT LENGTH   9

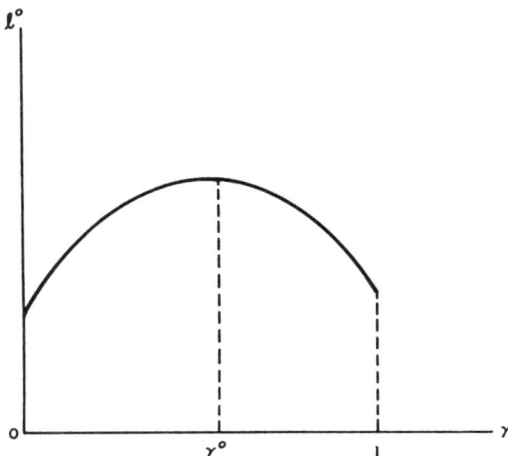

FIG. 1.—Relationship between optimal contract length and the degree of wage indexation

length, l^o, is plotted as a function of the indexing parameter, γ. Contract length reaches its maximum value when the indexing parameter assumes its optimal value, γ^o. Deviations of γ from γ^o in either direction bring about compensating reductions in contract length.[12] The curve depicting this relationship is drawn for given values of V_a and V_b. An increase in monetary variability will shift the curve down and to the right, while an increase in real variability will shift it down and to the left. Figure 1 illustrates one of the costs associated with government prohibition of indexing (or any regulation which prevents the economy from achieving a degree of indexing of γ^o)—reduced contract length. An additional cost not reflected in the figure is that associated with the larger deviations of actual from desired output brought about by any movement away from γ^o, a cost which is attenuated but not eliminated by the shortened contract length. These costs can be demonstrated formally by total differentiation of the loss function, Z, with respect to γ, an exercise which is left to the interested reader.

III. Varying Contract Lengths and the Cost of Indexing

The preceding sections developed an aggregate model from which a single, optimal contract length was derived. The present section focuses on a disaggregated version of the same model in which contract lengths vary by

[12] These results may be formally demonstrated by differentiating the expression for l^o (given by equation [B2] of Appendix B) with respect to γ. It is easily shown that the resulting expression for $dl^o/d\gamma$ is zero when γ is set equal to γ^o, positive when γ is less than γ^o, and negative for values of γ greater than γ^o.

industry in response to variations in the size of industry-specific disturbances. The framework becomes interesting when the assumption of
costless indexing is dropped, since it is then possible to demonstrate that
escalator clauses will appear only in longer contracts. Specifically, it is
shown that, if indexing involves a fixed per period cost,[13] there exists a
"cut-off" contract length above which index clauses will be incorporated
into agreements and below which they will not. An increase in monetary
variability reduces the cut-off contract length and consequently results in
an increase in the proportion of contracts indexed. So the analysis suggests
a positive correlation between monetary variability and the proportion of
contracts indexed. Finally, it is shown that the costs of monetary variability
are distributed differentially across industries, thereby imposing an additional cost on the system in the form of resource misallocation among
industries.

The framework used to demonstrate these results considers a single small
industry that is engaged in producing the (one) commodity of an economy
similar to that described in Sections I and II above. For simplicity, however, the variance of the aggregate real disturbance term is set equal to
zero, reducing the system at the aggregate level to an economy subject only
to monetary disturbances. The industry faces two kinds of uncertainty:
(i) an aggregate price level shock that it shares with all other industries,
and (ii) a relative real shock to its production function that is distributed
independently of the aggregate price level disturbance.[14] The variance of
the price level, V_ξ, is an increasing function of the variance of the money
supply, V_b. The variance of the real shock specific to industry i (denoted
V_i) may differ across industries. In all other respects, industries are assumed to be identical. Each industry operates in a labor market that is a
simple microcosm of the single aggregate market described in Section I.[15]
Similarly, in setting contract length and its indexing parameter, an industry seeks to minimize a loss function much like that employed in the
preceding sections.[16]

---

[13] This result is robust with respect to the specification of the indexing cost as long as
the per period cost of indexing does not increase with contract length more quickly than
the per period gains from indexing.

[14] A similar analysis could be carried out for industry-specific shocks that originate
from shifts in relative demand among industries. However, such an approach sacrifices
the analytical convenience of a one-commodity, one-price model.

[15] One of several problems involved in simply "scaling down" an aggregate model in
order to create a disaggregated world surfaces here. The resulting specification does not
permit interindustry labor mobility inside the contract period. That is, a worker whose
hours are reduced in a declining industry does not seek alternative employment in an
expanding industry.

[16] This measure of the losses due to unanticipated shocks to the system is undoubtedly
less satisfactory at the industry level than at the aggregate level. It does not, for example,
capture the costs incurred by an industry because it is not able to bid additional workers
away from other industries when it experiences an unanticipated increase in productivity
($u_{it} > 0$). However, the results of this section are not significantly altered by the particular
story told about the nature of the costs associated with being locked into a contract,

ON INDEXATION AND CONTRACT LENGTH   II

A formal description of the framework outlined above is contained in Appendix C. Solving this model for the optimal values of the indexing parameter, γ_i^o, and contract length, l_i^o, parallels the calculations of Section II. As expected in a regime where aggregate shocks are purely monetary and indexing is costless, full indexation is optimal for all industries ($\gamma_i^o = 1$ for all i). With full indexing, monetary shocks have no real effect on the economy, and consequently optimal contract length for industry i, l_i^o, is independent of the variance of monetary disturbances. If, however, γ_i were set at a value less than one, l_i^o would depend on the variance of money shocks (through V_ξ) as well as on the variance of the industry-specific shock, V_i. Specifically, optimal contract length for industry i is given by[17]

$$l_i^o = \frac{1}{\delta\eta}\left[\frac{2C/\lambda}{(1-\gamma_i)^2 V_\xi + (\eta/\varepsilon + \eta)^2 V_i}\right]^{\frac{1}{4}}. \quad (15)$$

If the industry is fully indexed ($\gamma_i = 1$), then optimal contract length is a function only of the variance of the industry-specific shock, V_i:

$$\left.l_i^o\right|_{\gamma_i=\gamma_i^o} = \frac{1}{\delta\eta}\left[\frac{2C/\lambda}{(\eta/\varepsilon + \eta)^2 V_i}\right]^{\frac{1}{4}}. \quad (16)$$

Note that, as discussed in Section II, any deviation of γ_i from its optimal value (in this case unity) results in a decrease in contract length.

Differentiation of equations (15) and (16) with respect to V_i establishes the proposition that optimal contract length is inversely related to the variance of the industry-specific shock. Thus industries that face a large variance of specific shocks will have short contracts, and those that face a small variance of specific shocks will have long contracts.

I now relax the assumption that indexing is costless and introduce a fixed per period cost of indexing, π. The cost is assumed to depend only on whether or not indexing takes place, not on the degree of indexing. Clearly, indexing will be adopted only if the gain from indexing exceeds its cost. The per period gain from indexing, G, is the difference between the value of the industry loss function corresponding to $\gamma_i = 0$ and the value calculated at $\gamma_i = \gamma_i^o = 1$:

$$G = \left.Z_i\right|_{\gamma_i=0} - \left.Z_i\right|_{\gamma_i=1}. \quad (17)$$

Appropriate substitution and manipulation result in the following expression for G:

$$G = (2C\lambda)^{\frac{1}{2}}\delta\eta\left\{\left[V_\xi + \left(\frac{\eta}{\varepsilon\eta}\right)^2 V_i\right] - \left[\left(\frac{\eta}{\varepsilon + \eta}\right)^2 V_i\right]^{\frac{1}{4}}\right\} > 0. \quad (18)$$

---

provided those costs are an increasing function of the size of the shocks faced by an industry.

[17] The symbols $\delta, \eta, \varepsilon, C, \lambda$, and γ retain their meanings from Sec. I, with the modification that they are here defined for an industry rather than the economy as a whole.

By differentiating this expression with respect to V_i, it can be shown that the gain from indexing is inversely related to the variance of relative shocks faced by an industry. This negative relationship implies that, for any given fixed per period cost of indexing (and a sufficiently large money variance, as discussed below), there exists a cut-off variance, V_i^c, and a corresponding cut-off contract length, l_i^c, for which the gain from indexing is exactly equal to the cost of indexing. In industries in which the variance of the industry-specific shock is less than V_i^c, wages will be indexed; while in industries in which the variance of the industry-specific shock exceeds V_i^c, wages will not be indexed.

These results are illustrated in figure 2, where the per period gain from indexing, the per period cost of indexing, and contract length for the cases of $\gamma_i = 0$ and $\gamma_i = \gamma_i^0 = 1$ are each drawn as a function of the variance of the industry specific shock. The cut-off variance, V_i^c, is determined by the intersection of the schedules labeled G and π, which depict, respectively, the gains and costs associated with indexing. Contracts are indexed in industries with a variance of industry-specific shocks less than V_i^c, and consequently contract length for these industries is given by the schedule labeled l_i^0 (indexed). Contract length for industries with a variance greater than V_i^c is given by the l_i^0 (nonindexed) schedule. Contract length for the full range of possible V_i, then, is represented by the solid portions of the two schedules.

Figure 2 is useful in illustrating two additional points. First, note that the position of the G schedule is determined, through the term V_ξ in equation (18), by the degree of monetary variability in the system. An increase

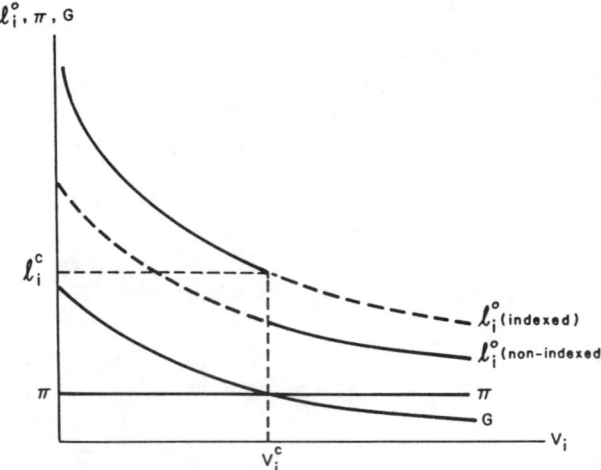

Fig. 2.—Determination of the "cut-off" value of the variance of industry-specific shocks

in the variance of money increases the variance of the price level and accordingly the gain from indexing, shifting the G schedule upward. Conversely, a decrease in the variance of money decreases the gain from indexing, shifting the G schedule downward. Clearly, for a sufficiently small money variance, the costs of indexing will exceed the gains from indexing for all values of V_i (the G schedule will lie below the π schedule for all V_i), and a nonzero cut-off variance will not exist. Thus, for sufficiently small values of V_b (and correspondingly small values of V_ξ), all contracts will be of the nonindexed variety. As monetary variability (and V_ξ) increase, the gains from indexing increase. At a sufficiently high level of monetary variability, the gains from indexing will exceed the fixed cost of indexing for industries with very low values of V_i, and these industries will index. Further increases in V_b will bring about corresponding increases in the proportion of contracts indexed. This point is illustrated in figure 3, where the percentage of contracts indexed is drawn as a function of the variance of monetary disturbances.

A second interesting point is the strong correspondence between indexed contracts and long contracts. As figure 2 demonstrates, this correspondence has two sources. The first is the negative relationship between industry-specific variance and the gains from indexing, which indicates greater gains from indexing for industries with longer contracts. The relationship is reinforced by the fact that, once indexing occurs, the costs associated with monetary variability are eliminated, and optimal contract length increases by a discrete amount. In figure 2 this second effect is represented by the shift from the l_i^o(nonindexed) schedule to the higher l_i^o(indexed) schedule that occurs at V_i^c as V_i decreases.

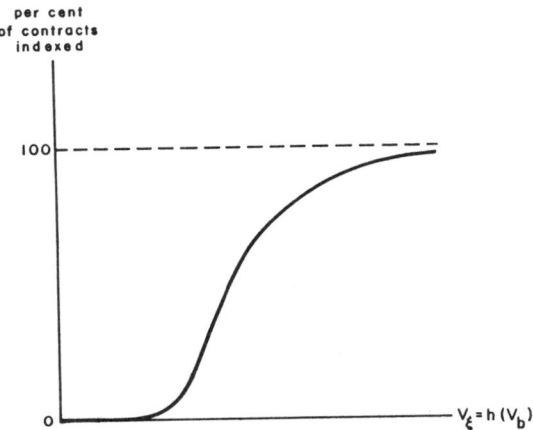

Fig. 3.—Relationship between the proportion of contracts indexed and the variance of monetary shocks.

Finally, it can be shown that the costs of monetary variability are distributed differentially across industries, thereby imposing an additional cost on the economy in the form of resource misallocation among industries.

The cost, ρ, associated with a given level of monetary variability, $\bar{V}_b$, is the difference between the value of the industry loss function corresponding to $V_b = \bar{V}_b$ and the value calculated at $V_b = 0$, plus the fixed cost of indexing if indexing occurs. Equations (19) and (20), then, give the costs of monetary variability for indexed and nonindexed industries, respectively:

$$\rho \bigg|_{\gamma_i = 1} = \pi \tag{19}$$

$$\rho \bigg|_{\gamma_i = 1} = (2C\lambda)^{\frac{1}{2}} \delta \eta \left\{ \left[V_{\xi} + \left(\frac{\eta}{\varepsilon + \eta} \right)^2 V_i \right]^{\frac{1}{2}} - \left[\left(\frac{\eta}{\varepsilon + \eta} \right)^2 V_i \right]^{\frac{1}{2}} \right\}, \tag{20}$$

where $\bar{V}_{\xi} = h(\bar{V}_b)$. For industries that are indexed, monetary variability does not effect the value of the industry loss function, but each industry incurs the fixed per period cost of indexing,[18] π. For industries that are not indexed, the costs of monetary variability are reflected in the value of the industry loss function and can be shown to be a decreasing function of V_i. These results are illustrated in figure 4, which depicts the total cost of money variance, ρ, as a function of the industry-specific variance, V_i. The $\bar{V}_i^c$ is the cut-off variance associated with $\bar{V}_b$, below which contracts are indexed. For industries to the left of $\bar{V}_i^c$, all of which are fully indexed, ρ is constant at a level equal to the fixed per period cost of indexing, π. For the nonindexed industries, to the right of $\bar{V}_i^c$, ρ is a decreasing function of V_i, with a maximum value of π.

Clearly, the costs of increased monetary variability differ across industries and, consequently, may result in misallocation of resources among industries.[19]

IV. Conclusions

This paper develops a framework for investigating the joint determination and interaction of contract length and the degree of wage indexation.

[18] The sole dependence of ρ on π in the case of indexed industries is peculiar to the present framework which does not incorporate aggregate real disturbances. A more general analysis that considered real as well as monetary shocks would, as Sec. II demonstrates, suggest an optimal degree of indexing less than one. Consequently, the value of the industry loss function would be affected by money variance for indexed as well as nonindexed industries and, in the case of indexed industries, ρ would depend on V_i as well as π. This would not, however, affect the conclusion that the costs of monetary variability are distributed differentially across industries.

[19] The marginal cost of an increase in monetary variability also differs across industries. Specifically, the cost is zero for industries that are indexed but positive and a decreasing function of V_i for nonindexed industries. Consequently, *changes* in monetary variability result in resource *reallocation* among industries, although not necessarily in greater *misallocation* among industries.

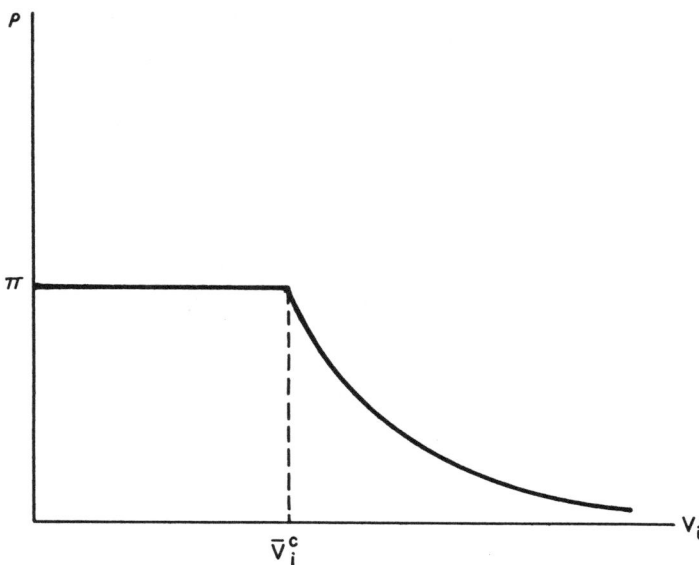

Fig. 4.—Relationship between the total per period costs of monetary variability and the variance of industry-specific shocks.

Within this framework, a number of propositions are demonstrated: optimal indexing, even if costless, will not completely insulate the real sector of an economy from the effects of unanticipated monetary shocks; thus policies that bring about increased monetary variability impose unavoidable costs on the economy. For any given degree of indexing, contract length is a decreasing function of the amount of uncertainty in the system and an increasing function of the cost of contracting. Any movement of the system away from the optimal degree of indexing involves a real resource cost, part of which is reflected in decreased contract length; thus in this model government regulation of indexing arrangements necessarily imposes social costs. It is shown that contract length may differ across industries in response to variations in the size of industry-specific shocks and that, if indexing is costly, indexing provisions will appear only in longer contracts. Further, as the variance of monetary disturbances increases, the proportion of contracts indexed will increase. Finally, the costs of monetary variability may differ across industries, causing resource misallocation among industries.

Appendix A

The Optimal Degree of Indexing

Equation (10) of the text may be developed as follows: from equation (7) of the text,

$$\phi_t = E[(\ln Y_t - \ln Y_t^0)^2].$$

The log of actual output (Y_t) is given by equation (1) of the text as a function of labor input, L_t, and the productivity factor, α_t. Actual labor input in turn is completely demand determined and therefore given by equation (5) of the text. Substituting equation (5) into (1) gives

$$\ln Y_t = -\delta\eta(\ln w_t - \alpha_t) + \alpha_t + \delta\eta \ln \delta. \tag{A2}$$

But the real wage rate, w_t, depends on the price level, P_t, and the value of the indexing parameter, γ:

$$\ln w_t = \ln W^* + \gamma_t(\ln P_t - \ln P^*) - \ln P_t = (\gamma - 1)(\ln P_t - \ln P^*), \tag{A3}$$

where $\gamma_t = (\ln W_t - \ln W^*)/(\ln P_t - \ln P^*)$. (Recall that asterisks denote certainty equivalents, or valuesc orresponding to $\alpha_t = \beta_t = 0$, and that $\ln w^* = \ln W^* - \ln P^* = 0$.) Equating equations (2) and (3) of the text yields expressions for $\ln P_t$ and $\ln P_t^*$:

$$\ln P_t = \ln \bar{M} + \beta_t - \ln k - \ln Y_t, \tag{A4}$$

$$\ln P^* = \ln \bar{M} - \ln k - \ln Y^*. \tag{A5}$$

But $\ln Y^*$ is given by

$$\ln Y^* = \delta \ln L^* = \delta\eta \ln \delta. \tag{A6}$$

(Recall that $\ln w^* = 0$.) Substituting this result into (A5) and subtracting (A5) from (A4) gives

$$\ln P - \ln P^* = \beta_t - \ln Y + \delta\eta \ln \delta. \tag{A7}$$

Substituting (A7) into (A3) and (A3) into (A2) and solving for $\ln Y_t$ produces

$$\ln Y_t = \delta\eta \left[\frac{(1 - \gamma_t)\beta_t + \gamma_t\alpha_t}{1 + \delta\eta(1 - \gamma_t)} \right] + \alpha_t + \delta\eta \ln \delta. \tag{A8}$$

The log of desired output $(\ln Y_t^o)$ is given by

$$\ln Y_t^o = \delta \ln L_t^o + \alpha_t = \delta\eta\alpha_t[\varepsilon/(\varepsilon + \eta)] + \alpha_t + \delta\eta \ln \delta, \tag{A9}$$

where desired labor input, L_t^o, is found by equating equations (5) and (6) of the text, solving for $\ln w_t$, and substituting the resulting expression back into (6).

Substitution of equations (A8) and (A9) into equation (A1) yields the desired expression for ϕ_t:

$$\phi_t = \delta^2\eta^2 \left\{ V_{\alpha_t} \left[\frac{\gamma_t}{1 + \delta\eta(1 - \gamma_t)} - \frac{\varepsilon}{\varepsilon + \eta} \right]^2 + V_{\beta_t} \left[\frac{(1 - \gamma_t)}{1 + \delta\eta(1 - \gamma_t)} \right]^2 \right\}. \tag{A10}$$

Differentiating equation (A.10) with respect to γ, setting the result equal to zero, and solving for γ_t^o gives

$$\gamma_t^o = \frac{V_a[\varepsilon\eta^2/(\varepsilon + \eta)] + V_b}{V_a[\varepsilon\eta^2/(\varepsilon + \eta)][(1 + \varepsilon)/\varepsilon] + V_b}. \tag{A11}$$

(Recall that $V_{\alpha_t} = tV_a$ and $V_{\beta_t} = tV_b$.) Since the expression for γ_t^o is independent of time (i.e., γ_t^o is the same for all t), it provides the general solution to equation (9) of the text and, with some manipulation, becomes equation (10) of the text.

Appendix B

Optimal Contract Length

The relevant first-order condition is

$$\lambda l \phi_l - \lambda \int_o^l (\phi_t) dt - c = 0. \tag{B1}$$

Substituting for ϕ_t and ϕ_l from equation (A10) of Appendix A, performing the necessary integration, and solving for the optimal value of l yields

$$l^o = \frac{1}{\delta\eta} \left\{ \frac{2C/\lambda}{V_a \left[\dfrac{\gamma}{1 + \delta\eta(1 - \gamma)} - \dfrac{\varepsilon}{\varepsilon + \eta} \right]^2 + V_b \left[\dfrac{(1 - \gamma)}{1 + \delta\eta(1 - \gamma)} \right]^2} \right\}^{\frac{1}{4}}. \tag{B2}$$

In a freely adjusting economy, the indexing parameter will assume the optimal value given by equation (10) of the text. Substituting this value into the preceding expression for l^o gives equation (11) of the text.

Appendix C

The Disaggregated Model

It is assumed that the price level, which is also the price faced by an individual industry, is generated by a Wiener process, ξ_t, which has zero mean and forecast variance tV_ξ:

$$\ln P_t = \bar{P} + \xi_t. \tag{C1}$$

In the absence of aggregate real shocks, V_ξ may be assumed to be an increasing function of V_b, the variance of monetary shocks:

$$V_\xi = h(V_b), \qquad h' > 0, \qquad h(0) = 0. \tag{C2}$$

Each industry can be described by a production relationship of the form

$$\ln Y_{ti} = \delta \ln L_{ti} + u_{ti}, \tag{C3}$$

where i is an index that runs across industries. The disturbance term u_{ti} is generated by a Wiener process with zero mean and forecast variance tV_i. All industries are identical except for the value of V_i.

Labor market conditions for the industry are given by equations (C4) and (C5), where L_t^D and L_t^S are the hours demanded from and supplied by the (fixed) number of workers who sign contracts with the industry. It is assumed that the industry faces an exogenously given nominal base wage, W^*, and that the number of workers who sign contracts with the industry is determined by the condition that, for $\beta_t = u_{ti} = 0$, the labor market clears at W^*.

$$\ln L_{ti}^D = -\eta(\ln w_t - u_{ti}) + \eta \ln \delta, \qquad \eta = 1/(1 + \delta), \qquad w_t = W_t/P_t, \tag{C4}$$

$$\ln L_{ti}^S = \varepsilon \ln w_t + \eta \ln \delta. \tag{C5}$$

Finally, the industry's loss function is given by

$$Z_i = 1/l_i \left[\lambda \int_o^{l_i} (\phi_{ti}) \, dt + C \right]. \tag{C6}$$

All symbols retain their meanings from Section I of the text, with the modification that they are here defined for an industry rather than the economy as a whole.

References

Barro, Robert J. "A Theory of Monopolistic Price Adjustment." *Rev. Econ. Studies* 39 (January 1972): 17–26.

———. "Indexation in a Rational Expectations Model." *J. Econ. Theory* 13 (October 1976): 229–44. (*a*)

———. "Rational Expectations and the Role of Monetary Policy." *J. Monetary Econ.* 2, no. 1 (January 1976): 1–32. (*b*)

Bernstein, E. M. "Indexing Money Payments in a Large and Prolonged Inflation." In *Essays on Inflation and Indexation*. AEI Domestic Affairs Study no. 197. Washington: American Enterprise Inst. Public Policy Res., 1974.

Fischer, S. "Wage Indexation and Macroeconomic Stability." *J. Monetary Econ.* 5, suppl. (1977): 107–47.

Fisher, Irving. *The Purchasing Power of Money; Its Determination and Relation to Credit, Interest and Crises.* New York: Macmillan, 1922.

Friedman, Milton. "Monetary Correction." In *Essays on Inflation and Indexation*. AEI Domestic Affairs Study no. 24. Washington: American Enterprise Inst. Public Policy Res., 1974.

Gray, Jo Anna. "Wage Indexation: A Macroeconomic Approach." *J. Monetary Econ.* 2, no. 2 (April 1976): 221–35.

Jevons, William S. *Money and the Mechanism of Exchange.* New York: Appleton, 1896.

Marshall, A. "Remedies for Fluctuations of General Prices." In *Memorials of Alfred Marshall*, edited by Arthur C. Pigou. London: Macmillan, 1925.

Pigou, Arthur C. *The Theory of Unemployment.* London: Macmillan, 1933.

[21]

A Theory of Exchange Rate Determination

Alan C. Stockman

University of Rochester

This paper develops an equilibrium model of the determination of
exchange rates and prices of goods. Changes in relative prices of
goods, due to supply or demand shifts, induce changes in exchange
rates and deviations from purchasing power parity. These changes
may create a correlation between the exchange rate and the terms of
trade, but this correlation cannot be exploited by the government to
affect the terms of trade by foreign exchange market operations.

I. Introduction

Exchange rates have recently exhibited considerable volatility and
together with prices have failed to conform to the predictions of the
purchasing power parity theory. Frequently, exchange rate changes
have failed to resemble contemporaneous changes in relative price
levels in either magnitude or direction. Exchange rates and their rates
of change have been more volatile than relative price levels and rates
of inflation. These features of exchange rate behavior have often
been regarded as inconsistent with equilibrium, and several disequilibrium interpretations of this anomalous behavior have been suggested.[1]

This paper proposes an alternative equilibrium explanation of exchange rate behavior. The explanation is based on a model of the
simultaneous determination of exchange rates and relative prices of

This paper draws on my Ph.D. dissertation at the University of Chicago. I wish to
thank Jacob A. Frenkel, Robert E. Lucas, Jr., Michael Mussa, and Maurice Obstfeld for
many helpful comments.
[1] See especially the papers by Dornbusch (1976a, 1976b) and Mussa (1976, sec. 4).
Wilson (1979) combines some features of these papers.

[*Journal of Political Economy*, 1980, vol. 88, no. 4]

different goods in international trade in an intertemporal framework with uncertainty and rational expectations. The model emphasizes the role of relative price changes, caused by real disturbances, in determining the behavior of exchange rates and integrates the important issues discussed by the traditional "elasticity theorists" into a general equilibrium framework.[2]

In the model developed in this paper, exchange rates may be volatile and can exhibit autocorrelated deviations from purchasing power parity, even though prices freely adjust to clear markets. Exchange rate changes may appear to cause relative price changes and generate additional uncertainty even when all markets are in equilibrium. Nevertheless, the relationship between the exchange rate and the terms of trade cannot be exploited by government exchange rate policies.[3]

The model shows how a change in the terms of trade caused by relative supply or demand shifts is divided between nominal price changes in each country and an exchange rate change, creating a correlation between the exchange rate and the terms of trade. The greater the changes in the terms of the trade and the larger the role of changes in the exchange rate in effecting these terms of trade changes, the greater the variability of exchange rates. The more persistent the shifts in the supplies or demands for goods, the more persistent the deviations from purchasing power parity.

Besides rationalizing exchange rate volatility and autocorrelated deviations from purchasing power parity, the model has several other implications. The correlation of the exchange rate with the terms of trade will be greater for countries with more homogeneous monetary policies. Exchange rate changes caused by monetary factors will not affect the terms of trade.[4] The model implies that deviations from purchasing power parity and changes in the terms of trade have roughly the same characteristics and bear approximately the same relationship to each other under both fixed and flexible exchange rate systems.

---

[2] These relative price changes were emphasized in the traditional literature on exchange rates but have been neglected in the recent exchange rate literature associated with the monetary approach.

[3] Government commercial policies such as tariffs or quotas can, however, affect the exchange rate by changing the terms of trade. Cassel (1922) discussed the role of commercial policies in causing deviations from purchasing power parity. Mussa (1974) examined the effects of commercial policies on the balance of payments, and his argument could be applied to a flexible exchange rate case; the effect he emphasizes is the change in real income and hence the domestic demand for domestic money due to a tariff.

[4] This paper abstracts from real effects of monetary shocks due to incomplete information. Saidi (1977) discusses this issue in an international context.

II. Purchasing Power Parity and the Terms of Trade

Large changes in exchange rates are generally associated with different rates of inflation in the countries concerned. A full model of the foreign exchange market is not required for the inference that a change in the stock of money will, other things the same, be associated with a corresponding increase in all nominal prices including the nominal price of foreign exchange. This result is guaranteed by the zero-degree homogeneity of demands and supplies with respect to all nominal prices. The purchasing power parity hypothesis, which states that there is a proportional relationship between the exchange rate and a ratio of foreign and domestic prices or price indexes, can be thought of as stating that other things *are* approximately the same. The accuracy of this hypothesis is independent of the accuracy of any particular theory of exchange rate determination.

A rough idea of the accuracy of purchasing power parity can be obtained from the percentage deviations from purchasing power parity with the U.S. dollar, from 1900–1904 to 1963–67, calculated by Gailliot (1970). These are, for Canada .04, France −.01, Germany .04, Italy −.11, Japan .26, Switzerland .14, and the United Kingdom .11 or .02.[5] Figure 1 shows the ratio of monthly consumer price indexes of France and the United States and the corresponding exchange rate for some recent years. It is apparent that deviations from purchasing power parity persist over time and that exchange rates vary more than ratios of price indexes. Neither phenomenon is unique to France during this time period.[6]

Monetary models of the exchange rate (Frenkel 1976, 1978; Frenkel and Johnson 1978) supplement the purchasing power parity relation with money demand functions and equilibrium conditions in the money markets. The equation for the exchange rate resulting from the basic monetary model is $d \ln e = d \ln (M^s/M^{*s}) - d \ln (m^d/m^{*d})$, where the exchange rate e is the domestic price of foreign money, M^s and M^{*s} are domestic and foreign nominal money supplies, and m^d and m^{*d} are the demands for real balances of domestic and foreign moneys, typically taken to be functions of real income and nominal interest rates. The success of the monetary models in explaining actual exchange rate behavior has been, perhaps not surprisingly,

[5] These are the percentage changes in exchange-rate-adjusted ratios of wholesale price indexes from the 1900–1904 average to the 1963–67 average.

[6] For example, Friedman and Schwartz (1963, p. 64) note that during the greenback period of 1861–79, the U.S.-U.K. exchange rate varied by about 2 to 1, while the ratio of price levels varied by only about 1.3 to 1. The French experience shown in fig. 1 can be regarded as representative.

Fig. 1

similar to the success of purchasing power parity. There remain substantial short-run variations in exchange rates unexplained by the monetary models.

In the explanations of exchange rate fluctuations proposed by Dornbusch (1976a, 1976b) and Mussa (1976), the prices of goods available to people in one country change relative to prices of those same goods in another country because domestic nominal prices are temporarily fixed in each country and a monetary shock causes a change in the exchange rate. A nominal shock therefore causes a change in relative goods prices in those models, even if real supplies and demands for goods are unaffected. Other economists (e.g., Balassa 1964) have emphasized changes in the relative prices of traded and nontraded goods. The relative price change that was emphasized most in the traditional literature on foreign exchange markets was the terms of trade.[7] Krueger (1969) noted that the traditional theory viewed the terms of trade as "the key variable," and the terms of trade also play an important role in the explanation presented by Friedman and Schwartz (1963) of deviations from pur-

---

[7] See Keynes (1930), Haberler (1949), Robinson (1949), and Machlup (1976). Keynes (1930, pp. 73–74) criticized the purchasing power parity hypothesis for assuming that the terms of trade are constant and suggested that variations in the terms of trade constitute "one of the greatest difficulties in the way of the maintenance of a country's external equilibrium."

chasing power parity during the U.S. greenback era, from the Civil War to 1879.[8] According to the price indexes reported in Graham (1922), the simple correlation coefficient between the log deviation from purchasing power parity (measured with general price indexes in the United States and the United Kingdom and with the greenback price of gold, to which the pound sterling was pegged) and the log terms of trade (measured with export price indexes converted at the current exchange rate) is −.68, calculated with 13 annual observations from 1866 through 1878.[9] The simple correlation coefficients between the monthly percentage changes in the exchange rate with the dollar and the monthly percentage change in the terms of trade (measured as the ratio of the domestic export price index divided by the import price index to the U.S. export price index divided by the U.S. import price index) from January 1974 through July 1977 are −.29 for the Canadian dollar, −.16 for the French franc, −.33 for the deutsche mark, −.15 for the lira, .21 for the yen, and −.24 for the guilder.[10] Dornbusch and Krugman (1976) have also presented evidence of this correlation, while Isard (1977) and Kravis and Lipsey (1978) have presented evidence that the exchange rate is correlated with changes in the terms of trade of even disaggregated categories of goods.[11] While the correlation between the exchange rate and the terms of trade is clear, the interpretation is not. In order to examine the equilibrium relationship between the exchange rate and the terms of trade, the next section presents a model in which both are endogenous.

[8] During the Civil War, U.S. cotton exports were cut off, resulting in a rise in the price of gold (foreign exchange) relative to purchasing power parity by 20 percent and affecting the terms of trade. After the Civil War, as the supply of goods for export rose again and reduced the terms of trade, the domestic currency appreciated from about 20 percent below purchasing power parity to about 10 percent above purchasing power parity. Later movements in the exchange rate may also have been related to changes in the terms of trade. See Friedman and Schwartz (1963, pp. 65–78).

[9] The sign indicates that currency depreciations are associated with increases in the relative price of a country's exports. This result does not seem to be due to spurious correlation induced by using the exchange rate in calculating the terms of trade, since the simple correlation between the log deviation from purchasing power parity and the log of the ratio of export price indexes, *not* converted at the exchange rate, is −.77, and the correlation between the log of the exchange rate and the log deviation from purchasing power parity, which would be negative if there were spurious correlation, is in fact .24.

[10] The number of monthly observations is 43, so the implied t-statistics are −1.9, −1.0, −2.2, −.9, 1.4, and −1.6.

[11] In Stockman (1979) I have outlined an explanation of why equilibrium models can be consistent with this evidence from disaggregated price data. Also, the terms of trade can apparently account for some of the residual variation in monetary models of the exchange rate (see Stockman 1978b).

III. A Model

Overview and Individual Optimization Problems

Consider a world with two countries, two goods, and two moneys. People in country one produce only good one but consume both goods one and two; people in country two produce only good two but consume both goods. Thus there is a complete specialization in production, and trade allows people to consume both goods.

Let $\{M_1^s, M_2^s\}_t$ be the nominal quantities of moneys one and two that have been issued by the governments of those countries and are used within those countries for domestic transactions. Let $\{P_1, P_2\}_t$ be the sequence of the money-one price of good one and the money-two price of good two, and let e_t be the price of money two in terms of money one. (I will refer to country one as the domestic country, so e is the price of foreign exchange.)

First suppose that M_1/P_1 and M_2/P_2 are constant over time (because demanders of each money want to maintain a money stock with constant purchasing power in terms of the corresponding good). The relative price of good one in terms of good two is $T \equiv P_1/eP_2$. Suppose now that a relative demand shift occurs: The demand for good one falls, the demand for good two rises, and the demands for moneys are unchanged. The ensuing fall in the terms of trade, T, must occur (solely) through a rise in the exchange rate, e, corresponding to a depreciation of domestic money.

By allowing money demands to depend on interest rates or expected inflation rates, one could study the effects of new information about future rates of monetary growth and inflation on the current exchange rate and price level, as in Mussa (1976) or Wilson (1979).[12] The effects depend on the serial-correlation properties of money and inflation, the interest or expected-inflation elasticity of the demand for money, etc. I will abstract from these important issues in order to concentrate on the relation between the exchange rate and relative prices. The model presented below introduces transactions and precautionary reasons for holding money and relaxes the assumption above that the real demand for money, in terms of the export good, is constant. The proposition illustrated above—that a shift in supplies or demands for goods induces a change in the exchange rate—continues to hold. But the result is generalized: A change in the relative price T due to a shift in supplies or demands for goods will

---

[12] Note that if prices adjust freely, then new information about future inflation affects current exchange rates and prices proportionally, so that no deviation from purchasing power parity results. Wilson (1979) examines the issue in a Dornbusch-type model with a slowly adjusting price level.

occur *partially* through a change in e and partially through changes in P_1 and P_2.

Another characteristic of the simple model above should be noted now. Since money supply changes have proportional effects on e and P_1/P_2, if the ratio of nominal money supplies is independent of the terms of trade, then the exchange rate will have greater variance than the nominal price ratio. In the model about to be presented, this result may or may not hold, depending on parameter values. However, deviations from purchasing power parity in this model may be autocorrelated even when due to temporary, serially independent shocks.

Let "individual one" be a representative individual in country one. He maximizes the quantity

$$E\left[\sum_{t=0}^{\infty}\beta^t U^1(c_{1t}^1, c_{2t}^1)\right] \qquad (1)$$

where $\{c_1^1, c_2^1\}_t$ is the sequence of individual one's consumption of goods one and two, $U^1(\cdot)$ is the current-period utility function of individual one, $\beta \in (0, 1)$ is a discount term, and E is an expected value operator.

Similarly, there is a representative individual in country two who maximizes the quantity

$$E\left[\sum_{t=0}^{\infty}\beta^t U^2(c_{1t}^2, c_{2t}^2)\right] \qquad (2)$$

where $\{c_1^2, c_2^2\}_t$ is the stochastic process describing individual two's consumption of goods one and two, $U^2(\cdot)$ (which need not be the same function as $U^1[\cdot]$) gives current-period utility of individual two, and β and E are as described before.

Production of goods one (in country one) and two (in country two) is exogenously given by the stochastic process $\{y_1, y_2\}_t$. Neither good is storable. Assume the process $\{y_1, y_2\}_t$ is generated by independent realizations of a random vector y_t from a stationary probability distribution with cumulative distribution function $F_y(\cdot)$, so the randomness in production is independent over time. The assumptions that output is exogenous, that goods are nonstorable, that production is specialized, and that shocks to production are independent both across goods and over time could all be relaxed with no important change in the results.

International transactions could in principle involve the use of either money for payments. Empirically, roughly two-thirds of international trade contracts appear to be denominated in the seller's currency (Grassman 1973). The choice of a currency for payments in international trade should depend on costs (in terms of depreciation uncompensated by interest payments on money) of holding each money and differential transactions costs in handling alternative currencies.[13] I assume here that all international transactions are financed with the seller's currency.

Since people demand foreign exchange because they want to purchase foreign goods or assets, the demand for foreign exchange is a derived demand. This was recognized in the traditional exchange rate literature.[14] The traditional elasticities approach formalized the derived demand for foreign exchange in a static model and developed specific formulas for certain cases (e.g., the Marshall-Lerner condition). The formulas obtained depended on the particular assumptions (Mundell 1971, pp. 94–97), but a unifying characteristic of the elasticity models was that they derived the demand for foreign exchange from the demand for foreign goods.

The demands for moneys can be derived from the demands for goods by specifying a simple transactions technology that prevents individuals from engaging in barter. The transactions technology involves a "liquidity constraint" on individual behavior that attempts to reflect the facts that money is held between the transactions for which it is used and that transactions would be more costly without money. The liquidity constraint in this paper requires that goods be purchased with money and that this money be held before it is spent. Expenditures during any period must be financed out of money available at the beginning of the period.[15] This ensures that an indi-

---

[13] If there are freely tradable international bonds with permissible short selling, then portfolio risks of currencies are irrelevant for money demands because the risk of each currency can be bought and sold in the bond market, thereby separating the decision to hold the money from the decision to hold the risk of the money. Risk elements then only affect bond holdings, not money holdings (see Fama and Farber 1977 and Stockman 1978a).

[14] References to the derived characteristic of demand for foreign exchange can be found in Cassel (1922, p. 138), Haberler (1949), Robinson (1949, p. 83), Friedman (1953, pp. 159, 162), Friedman and Schwartz (1963, pp. 161, 590, n. 35), Machlup (1972, pp. 29 ff.; 1976, pp. 111, 115, 119), and Mikesell and Furth (1974, pp. 6–17, 57).

[15] The formulation of the transactions technology used here is similar to that of Lucas (1977) and is one version of the formulation proposed by Clower (1967). Grandmont and Younes (1972, 1973) use a similar but more general formulation that allows some fraction of current income or other assets to be spent in the current period. The transactions technology in this paper is adopted as one way of introducing a transactions demand (and, due to uncertainty, a precautionary demand) for money into an optimization model. An alternative way to introduce money would be with an overlapping-generations model where money is the only store of value, as in Kareken and Wallace (1978). The transactions technology method permits the introduction of other assets (see Stockman 1978b) by asserting that only money—not bonds or capital—can be used to pay for goods, although it never addresses the source of this asymmetry.

vidual cannot sell his output for money and instantaneously spend that money for goods; that is, he cannot barter. He carries his receipts from current sales of output into the next period.

Since imports must be financed with foreign exchange (foreign money), the transactions technology applied to imports results in a demand for foreign exchange that is derived from the demand for imports. People, as importers, hold positive balances of foreign exchange, which they have purchased on the foreign exchange market at the price e.

Let the sequence of events each period be the following: The representative individual in country one enters each period with some domestic money, M_1^1, which he may use for domestic purchases, and some foreign exchange, M_2^1, for importing purposes. The superscripts denote the holder of the money (individual one or two); the subscripts denote money one or money two. Individual one then harvests his output, y_1, and takes it to market. (Individual two takes y_2 to market.) He observes the current equilibrium prices (p_1, p_2, and e) at which all trades take place. He purchases consumption goods, obtains the receipts from his sales, then goes to the foreign exchange market to purchase (or sell) foreign exchange to carry into the next period.[16]

Each period individual one chooses consumption of good one, c_1^1; consumption of good two, c_2^1; end-of-period holdings of domestic money (one), $M_1^{1'}$; and end-of-period holdings of foreign exchange, $M_2^{1'}$, subject to the constraints

$$p_1 y_1 + M_1^1 + \tau_1 + e M_2^1 - p_1 c_1^1 - e p_2 c_2^1 - M_1^{1'} - e M_2^{1'} = 0, \quad (3a)$$

$$p_1 c_1^1 \leq M_1^1 + \tau_1, \quad (3b)$$

$$p_2 c_2^1 \leq M_2^1, \quad (3c)$$

where M_1^1 and M_2^1 are predetermined (by last period's choices); y_1 is his output, which he sells at the price p_1 in terms of money one; and τ_1 and τ_2 are realizations of a stochastic process $\{\tau_1, \tau_2\}_t$ representing transfer payments of money one to individual one and of money two to individual two. (These are taxes if they take negative values.) These transfers occur overnight (between periods) and are available with other initial money holdings to finance current consumption. Equation (3a) is a budget constraint while (3b) and (3c) are liquidity constraints imposed by the assumed transactions technology. They state that current purchases of domestic goods are limited by initial holdings of domestic money and current imports are limited by initial

---

[16] Note that this individual receives payment for the sales of his own good after he has purchased goods this period; his current receipts are not available for financing current consumption. Note also that, as in other highly aggregated models, the individual is assumed to purchase on the market the goods he consumes.

holdings of foreign exchange. The analogous constraints for individual two's optimization problem are

$$ep_2y_2 + M_1^2 + eM_2^2 + e\tau_2 - p_1c_1^2 - ep_2c_2^2 - M_1^{2\prime} - eM_2^{2\prime} = 0, \quad \text{(4a)}$$

$$p_1c_1^2 \leq M_1^2, \quad \text{(4b)}$$

$$p_2c_2^2 \leq M_2^2 + \tau_2. \quad \text{(4c)}$$

The Role of the Government

The governments of each country have two roles: They determine $\{\tau_1, \tau_2\}_t$, the money supply changes financed by transfers to or taxes from their residents, and they may intervene in the foreign exchange market by buying or selling foreign exchange. Let θ_t denote purchases of money two with money one by the combined actions of the two governments on the foreign exchange market. The policies of the two governments can then be summarized by the stochastic process $\{\tau_1, \tau_2, \theta\}_t$.[17]

Let M_1^s and M_2^s denote the nominal quantities of moneys one and two outstanding at the beginning of the period. Then

$$M_1^s = M_1^1 + \tau_1 + M_1^2,$$
$$M_2^s = M_2^1 + M_2^2 + \tau_2. \quad \text{(5)}$$

At the end of the period the nominal money supplies are

$$M_1^{s\prime} = M_1^s + \theta,$$
$$M_2^{s\prime} = M_2^s - \frac{1}{e}\theta, \quad \text{(6)}$$

where θ is the foreign exchange market intervention undertaken by governments during the period. At the beginning of the following period nominal money supplies are

$$M_1^{s\prime} + \tau_1' \quad \text{and} \quad M_2^{s\prime} + \tau_2', \quad \text{(7)}$$

where the transfers τ_1' and τ_2' occur between periods.

---

[17] I assume that $\{\theta\}_t$ is the result of a joint decision of the governments of countries one and two. I therefore avoid game-theoretic aspects of the decisions to intervene in the foreign exchange market. Further, it is a matter of indifference (to this model) which country conducts the foreign exchange market intervention. If one country has insufficient reserves (of foreign currency) to sell all the foreign money that the intervention decision requires, the other country can always conduct the intervention since it can print the asset to be sold on the foreign exchange market. That is, there cannot be an international liquidity or reserve problem within this model. Such problems presumably arise in the real world because countries are unable to agree on a choice of $\{\tau_1, \tau_2, \theta\}_t$ and are unwilling to cooperate in the foreign exchange market operations required to achieve a target θ.

EXCHANGE RATE DETERMINATION   683

Let γ_i^j, $(i, j) = 1, 2$, denote the fraction of money j held by residents of country i. Notice that $\gamma_1^1 + \gamma_1^2 = 1 = \gamma_2^1 + \gamma_2^2$. These allocation parameters are endogenously determined.

Prices

At the beginning of any period the state of the world can be described completely by the state vector

$$s = (y_1, y_2, \gamma_1^1, \gamma_2^1, M_1^s, M_2^s, \theta) \tag{8}$$

and the probability distribution functions $F_y(\cdot)$, $F_t(\cdot)$, and $F_\theta(\cdot)$ which generate the stochastic processes $\{y_1, y_2\}$, $\{t_1, t_2\}$, and θ. Let $F(\cdot)$ denote the joint cumulative probability distribution function of these variables. The state vector s includes current outputs of each good, the nominal supplies of each money at the beginning of the period and their allocations, and the extent of government intervention in foreign exchange markets. A complete account of the state of the world includes both s and $F(\cdot)$, which individuals use to form their expectations about the future.

Individuals choose consumptions and end-of-period asset holdings to maximize (1) or (2) subject to (3) or (4). The equilibrium conditions require that all markets clear:

$$c_1^1 + c_1^2 = y_1,$$

$$c_2^1 + c_2^2 = y_2,$$

$$M_1^{1\prime} + M_1^{2\prime} = M_1^{s\prime}, \tag{9}$$

$$M_2^{1\prime} + M_2^{2\prime} = M_2^{s\prime}.$$

As only three of these four markets are independent, there are three prices, p_1, p_2, and e, that adjust each period to ensure equilibrium.

The demand functions of individual one for consumption and end-of-period money holdings depend on the prices he faces, p_1, p_2, and e; his initial money holdings, M_1^1 and M_2^1; his current income, y_1 (in terms of good one); and his beliefs about future prices and incomes. Given these beliefs about the future (which enter through the expected value operator in [1] and [2]), individual one's behavior can be described by the optimal policy or demand functions

$$c^1 = c^1(p_1, p_2, e, M_1^1 + \tau_1, M_2^1, y_1), \tag{10}$$

where c^1 is the vector $(c_1^1, c_2^1, M_1^{1\prime}, M_2^{1\prime})$. Similar demand functions describe individual two's behavior:

$$c^2 = c^2(p_1, p_2, e, M_1^2, M_2^2 + \tau_2, y_2), \tag{11}$$

where $c^2 = (c_1^2, c_2^2, M_1^{2\prime}, M_2^{2\prime})$.

The equilibrium price vector $p = (p_1, p_2, e)$, therefore, depends on (from [9], [10], and [11]) $M_1^1 + \tau_1, M_2^1, M_1^2, M_2^2 + \tau_2, y_1, y_2, M_1^{s\prime}$, and $M_2^{s\prime}$. So, using (5), (6), and the definition of γ_j^i, the price vector p depends on $y_1, y_2, \gamma_1^1, \gamma_2^1, M_1^s, M_2^s$, and θ, which are the elements of the state vector s. Let $p = \phi(s)$ give prices as a fixed function of the state of the world. The problem is now to investigate the function $\phi(\cdot)$ and the behavior of prices as the state vector changes over time.

Dynamics

Prices of goods and foreign exchange change over time as the state vector changes, and this relation is summarized by the function $\phi(s)$. The state vector changes for two reasons. First, new disturbances occur exogenously on initial money supplies, foreign exchange market intervention, and outputs (real incomes). Second, γ_1^1 and γ_2^1 change over time as people optimally adjust to past disturbances and to changes in expectations about the future. Given the expectations held by individuals about future variables and the exogenous transfers of taxes that will occur after the end of this period, the demand function and resulting market prices determine next period's allocation parameters $\gamma_1^{1\prime}$ and $\gamma_2^{1\prime}$.

Next period's state vector is

$$\underline{s}' = \left[y_1', y_2', \frac{z_1^{1\prime}(s) + \tau_1'}{M_1^s + \tau_1' + \theta}, \frac{z_2^{1\prime}(s)}{M_2^s + \tau_2' - (1/e)\theta}, \right.$$

$$\left. M_1^s + \tau_1' + \theta, M_2^s + \tau_2' - \frac{\theta}{e}, \theta' \right],$$

where $z_j^{1\prime}(s) = Z_j^{1\prime}[s, \phi(s)]$, $j = 1, 2$, and where $Z_j^{1\prime}[s, \phi(s)]$ is the (average) *aggregate* choice by people in country one of end-of-period balances of money j given s and $p = \phi(s)$. So s' depends on $y_1', y_2', \tau_1', \tau_2', \theta'$, and s, given the function $\phi(\cdot)$. That is,

$$s' = G(s, w'), \tag{12}$$

where $w' = (y_1', y_2', \tau_1', \tau_2', \theta')$. So the time path of goods prices and the exchange rate are determined by $p' = \phi(s') = \phi[G(s, w')] = $ function (s, w'). A similar line of reasoning shows that the price that will prevail j periods into the future is a function of the current state vector and the shocks $w', w'', \ldots, w^{(j)}$.

Expectations

The model can be completed with rational expectations imposed through the expected value operators in (1) and (2). Given the expectations held by individuals about the future values of the variables, individuals will be able to formulate demand functions, and prices will adjust to clear markets. These prices depend on the state of the world. However, the prices that occur in each state of the world affect expectations about future prices and therefore affect the demand functions today.

Before defining rational expectations it is useful to rewrite the individuals' optimization problems. Define an indirect utility function $V^1(\cdot)$ by the maximum value attained by the objective function in the solution to the problem

$$V^1(M_1^1 + \tau_1, M_2^{1\prime}, y_1, p) = \max \{U^1(c_1^1, c_2^1)$$

$$+ \beta \int V^1[M_1^{1\prime} + \tau_1', M_2^{1\prime}, y_1', \phi^e(s')]dF(w')\} \quad (13)$$

where maximization is with respect to $(c_1^1, c_2^1, M_1^{1\prime}, M_2^{1\prime})$ and subject to the constraints (3), and where $\phi^e(\cdot)$ maps the space of state vectors into the space of price vectors. Equation (13) says that individual one maximizes current-period utility plus the discounted expected value of future utilities given that he knows he will continue to behave optimally in the future. The optimization problem of individual two can be similarly reformulated. His indirect utility function will be

$$V^2(M_1^2, M_2^2 + \tau_2, y_2, p) = \max \{U^2(c_1^2, c_2^2)$$

$$+ \beta \int V^2[M_1^{2\prime}, M_2^{2\prime} + \tau_2', y_2', \phi^e(s')]dF(w')\} \quad (14)$$

where maximization is with respect to $(c_1^2, c_2^2, M_1^{2\prime}, M_2^{2\prime})$ and subject to the constraints (4).

Each individual may be assumed to have rational expectations in the following sense: (1) The function $F(\cdot)$ in (13) and (14) is the cumulative probability distribution function describing the behavior of $w \equiv (y_1, y_2, \tau_1, \tau_2, \theta)$, defined earlier. (2) The function $\phi^e(\cdot)$ in (13) and (14) is the same function $\phi(\cdot)$ that guarantees market clearing each period. (3) The individual knows that s' is determined by (12).

I assume that the information available to each individual includes the current state vector s. Each individual, since he knows s and $F(w')$, also knows the induced probability distribution function on s' and therefore the induced probability distribution on $p' = \phi(s')$. His current behavior is based on these expectations.

Each individual takes next period's state vector s' as exogenous to his own decisions (and random). Included in s' are $z_1^{1\prime}(s)$ and $z_2^{1\prime}(s)$ on which the individual has, through his knowledge of s and $G(\cdot)$, perfect foresight. This is a result of the individual's knowledge of the *aggregate* decisions that are made today in state of the world s. Now each individual chooses his own end-of-period balances optimally *given* $z_1^{1\prime}$ and $z_2^{1\prime}$. But $z_1^{1\prime}$ and $z_2^{1\prime}$ are just the (average) aggregates of the choices of all these individuals. It can be verified that, by construction of the Markov process $G(\cdot)$, the market-clearing prices $\phi(s)$ ensure that the consistency requirements

$$M_1^{1\prime}[\underline{s},\ \phi(\underline{s})] = Z_1^{1\prime}[\underline{s},\ \phi(\underline{s})] \tag{15}$$

and

$$M_2^{1\prime}[\underline{s},\ \phi(\underline{s})] = Z_2^{1\prime}[\underline{s},\ \phi(\underline{s})]$$

are met.

Equilibrium

An equilibrium requires both that people maximize expected utility given rational expectations, that is, that the demand functions solve (13) and (14) when $\phi^r(\cdot)$ is replaced by $\phi(\cdot)$ and s' by $G(s, w')$, where $G(\cdot)$ is such that (15) holds, and that prices clear markets, that is, that the equilibrium conditions (9) hold when the demand functions are inserted. It is straightforward to examine the consumer optimization problem *given* the behavior of prices as a function of the state vector (summarized by the function ϕ); the process generating the dynamic behavior of the state vector (summarized by the function G and the probability distribution function F); and, of course, the current state vector (see Stockman 1978*b*). The demand functions obtained from the maximization problem have some ambiguous signs for the usual reasons—wealth and substitution effects are not always reinforcing. But if substitution effects generally dominate wealth effects and both goods are normal, then increases in initial holdings of either money or in current income result in increases in the demand for both goods and both moneys. Increases in p_1 result in a decreased demand for good one but increases in the demand for the other good (in the absence of strong complementarity) and increases in the demand for both moneys. Increases in p_2 increase the demand for both moneys and the demand for good one while decreasing the demand for good two. Increases in the exchange rate, e, induce increases in the demand for good one and money one and decreases in the demand for good two and money two.[18] As each individual chooses consumption and money holdings taking as *given* the relation between prices and the state vector and the process generating changes in the state vector, the aggregate behavior of these individuals affects the things that each individual takes as given. While anticipations about the random part of the state vector are rational in the sense that the probability distribution on the exogenous variables is known, anticipations about the

---

[18] Some of these effects become zero when the liquidity constraints become binding as equalities. The optimization problem is analyzed in more detail in Stockman 1978*b*.

EXCHANGE RATE DETERMINATION   687

elements of next period's state vector that are the result of (aggregate) individual choices made today are rational in the sense that the individual knows with certainty these aggregate choices and makes his own plans accordingly. As all individuals do this, their choices *form* the aggregate choice that each takes as given. Market equilibrium therefore requires that both (9) and (15) hold.[19]

IV. Implications of the Model

Effect of a Real Shock

The initial effect of a real supply shock can be obtained by differentiating the equilibrium conditions (9). If the output of good one is increased, holding everything else constant including individuals' expectations of the probability distributions on future exogenous variables, then one obtains the exchange rate change

$$de = \frac{1}{\Delta}\{(c_{2_{p_1}}M'_{1_{p_2}} - c_{2_{p_2}}M'_{1_{p_1}})(1 - c^1_{1_{y_1}})$$

$$- (c_{1_{p_2}}M'_{1_{p_1}} - c_{1_{p_1}}M'_{1_{p_2}})c^1_{2_{y_1}}$$

$$- (c_{1_{p_1}}c_{2_{p_2}} - c_{1_{p_2}}c_{2_{p_1}})M^{1'}_{1_{y_1}}\}dy_1$$

where $c_{1_{p_1}} \equiv \dfrac{\partial c^1_1}{\partial p_1} + \dfrac{\partial c^2_1}{\partial p_1}$ and so on, and

$$\Delta \equiv c_{1_{p_1}}c_{2_{p_2}}M'_{1e} + c_{1_{p_2}}c_{2e}M'_{1_{p_1}} + c_{1e}c_{2_{p_1}}M'_{1_{p_2}} - c_{1_{p_2}}c_{2_{p_1}}M'_{1e}$$

$$- c_{1e}c_{2_{p_2}}M'_{1e} - c_{2e}c_{1_{p_1}}M'_{1_{p_2}}$$

[19] I have not been able to characterize the full steady-state solution to the model in the infinite-horizon case. The problem is the following: There are functions $V^1(\cdot)$, $V^2(\cdot)$, $d^1(\cdot)$, and $d^2(\cdot)$ with the desired properties for *each* $\phi(\cdot)$ and $G(\cdot)$, and there is some $\phi(\cdot)$ that satisfies (9) (the equilibrium conditions) for each $d^1(\cdot)$, $d^2(\cdot)$, and $G(\cdot)$. So the set of functions (17) with the desired properties exists if there is a function $G(\cdot)$ satisfying (15). Denote $z' \equiv G^*(s)$, a subvector of $s' = G(s, w')$ since z' does not depend on w', but only on choices made today, prior to the realization of new shocks. Current prices for each $F(\cdot)$ depend on both the state of the world s and the function $G^*(\cdot)$. Denote this correspondence by $\rho[s, G^*(\cdot)]$. The problem is to find a function $\bar{G}^*(\cdot)$ from the space of the state vector to R^2_+ such that

$$\begin{pmatrix} M^{1'}_1\{s, \rho[s, \bar{G}^*(s)]; \bar{G}^*(s)\} \\ M^{1'}_2\{s, \rho[s, \bar{G}^*(s)]; \bar{G}^*(s)\} \end{pmatrix} = \bar{G}^*(s).$$

Then (15) will hold with $\phi(s) \equiv \rho[s, \bar{G}^*(s)]$. Unfortunately, the above equation that implicitly gives $\bar{G}^*(\cdot)$ is a fixed point problem in a space of *functions* and little is known (by me) about its solution. However, the equilibrium can be described for an *n*-period version of the model for arbitrary *n*. It seems unlikely that the properties of the steady-state equilibrium, if it exists, will be different from the equilibrium of an *n*-period version of the model, for which an equilibrium *does* exist (Stockman 1978*b*).

688   JOURNAL OF POLITICAL ECONOMY

or

$$\frac{de}{dy_1} = a_1 + a_2 c^1_{1_{y_1}} + a_3 c^1_{2_{y_1}} + a_4 M^{1'}_{1_{y_1}}.$$

The effect of a change in income on the demand for domestic money, given p_1, p_2, and e, is captured in the fourth term, which gives the consequent appreciation of the exchange rate. This is the term emphasized in the monetary approach to the exchange rate and balance of payments. The first term, which does not depend on income elasticities of demand, gives the effect on the exchange rate as the relative price of goods changes due to an increase in the supply of good one. This term is generally positive (the exception obviously being a case in which income effects of a price change dominate substitution effects). The second and third terms give the effect on e of changes in the demands for each good induced by the change in income. These terms comprise two effects. First, given the demands for moneys (as in the example at the beginning of Section III), shifts in demands for goods due to a change in income may induce a change in the relative prices of goods and hence in the exchange rate. Second, the budget constraint guarantees that, given $c^1_{2_{y_1}}$ and $M^{1'}_{1_{y_1}}$, the larger $c^1_{1_{y_1}}$ the smaller the increase in the demand for foreign exchange as income rises, therefore the larger the appreciation of domestic money due to a rise in y_1. Note that the magnitude of the exchange rate change, which is associated with the relative price change caused by the supply shock, depends (in a somewhat complicated way) on the elasticities of demand for both goods and moneys.

A similar expression can be derived for the change in the exchange rate due to an increase in y_2. These expressions give the changes in the exchange rate and prices of goods given the other elements of the state vector. They may be regarded as expressions for the change in prices, from one period to the next as a new realization of y is realized, that would occur if the only change in s were the change in y. But this will not generally be the case: Aside from changes in money supplies through transfer payments and the extent of government transactions on the foreign exchange market, γ^1_1 and γ^1_2 will generally change over time, reflecting changes in the international distribution of wealth occurring through international capital flows.[20] Windfall gains in income will be dissipated slowly over time and will cause s to change even in the absence of new shocks (in a manner somewhat analogous to the process described in Dornbusch [1976c]), as described by the Markov process $G(\cdot)$. The terms of trade will change slowly over time

---

[20] In this paper these are money flows. The model can be extended to include domestic and foreign bonds as in Stockman (1978b).

and the deviation from purchasing power parity will persist, though diminish, over time. So deviations from purchasing power parity may be autocorrelated even when the underlying shocks are serially independent.

A Special Case

Suppose y, τ, and θ are perfectly predictable; in particular let y be a constant vector and $\tau_1 = \tau_2 = \theta = 0$. Then the optimization problem of representative individual one can be represented by $V^1[M_1^1, M_2^1, y_1, \phi(s)] = \max \{U^1(c_1^1, c_2^1) + \beta V^1[M_1^1{}', M_2^1{}', y_1, \phi(s')]\}$ subject to (3). The path of the state vector is determined by $s_{t+1} = G(s_t, \bar{y}, 0) \equiv H(s_t)$, where $\bar{y}$ is the fixed value of the output vector. This is a special case of (12). If this difference equation has a solution $\bar{s}$ then this vector characterizes the steady state of this special case of the model. The issue is what determines the steady-state level of goods prices and the exchange rate.

In this special case neither individual will find it useful to hold precautionary money balances. When each individual spends his entire initial money holdings on goods, the prices of goods follow a simple quantity theory: $M_1^s = p_1 y_1$ and $M_2^s = p_2 y_2$.

The first-order conditions for the representative individuals' optimization problems become (with superscripts omitted)

$$\lambda_0 = \frac{U_1(c_1, c_2)}{p_1} - \lambda_1 = \frac{U_2(c_1, c_2)}{ep_2} - \lambda_2 \frac{1}{e}$$

$$= \beta V_1[M_1', M_2', \bar{y}, \phi(\bar{s})]$$

$$= \frac{1}{e} \beta V_2[M_1', M_2', \bar{y}, \phi(\bar{s})].$$

The last equality shows that the exchange rate is equal to the ratio of the marginal values of each money for purchasing goods next period. The exchange rate can also be expressed in terms of the current-period variable by using the above first-order conditions, the budget constraint, and the definition of $V(\cdot)$ to show that $\lambda_1 = \lambda_2/e$. Hence $U_1/p_1 = U_2/ep_2$ in this special case, and the exchange rate can be written as

$$e = \frac{M_1^s}{M_2^s} \frac{y_2}{y_1} \frac{U_2}{U_1} = \frac{p_1}{p_2} \frac{U_2}{U_1}.$$

That is, the exchange rate is related to nominal money supplies, real outputs, and the marginal rate of substitution in consumption between foreign and domestic goods. Both real and nominal variables affect the exchange rate. If a ratio of production price indexes is used

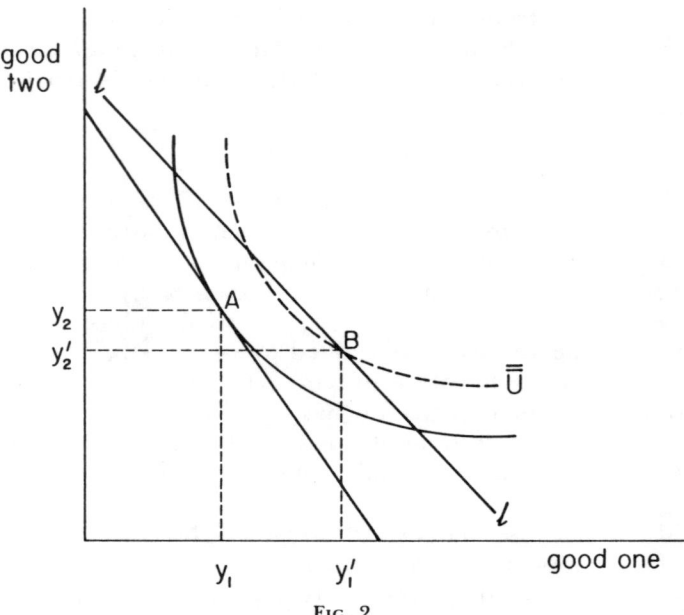

FIG. 2

to calculate purchasing power parity, then deviations of the exchange rate from this value can occur through changes in the marginal rate of substitution between the goods.

A change in the terms of trade will generally occur through changes in each of p_1, p_2, and e. Suppose that equilibrium initially occurs at point A in figure 2. Then let production conditions (endowments) change so that the new production point is B. Given nominal money supplies, the new values of p_1 and p_2 are determined by M_1^s/y_1' and M_1^s/y_2'. Suppose that *at the old exchange rate* this results in a relative price p_1/ep_2 shown by the slope of line ℓ through the equilibrium point B. The highest indifference curve that can be attained at B is $\bar{\bar{U}}$ (I am assuming for simplicity that the utility functions of the two representative individuals are identical and homothetic). If the exchange rate were unchanged, people would attempt to move along a budget line ℓ to a preferred position by purchasing less of good one and more of good two. Individuals in country one therefore increase their demand for foreign exchange to purchase these imports; individuals in country two supply less foreign exchange because of their reduced demand for country one's good at this relative price. Consequently, the price of money two in terms of money one will rise until the relative price of good one, p_1/ep_2, has fallen to a point where ℓ is tangent to $\bar{\bar{U}}$ at B. Then the foreign exchange market (and each goods market) clears. The change in the terms of trade has been divided between changes in nominal export prices and the exchange rate.

Suppose the utility function of each individual is $U = 5(c_1 + c_2) - (c_1^2 + c_2^2) + 5c_1c_2$. Suppose that initial production is at $y_1 = 2, y_2 = 3$. Now let production change to $y_2 = 3, y_2 = 2$. Initially the relative price of the two goods is 16/9. Now, since each nominal price is determined by a simple quantity theory with unit velocity, the exchange rate is

$$e = \frac{M_1^s}{M_2^s} \frac{3}{2} \frac{9}{16} \propto \frac{27}{32}.$$

With the production change and constant money supplies, the exchange rate becomes proportional to 2/3 times 16/9, or 32/27. The new relative price of good one in terms of good two is 9/16. The money-one price of good one is reduced by about one-half, while the money-two price of good two is increased by about one-third. The increase in the exchange rate of about two-fifths accounts for the remainder of the reduction in the relative price of good one by about two-thirds. The depreciation of money one is associated in this example with a "worsening" of country one's terms of trade, that is, a decrease in the relative price of its export good.

Other things the same, the lower the marginal rate of substitution between goods one and two the larger the depreciation of money one relative to money two required for equilibrium. If the marginal rate of substitution between the goods is greater in the long run than in the short run then the exchange rate will depreciate more in the short run than in the long run even if production remains at point B. This "overshooting" by the exchange rate of its long-run value resembles a conclusion reached by Dornbusch, but here it can occur as an *equilibrium* phenomenon.

While a change in the terms of trade is associated with a change in the exchange rate, government exchange market transactions cannot succeed at affecting the terms of trade. If the government of country one were to attempt to depreciate domestic money by purchasing foreign money on the foreign exchange market, M_2^s would fall and M_1^s would rise. As a result, p_1 and e would rise and p_2 would fall, but p_1/ep_2 would remain approximately unchanged. (The qualifier is necessary because of the distribution effects associated with changes in the values of moneys caused by the government transactions.) The reason that government exchange market transactions cannot exploit the relationship between the exchange rate and the terms of trade is that the exchange rate change did not "cause" the terms of trade change (although it may appear that way to some people living in this hypothetical world) but was merely one way in which the terms of trade change occurred.

A producer of good one (individual one) may reasonably regard the exchange rate increase as undesirable in the sense that he would prefer to be producing a relatively more valuable good. These same individuals would be roughly indifferent to a change in the exchange rate that was accompanied by changes in all other nominal prices. In an extended model in which people are uncertain about whether an exchange rate change is associated with a "real" or "nominal" disturbance, people may reasonably be concerned about *any* exchange rate change, since people will rationally impute some part of that change to real factors and some part to nominal factors. Although in this model people were assumed to know the current state vector, in a more general model with incomplete current information, monetary changes, including those due to foreign exchange market operations, might have some real effects. It seems unlikely, however, that such a model would imply that monetary policy could have any systematic effect on relative prices that could provide a theoretical justification for any particular government foreign exchange market policy.

If the government of country one were to peg the exchange rate, then figure 1 would be unchanged but nominal money supplies would change by $dM_1^s + edM_2^s = 0$, M_1^s rising in the example above. Thus p_1 and p_2 would change proportionally to the money supply changes in addition to the changes due to the real disturbance. So p_1 will rise more than if the exchange rate had been flexible and money supplies constant, and p_2 will fall more than in that case. The deviation from purchasing power parity will, therefore, be roughly the same under either exchange rate system, although in the flexible exchange rate case it will occur partially through exchange rate changes while in the pegged exchange rate case it will occur solely through changes in nominal export prices.

V. Conclusions

There are two interpretations of the relationship between changes in the terms of trade and changes in the exchange rate. According to one interpretation, the forces that cause the change in the exchange rate also cause a change in the terms of trade because prices of goods do not adjust to clear markets. The change in relative prices is therefore a disequilibrium phenomenon. This interpretation can be found in Dornbusch (1976a, 1976b), Dornbusch and Krugman (1976), and Isard (1977). Another version of the disequilibrium interpretation can be found in Negishi (1968) and Kemp (1969, chap. 14). This version begins with a two-country, two-good, two-money model with complete specialization in production and formally differentiates the system with respect to the exchange rate, allowing prices to change but not allowing asset stocks to change. That is, the exchange rate is assumed to change even though no policy variables have changed: There is no change in either money supply and there are no government foreign exchange market actions. This "short-run" analysis allows one to derive some of the formulas presented by earlier foreign exchange market theorists. The associated "long-run analysis" involves changes in policy variables and hence money supplies, but then either the elasticities of demand and supply of goods have *no effect* on the final equilibrium or they affect it only insofar as shifts in demand cause changes in real incomes and hence changes in the demands for domestic moneys (Mussa 1974).

This paper has presented an alternative *equilibrium* interpretation of the elasticity approach to the foreign exchange market and of the relation between the terms of trade and the exchange rate. Domestic money is demanded because it provides the particular services of allowing people to transact (cheaply) in domestic markets to purchase goods, and foreign exchange is demanded by importers because it is used to finance imports, purchase foreign assets, and so on. Other things the same, the demand for foreign exchange depends on the exchange rate. But as Friedman (1953, pp. 159–60) noted: "The changes continuously taking place in the conditions of international trade alter the 'other things' and so the desirabilities of using the currencies of various countries for each of the purposes listed. The aggregate effect is at one time to increase, at another to decrease, the amount of a country's currency demanded at any given rate of exchange relative to the amount offered for sale at that rate."

Real supply and demand shocks affect both relative prices and the derived demand for foreign exchange. A shock that increases the demand for Japanese television sets may also increase the derived demand for yen to import those sets, so the derived demand for foreign exchange is affected as people substitute between domestic and foreign goods (Machlup 1972, p. 35). Friedman and Schwartz (1963, p. 78), in explaining why the U.S. dollar did not depreciate by even more than it did during the greenback era, suggest that economic growth improved "the competitive position of the United States in exports more than it had expanded its demand for imports, which is to say, had increased the demand for U.S. dollars by foreigners (to buy U.S. exports) more than it had increased the demand for foreign currency by U.S. residents (to buy imports). The effect of such a shift in comparative advantage would be to raise the value of the U.S. currency in terms of foreign currencies at which trade would balance," that is, relative to purchasing power parity. The changes in the demand for foreign exchange that result from real supply and demand shocks affect the equilibrium exchange rate. Therefore changes in the terms of trade are associated with changes in the exchange rate.

This paper has shown that deviations from purchasing power parity and exchange rate volatility can be consistent with an equilibrium framework with strong roots in traditional theory of foreign exchange markets (e.g., Friedman 1953 and Machlup 1972). The theory also accounts for a correlation between the exchange rate and the terms of trade. In contrast to pure monetary models of the exchange rate, the theory provides a rationale behind the frequently encountered popular statements that appreciation of a currency is related to a fall in the country's import prices and a rise in the foreign price of its exports, and that a balance of trade deficit or the anticipation of a balance of trade deficit may be associated with a currency depreciation. Since changes in relative prices occur partially through changes in exchange rates, people may care about the level of the exchange rate in the sense that they care about the relative price of domestic and foreign export goods. People may blame a relative price change on the exchange rate for the same reason they may blame inflation on whatever good happened to suffer the greatest relative price increase during the inflation. Since exchange rate changes are simply one of the ways in which the terms of trade change occurs, the equilibrium version of the elasticities approach leads to an entirely different interpretation of the correlation between the exchange rate (or deviations from purchasing power parity) and the terms of trade than is suggested by the disequilibrium models.

While changes in the terms of trade occur partially through changes in the exchange rate, not all changes in the exchange rate are associated with changes in the terms of trade. A currency reform in one country that left unchanged the distribution of wealth would change the price of foreign exchange along with all other nominal prices. In this sense, changes in the exchange rate may be caused by either real or monetary factors.

It follows that government foreign exchange market policies will not be able to exploit the relationship between the exchange rate and the terms of trade in order to achieve a desired terms of or balance of trade. If the relationship between the exchange rate and the terms of trade is due to shifts in the underlying real supplies and demands for foreign or domestic goods, it will not be substantially affected by government foreign exchange market transactions. When a change in the exchange rate is due to such changes in real conditions, government foreign exchange market policies can reverse the change in the exchange rate only by affecting general price levels—it cannot reverse the changes in real conditions that originally caused the exchange rate movement. Other policies such as tariffs, quotas, and controls on foreign exchange transactions may affect the exchange rate indirectly by directly affecting the terms of trade (Cassel 1922, pp. 147–62; Friedman 1953, pp. 167–69) but foreign exchange market transactions cannot be used as a tool by policymakers to exploit the exchange rate–terms of trade correlation.

There appear to be several types of empirical evidence that could be used to discriminate between the equilibrium explanation of exchange rate determination presented in this paper and the disequilibrium explanations that were discussed above, short of estimating an entire general equilibrium structural model. First, the equilibrium theory implies that deviations from purchasing power parity and changes in the terms of trade are essentially real phenomena that will not be systematically related to the exchange rate system (except insofar as different exchange rate systems are associated with different characteristics of monetary policy—e.g., greater variability in the unanticipated component of the money supply might be associated with greater variability of relative prices along the lines of Barro [1976]). Ignoring the distribution effects of money supply changes and the consequent effects on relative prices, a change in the money supply affects the exchange rate only by affecting the general level of nominal variables and cannot reverse the change in real factors that caused the changes in the terms of trade and the exchange rate. Government monetary or exchange rate policy can, therefore, only add a nominally induced change in the exchange rate to a relative-price-induced change in the exchange rate and, hence, cannot affect the terms of trade or the deviation from purchasing power parity. In pairs of countries with relatively greater differences in monetary policies and inflation rates, a greater fraction of exchange rate changes will be due to monetary rather than real changes and the correlation between the exchange rate and the terms of trade will be less pronounced, but the terms of trade and the deviations from purchasing power parity will be unaffected.

Second, the expected rate of change of the exchange rate, as revealed on the forward foreign exchange market (Stockman 1978a) should be related to anticipated changes in the terms of trade or factors associated with the terms of trade as well as to the anticipated inflation differential. (This may explain the widely discussed role of the recent U.S. trade deficits in affecting the performance of the dollar on foreign exchange markets.) Third, applied work on the "real side of international trade" should, according to the equilibrium theory, be able to explain relative prices of goods in international trade without making important reference to monetary variables or to the exchange rate system. The exchange rate should enter such studies only as part of measured relative prices.

Further work on the theory presented here might focus on a more detailed characterization of the properties of the equilibrium exchange rate. Another extension would be to include more goods or introduce information, search, or transportation costs that prevent perfect arbitrage in the markets for each good. Other extensions might involve an explicit consideration of prior contracting in international trade or the separation of individual consumers and firms that import foreign goods.

If the theory presented here is true, then government foreign exchange market and monetary policy cannot exploit the relationship between the exchange rate and the terms of trade. Government policies should therefore be directed at other goals not discussed in this paper, such as minimizing the amount of noise in the signals carried by market prices. The choice of a pegged versus flexible exchange rate system can then be based on the classic arguments for each system, such as disciplining the monetary authorities or minimizing adjustment costs (Friedman's "daylight-savings-time" argument) or choosing some rate of inflation that may differ from the foreign rate. A persuasive argument for flexible rates might be to eliminate a constraint on monetary policy in order to make that policy steady and predictable. Although people may quite rationally care about the level of the exchange rate, its changes are only associated with, not causes of, the relative price changes which are really important.

References

Balassa, Bela. "The Purchasing-Power Parity Doctrine: A Reappraisal." *J.P.E.* 72, no. 6 (December 1964): 584–96.
Barro, Robert J. "Rational Expectations and the Role of Monetary Policy." *J. Monetary Econ.* 2, no. 1 (January 1976): 1–32.
Cassel, Gustav. *Money and Foreign Exchange after 1914.* New York: Macmillan, 1922.
Clower, Robert W. "A Reconsideration of the Microfoundations of Monetary Theory." *Western Econ. J.* 6, no. 1 (December 1967): 1–8.
Dornbusch, Rudiger. "The Theory of Flexible Exchange Rate Regimes and Macroeconomic Policy." *Scandinavian J. Econ.* 78, no. 2 (May 1976): 255–75. (a)
———. "Expectations and Exchange Rate Dynamics." *J.P.E.* 84, no. 6 (December 1976): 1161–76. (b)
———. "Exchange Rate Expectations and Monetary Policy." *J. Internat. Econ.* 6, no. 3 (August 1976): 231–44. (c)
Dornbusch, Rudiger, and Krugman, Paul. "Flexible Exchange Rates in the Short Run." *Brookings Papers Econ. Activity*, no. 3 (1976), pp. 537–75.
Fama, Eugene F., and Farber, Andre. "Money, Exchange Rates, and Capital Market Equilibrium." Working Paper, Univ. Chicago, Graduate School Bus., 1977.

EXCHANGE RATE DETERMINATION   697

Frenkel, Jacob A. "A Monetary Approach to the Exchange Rate: Doctrinal Aspects and Empirical Evidence." *Scandinavian J. Econ.* 78, no. 2 (May 1976): 200–224.

———. "The Purchasing Power Parity: Doctrinal Perspective and Evidence from the 1920s." *J. Internat. Econ.* 8, no. 2 (May 1978): 169–91.

Frenkel, Jacob A., and Johnson, Harry G., eds. *The Economics of Exchange Rates: Selected Studies.* Reading, Mass.: Addison-Wesley, 1978.

Friedman, Milton. "The Case for Flexible Exchange Rates." In *Essays in Positive Economics.* Chicago: Univ. Chicago Press, 1953.

Friedman, Milton, and Schwartz, Anna J. *A Monetary History of the United States, 1867–1960.* Princeton, N.J.: Princeton Univ. Press, 1963.

Gailliot, Henry J. "Purchasing Power Parity as an Explanation of Long-Term Changes in Exchange Rates." *J. Money, Credit, and Banking* 2, no. 3 (August 1970): 348–57.

Graham, Frank D. "International Trade under Depreciated Paper, the United States, 1862–79." *Q.J.E.* 36, no. 2 (February 1922): 220–73.

Grandmont, Jean-Michel, and Younes, Yves. "On the Role of Money and the Existence of a Monetary Equilibrium." *Rev. Econ. Studies* 39, no. 119 (July 1972): 355–72.

———. "On the Efficiency of a Monetary Equilibrium." *Rev. Econ. Studies* 40, no. 122 (April 1973): 149–65.

Grassman, Sven. "A Fundamental Symmetry in International Payment Patterns." *J. Internat. Econ.* 3, no. 2 (May 1973): 105–16.

Haberler, Gottfried. "The Market for Foreign Exchange and the Stability of the Balance of Payments: A Theoretical Analysis." *Kyklos* 3, no. 3 (1949): 193–218.

Isard, Peter. "How Far Can We Push the 'Law of One Price'?" *A.E.R.* 67, no. 5 (December 1977): 942–48.

Kareken, John H., and Wallace, Neil. "Samuelson's Consumption-Loan Model with Country-Specific Fiat Monies." Staff Report, Federal Reserve Bank of Minneapolis, July 1978.

Kemp, Murray C. *The Pure Theory of International Trade and Investment.* Englewood Cliffs, N.J.: Prentice-Hall, 1969.

Keynes, John Maynard. *A Treatise on Money.* London: Macmillan, 1930.

Kravis, I., and Lipsey, R. "Price Behavior in the Light of Balance of Payments Theories." *J. Internat. Econ.* 8, no. 2 (May 1978): 193–246.

Krueger, Anne O. "Balance-of-Payments Theory." *J. Econ. Literature* 7, no. 1 (March 1969): 1–26.

Lucas, Robert E., Jr. "Notes on Monetary Theory." Lecture Notes, Univ. Chicago, 1977.

Machlup, Fritz. *The Alignment of Foreign Exchange Rates.* New York: Praeger, 1972.

———. "The Theory of the Foreign Exchanges." In *International Payments, Debts, and Gold.* New York: New York Univ. Press, 1976.

Mikesell, Raymond F., and Furth, J. Herbert. *Foreign Dollar Balances and the International Role of the Dollar.* New York: Columbia Univ. Press (for Nat. Bur. Econ. Res.), 1974.

Mundell, Robert. *Monetary Theory.* Pacific Palisades, Calif.: Goodyear, 1971.

Mussa, Michael. "A Monetary Approach to Balance-of-Payments Analysis." *J. Money, Credit, and Banking* 6, no. 3 (August 1974): 333–51.

———. "The Exchange Rate, the Balance of Payments, and Monetary and Fiscal Policy under a Regime of Controlled Floating." *Scandinavian J. Econ.* 78, no. 2 (May 1976): 229–48.

Negishi, Takashi. "Approaches to the Analysis of Devaluation." *Internat. Econ. Rev.* 9, no. 2 (June 1968): 218–27.

Robinson, Joan. "The Foreign Exchanges." In *Essays in the Theory of Employment.* Oxford: Basil Blackwell, 1949.

Saidi, Nasser. "Rational Expectations, Purchasing Power Parity, and the Business Cycle." Working Paper, Univ. Chicago, Dept. Econ., September 1977.

Stockman, Alan C. "Risk, Information, and Forward Exchange Rates." In *The Economics of Exchange Rates: Selected Studies*, edited by Jacob A. Frenkel and Harry G. Johnson. Reading, Mass.: Addison-Wesley, 1978. (*a*)

———. "A Theory of Exchange Rate Determination." Ph.D. dissertation, Univ. Chicago, 1978. (*b*)

———. "On Explaining the Behavior of Exchange Rates: A Comment on Papers by Mussa and Bilson." In *Carnegie-Rochester Conference Series, 11*, edited by Karl Brunner and Allan H. Meltzer. *J. Monetary Econ.*, vol. 5 (suppl.; November 1979).

Wilson, Charles A. "Anticipated Shocks and Exchange Rate Dynamics." *J.P.E.* 87, no. 3 (June 1979): 639–47.

[22]

Economica, **51**, 109–127

The Gibson Paradox: A Cross-Country Analysis

By Gerald P. Dwyer, Jr

Emory University, Atlanta, Georgia

Introduction

A positive correlation between the levels of interest rates and prices has been pointed out many times. Thomas Tooke (1844, pp. 76–78) was probably the first to notice this positive correlation; John Maynard Keynes (1930, pp. 198–208) christened it the "Gibson paradox"; most recently, Thomas J. Sargent (1973), Robert J. Shiller and Jeremy J. Siegel (1977), as well as Milton Friedman and Anna J. Schwartz (1982, pp. 477–587) have examined explanations of this positive correlation.

The aspect of this correlation emphasized by Keynes was that it appeared to hold over long periods of time. As A. H. Gibson (1923) had pointed out, interest rates rose and fell roughly concurrently with the level of prices for over 150 years in the United Kingdom. Since there was no theoretical reason to expect what the data indicated, and some reason to expect no relationship whatsoever between the level of interest rates and the price level, Keynes labelled it a "paradox".

Whether or not this positive correlation can be called a paradox, numerous explanations of it have been advanced. Knut Wicksell (1899, pp. 78–81, 167) and Keynes (1930, pp. 198–208) suggest that increases in the demand for loans raise interest rates and result in an increased money supply and level of prices; and conversely for decreases in the demand for loans. Sargent (1973) generalizes this explanation to changes in aggregate supply and demand which result in a positive correlation of interest rates and prices. As Philip Cagan (1965) and Shiller and Siegel (1977) note, if increases in the demand for loans increase the money supply but not the supply of high-powered money, then this hypothesis suggests a positive correlation of the money multiplier and the price level. They do not find such a positive correlation.

Irving Fisher (1930) suggests that the positive correlation may simply be an "accidental" result of his fundamental hypothesis that nominal interest rates reflect expected inflation combined with imperfect foresight concerning inflation and the upward and downward movement of prices historically. This explanation has been found inadequate by some because the estimated distributed lag of inflation rates to explain interest rates seems too long when estimated with data over long periods of time (Cagan, 1965; Macauley, 1938, pp. A311–323; Sargent, 1973, pp. 386–387). Harley (1977) presents some evidence that expected inflation explains at least part of the positive correlation of interest rates and prices in Great Britain from 1873 to 1913. Milton Friedman and Anna J. Schwartz (1982) also present evidence that interest rates reflect expected inflation for sub periods with a positive correlation. Overall, the evidence concerning Fisher's hypothesis is mixed.[1]

Despite this research, neither the generality nor the stability of any positive correlation between interest rates and prices has been examined in detail.

With one exception (Wicksell, 1899, p. 87), all of the research has focused on the United Kingdom and the United States. Comparable data for European countries in the same period do exist. Do the positive correlations generalize, and to what extent do they hold even for the United Kingdom and United States? Furthermore, are these positive correlations stable over time or does the relationship change over time? With the exceptions of David Meiselman (1963) and Friedman and Schwartz (1982, pp. 527–573), the stability of any relationship has been largely ignored.

The purpose of this paper is to answer these questions and to test the ability of one version of Fisher's hypothesis to explain it. In the first section, data on interest rates and price levels are examined for evidence of a positive correlation of the two series. In the second section, the stability of any such relationship is examined. In the third section, a test of Fisher's hypothesis using rational expectations is outlined; a summary of the results is then presented.

I. THE GIBSON PARADOX

Data on nominal interest rates and prices for the United Kingdom, the United States, France and Belgium are presented in this section. The technical details concerning the construction of the series and their sources are included in a Data Appendix available on request. In order to facilitate the interpretation of the data, two restrictions are met by the interest rates: (1) they are a continuous series for some period, not just scattered observations from ledgers for example; and (2) they are determined in more or less free markets between borrowers and lenders. Despite the consequent limitation of the sample to Western European and American interest rates since 1729, a broad range of experience is included. In this section, the price indexes are wholesale price indexes for the years through 1913 and consumer price indexes thereafter.[2]

The United Kingdom

The data underlying Gibson's original observations of a positive correlation of bond yields and the price level illustrate it best. Graphs of the data and summary statistics for the United Kingdom are presented in Figure 1 and Table 1. As can be seen in Figure 1, the correlation of the consol yield and the price level is positive. For the period covered by the graph, 1729–1975, the correlation is $0·78$.[3] If 1914–1975 are deleted, the correlation is a somewhat lower $0·67$; the correlation for 1914–1975 is $0·84$. With the estimated standard deviations in Table 1, it is possible to test if these correlations are significantly different from zero.[4] The first two correlations are statistically significant at the 5 per cent significance level. The correlation for 1914–1975 is not statistically significant even though it is the largest of the three, because there are too few effective degrees of freedom in the data.

Figure 1 suggests that wars might contribute a significant component of the Gibson paradox. Without any knowledge of the wars that the United Kingdom engaged in during the eighteenth and nineteenth centuries, it generally is possible to pick them out by looking for years with high consol yields. None the less, the correlation of the consol yield and the price level is $0·83$ if war years are excluded from the correlation, which is slightly greater than

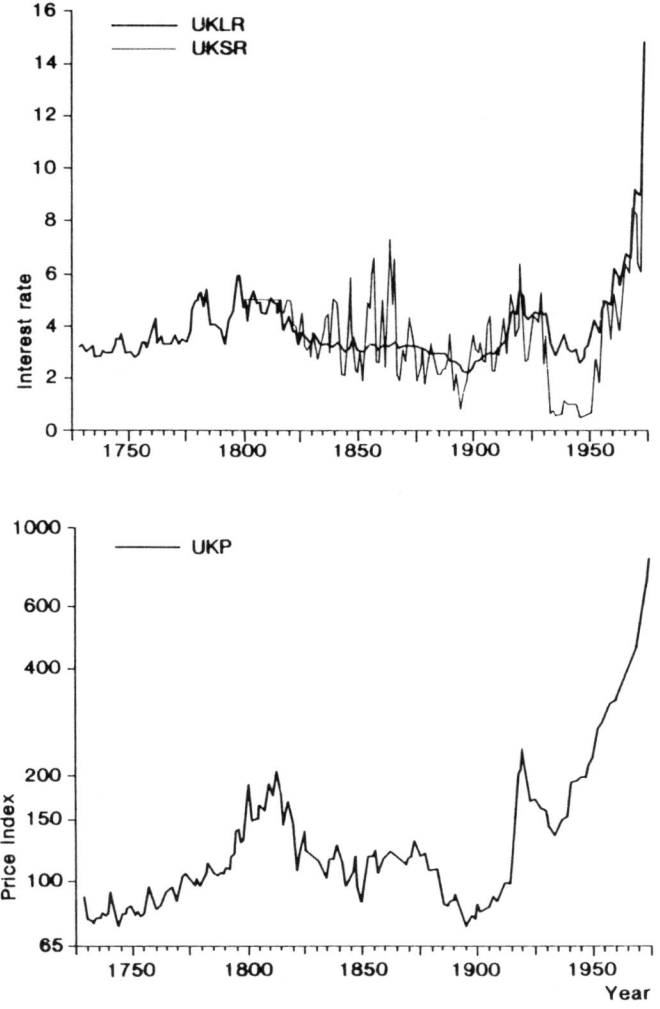

FIGURE 1.   Prices and interest rates in the United Kingdom.

its value including wars. For the period before the First World War the correlation is less with wars excluded than for the period as a whole, but the decrease from 0·67 to 0·58 is not substantial.

The correlations of the price level with the market discount rate on three-month bills in London are not as high as the correlations with the yield on consols. This is consistent with Keynes's original observation (1930). None the less, the correlation of the discount rate and the price level for 1833–1975 is 0·52, which is statistically significant at the 5 per cent level.[5]

TABLE 1

THE CORRELATION OF PRICES AND INTEREST RATES IN THE
UNITED KINGFOM

	War and peace		Peace		War	
	UKLR	*UKSR*	*UKLR*	*UKSR*	*UKLR*	*UKSR*
*Entire series**						
Mean (X)[†]	0·039	0·035	0·039	0·035	0·040	0·030
SD (X)	0·016	0·021	0·017	0·020	0·009	0·017
Cor (X, X_{-1})	0·96	0·80	0·96	0·76	0·91	0·83
Corr (X, LP)	0·78	0·52	0·83	0·55	0·45	−0·48
SD (Corr)	0·06	0·08	0·07	0·09	0·12	0·23
CSD (CORR)	0·37	0·24	0·45	0·24	0·47	0·59
Before First World War						
Mean (X)	0·035	0·033	0·033	0·032	0·041	0·041
SD (X)	0·007	0·013	0·005	0·013	0·009	0·011
Corr (X, X_{-1})	0·93	0·49	0·92	0·43	0·89	0·63
Corr (X, LP)	0·67	0·50	0·58	0·50	0·70	0·94
SD (Corr)	0·07	0·11	0·09	0·12	0·13	0·38
CSD (Corr)	0·30	0·18	0·36	0·18	0·47	0·61
1914–1975						
Mean (X)	0·051	0·037	0·054	0·041	0·036	0·024
SD (X)	0·025	0·028	0·027	0·029	0·006	0·017
Corr (X, X_{-1})	0·94	0·87	0·93	0·85	0·77	0·75
Corr (X, LP)	0·84	0·75	0·85	0·80	−0·26	−0·51
SD (Corr)	0·13	0·13	0·14	0·14	0·30	0·30
CSD (Corr)	0·55	0·42	0·55	0·44	0·62	0·61

* The long-term yield, *UKLR*, is the consol yield continuously available since 1729. The natural logarithm of the price index, *LP*, covers the same period. The short-term interest rate, *UKSR*, is the discount rate on three-month bills and is used for 1833–1975.
† "Mean (X)" is the mean of each variable, X; "SD (X)" is the standard deviation of each variable; "Corr (X, X_{-1})" is the first-order serial correlation coefficient; "Corr (X, LP)" is the correlation of each variable with the logarithm of the price level; "SD (Corr)" is the asymptotic standard deviation of each correlation on the hypothesis that X and LP are serially uncorrelated; and "CSD (Corr)" is the approximately corrected standard deviation on the hypothesis that X and LP are first-order autoregressive processes.

The United States

A graph of the data and summary statistics for the other country sometimes used in discussions of the Gibson paradox—the United States—are presented in Figure 2 and Table 2. The long-term rate of interest for the United States from 1857–1975 in Figure 2 is positively correlated with the price level, but the correlation is a relatively trivial 0·22 for the period as a whole. If the data are broken into periods before the First World War and since, the correlations increase to 0·71 and 0·53.

Figure 2 also does not show a substantial correlation of the short-term interest rate and the price level in the United States. The correlation for the data as a whole is virtually zero, −0·07, but is positive if the data are divided at the First World War. The correlations are 0·65 for the earlier period and 0·49 for the later period. The substantial difference between the overall correlations and the correlations for the separate periods is consistent with the visual impression that the relationship between the price level and interest rates, if any, is not constant over time.

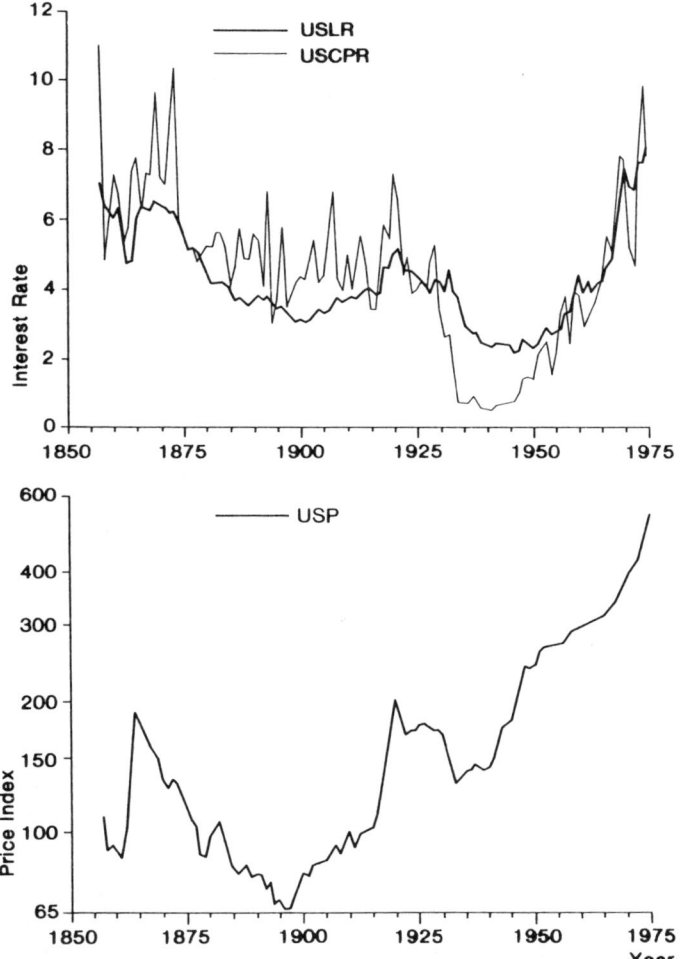

FIGURE 2.   Prices and interest rates in the United States.

These differences between the correlations for the United Kingdom and the United States occur even though, as would be expected because the countries generally have been on the same monetary standard, the interest rates and price levels in the two countries are highly correlated. For 1857–1975, the correlation of the long-term interest rates is 0·53, the correlation of the short-term interest rates is 0·62, and the correlation of the price levels is 0·96.

France and Belgium

The data for France, presented in Figure 3 and Table 3, show even further variation of these correlations. As a quick glance at Figure 3 suggests, and

TABLE 2

PRICES AND INTEREST RATES IN THE UNITED STATES

	War and peace		Peace		War	
	USLR	USCPR	USLR	USCPR	USLR	USCPR
Entire series*						
Mean (X)†	0·043	0·045	0·044	0·047	0·037	0·033
SD (X)	0·014	0·022	0·014	0·021	0·013	0·025
Corr (X, X_{-1})	0·95	0·80	0·96	0·75	0·85	0·83
Corr (X, LP)	0·22	−0·07	0·26	−0·06	−0·47	−0·40
SD (Corr)	0·09	0·09	0·10	0·09	0·24	0·24
CSD (Corr)	0·48	0·26	0·53	0·21	0·63	0·60
Before First World War						
Mean (X)	0·046	0·057	0·045	0·056	0·049	0·058
SD (X)	0·012	0·016	0·012	0·017	0·011	0·014
Corr (X, X_{-1})	0·94	0·46	0·95	0·43	0·57	0·30
Corr (X, LP)	0·71	0·65	0·78	0·66	0·18	0·74
SD (Corr)	0·13	0·13	0·14	0·14	0·45	0·45
CSD (Corr)	0·47	0·21	0·59	0·21	0·64	0·54
1914–1975						
Mean (X)	0·040	0·035	0·042	0·038	0·031	0·022
SD (X)	0·015	0·022	0·015	0·022	0·009	0·021
Corr (X, X_{-1})	0·94	0·85	0·93	0·82	0·80	0·78
Corr (X, LP)	0·53	0·49	0·54	0·54	−0·67	−0·61
SD (Corr)	0·13	0·13	0·14	0·14	0·29	0·29
CSD (Corr)	0·56	0·40	0·58	0·40	0·65	0·62

* The long-term interest rate, *USLR*, the short-term interest rate, *USCPR*, and the logarithm of the price index, *LP*, are for the years 1857–1975.
† See note to Table 1 for definition of measures.

Table 3 shows, the correlation of the long-term yield with the price level is virtually zero, −0·01, for 1798–1975. The correlation for the period before the First World War is 0·43; the correlation of the *rentes* yield and the price level is only 0·11 for 1914–1975. The correlation of the long-term yield with the price level across all wars is negative.

The French market rate of discount is also presented in Figure 3 for 1863–1975. As is by now usual, the correlations rise for sub-periods: the correlation for 1863–1975 is 0·51, the correlation for 1863–1913 is 0·63, and the correlation for 1914–1975 is 0·55. The higher correlation of the price level with the short-term interest rate than with the *rentes* yield for 1914–1975 is due partly to the lack of data for the short-term interest rate for 1915–1924, but the correlation of the price level with the *rentes* yield is still only 0·28 for the same period. Therefore, these data are inconsistent with the common conclusion that the Gibson paradox is more pronounced for long-term interest rates than for short-term interest rates (Keynes, 1930; Shiller and Siegel, 1977).

The Belgium data are presented in Figure 4 and Table 4. The Belgium data on *rentes* yields and price indexes can be usefully compared with the French data. There are only two observations for years in which Belgium was at war; the statistics without these observations are not presented. Events that affected mainly France, such as the 1848 Revolution and the Franco-Prussian War, appear in movements of the Belgian *rentes* yields as they do in movements

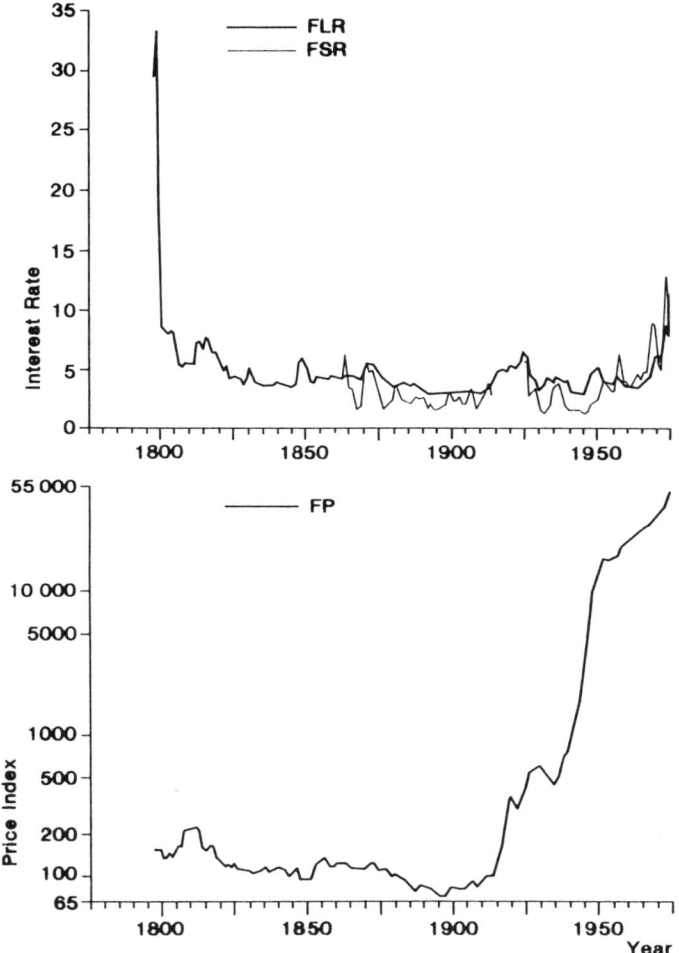

FIGURE 3.   Prices and interest rates in France.

of the French *rentes* yield, even though Belgium was not directly involved in them. The movements of the Belgian price index also largely parallel those of the French price index, which is not surprising, because they generally have a common currency with the same denominations and metallic content when on metallic standards. There is, however, one dramatic exception. Towards the end of and after the Second World War, France and Belgium have substantially different rates of inflation. By 1952, the French consumer price index is 19·3 times its level in 1940, while the Belgian consumer price index is only about 3·5 times its level in 1940. Despite this differential change in the price level, after the French devaluation relative to Belgium with subsequent maintenance of a fixed exchange rate, their interest rates return to

TABLE 3

THE CORRELATION OF PRICES RATES IN FRANCE

	War and peace		Peace		War[‡]	
	FLR	*FSR*	*FLR*	*FSR*	*FLR*	*FSR*
*Entire series**						
Mean (X)[†]	0·048	0·033	0·042	0·034	0·067	0·024
SD (X)	0·032	0·019	0·010	0·019	0·059	0·014
Corr (X, X_{-1})	0·87	0·79	0·91	0·79	0·83	0·76
Corr (X, LP)	−0·01	0·51	0·27	0·57	−0·21	−0·91
SD (X)	0·07	0·10	0·09	0·10	0·15	0·33
CSD (Corr)	0·27	0·28	0·37	0·29	0·44	0·66
Before First World War						
Mean (X)	0·050	0·028	0·041	0·027	0·087	—
SD (X)	0·039	0·010	0·010	0·010	0·074	—
Corr (X, X_{-1})	0·87	0·67	0·92	0·67	0·77	—
Corr (X, LP)	0·43	0·63	0·77	0·60	−0·02	—
SD (Corr)	0·09	0·14	0·10	0·14	0·20	—
CSD (Corr)	0·30	0·29	0·41	0·30	0·48	—
1914–1975						
Mean (X)	0·045	0·039	0·046	0·043	0·039	0·017
SD (X)	0·011	0·024	0·011	0·024	0·008	0·002
Corr (X, X_{-1})	0·85	0·78	0·83	0·74	0·76	0·35
Corr (X, LP)	0·11	0·55	0·07	0·50	−0·82	−0·86
SD (Corr)	0·13	0·14	0·14	0·15	0·29	0·38
CSD (Corr)	0·40	0·37	0·42	0·36	0·61	0·49

* The long-term interest rate, *FLR*, covers 1798–1975; the short-term interest rate, *FSR*, covers 1863–1975 with 1915–1924 missing; and the logarithm of the price index, *LP*, covers 1798–1975.
† See note to Table 1 for definition of measures.
‡ The French Revolutions of 1830 and 1848 are counted as war periods.

their rough former equality as would be expected. As a consequence, the relationship between the bond yield and the price level, which would be roughly the same in the countries before this relatively greater inflation in France, would have different constant terms now. This shows the correctness of an argument that goes back to Fisher: any relationship between the bond yield and the price level is accidental in the sense that it is not independent of the movements of the price level.

The Belgian short-term interest rate is available before 1863, in fact back to 1848, which is some advantage. As can be seen in Figure 4, with substantial fluctuations this rate declined from 1848 to 1896 even though the price level had no such trend. This difference in the behaviour of the series is reflected in the low correlation of 0·38 between the interest rate and price level for 1848–1913. The correlation for the postwar data is also hardly substantial, 0·32, and the correlation for the entire series is only 0·26.

Summary

The most prominent conclusion to be drawn from this examination of the data is that interest rates and price levels are not invariably positively correlated. For the available data for the United States, the correlation of the long-term bond yield and the price level is 0·22, which pales by comparison with the high correlations for the United Kingdom; the correlation of the

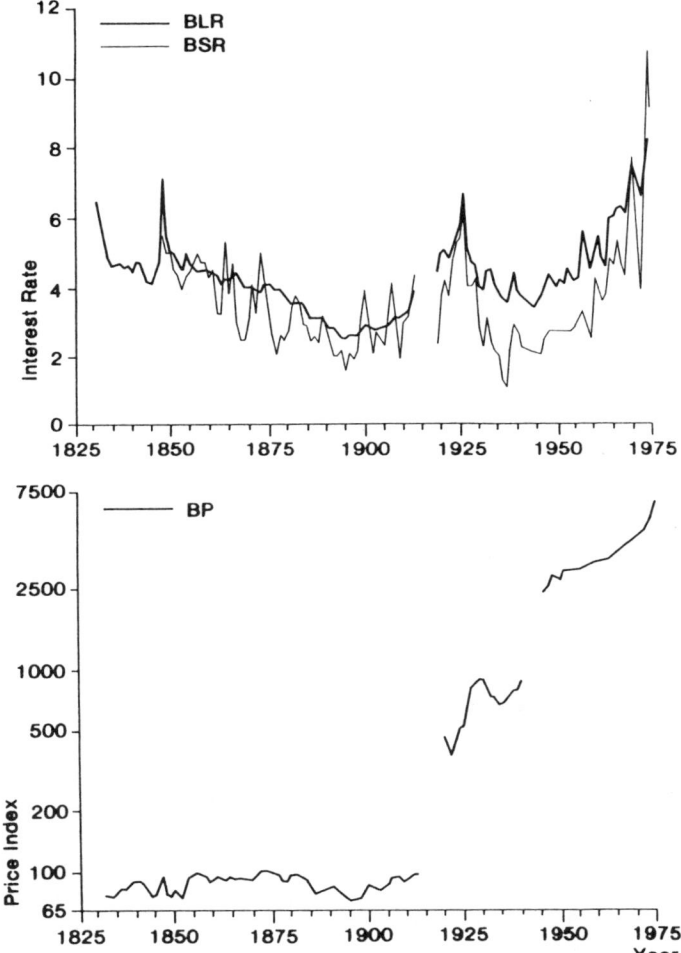

FIGURE 4.   Prices and interest rates in Belgium.

short-term interest rate and the price level is negative. For France, the correlation of the bond yield and the price level is a trivial -0.01. These results arise without any pre-selection of periods to obtain a positive or negative correlation. It is possible to select periods and to divide the sample in order to increase these correlations, but some criteria for believing that the empirical generalisation of the Gibson paradox is important would be necessary.

The second important conclusion to be drawn from this analysis is that the relationship between interest rates and price levels is such that any relationship is not independent of the movements of the price level. A period of inflation, once terminated, will not leave a permanent mark on the interest rate.

TABLE 4

THE CORRELATION OF PRICES AND INTEREST
RATES IN BELGIUM

| | War and peace | |
	BLR	BSR
*Entire series**		
Mean (X)[†]	0·044	0·036
SD (X)	0·012	0·014
Corr (X, X_{-1})	0·91	0·73
Corr (X, LP)	0·57	0·26
SD (Corr)	0·09	0·09
CSD (Corr)	0·37	0·22
Before First World War		
Mean (X)	0·039	0·034
SD (X)	0·009	0·010
Corr (X, X_{-1})	0·89	0·71
Corr (X, LP)	0·08	0·38
SD (Corr)	0·11	0·12
CSD (Corr)	0·29	0·25
1941–1975		
Mean (X)	0·051	0·039
SD (X)	0·012	0·017
Corr (X, X_{-1})	0·86	0·69
Corr (X, LP)	0·46	0·32
SD (Corr)	0·14	0·14
CSD (Corr)	0·45	0·31

* The long-term interest rate, BLR, covers 1832–1975 with 1914–
1918 missing. The short-term interest rate, BSR, is available for
1848–1975 with 1914–1918 missing; and the price index, LP, is
available for 1832–1975 with 1914–1919 and 1941–1945 missing.
† See note to Table 1 for definition of measures.

In addition, the hypothesis that the price level is more highly correlated
with the long-term interest rate than with the short-term interest rate does
not generalize beyond the source of the observation—the United Kingdom.
The higher serial correlation of the long-term than the short-term interest
rate aside, the examination of data for countries in the same geographic area
and the same historical period produces counter-evidence.

Finally, it is clear that the positive correlations of interest rates and price
levels are not due solely to the movements of the series during wars. The
positive correlations of price levels with bond yields or short-term interest
rates persist when war years are deleted.

II. THE STABILITY OF THE RELATIONSHIP BETWEEN PRICE LEVELS AND INTEREST RATES

The increase of correlations as data are divided into sub-periods suggests
that the correlations between nominal interest rates and price levels are not
stable. Two hypotheses concerning the instability of the relationship between

interest rates and price levels are tested in this section. The first is that the relationship is different in periods of peace than in periods of war. The second is that changes in the monetary system, in particular changes from commodity money to fiat money, result in a different relationship. Breaks based on these divisions are plausible because these events may be associated with structural changes in the economy.

The relationship between interest rates and price levels is specified as a bivariate autoregression instead of as a simple correlation or regression. This specification can be written as

$$
\begin{aligned}
p_t &= \mu_1 + \sum_{j=1}^{k} \alpha_j^p \, p_{t-j} + \sum_{j=1}^{k} \alpha_j^i i_{t-j} + \varepsilon_t^p \\
i_t &= \mu_2 + \sum_{j=0}^{k} \beta_j^p p_{t-j} + \sum_{j=1}^{k} \beta_j^i i_{t-j} + \varepsilon_t^i
\end{aligned}
$$

(1)

where p_t is the natural logarithm of the price level at time t, i_t is the nominal interest rate, μ_1 and μ_2 are constant terms, the α's and β's are parameters, and the ε's are error terms. The current price level at time t is introduced into the second regression in order to allow contemporaneous correlation to be explicitly included in the set of equations. For convenience, the number of lags of each variable has been set equal to one number, k.[6] A simple contemporaneous relationship between the price level and the interest rate is a special case of (1) with all α's and all β's except β_0^p equal to zero. The main practical advantage of this specification over simple correlations is that the residuals in (1) are serially uncorrelated whereas the residuals in simple regressions, a special case, are highly serially correlated. This vector autoregression can be interpreted as a representation that results from a covariance–stationary model of the economy.[7]

In order to minimize problems associated with changes in the data, only selected series are used in the tests of stability. The most useful interest rates are consol yields and open-market discount rates for the United Kingdom, the adjusted railroad bond yields and commercial paper discount rates for the United States, and the Yields on French 3 per cent *rentes*. Each of these series is available for a relatively long period of time (the shortest being the adjusted railroad bond yield available from 1857 to 1936 and is relatively homogeneous over time. The price indexes are wholesale price indexes throughout. Consumer price indexes are available for shorter periods of time; there is no reason to think that duplication of the regressions with them would alter the results in any important way.

Table 5 contains the F-ratios to test the stability of the bivariate autoregressions.[8] The F-ratios to test the hypothesis of stability across periods of war and peace are presented in the first row of the table. These data are not consistent with the hypothesis that there is a stable relationship between prices and interest rates across all periods of war and peace. In every case, the hypothesis of stability can be rejected at least at the 5 per cent significant level. The F-ratios to test the hypothesis of stability across changes in monetary standard are presented in the lower part of Table 5. With only one exception, the hypothesis of stability can be rejected in every case.[9]

TABLE 5

F-RATIOS FOR TESTS OR STABILITY OF AUTOREGRESSIONS

| Basis of division | United Kingdom | | | | United States | | | | France 3% *rentes* yields | |
| | Consol yield | | Discount rate | | Adjusted railroad bond yield | | Commercial paper rate | | | |
	Price index	Interest rate	Price index	Interest rate	Price index	Interest rate	Price index	Interest rate	Price index	Interest rate
War and peace	1·507* (103,134)†	2·412* (112,124)	3·045* (39,90)	1·968* (42,90)	1·785* (25,45)	2·562* (27,42)	2·670* (39,70)	1·593* (42,66)	1·893* (56,97)	2·203* (60,74)
Monetary standards	3·887* (35,202)	3·368* (39,197)	3·972* (21,112)	2·382* (24,109)	1·115 (23,47)	4·714* (25,44)	2·077* (26,83)	2·295* (29,79)	3·293* (45,90)	2·502* (50,84)

* The F-ratio is greater than 5 per cent significance level.
† Degrees of freedom are in parenthesis below each F-ratio.

The results are inconsistent with the hypothesis that there is a stable relationship between interest rates and price levels over all of the available data. There is no puzzling stable relationship between interest rates and price levels that persists over long periods of time.

This indicates that many attempts to test Fisher's explanation of the Gibson paradox are misguided. The consistency of Fisher's hypothesis with the data for sub-periods is sufficient as an explanation of what does appear for sub-periods: a stable relationship and a positive correlation. In the next sections, the results of test of a version of Fisher's hypothesis combined with rational expectations of inflation are presented.

III. A TEST OF FISHER'S HYPOTHESIS

The version of Fisher's hypothesis to be tested has three components: (1) the nominal interest rate equals the expected rate of return from commodities including the expected increase of prices; (2) expectations are rational in the sense of Muth (1961); and (3) variation of the expected real interest rate cannot be predicted by the variables used to predict the expected inflation rate. The first and second components of this hypothesis imply that

(2) $i_t = E(r_t|\Omega_t) + E(\Delta p_t|\Omega_t)$

where i_t is the nominal interest rate on a security in period t, r_t is the real interest rate on commodities, Δp_t is the rate of inflation, Ω_t is the set of information available at time t, and $E(X_t|\Omega_t)$ is the expected value of X_t conditional on Ω_t. The third component is that the information set used in the tests, ψ_t, which is a subset of r_t and excludes i_t, does not help to predict r_t, or

(3) $E\{E(r_t|\Omega_t)|\psi_t\} = \mu_r$

where μ_r is the mean real interest rate. This is somewhat less restrictive than assuming that the expected real interest rate is constant as in Fama (1975). Application of the law of iterated expectations and use of (3) in (2) yields

(4) $E(i_t|\psi_t) = \mu_r + E(\Delta p_t|\psi_t)$.

Because the focus of interest is a correlation of interest rates and price levels, it is useful to rewrite equation (4) as[10]

(5) $E(i_t|\psi_t) = \mu_r + E(p_{t+1}|\psi_t) - E(p_t|\psi_t)$.

Implementation of the test only requires the specification of an information set and testing the constraints across the interest rate and price level expectations. In order to have a tractable test, linear regressions instead of mathematical expectations are used in the tests. This can be justified either by assuming normal distributions for the fundamental innovations generating the interest rate and the price level, or by interpreting the expectations operator above as a regression operator. The restrictions imposed by (5) can be tested by a standard likelihood ratio test based on a statistic asymptotically distributed as a chi-square variable under the hypothesis that the restrictions are correct.[11]

Although the hypothesis is formulated as if the data are measured at points in time, the hypothesis can be tested using the averaged data that are actually available. With exceptions, the data available are annual averages of interest rates and annual averages of price levels. This averaging of the data creates no problem for the subset of information used, ψ_t, because the subset can include averaged data. Furthermore, equation (5) can be applied to averaged logarithms of the monthly price levels. The only approximation involved is that the tests are run with the logarithms of the annual average price levels instead of the annual average of the logarithm of the price levels. To a first-order of approximation, these are the same.

A more interesting aspect of the data than the averaging is that the interest rates are three-month interest rates that include three-month forecasts of inflation and the inflation rates are annual inflation rates. Can these be used as they are in (5)? The average nominal interest rate includes an annual average of expected monthly inflation rates, which can be written

$$(6) \qquad \tfrac{1}{12} \sum_{m=1}^{12} E\{(p_{t,m+1} - p_{t,m})|\Omega_m\}$$

where $p_{t,m}$ is the logarithm of the price level in month m of year t and Ω_m is the set of information available in month m. Taking the expectation of (6) conditional on information available through the previous year and cancelling terms yields

$$(7) \qquad \tfrac{1}{3} \sum_{m=1}^{3} E\{(p_{t+1,m} - p_{t,m})|\psi_{t-1}\},$$

since intervening expected price levels conditioned on ψ_{t-1} cancel. For the test to be appropriate, the expected inflation rate has to reduce to a similiar term. The price level for each year generally is an arithmetic mean of monthly values which to a first order of approximation equals the geometric mean of the monthly values. Therefore, the inflation rate, which is calculated as the difference of the logarithms of the average price levels, approximately equals

$$(8) \qquad \tfrac{1}{12} \sum_{m=1}^{12} (p_{t+1,m} - p_{t,m}).$$

If the expected value of (8) is taken conditional on ψ_{t-1}, this expression differs from (7) by the inclusion of nine additional annual inflation rates. If the information set, the annual averages of previous years' data, predicts the same annual inflation rate for the first three months of the year as for the last nine, then the test, (4) or (5), is completely appropriate.

IV. EMPIRICAL RESULTS

The empirical evidence indicates that there is no stable long-run relationship between interest rates and price levels. As a consequence, the hypothesis is tested only for sub-periods. If the First and Second World Wars are excluded because of the substantial controls on the economies, the nineteenth and early twentieth century is the only period of time for which more than about 20 annual observations are available.[12] This is a period in which a positive correlation of interest rates and price levels has been of substantial interest (Saul, 1969; Harley, 1977).

Before examining the ability of the hypothesis to explain any correlation of interest rates and price levels, it is necessary to determine the periods that

TABLE 6

F-TESTS FOR COMBINING PERIODS IN THE NINETEENTH AND EARLY TWENTIETH CENTURIES

	United Kingdom	United States	France
Initial years	1857–1898	1865–1897	1872–1913
Added years	1899–1902	1898	1870–1871
F-ratios			
Price level	0·927	0·218	0·896
Interest rate	0·296	0·031	6·975*
Added years	1903–1913	1889–1913	
F-ratios			
Price level	1·390	6·421	
Interest rate	0·481	0·540	
Added years	1854–1856		
F-ratios			
Price level	0·388		
Interest rate	1·415		
Added years	1836–1853		
F-ratios			
Price level	3·486*		
Interest rate	0·952		
Final periods	1854–1913	1865[†]–1913	1872–1913

* Statistically significant at the 5 per cent significance level.
† Despite the rejection of the hypothesis of the same regression for 1865–1898 as for 1899–1913, these periods will be combined because a similar period is combined for the United Kingdom and because tests starting from resumption in 1880–1897 are consistent with the use of this period.

have a stable relationship of the two series. This is accomplished by dividing the data into periods based on wars. Then, using a series of sequential F-tests, I combine periods until rejection of a constant relationship is indicated.

The F-ratios are presented in Table 6. The F-ratios are based on bivariate autoregressions with three lags of each variable. Wholesale price indexes are used in order to maintain comparability over time and to maximize the possible lengths of the overall time periods. Belgium is not included in the table because it is not directly involved in any war from 1848 to 1913. All of the tests start from a base period that includes at least the "Great Depression" from 1873 to 1896. The resulting periods are 1854–1913 for the United Kingdom, 1865–1913 for the United States, and 1872–1913 for France.

The likelihood ratio test statistics and marginal significance levels for testing the hypothesis are presented in Table 7.[13] These results are based on bivariate autoregressions.[14] Results for the periods indicated by the F-tests in Table 6 are presented in the first three rows. At usual significance levels, the results are consistent with the hypothesis for the United Kingdom, marginally consistent with the hypothesis for France and Belgium, but not consistent with the hypothesis for the United States. To what extent can the divergent results be explained?

TABLE 7

TEST STATISTICS BASED ON PRICES AND INTEREST RATES FOR THE
NINETEENTH AND EARLY TWENTIETH CENTURIES

	United Kingdom	United States	France	Belgium
Dates	1854–1913	1865–1913	1872–1913	1850–1913
Likelihood ratio test statistic*	8·616	16·607	9·781	11·490
Marginal significance level	0·071	0·002	0·044	0·022
Dates	1872–1913	1882–1913		1872–1913
Likelihood ratio test statistic	2·563	4·860		9·323
Marginal significance level	0·633	0·302		0·054

* Test statistics are asymptotically chi-square with 4 degrees of freedom under the null hypothesis.

    The period for the United States includes 14 years before resumption of the gold standard in 1879. As the figures in the second three rows of Table 8 indicate, the relationship between the interest rate and the price level is consistent with the hypothesis for the period when the United States is on the gold standard.[15]

    Belgium's data are not divided into sub-periods because it is not directly involved in wars. None the less, its interest rates mirror events, including wars, in France. This suggests that the test be done for the same period as for France. As is shown in Table 7, the results for Belgium are very close to those for France when the test is run for the same period. For comparison, results also are presented for the United Kingdom for 1872–1913.

    Table 8 contains likelihood ratio test statistics and marginal significance levels for testing the hypothesis with information besides past price levels and interest rates. Besides these two series, the money stock and real income (both

TABLE 8

TEST STATISTICS WITH ADDITIONAL SERIES FOR THE LATE NINETEENTH AND
EARLY TWENTIETH CENTURIES

	United Kingdom	United Kingdom	United States	United States
Additional series	Money	Real income	Money	Real income
Years	1874–1913	1854–1913	1882–1913	1882–1913
Likelihood ratio test statistic*	6·302	9·328	9·282	8·232
Marginal significance level	0·390	0·456	0·158	0·222

* Test statistics are asymptotically chi-square with 6 degrees of freedom under the null hypothesis.

detrended), are each used to help predict the interest rate and the price level in trivariate autoregressions for the United Kingdom and the United States—countries with available data. The period used for the United States is that in which the simple hypothesis works. At usual significance levels, the results continue to be consistent with the hypothesis when these variables are added to the information used to predict the price level and the interest rate.

Why are these results favourable to Fisher's hypothesis when past analyses summarized by Sargent (1973) raise serious questions about the hypothesis? Part of the reason for a favourable verdict is that no attempt is made to characterize all of the available data with one constant-coefficient bivariate autoregression. For example, this version of Fisher's hypothesis can be rejected at the resounding significance level of $0 \cdot 129 \times 10^{-5}$ with US data for 1860–1975. Friedman and Schwartz (1982, pp. 546–563) and Harley (1977) also find that versions of Fisher's hypothesis can explain some periods, which is further evidence that the attempt to characterize all of the available data is a source of the earlier negative results.

V. Conclusion

A positive correlation of the levels of prices and interest rates was first observed in data for the United Kingdom. Even after allowing for the serial correlation of the prices and interest rates, the correlations between prices and long-term or short-term interest rates are statistically significant.

This positive correlation does not generalize beyond the source of the observation. Neither the United States, France nor Belgium has a statistically significant correlation when all of the available data are used. Indeed, two of the six correlations are negative. When data for the period before the First World War are used, the only statistically significant correlations are the correlations of prices and short-term interest rates in the United States and France.

The hypothesis that there is a stable correlation, which is examined in the more general context of a bivariate autoregression, is not consistent with available data. Wars and changes in monetary standards, possibly related to structural changes in the economy, are used to divide the sample data into sub-periods. The results are uniformly inconsistent with a stable relationship. Therefore, in the sense of a stable relationship that persists over long periods of time, there is no Gibson paradox.

Irving Fisher's hypothesis is able to explain the stable positive correlation of interest rates and price levels for a period in which it has been of substantial interest—the last half of the nineteenth century and the early twentieth century. The hypothesis tested is based on assumptions that the expected real interest rates vary unpredictably and that expectations of inflation are rational. The restrictiveness of the hypothesis reinforces the strength of the results.

ACKNOWLEDGMENTS

I would like to thank Milton Friedman, Robert E. Lucas, Jr, Sam Peltzman, Raymond C. Battalio, Michael D. Bordo, Paul Evans, Thomas Gittings, Robert D. Laurent, Larry C. Mote, Thomas J. Sargent, G. William Schwert, Robert Shiller, Jeremy J. Siegel and Alan Stockman for helpful comments. The Federal Reserve Bank of Chicago provided substantial financial assistance at an early stage of the work. No part of the analysis or any conclusion can necessarily be attributed to the Federal Reserve Bank of Chicago or the Federal Reserve System.

NOTES

[1] Shiller and Siegel (1977) suggest that distribution effects arising from unexpected price changes may explain the positive correlation. To date, there are no empirical tests of this hypothesis.

[2] In part, this use of consumer price indexes is forced by problems associated with wholesale price indexes since the Second World War. The treatment of value added taxes changes over time in the continental European countries, and comparable wholesale price indexes cannot be calculated for the United Kingdom and France since 1955 and 1974, respectively.

[3] The graphs have a ratio scale for the price level, and all correlations are in terms of the logarithms of variables. Shiller and Siegel (1977) also use the logarithm of the price level. References to "the natural logarithm of the price level" often are abbreviated to "the price level" in the text.

[4] The standard deviations of the correlations "SD(Corr)", presented in Tables 1-4, are $T^{-1/2}$, where T is the number of observations in the series. This is the asymptotic standard error based on the hypothesis that one of the two series is serially uncorrelated.

The "corrected" standard deviations of the correlations, CSD (Corr), are $T^{-1/2}.\{(1 + r_x r_y)/(1 - r_x r_y)\}^{1/2}$ where the r's are the estimated first-order serial correlation coefficients of the series. This estimator of the standard deviation is based on the hypothesis that both series are first-order autoregressive processes. For discussion of this estimator, see Bartlett (1935, 1946).

At least for the long-term bond yields and the price level, the assumption that the time series are adequately characterized by first-order autoregressive processes is closer to correct than the assumption that they are serially uncorrelated. For example, for 1729-1913, the first 12 autocorrelations of the consol yield are 0·94, 0·88, 0·83, 0·77, 0·72, 0·69, 0·66, 0·63, 0·61, 0·59, 0·57, 0·56; for 1725-1913, the first 12 autocorrelations of the price level are 0·96, 0·91, 0·87, 0·85, 0·84, 0·82, 0·79, 0·76, 0·72, 0·68, 0·65, 0·61. For 1833-1913, the short-term interest rate is less adequately characterized by a first-order autoregressive process, with autocorrelations of 0·69, 0·55, 0·51, 0·41, 0·45, 0·43, 0·42, 0·48, 0·49, 0·41, 0·32, 0·31. The autocorrelations for the other countries are consistent with these for the United Kingdom.

[5] The application of the usury law to three-month bills ends in 1833. Even though the average annual rate is below five percentage points from 1822 to 1833, it seems best to exclude these years. Inclusion of these years has little effect on the correlations.

[6] Successive F-tests indicate that the order of the distributed lags can be reduced from ten to three lags—the lag length used in this test. The restriction of the number of lags is based on both variables in order to have a simple, well-defined test procedure. The t-values suggest that too many lags of the price level have been included. If anything, this biases the following tests in favour of the hypothesis of stability.

[7] If the interest rate and the price level are covariance-stationary, then by Wold's theorem (1938) there exists a moving average representation of the two series. If this moving-average representation is invertible, then there exists an autoregressive representation (possibly with infinite lags) such as (1). If the underlying series are covariance-stationary, then the failure of (1) to pass the tests of stability may be due to changes in structural parameters relating the interest rate and the price level, changes in the relationship between these two variables and other variables, or changes in the distribution of the fundamental innovations.

[8] No test of the stability of a subset of the coefficients is performed, because, excluding the intercept, a change of the lagged interest rates' or lagged price levels' coefficients in either regression generally will change the long-run relationship between the interest rate and the price level.

[9] Attempts to locate the source of the instability by combining periods based on monetary standards were unsuccessful in locating a consistent source of the breaks.

[10] When price levels are used, some of the estimated bivariate and trivariate autoregressions are almost unstable, i.e. have eigenvalues of the system close to one. As a consequence, it may be useful to estimate the autoregressions in terms of the inflation rate. These autoregressions

have much smaller eigenvalues. The results based in inflation rates invariably are more consistent with the hypothesis than the results based on price levels.

[11] Details of the calculation of the restrictions and the justification for the chi-square test statistic are provided in Dwyer (1981).

[12] Test results using this data for 1953–1975 are consistent with the results obtained with point-in-time data available for the United States in this period.

[13] Following a suggestion by Sims (1980), I calculate the test statistic as $(T - k) \ln (D_r / D_u)$, where T is the number of observations, k is the average number of variables in the autoregressions, D_r is the determinant of the covariance matrix of the residuals from the restricted estimation, and D_u is the determinant from the unrestricted estimates.

[14] Two lags appear to be sufficient to characterize the series in the sub-periods. The detailed estimates are available on request. Results based on three lags are generally much more consistent with the hypothesis.

[15] The price level and interest rate for the first year after resumption, 1879, are excluded from the calculations for reasons explained by Friedman and Schwartz (1982, p. 104).

REFERENCES

BARTLETT, M. S. (1935). Some aspects of the time-correlation problem in regard to tests of significance. *Journal of the Royal Statistical Society*, **98**, 536–543.

—— (1946). On the theoretical specification and sampling properties of autocorrelated time series. *Supplement ot the Journal of the Royal Statistical Society*, **8**, 27–41.

CAGAN, PHILLIP (1965). *Determinants and Effects of Changes in the Stock of Money, 1875–1960*. New York: Columbia University Press for the National Bureau of Economic Research.

DWYER, GERALD P., JR (1981). Are expectations of inflation rational? Or, is variation of the expected real interest rate unpredictable? *Journal of Monetary Economics*, **8**, 59–84.

FAMA, EUGENE F. (1975). Short-term interest rates as predictors of inflation. *American Economic Review*, **65**, 269–282.

FISHER, IRVING, (1930). *The Theory of Interest*. New York: Macmillan.

FRIEDMAN, MILTON and SCHWARTZ, ANNA J. (1982). *Monetary Trends in the United States and the United Kingdom*. University of Chicago Press.

GIBSON, A. H. (1923). The future course of high-class investment values. *The Bankers', Insurance Managers', and Agents' Magazine*, **115**, 15–34.

HARLEY, C. KNICK (1977). The interest rate and prices in Britain, 1873–1913: A study of the Gibson paradox. *Explorations in Economic History*, **14**, 69–89.

KEYNES, JOHN MAYNARD (1930). *A Treatise on Money*, Vol. II. New York: Harcourt, Brace and Company.

MACAULEY, FREDERICK R. (1938). *The Movements of Interest Rates, Bond Yields and Stock Prices in the United States Since 1856*. New York: National Bureau of Economic Research.

MEISELMAN, DAVID (1963). Bond yields and the price level: the Gibson paradox regained. In Deane Carson (ed.), *Banking and Monetary Studies*, Homewood, 111.: Richard D. Irwin, Inc.

MUTH, JOHN F. (1961). Rational expectations and the theory of price movements. *Econometrica*, **29**, 315–335.

SARGENT, THOMAS J. (1973). Interest rates and prices in the long run: a study of the Gibson paradox. *Journal of Money, Credit and Banking*, **5**, 395–449.

SAUL, S. B. (1969). *The Myth of the Great Depression 1873–1896*. New York: St Martin's Press.

SIMS, CHRISTOPHER A. (1980). Macroeconomics and reality. *Econometrica*, **48**, 1–48.

SHILLER, ROBERT J. and SIEGEL, JEREMY J. (1977). The Gibson paradox and historical movements in real interest rates. *Journal of Political Economy*, **85**, 891–907.

TOOKE, THOMAS (1844). *An Inquiry into the Currency Principle*. London: Longman, Brown, Green, and Longmans.

WICKSELL, KNUT (1899). The influence of the rate of interest on commodity prices. In Erik Lindahl (ed.), *Selected Papers on Economic Theory*. Cambridge: Harvard University Press, 1958.

WOLD, H. (1938). *A Study in the Analysis of Stationary Time Series*, 1st ed. Uppsala: Almquist and Wicksell.

Name Index